ROME Splendours of an Ancient Civilization

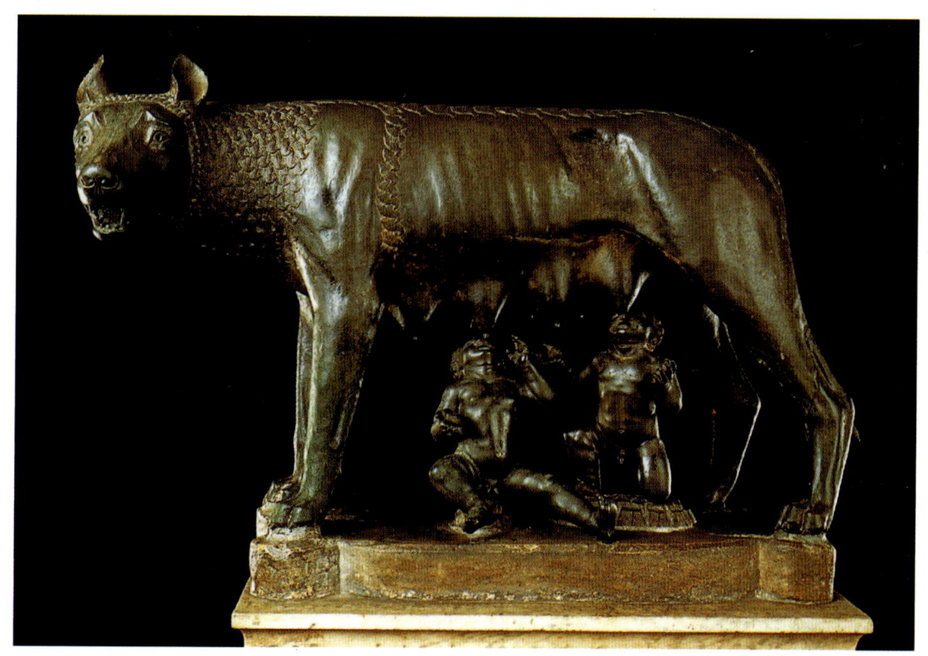

Thames & Hudson

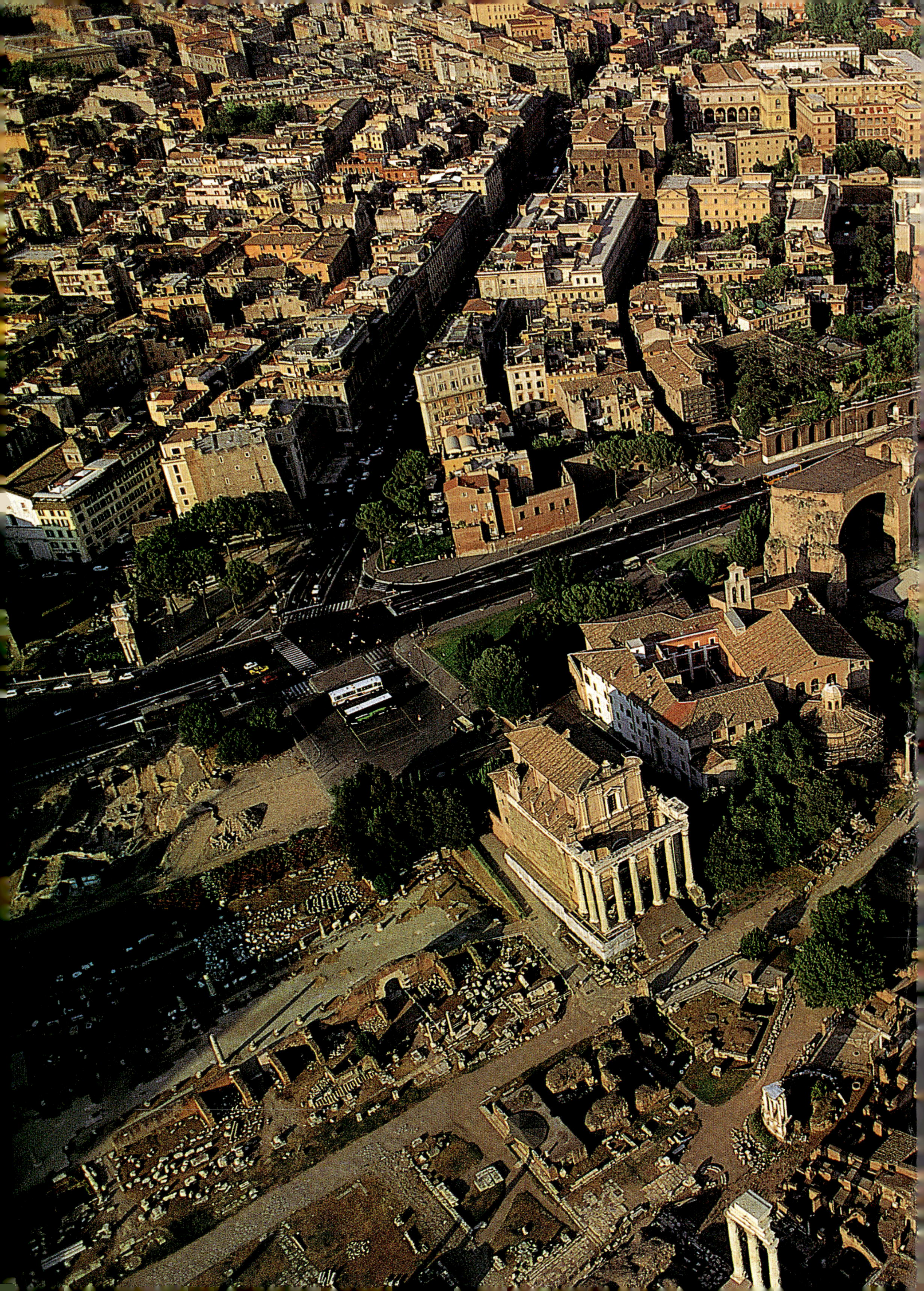

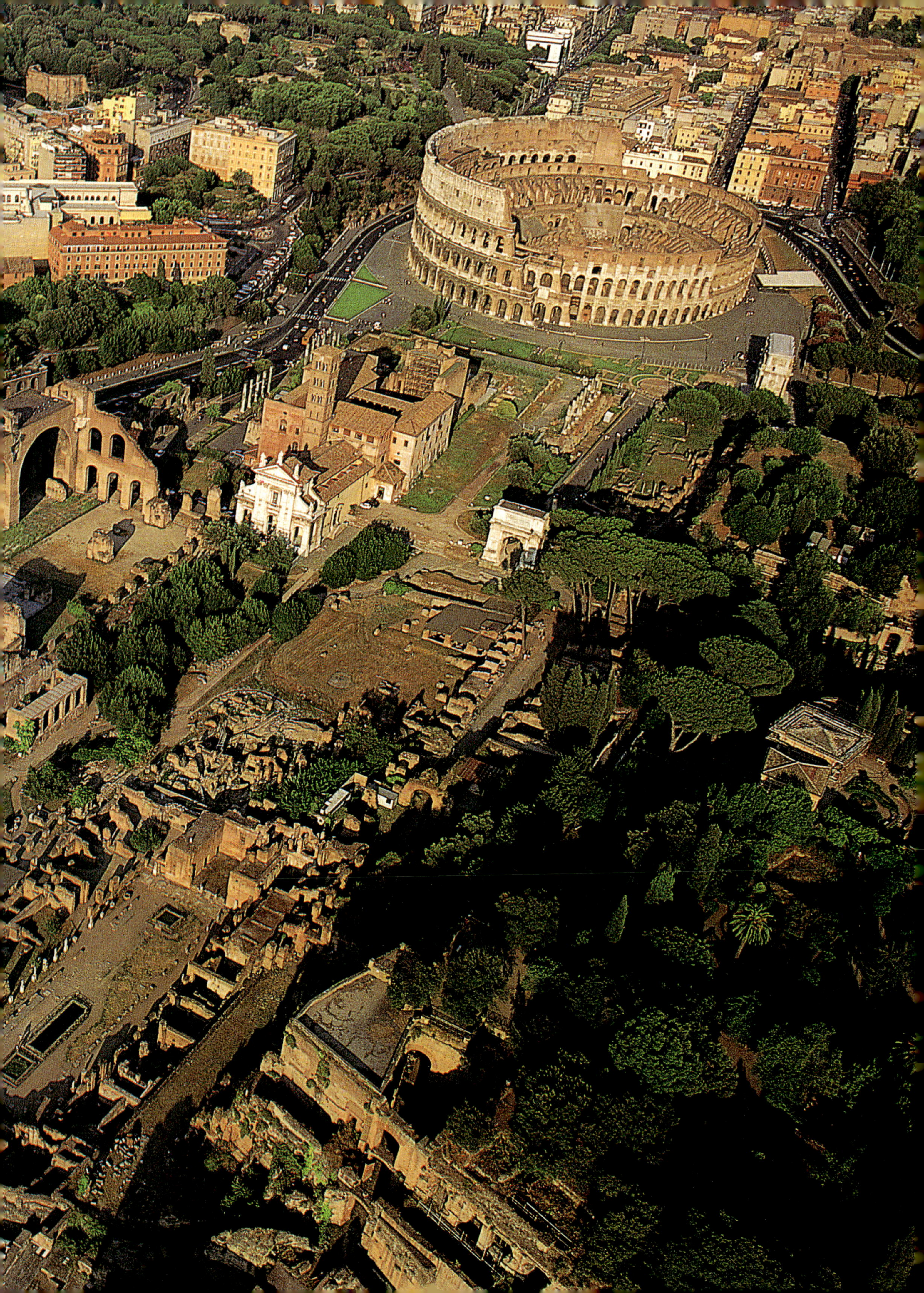

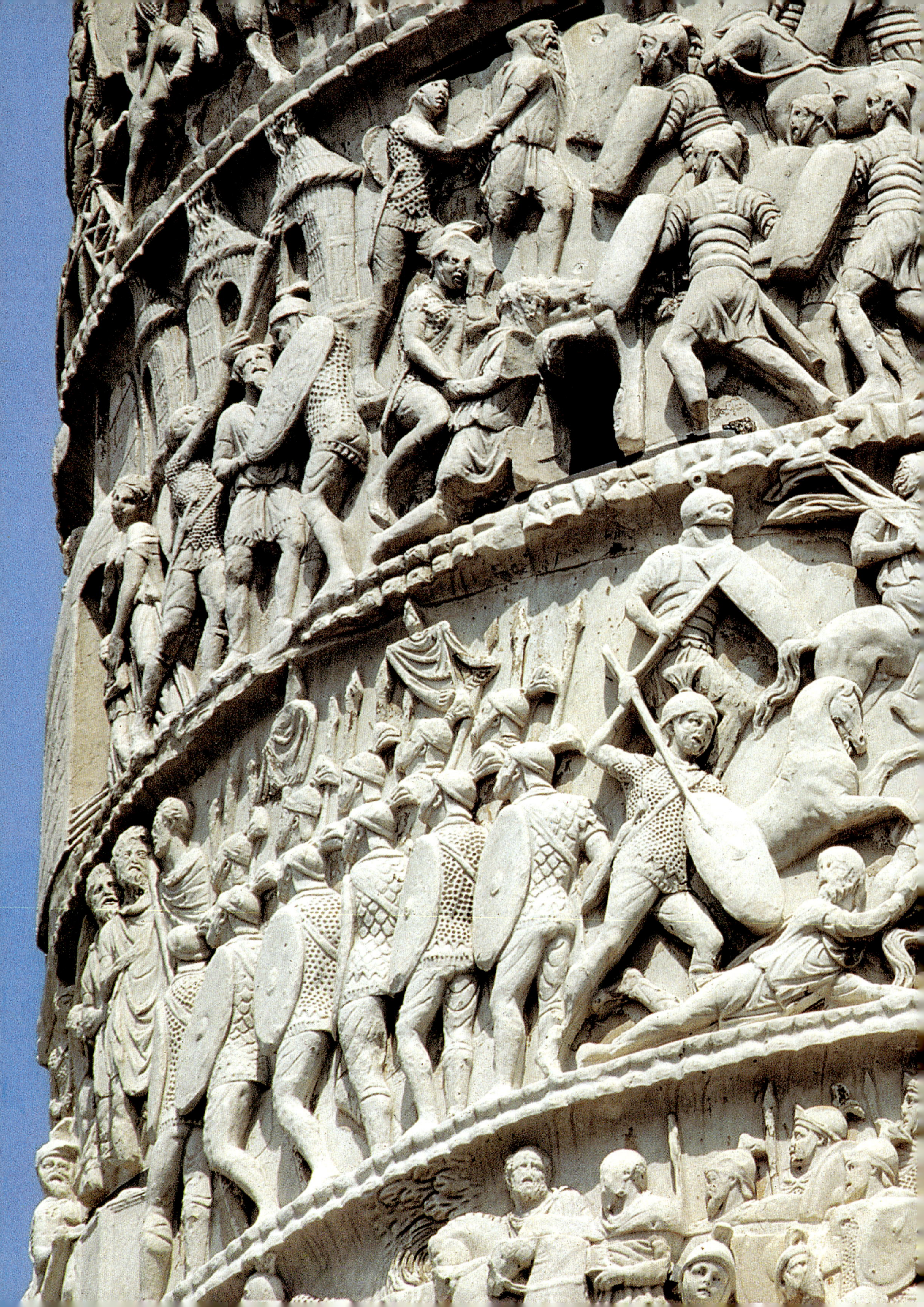

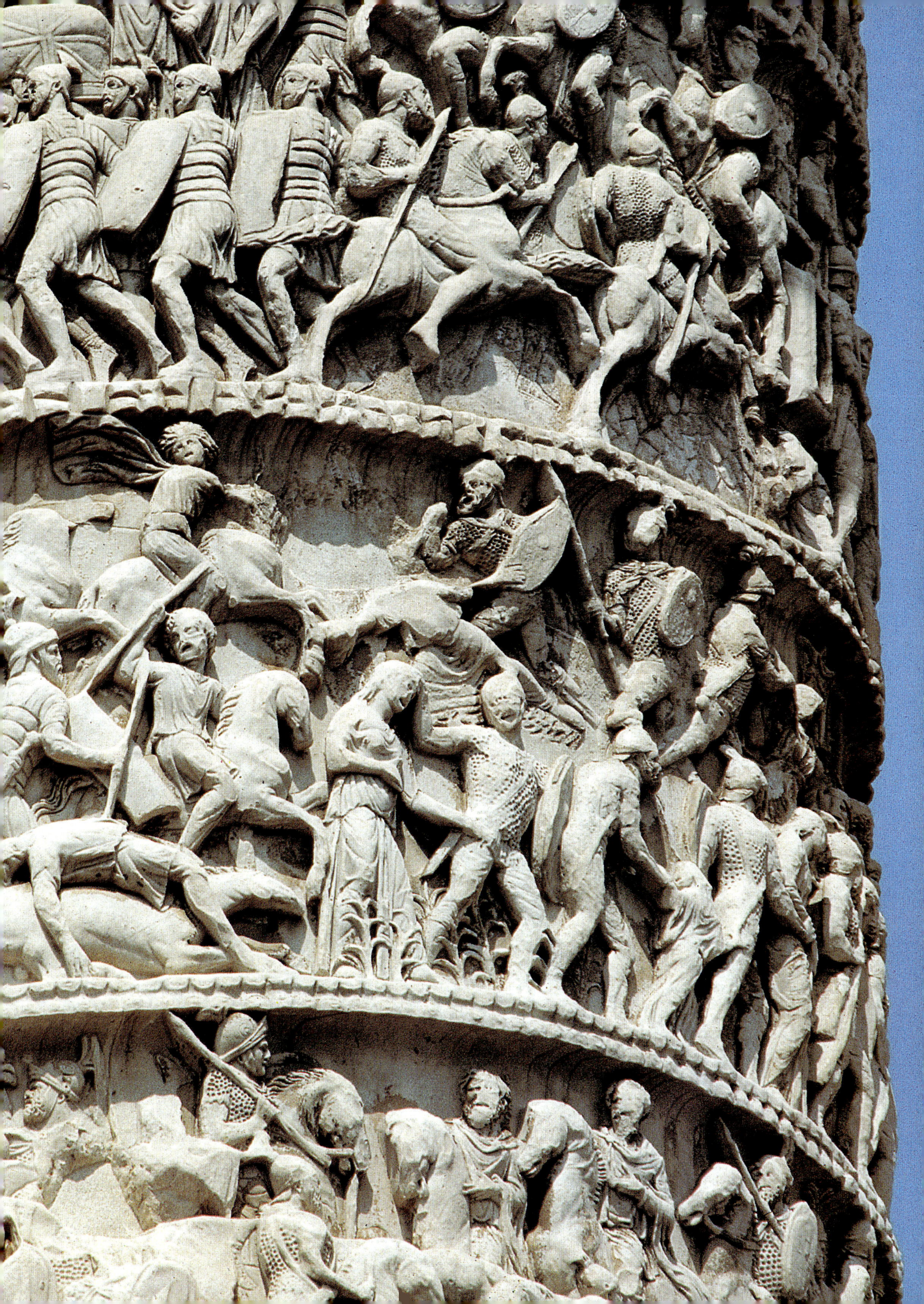

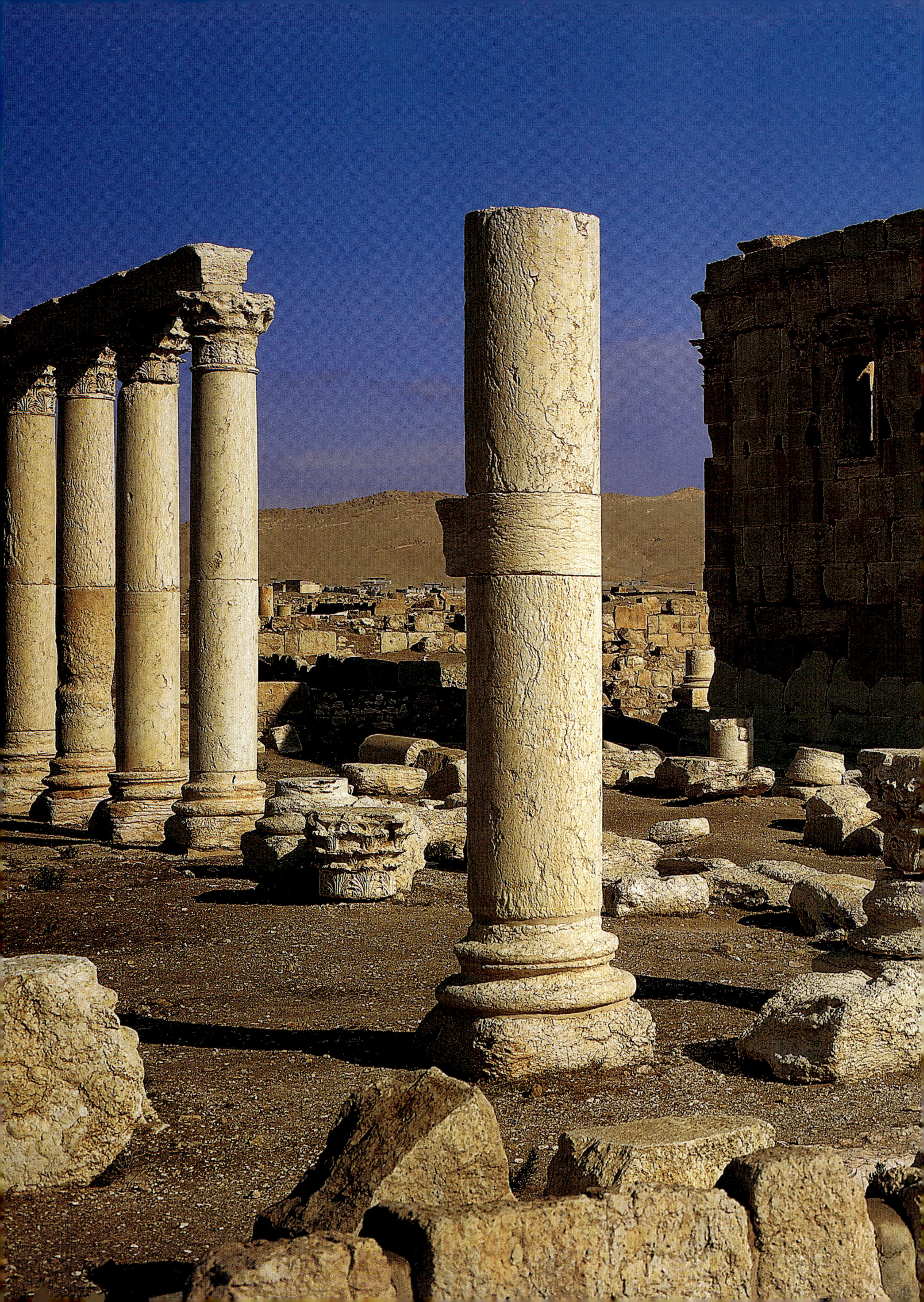

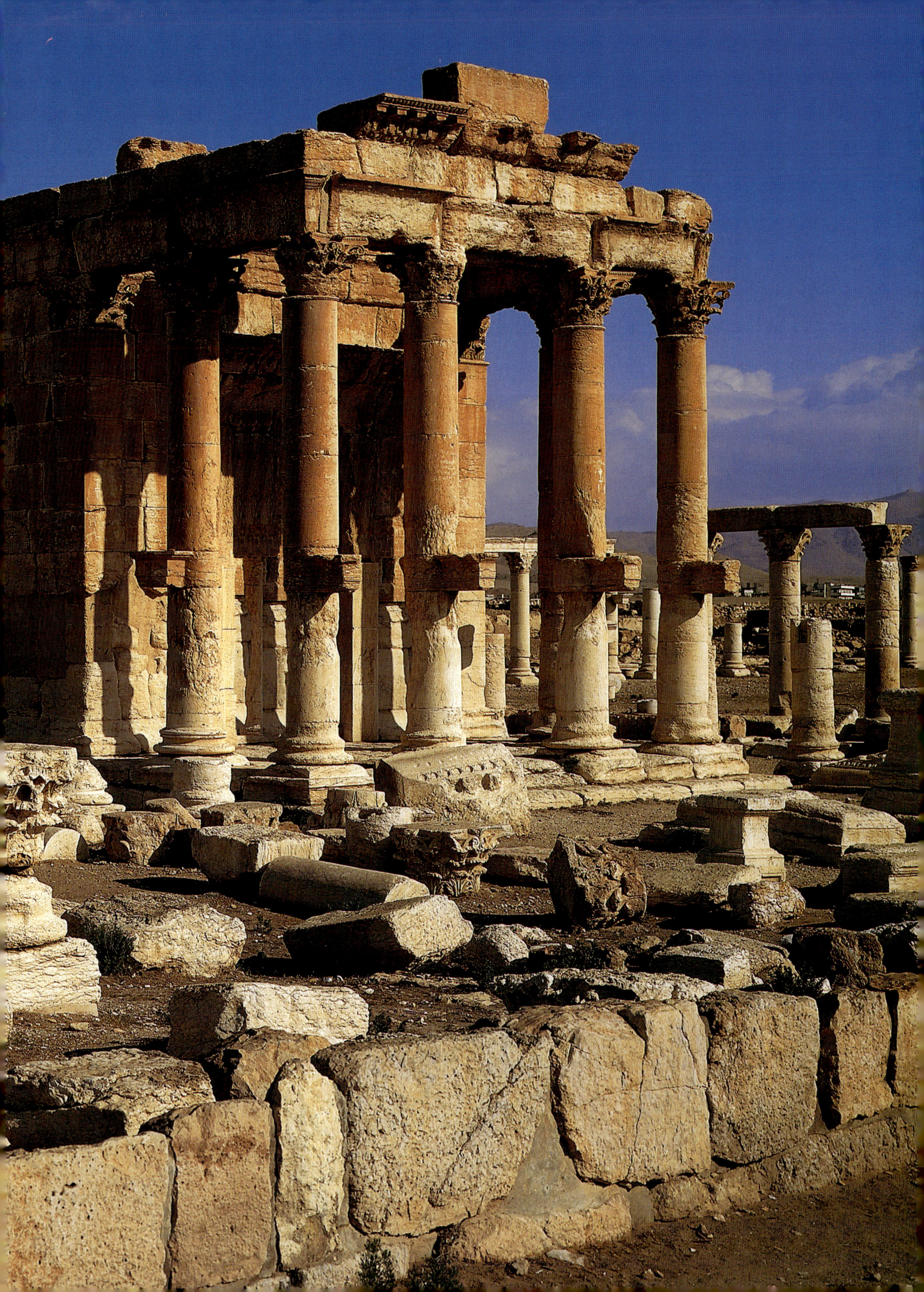

Contents

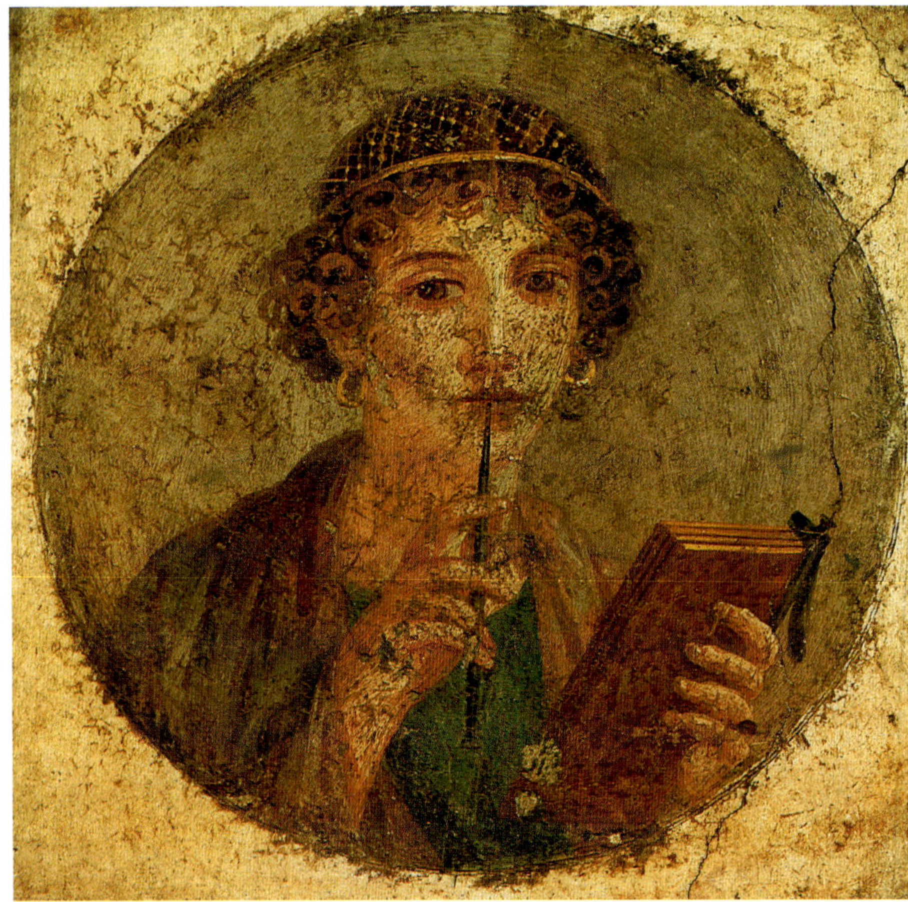

(Note: caption numbers refer to the pages where the illustrations appear.)

1 The Capitoline she-wolf symbolizes the mythical origins of Rome. This Etruscan bronze dates from the 5th century BC*, while the twins – Romulus and Remus – are an addition by the Renaissance sculptor Pollaiuolo.*

2–3 For centuries the Roman Forum, standing in the valley at the foot of the Palatine Hill, was the heart of public life in Rome. Temples, basilicas, triumphal arches and votive columns were added at different times.

4–5 The Column of Marcus Aurelius, which stands in front of the Palazzo Chigi in Rome, was erected between AD *176 and 193 to celebrate the emperor's victories against the Germans and the Sarmatians. It is just under 30 m (98 ft) tall and decorated with spiral reliefs depicting the various stages of the military campaigns.*

6–7 The Temple of Ba'alshamin is one of the most outstanding monuments in Palmyra. This flourishing Syrian caravan town became part of the Roman empire under Hadrian in the 2nd century AD*.*

8 A delicate fresco from Pompeii shows a girl in a pensive attitude. Because of the quill pen resting on her lips and the wax tablet she is holding in her left hand, she is known as the Poetess.

9 This intense portrait of Augustus, a detail from the Prima Porta statue, named after the site where it was found, shows the founder of the Roman empire at the peak of his strength and wearing the commander's breastplate.

10–11 The Villa of the Mysteries in Pompeii contains the most famous cycle of frescoes from Roman times, dating from the 1st century BC*. The figures are depicted life-size.*

12–13 The statue known as the Boxer is a masterpiece of the so-called Neoattic school of the 1st century BC*, which had a pronounced influence on Roman statuary.*

14–15 A superb and highly accomplished mosaic from Hadrian's Villa at Tivoli portrays two theatrical masks. These were worn by actors to emphasize the more grotesque features of the various characters they portrayed.

Texts and captions
Anna Maria Liberati
Fabio Bourbon

Editor
Valeria Manferto De Fabianis

Graphic design
Patrizia Balocco Lovisetti

Editorial co-ordination
Fabio Bourbon

Colour and black-and-white drawings
Roberta Vigone
Monica Falcone

The Publisher would like to thank the Commander Vincenzo Calabrese and Augustín Velázquez Jiménez, Director of the Museo Nacional de Arte Romano of Merida, Spain, for their valuable contributions to this book.

First published in the United Kingdom in hardback in 1996 by Thames & Hudson Ltd, 181A High Holborn, London WC1V 7QX

www.thamesandhudson.com

Paperback edition published in 2001,
This new smaller format hardback edition first published 2005

British Library Cataloguing-in-Publication Data
A catalogue record for this book is available from the British Library

ISBN 0-500-51205-1

Printed and bound in China

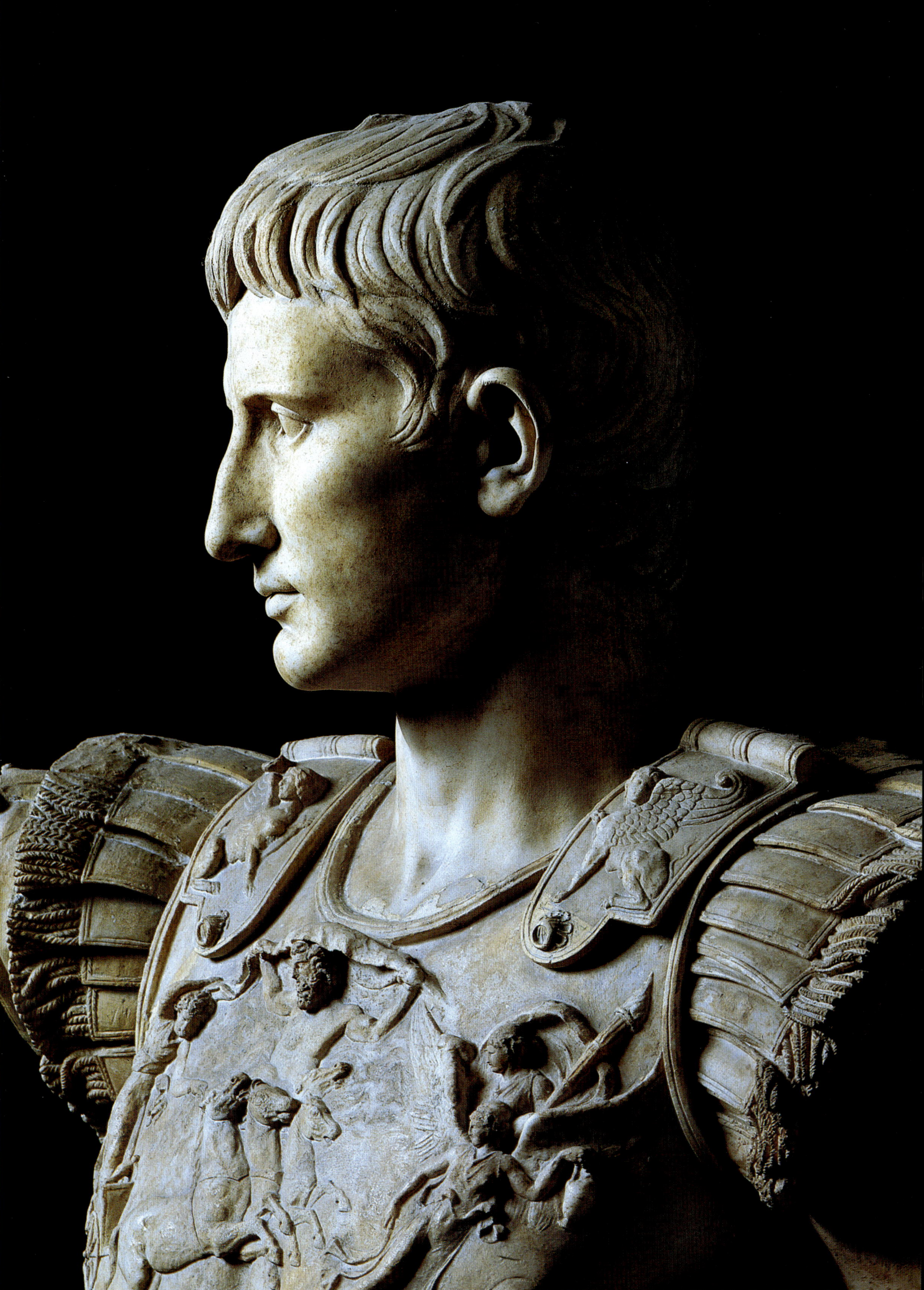

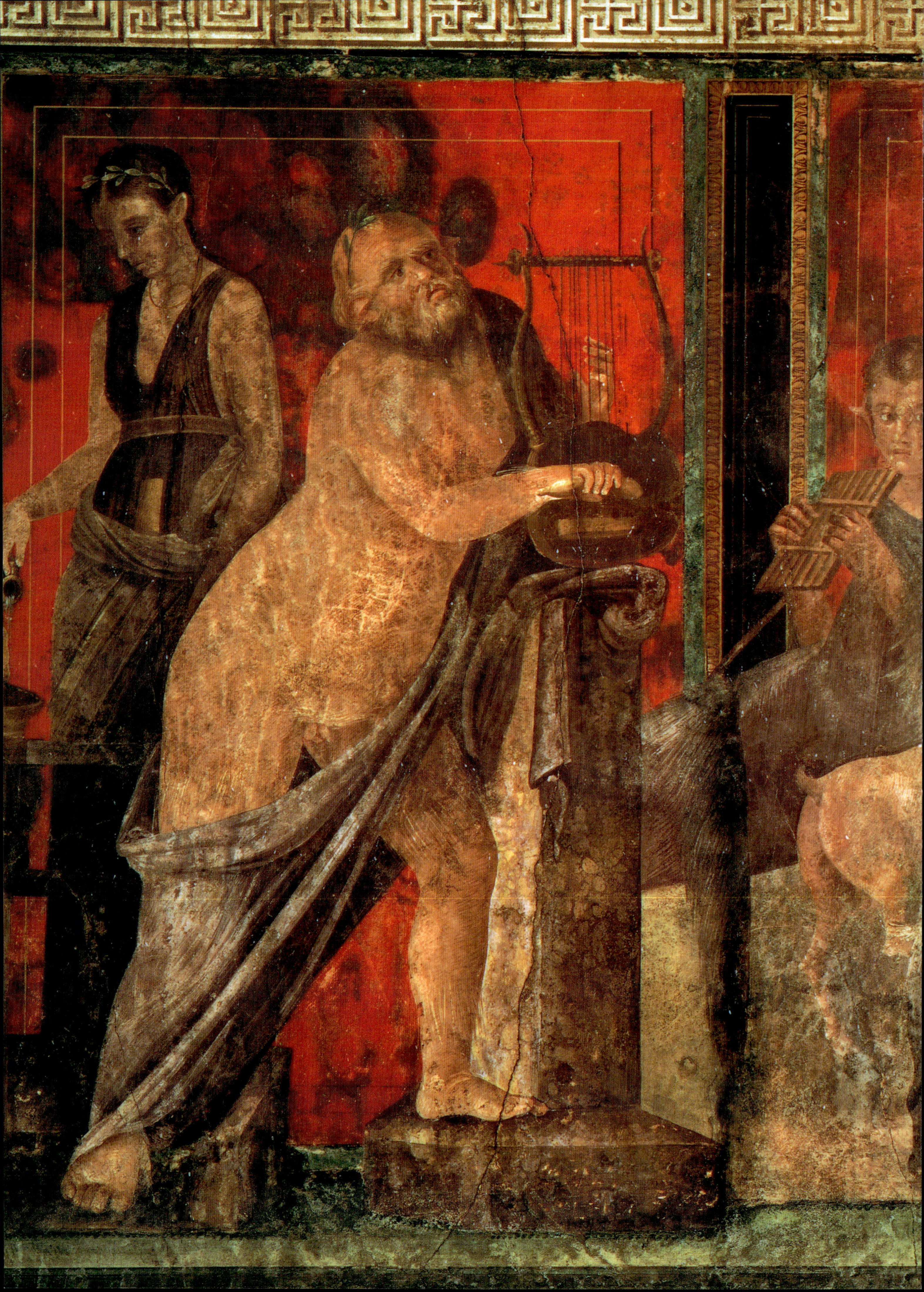

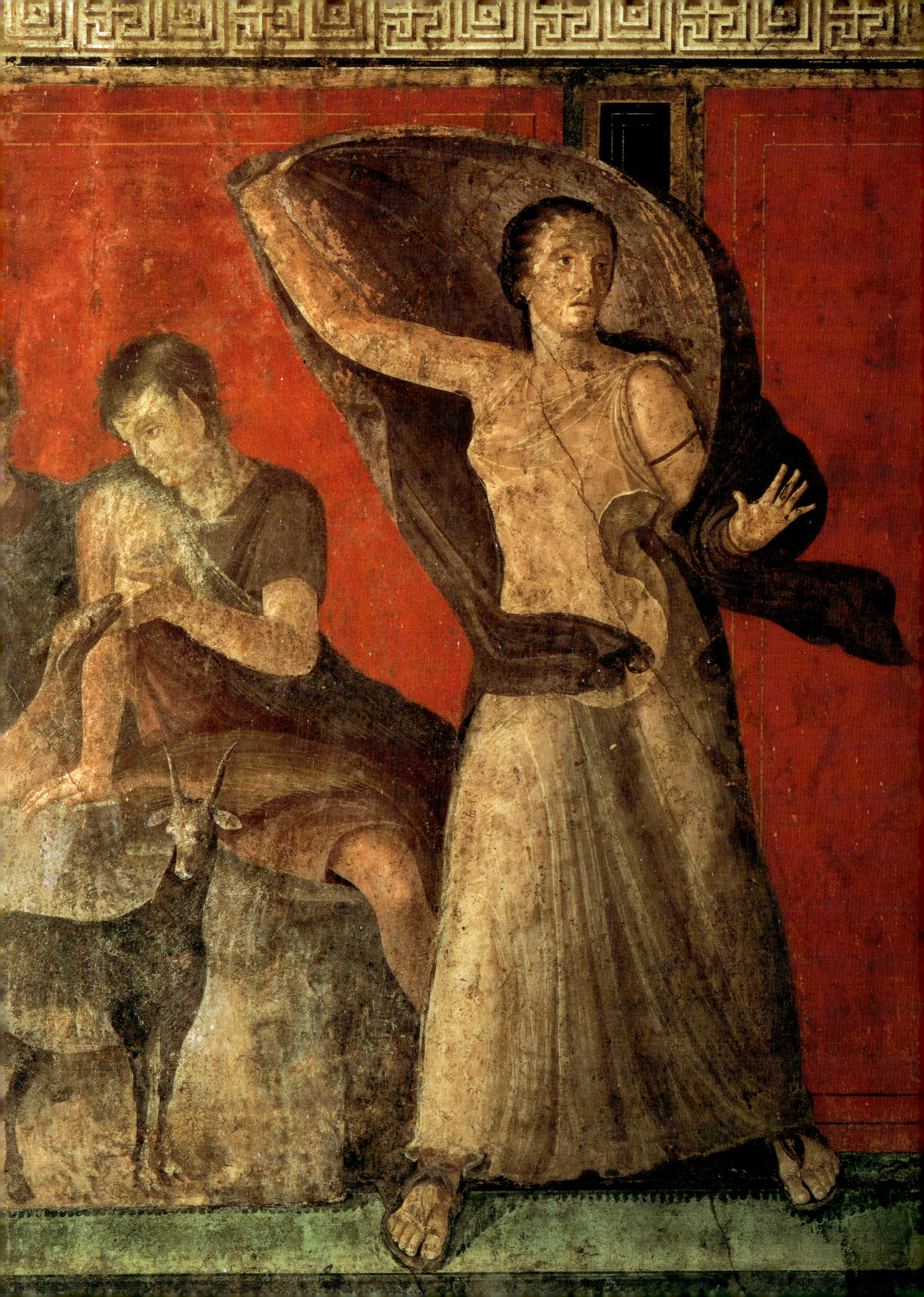

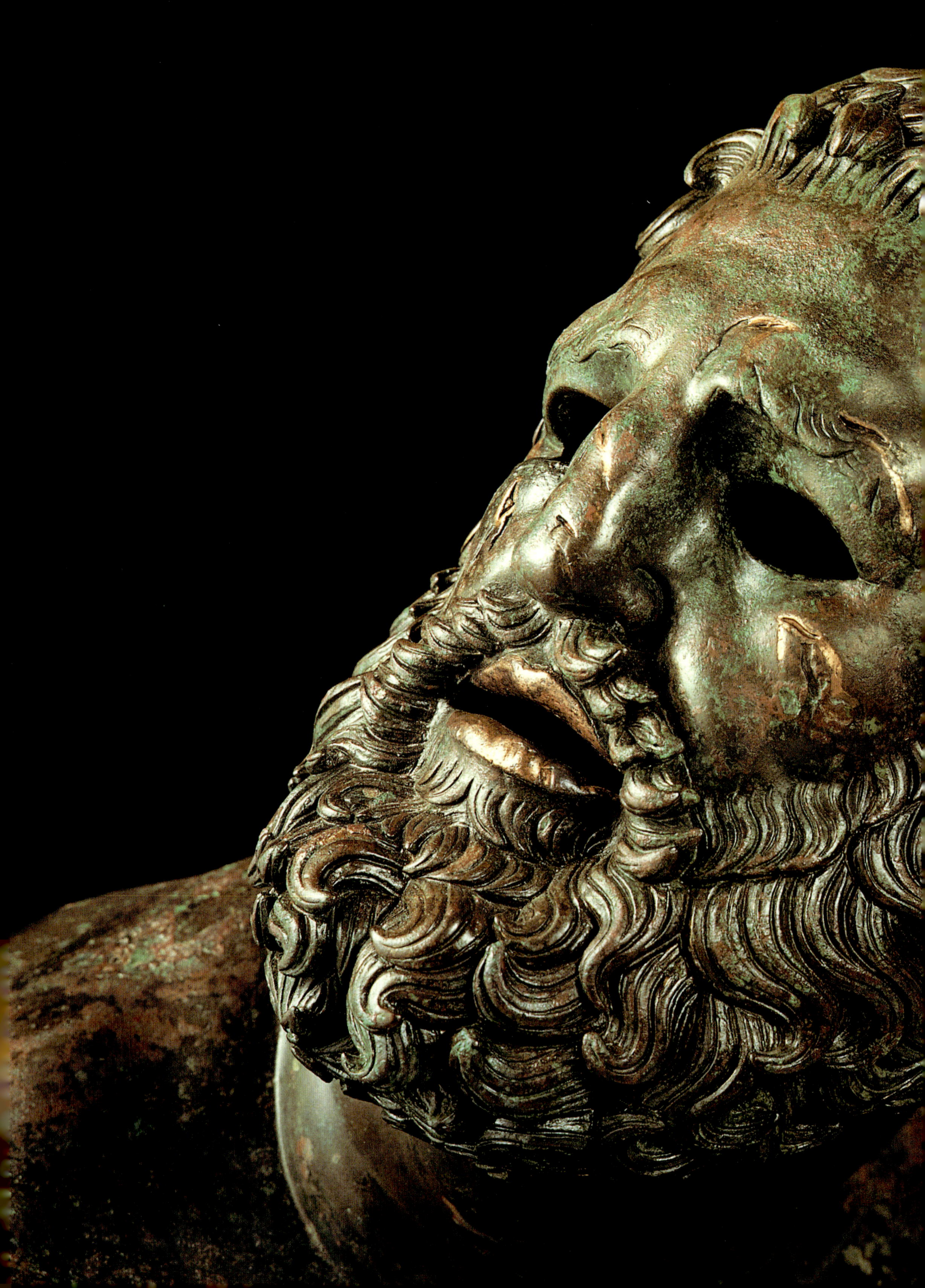

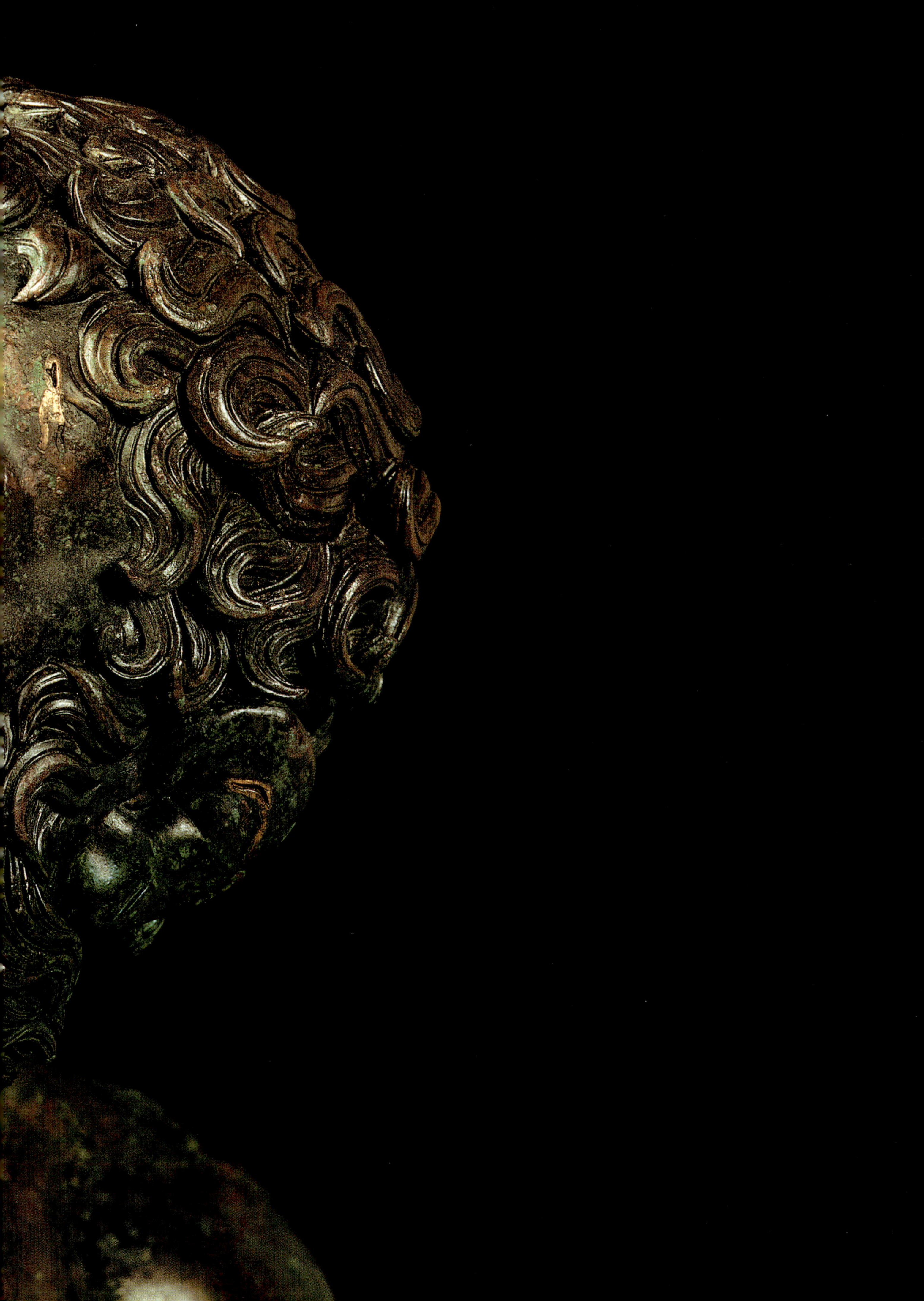

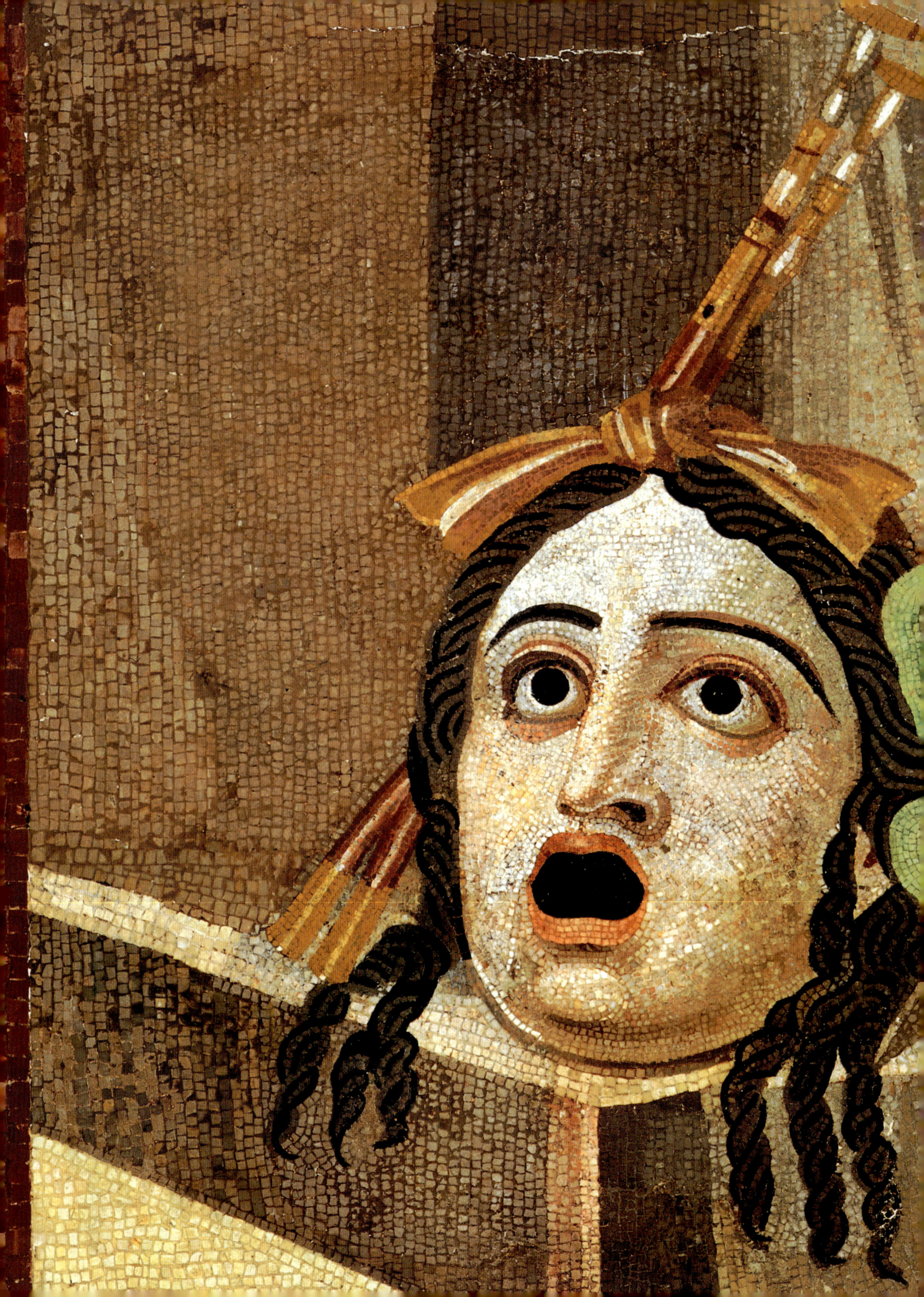

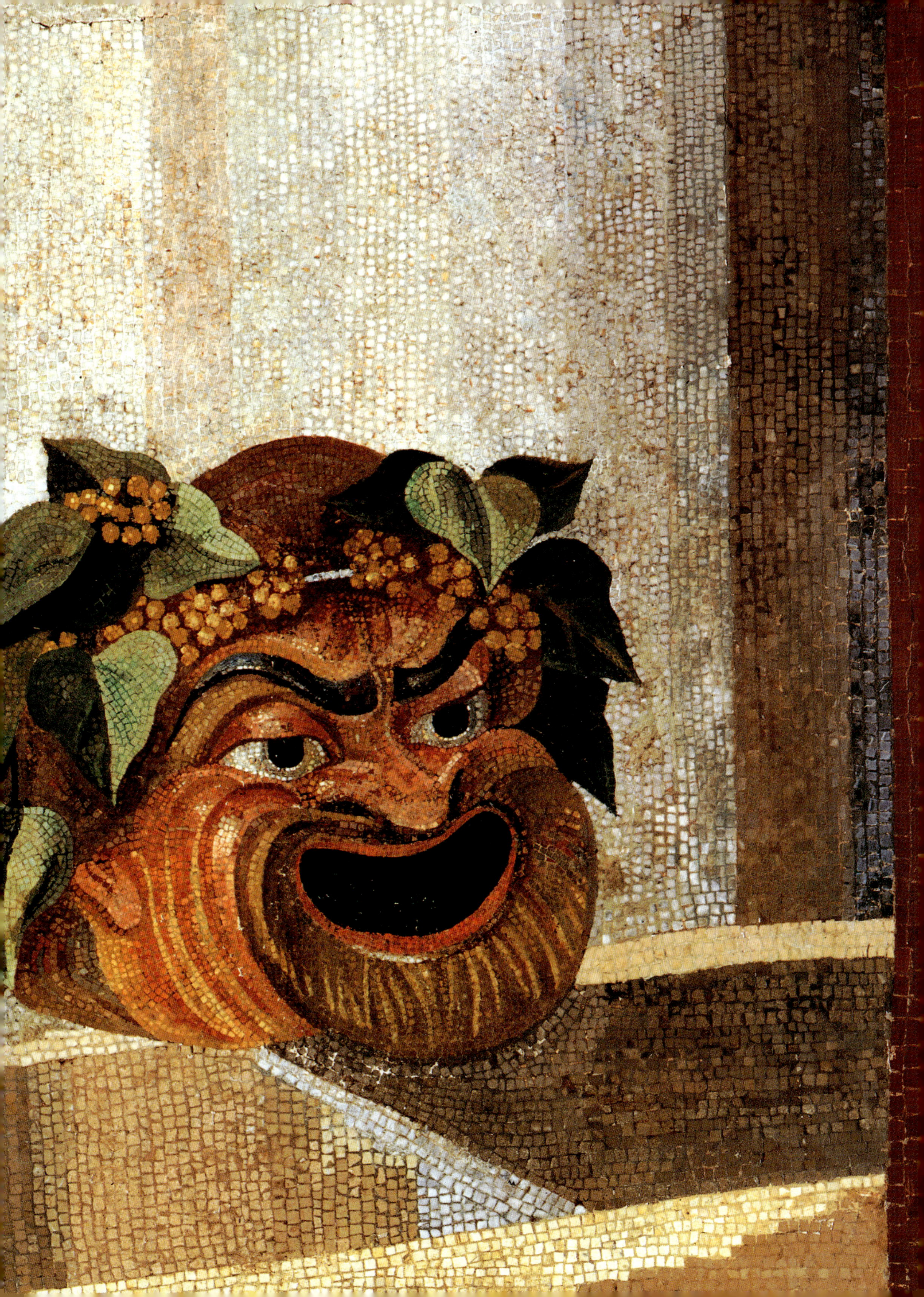

PREFACE

Roman civilization still holds an irresistible attraction, even in today's technological world. It has survived through the centuries not only in the form of archaelogical remains and abstract ideas, but above all as a tangible heritage which is still active in the world in which we live.

The complex water supply systems found from Britannia to Syria, the efficient road network which connected even the most distant towns to the heart of the empire and the residential districts discovered in Ostia all bear witness to a society which was highly technically advanced. Methods of construction, and styles of architecture and decoration from the Roman world are extensively reflected in the artistic languages we are most familiar with, from Renaissance to postmodern. Even the social issues - the constant struggle for political power, the excesses and decadence of the ancient Roman lifestyle - are by no means alien to us.
For better or worse, the long shadow cast by Rome permeates many aspects of our daily lives. We are often only subconsciously aware of this heritage, and it is perhaps not surprising that we fail to remember every time we turn on a tap to quench our thirst that we have just used a mechanism designed 2000 years ago. Equally, we do not consider every day te fact that the origins of the legal system that protects our rights date back to the work of the Roman jurists.

Recounting the history of Rome and its civilization - which influenced the culture of a large part of the world for over 1000 years - is no easy task. We have therefore tried to bring ancient Rome to life by describing its social, political, cultural and artistic aspects as clearly and succinctly as possible. We hope that the various chapters are structured in such a way as to familiarize even the least expert with this highly complex world, while still entertaining the more demanding readers who, we trust, will still find plenty to interest them in this volume.

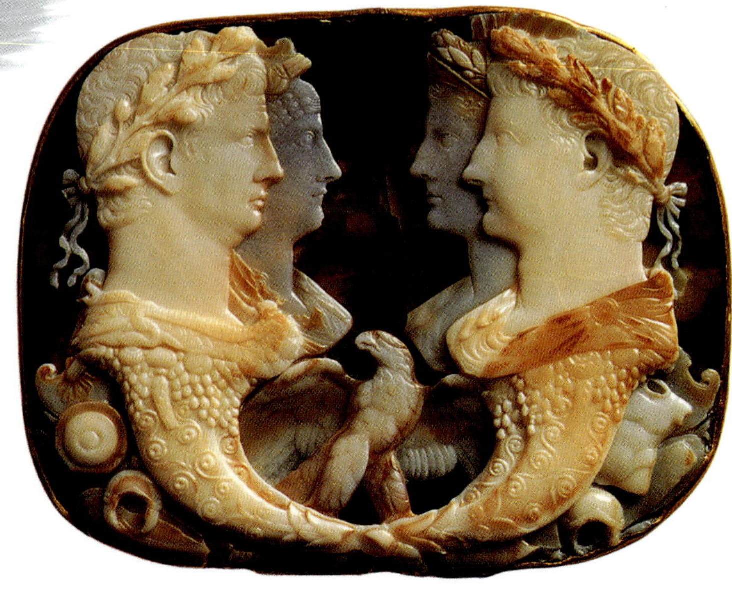

16 Cameos, often exquisitely carved from semiprecious stones, were designed to immortalize leading personalities and emphasize key aspects of imperial court life. The 'Gemma Claudia' portrays the emperor Claudius with his wife Agrippina the Younger on the left, and Germanicus, a valiant commander and adopted son of Tiberius, with his wife Agrippina the Elder, on the righ.

The underlying characteristics of Roman civilization are explored by an overview of the various stages of its history, from archaic times to the decline of the empire, and the most interesting aspects of everyday life. The remains of Roman civilization in Italy and the various provinces of the empire are given particular attention, by a detailed look at important archaeological sites in each region, demonstrating the influence exerted by Rome – sometimes overwhelming local cultures, but often incorporating them with interesting results.

Many new aerial photographs have been specially taken to highlight details of monuments or town planning which would otherwise be difficult to appreciate. These, together with diagrams, plans, drawings and reconstructions all contribute to a full understanding of the splendours of a civilization which conquered the world.

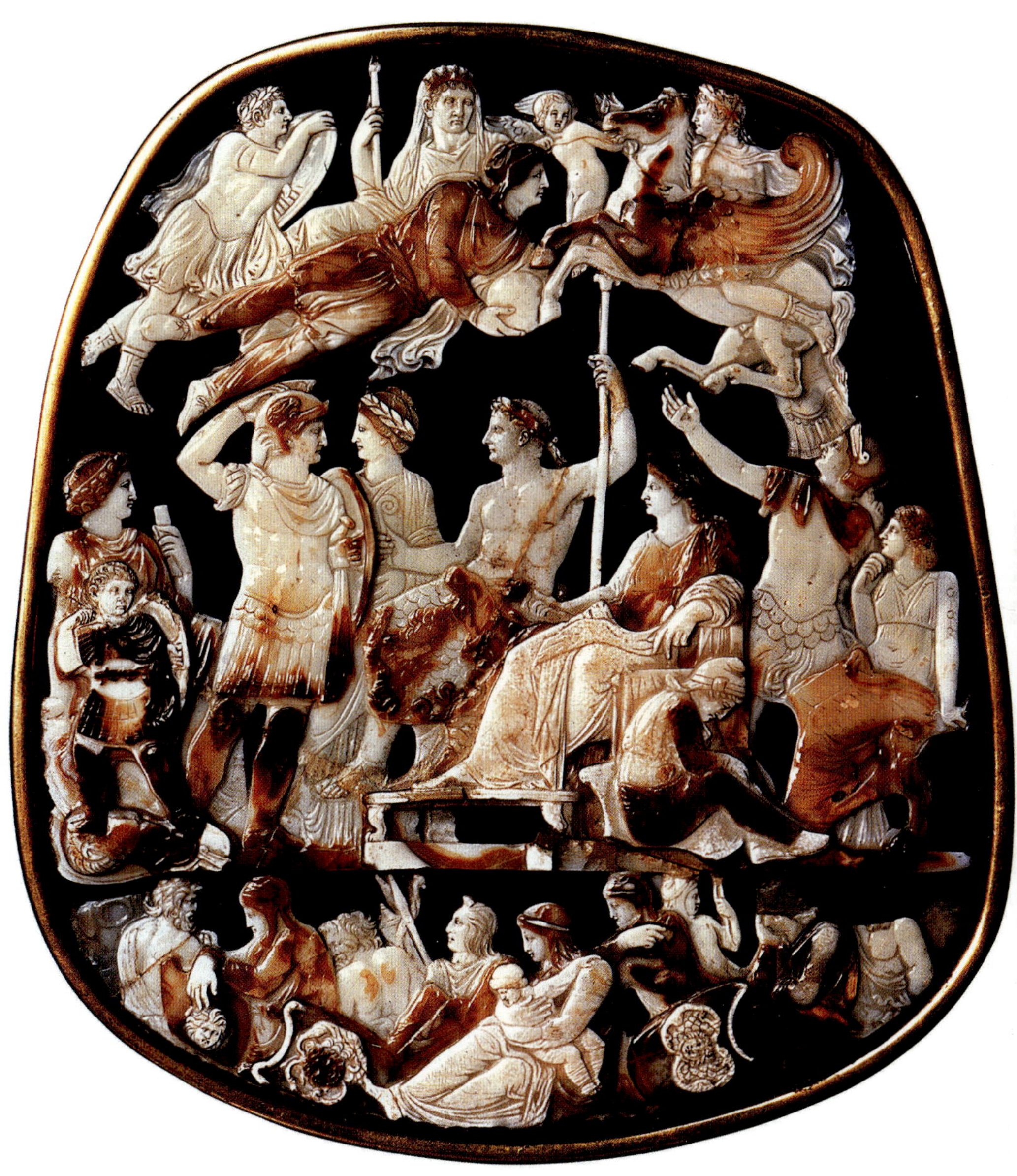

17 A masterpiece of the jeweler's art, this sardonyx cameo from the 1st century AD, known as the 'Grand Camée de France', portrays Tiberius in the midst of members of the Julio-Claudian family, including his mother, Livia.

18–19 (overleaf) Designed for gladiatorial games and wild beast hunts, the Colosseum was inaugurated in AD 80; it was the largest amphitheatre in the Roman world. In this aerial photo the inner structure of the building is revealed, including the complex system of underground chambers. The load-bearing structures of this edifice were made of travertine blocks, with lighter tufa and brick masonry filling the sections between.

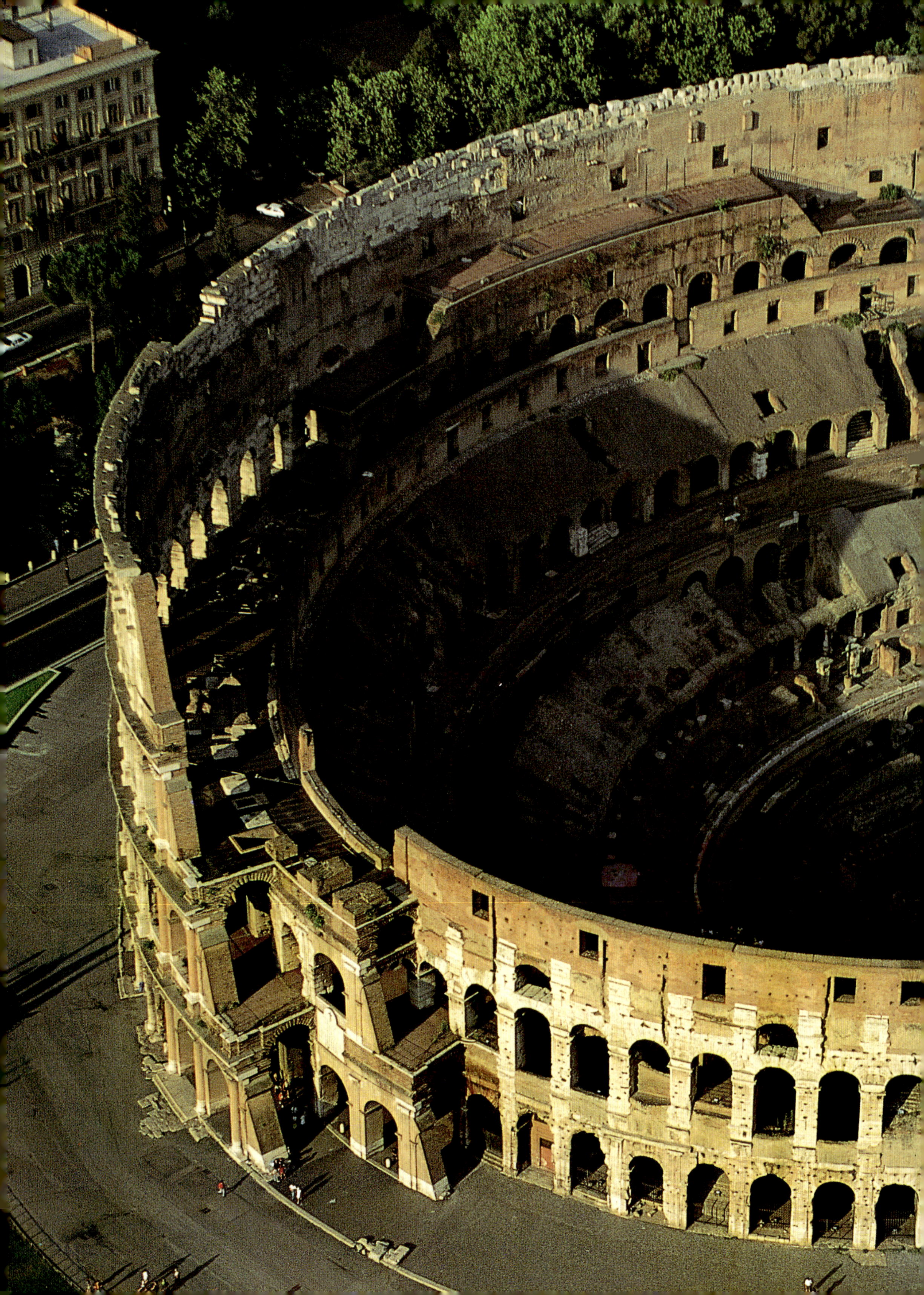

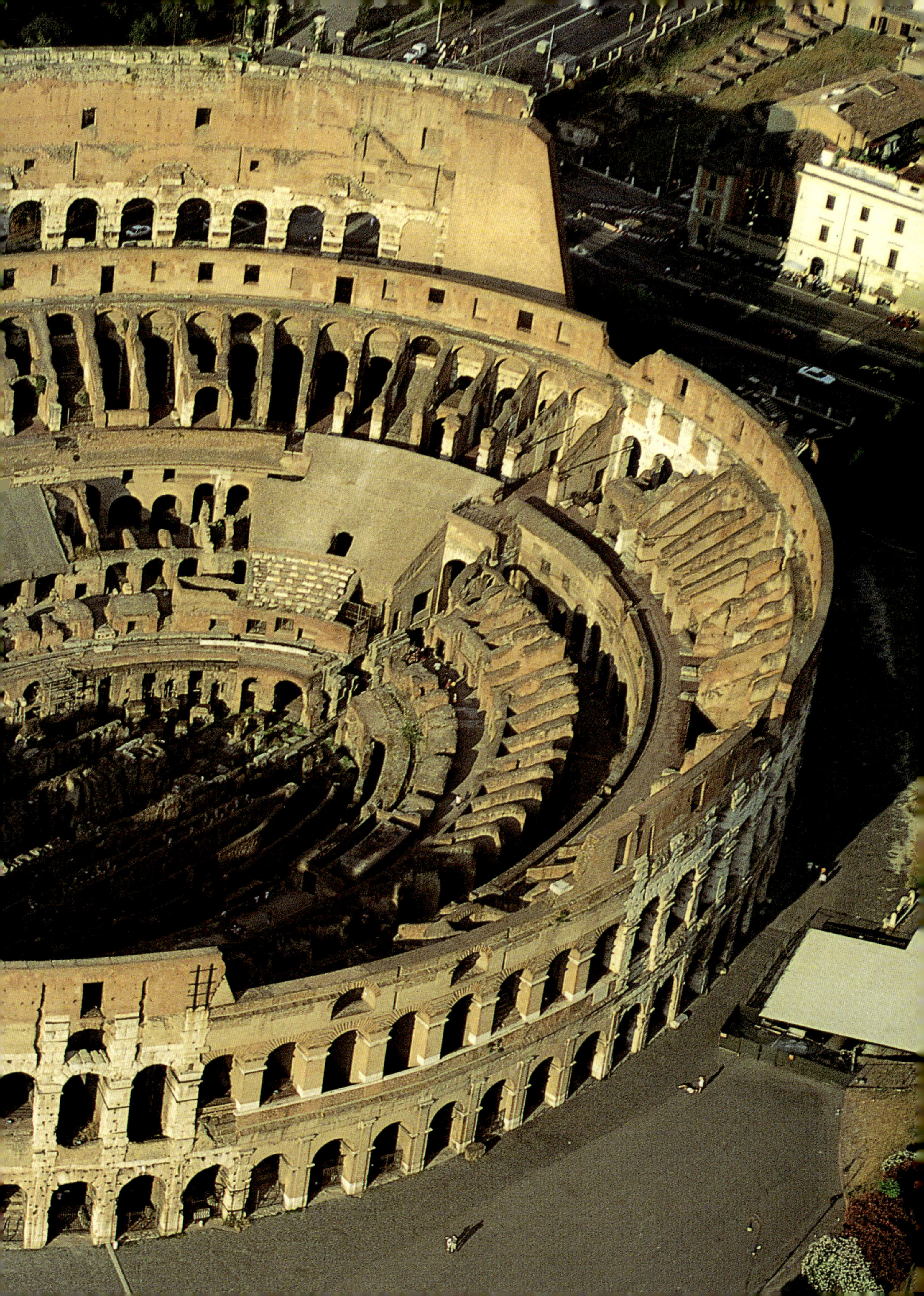

ROME:
FROM ITS ORIGINS TO THE FALL OF THE EMPIRE

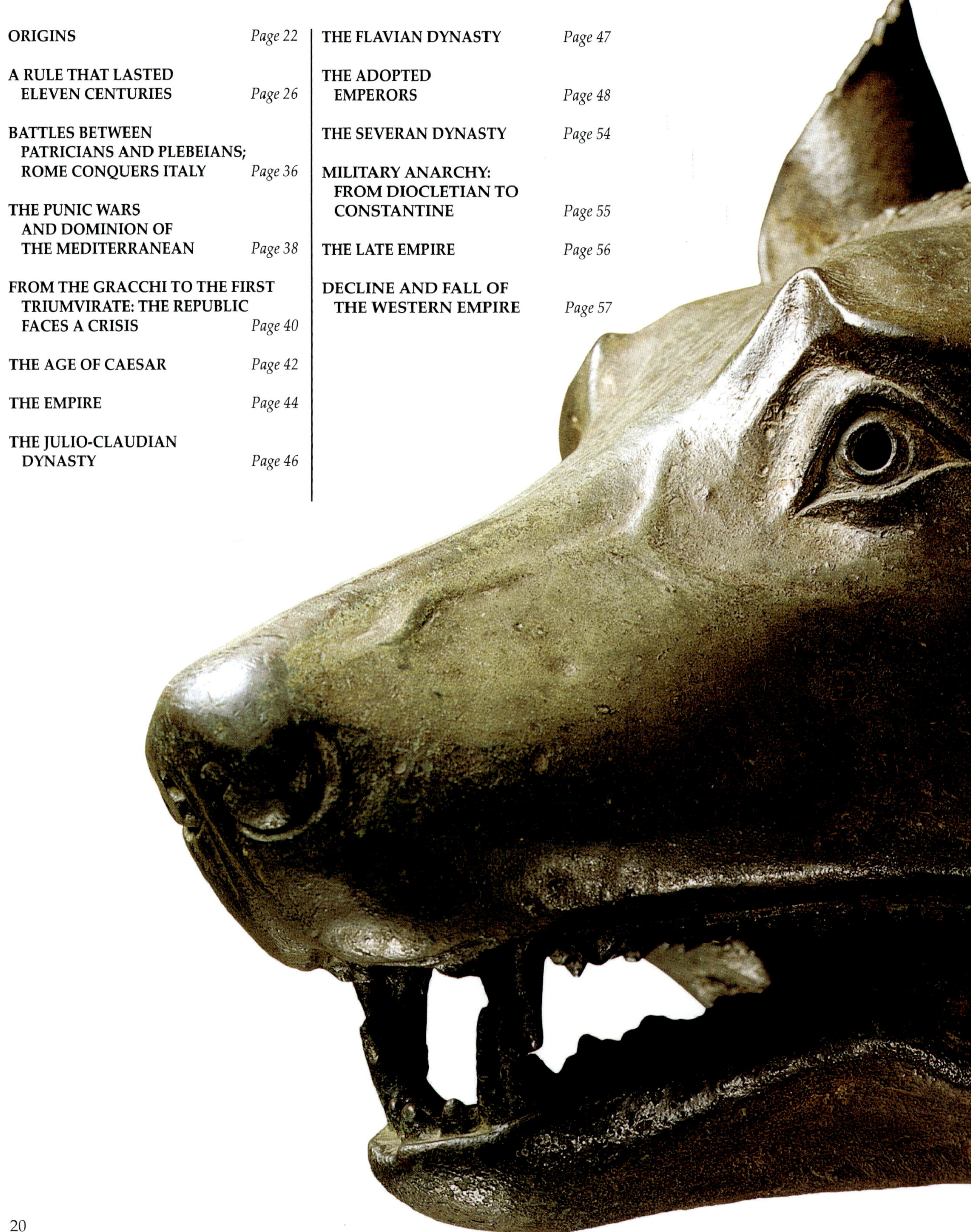

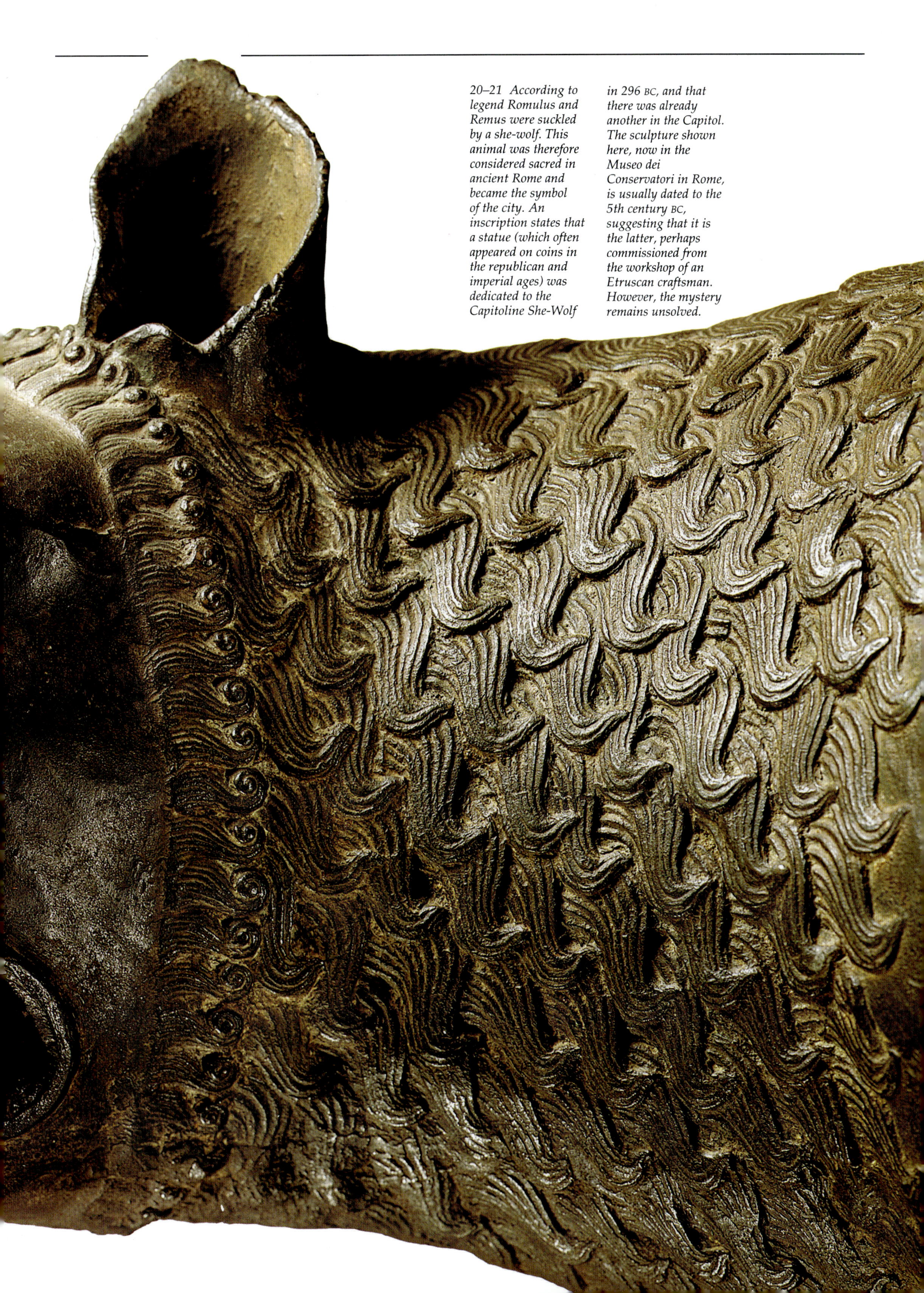

20–21 According to legend Romulus and Remus were suckled by a she-wolf. This animal was therefore considered sacred in ancient Rome and became the symbol of the city. An inscription states that a statue (which often appeared on coins in the republican and imperial ages) was dedicated to the Capitoline She-Wolf in 296 BC, and that there was already another in the Capitol. The sculpture shown here, now in the Museo dei Conservatori in Rome, is usually dated to the 5th century BC, suggesting that it is the latter, perhaps commissioned from the workshop of an Etruscan craftsman. However, the mystery remains unsolved.

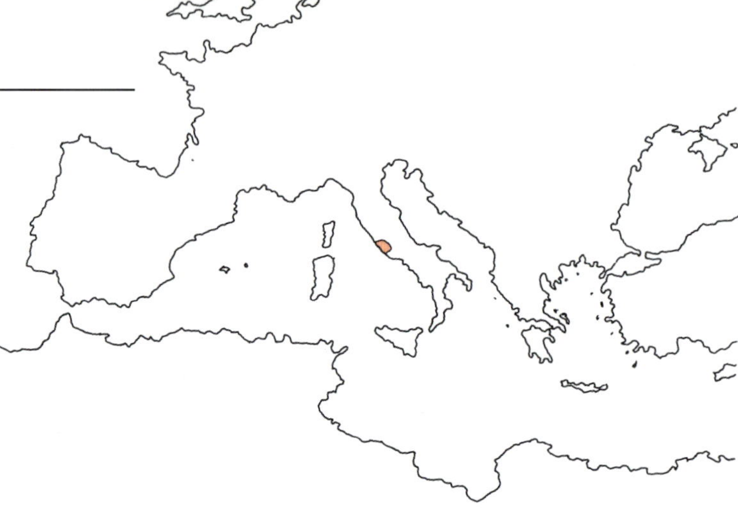

ORIGINS

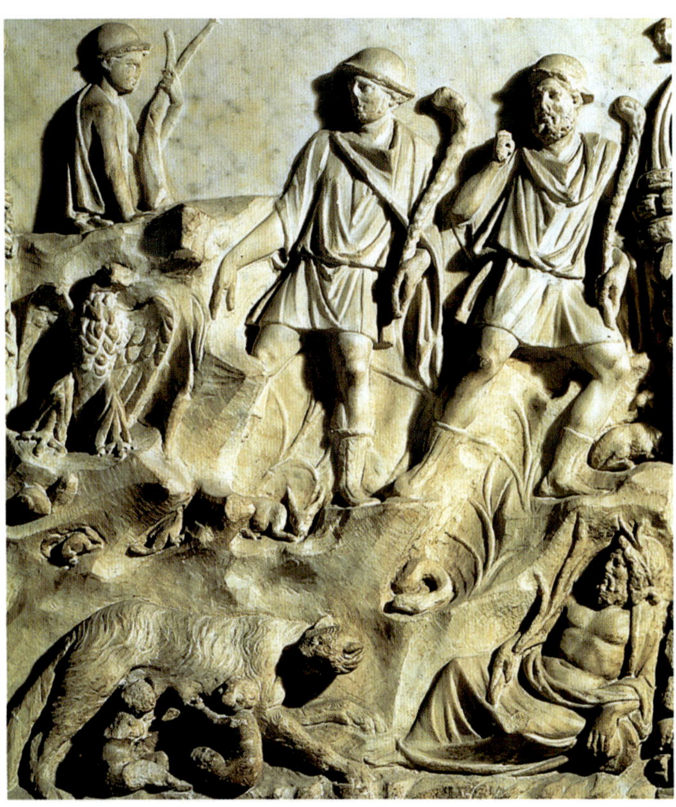

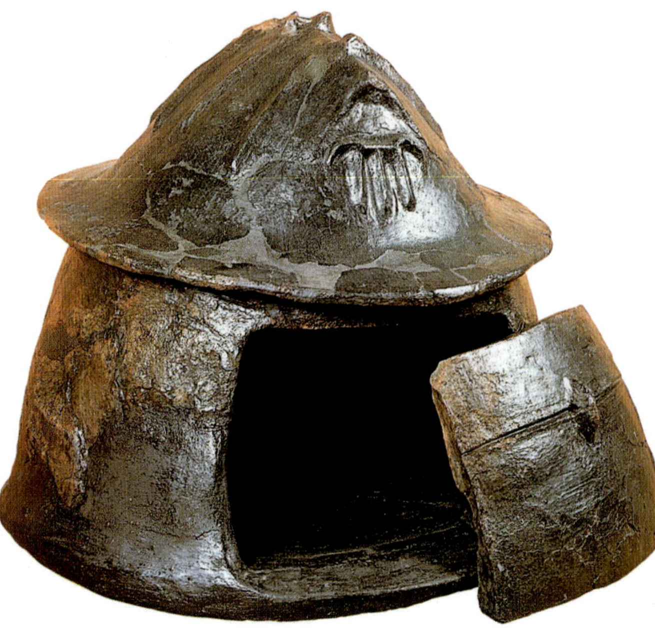

In the 8th century BC, Latium was inhabited by a population of shepherds and farmers, the Latins. They occupied the plains and coastal areas of the region in numerous scattered villages. Independent from one another, they were united in religious associations and open to cultural influences from the Etruscans and Greeks who had settled in the neighbouring areas.

One of these villages, Rome, was built in a favourable position for trade, situated on the River Tiber at a point where it was particularly easy to ford. Ruled by a king, Rome reached a level of development that already distinguished it from the other Latin communities. The four legendary pre-Etruscan kings are said to have been responsible for various acts which, though difficult to date, paved the way for the future power of Rome.

Tradition has it that Romulus, after founding the city in 753 BC (the conventional date proposed by Varro, a scholar of the time of Julius Caesar), established the senate and increased the population by allowing the Sabines to settle in Rome; Numa Pompilius organized religious life, set up the Colleges of Priests and reformed the calendar by dividing the year into 12 months; Tullius Hostilius (673–642 BC) destroyed the rival city of Alba Longa, thereby extending Rome's rule; and Ancus Martius (641–617 BC) built the first bridge over the Tiber and founded the colony of Ostia at its mouth, thus creating a port for Rome.

Towards the end of the 7th century BC Rome came under the dominion of the Etruscans, who pushed through Latium to Campania. Tradition tells of three Etruscan

22 (left, above) The origins of Rome are still shrouded in mystery. Greek historians included Rome among the towns founded by the Trojan hero Aeneas, who fled to Italy after the fall of Troy, while the first Roman historian, Fabius Pictor, recounted the legend of Romulus and Remus, which is illustrated on this altar dating from the 2nd century AD. The twins, who were the sons of Mars and Vestal Virgin Rhea Silvia, were abandoned in a basket on the Tiber but were saved by a she-wolf and brought up by the shepherd Faustulus. When they grew up they punished the usurper Amulius, and Romulus, who laid the foundations of Rome, became the first king of the city.

22 (left, below) Numerous hut-shaped cremation urns, such as this one, have been found in tombs excavated in the area of the Roman Forum. Dating from the 10th to 8th centuries BC, they are of particular interest because they portray, in a stylized way, the homes typical of the earliest Roman settlement.

23 (opposite) The famous Apollo of Veii is attributed to Vulca, the only Etruscan artist whose name survives; he was summoned to Rome by Tarquinius Priscus to create the statue of Jupiter for the Capitoline Temple.

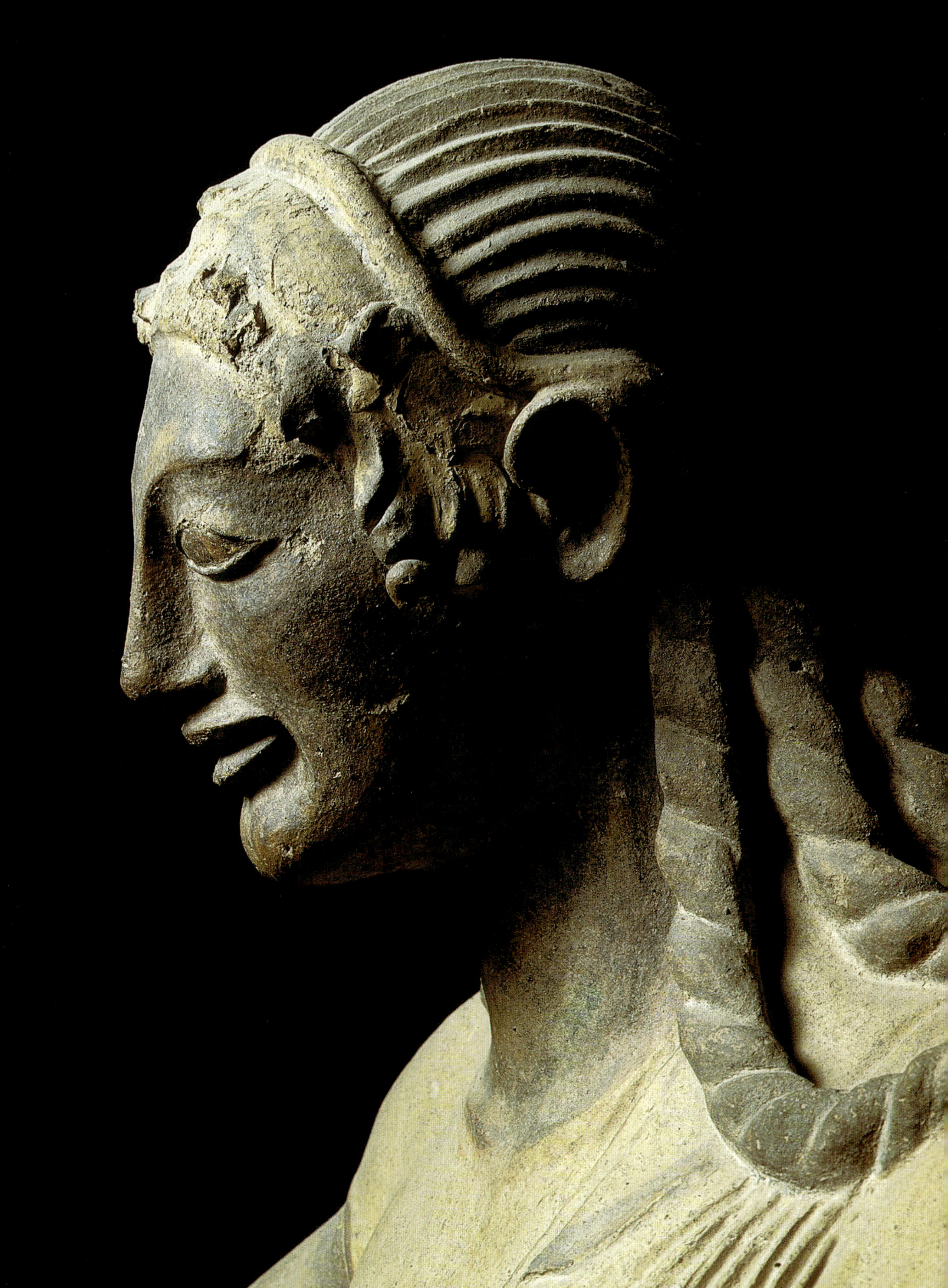

kings: Tarquinius Priscus (616–579 BC), Servius Tullius (578–535 BC) and Tarquinius Superbus (Tarquin the Proud, 534–509 BC). Rome was prospering, and was transformed from an agricultural town into a centre of trade and commerce. Society was made up of patricians – members of rich and powerful families – and plebeians – the humbler sections of the population.

The king exercised power in the religious, political, military, judicial and legislative fields, but left some authority to two consultative bodies: the senate (representatives of the leading families) and the *comitia curiata*, an assembly of citizens divided into 30 *curiae*, grouped into three clans and controlled by the patricians. By setting up the *comitia centuriata*, based on the division into centuries, Servius Tullius tried to limit the power of the patricians and help the middle-classes improve their status.

Rome was now extending its rule to the surrounding territory. The city, fortified by walls and embellished with temples and public buildings, was much larger than the other major cities of Latium and Etruria. The expulsion of Tarquin the Proud marked the end of Etruscan rule and the advent of a patrician regime hostile to the rise of the new classes the monarchy had favoured.

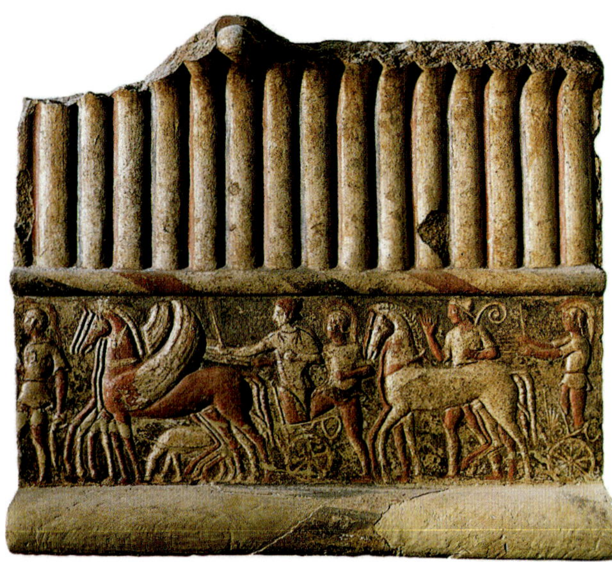

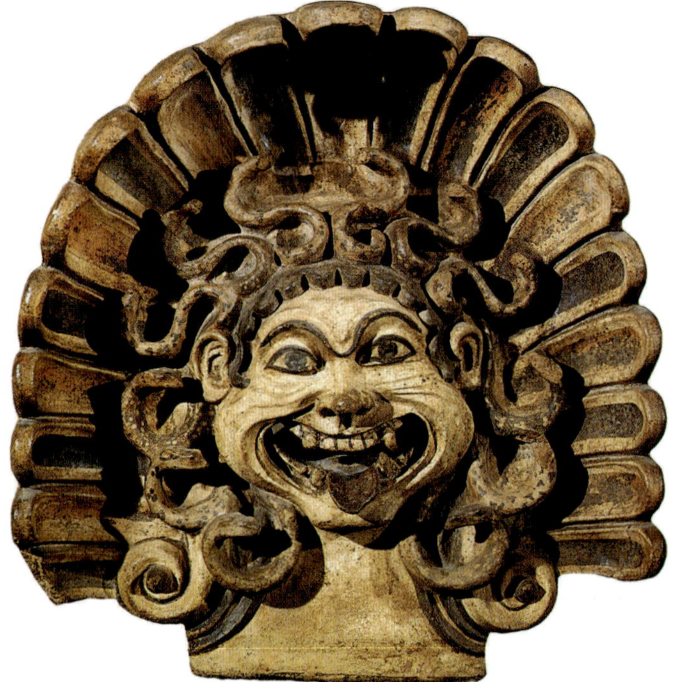

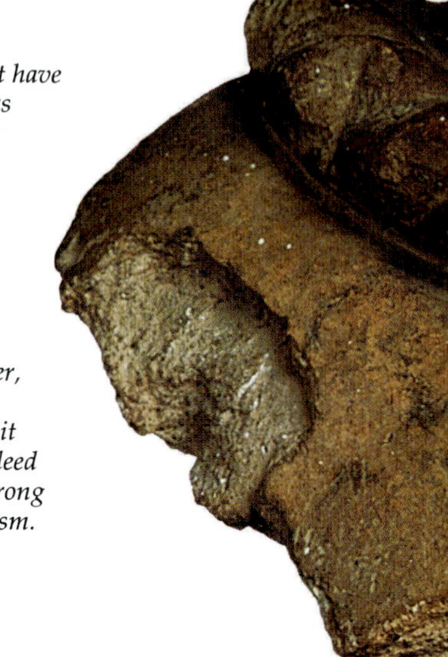

24 Although the last kings of Rome were of Etruscan origin, the city always maintained its independence. It is clear, however, that Roman culture, art and architecture were strongly influenced by their Etruscan counterparts at this early stage. As well as adopting Etruscan ceremonies, symbols of authority, such as the fasces, *and some religious practices, the Romans imported many goods from Etruria. It is clear that numerous Etruscan craftsmen were also summoned to Rome to construct public works and decorate the main temples. The two antefixes and the multicoloured terracotta frieze shown here give some idea of what these decorations must have looked like. It was not until the 4th century BC that Roman art began to break away from Etrusco-Italic art and develop its own original features. However, especially in the case of statuary, it retained, and indeed emphasized, a strong tendency to realism.*

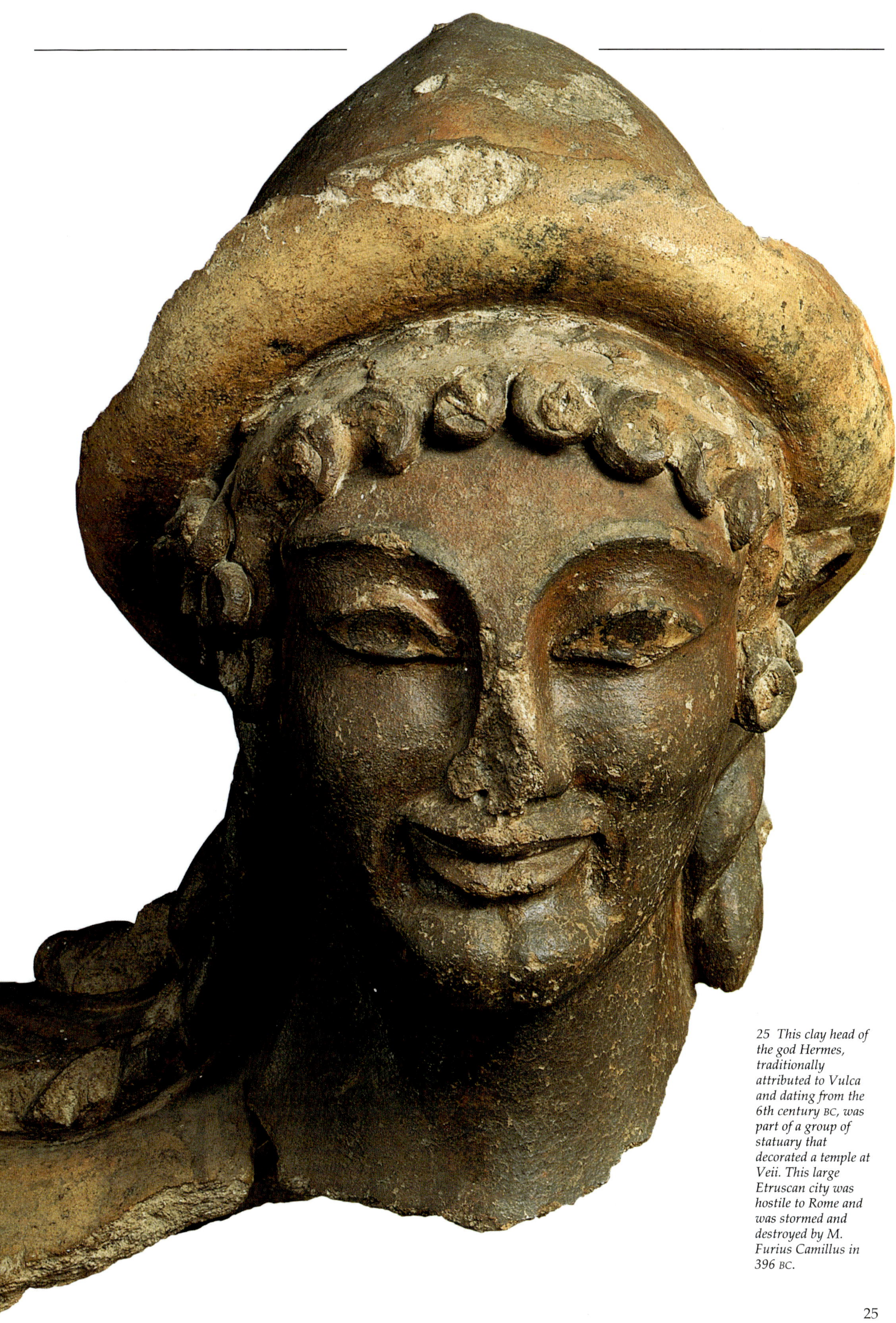

25 This clay head of the god Hermes, traditionally attributed to Vulca and dating from the 6th century BC, *was part of a group of statuary that decorated a temple at Veii. This large Etruscan city was hostile to Rome and was stormed and destroyed by M. Furius Camillus in 396* BC.

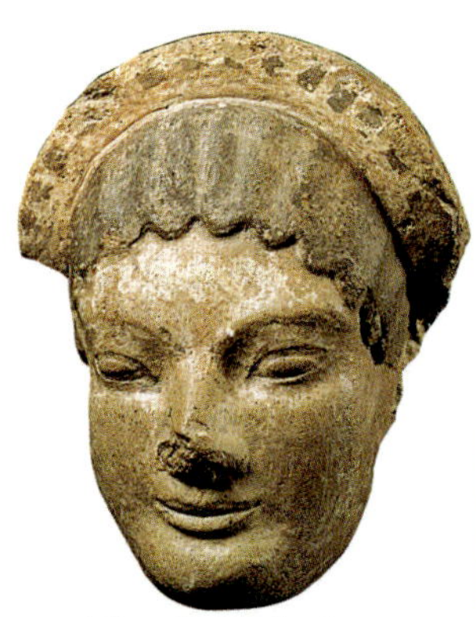

The foundation of Rome and the age of kings: 753–509 BC

According to legend Rome was founded by Romulus, brother of Remus, on 21 April 753 BC. From that date until 509 BC, seven kings are traditionally said to have reigned. Archaeological excavations date the remains of the first settlement of huts on the Palatine Hill, the original nucleus of the Urbs, to the 10th century BC. Around 575 BC two marshy areas by the Tiber were levelled for the construction of the Roman Forum and the Forum Boarium. Rome expanded into Latium, destroying the rival city of Alba Longa. The colony of Ostia was founded at the mouth of the Tiber. Under Tarquinius Priscus, Etruscan domination of Rome and expansion towards Campania began. Society was divided between patricians and plebeians.

Foundation of Rome (753 BC)

Reign of Romulus (753–715 BC)

Reign of Numa Pompilius (715–673 BC)

Reign of Tullius Hostilius (673–642 BC)

Reign of Ancus Martius (641–617 BC)

Reign of Tarquinius Priscus (616–579 BC)

Reign of Servius Tullius (578–535 BC)

Reign of Tarquin the Proud (534–509 BC)

Expulsion of Tarquin the Proud and beginning of the republic (509 BC)

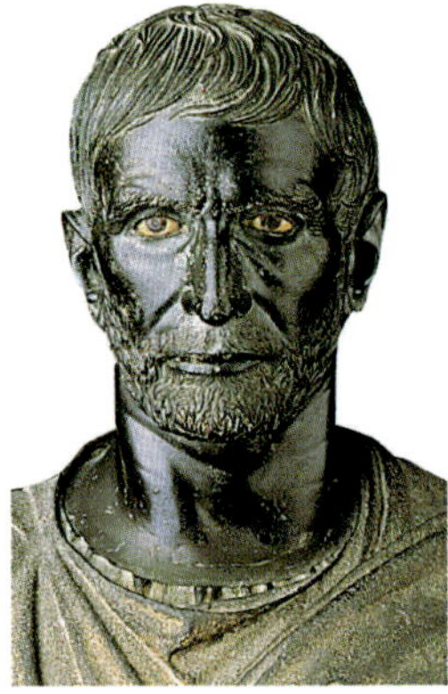

The republic; patricians and plebeians: 509–343 BC

With the expulsion of the Etruscan kings and the election of the first consuls, Lucius Junius Brutus and Lucius Tarquinius Collatinus, the Roman republic came into being. A long period of social strife between patricians and plebeians began. In 493 BC Rome joined the Latin League. In 494 BC the tribunes of the plebs were created and the comitia tributa *established to defend the rights of the less wealthy. The organization of the army into centuries dates to 451 BC. In the same year the first decemvirs were elected, and the Twelve Tables of the Law enacted. The city of Veii was destroyed in 396 BC. Rome was sacked by the Gauls in 390 BC, but soon recovered and continued its policy of expansion. In 367 BC the plebeians gained the right to appoint their own consuls and, later, admission to the main magistratures.*

Roman victory against the Latins at Lake Regillus (496 BC)

Creation of the tribunes of the plebs (494 BC)

The Twelve Tables of the Law (451 BC)

Marriage between patricians and plebeians allowed (445 BC)

Destruction of Veii (396 BC)

The Gauls burn Rome (390 BC)

Plebeians allowed to hold consular office (367 BC)

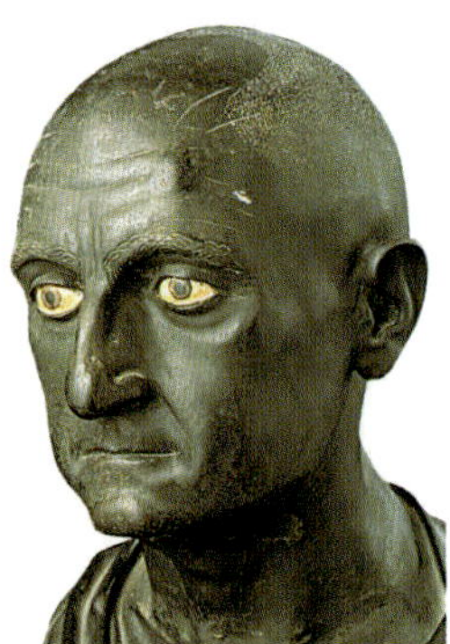

The conquest of Italy and the Punic Wars: 343–146 BC

Between 343 and 341 BC the Romans fought the first war against the Samnites, whose rule extended over southern Italy. In 338 BC the Latin League was dissolved by Rome. During the Second Samnite War the Romans were defeated at the Caudine Forks, but the third and decisive war concluded in 290 BC with victory for Rome. Pyrrhus, King of Epirus, invited to Italy by Tarentum in 280 BC, was defeated five years later at Beneventum. Rome, now expanding rapidly, clashed with Carthage; at the end of the Second Punic War in 201 BC, Rome controlled the Mediterranean. In 146 BC Carthage was razed to the ground; Rome annexed Greece and Macedonia.

Samnite Wars (343–290 BC)

Victory over Pyrrhus (275 BC)

The First Punic War (264–241 BC)

The Romans occupy Sardinia and Corsica (238 BC)

The Romans occupy Cisalpine Gaul (222 BC)

The Second Punic War (218–201 BC)

The Romans institute the Hispanic provinces (197 BC)

The Third Punic War and the destruction of Carthage (149–146 BC)

The destruction of Corinth; Macedonia and Greece become Roman (146 BC)

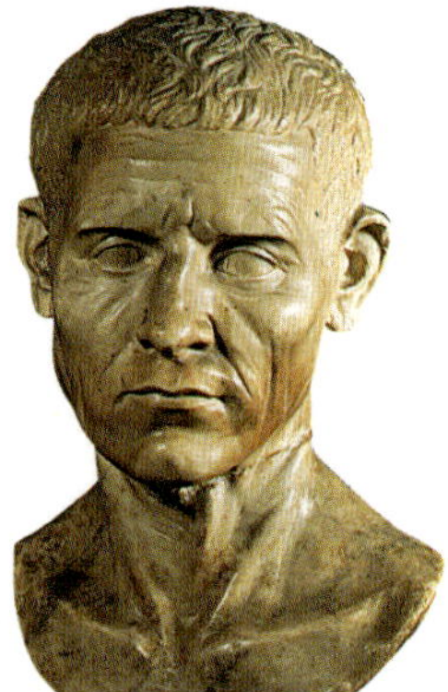

The crisis facing the republic: 146–78 BC

The province of Asia was constituted in 130 BC. The republic was racked by social conflict – Tiberius Gracchus, the tribune, challenged the authority of the senate and endeavoured to introduce agricultural reforms, but was assassinated. Gaius Gracchus, tribune of the plebs in 123 and 122 BC, confirmed the laws proposed by his brother, but was also killed. Transalpine Gaul was conquered between 125 and 121 BC. The Jugurthine War was won in 105 BC by Gaius Marius, who reorganized the army in the same year. Between 91 and 88 BC Rome fought the Social War against its Italic allies, to whom Roman citizenship was eventually granted. General Lucius Cornelius Sulla became dictator and reformed the constitution, re-establishing the absolute authority of the senate.

Assassination of Tiberius Gracchus (133 BC)

Assassination of Gaius Gracchus (121 BC)

War against Jugurtha (111–105 BC)

Marius defeats the Teutones and Cimbri (102–101 BC)

Social War (91–88 BC)

Death of Gaius Marius (86 BC)

Sulla wins the First Mithradatic War (87–85 BC)

Sulla becomes dictator (82 BC)

Sulla dies at Pompeii (78 BC)

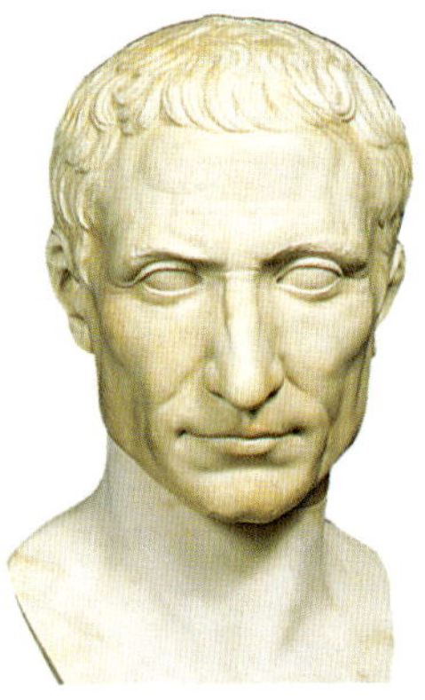

The age of Caesar and the end of the republic: 78–44 BC

Rome experienced a period of social upheaval, and the senatorial oligarchy was increasingly weakened. Pompey, elected consul in 70 BC, conquered Pontus, Bithynia and Palestine in 64 BC. In 63 BC Cicero foiled the Catiline conspiracy. Caesar, Pompey and Crassus formed the First Triumvirate, a coalition against the power of the senate, in 60 BC. Between 58 and 51 BC Caesar conquered Gaul. On the death of Crassus in 52 BC, Pompey became sole consul, with the support of the senatorial party. In 49 BC the senate ordered Caesar to disband the legions, but he crossed the River Rubicon and marched on Rome, thus initiating the Civil War. Pompey was defeated at Pharsalus and fled to Egypt, where he was killed. In 45 BC Caesar finally defeated Pompey's supporters at Munda. In February of 44 BC he was appointed dictator for life, but was assassinated on 15 March by conspirators led by Brutus and Cassius.

Consulship of Pompey and Crassus (70 BC)

Conspiracy of Catiline (63 BC)

First Triumvirate (60 BC)

Caesar conquers Gaul (58–51 BC)

Civil War breaks out (49 BC)

Battle of Pharsalus and death of Pompey (48 BC)

Caesar defeats Pompey's supporters at Munda (45 BC)

Caesar assassinated (44 BC)

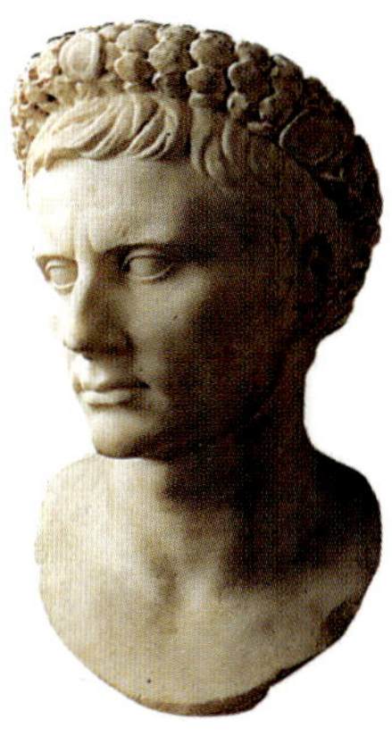

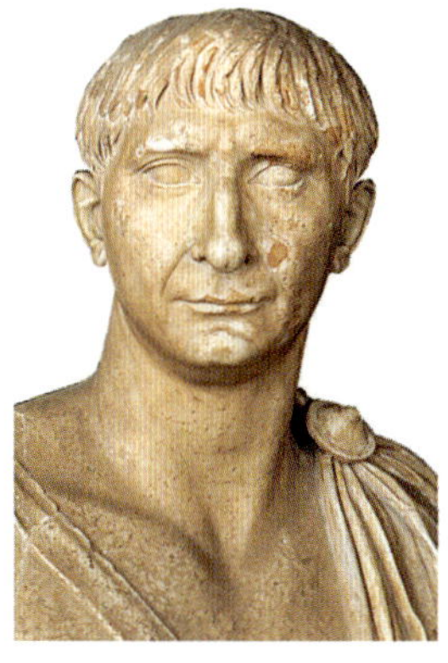

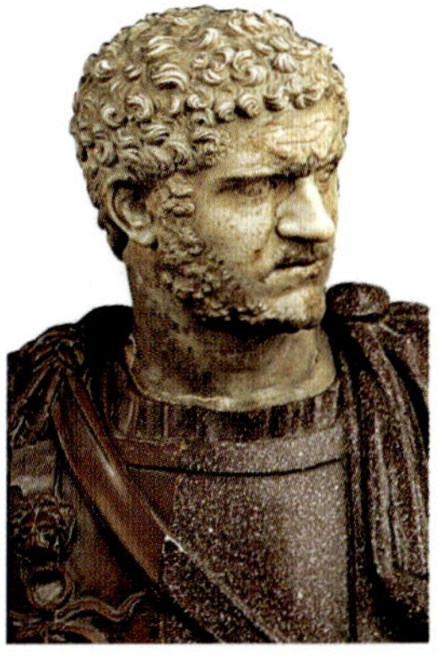

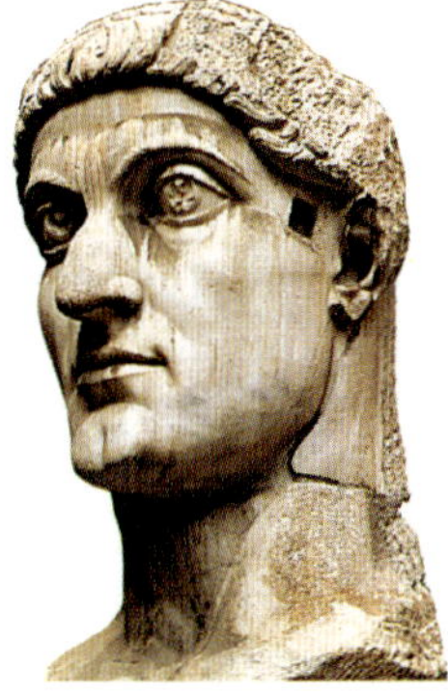

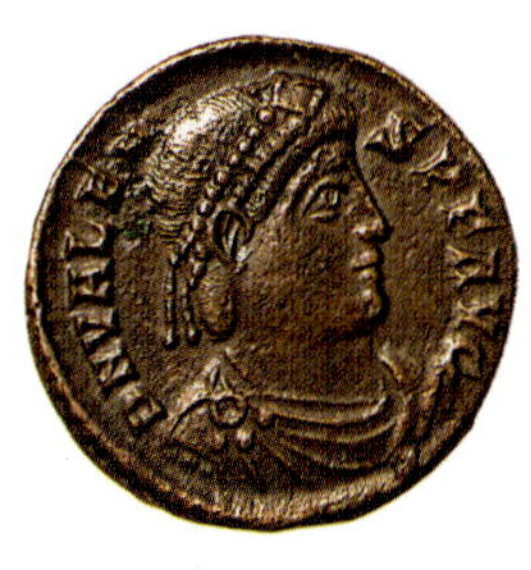

Augustus and the Julio-Claudian dynasty: 44 BC–AD 68

With the battle of Actium, when the forces of Octavian defeated those of Antony and Cleopatra, the struggle for the succession to Caesar ended and the imperial age began. Octavian, who received the title of Augustus from the Senate in 27 BC, reorganized the political structures of the state and concentrated all the major powers in his own hands; he limited the role of the senate, reorganized the provinces, strengthened the borders and boosted the economy. On his death in AD 14 he was succeeded by Tiberius, who was a good administrator and skilled diplomat. After the troubled reign of Caligula, Claudius undertook bureaucratic and financial reform of the state and the Romanization of the provinces. His successor, Nero, is infamous for his excesses and is accused of the burning of Rome.

Second Triumvirate (43 BC)

Battle of Actium (31 BC)

Octavian receives the title of Augustus (27 BC)

Death of Augustus (AD 14)

Reign of Tiberius (AD 14–37)

Crucifixion of Jesus Christ (AD 33)

Reign of Caligula (AD 37–41)

Reign of Claudius (AD 41–54)

Reign of Nero (AD 54–68)

The Flavian dynasty and the adopted emperors: AD 68–192

On the death of Nero a period of military anarchy ensued, during which the emperors Galba, Otho and Vitellius reigned in quick succession. After Vespasian seized power, he conquered Judaea and reorganized the administration of the state. After the brief reign of Titus, Domitian consolidated the Roman conquests in Britannia and Germany. By adopting Trajan, Nerva initiated the series of adopted emperors. The victorious military campaigns of Trajan took the empire to the its greatest extent. Hadrian reversed the expansionist policy of his predecessor and built Hadrian's Wall in Britannia. The reign of Antoninus Pius coincided with a long period of peace, while Marcus Aurelius had to put down a number of revolts in Africa, Spain and Britannia. With the accession of Commodus, a serious political crisis began.

Reign of Vespasian (AD 69–79)

Reign of Titus (AD 79–81)

Eruption of Vesuvius (AD 79)

Reign of Domitian (AD 81–96)

Reign of Trajan (AD 98–117)

Dacian Wars (AD 101–106)

Reign of Hadrian (AD 117–138)

Reign of Antoninus Pius (AD 138–161)

Reign of Marcus Aurelius (AD 161–180)

Reign of Commodus (AD 180–192)

The Severan dynasty and the period of anarchy: AD 193–284

After the short reign of Pertinax, Septimius Severus became emperor with the support of his legions. He promoted the policy of appointing Romanized provincials to government office, but this reform and an increase in military expenditure created discontent and weakened the economy. On his death, his despotic, bloodthirsty son Caracalla became emperor. In order to rule he bought the favour of the army, thus further depleting the state coffers. In AD 212, with the Constitutio Antoniniana, he granted Roman citizenship to all free citizens of the empire. His assassin Macrinus reigned for only a short time. Heliogabalus introduced the worship of oriental gods to Rome. The rule of the mild Alexander Severus was marked by wars against the Persians. In AD 235 a long period of military anarchy began; the title of emperor was disputed by numerous generals, while barbarians massed at the borders.

Reign of Septimius Severus (AD 193–211)

Reign of Caracalla (AD 211–217)

Enactment of the Constitutio Antoniniana (AD 212)

Reign of Macrinus (AD 217–218)

Reign of Heliogabalus (AD 218–222)

Reign of Alexander Severus (AD 222–235)

Period of anarchy and disorder (AD 235–284)

The late empire and the division of power: AD 284–337

In AD 284 the reign of Diocletian began. He initiated a series of reforms, culminating in the division of the empire and the institution of the Tetrarchy. However, when he retired to Split, persuading Maximian (to whom he had entrusted the west) to abdicate too, the succession mechanism failed to work, and a struggle for power began. The usurpers Constantine and Maxentius took to the field of battle (AD 312); Constantine was the victor and proclaimed freedom of worship for the Christians in the Edict of Milan. His agreement with Licinius, Augustus of the east, was short-lived. The rivalry between the two degenerated into civil war, and in AD 324 Constantine eliminated his rival and took the title of the sole Augustus. In AD 330 he proclaimed Constantinople the capital of the empire. On his death, the empire was divided between his sons.

Reign of Diocletian (AD 284–305)

Diocletian institutes the Tetrarchy (AD 293)

Collapse of the Tetrarchy (AD 306)

Battle of the Milvian Bridge (AD 312)

Edict of Milan (AD 313)

Constantine unifies east and west (AD 324)

Constantinople becomes the capital (AD 330)

Death of Constantine; division of the empire between Constantius II, Constantine and Constans (AD 337)

The decline and fall of the empire in the west: AD 337–476

Constantius II, who fought against the Persians, was succeeded by Julian the Apostate, who attempted to restore paganism. Valens was killed at the battle of Hadrianopolis (AD 378) against the Goths. Theodosius reunited the empire and allowed numerous barbarian communities to settle inside its borders as foederati *(allies). In the Edict of Thessalonica (AD 380) he proclaimed Christianity to be the only state religion. On his death, the empire was divided between his sons: Honorius took the west, and Arcadius the east. The western capital was transferred to Ravenna (AD 402). Rome was sacked by the Goths in AD 410. Valentinian III reigned under the regency of his mother, Galla Placidia, but by now the unity of the empire in the west was disintegrating. In AD 452 the Huns invaded Italy. The deposition of Romulus Augustulus (AD 476) marked the end of the Roman empire in the west.*

Constantius II reunites the empire (AD 353–361)

Reign of Julian the Apostate (AD 361–363)

Valens defeated at Adrianopole (AD 378)

Reign of Theodosius (AD 379–395)

Alaric sacks Rome (AD 410)

Attila invades Italy (AD 452)

The fall of the Roman empire in the west (AD 476)

BATTLES BETWEEN PATRICIANS AND PLEBEIANS; ROME CONQUERS ITALY

Tarquin's expulsion was followed by a period of internal and external conflicts. Internally, a struggle took place between the patricians – whose power had increased by exiling the king – and the plebeians who, though they had lost the support of the monarchy, were becoming aware of their own strength. In addition to economic power, the patricians held political power through the senate, the civil and religious magistratures and control of the law, which was handed down by oral tradition.

Important stages in the plebeians' campaign to participate in political life were the election of their own assembly and magistrates – tribunes of the plebs; the appointment of the decemvirs to draft a written code of laws, the Twelve Tables; the setting up of the *comitia tributa*, which had a legislative function and was open to the plebeians; and gaining access to various magistratures. A series of laws limited the power of the rich through the gradual elimination of their political and economic domination and allowed the rise of a nobility – *nobiles* – which included the wealthier plebeian families.

The young republic was soon forced to defend itself against its neighbours. At the same time an expansionist drive enabled it to dominate the entire peninsula in just over two centuries. The political and military rise of Rome had two main phases: first in Latium, between the fall of the monarchy and the Gallic invasion (509–390 BC); and then over the entire peninsula, against the Etruscans and Gauls in the north, and the Umbrians, Samnites and Greek towns further south. A significant event was the defeat of the Latins at Lake Regillus in 496 BC. This was followed by gradual domination of neighbouring populations (the Aequi, Volsci and Hernici), the elimination of the Etruscan threat culminating with the destruction of Veii in 396 BC, and finally the three Samnite wars between 343 and 290 BC. One consequence of this was the constitution of a Roman-Latin federal state and dominion over a huge territory with numerous flourishing colonies. The conquest of the Samnites brought the Romans into contact with the Greek towns on the Ionian Sea, on which the nearby Hellenistic kingdom of Epirus had also set its sights. In 280 BC Pyrrhus of Epirus landed in Italy with his army to support Tarentum and other minor towns. However, the Romans, despite some setbacks, eventually prevailed, forcing the enemy to retreat and the Greek towns to submit. By the second half of the 3rd century BC, Rome had become the ruler of Italy, from the Arno and the Rubicon in the north to the Strait of Messina in the south. Meanwhile, the struggle between patricians and plebeians and the transformation of Rome from small city-state to the capital of a confederation of peoples radically modified the Roman state. The power base was theoretically held by various people's assemblies – the *comitia curiata, comitia centuriata, comitia tributa* and the council of the plebs; in practice, however, real power was exercised by the senate, made up of members of the richest and most important families. Executive power was held by the magistrates: consuls, praetors, censors, aediles, quaestors and tribunes of the plebs.

36 The obverse of this republican gold coin, minted in Rome, portrays Mars, god of war, while the reverse shows an eagle. Mars was originally the god of spring and the harvest, and his transformation from tutelary deity of agriculture to war god graphically reflects the development of the Roman people from a settled population of farmers to an expansionist race.

37 (opposite) Lucius Junius Brutus was honoured as the man who freed Rome from the tyranny of the Etruscan kings and initiated the republic. This sculpture, by an Italic bronze worker of the 4th century BC, is traditionally identified as a portrait of him. In practice, as with all supposed images of leading figures from the earliest period of Roman history, this is entirely conjectural.

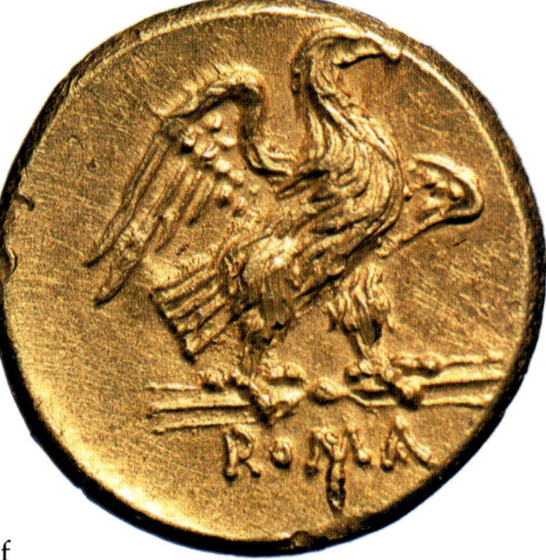

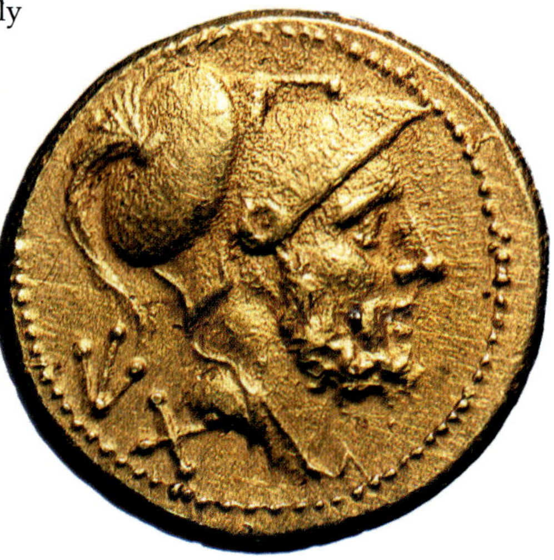

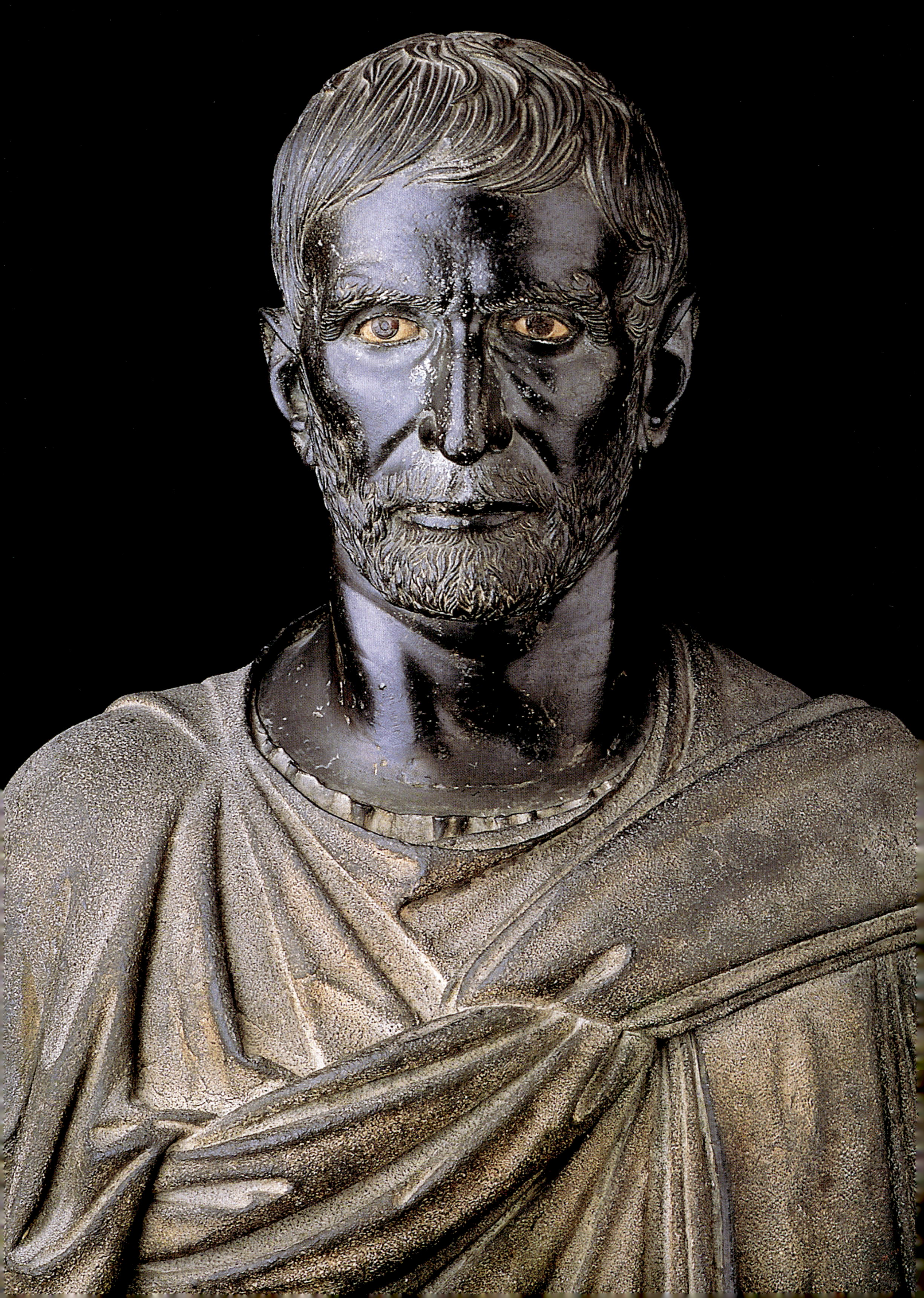

THE PUNIC WARS AND DOMINION OF THE MEDITERRANEAN

Having extended its rule to the Greek towns of Italy, Rome inevitably soon came into conflict with the power that held sway over much of the Mediterranean – Carthage. By the beginning of the 3rd century BC, Carthage dominated the African coast as far as Egypt and also the Spanish coast in the west; its contacts reached south along the Atlantic coast of Africa and north as far as Cornwall. Carthaginian interests mainly revolved around trade, served by a great fleet which was also equipped for military actions, ready to intervene whenever required. Sardinia, Corsica and western Sicily were under the control of Carthage, but it left the coasts of Italy alone under the terms of treaties concluded first with the Etruscans and then with the Romans.

Conflict between the two powers began in Sicily, home of Greeks who had been rivals of the Carthaginians for centuries and were allied with their fellow-citizens in southern Italy, now ruled by Rome. The Punic Wars were fought over several decades, with the Romans gaining the upper hand on land and sea. During the first war, the Romans won great naval victories at Mylae in 260 BC and the Aegates Islands in 241 BC. Sicily, and later Sardinia and Corsica, thus came under Roman control. The Second Punic War was dominated by the genius of the Carthaginian general Hannibal; the Roman armies achieved some victories but also suffered some resounding defeats, culminating in the battle of Cannae in 216 BC. Only the intervention of the Scipio family, especially Publius Cornelius Scipio, reversed the fortunes of the war in favour of Rome, which finally defeated Carthage at Zama in 202 BC.

The Roman victory established a new balance of power in the Mediterranean. In the western sector Rome replaced Carthage in control of Spain, while the eastern half was still dominated by the kingdoms of Macedonia, Syria and Egypt, often themselves in conflict. Greece was made up of city-states and leagues of towns in a very unstable system of alliances. Rome could not remain indifferent to such an international situation which, though it presented cause for concern, also offered great opportunities for intervention and expansion. The Romans thus initiated a series of diplomatic and military operations which, in a few years (between 201 and 133 BC), made them the rulers of the entire Mediterranean. These included the Macedonian Wars, culminating in 168 BC with victory at Pydna, the destruction of Corinth in 146 BC, and the siege of Numantia in 133 BC.

Initially Rome governed with a degree of tolerance for the populations under its rule. However, after 168 BC it adopted an unscrupulous policy of direct annexation of territories in line with the capitalist interests of the dominant Roman groups, involving the subjugation and destruction of possible competitors and intensive exploitation of the lands conquered.

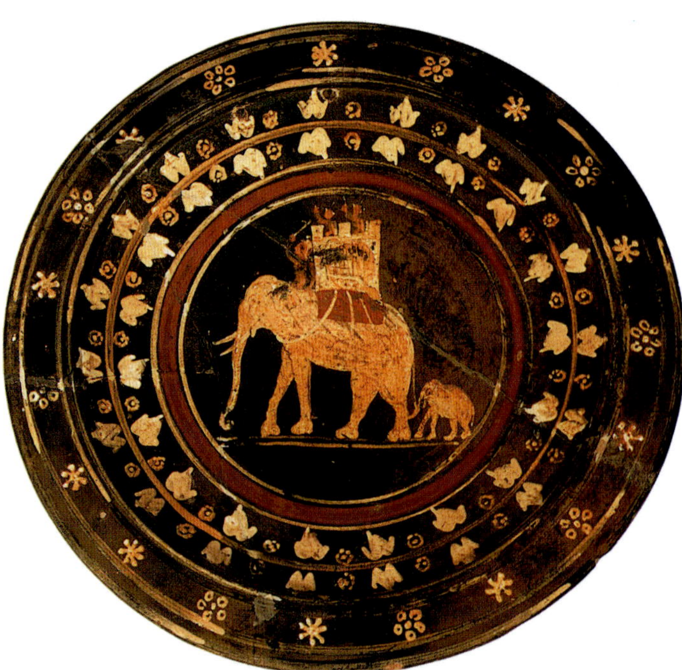

38 (left) Elephants, as portrayed on this Campanian plate of the 3rd century BC, were used for the first time against the Romans by Pyrrhus, King of Epirus. They were also used later by Hannibal, the Carthaginian general who invaded Italy after crossing the Alps in the Second Punic War.

39 (opposite) Publius Cornelius Scipio, shown here in a portrait which emphasizes his strong character, was nicknamed 'the African' after he defeated Hannibal at the battle of Zama, south of Carthage, on 19 October, 202 BC.

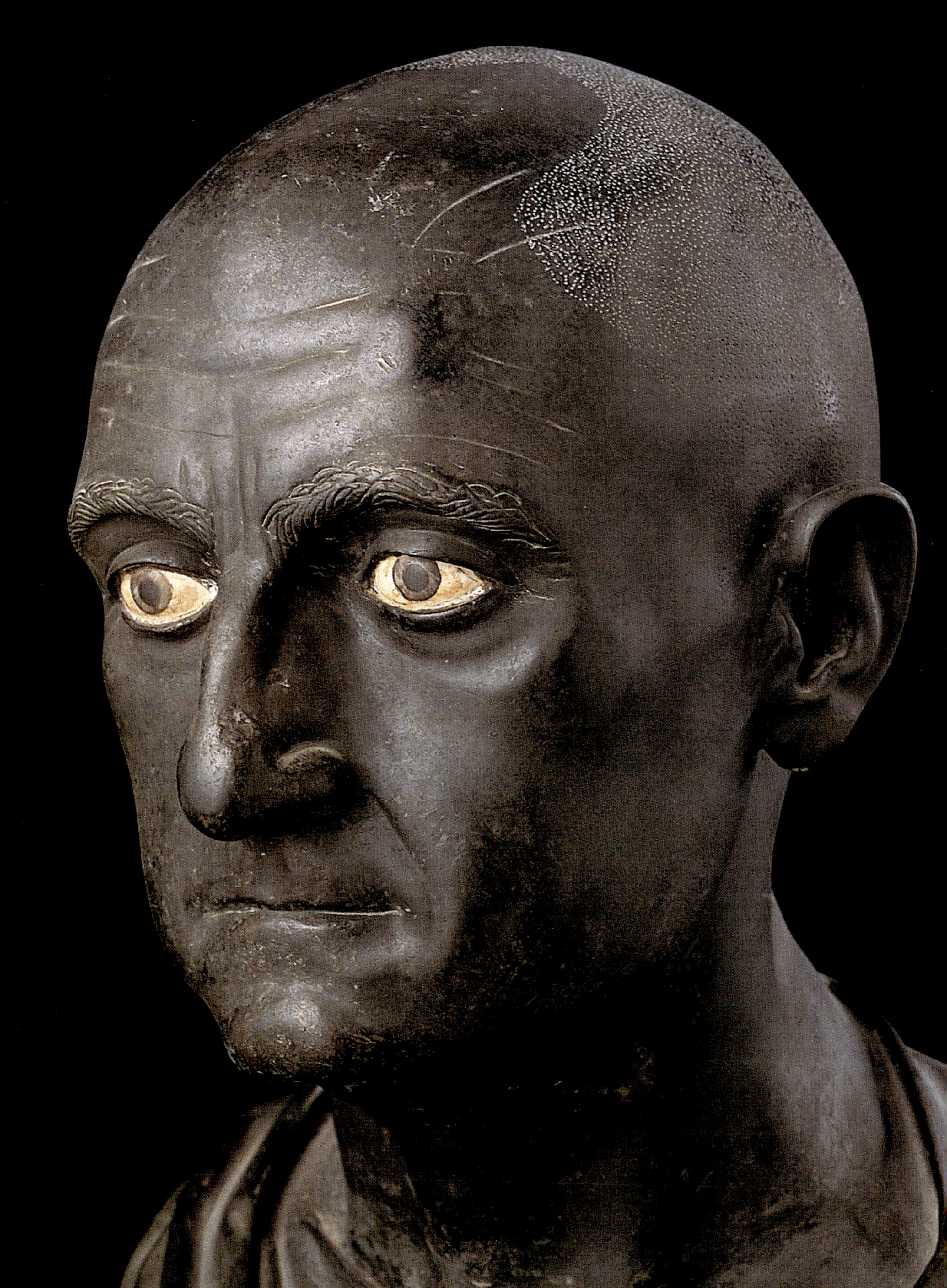

FROM THE GRACCHI TO THE FIRST TRIUMVIRATE: THE REPUBLIC FACES A CRISIS

40 (right) This bronze statue by a Romanized Etruscan craftsman, dating from the 2nd or 1st century BC, portrays a virile character in an oratorical attitude, with his right arm raised in a gesture common among Roman politicians. It is easy to imagine Tiberius Gracchus in the same pose.

40 (below) The great orator and author Marcus Tullius Cicero became the champion of the senatorial class when he thwarted the conspiracy of Catiline, who was supported by the lower classes. On Caesar's death he mistakenly thought he could defend the republic against Antony, who had him killed.

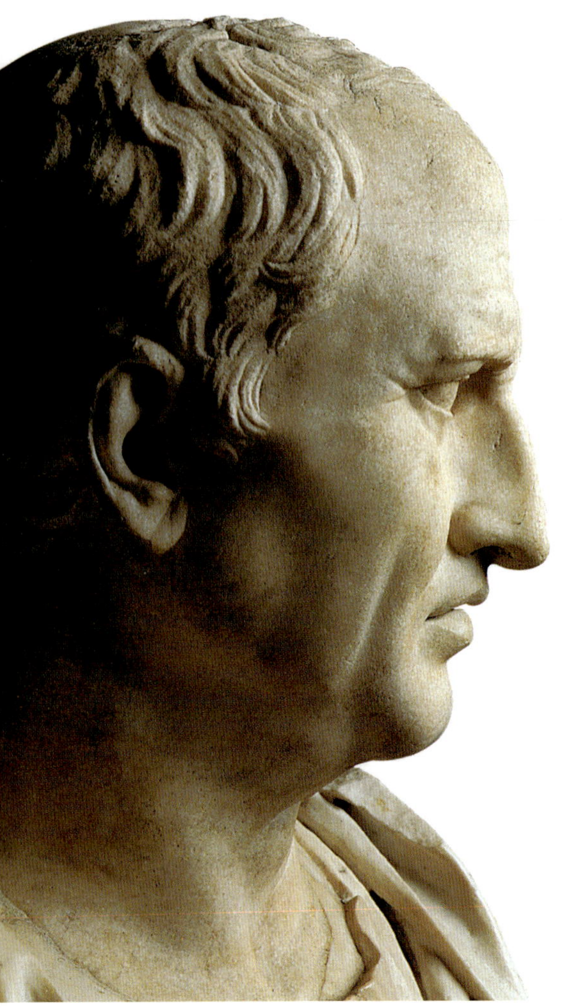

The republic, transformed from a small state to a great Mediterranean power in a very short time, was faced by growing social inequality caused by its conquests. A series of civil clashes paved the way for social and constitutional changes. In 133 BC Tiberius Gracchus, tribune of the plebs, was assassinated, together with many of his supporters, after arousing the violent opposition of the senate. A serious crisis in Roman society followed, with Italics and other provincials aspiring to political power; even Roman citizens, especially small landowners forced into debt by an economic policy which ran contrary to their interests, were pressing for the extension of privileges that had so far only been granted to a few groups. Two personalities emerged during this troubled time: Marius and Sulla. Gaius Marius, an energetic man with no connections to the senatorial class, had been elected consul by the people's party (*populares*), while Lucius Cornelius Sulla was a representative of the conservatives (*optimates*).

Sulla undertook a reform of the state with a conservative, even authoritarian tone. This reform, imposed by force, ignored the serious social problems and did not long survive the death of its creator.

The subsequent period was one of extraordinary vitality for Roman society; major socio-political transformations took place, and the economy and intellectual life both flourished. Sulla's constitution was the last attempt to organize the state on the basis of the domination of the senatorial oligarchy. But the state

41 (opposite, above) Sulla, of patrician origins, had already demonstrated his skills as a general when he was elected consul. In 87 BC he led a Roman expedition against Mithridates in Asia Minor, and in his absence the policies of the people's party brought him into conflict with Gaius Marius. At the end of the ensuing civil war, after eliminating his opponents (partly by the use of proscription lists), he reformed the constitution, which then became more like an oligarchy.

41 (opposite, centre) A skilled general, Gnaeus Pompey received military appointments from Sulla and won a series of outstanding victories against the supporters of the democratic party. On Sulla's death in 78 BC Pompey continued to defend his policies. Having reached an agreement with Crassus in 72 BC, however, he became consul and undertook to abolish Sulla's constitution. In 70 BC he formed the First Triumvirate with Crassus and Caesar, but soon came into conflict with them.

could not survive without the representation of other social forces – the proletariat, soldiers, small businessmen and provincials – all excluded from the exercise of power, to which they could only gain access by joining the dominant class. A different balance could only be achieved by creating a new centre of power to control the senate and guarantee full participation in society to the emerging groups. Notwithstanding resistance from a senatorial class unwilling to relinquish its status, this was achieved, in part by men who were appointed by the senate to protect its interests but who were eventually able to create a consensus – though often in conflict with the senate.

Gnaeus Pompey is emblematic of this period. Despite his earlier allegiances, he was responsible for the abolition of the constitution of Sulla, allowing the traditional political forces to take the field once more. Following some major foreign appointments obtained from the tribunes of the plebs, whose role had been restored, Pompey also annexed new territories. In 63 BC Cicero, a consul and leading representative of the declining senatorial domination, defeated an attempt by Catiline to seize power with a display of oratory that has gone down in history. This did not prevent the men who held the real power, supported by the people's party and their armies, from joining in an alliance against the senate.

The First Triumvirate of Julius Caesar, Crassus and Pompey was formed. With the formal consent of the senate, power was shared with the knights, the people and the army. One outcome of this was the appointment of Caesar as proconsul of Gaul for five years.

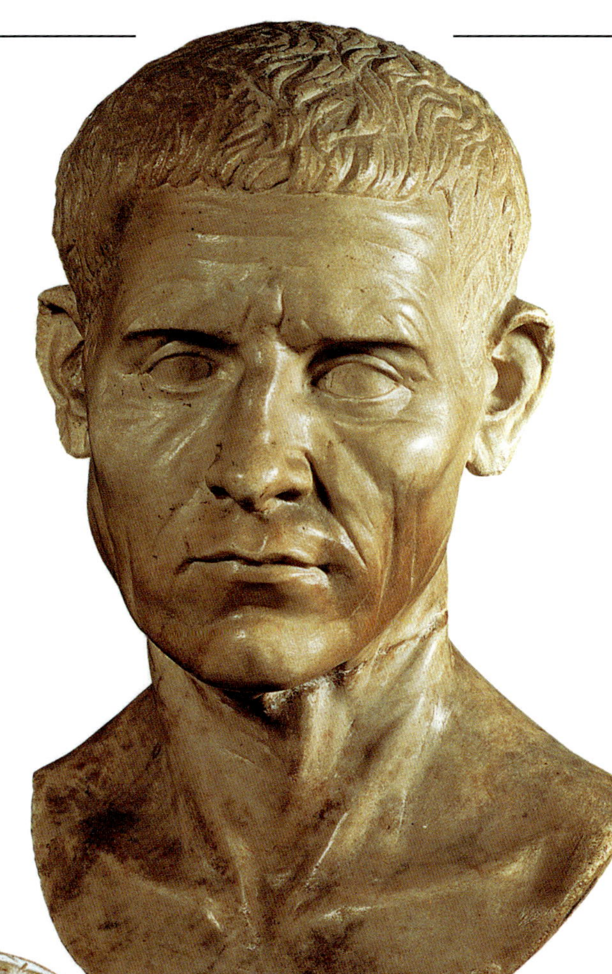

41 (below) Gaius Marius, who came from a peasant family, won major victories against the Cimbri and Teutones, and in the political sphere aimed at striking a balance between the opposing forces. He became a leader of the democrats and found himself in conflict with Sulla (against whom he triumphed for a short period) in a tragic climate of violence. Marius' death in 86 BC, shortly after his election as consul, left the field clear for Sulla, who brutally eliminated all opposition and initiated a reign of terror.

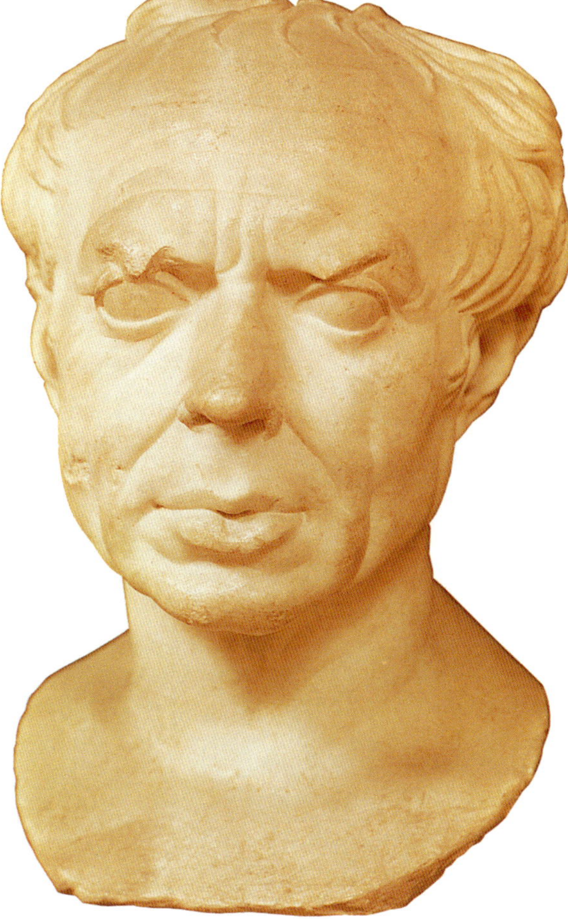

THE AGE OF CAESAR

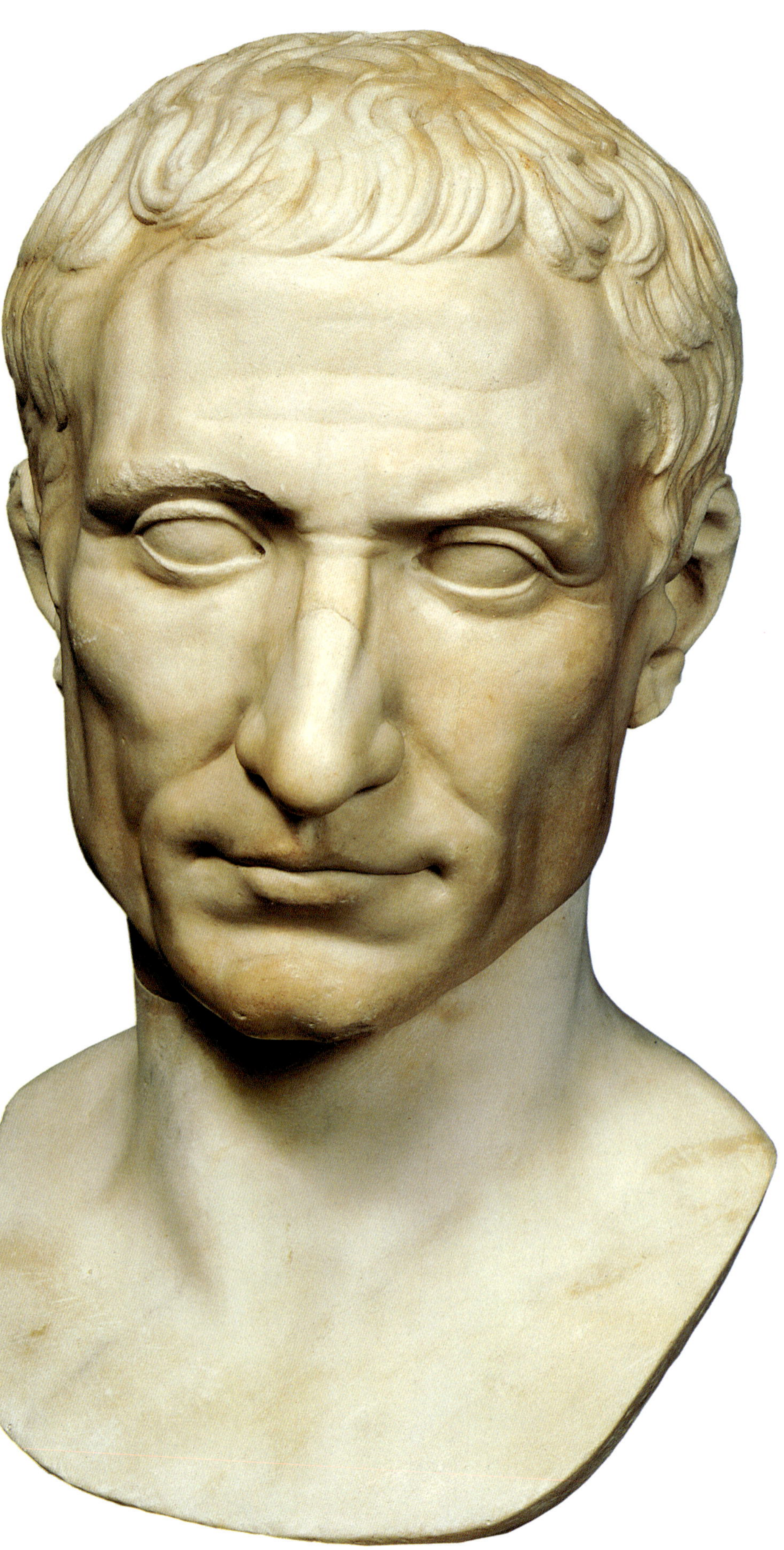

Caesar's conquest of Gaul formed a major extension of Roman rule, and also provided him with the military base for political power. He obtained a five-year extension of his appointment, and went on to win many brilliant military victories, even leading his troops into Britannia and across the Rhine.

In Rome, in the meantime, events which would lead to civil war were unfolding. After the death of Crassus at the battle of Carrhae against the Parthians in 53 BC the Triumvirate was dissolved, and conflict grew between Caesar, whose strength lay in his victories and the support of the people's party, and Pompey, allied with the senatorial party, whose leading representatives were Cicero and Cato.

In 49 BC civil war broke out. The first symbolic act was the crossing of the Rubicon by Caesar, who then marched on Rome with his army. Rapid victories in various parts of the Mediterranean made Caesar the unchallenged victor and enabled him to concentrate all power on himself, resulting in a decline of the senatorial class. However, he was assassinated on 15 March, 44 BC by a group of conspirators led by Brutus and Cassius. The conspirators were vainly attempting to halt a historical process, but now the ball was rolling it could not be stopped merely by the physical elimination of one man, however outstanding. Caesar's heirs were Mark Antony, a consul, and his nephew and adopted son Octavian. These men had very different temperaments. Octavian thought that power should not be based on the model of a Hellenistic type of

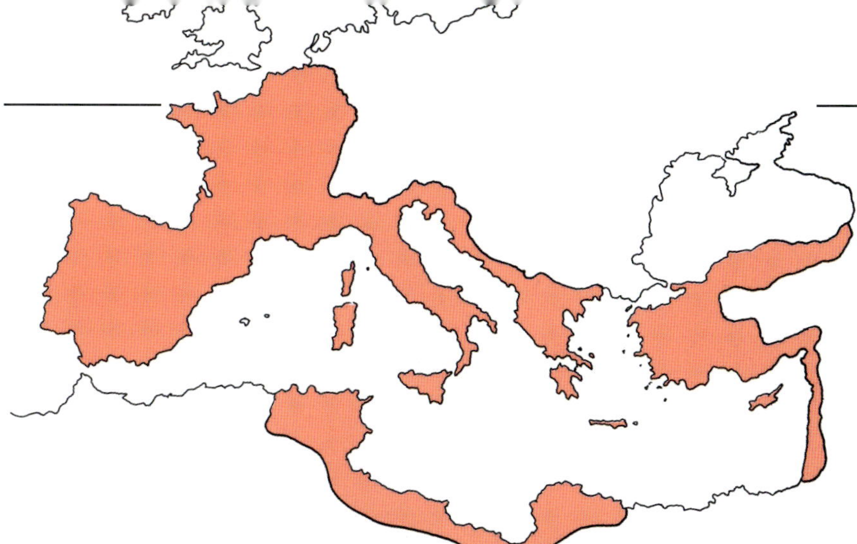

monarchy, but should be supported by as wide a consensus as possible, with formal obedience paid to the senate and the republican magistratures. The great orator Cicero made an anachronistic attempt to re-establish the authority of the senate by declaring Antony an enemy of the state, but paid for it with his life. Octavian and Antony, together with Aemilius Lepidus (who was soon excluded), formed the Second Triumvirate. After defeating the assassins Brutus and Cassius at Philippi in 42 BC, they divided the empire: Octavian took the west, and Antony the east.

The time was now ripe for government by one man – the most able. Octavian triumphed by defeating Antony at Actium in 31 BC, and skilfully began the task of reconstructing the state.

42 (opposite) Julius Caesar, born in 100 BC, came from an ancient patrician family. He soon attracted the enmity of Sulla, but after the latter's death he embarked on an outstanding political and military career. In 60 BC he joined forces with Pompey and Crassus, and two years later he began the Gallic campaign, which ended victoriously in 52 BC. After the death of Crassus he came into conflict with Pompey, who died in the attempt to oppose him. He won the civil war at the battle of Munda but was assassinated in 44 BC after being made dictator for life.

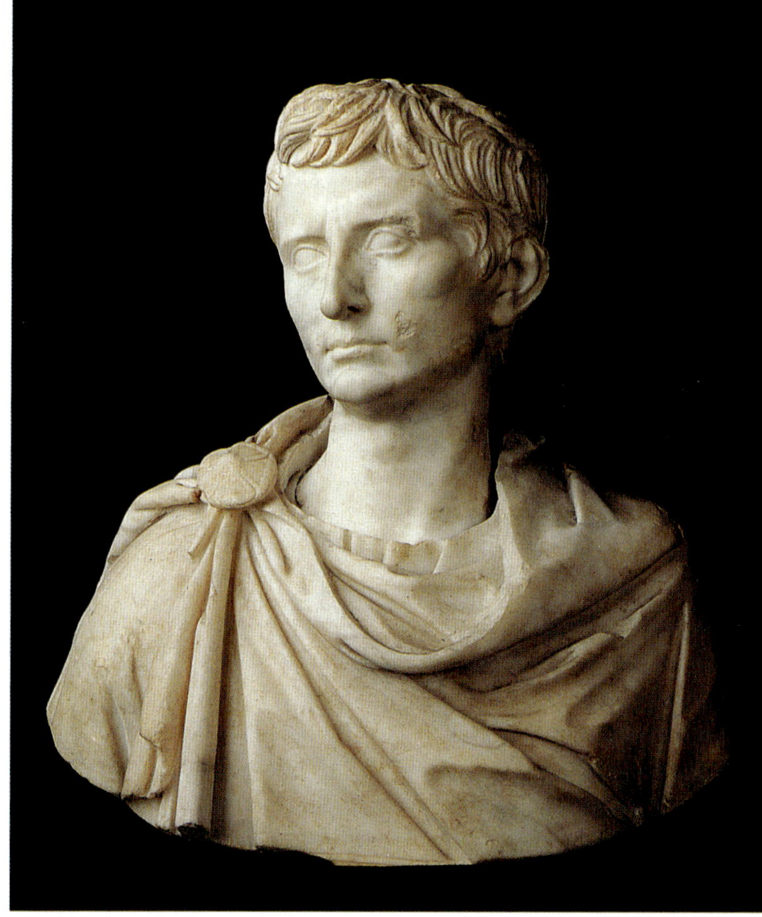

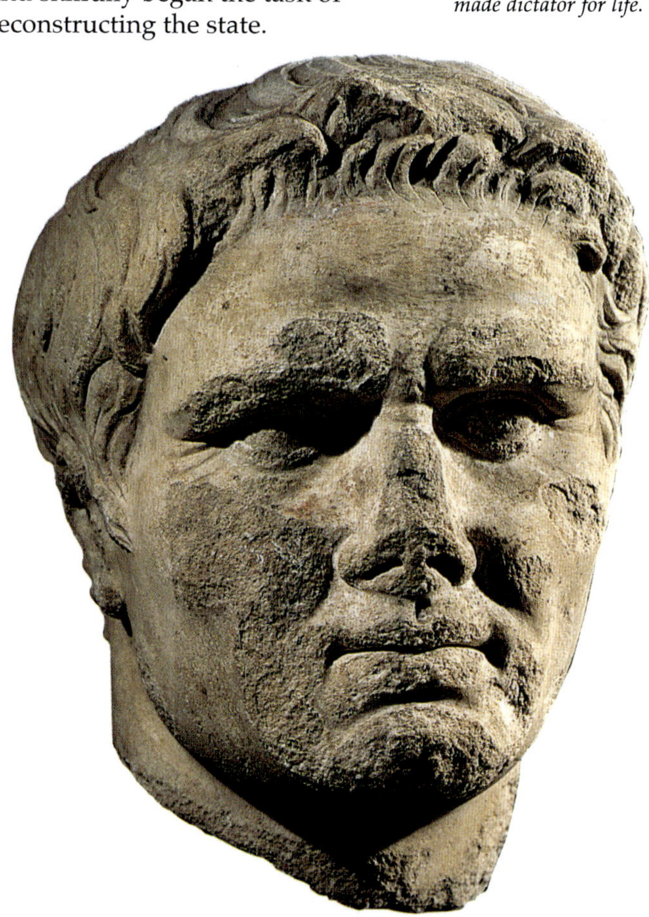

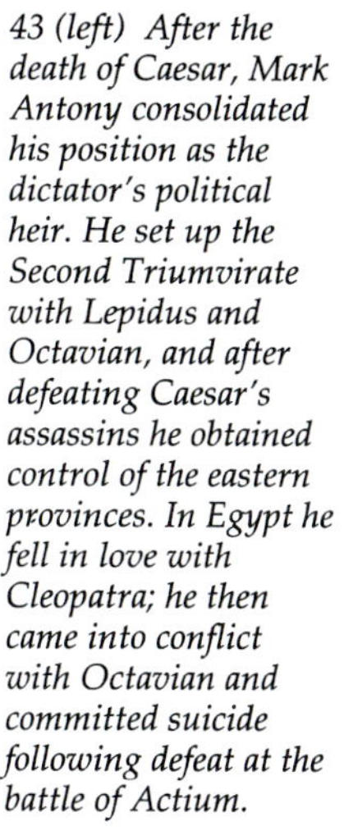

43 (left) After the death of Caesar, Mark Antony consolidated his position as the dictator's political heir. He set up the Second Triumvirate with Lepidus and Octavian, and after defeating Caesar's assassins he obtained control of the eastern provinces. In Egypt he fell in love with Cleopatra; he then came into conflict with Octavian and committed suicide following defeat at the battle of Actium.

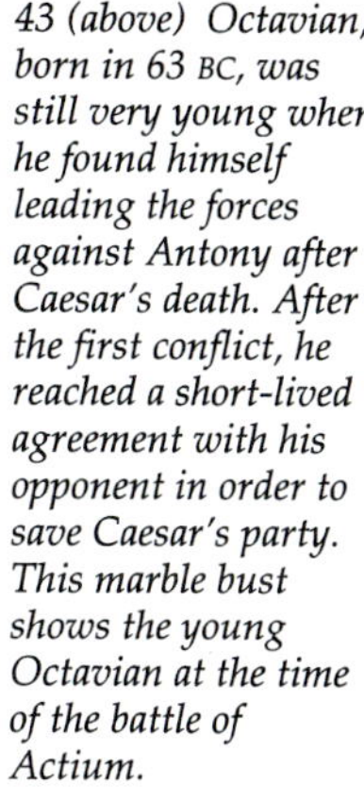

43 (above) Octavian, born in 63 BC, was still very young when he found himself leading the forces against Antony after Caesar's death. After the first conflict, he reached a short-lived agreement with his opponent in order to save Caesar's party. This marble bust shows the young Octavian at the time of the battle of Actium.

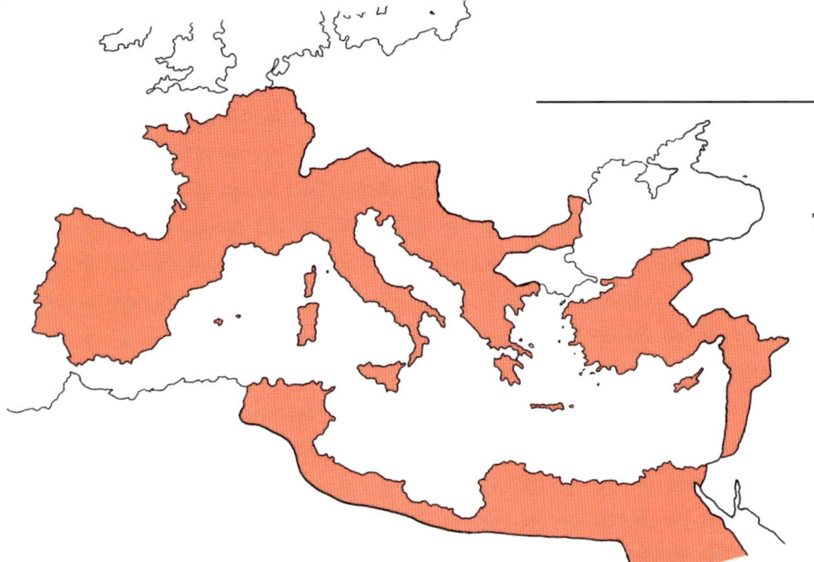

THE EMPIRE

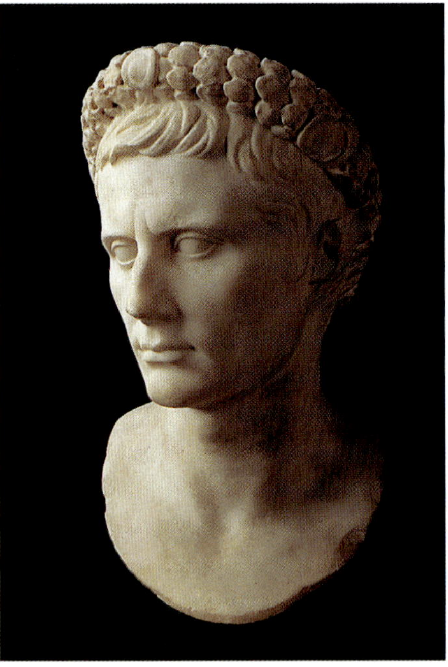

44 (right) After defeating Mark Antony in battle, Octavian returned to Rome, celebrated his victory and declared the period of the civil wars over. From that time onwards he worked to consolidate his personal power, moving the Roman state towards the status of an empire. The title of Augustus, taken from religious vocabulary and bestowed on him by the Senate in 27 BC, *remained the official title for all the Roman emperors.*

44 (below) This magnificent onyx cameo dating from the reign of Augustus portrays an eagle holding the symbols of victory in its claws. The great bird of prey was considered the emblem of imperial strength. The gold and silver frame dates from the second half of the 16th century.

45 (opposite) Over 80 statues were erected in honour of Augustus in Rome alone, the most famous of which is the Prima Porta statue, named after the place of its discovery. The reliefs on the breastplate allegorically evoke his feats of arms; in particular, the central scene portrays a defeated barbarian delivering a Roman banner, probably lost in battle by another commander, into the hands of the emperor. Octavian's rise to power was facilitated by his influence over the army; his prestige was won on the battlefield, where he consistently demonstrated his skill as a great strategist. By the time of his death in AD *14, the Roman empire was firmly consolidated.*

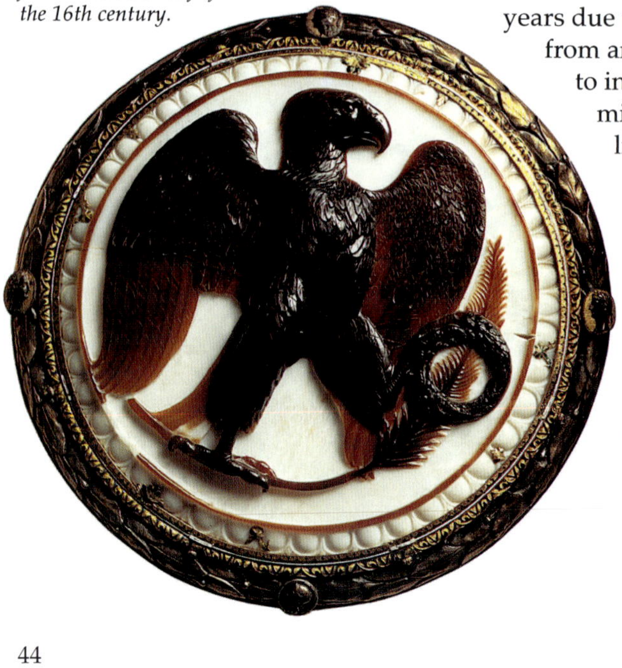

Octavian astutely transformed the Roman state without bloodshed and reigned over an era of internal peace which facilitated the economic and cultural development of the entire empire. As Julius Caesar had done before him, Octavian maintained the appearance of retaining all the magistratures, but actually held the reins of power by conferring a number of key titles and functions on himself. The most important were the *potestas tribunicia*, which gave him the rights of the tribunes such as inviolability and the prestige of representing the people, and the command of the army – *imperium*, hence the title *imperator* (emperor). He accepted the name of Augustus to symbolize his exceptional role.

Augustus reorganized the senatorial and equestrian orders, and divided the provinces into two classes – senatorial and imperial. He set up a special corps of personal bodyguards called the Praetorian Guard, and began a programme of restoration of Rome, neglected for years due to the civil wars. Apart from an unsuccessful attempt to invade Germany his military activities were limited to consolidating the borders, only intervening where resistance remained. As the success of his complex political and administrative reorganization of the state required maximum support from its citizens, instead of focusing on innovations Augustus emphasized the continuity of his political views with those of republican Rome, presenting himself as the restorer of traditional values. In this context he promoted the worship of specifically Roman divinities, and revived forgotten practices and ceremonies. However, this did not prevent the spread of new religious sects, including Christianity, which would change the face of the empire.

Augustus' programme of peace and restoration was widely supported by the intellectuals of the age. The universal peace maintained by Augustus – celebrated in the altar of peace, the *Ara Pacis Augustae* dedicated to him by the Senate in 13 BC – appealed to them by enhancing the civil and moral role they felt to be their due. Some of the greatest Latin literature was written under Augustus: Virgil, Horace, Ovid, Propertius, Tibullus and Livy were its leading representatives. By the death of Augustus in AD 14, Rome had been transformed into an empire, and the framework to support it in the centuries to come had already been established.

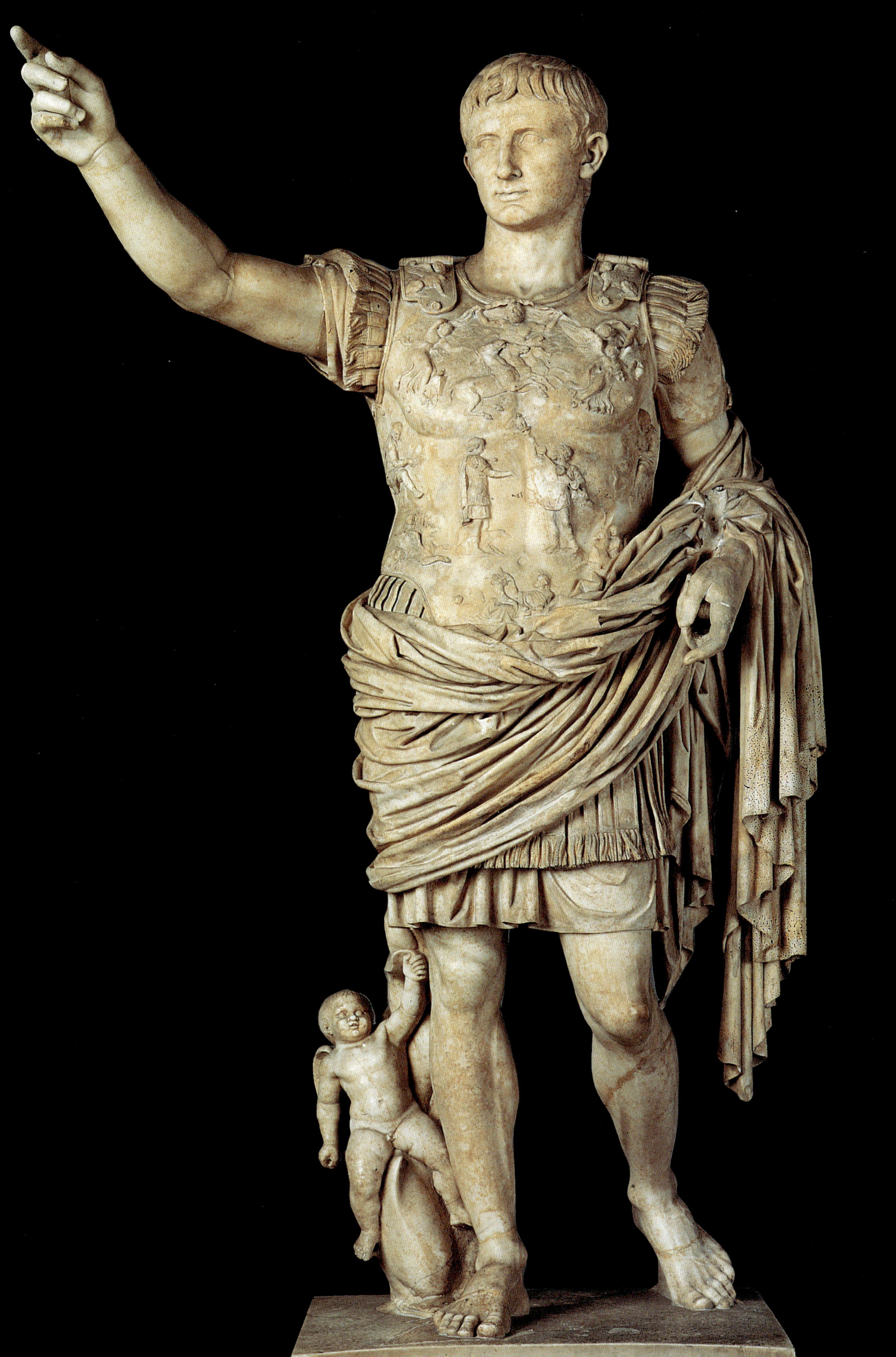

THE JULIO-CLAUDIAN DYNASTY

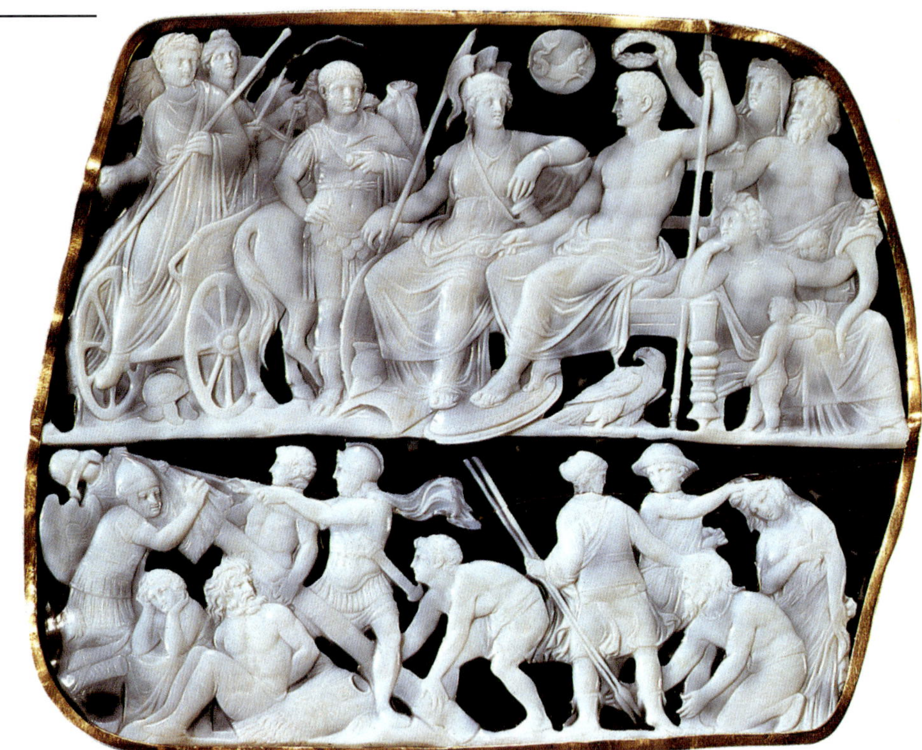

The unknown factor in the new political system was the method of succession, due to the unusual position of the emperor, who formally received his powers from the senate. Augustus overcame this problem by introducing a cleverly disguised system of dynastic succession which enabled four members of the Julio-Claudian family to rule the empire. Tiberius (AD 14–37) was designated as his successor by Augustus, Caligula (AD 37–41) was proposed by the prefect of the Praetorian Guard, Claudius (AD 41–64) was imposed by the Praetorian Guard, and Nero (AD 54-68) was the choice of Claudius' wife Agrippina, again supported by the Praetorian Guard.

The position of these early successors of Augustus was rather precarious. Caligula and Nero both died as a result of conspiracies by the Praetorian Guard, and Claudius may have been poisoned. Nevertheless, the empire continued to expand during this period, accompanied by economic and social consolidation and a growth of agriculture, trade and commerce. The roads, built for commercial and military purposes, now formed a vast network covering the whole empire, connecting the provinces with one another and with Rome. Under Claudius, not only did the organization of the imperial administration considerably improve, but a new province was also added to the empire – Britannia.

46 (above) The 'Gemma Augustea', an onyx cameo dating from the 1st century AD, shows Tiberius in triumph before Augustus and the personification of Rome. Below, some Roman soldiers are hoisting aloft spoils won from defeated enemies in front of a group of prisoners. Tiberius had already demonstrated his abilities as a brave commander before Augustus designated him as his successor.

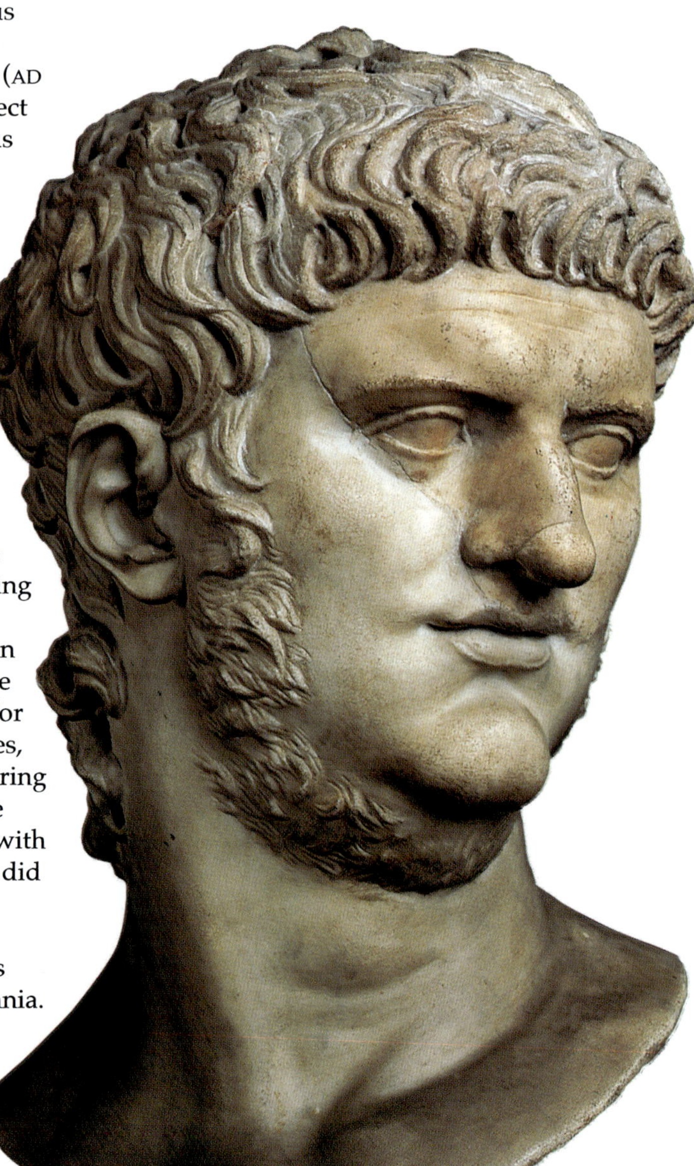

46 (below) Nero became emperor as a result of the intrigues of his mother Agrippina, who did not hesitate to assassinate Claudius in order to achieve her purpose. He originally reigned with moderation, but soon indulged in every kind of excess. Encouraged by Tigellinus, prefect of the Praetorian Guard, he initiated a reign of terror and embarked on exorbitant spending which dealt a crippling blow to the economy of the state. After the fire of Rome, a series of conspiracies and revolts against him began, and eventually he was forced to commit suicide.

THE FLAVIAN DYNASTY

47 (left) *Titus demonstrated his outstanding military abilities during the Judaean War, conducted by his father Vespasian. He became emperor in* AD *79, but died only two years later, after strengthening Roman hold on Britannia.*

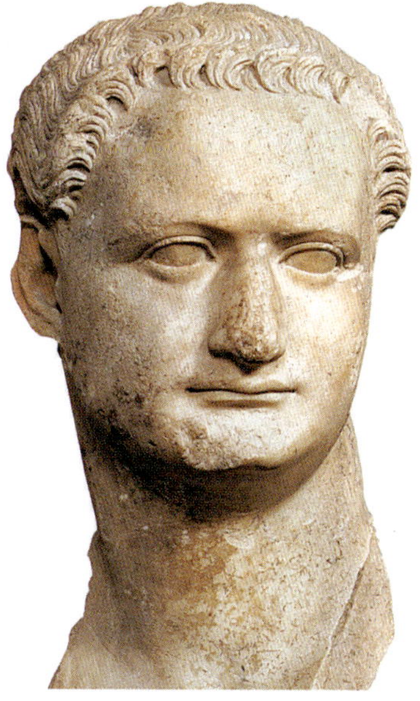

47 (below) *Domitian, the son of Vespasian and younger brother of Titus, was acclaimed Emperor although he had demonstrated little aptitude for command. His reign was characterized by an accentuated form of absolute rule.*

After Nero's death, the political situation became increasingly complex. During the year AD 69 the empire was racked by military anarchy, which led to civil war. Three emperors, elected on each occasion by the legions stationed in various parts of the empire, were assassinated in turn. Eventually, T. Flavius Vespasianus (AD 69–89) prevailed, with the support of the eastern and Danube legions, and his proclamation was ratified by the senate. Vespasian thus began the Flavian dynasty. He proved an excellent administrator, reorganizing the state treasuries and giving special priority to the provinces, improving the army, and strengthening the borders.

He was succeeded by his sons: first Titus (AD 79–81), then Domitian (AD 81–96). During the brief reign of Titus the Temple in Jerusalem was destroyed and the eruption of Vesuvius buried Pompeii, Stabiae and Herculaneum.

Domitian attempted (like Caligula before him) to institute a true absolute monarchy. During this period the senate finally lost its power as a decision-making body, increasingly becoming an elite group from which the emperors obtained useful candidates for administrative office. Numerous members of the equestrian order who were natives of Italic towns, and even the provinces, were given high office. This policy, designed to introduce new blood into the Roman administration, was continued by subsequent emperors.

Major new monuments were built in Rome under the Flavians, the most famous being the Colosseum. The borders were strengthened by modest conquests, and the empire enjoyed a period of calm. There was no lack of strong opponents to the policies of the Flavians, however, especially under Domitian; his attempt at self-deification was strongly opposed in cultural circles and by believers in Christianity, against which he unleashed a ruthless persecution. In AD 96 Domitian was assassinated.

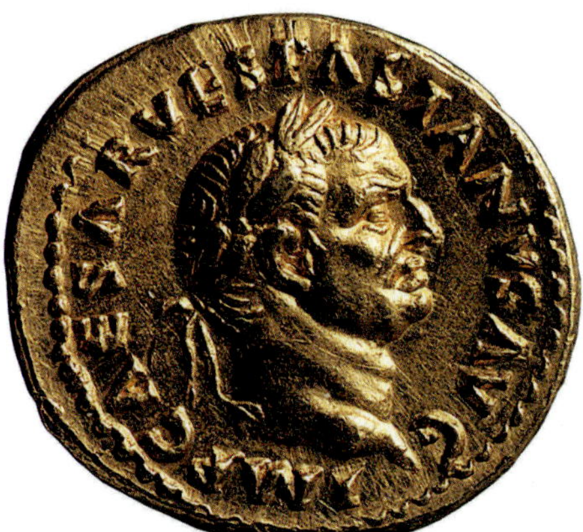

47 (below) *On Nero's death, Vespasian was proclaimed emperor by his soldiers in Judaea. A man of great character, he energetically defended the borders of the empire, undertook to replenish the state finances, reorganized the administration of the provinces and, above all, guaranteed the dynastic continuity of power through his sons, Titus and Domitian.*

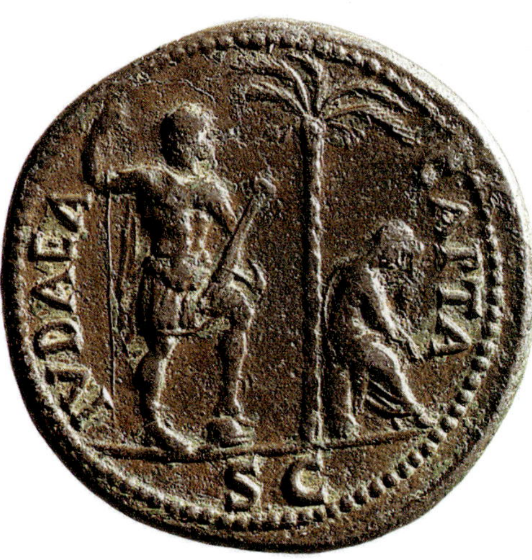

47 (left) *This coin was minted by Vespasian in* AD *70 to celebrate the conquest of Judaea (portrayed as a woman with bowed head) by his son Titus. With the fall of Jerusalem and the destruction of the Temple there, commemorated on the triumphal arch erected in the Roman Forum, the second Jewish Diaspora began.*

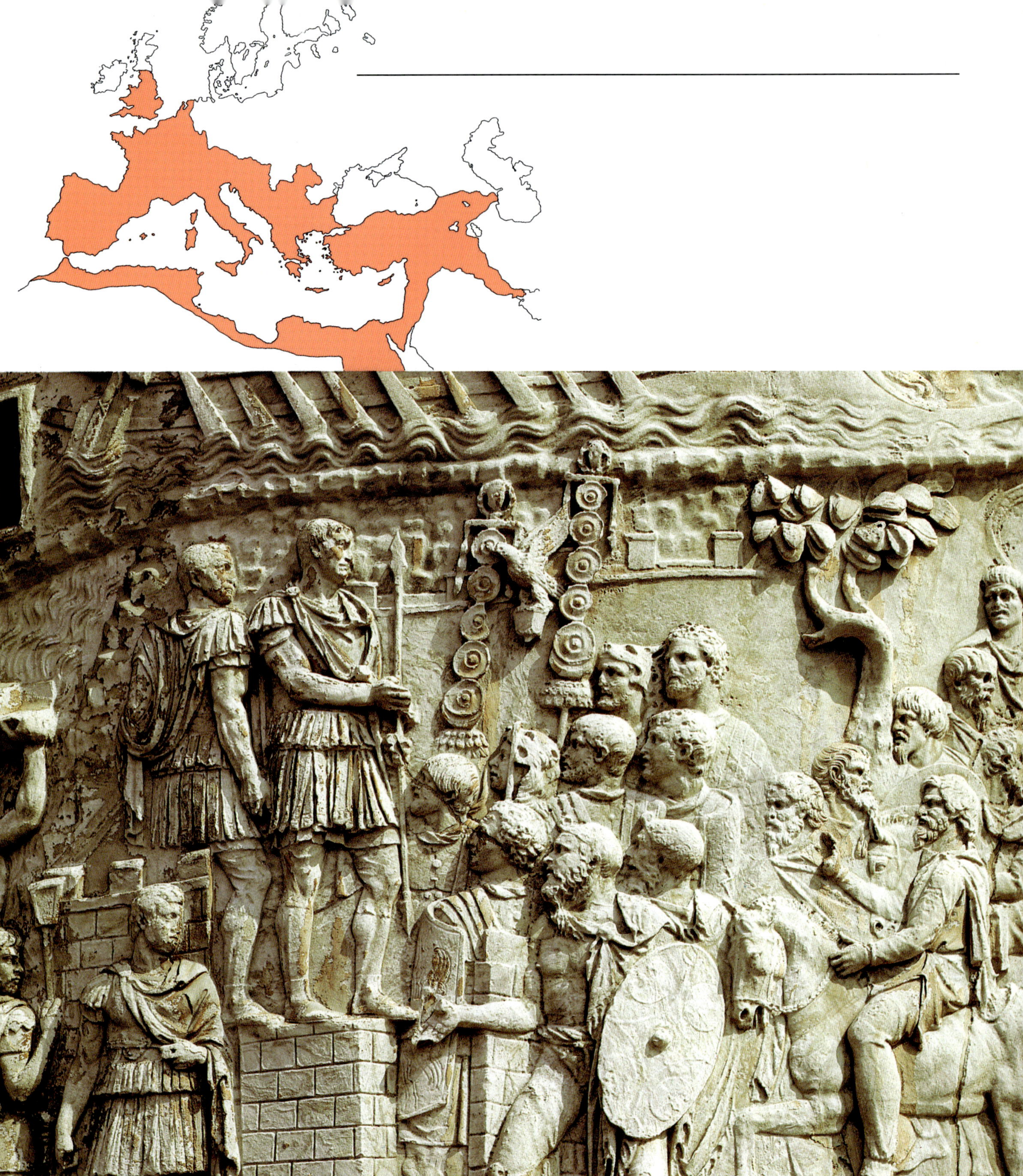

THE ADOPTED EMPERORS

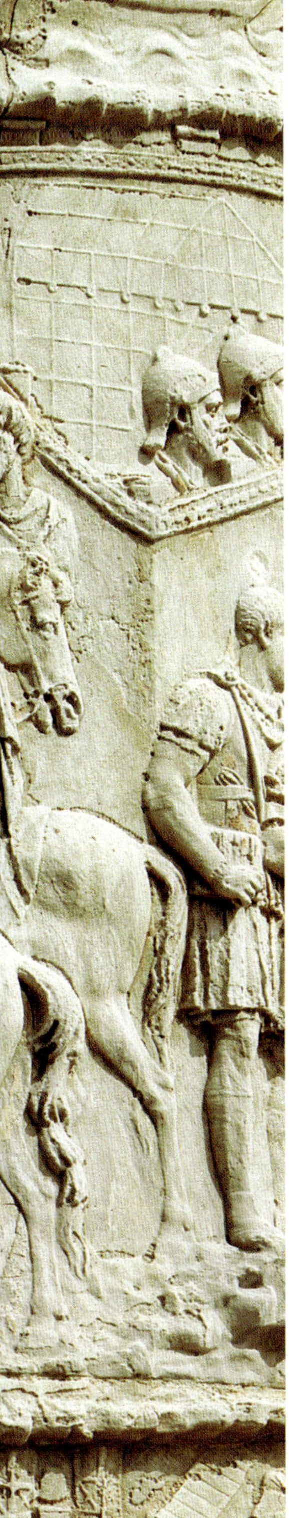

48–49 *The reign of Trajan was long remembered as a golden age; mining and farming expanded, and, because of the security of the borders, trade flourished. Above all, as a result of his conquests, the Roman empire reached its greatest extent. Trajan succeeded in conquering Dacia and occupying Ctesiphon, the capital of the Parthian empire, which had been an enemy of Rome for centuries. He also promoted extensive monumental building work in Rome, commissioning the construction of a new forum from the architect Apollodorus of Damascus. A triumphal column was erected here to commemorate his victories over the Dacians. The shaft of Trajan's Column, which stands 30 m (98 ft) tall, is decorated with a spiral frieze with reliefs illustrating the major episodes of the war. The scene reproduced here shows the emperor standing in front of the Roman fortifications as he addresses the troops and receives a delegation.*

In the 2nd century AD a general state of political stability allowed manufacturing and commercial activities to expand and culture to thrive throughout imperial society. A new system of succession – by adoption – replaced the previous dynastic structure: each emperor chose his successor from outside his family on the basis of the qualities of the individual. Emperors now often came from the provinces – beginning with Trajan, a native of Italica in Baetica, Spain – demonstrating that these regions were now on a par with Italy, and were vital to the prosperity and unity of the empire.

Nerva (AD 96–98) was the emperor responsible for the new method of succession. He had been elected by the senate when already elderly and immediately adopted M. Ulpius Traianus (Trajan, AD 98–117), a young consul who proved to have outstanding political and military gifts. The conquest of Dacia and the defeat of the Parthians are evidence of Trajan's ability as a general. His successor Hadrian (AD 117–138) preferred a policy of consolidation. Abandoning the lands beyond the Euphrates, he built a strong system of defensive fortifications along the borders of the empire, including Hadrian's Wall in Britannia, and devoted his attention to solving the administrative problems of the empire and achieving its complete Romanization.

The policy of Antoninus Pius (AD 138–161) was inspired by that of his predecessor, and he built a new wall north of Hadrian's in Britannia. He was succeeded to the throne by Marcus Aurelius (AD 161–180), a valiant general and philosopher who was an adherent of Stoicism. He abandoned the adoptive principle of succession, and returned to the dynastic system, a decision that turned out to be a serious mistake. His son Commodus (AD 180–192), who succeeded to the throne at an early age, broke the pattern of good government and was distinguished only by his ambition and cruelty. On the brink of the 3rd century AD, one of the last periods of splendour of the Roman empire came to an end.

Although highly complex, imperial administration had reached a level of unparalleled efficiency. Grants of citizenship in the provinces had increased, the general economy was at an excellent level and numerous

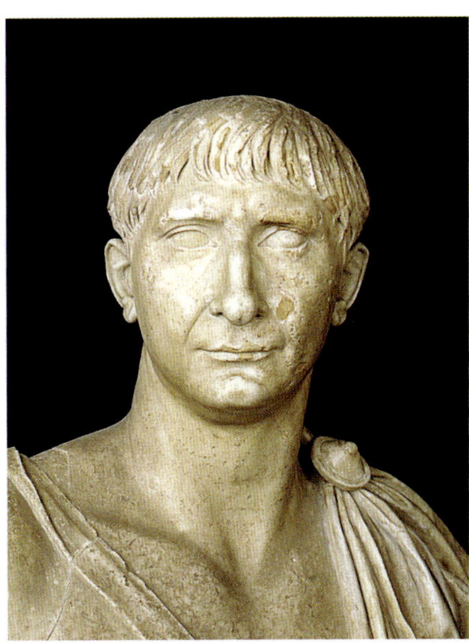

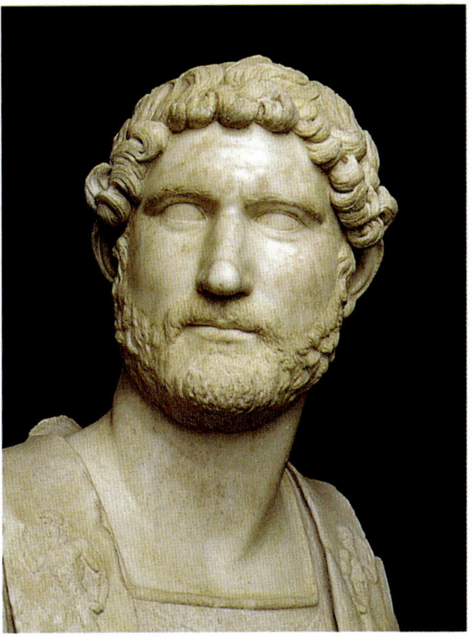

49 (right, above) Trajan, born in the part of Spain known as Baetica, succeeded Nerva. He undertook the conquest of Dacia after strengthening the Rhine border. An excellent government and financial administrator, he was popular with all classes of society. He died in the course of his campaigns against the Parthians.

49 (right, below) Hadrian, acclaimed emperor after Trajan's death, immediately made peace with the Parthians and pursued a policy designed to strengthen the borders of the empire, renouncing the expansionism of his predecessors. An admirer of Greek civilization, he delighted in poetry and meditation.

measures aiding the poor were instituted, such as benefits for needy children and alms for the plebeians.

At the same time, however, there was a growing spiritual restlessness among both intellectuals and the masses, with a move away from political life towards a search for inner happiness and salvation of the soul that could find no answer in the official state religion. Interest in the philosophical schools of Stoicism and Cynicism spread among the educated classes, as did worship of the mystery cults of Isis, Serapis and Mithras among the poorer people. Christianity was growing in popularity as it met the needs of the deprived sections of society and satisfied the questioning of the more sensitive, reflective spirits. The political authorities were generally tolerant of all forms of religion and thought, provided they did not represent a threat to the established order, for instance by denying the official state religion. For this reason, despite the climate of tolerance, a programme of severe repression was instituted against the Jews in AD 135, whose monotheism was an ideological challenge to the empire.

Christianity appeared different: it was based on simple, easily understood rites and preached brotherly love, and immediately attracted followers from all walks of life. The authorities looked on with increasing consternation at the growth of a religion that considered itself to be the sole repository of truth, and viewed loyalty to the empire as subordinate to the Word of God. The biblical expression 'render unto Caesar the things that are Caesar's, and unto God the things that are God's' indicated that although Christians did not reject human laws, they obeyed their faith absolutely. This brought about the systematic persecutions beginning in the 3rd century AD.

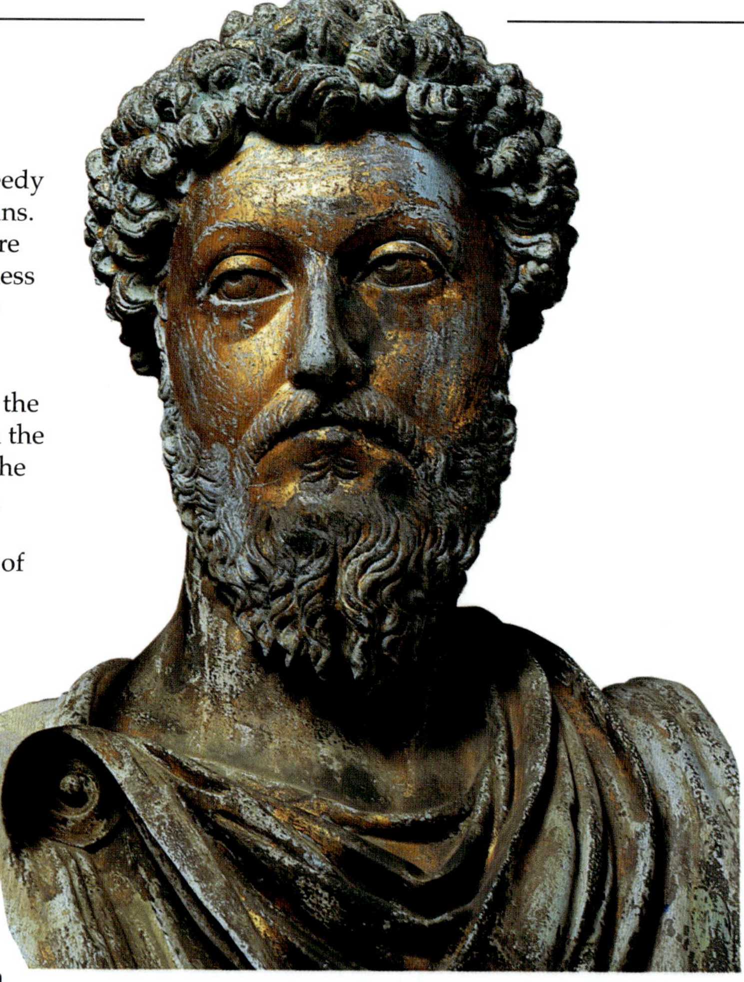

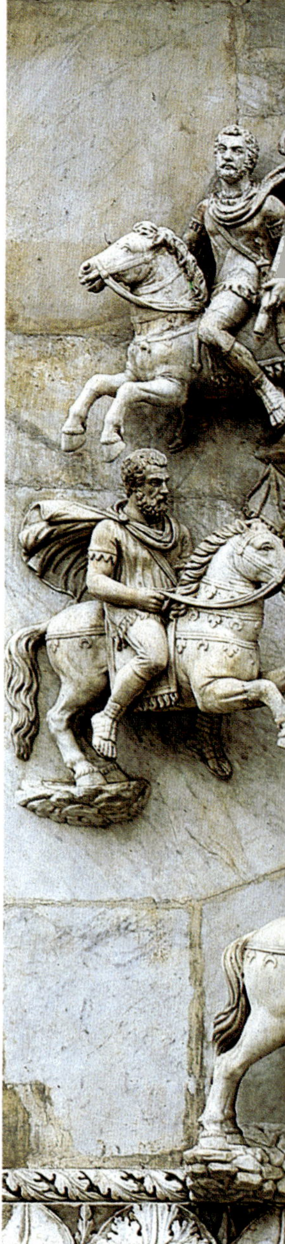

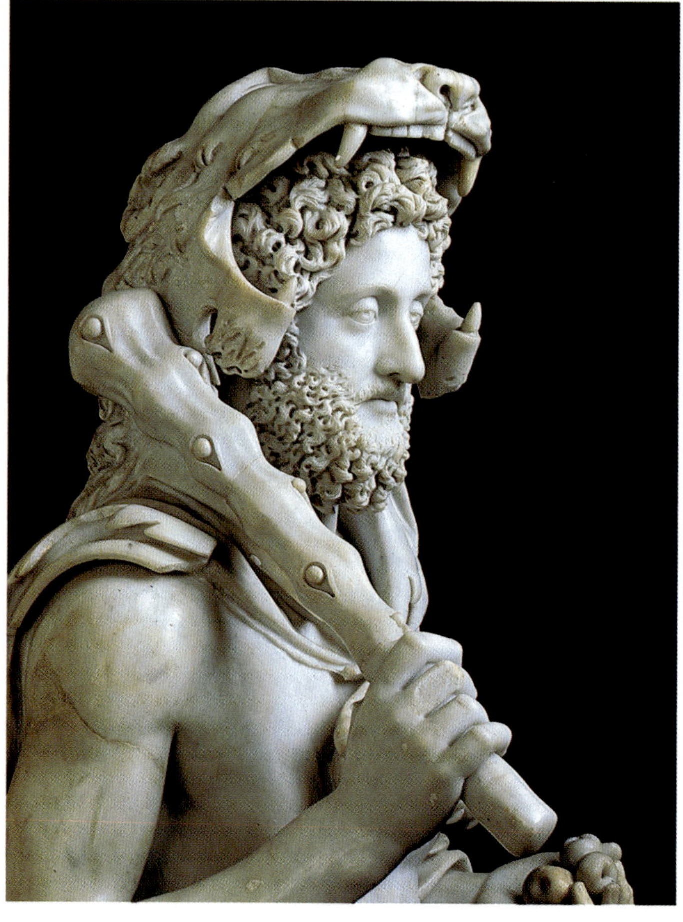

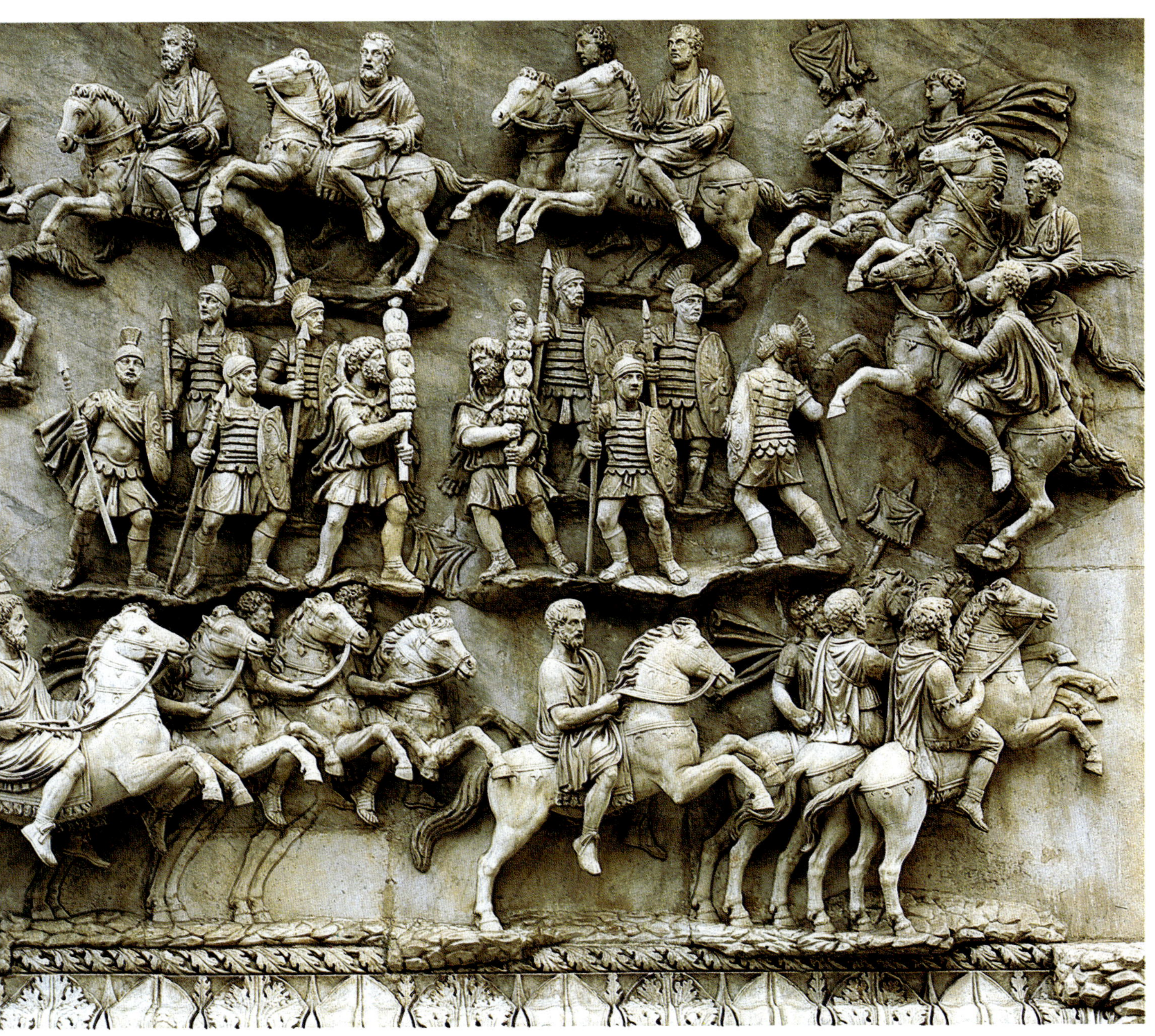

50 (opposite, above) Marcus Aurelius kept the peace within the state and suppressed revolts which broke out on the empire's borders. A decisive commander and a philosopher of Stoic and Epicurean inspiration, he is remembered as a very humane man. His equestrian statue in the Capitol (a detail is shown here) is the only one of an emperor to have survived intact from the Roman era.

50 (opposite, below) Commodus became emperor at an early age, on the death of his father Marcus Aurelius, whose virtues he failed to inherit. His reign was tragically famous for acts of senseless cruelty and tyranny; an exhibitionist, he identified with Hercules and liked to be portrayed in that guise. Unpopular even with the aristocracy, he eventually fell victim to a conspiracy.

50–51 (above) The base of the triumphal column in Rome dedicated to Antoninus Pius is magnificently decorated; one of the two splendid reliefs on the short sides depicts a parade of Roman soldiers and knights, with great effects of light and shadow. Antoninus Pius, who succeeded Hadrian, was universally admired for his good and competent rule. A resolute man and a capable government administrator, he consolidated domestic peace and at the same time firmly crushed uprisings in Africa and in Britannia, where he built his own defensive wall to the north of Hadrian's. He also reduced taxes and was responsible for numerous charitable foundations. His long reign marked the height of the stability of Rome's institutions and military power.

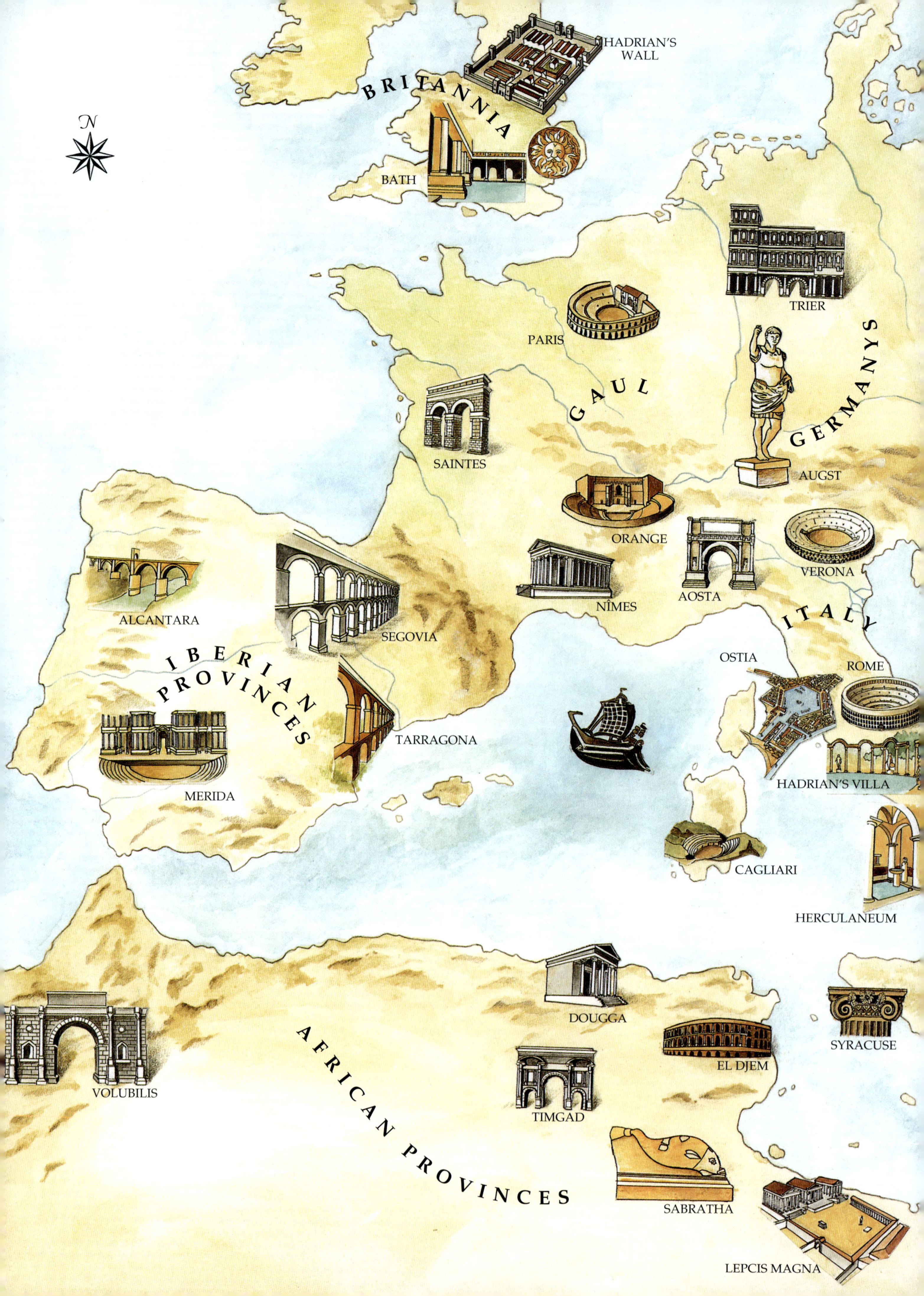

N
BRITANNIA
HADRIAN'S WALL
BATH
PARIS
TRIER
GAUL
GERMANYS
SAINTES
AUGST
ORANGE
VERONA
AOSTA
NÎMES
ITALY
ALCANTARA
SEGOVIA
IBERIAN PROVINCES
TARRAGONA
MERIDA
OSTIA
ROME
HADRIAN'S VILLA
CAGLIARI
HERCULANEUM
DOUGGA
SYRACUSE
EL DJEM
VOLUBILIS
TIMGAD
AFRICAN PROVINCES
SABRATHA
LEPCIS MAGNA

THE ROMAN EMPIRE IN THE 2ND CENTURY AD, AT ITS GREATEST EXTENT

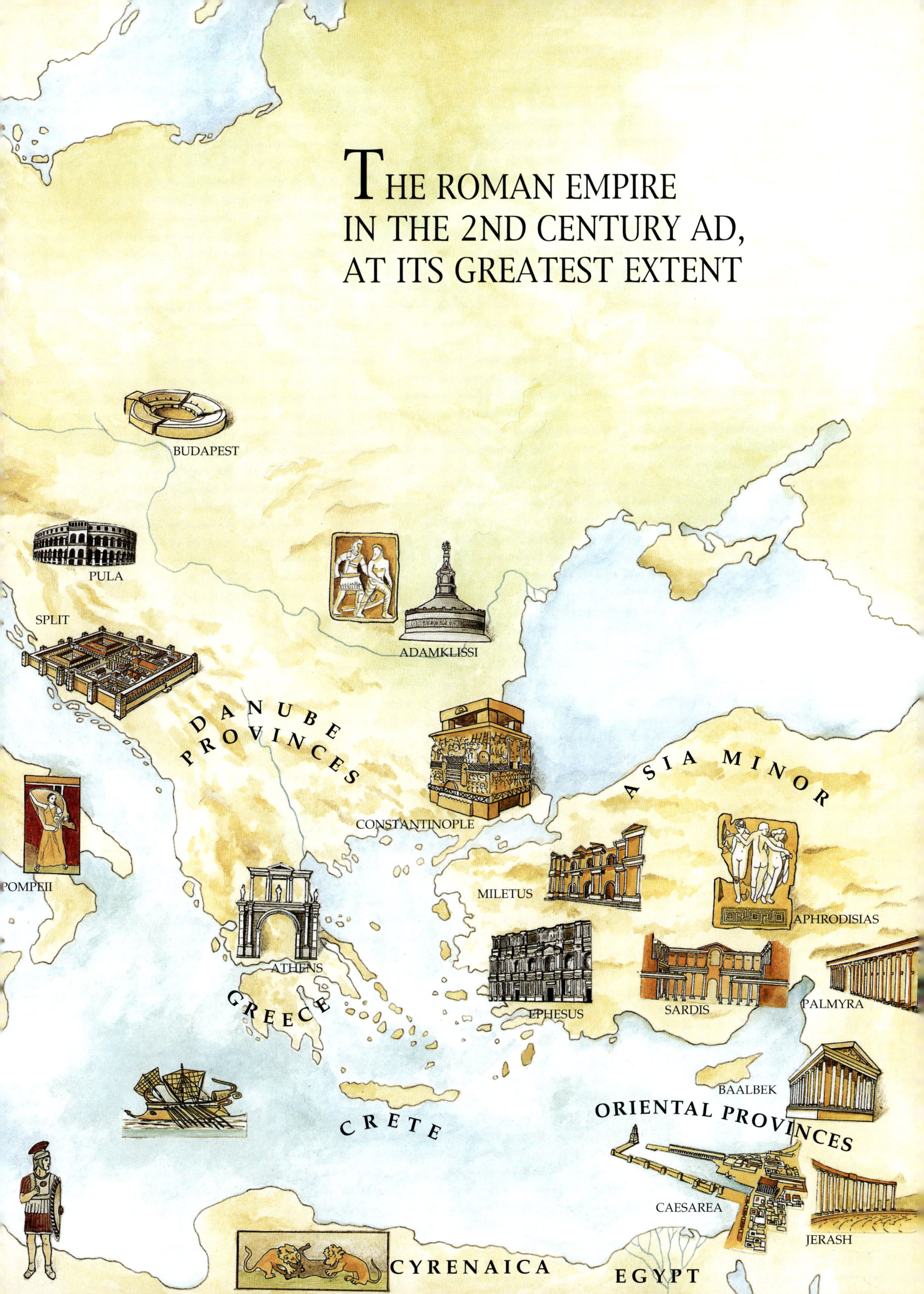

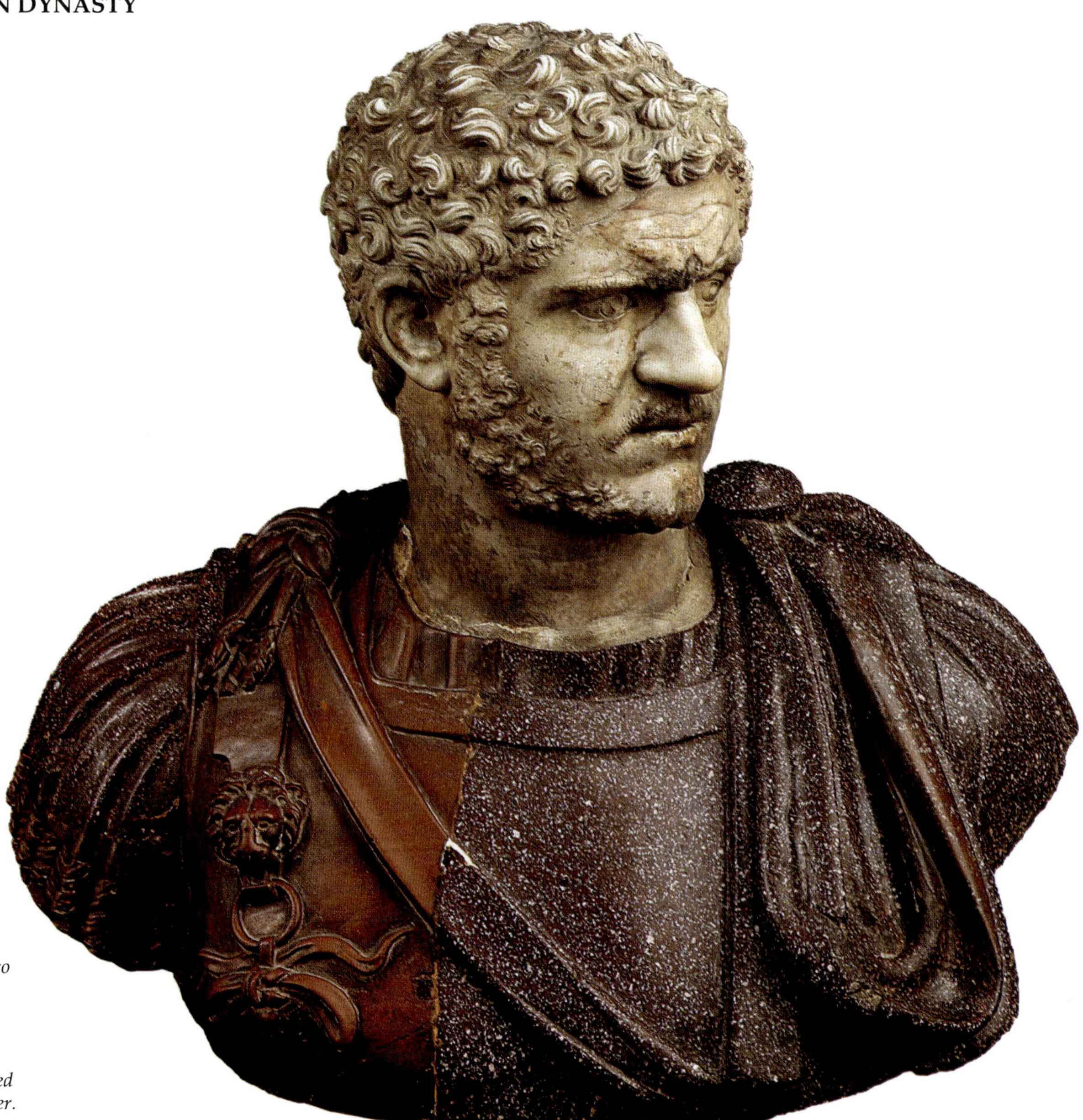

54 Caracalla liked to be shown in his official portraits with a menacing expression, and his head slightly inclined towards one shoulder.

At the beginning of the 3rd century AD, after the reign of Commodus and the ensuing five years' civil war, the empire took on an increasingly military bias. This development was due to the concentration of authority in the hands of the emperor. The senate was deprived of its legislative and judicial powers to the advantage of the emperor's private counsellors. Merchants and manufacturers were organized into guilds, and the state began to intervene widely in economic life.

Septimius Severus (AD 197–211), supported by the legions of Pannonia and Germany, was the first emperor of the Severan dynasty, ushering in a new era of prosperity. He defeated the Parthians, reformed the province of Mesopotamia, made the city of Palmyra into a colony, and generally strengthened the empire's defences. In Africa, the frontiers were pushed south to Mauretania and Tripolitania, with its flourishing cities such as Sabratha and Lepcis Magna. The latter was the birthplace of the emperor, who lavished great attention on the city, embellishing it with magnificent buildings.

Septimius Severus was succeeded by his son, M. Aurelius Antoninus, nicknamed Caracalla (AD 211–217). During his brief reign a decree of great civil importance, the Constitutio Antoniniana, was issued, which granted Roman citizenship to all free inhabitants of the empire. Caracalla, who had already had his brother Geta murdered to avoid sharing power with him, was himself assassinated and Avitus Bassianus, better known as Heliogabalus (AD 217–222), was acclaimed emperor. His reign was short-lived, and the last descendant of the dynasty, Severus Alexander (AD 222–235), came to power. He was not a total failure, but, especially because of increasing pressure from the barbarians, found it increasingly difficult to defend the borders. This caused disorder and unrest in the army which reached such a peak that the emperor was assassinated.

MILITARY ANARCHY: FROM DIOCLETIAN TO CONSTANTINE

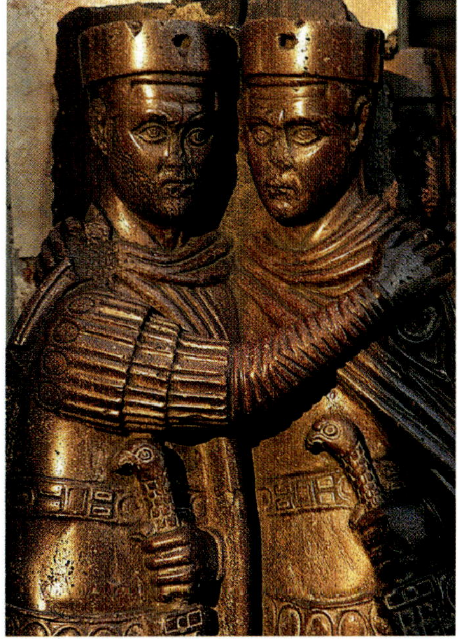

55 (left) *It is generally thought that the statue group in red porphyry built into a corner of the Treasury of St Mark's in Venice portrays the Augustuses– Diocletian and Maximian – and the Caesars – Galerius and Constantius.*

55 (below) *Constantine revolutionized the Roman world by granting freedom of worship to the Christians and proclaiming Byzantium, renamed Constantinople, the new capital of the empire.*

In the years between AD 235 and 284, a profound constitutional and social crisis took place. The economy was almost paralysed and debasement of the coinage caused intolerable inflation. Border areas were under increasing pressure from numerous barbarian populations. The army, having almost entirely deprived the senate of its power, became the *de facto* ruler of the empire. The many emperors in this period include M. Junius Philippus, or Philip the Arab (AD 244–249), who celebrated the 1000th anniversary of Rome's foundation with great pomp; Decius (AD 249–251), who was responsible for the first great persecution of the Christians in AD 250; Valerian (AD 253–260), taken prisoner by the Parthians, and his son Gallienus (AD 260–268) who, like his father, fought to defend the borders; and finally Aurelian (AD 270–275), who regained and destroyed Palmyra (guilty of rebelling against Rome and creating a powerful independent kingdom), and surrounded Rome with a ring of strong walls. But no sooner had the unity of the empire been restored than Aurelian was assassinated.

After further short-lived reigns, the troops in the east proclaimed Diocletian emperor (AD 284–305). He put an end to the period of anarchy and initiated a series of reforms which ensured the empire's survival for another century. The continual pressure of the barbarians on the borders led him to make defence a priority. First he decided that the emperor should no longer live in Rome, but as close as possible to the border; and he also considered that the complex political problems could no longer be handled by a single ruler. He thus formed the Tetrarchy. Power was now shared between two Augustuses aided by two Caesars, who would later come to power and appoint two Caesars to replace them. Jurisdiction was on a territorial basis and the aim was to prevent the disintegration caused by the increasing problems in various parts of the empire. The benefits of the Tetrarchy were felt immediately: defence of the borders became easier and more effective, and various attempts at rebellion were stifled at birth. In practice, however, it already heralded the division of the empire into east and west. The system of succession proved excessively complicated, and failed when Diocletian retired to private life in AD 305 and persuaded his colleague Maximian to do the same. The two Caesars, Galerius and Constantius, became Augustuses, but a fierce battle arose between the two aspiring Caesars thereby excluded from that office, Maxentius and Constantine. Constantine, who declared that the Christian God was on his side, confronted Maxentius in Italy. This was a turning point in the history of both the empire and Christianity, which had suffered persecution under Valerian and Diocletian. Maxentius' troops were defeated in AD 312 in a battle at the Milvian Bridge at the gates of Rome, and Constantine proclaimed his devotion to the cross, the symbol of Christianity. This was undoubtedly a political gesture, which allowed the victor to promote the unity of the empire with the support of the new religion. Constantine and Licinius, the legitimate Augustus of the east, shared power. However, in AD 324, Constantine defeated his colleague and reunited the empire. This action, which proved to have far-reaching consequences, in many respects followed the route begun

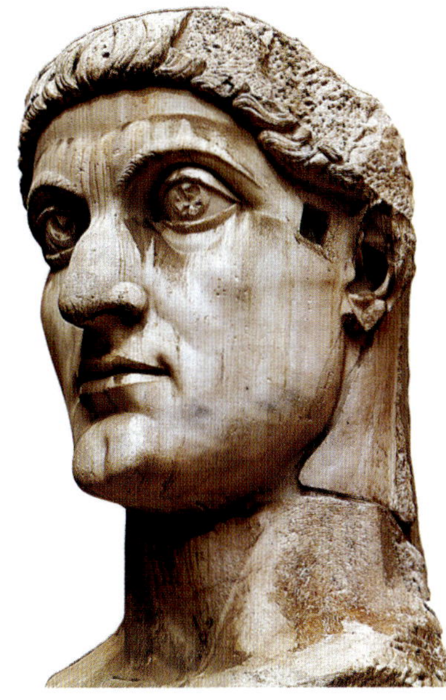

by Diocletian. Constantine passed laws of major importance. The Edict of Milan, of AD 313, ended the tragic persecutions of the Christians, and gave full freedom to the Church. In AD 330 the capital was transferred from Rome to Byzantium, renamed Constantinople, so that the seat of power was close to the threatened borders. In practice, this led to the decline of the western empire.

Finally, wishing the Church to preserve its unity, Constantine (who was not only the emperor but also effectively head of the Christian Church), presided over the Ecumenical Council of Nicea in AD 325. This Council produced the Nicene Creed, which would heal the split between Catholics and Arians, thus reuniting the Christian world.

THE LATE EMPIRE

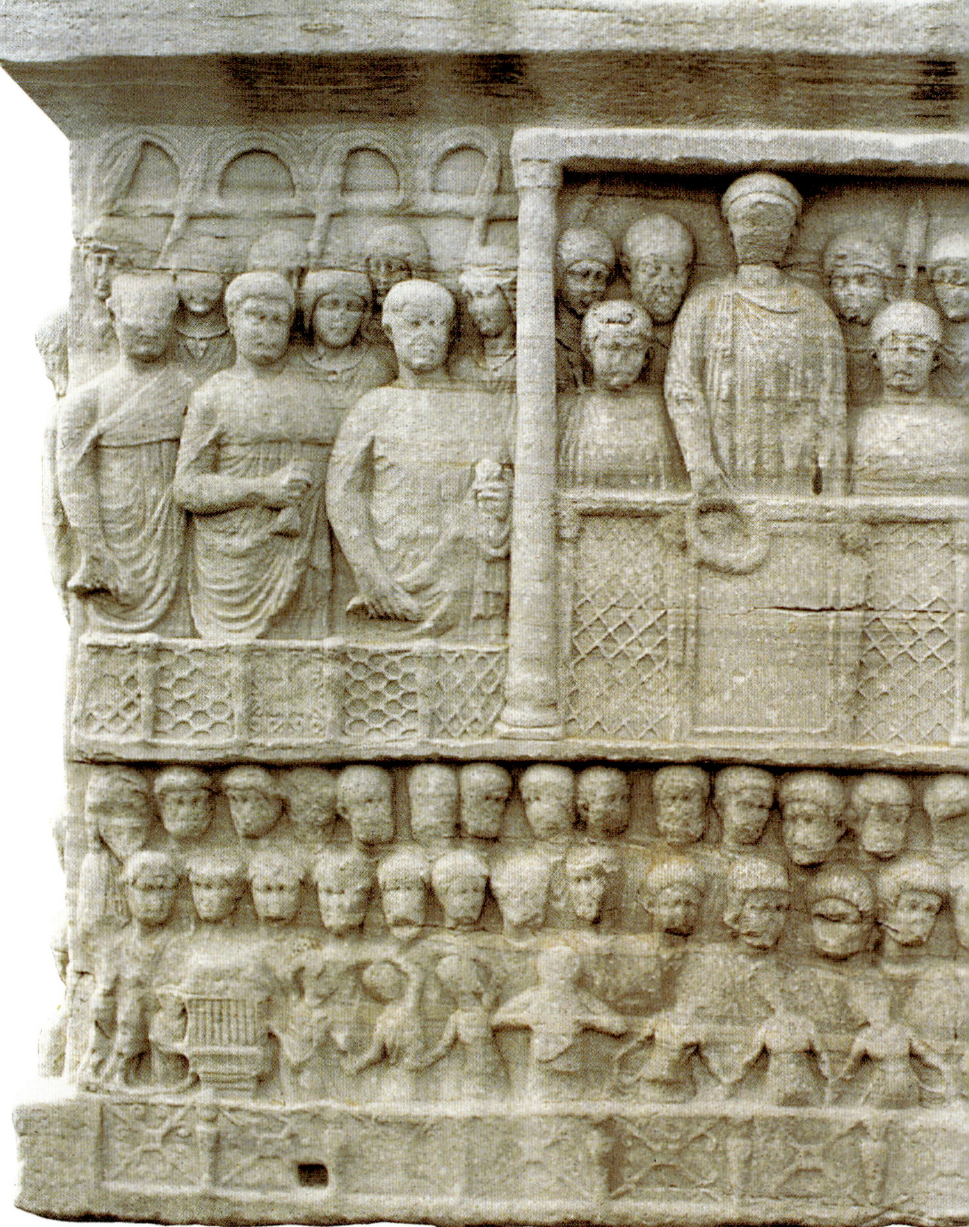

The move of the capital of the empire to the east marked the beginning of the period known as the late empire. At this stage the decadence of the western world was evident, although Rome still maintained some dignity, and it was a period in which architecture flourished.

The eastern and western parts of the empire were by now two completely different worlds, with little communication between them. On the edges of the empire there was increasing pressure from barbarian populations, who confronted an ever weaker army.

On Constantine's death the empire was once more divided between squabbling heirs, then reunited in AD 353 under Constantius. In AD 361, Julian was proclaimed emperor by the troops in Gaul. Julian, called the Apostate by the Christians, pursued his aim of restoring the greatness of the empire by a return to the ancient cultural values of paganism. He died in AD 363 fighting against the Parthians while trying to conquer the east, believing he was following in the footsteps of Alexander the Great. Thus ended his hopeless attempt to restore the greatness of Constantine's dynasty.

In AD 364 the empire was divided between Valentinian and Valens, who defended it bravely until the disastrous defeat at Hadrianopolis in AD 378, in which Valens died. After their victory the Goths invaded the Balkans, and never withdrew.

Under Valentinian the western capital of the empire, Trier (Trèves), a city in Gaul, reached its greatest splendour. In AD 375 Valentinian was succeeded in the west by his son Gratian, who called on a man of great merit, Theodosius, to replace Valens in the east.

Under this emperor the last great move towards the Church took place, when Catholicism was declared the state religion. The empire was reunited for a short period under Theodosius; he died in AD 394, leaving as heirs his sons Honorius for the west and Arcadius for the east. Thereafter, however, the two empires moved rapidly towards separate destinies.

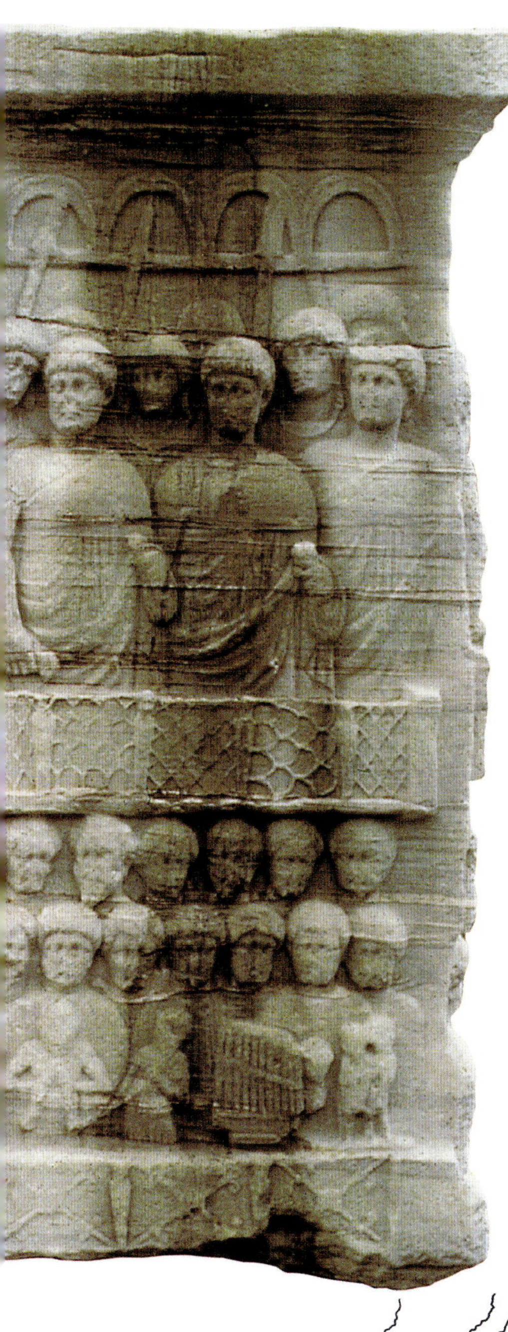

DECLINE AND FALL OF THE WESTERN EMPIRE

Ruling the empire in the west was no easy task. In practice, power was held by the military leaders, often barbarians, and large landowners; the Church asserted its political authority, the economy was experiencing a serious recession and there was a sharp decline in the population. Under these circumstances, the empire became increasingly open to barbarian invasion. With the empire breaking up, the emperor's sovereignty was effectively limited to Italy alone.

In the east, however, the emperor had no such difficulties: he could rely on an efficient bureaucracy, more pliable military commanders and a Church which submitted to the imperial will. The economy and trade were flourishing and, save for rare exceptions, the barbarians were unable to make lasting breaches in the unity of the empire. Separation from the west was emphasized when Greek became the official language in AD 440, with Latin no longer used for the administration.

In the west, the barbarian general Stilicho, loyal to Honorius, strenuously defended Italy against the barbarian hordes. However, after his death the Visigoths under Alaric attacked and sacked Rome in AD 410, to the horror of the civilized world.

Barbarian kingdoms were now found on Roman soil, and though they declared themselves subjects of the emperor, they did not recognize his authority. The Roman general Aetius was the last bulwark against the mounting tide. He reunited inhabitants of the empire, old and new, in a campaign against Attila and the Huns, who were beaten in the epic battle of Châlons in AD 451. A few years later, however, Genseric's Vandals again sacked Rome. This, together with the death of emperor Valentinian III, marked the end of the Roman empire in the west. In the year AD 476, Odoacer, chief of the Heruli, deposed the last emperor, Romulus Augustulus, seized power and sent the imperial insignia to the eastern emperor.

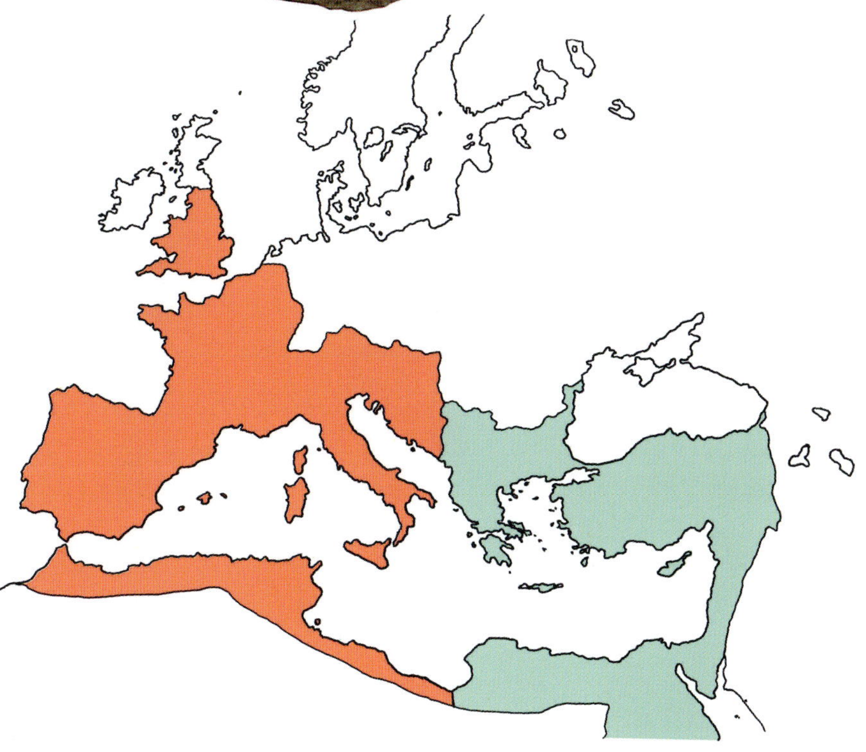

56–57 Theodosius, Augustus of the east from AD 379, reunited the empire, but only for a short period. His policy of religious intransigence, which culminated in AD 392 with a ban on the private worship of pagan gods, led to an uprising in the west, which was still attached to the traditional deities. Although Theodosius won the day he was forced, just before his death, to divide the empire again between his sons Arcadius and Honorius. An obelisk erected by Theodosius in the Hippodrome in Constantinople was decorated on the base with four great reliefs. This one depicts the imperial family and some court dignitaries watching the games. The rigidly frontal composition and static poses herald the basic characteristics of Byzantine art.

Aspects of Roman Civilization

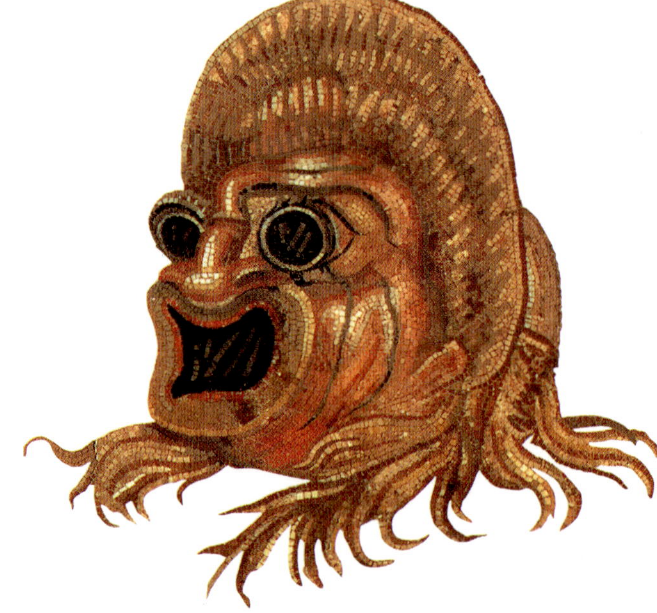

58 Women were not usually allowed to act in the theatre; female masks were therefore worn by male actors when the action required it. Designs similar to this Pompeiian mosaic also appear on ivory or stone theatre 'tickets' found in numerous archaeological excavations.

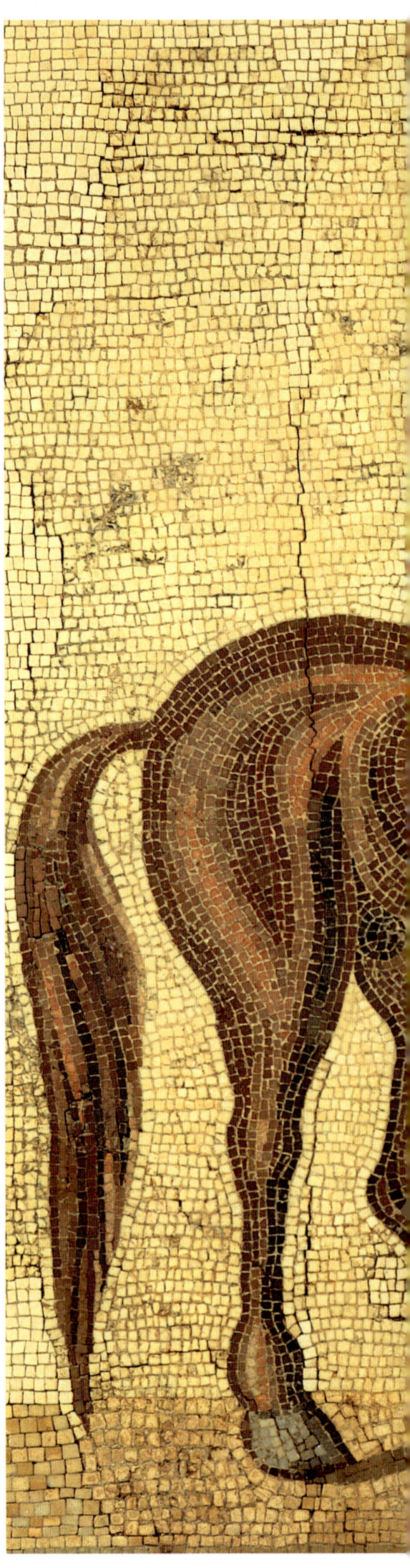

58–59 This famous mosaic, discovered in Rome, portrays a circus charioteer with his steed. On his head he wears a kind of rigid leather helmet, and his chest is protected by woven leather strips. The Romans were so fond of circus contests that these events became an essential part of society during the empire.

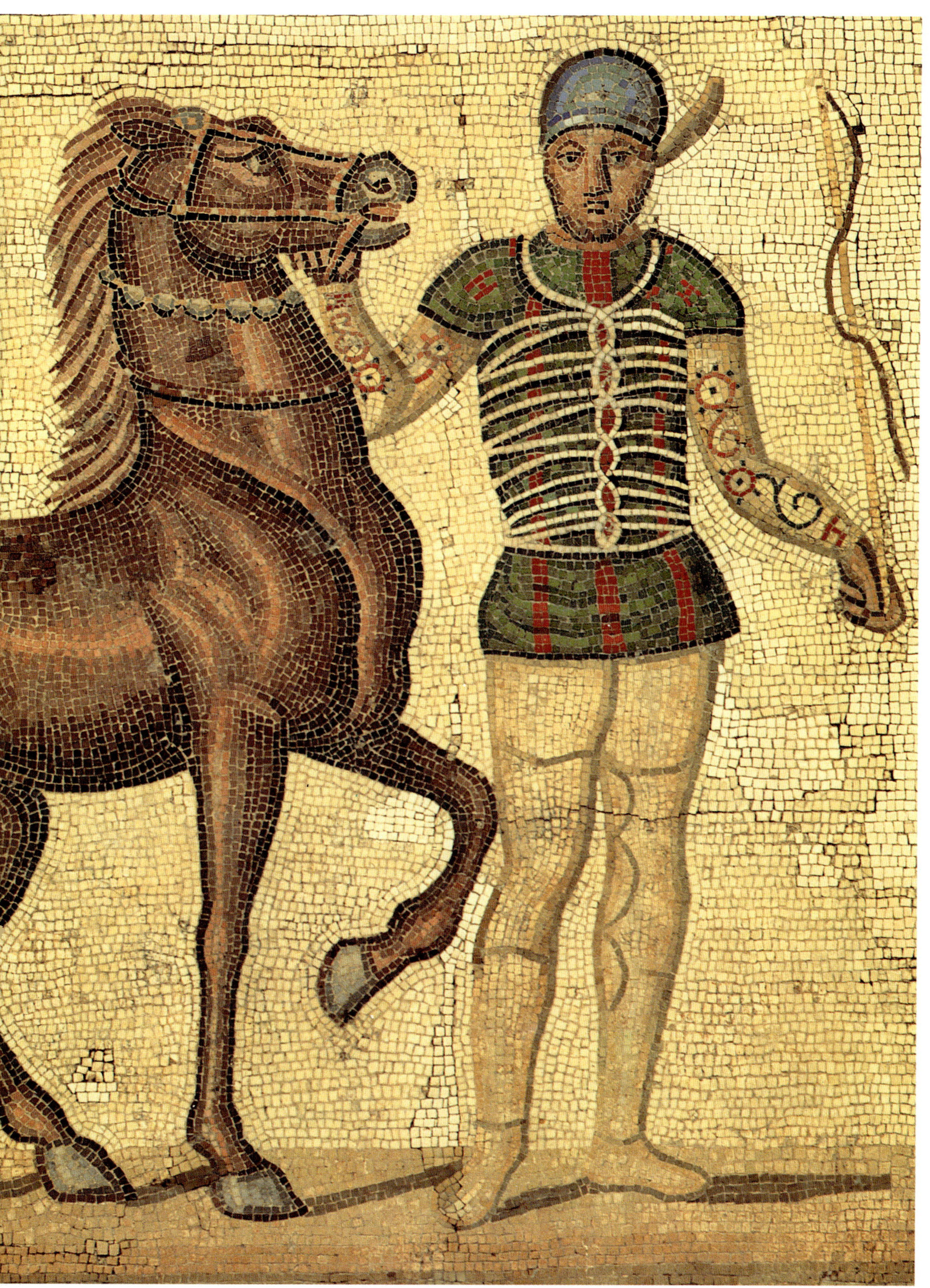

In the age of Cicero, Rome looked as though it was suspended in the air because of its superimposed buildings. Under Augustus the city was built even higher and, as Vitruvius wrote, 'The majesty of the Urbs and the considerable growth of its population necessitated an exceptional extension of its homes. The result of this situation was that a remedy was sought in the height of the buildings.'

The government occasionally intervened in town planning, but usually with poor results. Augustus himself, though he boasted that he had found a city of brick and left a city of marble, was unable to improve the overcrowding, unhealthiness and congestion of the poorer districts. Fires and building collapses were the most common disasters. The addition of upper storeys allowed more people to

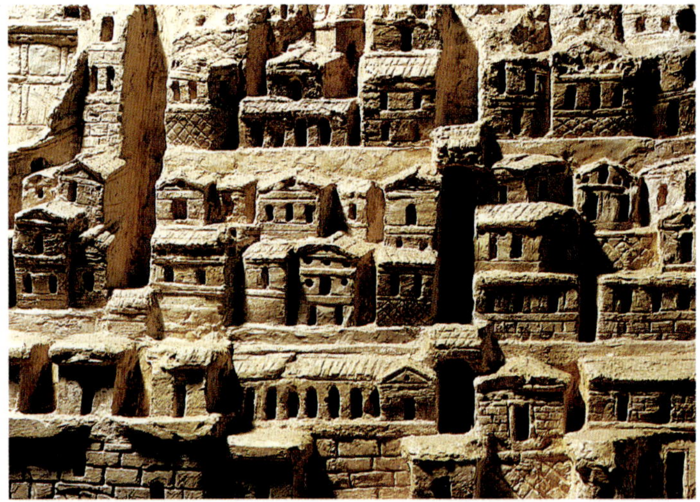

60 (left, above) This marble relief dating from the 1st century BC, *found in the area of Lake Fucino, shows a Roman town surrounded by walls; the* insulae *appear to be arranged in a strictly geometrical layout. Roman surveyors used some quite advanced technical instruments for the purposes of town planning.*

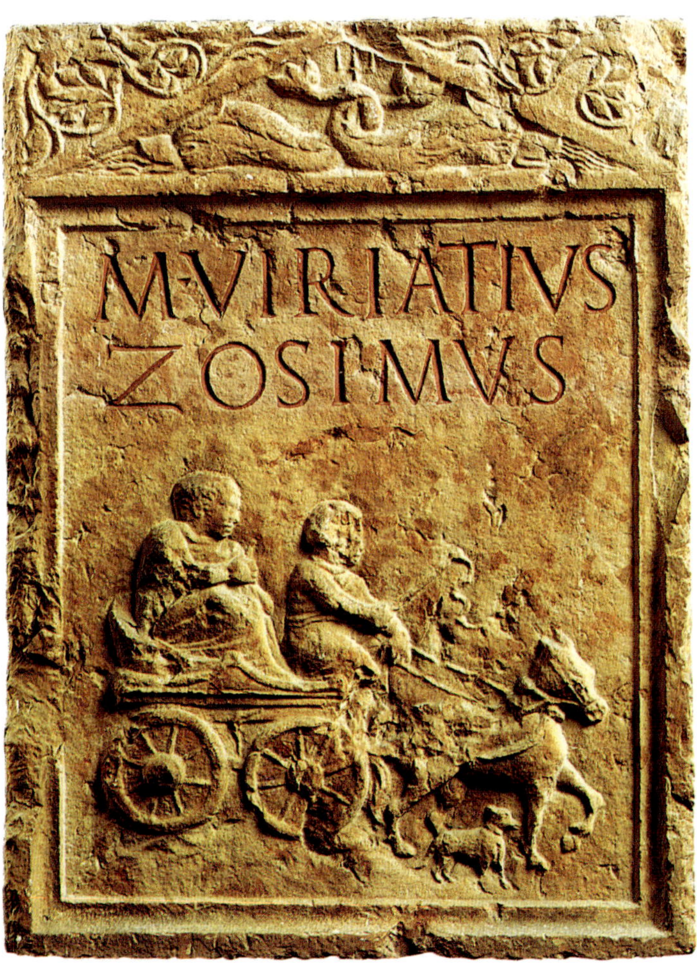

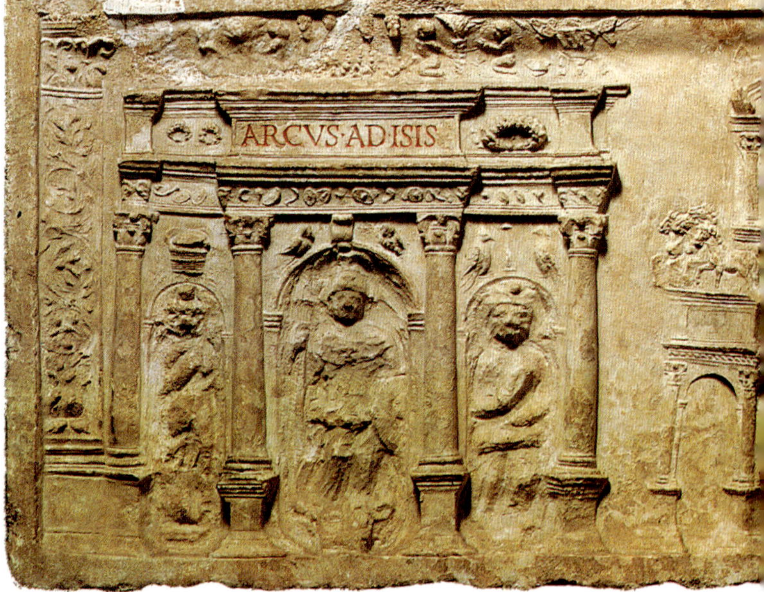

60 (left) Traffic in Roman towns was extremely busy. Four-wheeled passenger coaches (raedae) *similar to the one depicted in this bas-relief jostled with the much heavier four-wheeled goods carts* (sarraca) *and the only slightly smaller carts with two solid wheels* (plaustra) *used mainly by farmers to take their produce to market. A kind of light* raeda *was used for the* cursus publicus velox, *the rapid, state-run transport service. The most suitable vehicle for long journeys was the* carruca dormitoria, *in which passengers could travel and sleep in relative comfort under cover.*

crowd into a small space, but, being built of wooden materials with light masonry – quick to build, extremely cheap and highly profitable – they were fragile and easily caught fire.

Paradoxically, the person responsible for alleviating this catastrophic state of affairs and partly renovating the city was Nero. The terrible fire of AD 64, which destroyed three Augustan regions and seriously damaged many others, led to the passing of regulations which prohibited unauthorized and makeshift constructions. The height of private properties was controlled; porticoes were built; wooden ceilings were prohibited; and the separation of buildings from one another was made compulsory.

In the imperial age Rome became a true metropolis of the ancient world. However, despite the magnificent setting provided by its monuments, the city was chaotic. There had never been any real town plan, and its inhabitants were crowded into the small space left over by imperial palaces, markets, gardens and numerous public buildings.

In the 4th century AD the city contained some 44,000 tenement blocks (*insulae*) and 1800 houses (*domus*). The population amounted to almost a million, not counting slaves and the huge, variegated, cosmopolitan mass of immigrants. All these people crowded inside the city walls in the most amazing muddle, and the untidy layout of the town was accentuated by an inadequate road network. There were no rigid territorial divisions between the various districts of the city; uncomfortable, flimsy buildings connected by narrow, dark alleys, often coexisted with splendid mansions.

Only a few fortunate citizens had comfortable houses, while the majority lived in small *domus* and in large rented apartments of varying degrees of decency. Mostly the plebs found themselves in conditions barely fit for human habitation: there were attics inhabited by slaves and ordinary people; cellars, such as that in which a poet friend of Martial's lived; rooms under staircases; and shops with garrets used as dwellings for the humbler people.

Large number of shops – *tabernae* – gave the city the appearance of a huge bazaar, accentuated by the presence of numerous pedlars who mingled with the crowd looking for potential customers. All sorts of goods were sold in the *tabernae*, from foodstuffs, fabrics and crockery to jewelry and books. There were also premises used for businesses such as laundries, dyers, tanners and

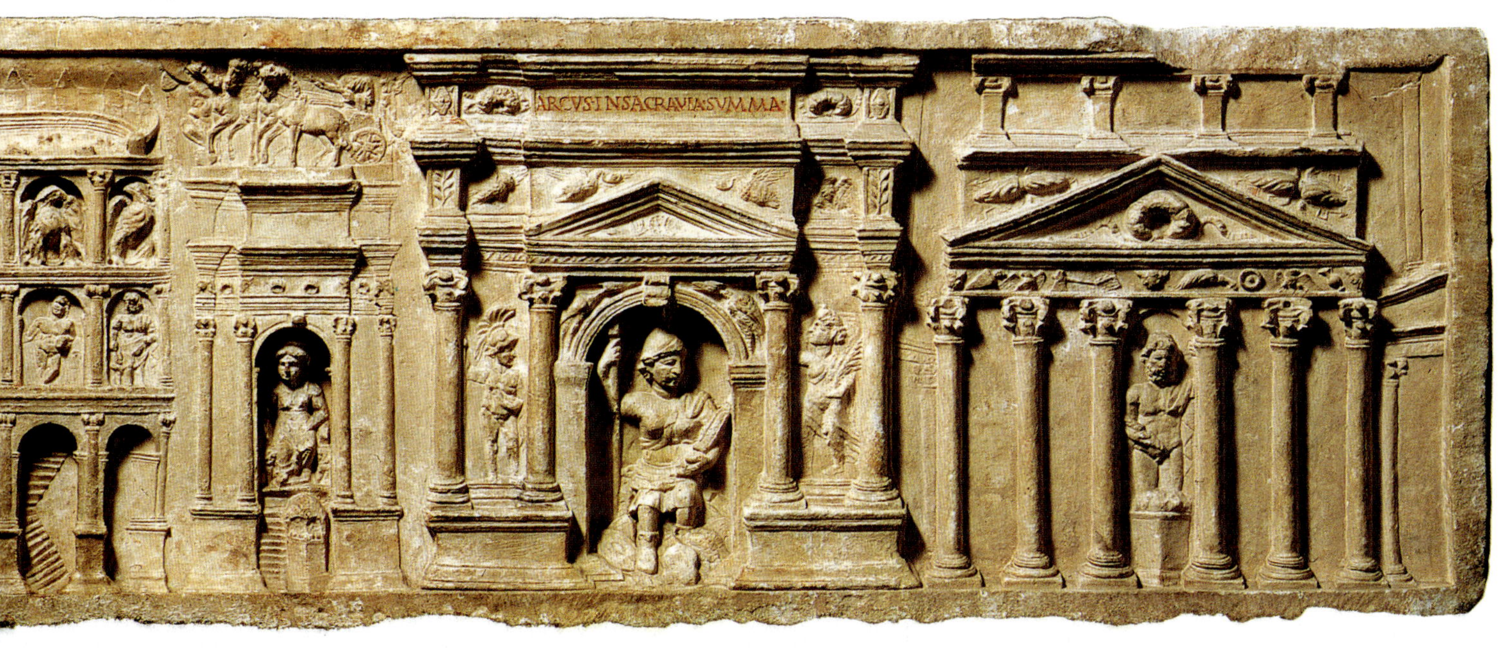

60–61 This relief shows a view of the monuments of ancient Rome. Although the splendour of its buildings made it a unique metropolis, Rome faced many of the problems which beset modern cities. In order to cope with the terrible traffic congestion, for example, carts were not allowed on the streets during the day, with the sole exception of those transporting refuse or building materials for public works. It thus became necessary to provide large parking areas for vehicles and horses (areae carruces), *and parking attendants were employed. Refuse disposal and road cleaning involved considerable problems for the city's administrators, and fire prevention was also a major task. It was handled by a corps of* vigiles *organized along military lines, who were equipped with ladders, buckets, fireproof blankets and pumps which could be connected to the public fountains.*

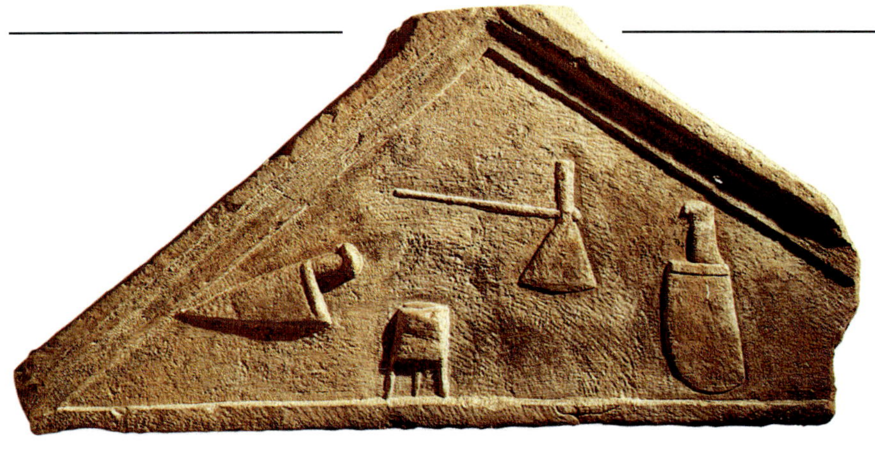

62 (left) A relief showing the tools of a butcher. Trades such as this in ancient Rome were organized in a way that is still familiar in the present day: there were wholesalers, retailers and even salesmen who travelled all year round to sell and advertise the goods of the major firms.

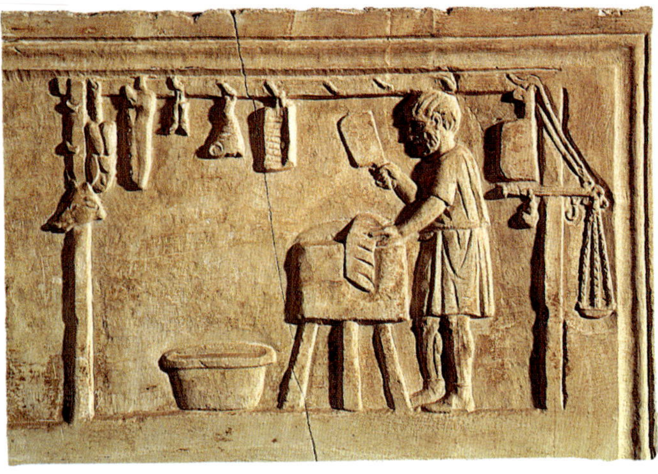

62 (above) In this relief of the interior of a butcher's shop the artist has paid great attention to detail. Note the steelyard behind the shopkeeper, the various cuts of meat, and the basin to catch the blood. From the 2nd century BC the Romans ate more meat, especially lamb and pork.

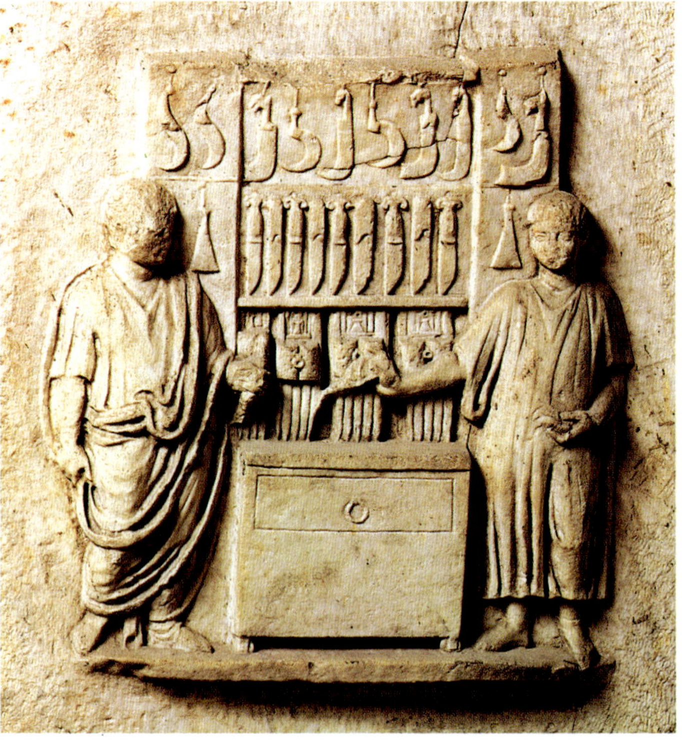

62 (above) This relief, dating from the 1st century AD, shows the workshop of a knife-maker. The first tradesmen's guilds, which played an important part in the development and management of the Roman economy, were founded in the age of the kings. Under Augustus, when there were already over 150 of them, they were subjected to government regulation, requiring them to hold imperial authorization.

bakeries, together with those where blacksmiths, shoemakers, potters, carpenters, glaziers and stone-dressers worked. The *tabernae argentariae* were 'banks' which primarily dealt in currency exchange. All these traders usually conducted their business out of doors, and their stalls obstructed the streets, increasing traffic problems.

Litters, sedan chairs and vehicles of all kinds also thronged the streets, as well as flocks of sheep and herds of cattle. At night the streets were dark and dangerous places as there was no public lighting, except in the central area, and anyone venturing out had to go about in groups, or be preceded by slaves bearing torches or lanterns.

There was a continual hum of noise both by day and by night, when carts carrying heavy goods were allowed to circulate freely in the city streets, now finally empty. Life was mainly lived out of doors, and there was an incessant babble of voices, and, as Martial wrote, 'the schoolmasters won't leave you in peace in the morning or the bakers by night, and at all hours of the day the coppersmiths are beating with their hammers. Here there's a moneychanger who, having nothing else to do, overturns a pile of coins on his filthy table; over there is a workman with a gleaming hammer beating gold ore from Spain, already smashed to pieces, while the fanatical rabble of initiates of the cult of Bellona never ceases its bawling. The shipwrecked sailor, all bandaged up, will insist on repeating his story...the rheumy-eyed match-seller will insist on barking his wares...and who can tell how many hands beat copper receptacles in the city when, during an eclipse of the moon, spells are cast and magic rites practised?'

Despite this somewhat depressing picture, in many respects Rome, and Roman towns in general, provided their inhabitants with a quality of life which was unimaginable for many centuries, at least until the end of the Age of Enlightenment in the 18th century. The complexities of supplying water for so many people is a good example. It has been calculated that between the 3rd and 4th centuries AD the city of Rome had 11 aqueducts, which provided over one million cubic metres of water a day to meet the needs of a population of around one million. This allowed a daily consumption per person twice as high as in the present. However, the baths, fountains and other public installations absorbed a high percentage of the total supply. At the height of its glory, Rome boasted 11 large thermae (baths complexes), 856 public baths, 15 nymphaea (fountain-houses), 2 naumachiae (for mock naval battles) and 1352 fountains and basins.

The amount of water used in Pompeii was also high; only the houses of the less well-off citizens were not connected to the town water supply, but numerous fountains, usually situated at crossroads, provided for the needs of the poor. Finally, in most towns, waste water was efficiently removed by complex sewage systems.

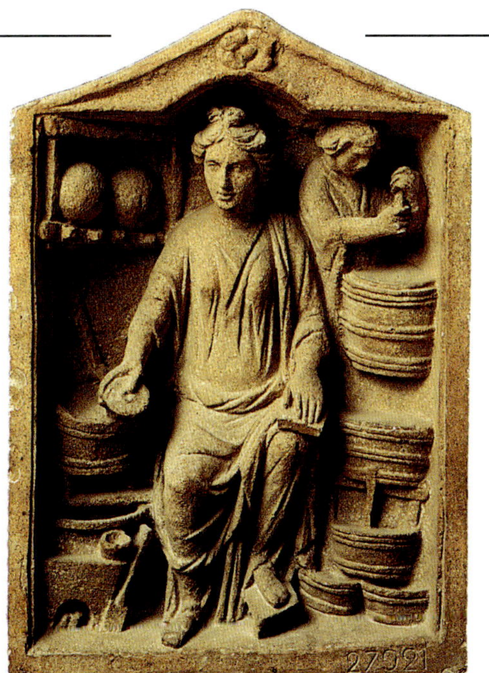

63 (right, above) Roman doctors were able to diagnose numerous illnesses, they also performed surgical operations, gave dental treatment and prescribed medicines. This relief shows a pharmacy.

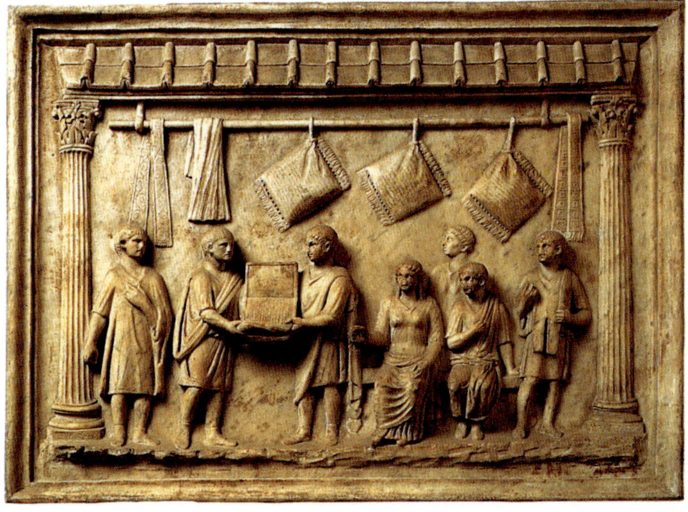

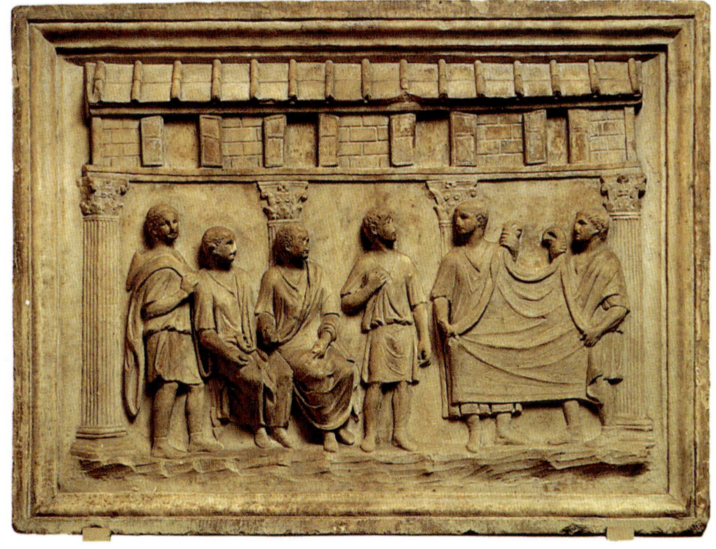

63 (above and centre) Fabric merchants display their goods to customers. Note the three fringed cushions hanging from the ceiling in the left-hand relief. The Romans were always very fond of these luxury items, preferably brightly coloured, which played an important part in home furnishings.

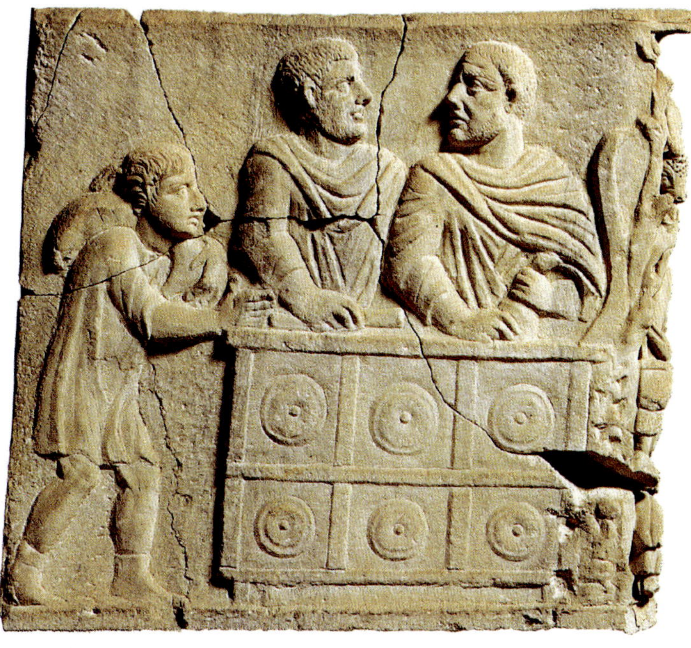

63 (right, below) A marble bas-relief of an argentarius *(banker) in his office. The* tabernae argentariae *were the equivalent of modern banks; the transactions included deposits, loans liable to interest, investments and exchange of foreign currency. Each operation was recorded in account books.*

DWELLINGS AND FURNISHINGS

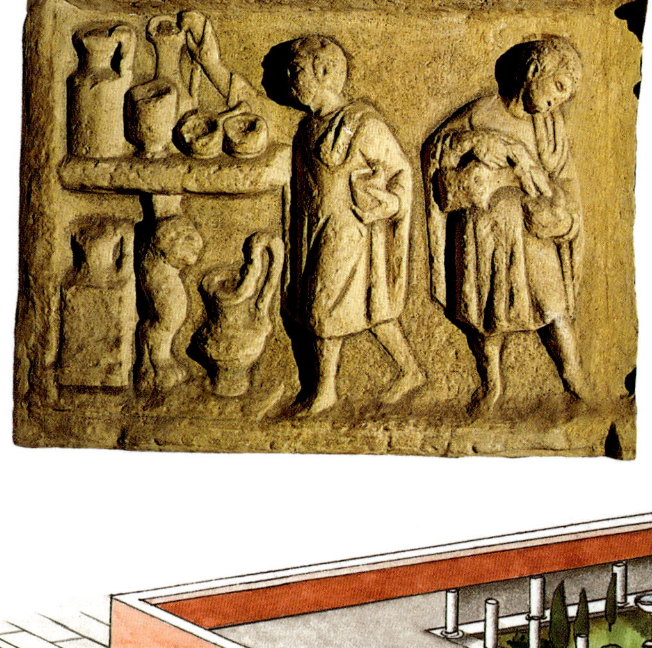

Many centuries separate the prehistoric huts of Latium from the complex, well-designed homes of Pompeii, during which time the primitive layout was transformed into the well-known Roman type. The earliest Roman house is represented by older Pompeiian homes, such as the House of the Surgeon. This consisted of an entrance (*fauces*) leading to a central courtyard (atrium) equipped with an *impluvium*, a tank to collect rainwater. The *cubicula* (bedrooms) lined the sides of the atrium and on the third side, opposite the main entrance, was the *tablinum* (dining room). Nearby were the minor rooms (*alae*). From the *tablinum* a corridor led to the garden (*hortus*).

There were variations on this basic layout, but classic examples can be found in the homes of the Etruscans, Romans and Campanians, at least until the end of the 3rd century BC. From the 2nd century BC, the model changed to the Graeco-Roman type, and houses became larger and more luxurious – one of the best examples is the House of Pansa in Pompeii. In addition to the traditional Roman layout, a second one was added, extending existing rooms and increasing the size and potential use of the house. This is the 'peristyle house', so called because its characteristic feature is a large garden surrounded by a colonnaded portico, which is mainly found in Pompeii. Such houses, which reached the height of popularity during the later republican period, sometimes featured double peristyles, bathrooms, libraries, cryptoporticuses (ground-level or underground passages), *triclinia* and other rooms whose names revealed their Greek origin.

Works of art, statues and marble ornaments were displayed in the peristyle. Herms, busts and reliefs representing theatrical masks, satyrs and cherubs were also placed in the central area, often occupied by a *viridarium*. The flowerbeds contained low espaliers of myrtle, rosemary and thyme. Acanthus was planted around the fountains and nymphaea, and other flowers added to the charm of the area. Trees included pines, fir trees, olives, oleanders and laurels, together with fruit trees such as pomegranates and apples. Vines and ivy shaded the pergolas. Roman gardeners specialized in clipping evergreen plants into animal forms or geometric shapes, called *ars topiaria*. Nymphaea, fountains and pools increased the delights of the peristyle, whose architectural settings featured niches and apses decorated with mosaics.

Another room typical of these new homes was the *triclinium*. Situated near the peristyle, it was used only as a dining room, and came into use when the practice of eating in a reclining position was introduced in Rome. The *triclinia* of the Pompeiian *domus* give only an impression of those to be found in the mansions of Rome, which could seat large numbers of guests. There were many open-air *triclinia* situated around attractive water features under pergolas, for use in warm weather.

The true Roman home, however, was not the rich *domus* but the *insula*, the large tenement block with numerous occupants. They were built of masonry with a brick curtain wall; usually with shops on the ground floor and the most comfortable, luxurious apartments near the inner courtyard. On the upper storeys were further dwellings, whose structure became less and less stable towards the top.

The *insulae* of Rome have nearly all disappeared, but many examples still exist in Ostia, like the House of

64 (opposite) Two servants performing household tasks. Roman society was rigidly divided into free men and slaves (prisoners of war, debtors and offenders whose crimes involved loss of liberty), whose masters had the right of life and death over them. They were sold in slave markets and were employed in a wide variety of tasks (from farm work to teaching mathematics) depending on their abilities; some fetched exorbitant prices. Sometimes, for special merits, slaves were granted the status of freedmen; many freedmen were able to accumulate large fortunes as a result of their skills, and bought other slaves in turn.

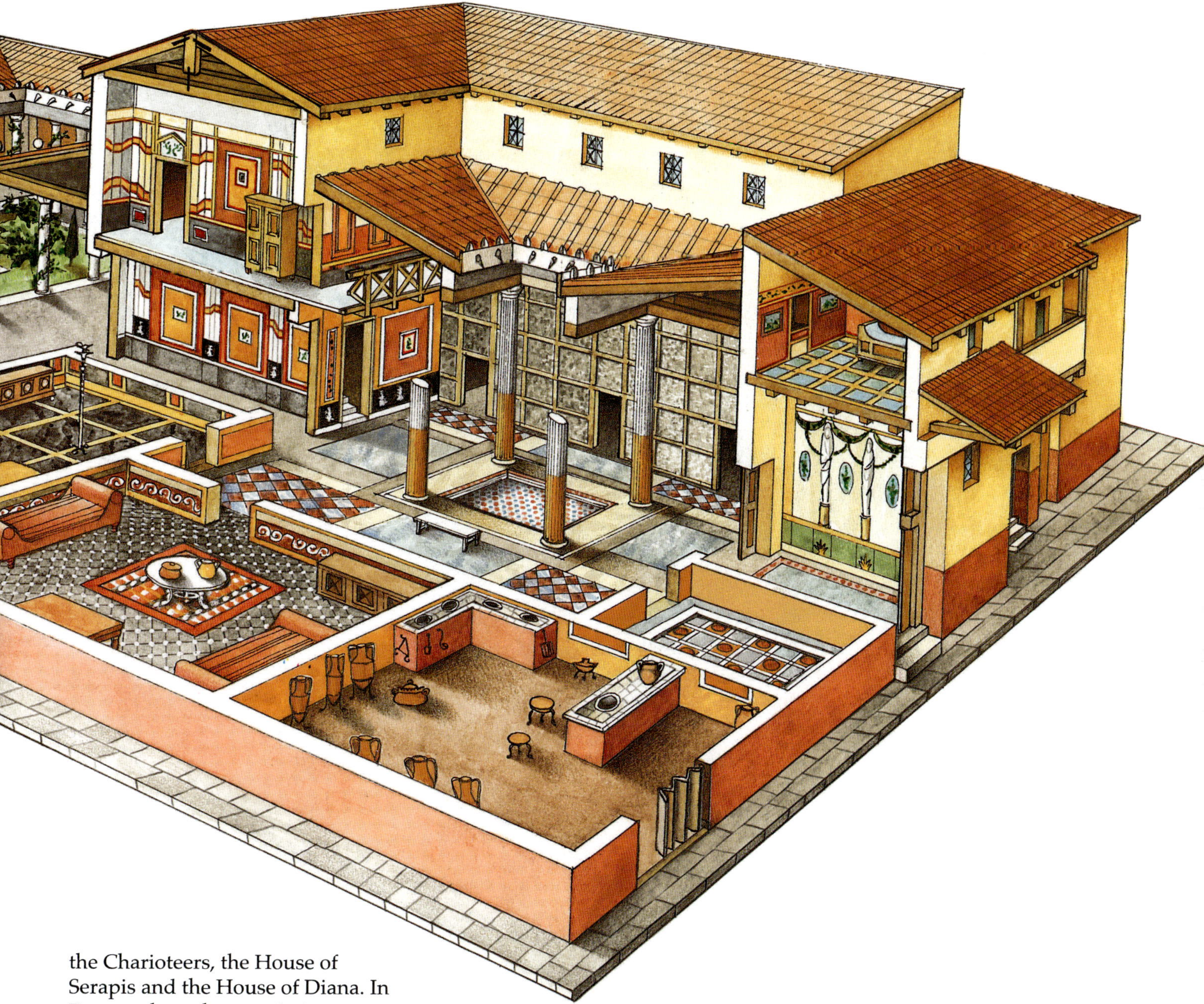

the Charioteers, the House of Serapis and the House of Diana. In Rome, where the population was much greater than elsewhere, they often reached a height of 30 m (98 ft). Rents were very high, often impossibly so, especially in Rome, where they amounted to four times those paid in other towns. More than once a rent amnesty was granted to the poorer citizens. The greed of the owners often forced tenants to sub-let their homes. Property speculation was rife, and the buyers of these buildings often deliberately caused them to collapse and started fires.

64–65 Reconstruction of a typical Pompeiian domus*: the door opened on to a passage (*fauces*) which led to an unroofed courtyard (the* atrium*), shown here partly without its plaster to reveal the structure of the masonry. In the centre was a basin (the* impluvium*) which collected rainwater and conveyed it to a cistern below. The atrium was surrounded by bedrooms (*cubicula*); at the end there were sometimes two open rooms, the alae, used for various purposes. In front of the entrance was the* tablinum*, where the owner received guests; next to it was the* triclinium*, the family dining room. The kitchen, with the toilet nearby, was a small room overlooking the atrium. Upstairs rooms were used for various purposes (study, library) and as servants' quarters. At the rear was the* peristylium*, a garden surrounded by porticoes, often with a fountain. One of the rooms overlooking the main road was often used as a shop. Unlike modern homes, the Roman* domus *was almost entirely inward-facing; light and air entered through the atrium and peristyle, and there were very few windows in the walls on the street side.*

Other discomforts had to be suffered in the *insulae*: the poorer people who lived on the upper floors enjoyed few essential services. As none of these buildings survive above the second floor, we have no evidence of running water; in any case, there were financial difficulties involved in using the city water supply. Toilets were reduced to the bare minimum, and hazardous braziers were used for heating.

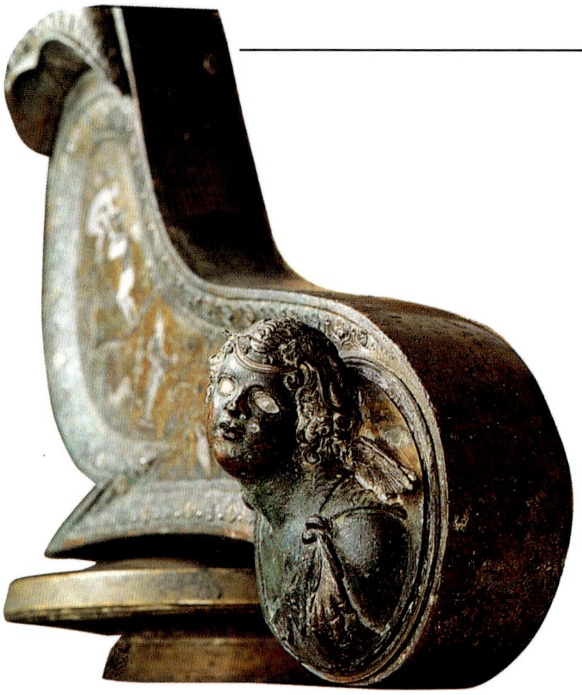

66 After the conquest of the Hellenistic kingdoms, a stream of luxury goods arrived in Rome and the city enjoyed a period of great elegance. This was reflected in furniture, numerous examples of which have survived. On this page are details of a bronze bed of the late 1st century BC*, from Amiterno in Abruzzo. The wooden parts have been reconstructed.*

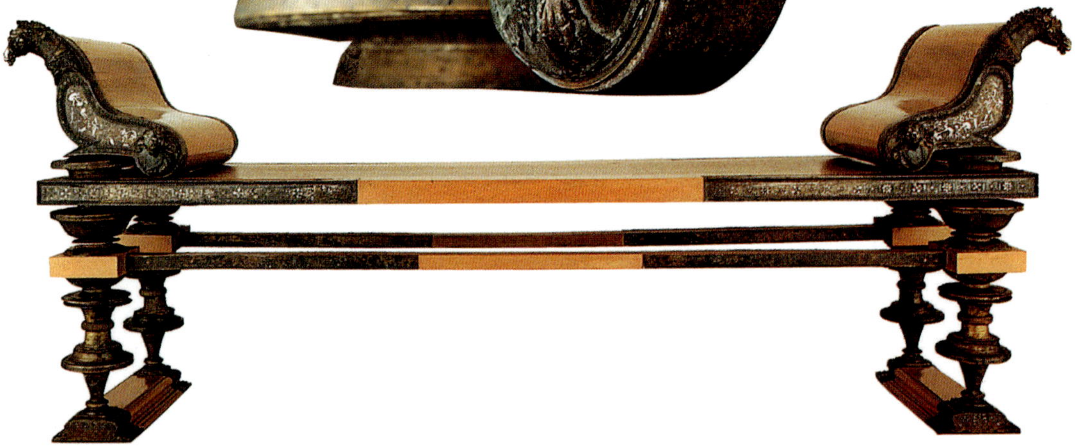

Ordinary people did not cook much at home but ate in the streets at no particular time. Hawkers offered roast meat, sausages, fried fish, olives and sweetmeats. Food could also be found in the inns – those of Ostia were particularly famous. In addition to a counter there were pitchers sunk into the floor for food storage, an oven, fireplaces and braziers. These places, called *popinae*, had a bad reputation, and were frequented by people of all kinds and gambling was common.

The culinary habits of the rich, who enjoyed magnificent banquets, must have been very different: the main dish was usually based on meat and its cooking was often elaborate, with complicated stuffings and strong flavourings.

While it may seem odd that only a small space was devoted to the kitchen in Roman homes, it is perhaps even more surprising that furnishings in general were few and far between. Niches and cupboards

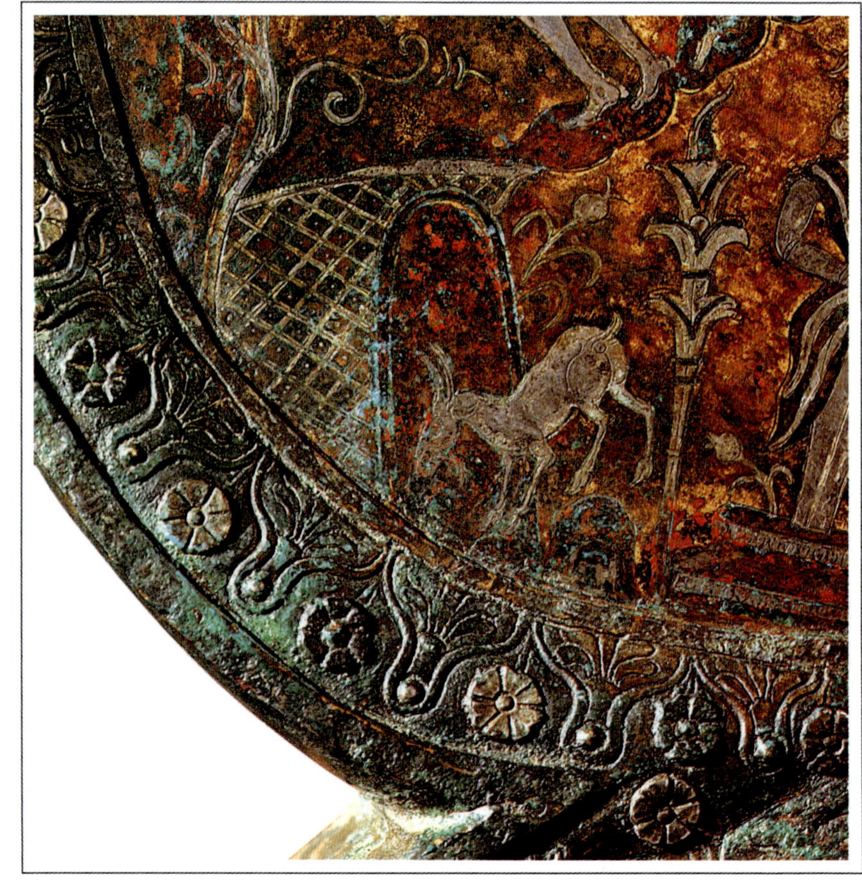

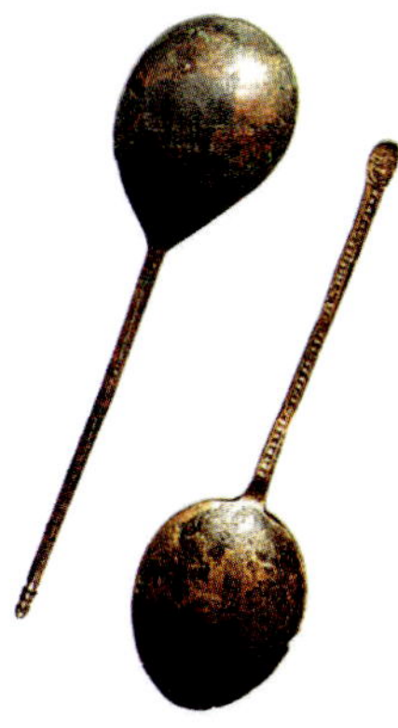

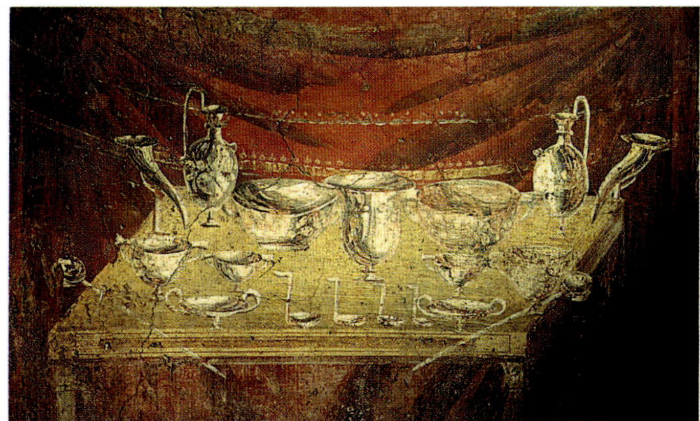

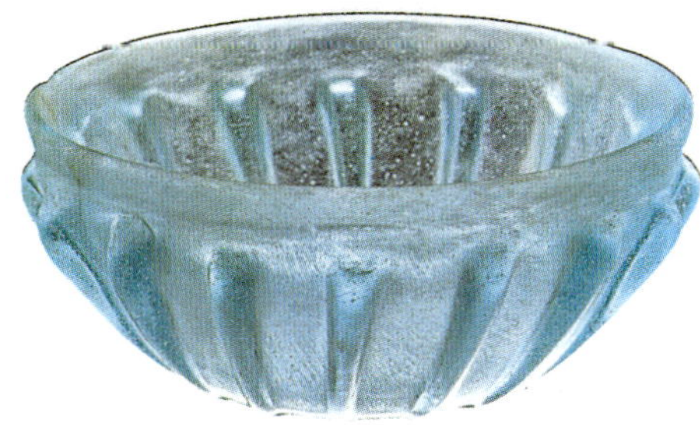

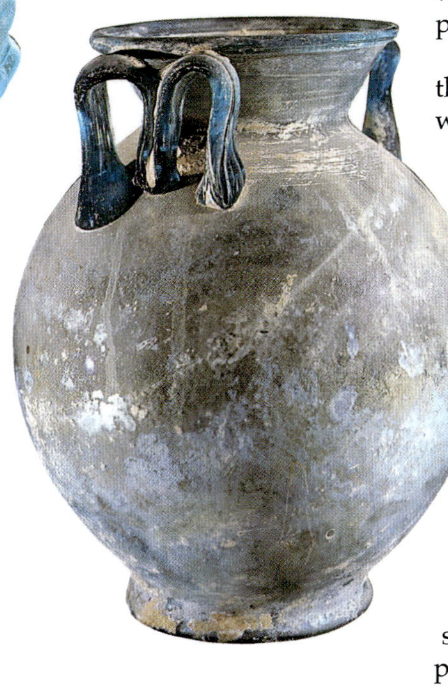

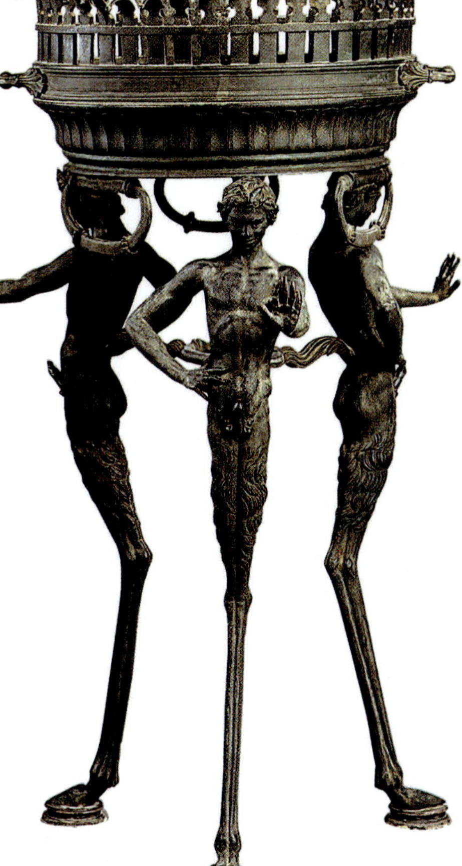

were hollowed out in the walls to hold objects and household goods. Beds and tables were often made of masonry. In the *insulae*, because of the limited space available, furniture consisted of little more than a pallet, a table and a few chairs.

An important feature of the *domus*, near the entrance, in the atrium or next to the kitchen, was the *lararium*, the shrine dedicated to the Lares – who were the household gods who protected the family. Food and libations were placed in front of their images and alongside them were kept the *imagines maiorum*, wax portraits representing the ancestors.

Characteristic items of furniture in the dining rooms of wealthy homes were the couches. They were usually arranged in a horseshoe shape, each one accommodating three people. The most attractive examples were made of high quality wood with legs and headrests (*fulcra*) made of bronze and bronze decorations. Food was placed on a round, three-legged table. An *abacus* (a sideboard of Etruscan origin) was used to display the best crockery. Tables came in numerous shapes; particularly exquisite were the *monopodia*, single-legged tables made of highly prized woods such as cedar and maple, introduced after the conquest of Asia Minor. Different types of chair included the *solium*, used by the *paterfamilias* (head of the family) and the *cathedra*, the typical woman's chair, with no arms and a high, curved back. Cupboards and chests containing a variety of objects completed the furniture of the home. Decorative objects included candlesticks of different shapes and sizes, carpets and curtains. Mosaics and paintings were also important in richer homes. In frescoes, the artists used perspective effects to create the illusion of space. Wealthier citizens collected statues, objets d'art and sometimes rare books.

67 (top) The wealthier families owned entire dinner services made of finely worked silver, comprising jugs, plates, drinking horns and cutlery; the less wealthy used bronze or pottery.

67 (centre) The Romans called everything used to furnish the home (from crockery to wall frescoes) suppellex. *Glassware was very popular, and its manufacture reached very high levels of accomplishment.*

67 (below) Braziers of various shapes and sizes were used to heat the rooms of the home. This one, with legs in the form of young satyrs, was found in Herculaneum, and is of a particularly elegant design. The ithyphallic representation, which was not considered in the least vulgar, had an auspicious and even apotropaic function in Roman times. For this reason painted or carved phalluses, intended to ward off the evil eye, appear on the walls of many homes in Pompeii.

68 In the baths the women entered the palaestra and bathed wearing a brassière (fascia pectoralis) *and briefs* (subligar), *similar to the modern bikini. In this detail of the famous mosaic . decorating the 'bikini girls room' in the Piazza Armerina villa in Sicily, two young women are engaged in gymnastic exercises to warm up before the various stages of bathing. The baths, which were patronized by all classes of society and were the hub of the city's social life, not only contained the facilities required for personal hygiene, but also served as a meeting place and reading room and were used for conferences and sports contests.*

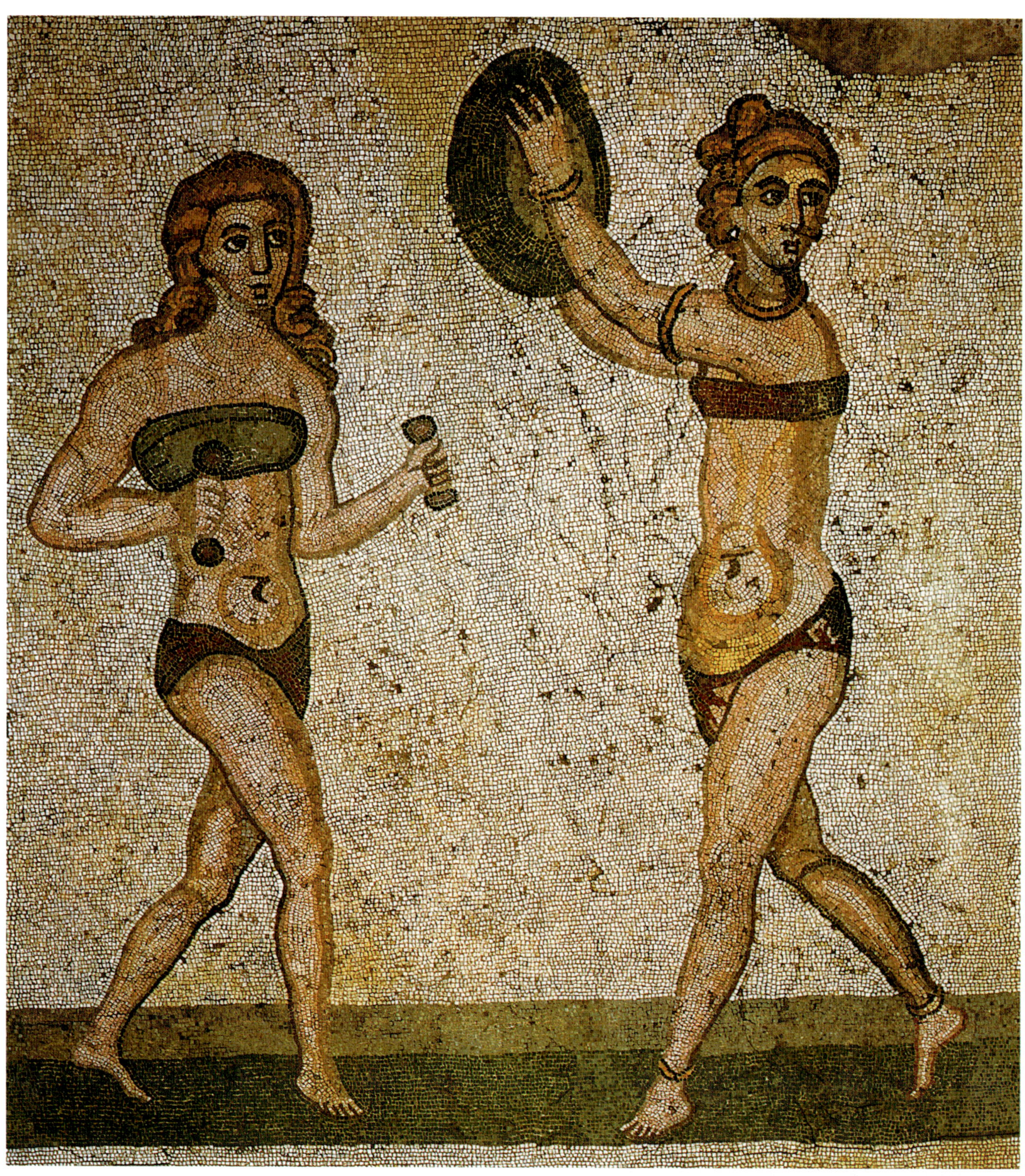

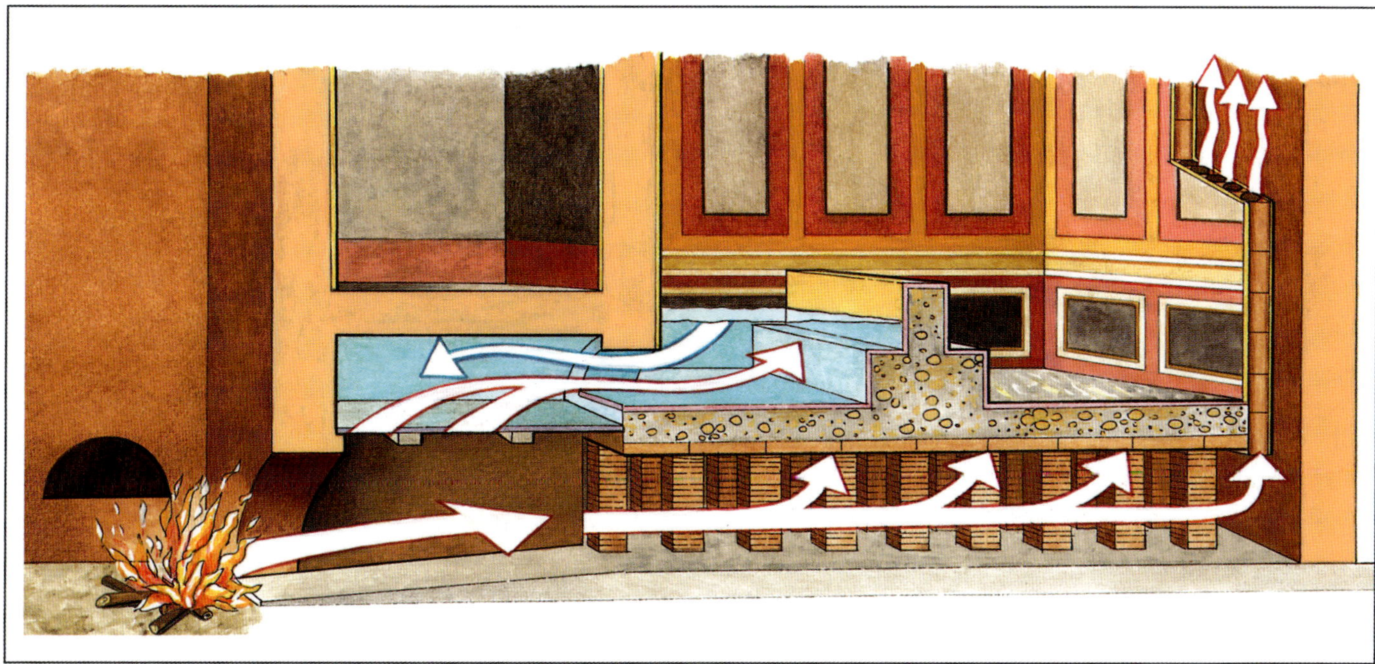

As today, the problem of occupying one's free time also arose in ancient Rome. For the mass of loafers, unemployed, immigrants and adventurers there was an endless choice: they could roam around the forums, basilicas and porticoes, and drink and gamble in the inns. For ordinary citizens the working day ended quite early and it was impossible to go out at night because the city was a dangerous place when darkness fell, so they had to find something to do until supper time.

A good solution for all was a visit to the baths – a daily routine for rich and poor, young and old, men and women alike. In the imperial age they were free of charge; at other times entrance might cost a *quadrans* at most, far less than a litre of wine or a loaf of bread.

The various rooms were laid out in accordance with the sequence of operations. First came the changing room (apodyterium), followed by the hot bath room (caldarium) then a moderately heated intermediate room (tepidarium), and finally the cold bath room (frigidarium), completed by the swimming pool (natatio), usually situated in the open air. All around were other rooms for saunas, massage and depilation. There were also gymnasiums, libraries, reading rooms, lounges and even places to eat a snack. The baths thus not only met the needs of physical fitness, but also provided opportunities for social contact, where people met for the pleasure of the encounter as well as to talk about politics, sport and business.

Ball games were one of the most popular activities at the baths and depending on whether they were played outdoors or in special closed rooms called *sphaeristeria*, the ball would be filled with feathers, sand or air. The most common game was *trigon*, played by three people; another was *harpastum*, similar to modern rugby, in which a player had to obtain control of the ball and keep it, withstanding pushes and shoves by a crowd of opponents.

Other great attractions were the circus and the amphitheatre. Public performances had always been used as a means of political and electoral propaganda in Rome, and in the imperial age were essential to the absolute rule of the emperor. Along with periodic corn doles they served to keep the population under control: satiated bodily and

69 Water for the baths was supplied by an aqueduct, then collected in large cisterns and conveyed through pipes regulated by valves and taps direct to the cold bathing pools. The water for the hot bathing pools was diverted to the boilers, then mixed with more cold water if necessary. Another method, shown in the reconstruction, provided both hot water and room heating in the caldarium. From the oven, hot air passed under a section of the pool (testudo alvei)*, maintaining it at a constant temperature because of the convective flow characteristic of fluids, by which cold water tends to sink and warm water to rise. The hot air was conveyed to the hypocaust (the cavity under the floor supported by pillars) and then rose to vents in the roof of the building, flowing through brick pipes in the walls of the caldarium. Although the floor was formed of a thick insulating* suspensura*, it was often too hot, and the bathers therefore wore wooden-soled clogs. Similar heating systems were also used in private villas.*

mentally, the people had little desire to think. Having acquired this role, entertainments, called *ludi* (games), multiplied over the years, and the feast days with which they were originally associated increased, rising to a record number of 182 a year by the imperial age.

The games were generally held by day, but sometimes they also took place at night, by torchlight. They might last for hours and even, with intervals and interruptions, a whole day. The *ludi* constituted a social event – people went there 'to see and be seen', wearing elegant clothes, hairstyles and jewelry and attended by maids, even at the price of getting into debt or squandering their fortunes. The circus games (*ludi circenses*), the oldest of all, were held in the Circus Maximus. This huge structure could hold over 250,000 spectators because of its special construction which allowed wooden stands to be erected in addition to the stone terraces. Its main feature was the *spina*, a low, straight wall 340 m (1115 ft) long, with a wealth of architectural and decorative elements, such as the gigantic obelisk of Ramesses II brought to Rome to commemorate the conquest of Egypt. At each end there was a group of seven, large, gilded bronze eggs and another of seven bronze dolphins; an egg or a dolphin was removed from each alternately to indicate the number of laps run by the chariots during races.

Light, fast chariots drawn by two, three or four horses competed in the chariot races held in the circus. Charioteers had to drive seven laps of the circuit anticlockwise at the greatest possible speed, very close to the *spina* and rounding it at the *metae* (sets of three conical pillars at either end). During the race all kinds of dirty tricks were not only acceptable but positively encouraged by the crowd, such as the right-hand chariots crowding the left-hand ones as close as possible with the aim of making them crash into the *spina*.

The horses and charioteers were divided into factions, each with their own colour. There were originally two, but the number was later increased to four: *Russata* (red), *Albata* (white), *Veneta* (blue) and *Prasina* (green). *Russata* usually raced with *Veneta*, and *Albata* with *Prasina*. During races the charioteers wore clothing in the colour of their faction. It consisted of a tunic with a band of leather straps tightly bound round the chest to prevent fractures of the ribs, leggings to protect shins and thighs, and a helmet to protect the head. The charioteers were very popular, and often accumulated huge fortunes. The horses also had their fans, who gave them grand names like Victor or Adorandus, or jokey ones like Piripinus.

Spectacles in the amphitheatre were also hugely popular. The Flavian amphitheatre, better known

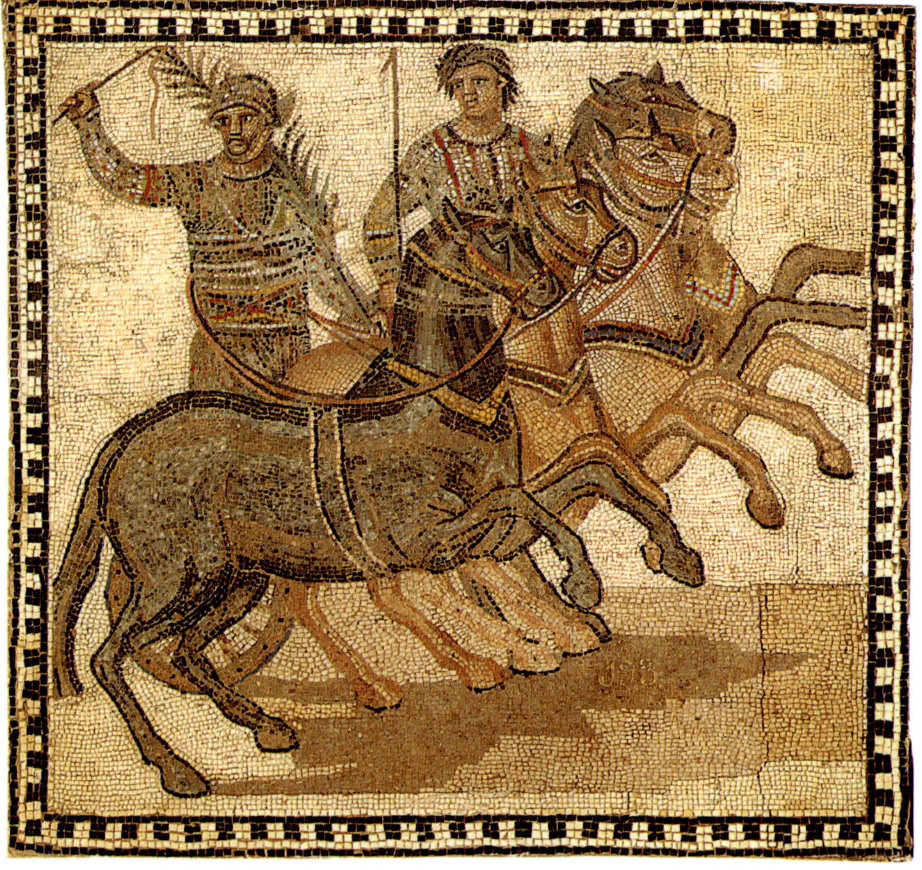

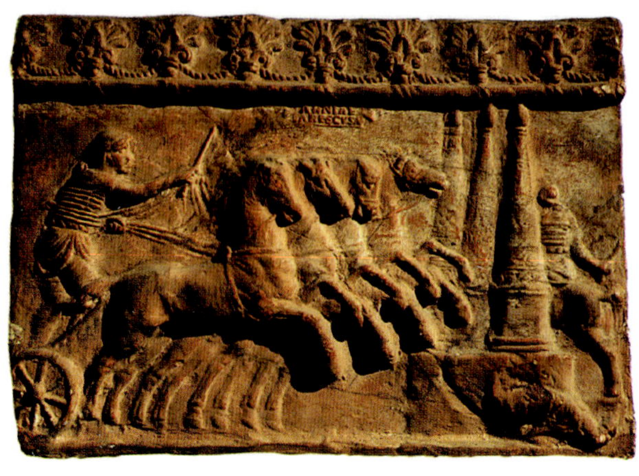

70 (above) Circus scenes are very common among the wealth of mosaics produced in the late imperial period, attesting to the great popularity of this type of entertainment. The actual races alternated with contests of skill and comedy shows, but the audience went wild when the charioteers of the four official teams appeared.

70 (below) This lively terracotta bas-relief shows a charioteer about to drive round one of the metae. *The contestants most popular with the public were those who demonstrated their courage and skill by performing reckless stunts; these feats were also generously rewarded by the managers of the various teams.*

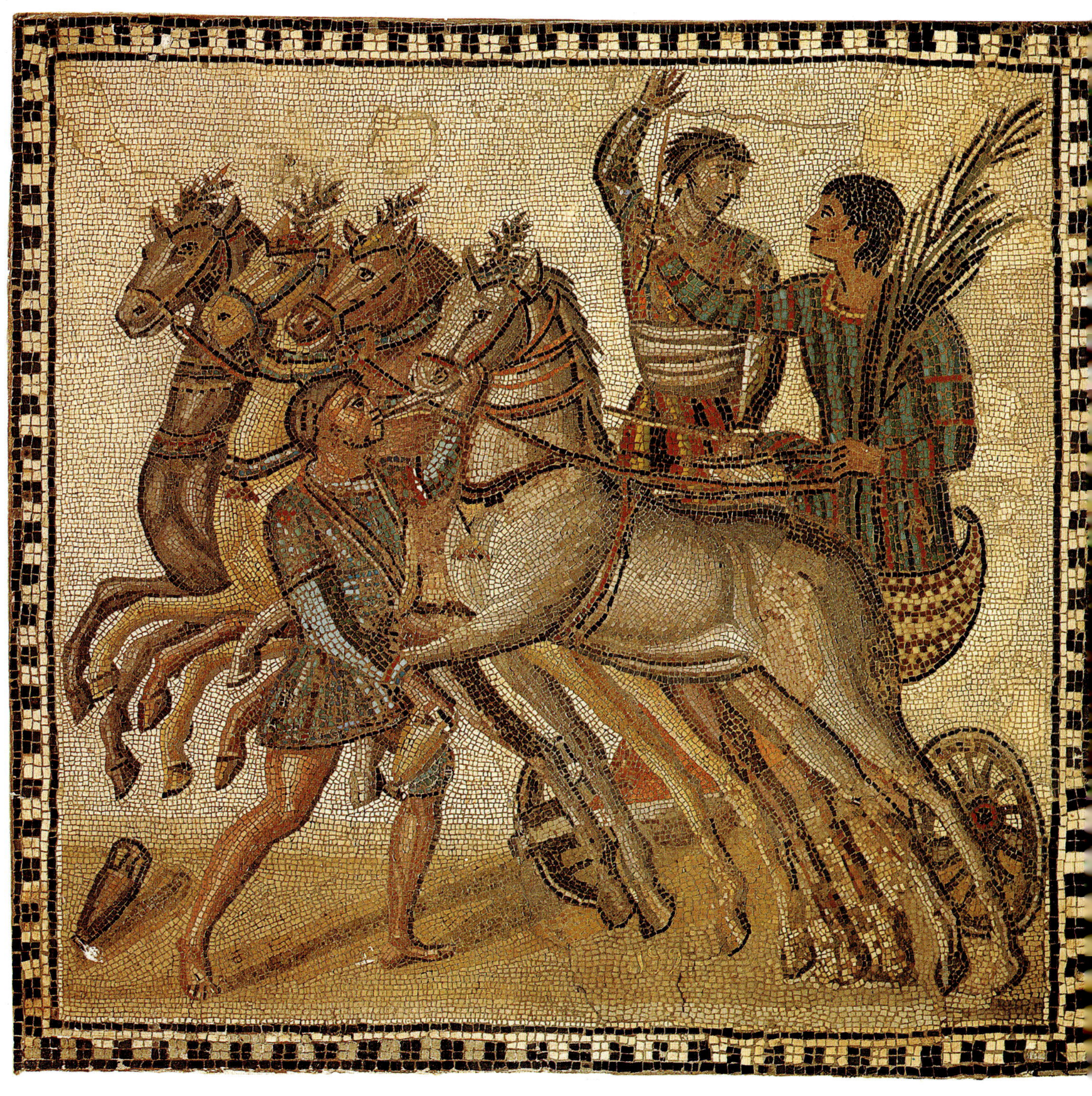

71 (above) Individual charioteers were very popular, and often amassed huge fortunes. The horses also had their fans, who gave them impressive names such as Victor or Adorandus, or jokey ones like Piripinus. Furious disputes often broke out between the supporters of the various teams.

72–73 (overleaf) Life and death in the amphitheatre, in a mosaic dating from the 4th century AD. *Gladiatorial combat originated with the Etruscans – slaves or prisoners were forced to fight at the funerals of notable figures to satisfy the blood-lust of the gods. The custom was then adopted in ancient Rome, where its significance gradually changed, and the combats became increasingly grandiose public entertainments. The* munera *were held in purpose-built structures and financed by emperors and politicians seeking to win the people's favour. They spread to every province of the empire.*

73 Gladiators were classed according to the weapons and equipment they used. The performances required considerable organization, and there were special schools where all the tricks of the trade where taught. The most famous school for gladiators, called the Ludus Magnus, *was in Rome, near the Colosseum.*

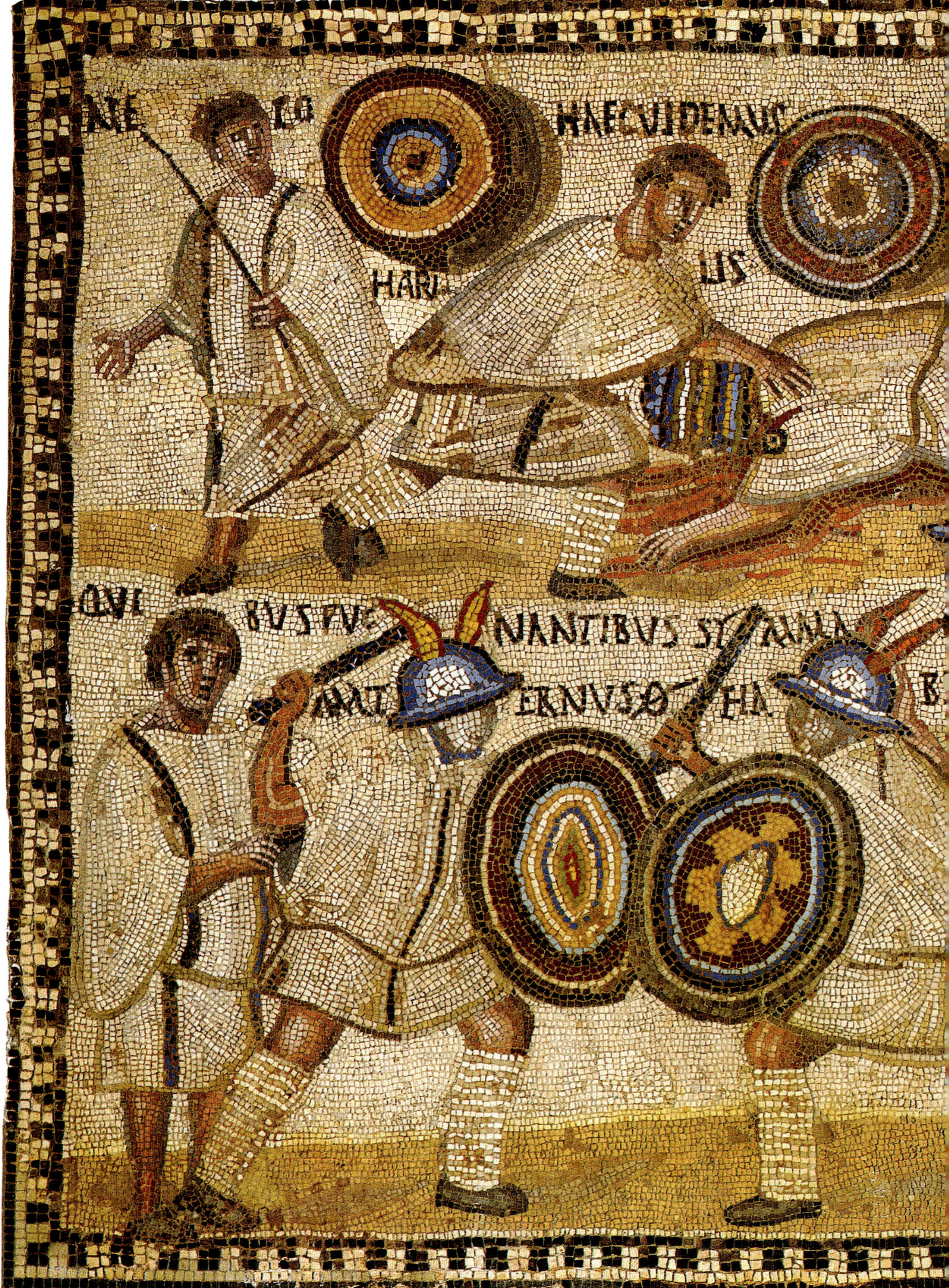
HAEC VIDEMUS
QVI
BVS PVG
NANTIBVS
ERNVS

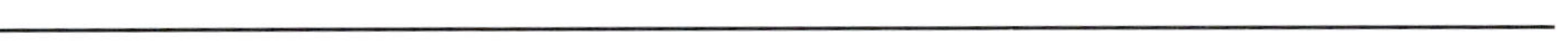

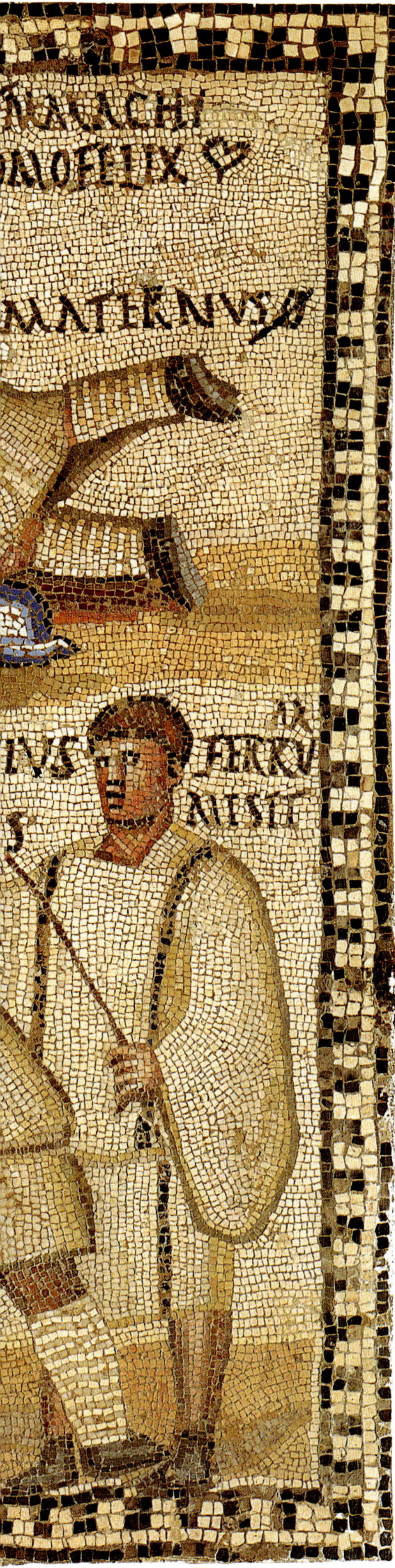

as the Colosseum, was a building truly worthy of a city like Rome, combining grandiosity with functionality. Inaugurated in AD 80 it had an elliptical plan, with a circumference of 537 m (1762 ft) and it was 50 m (165 ft) high. Below the arena, the floor of which was made of wooden boards covered with sand, was a basement where wild animals and scenery for the events were kept, as well as the machinery used to lift them to arena level. A huge canvas canopy which was hauled up from the outside by special naval squads served to protect spectators from the heat. The inaugural celebrations went on non-stop for 100 days, during which hundreds of gladiators and 5000 animals died.

Gladiatorial fights consisted of a series of duels between pairs of opponents who were specially trained in various types of combat, for which particular weapons and techniques were used. After various preambles, accompanied by an orchestra which highlighted the most important moments with music, the show began. Duels between several pairs of gladiators took place simultaneously; those who were not killed but were unable to continue laid down their weapons, and could ask for mercy by raising an arm. The decision rested with the emperor, who usually complied with the demands shouted by the crowd: '*mitte!*' (send him back) or '*iugula!*' (cut his throat).

The gladiators were divided into various categories: *samniti*, *secutores*, *oplomachi*, *provocatores*, *retiarii*, *murmillones* and *thraces*. The *retiarius* was an intriguing figure – his only defence was a kind of 'sleeve' of metal strips protecting his left arm and he was armed with a trident and a net. With these he tried to immobilize his opponent, usually the *murmillon*, a heavily armed

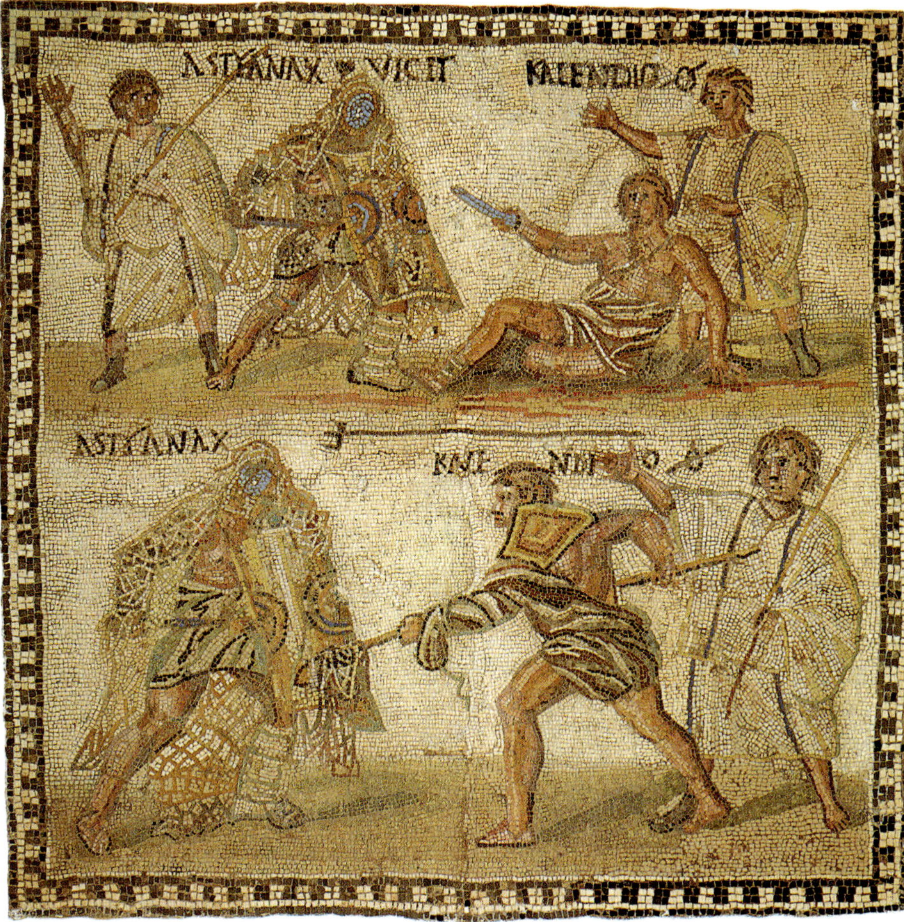

74–75 *It took just five years to complete the Flavian amphitheatre, better known as the Colosseum – from* AD *75 to 80, when it was inaugurated with 100 days of* munera *and* venationes *(games and wild beast hunts). It is an architectural wonder, especially if its extraordinary dimensions are considered: it is 50 m (165 ft) high and 188 m (617 ft) long on its major axis, and held 50–70,000 spectators. It is estimated that its construction required 100,000 cubic metres of travertine, 6000 tons of concrete and 300 tons of iron for the brackets which held the blocks together. To ensure the maximum possible speed of construction, the site was divided into four sectors, each commissioned from a different contractor. The sectors were further organized according to the materials and the height required, in accordance with a detailed plan, in order to optimize costs. The Colosseum consists of 80 radial walls,*

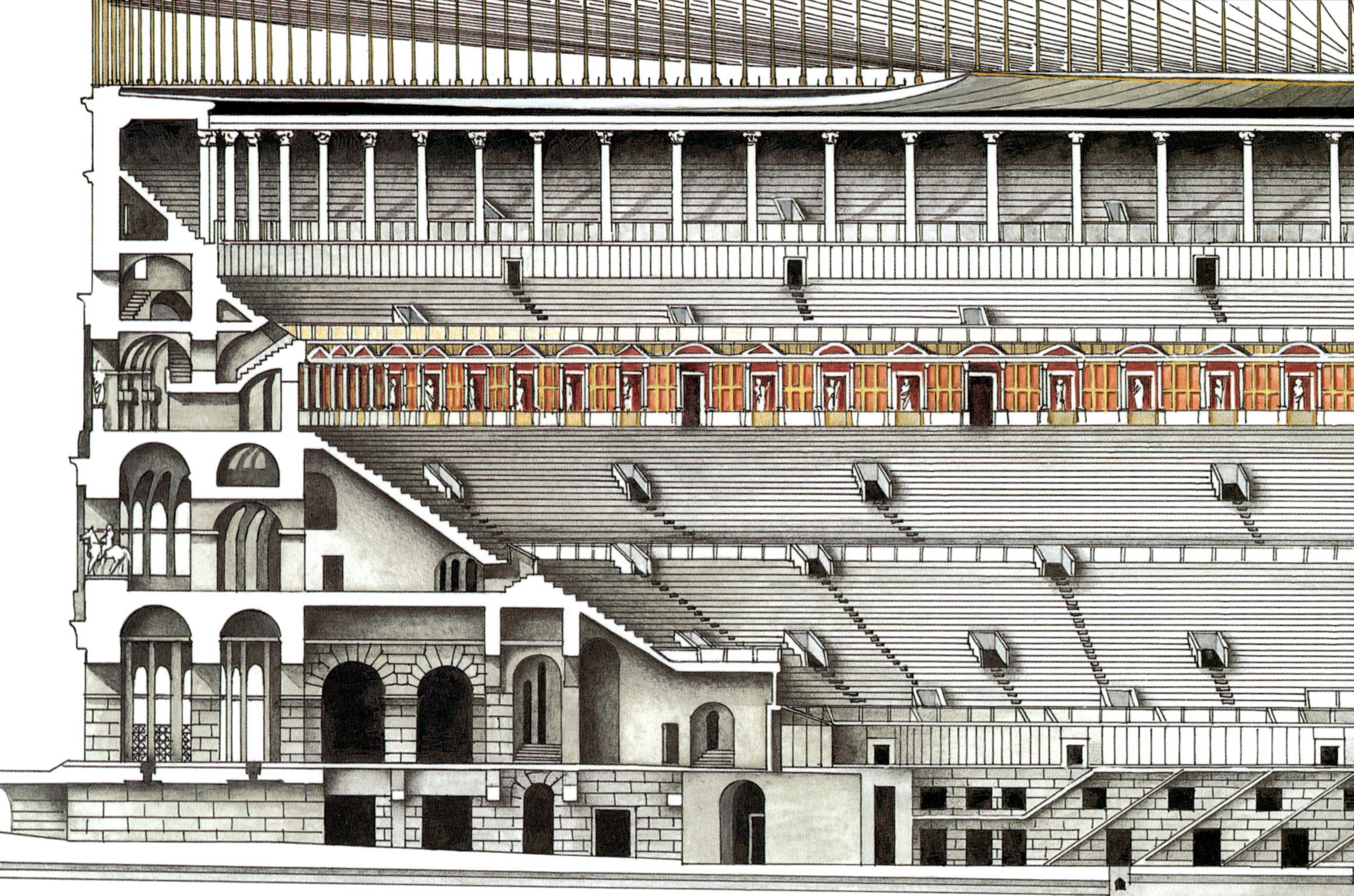

opponent who wore a helmet emblazoned with a fish (*murma*). The combat thus symbolized the battle between fish and fisherman. Gladiators were usually slaves, war captives or prisoners condemned to death, but some free men were attracted, perhaps by hunger, to this terrible career.

Wild beast hunts (*venationes*) were a popular event in the amphitheatre. The animals, starving after a long period in the dark without food, were flung into the arena. Their death had to be spectacular, so various events were arranged, such as fights with bulls or rhinoceroses, or battles between different animals, or animals chasing totally unarmed men, who were inevitably torn to pieces. The scenery was carefully designed to reproduce the natural environment of the wild beasts.

There were other, minor kinds of entertainment ranging from exhibitions of tamed animals and parodies of *venationes*, with hares chased by dwarfs, to acts by jugglers, acrobats and illusionists. Some popular shows re-enacted mythical and historical episodes and folk stories, like that of a brigand who was captured and crucified or torn to pieces by a bear. All these bloodthirsty spectacles were taken very seriously and watched enthusiastically by the excited crowds. In particularly permissive periods some ladies of good society took part: 'Mervia, bare-breasted and brandishing a skewer, chases a Tuscan wild boar around the arena'. Accustomed to such excitement, the populace was less interested in more decorous forms of entertainment. Athletic contests and gymnastic exhibitions were actually considered immoral, despite the fact that Domitian built a magnificent stadium on the Campus Martius intending to revive the sporting contests of ancient Greece. He also built an Odeum next to it for musical performances.

converging from the outer to the inner ring, which supported the great auditorium made of travertine blocks, and the complex system of tunnels and staircases which allowed the audience to exit the huge building in just a few minutes. The load-bearing structure is made of carved stone blocks, while the vaults between one wall and the next were cast in concrete. The outer perimeter ring consists of four storeys: the first three each had 80 arches which supported one another, distributing the weight of the building on the foundations in a perfectly balanced way. The 240 poles which supported the ropes of the great canopy used to shade the auditorium were driven into the perimeter of the fourth storey, with its square windows. The huge canopy, which consisted of numerous strips of canvas joined together, was hauled up by 100 sailors from the fleet at Misenum.

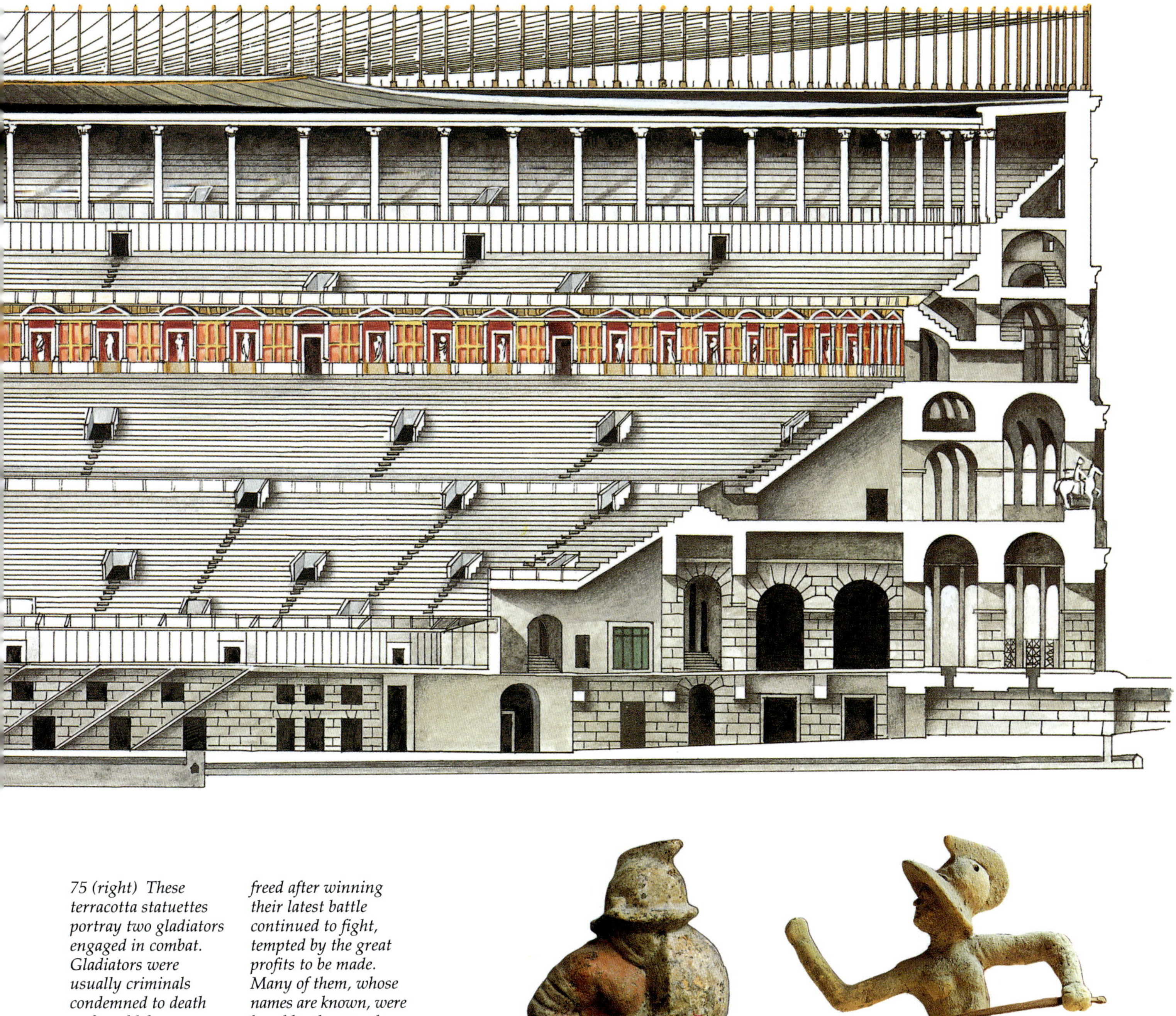

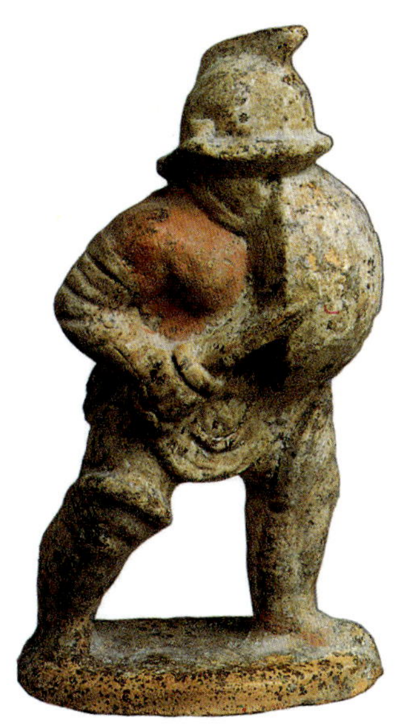

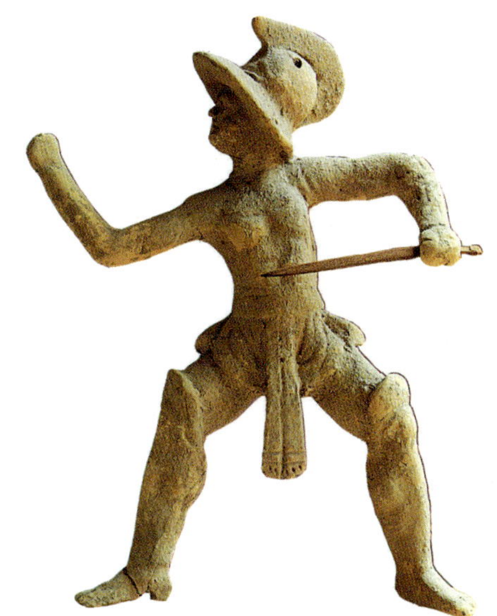

75 (right) These terracotta statuettes portray two gladiators engaged in combat. Gladiators were usually criminals condemned to death or forced labour, or slaves who had committed serious offences; sometimes, however, they were free men attracted by the chance of becoming famous and earning large sums of money. Incredible as it may seem, numerous gladiators who were freed after winning their latest battle continued to fight, tempted by the great profits to be made. Many of them, whose names are known, were loved by the crowds, and ended their long careers with a fair amount of wealth. It is believed that the most famous gladiators minimized the risks when they fought, sending the crowd wild with consummate skill, rather as in present-day wrestling.

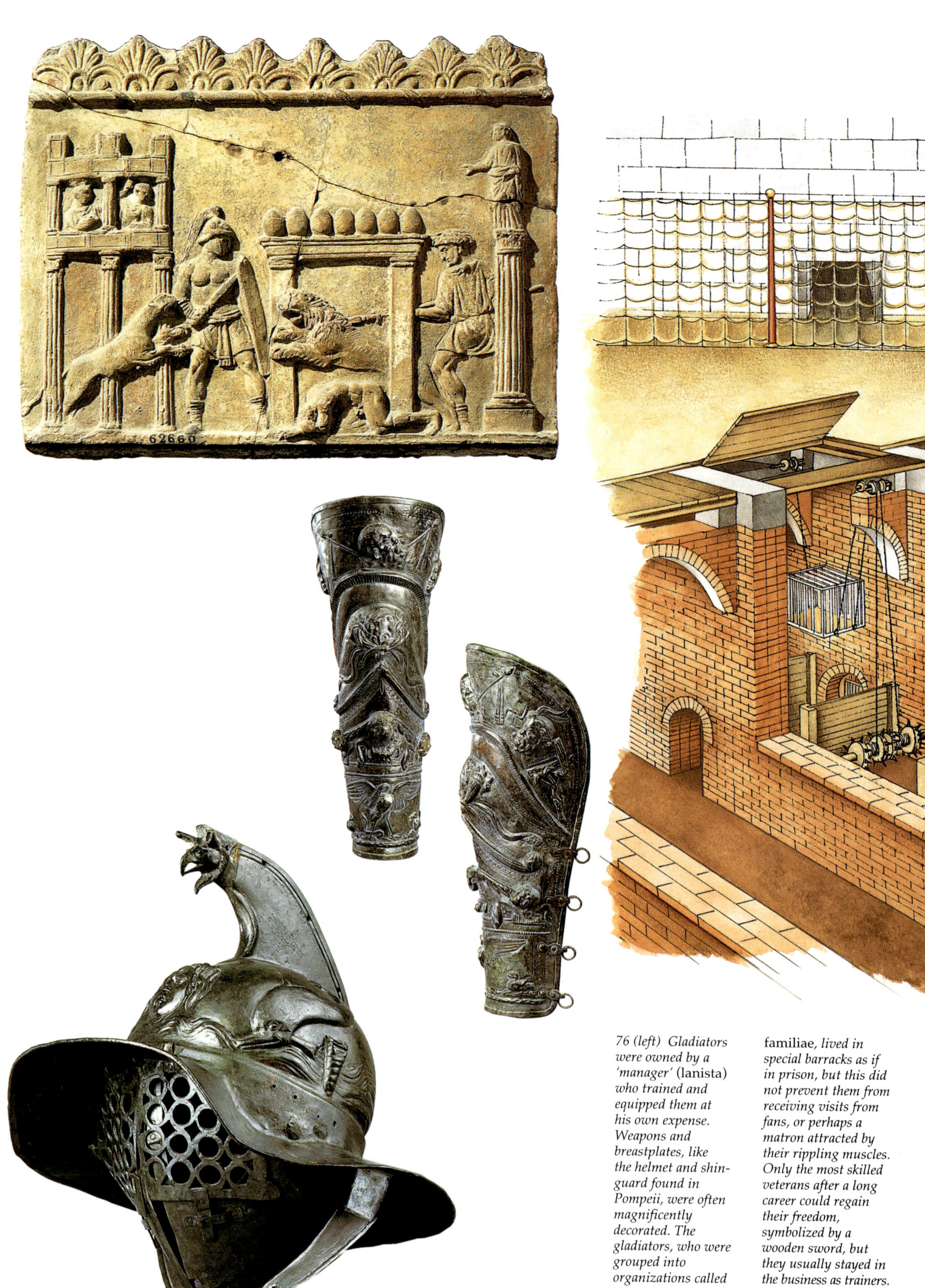

76 (left) Gladiators were owned by a 'manager' (lanista) *who trained and equipped them at his own expense. Weapons and breastplates, like the helmet and shin-guard found in Pompeii, were often magnificently decorated. The gladiators, who were grouped into organizations called* familiae, *lived in special barracks as if in prison, but this did not prevent them from receiving visits from fans, or perhaps a matron attracted by their rippling muscles. Only the most skilled veterans after a long career could regain their freedom, symbolized by a wooden sword, but they usually stayed in the business as trainers.*

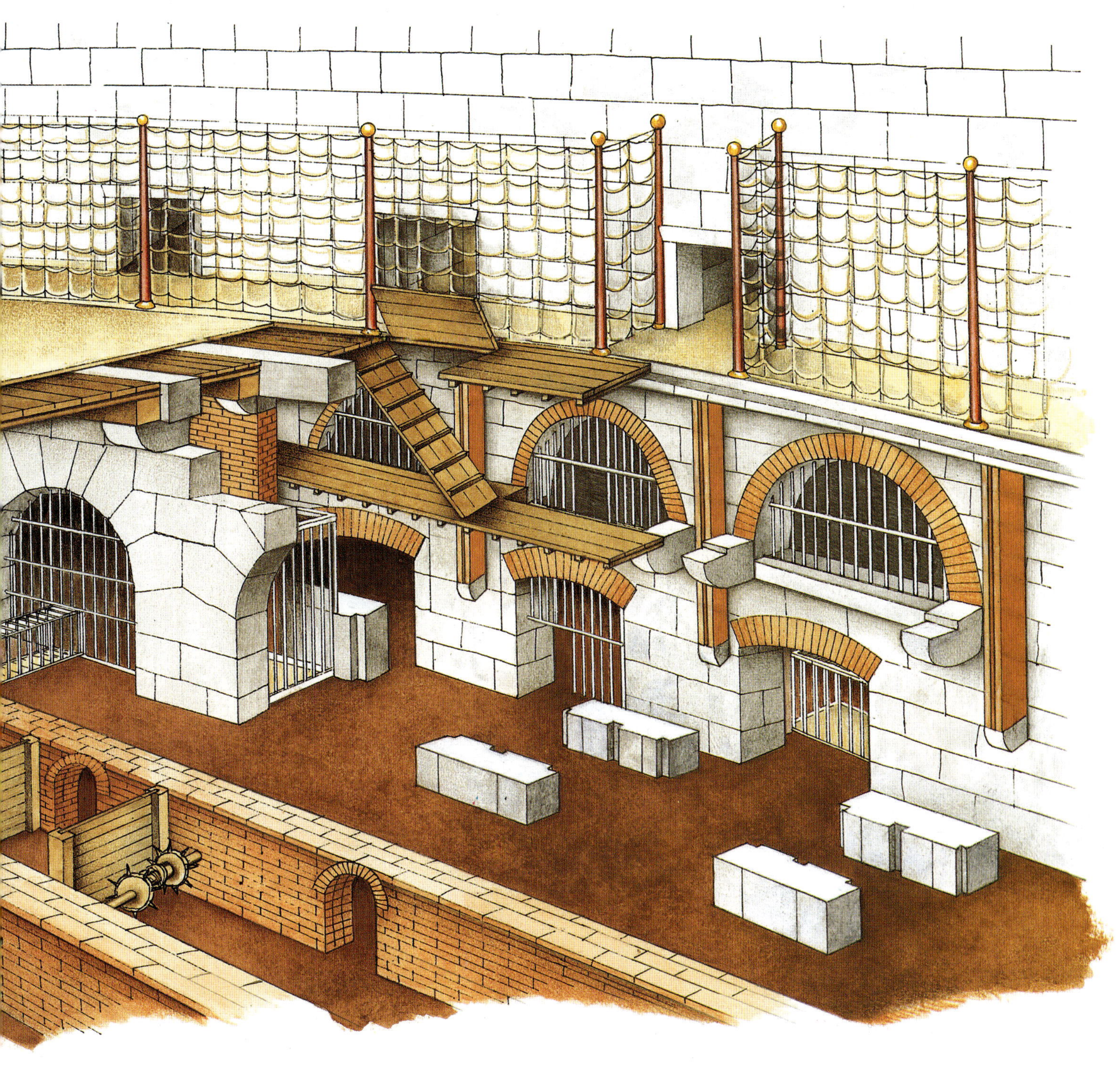

76–77 Domitian ordered the construction of the Colosseum basements as he decided to use other purpose-built structures for the naumachiae (miniature naval battles for which the arena was flooded). With the aid of this maze of tunnels, cells and service corridors, the amphitheatre reached the height of its glory: wild beasts and gladiators could be made to appear suddenly in the middle of the arena by the use of ramps and elevators operated by winches and counterweights, together with scenery portraying temples, woods or mountains. Passages between cages could be closed with partitions to reduce the risk of escape. The basement was roofed with wooden boards covered with fine sand in which various trapdoors were concealed. A strong net surrounded the entire perimeter of the arena to protect the spectators in the front rows from the wild beasts.

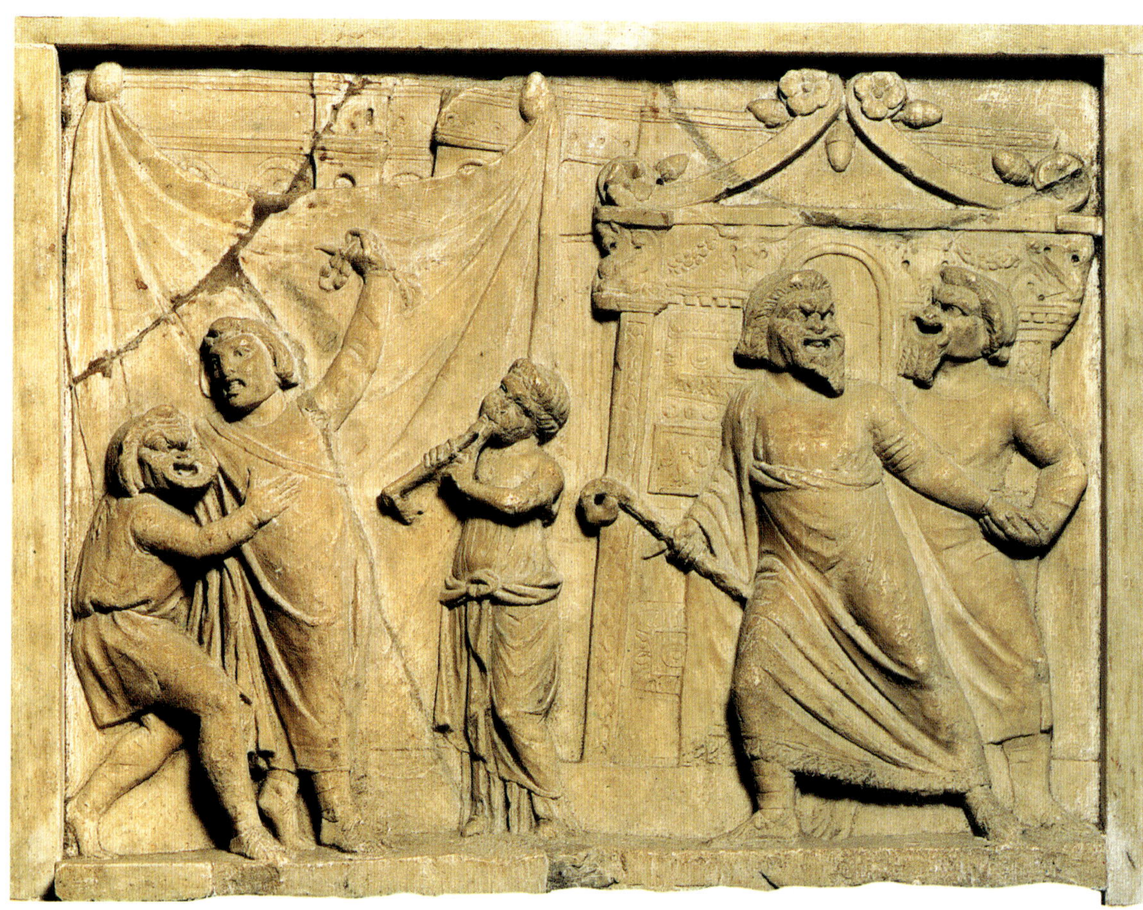

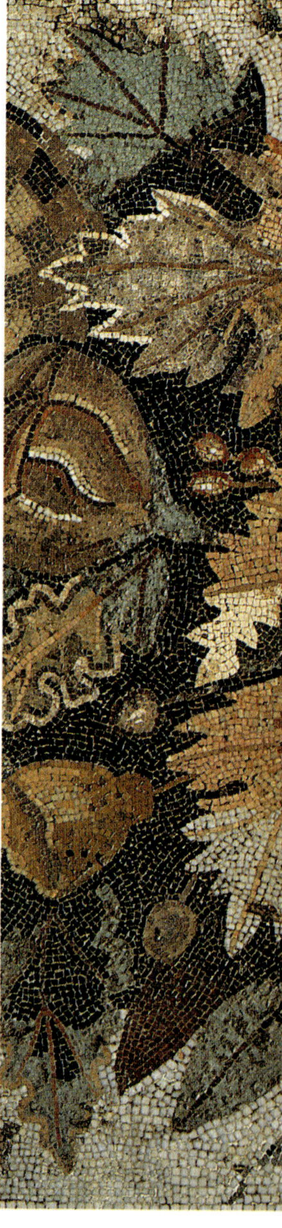

78 (above) *A comic scene, portrayed in a relief from the 1st century* AD. *After a distinguished period of the great names of Roman theatre (Livius Andronicus, Ennius, Plautus and Terence), the public lost interest in this kind of performance. They now preferred simple shows based on spontaneous gags and dirty jokes to the traditional Greek style of theatre. In the imperial age dramas were no longer staged but were read in private drawing rooms before an élite audience.*

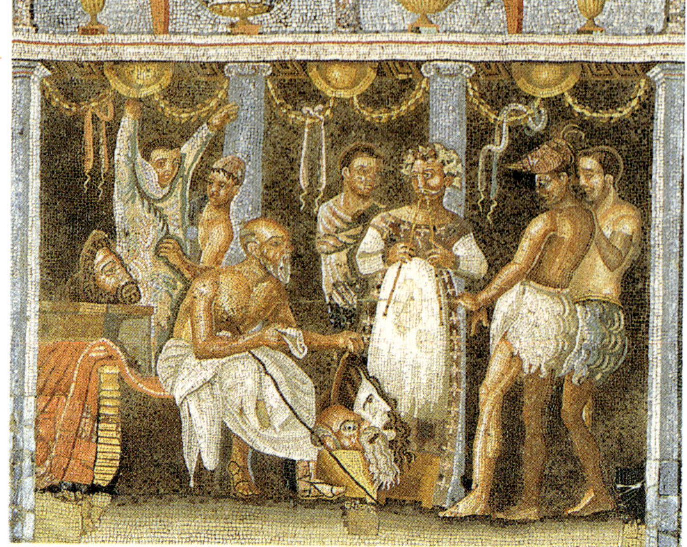

78 (left) *Staging a theatrical performance could be an expensive business, although the government paid a generous grant. The most famous theatrical companies could command very high fees and they imposed their own terms on impresarios, who also had to pay the wages of stagehands, dressmakers and set designers. In this mosaic, found in Pompeii, actors are preparing for a play; one of them is playing the* tibia, *a wind instrument similar to the flute.*

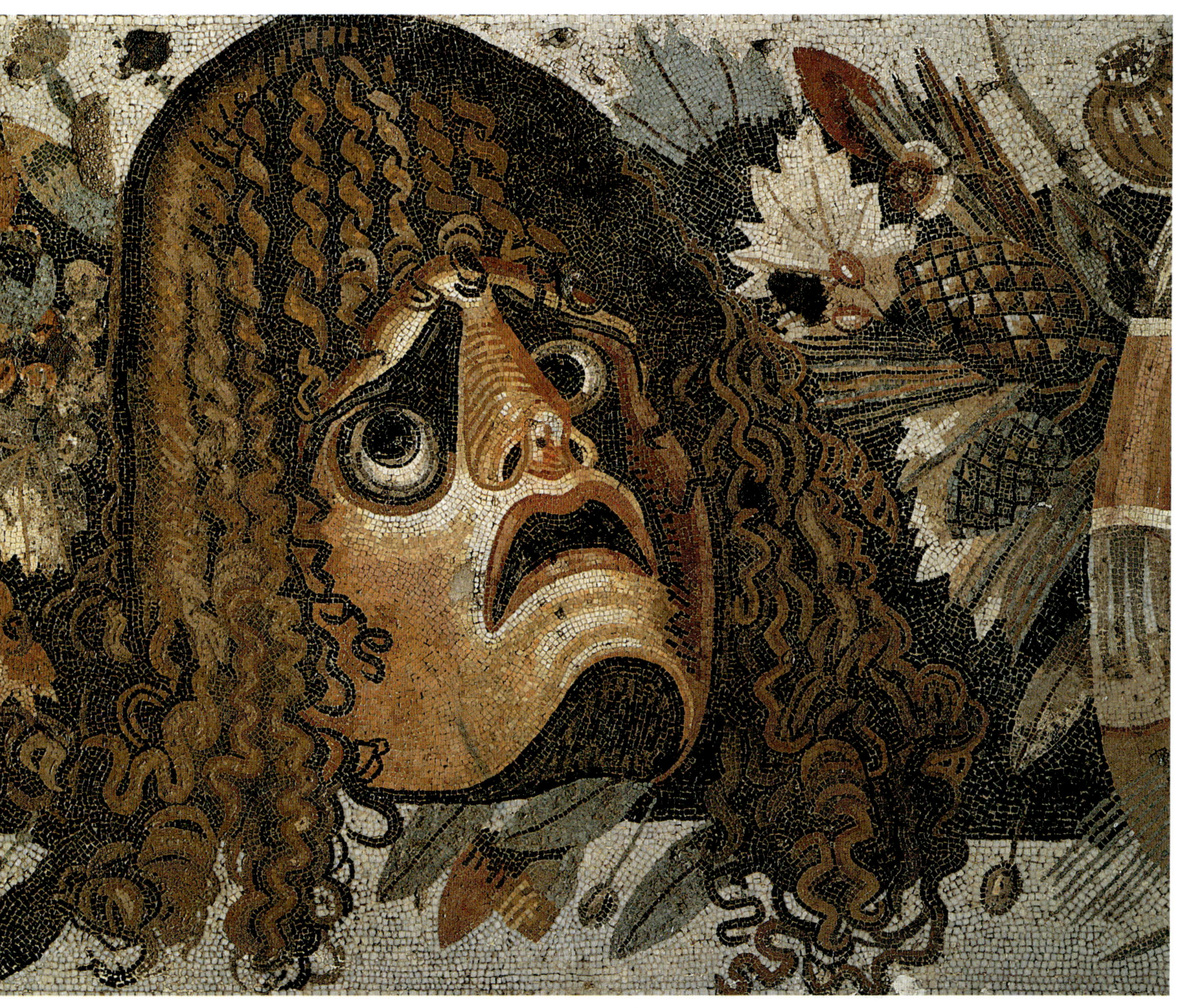

78–79 The Romans preferred circus races and gladiatorial contests to theatrical performances. This was at least partly a result of a decree of the 2nd century BC, *issued by the aristocracy preventing the construction of permanent theatres; a ban which lasted until the time of Pompey. Their hostility stemmed from the risk they perceived in concentrating a large number of people in a place where an author might rouse the rabble with excessively libertarian or otherwise dangerous subjects. Even in the imperial period the plays staged were carefully controlled.*

The naumachiae, miniature mock naval battles fought in the artificial lakes of the same name, in which the combatants fought to the death, were more popular. Augustus' naumachia in Trastevere, 536 m (1758 ft) long and 357 m (1170 ft) wide, was famous; it was supplied with water by a special aqueduct and inaugurated with a performance in which 3000 fighting men took part, plus the crews of the ships.

The glorious old tragedies were not very popular with the Romans in the imperial age, who preferred mime shows to traditional theatrical performances. These were episodes taken from the theatrical repertoire, and adapted to highlight their macabre, mysterious or grosser aspects. The mimic alone portrayed all the action, accompanied by musicians and dancers. Some of these actors became true idols and made their fortune.

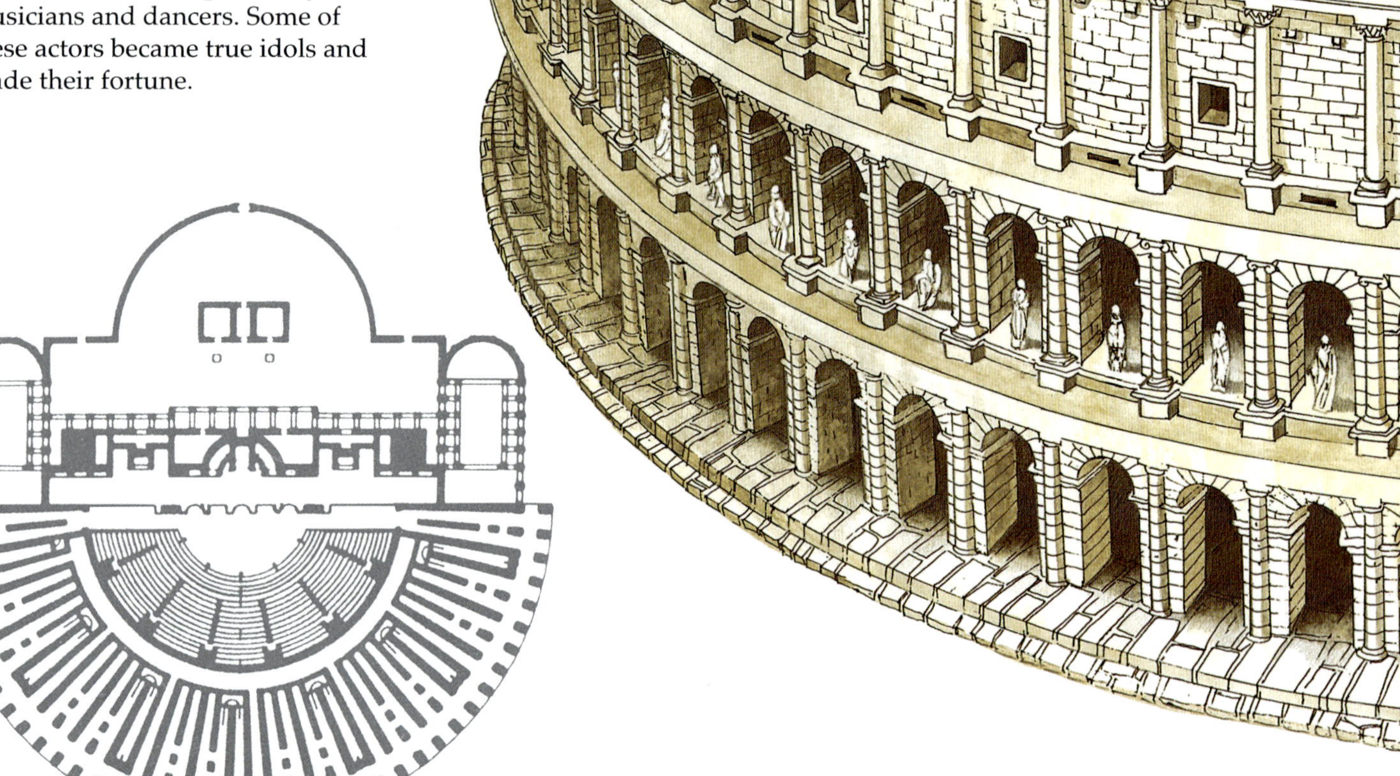

*80–81 Until 55 BC Rome had no stone theatre but only temporary structures built of wood. A century earlier, a proposal to build a permanent structure had met with strong opposition from the senate, which was convinced that such a project would be lead to moral corruption. The construction of a theatre in Rome by Pompey and the extension of the range of leisure activities offered to the plebs by Caesar changed the situation, and theatrical buildings were soon erected in many parts of Italy and the provinces of the empire. In Roman theatres, such as the Theatre of Marcellus in Rome (above), unlike Greek ones, the auditorium was usually not built into a natural hillside but supported by special masonry structures. The stage front was also much higher and more elaborate, so that it had the appearance of a two- or three-storey monumental wings containing the three entrances for the actors. The central entrance (*regia*) was used by the leading actors, and the two side entrances (*hospitalia*) by the supporting cast; the side of the stage from which they entered (right or left) indicated the origin of the character (town or country). Sets and stage machinery added to the interest of the performance, which was accompanied by an orchestra seated in the orchestra pit at the foot of the stage.*

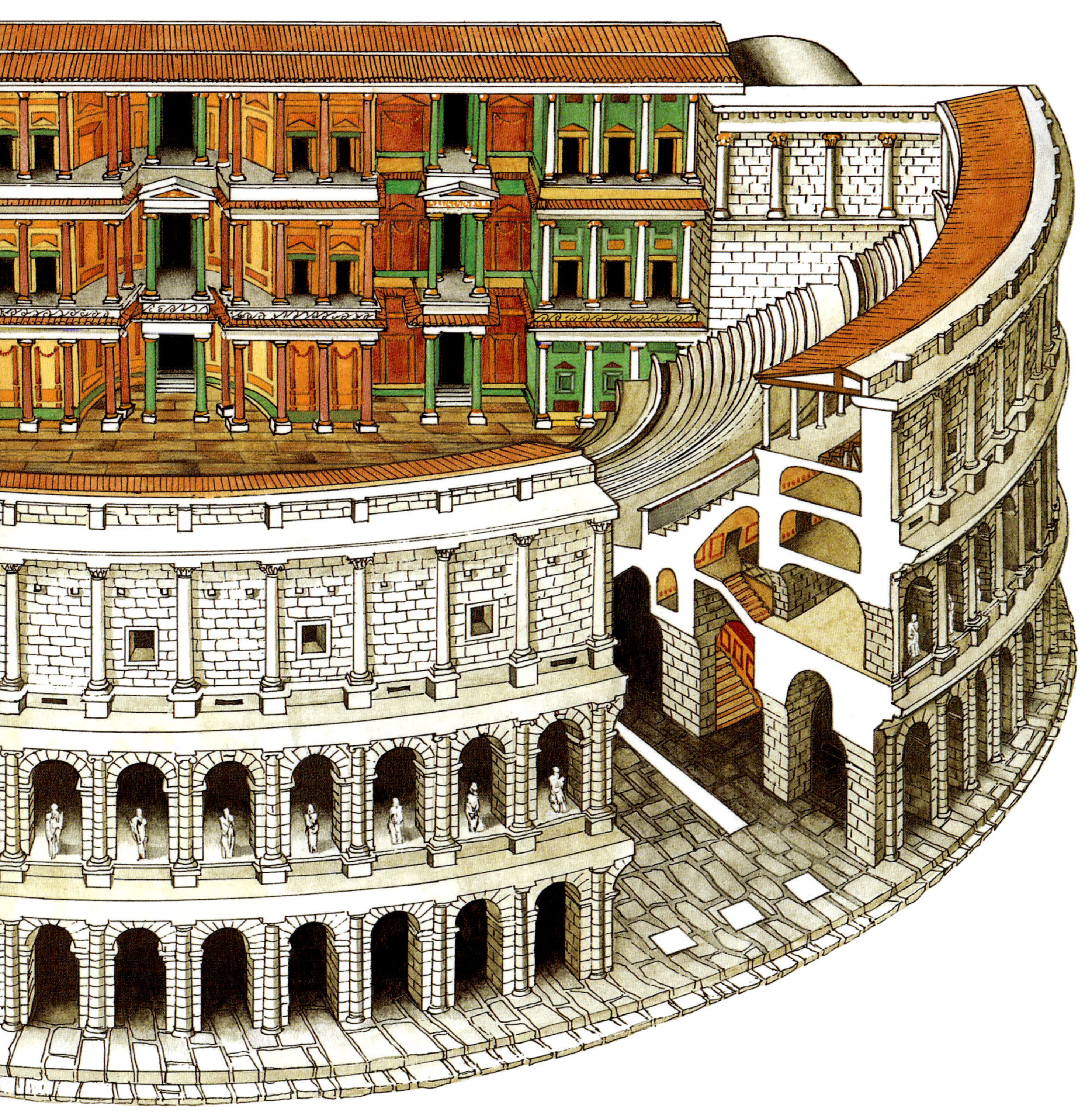

82–83 (overleaf) This famous mosaic dating from the 1st century BC *and signed by an artist of Greek descent – Dioscurides of Samos – was found in the house known as the 'Villa of Cicero' in Pompeii. It portrays some New Comedy characters, strolling players who belonged to the cult of Cybele. From the 1st century* BC*, two genres destined to supplant Greek tragedy – mime and pantomime – became increasingly popular. In the former, which featured comic and erotic subjects sometimes tinged with political and social satire, acting alternated with dancing, and masks were not used. Woman also took part in these performances, usually scantily clad, and they were sometimes called on to perform a virtual striptease; in view of which they were considered little better than prostitutes. Pantomime, which featured tragic subjects, was inspired by mythology and history; an actor danced and acted, his gestures emphasized by a narrator and background music.*

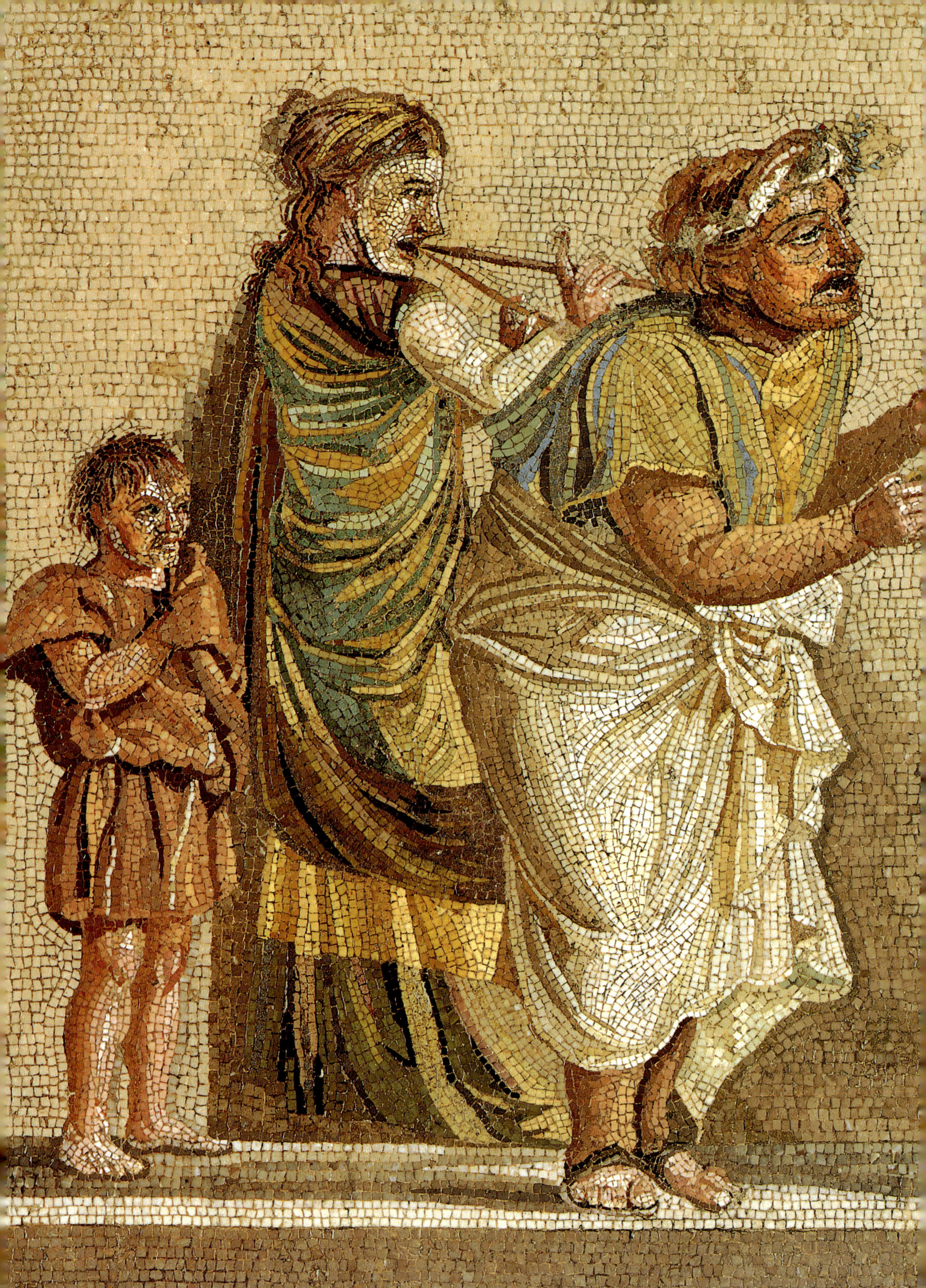

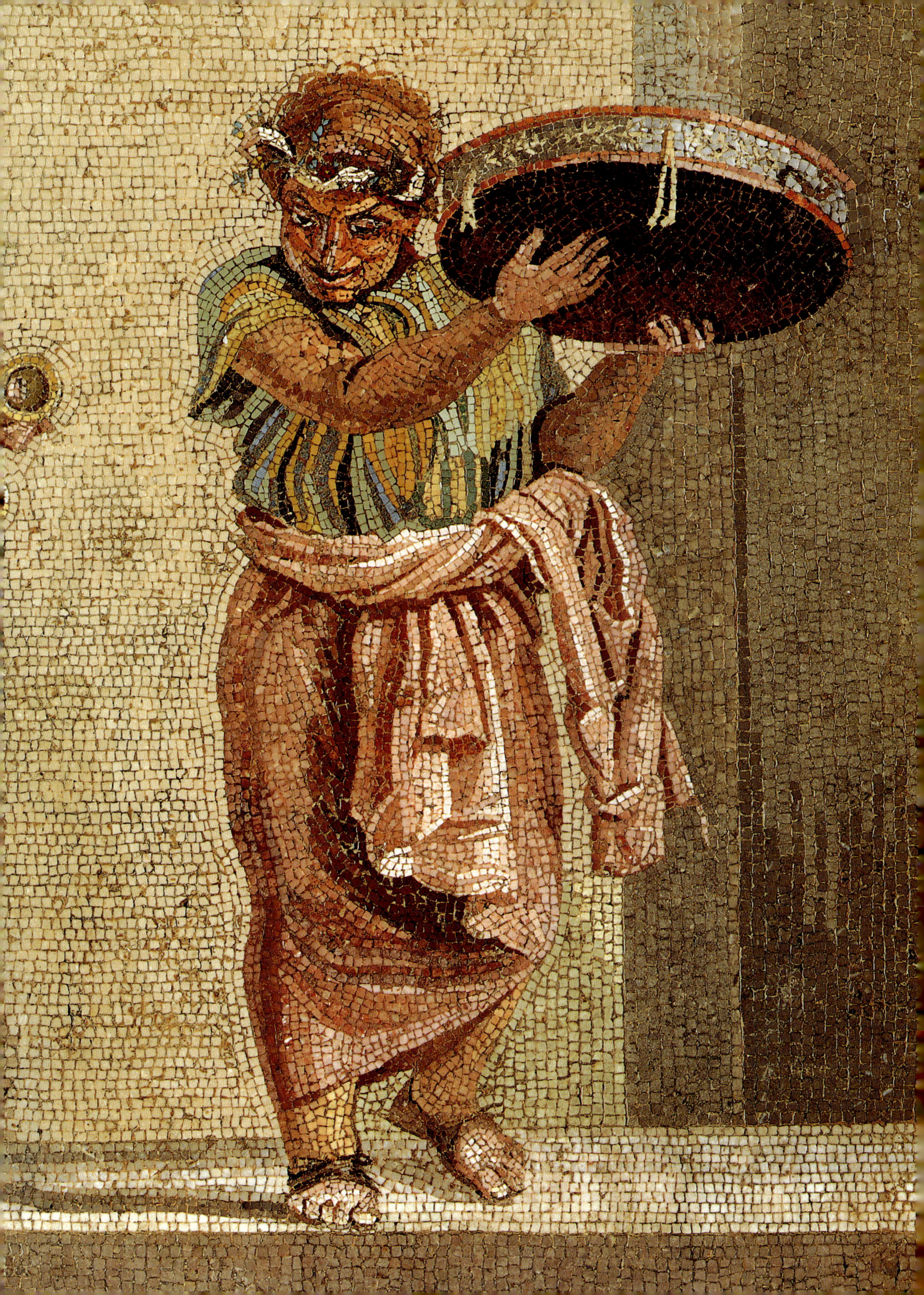

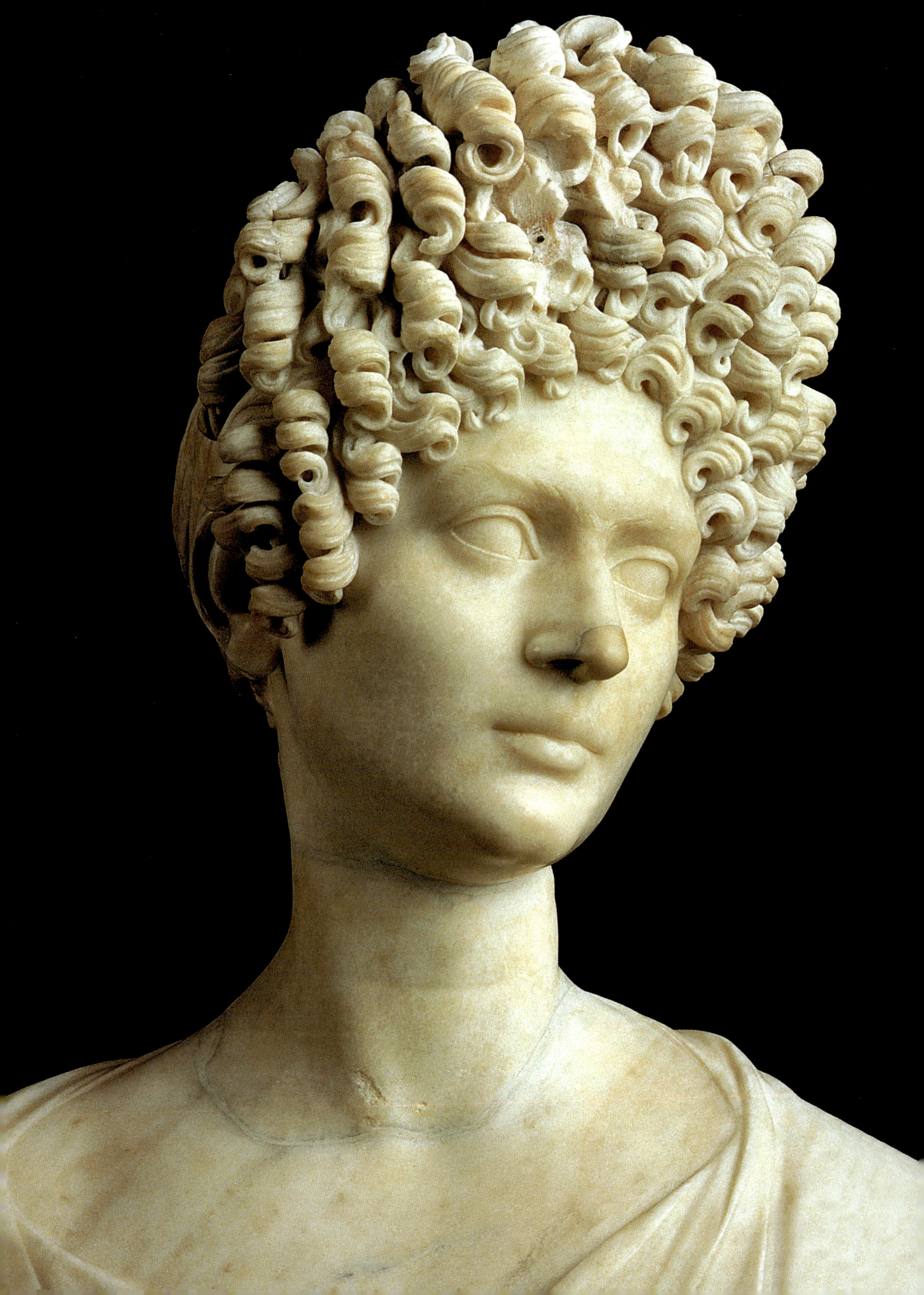

CLOTHING AND HAIRSTYLES

Roman clothing was quite simple: the basic garment was the *tunica*. Usually sleeveless and tight-waisted, it was knee-length or calf-length and decorated with a strip of purple (*clavus*): wide for senators, narrower for knights. The *tunica* was covered by the *toga*, a large, white, woollen cloak which was wrapped round the body, leaving the right arm free. Boys up to the age of 16 wore the *toga praetexta* decorated with a strip of purple; only on reaching their majority were they clad in the white *toga virilis* at a special ceremony.

Over the *tunica* women wore a *stola*, a short-sleeved dress fastened at the waist by a belt and draped to form elegant pleats. Outdoors they wore a cloak (*palla*), which could be used to cover the head. The most common type of footwear were *calcei*, like ankle boots.

Ladies' hairstyles varied from period to period, thus providing useful dating evidence. In ancient times they were simple: hair was worn with a central parting and gathered in a bun or in a ponytail, sometimes embellished with a thin fringe of curls on the forehead. Hairstyles grew more elaborate in the Augustan period, and reached the peak of sophistication in the Flavian era, when they became monumental constructions of curls. Indispensable tools were the comb, of bronze, bone or ivory, and the *calamistrum*, hollow curling tongs heated on a brazier. Women also used hairpins, ribbons, nets, wigs and hairpieces which increased the bulk and volume of their hairstyles. Dyes and bleaches were also used. A dye called *Spuma Batava* was used to colour the hair copper-blonde.

85 (above) This bust of Faustina the Younger, daughter of Antoninus Pius, shows her wearing a hairstyle which frames the face with broad waves; the hair was gathered on the head in what was known as the 'melon' style, then formed into a chignon of rolled plaits.

85 (below) Hairpieces were widely used to add volume to the more complex creations; at the nape of the neck the hair was gathered into complicated 'doughnut' style buns. The wealthier matrons had their hair and cosmetics done for them by an ornatrix, *a slave who specialized in beauty treatments.*

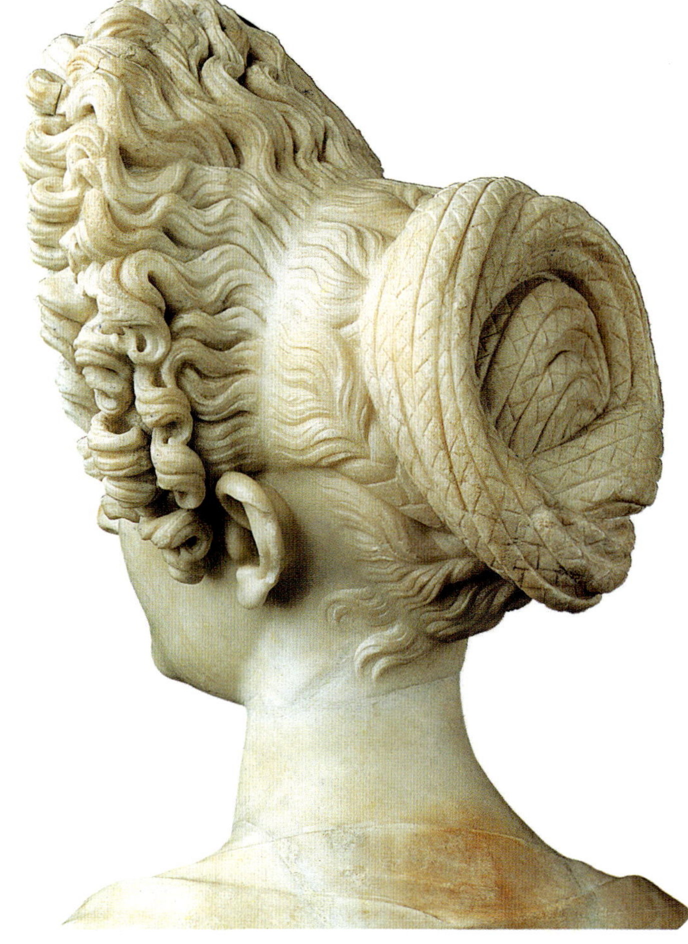

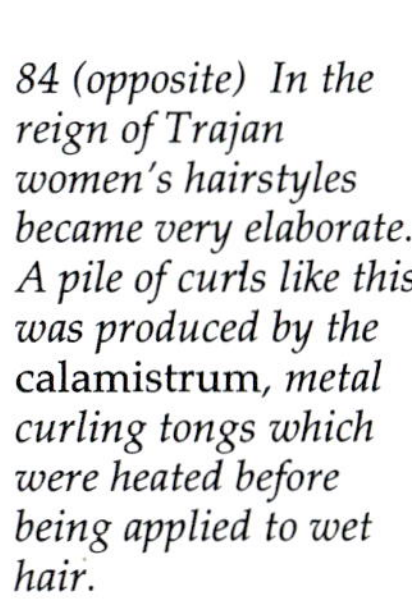

84 (opposite) In the reign of Trajan women's hairstyles became very elaborate. A pile of curls like this was produced by the calamistrum, *metal curling tongs which were heated before being applied to wet hair.*

JEWELRY AND COSMETICS

86 (top) An inset with embossed relief decoration, surrounded by a beaded edge, ornaments this gold bracelet. A naked cherub holds a mirror in front of a female figure wearing a long gown; the subject, known as the 'Venus of Pompeii', also appears in some wall paintings found in the buried town.

True Roman jewelry was first made in the 1st century BC. The spoils of war had brought to Rome not only works of art, but also pearls and precious gems. Personal ornaments from Pompeii, Herculaneum, Stabiae and Oplontis give some idea of the jewelry common in early imperial times. The preference was for colourful, though not very elaborate pieces; pearls, gems and glass paste contrasted with the bright yellow gold to produce jewels of great effect and ostentation, beloved of the nouveaux riches like Fortunata, the wife of Trimalchio. Earrings (*inaures*) of all shapes and sizes were very popular. According to Pliny, 'People nowadays go to buy clothes in China, look for pearls in the depths of the Red Sea, and emeralds in the bowels of the earth. Moreover, the practice of piercing the ears has been invented: it evidently did not suffice to wear jewels round the neck, in the hair and on the hands; they also have to be stuck in the body'.

Cosmetics were the object of a flourishing trade. Ointments and perfumes were contained in small, elegant pottery or alabaster jars or glass bottles. All Romans made immoderate use of them, and women devoted a lot of time to their make-up and to concocting face-masks with various ingredients, such as plants and organic materials, some of which are unspeakable.

86 (centre) This type of ring, formed by a beaded strand of solid gold set with a pearl, became very common in Roman jewelry from the 1st century AD; the pearl might be replaced by a brightly coloured semiprecious stone.

86 (below) The small settings which make up this unusual pair of earrings contain fragments of quartz. These jewels are among the numerous valuable pieces of Roman jewelry found at Oplontis, near Pompeii.

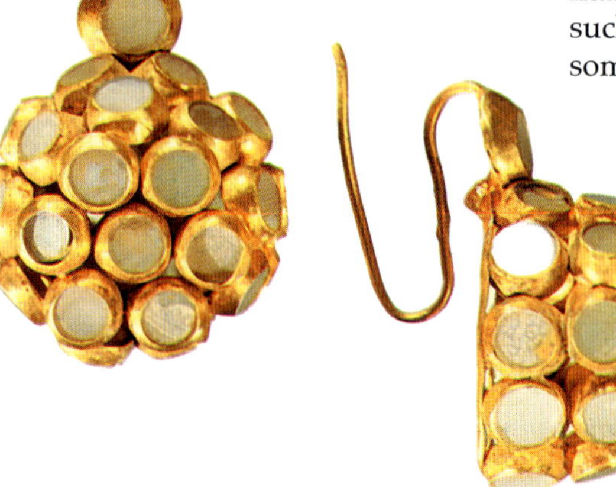

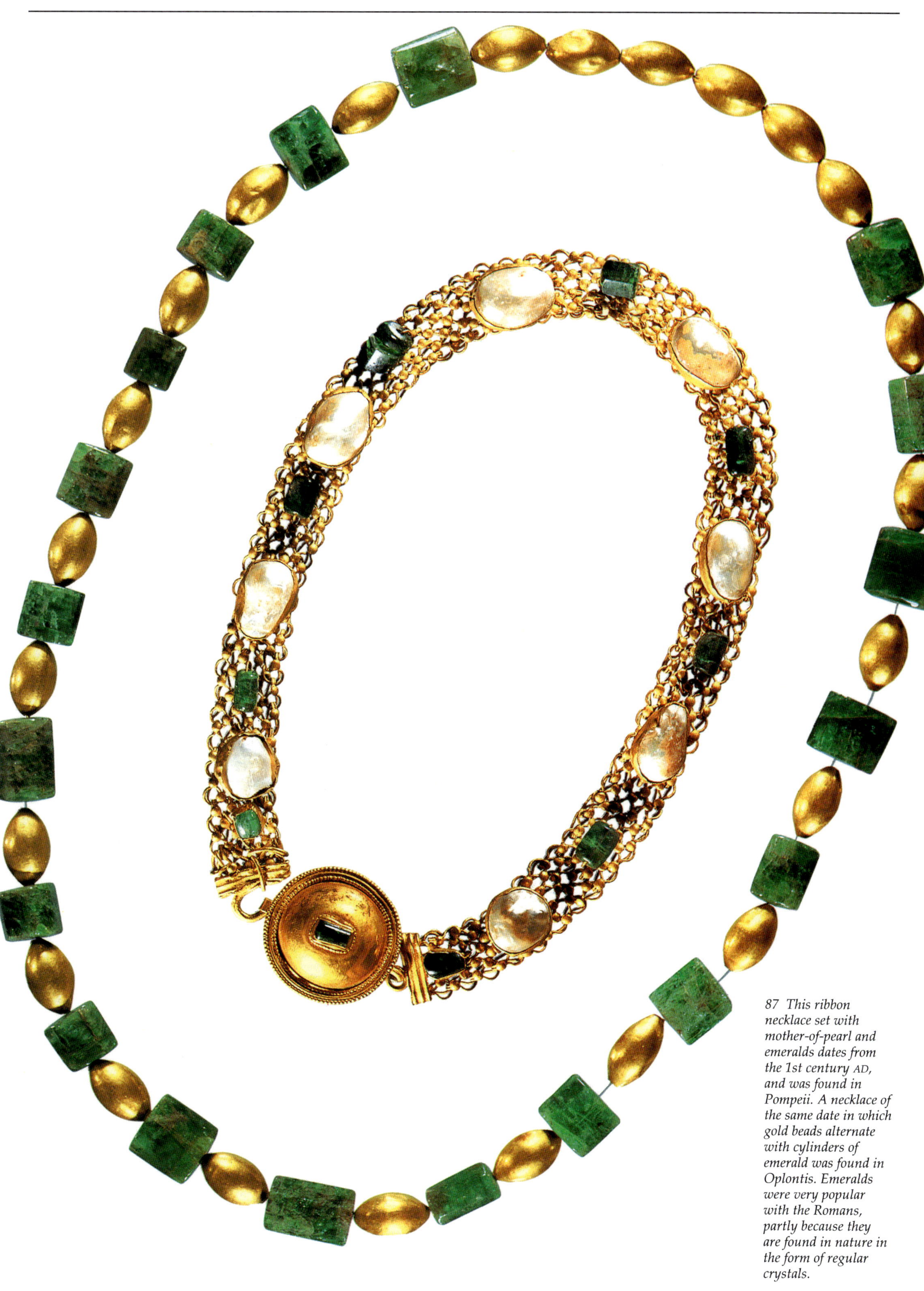

87 This ribbon necklace set with mother-of-pearl and emeralds dates from the 1st century AD, *and was found in Pompeii. A necklace of the same date in which gold beads alternate with cylinders of emerald was found in Oplontis. Emeralds were very popular with the Romans, partly because they are found in nature in the form of regular crystals.*

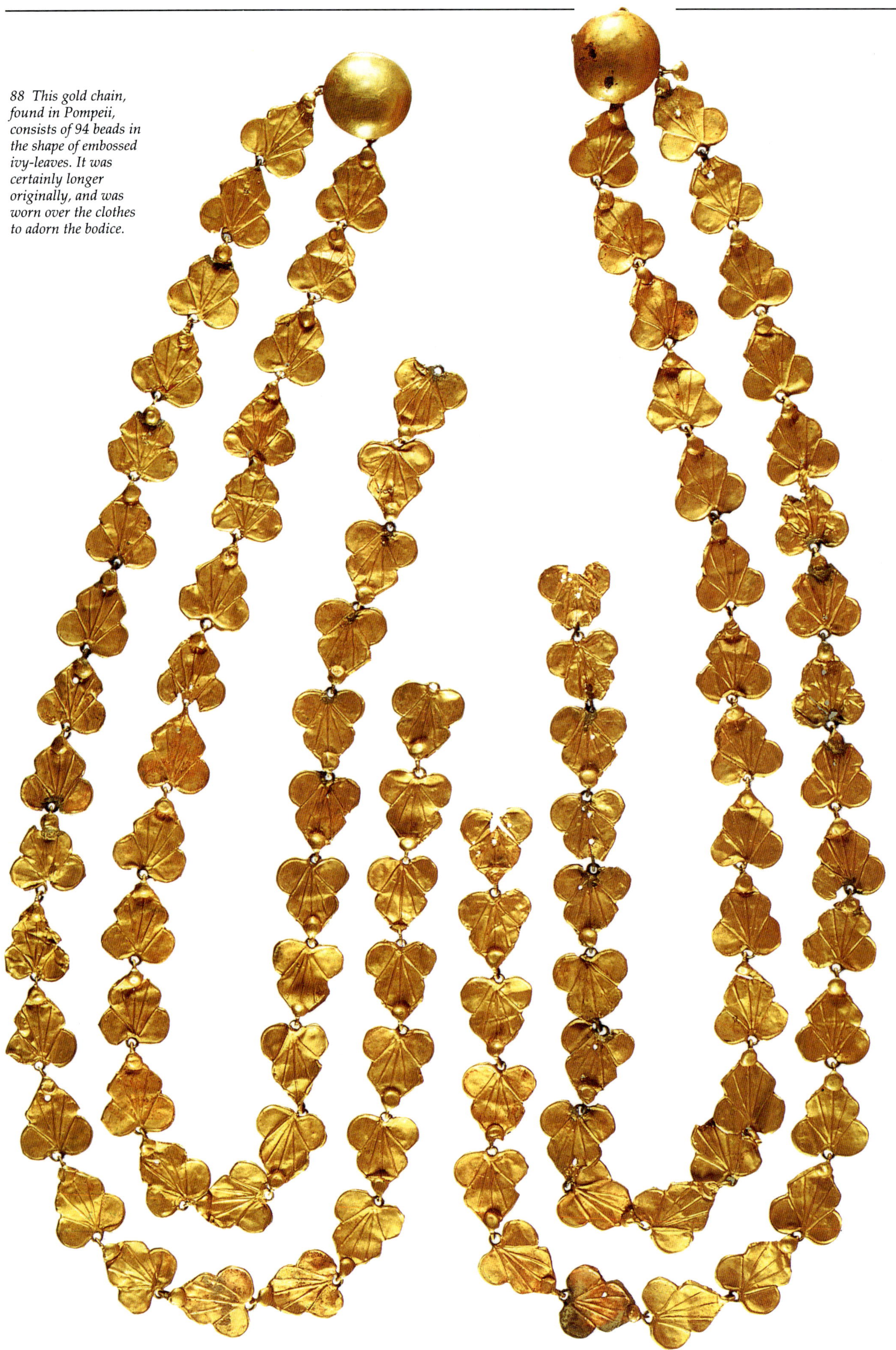

88 This gold chain, found in Pompeii, consists of 94 beads in the shape of embossed ivy-leaves. It was certainly longer originally, and was worn over the clothes to adorn the bodice.

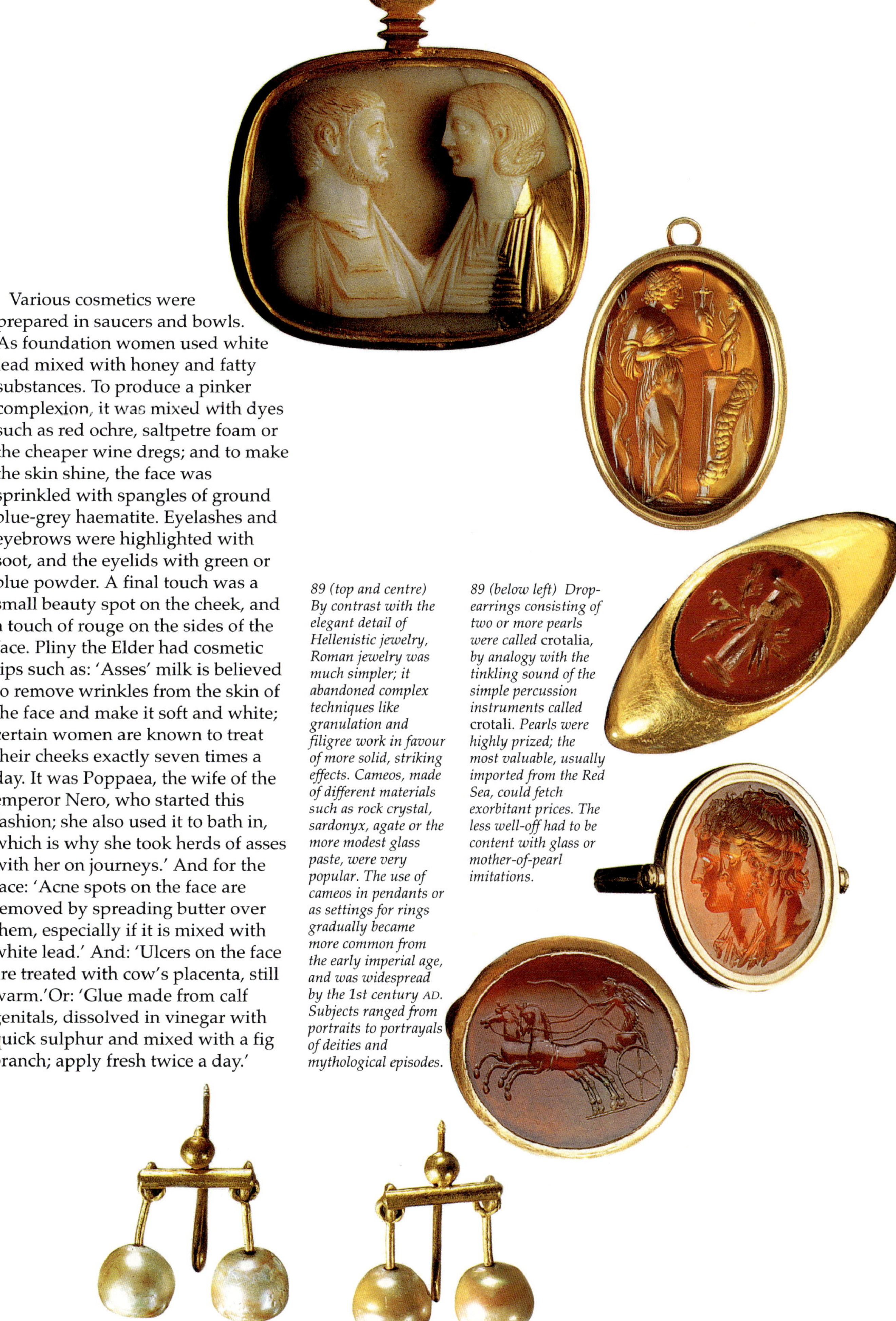

Various cosmetics were prepared in saucers and bowls. As foundation women used white lead mixed with honey and fatty substances. To produce a pinker complexion, it was mixed with dyes such as red ochre, saltpetre foam or the cheaper wine dregs; and to make the skin shine, the face was sprinkled with spangles of ground blue-grey haematite. Eyelashes and eyebrows were highlighted with soot, and the eyelids with green or blue powder. A final touch was a small beauty spot on the cheek, and a touch of rouge on the sides of the face. Pliny the Elder had cosmetic tips such as: 'Asses' milk is believed to remove wrinkles from the skin of the face and make it soft and white; certain women are known to treat their cheeks exactly seven times a day. It was Poppaea, the wife of the emperor Nero, who started this fashion; she also used it to bath in, which is why she took herds of asses with her on journeys.' And for the face: 'Acne spots on the face are removed by spreading butter over them, especially if it is mixed with white lead.' And: 'Ulcers on the face are treated with cow's placenta, still warm.'Or: 'Glue made from calf genitals, dissolved in vinegar with quick sulphur and mixed with a fig branch; apply fresh twice a day.'

89 (top and centre) By contrast with the elegant detail of Hellenistic jewelry, Roman jewelry was much simpler; it abandoned complex techniques like granulation and filigree work in favour of more solid, striking effects. Cameos, made of different materials such as rock crystal, sardonyx, agate or the more modest glass paste, were very popular. The use of cameos in pendants or as settings for rings gradually became more common from the early imperial age, and was widespread by the 1st century AD. *Subjects ranged from portraits to portrayals of deities and mythological episodes.*

89 (below left) Drop-earrings consisting of two or more pearls were called crotalia, *by analogy with the tinkling sound of the simple percussion instruments called* crotali. *Pearls were highly prized; the most valuable, usually imported from the Red Sea, could fetch exorbitant prices. The less well-off had to be content with glass or mother-of-pearl imitations.*

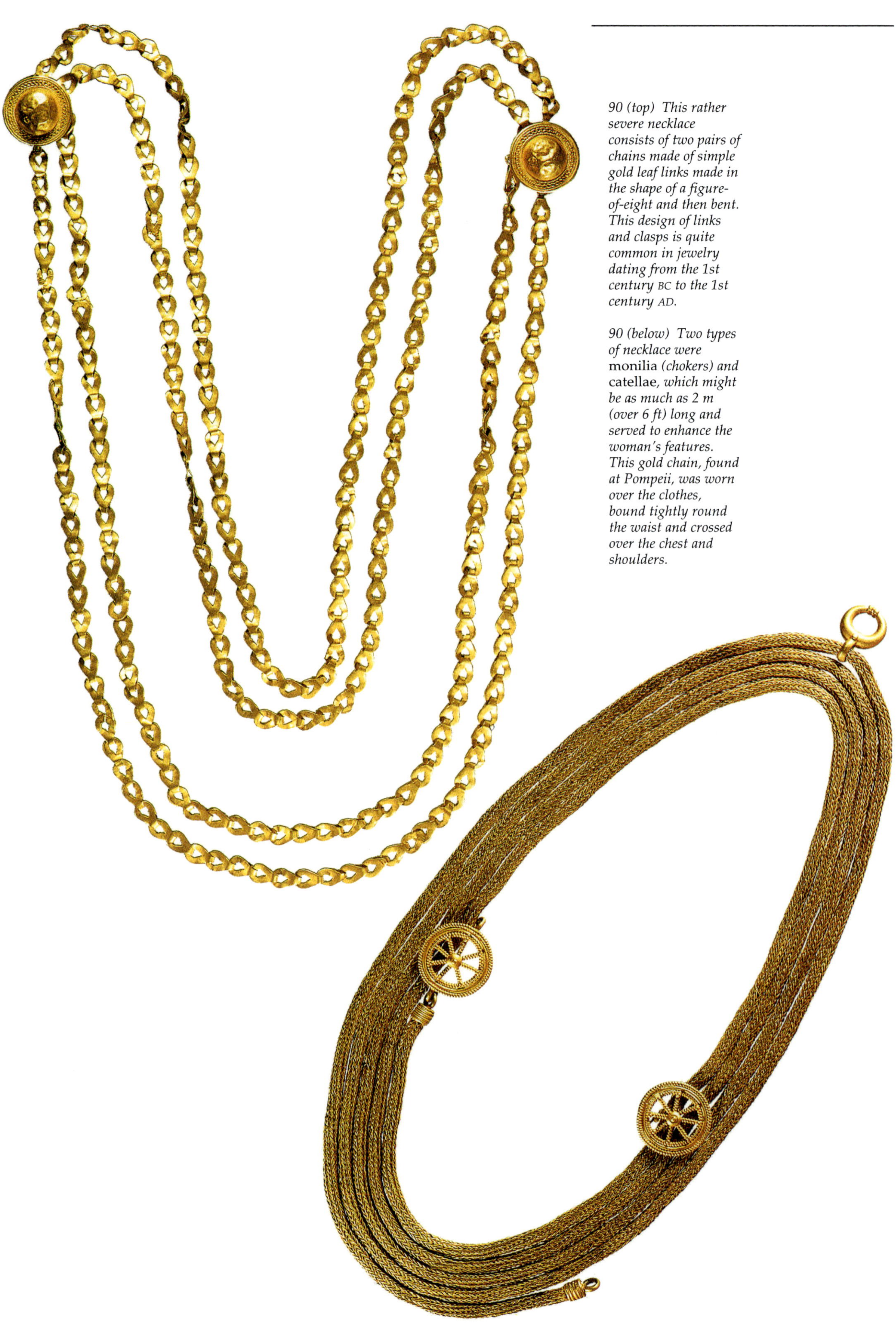

90 (top) This rather severe necklace consists of two pairs of chains made of simple gold leaf links made in the shape of a figure-of-eight and then bent. This design of links and clasps is quite common in jewelry dating from the 1st century BC *to the 1st century* AD.

90 (below) Two types of necklace were monilia *(chokers) and* catellae, *which might be as much as 2 m (over 6 ft) long and served to enhance the woman's features. This gold chain, found at Pompeii, was worn over the clothes, bound tightly round the waist and crossed over the chest and shoulders.*

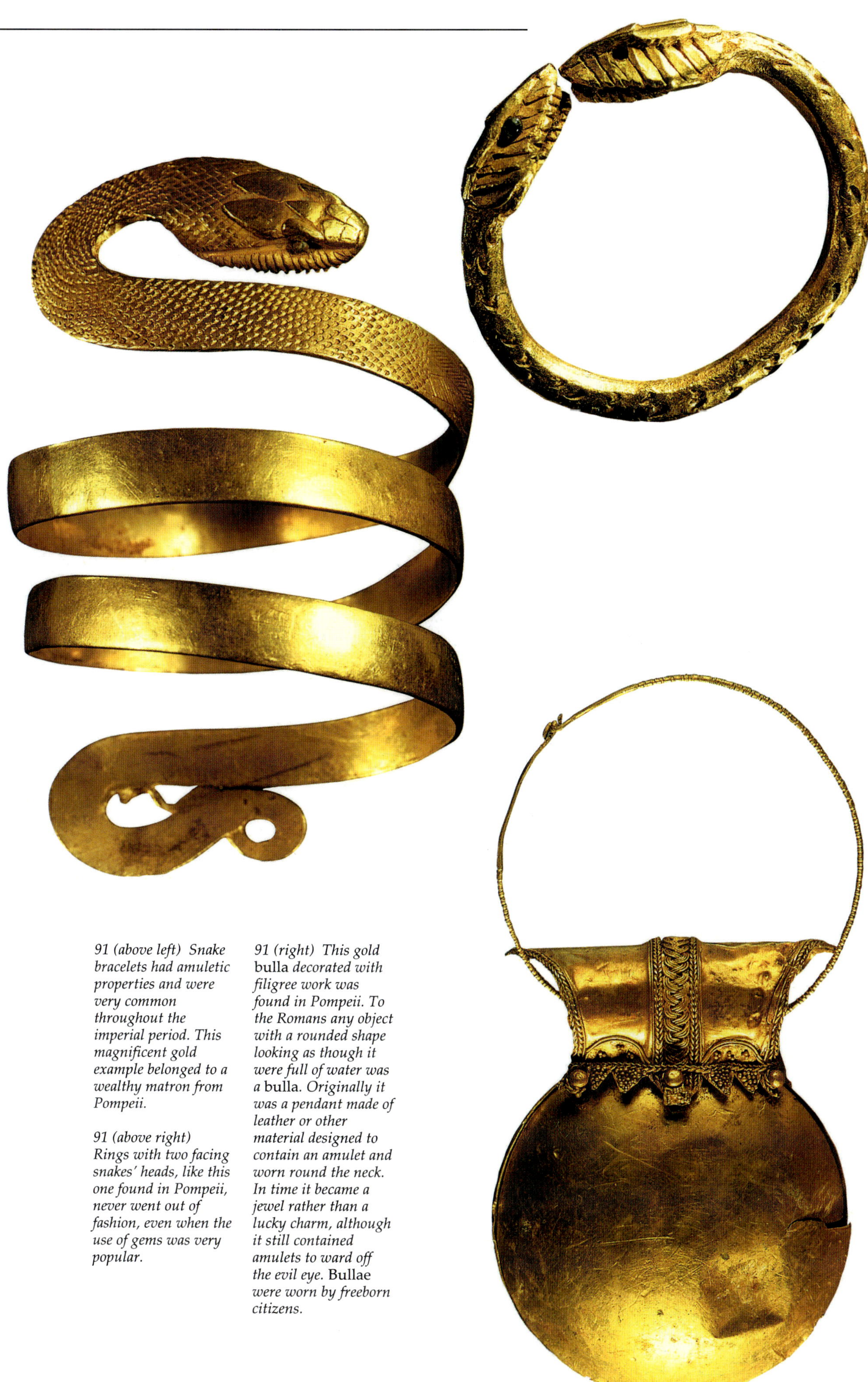

91 (above left) Snake bracelets had amuletic properties and were very common throughout the imperial period. This magnificent gold example belonged to a wealthy matron from Pompeii.

91 (above right) Rings with two facing snakes' heads, like this one found in Pompeii, never went out of fashion, even when the use of gems was very popular.

91 (right) This gold bulla *decorated with filigree work was found in Pompeii. To the Romans any object with a rounded shape looking as though it were full of water was a* bulla. *Originally it was a pendant made of leather or other material designed to contain an amulet and worn round the neck. In time it became a jewel rather than a lucky charm, although it still contained amulets to ward off the evil eye.* Bullae *were worn by freeborn citizens.*

92 (above) Numerous sarcophagi dating from the imperial age were decorated with scenes of battle. From the beginning, Roman society was strongly permeated with a military spirit, which influenced its entire development.

92 (below) Roman legionaries were true professionals able to fight in any situation and cope with various logistical necessities. In this relief on Trajan's Column, the soldiers are engaged in building a fort.

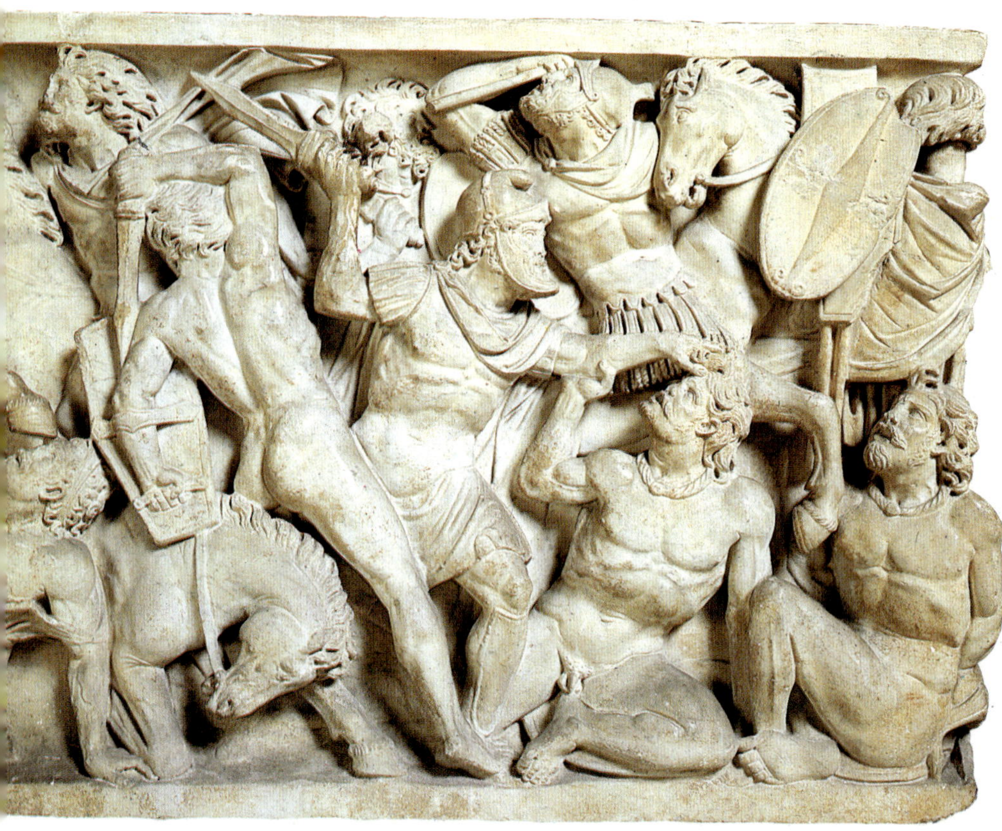

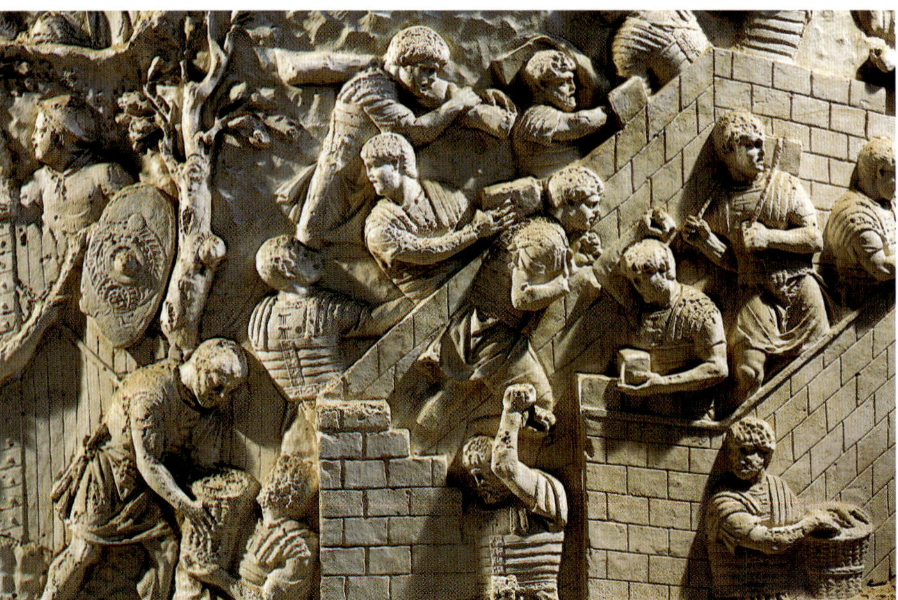

Rome's economic and cultural power, first achieved by force of arms, was strenuously defended by force of arms until the final collapse of the empire. In many respects it is therefore true to say that Rome's authority depended on the strength of its legions. When threatened by waves of barbarian attacks, Roman society, already facing a serious crisis, was no longer able to muster the material or spiritual resources to halt the dreadful momentum.

Until the fall of the empire, the Roman army was the best-organized and most efficient military machine in the ancient world. Excellent training and the specialization of its troops, together with an extensive network of logistical support and technologically advanced weaponry made it a perfect tool, whose lethal strength was placed at the service of able strategists for over 800 years.

Although information about the early age of the kings is somewhat fragmentary, it is known that society was divided between free citizens and those who did not enjoy full rights, and were therefore not called up for military service. At that time the Roman army was drawn from three tribes, which provided 1000 infantrymen and 100 horsemen each in case of need. Their equipment consisted of a leather breastplate, helmet and greaves, a wooden shield, a long spear and a sword. As the soldiers were equipped at their own expense, weapons and equipment were not standard, and varied according to income.

The first reform of the army, by Servius Tullius, had major military, and political repercussions. The

93 (opposite) The Praetorian Guard was founded by Augustus as his personal bodyguard, and was the main military system for controlling the capital for his successors. Quartered in barracks on the outskirts of the city, the Praetorians wore special uniforms, received more pay than the legionaries, and served for a shorter period. For over two centuries they were the only troops stationed in Italy, and they had a part in the rise and fall of several emperors.

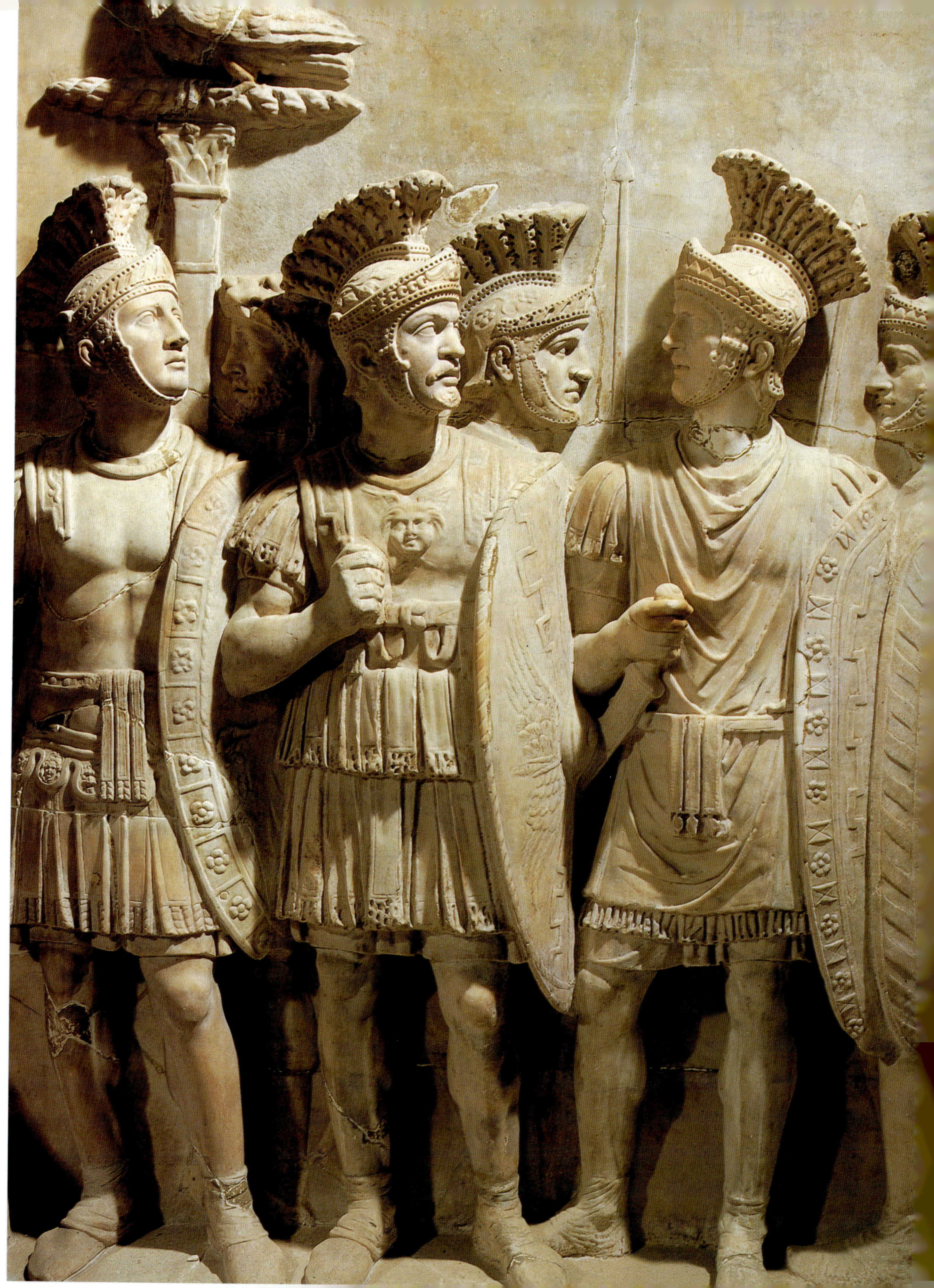

96 (top) *The triumph was the greatest honour paid to a general who had won a decisive victory over an enemy. He was entitled to ride through the streets of Rome on a quadriga (chariot), his head crowned with a laurel wreath, between lines of applauding crowds, followed by the war booty, including enemy weapons and chained prisoners, as shown in this relief.*

were also taught the most effective combat techniques in attack and defence; in particular, they learned how to form the *testudo*, the best-known Roman military formation. This 'tortoise', formed by the soldiers with their shields, protected the unit from above and on the two most exposed flanks, so that they could advance even under a violent hail of enemy fire.

When the training period was over the soldiers began their regular military life. Although marches and simulated combats were far less frequent, leisure time was still a luxury, as the legionaries were called on to perform numerous tasks such as maintenance work on their quarters, guard duty and, if they were stationed in recently conquered territory, building roads, bridges, aqueducts and even new towns. Some reliefs on Trajan's Column show squads of sappers assembling pontoon bridges over the Danube and legionaries erecting the fortifications of a new camp.

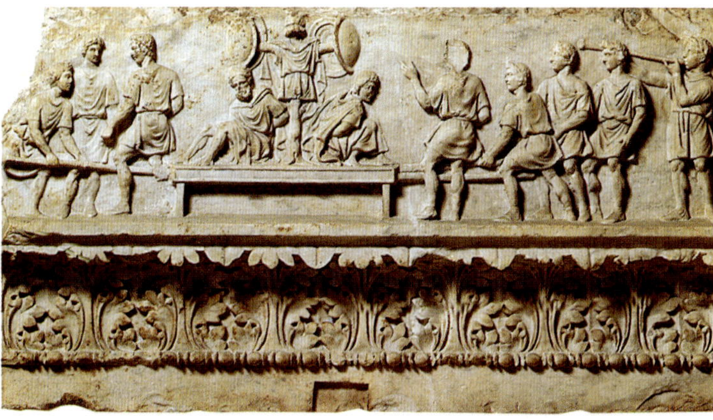

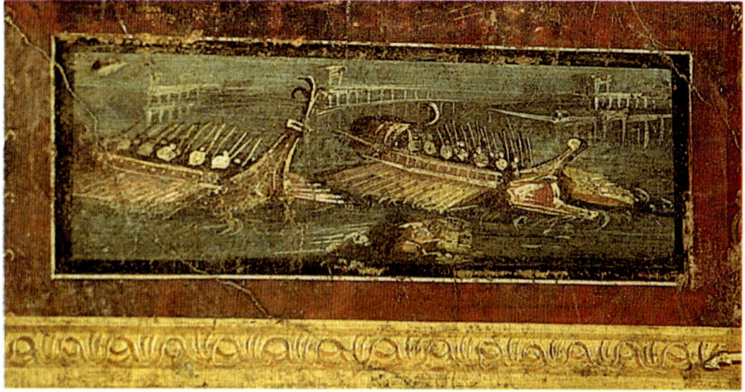

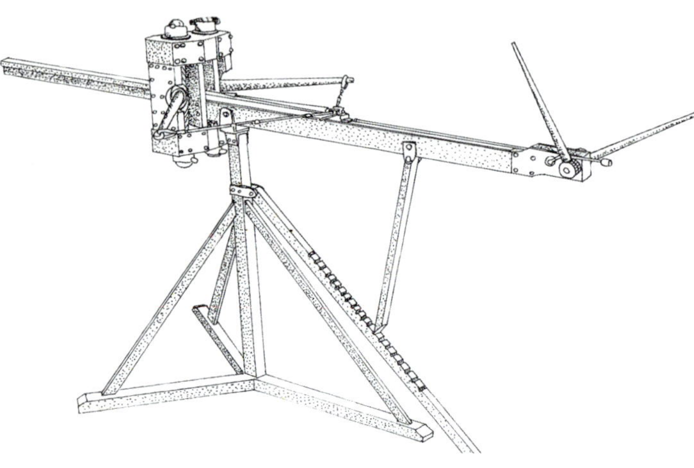

Roads played an essential part in achieving the rapid pacification, control and Romanization of recently subjugated territories. The extent and efficiency of the road network, even in the remotest areas, was one of the distinguishing features of Roman civilization.

Soldiers might also be required to perform policing tasks or patrol duties; in any event, being professionals, training continued throughout their military careers. The historian Flavius Josephus praised Roman military organization on several occasions, highlighting its outstanding discipline and the speed with which the men obeyed orders.

Large-scale military manoeuvres were regularly held, especially when the territorial expansion of the empire began to slow down, so that troops stationed along the borders maintained their high level of training. Often, if time allowed, the commanders performed a rapid check on their men's abilities before going into battle. In combat, especially in sieges, the Roman army used a range of heavy equipment, from *vineae* (strong, mobile shelters used to protect soldiers approaching the city walls) to the various types of catapult and *ballistae*; the latter, resembling large crossbows, were long-range precision weapons. Some horse-drawn mobile types could fire a projectile for a distance of around 500 m (1640 ft).

Roman legionaries were usually supported by auxiliary troops, who were not required to perform the same duties as the legions, and could carry out specific tasks requiring great flexibility and versatility. Their numbers were always large, equalling and perhaps

96 (centre) *Roman naval power had its origins in the First Punic War, when the Romans realized they needed a fleet to defeat the Carthaginians, who were excellent sailors. Taking a captured enemy ship as their model, they soon managed to build a large number of their own, and won their first naval battle at Mylae in 260* BC. *A typical feature of Roman warships was the rostrum, a pointed beam usually covered with thick bronze plates which projected from the prow of the hukl at water level; this lethal weapon served to ram enemy ships, opening great breaches in their planking. The rostra of ships caputred in battle were prized military trophies; they were displayed in the forum, on a dais named the Rostra after them.*

96 (bottom) *The Roman army had various long-range artillery weapons which were particularly effective during sieges. In addition to the missile launcher illustrated here, called the* scorpio, *which could hurl a javelin, there were various kinds of catapult. The most powerful, called the* onager, *could hurl a projectile weighing 50 kg (110 lb) a distance of 400 m (1312 ft), with devastating effects.*

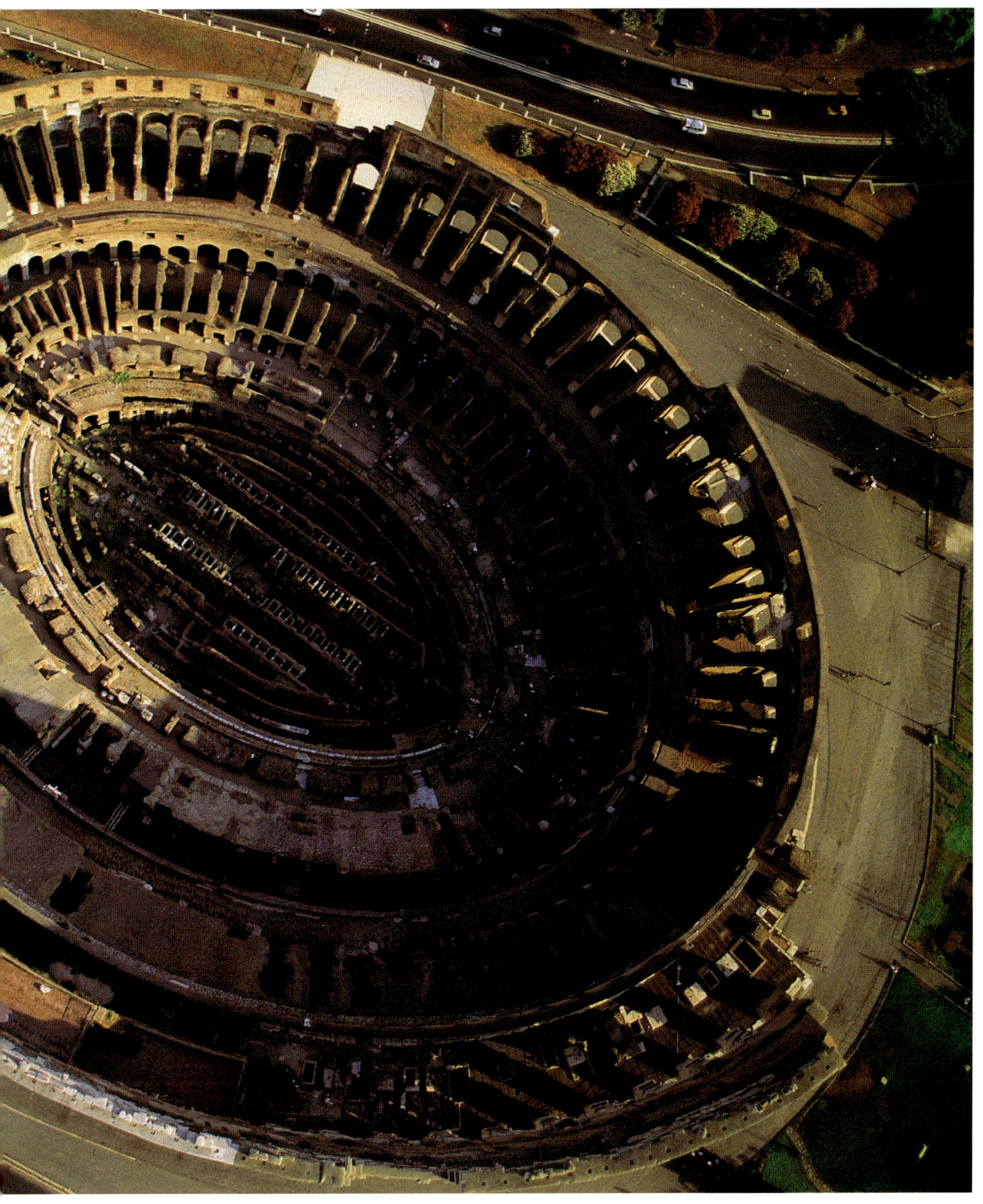

THE IMPERIAL FORUMS

A Temple of the Divine Trajan
B Trajan's Column
C Basilica Ulpia
D Trajan's Markets
E Forum (AD 113)
F Temple of Venus Genetrix
G Forum of Julius Caesar (42 BC)
H Temple of Mars Ultor (the Avenger)
I Forum of Augustus (2 BC)
J Temple of Minerva
K Forum of Nerva or Forum Transitorium (AD 97)
L Forum of Vespasian or Forum of Peace (75 BC)
M Temple of Peace

In antiquity Rome looked very different from today: high, steep hills surrounded deep ravines and impassable valleys. Lush vegetation, including centuries-old woods, covered the hillsides and the outskirts of the city, together with fields of cereals, vegetable gardens and vineyards. Numerous streams flowed through the valleys often becoming marshland, with ponds and small lakes. Villages stood on the hilltops, marking out the various communities that lived in the area.

In the age of the kings Rome was densely populated; even then it was one of the largest cities in the western Mediterranean. Alongside the clay and straw huts dating from earlier periods, masonry houses began to be built, with tiled roofs and inner courtyards, similar to the contemporary Etruscan houses. Patrician houses, built on the hilltops, were often surmounted by high towers. Royal mansions – including those of Ancus Martius, Tarquinius Priscus and Tarquin the Proud (built on the Velia), and Servius Tullius (on the Oppian Hill) – must have been of this type.

The monumental part of the city was limited in size. On its outskirts were vast open spaces used for cemeteries; the Campus Martius where men assembled for weapons training and military exercises; and areas for clay extraction and brick kilns, near which the fortified Janiculum stood. A massive wall ran along the ridges of the hills, forming a continuous route nearly 11 km (7 miles) long and enclosing an area of almost 400 ha (988 acres). At an early stage a formal square had been laid out in the town centre – the Forum – around which the first public buildings gradually sprang up.

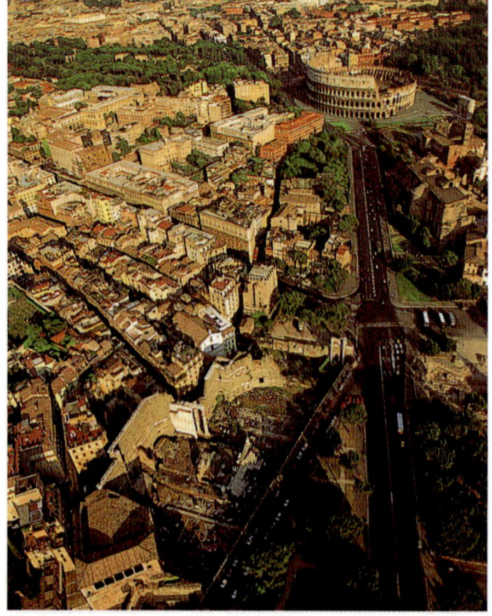

100 (top) An aerial view showing the remains of the Forum of Augustus and the Forum of Nerva, both of which are part of the huge imperial forum complex. They were built next to the older Roman Forum with the intention of creating larger and more rational monumental spaces designed not only for the emperors' personal ceremonies, but above all for the public life of Rome. They were used for business and political discussions, religious ceremonies and markets.

101 (opposite) In this aerial view the area of the Forum of Augustus and the foundations of the Temple of Mars Ultor are visible in the foreground and, in the background, are the remains of the Forum of Trajan and the adjacent Markets. Dozens of shops selling foodstuffs were crowded into this structure. Occasional free handouts of food to the plebs were also held here.

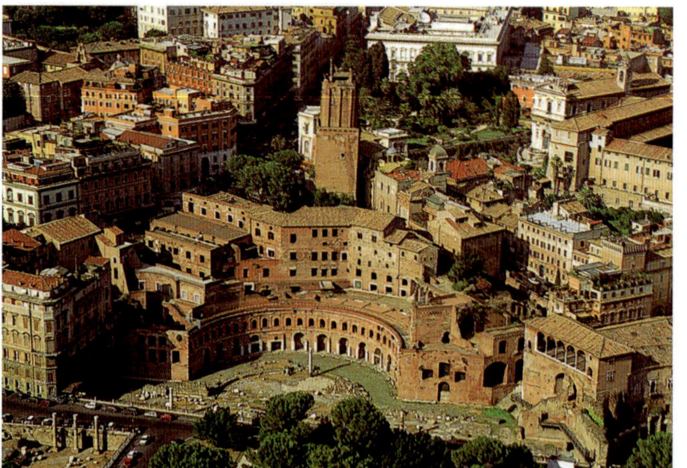

100 (centre) The Forum of Trajan, funded by booty from the Dacian wars, was the last to be built in Rome. It was also the most grandiose in design and its use of valuable materials. Apollodorus of Damascus, the architect, introduced new features, such as the transverse position of the Basilica Ulpia in relation to the rest of the complex, and the semicircular Markets of Trajan, a complex of tabernae *on six floors.*

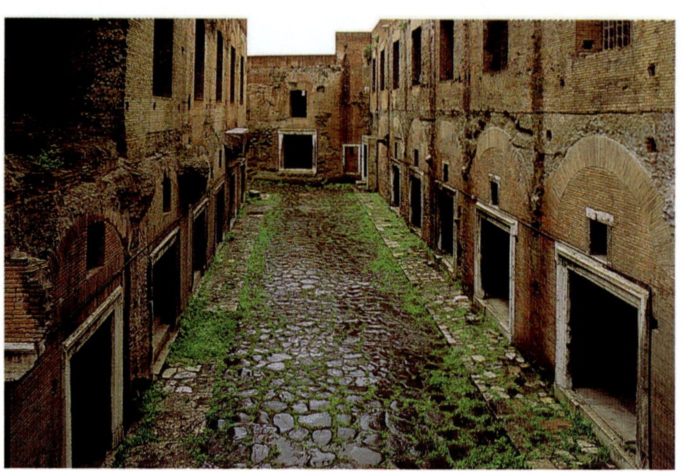

100 (bottom) For the construction of the Forum of Trajan the Quirinal Hill was carved out to a height equal to the column. Apollodorus of Damascus used the excavated area to build the Markets, which also acted as a retaining wall for the hillside behind. The best-preserved part of the complex is the section known as Via Biberatica.

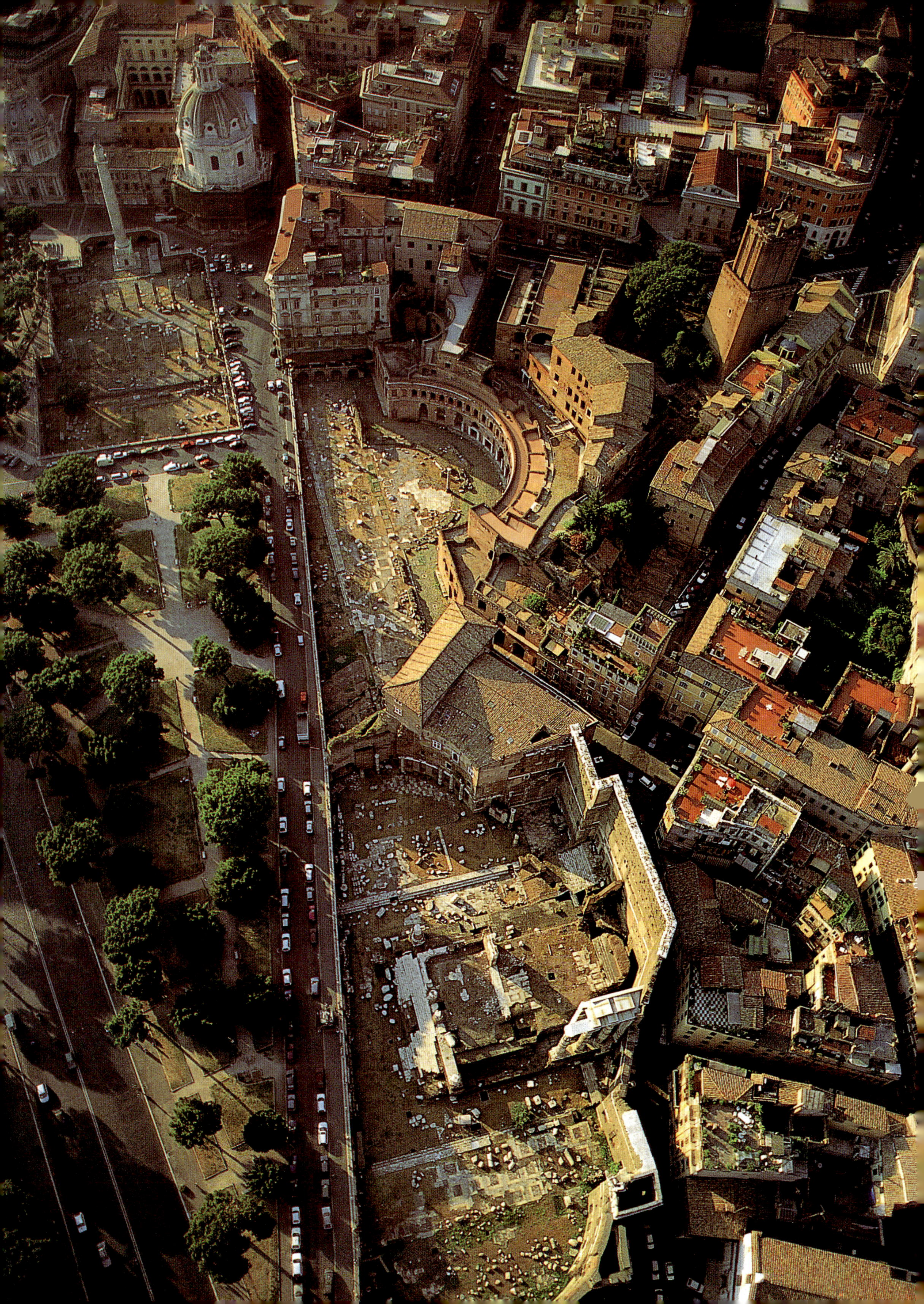

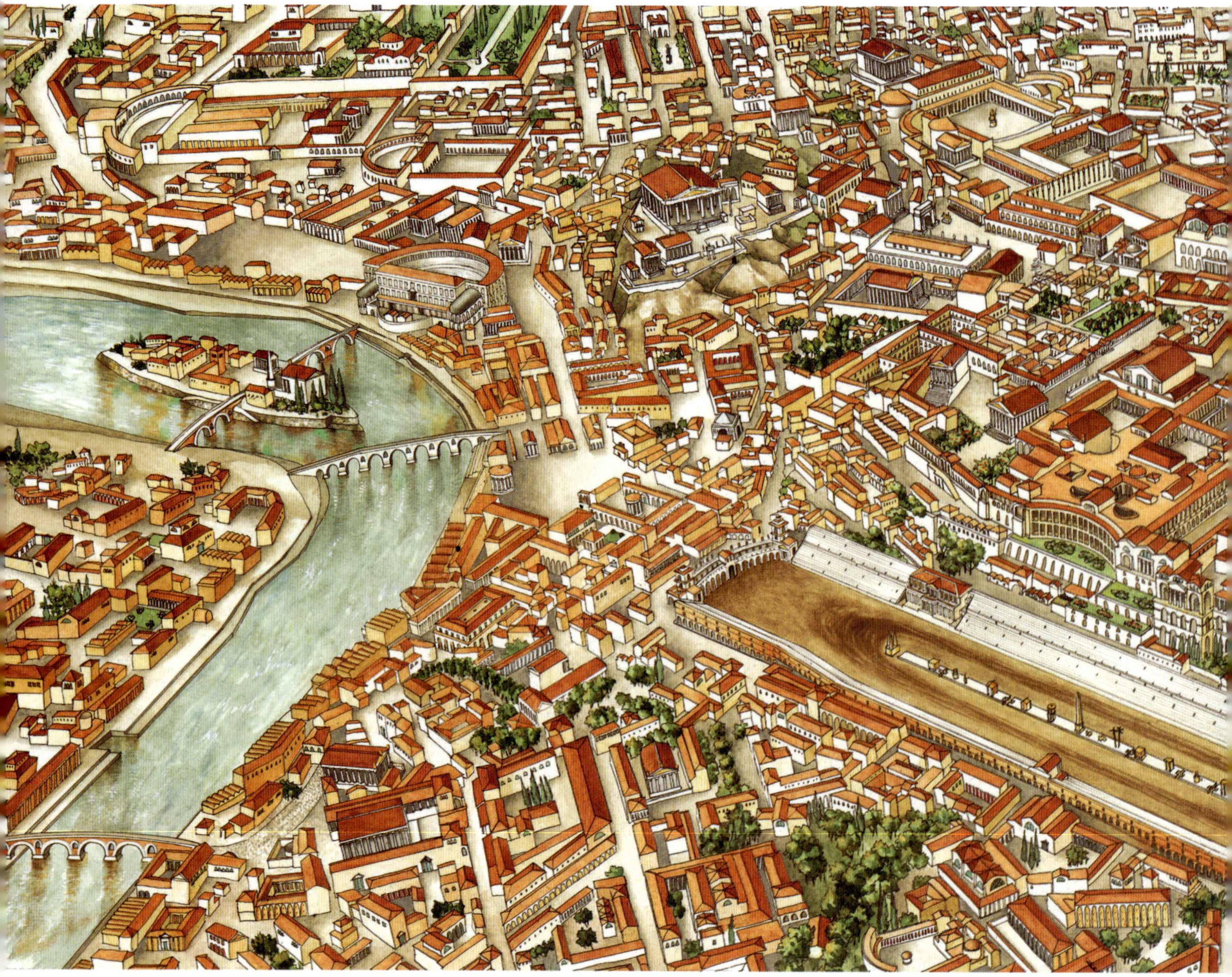

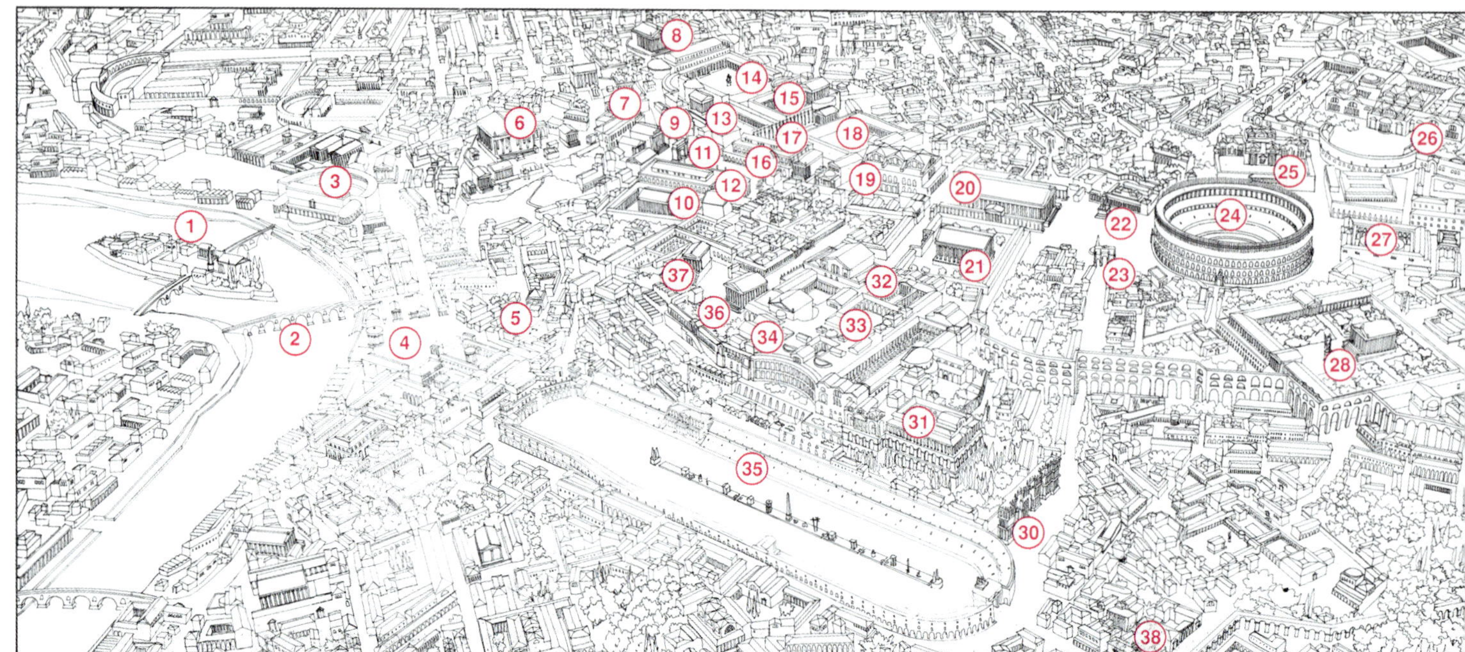
1
2
3
4
5
6
7
8
9
10
11
12
13
14
15
16
17
18
19
20
21
22
23
24
25
26
27
28
30
31
32
33
34
35
36
37
38

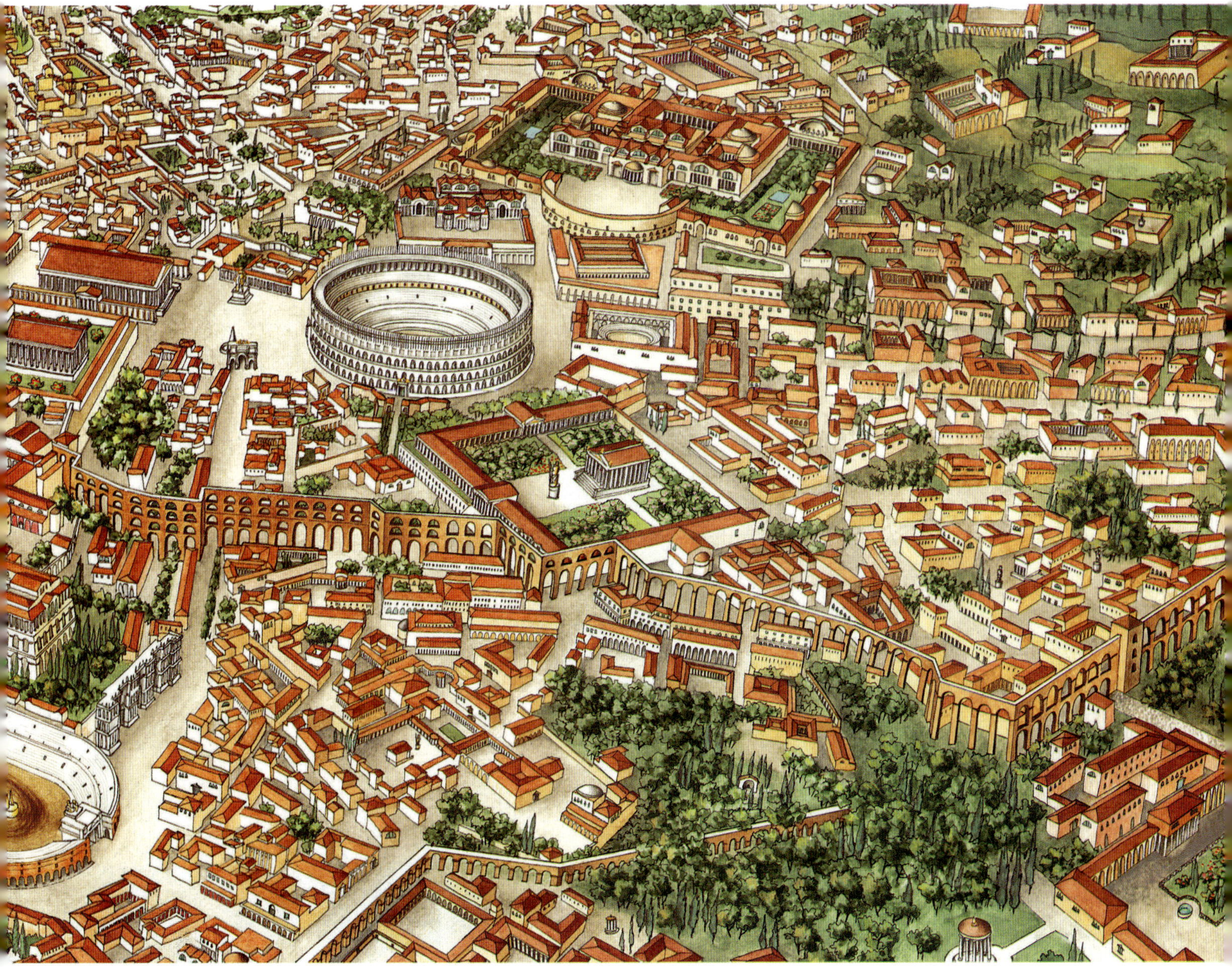

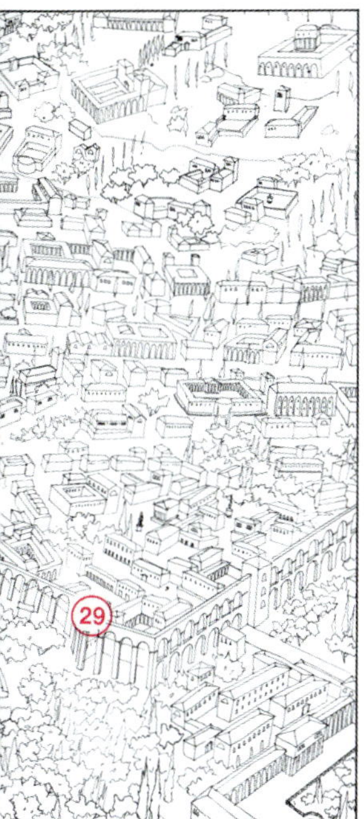

1 Tiber island
2 Aemilian Bridge
3 Theatre of Marcellus
4 Forum Boarium
5 Arch of Janus
6 Temple of Jupiter Capitolinus
7 Tabularium
8 Temple of the Divine Trajan
9 Arch of Septimius Severus
10 Basilica Julia
11 Curia
12 Roman Forum
13 Forum of Caesar
14 Forum of Trajan
15 Forum of Augustus
16 Basilica Aemilia
17 Forum of Nerva or Forum Transitorium
18 Forum of Vespasian or Forum of Peace
19 Basilica Nova or Basilica of Maxentius
20 Temple of Venus and Rome
21 Temple of the Caesars
22 Colossus of Nero
23 Arch of Constantine
24 Flavian amphitheatre or Colosseum
25 Baths of Titus
26 Baths of Trajan
27 Ludus Magnus
28 Temple of the Divine Claudius
29 Aqua Claudia
30 Septizodium
31 Palace of Septimius Severus
32 Domus Flavia
33 Domus Augustana
34 Palatine Hill
35 Circus Maximus
36 Temple of Apollo
37 Temple of Cybele
38 Aqua Marcia

102–103 Rome in the mid-4th century AD *was a city of over a million inhabitants, which had grown up without a precise town plan. Its crowded urban fabric was dominated by the great imperial palaces on the Palatine Hill, large public buildings and huge aqueducts. This was how Rome might have looked a few years after Constantine's victory at the Milvian Bridge and before the long period of decadence which was to see the proud monuments of the greatest city in the ancient world fall into decay and ruin.*

The city was dominated by the huge Temple of Jupiter Capitolinus built by Tarquin the Proud, who also modified the Circus Maximus for chariot races. However, it was Servius Tullius who was responsible for much of the monumental layout of the city. It was divided for administrative purposes into four regions, and trade was boosted by the construction of the Tiber Port near the Forum Boarium. The Temples of Fortune and Mater Matuta were built close by. The construction of the Temple of Diana on the Aventine Hill, the shared cult centre of the federated Latin states is also attributed to Servius Tullius; earlier, Ancus Martius had built the first fixed bridge over the Tiber (the Pons Sublicius). Tarquinius Priscus reclaimed the valley floor by draining water into the Cloaca Maxima.

During the republican age work begun previously was completed, and new buildings were constructed, including the Temple of Jupiter Capitolinus on the Capitol, the temples of Saturn and Castor and Pollux in the Forum, the temples of Ceres, Liber and Libera on the Aventine Hill, and the Temple of Semus Sancus on the Quirinal Hill.

From the beginning of the 5th century BC building work was greatly curtailed because of continual wars against the Latins, Etruscans and Volsci. In 390 BC the Gauls defeated the Romans at the Allia river, entered Rome and sacked it. Though devastated the city was rebuilt. As reported by the historian Livy, however, the work was done in such haste that no town plan was imposed. An already difficult urban situation thus became even more complicated, and Rome, unlike its colonies and the newly built towns – which had wide streets and a regular layout – increasingly resembled 'an agglomeration of houses rather than a properly built city'. A few years later, in 378 BC, the old city walls were strengthened and their defensive capacity improved. New temples included that of Juno the Admonisher on the Arx, the Temple of Salus on the Quirinal Hill, one consecrated to Jupiter Victor on the Palatine Hill and that of Quirinus on the Quirinal Hill. In 312 BC the first aqueduct was built by the censor Appius Claudius, and in 291 BC a Temple of Aesculapius, god of healing, rose on the Tiber island.

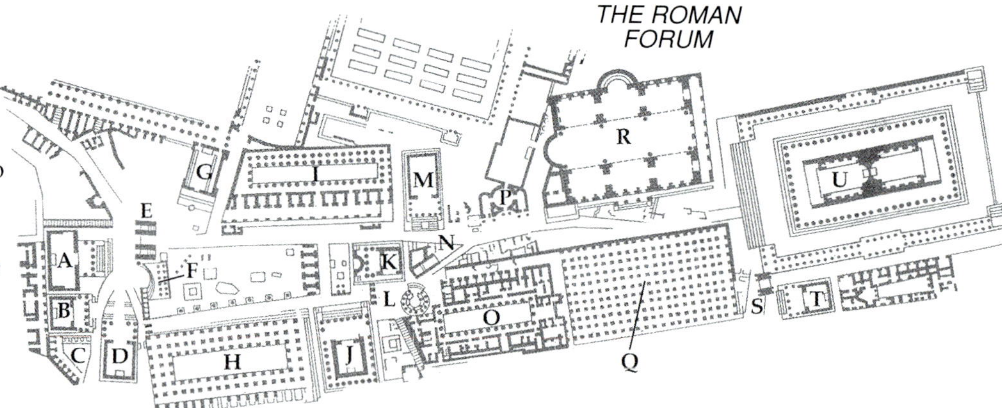

A Temple of Concord
B Temple of Vespasian
C Portico of the Twelve Gods
D Temple of Saturn
E Arch of Septimius Severus
F Rostra
G Curia
H Basilica Julia
I Basilica Aemilia
J Temple of Castor and Pollux
K Temple of the Divine Julius
L Temple of Vesta
M Temple of Antoninus and Faustina
N Regia
O House of the Vestals
P Temple of the Divine Romulus
Q Porticus Margaritaria
R Basilica Nova or Basilica of Maxentius
S Arch of Titus
T Temple of Jupiter the Messenger
U Temple of Venus and Rome

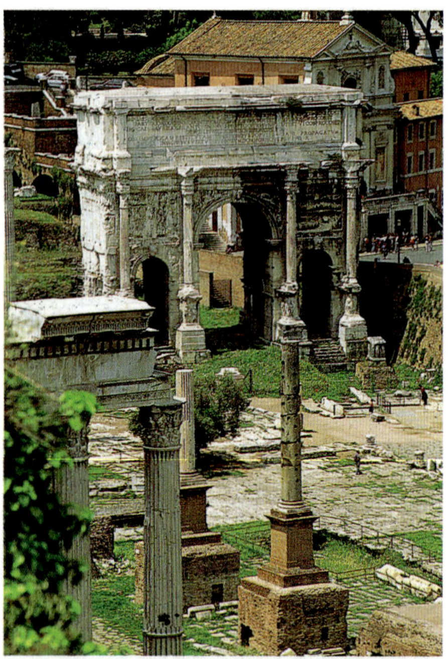

104 (left above) The Arch of Septimius Severus was erected in the Roman Forum to commemorate the emperor's victories in the east. The various episodes of the war are depicted in great detail in the numerous reliefs decorating the monument.

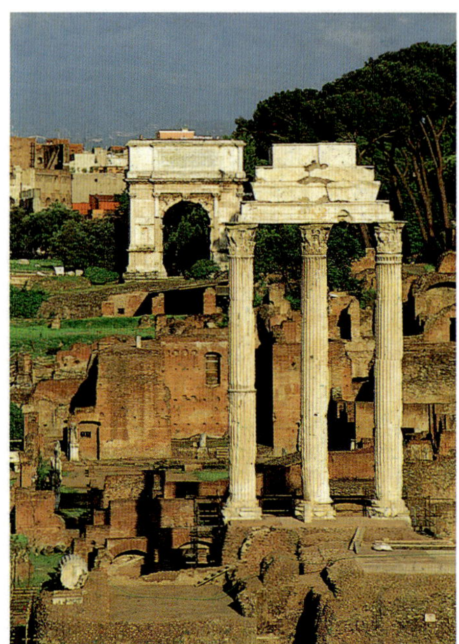

104 (left below) Behind the surviving columns of the Temple of Castor and Pollux (dating from the age of Tiberius) stands the white form of the Arch of Titus, erected in AD 81 to celebrate the victory of Vespasian and his son over the Judaeans.

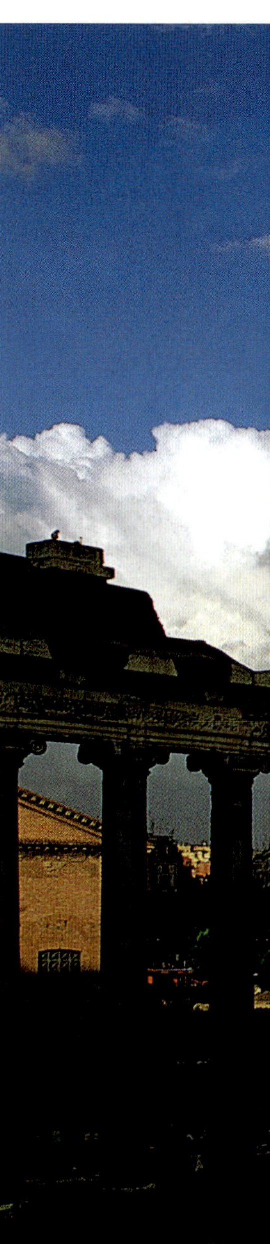

104–105 The Roman Forum was the centre of the city's public life for centuries. The columns of the Temple of Saturn can be seen on the left, the Temple of Antoninus and Faustina in the centre, and the Temple of Castor and Pollux on the right.

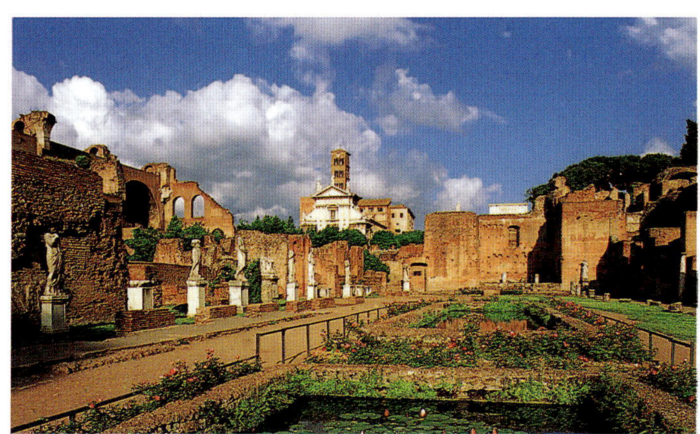

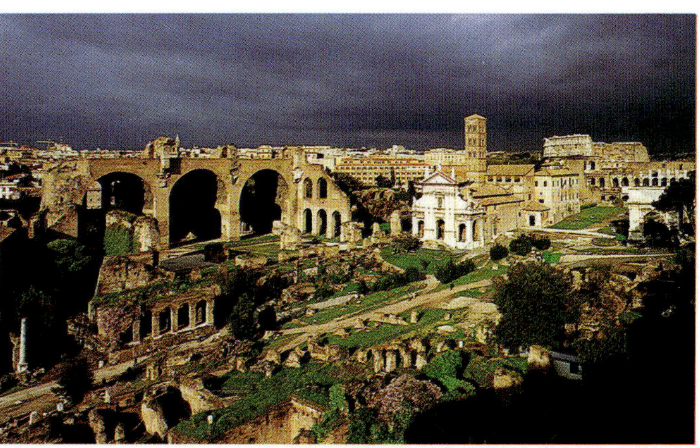

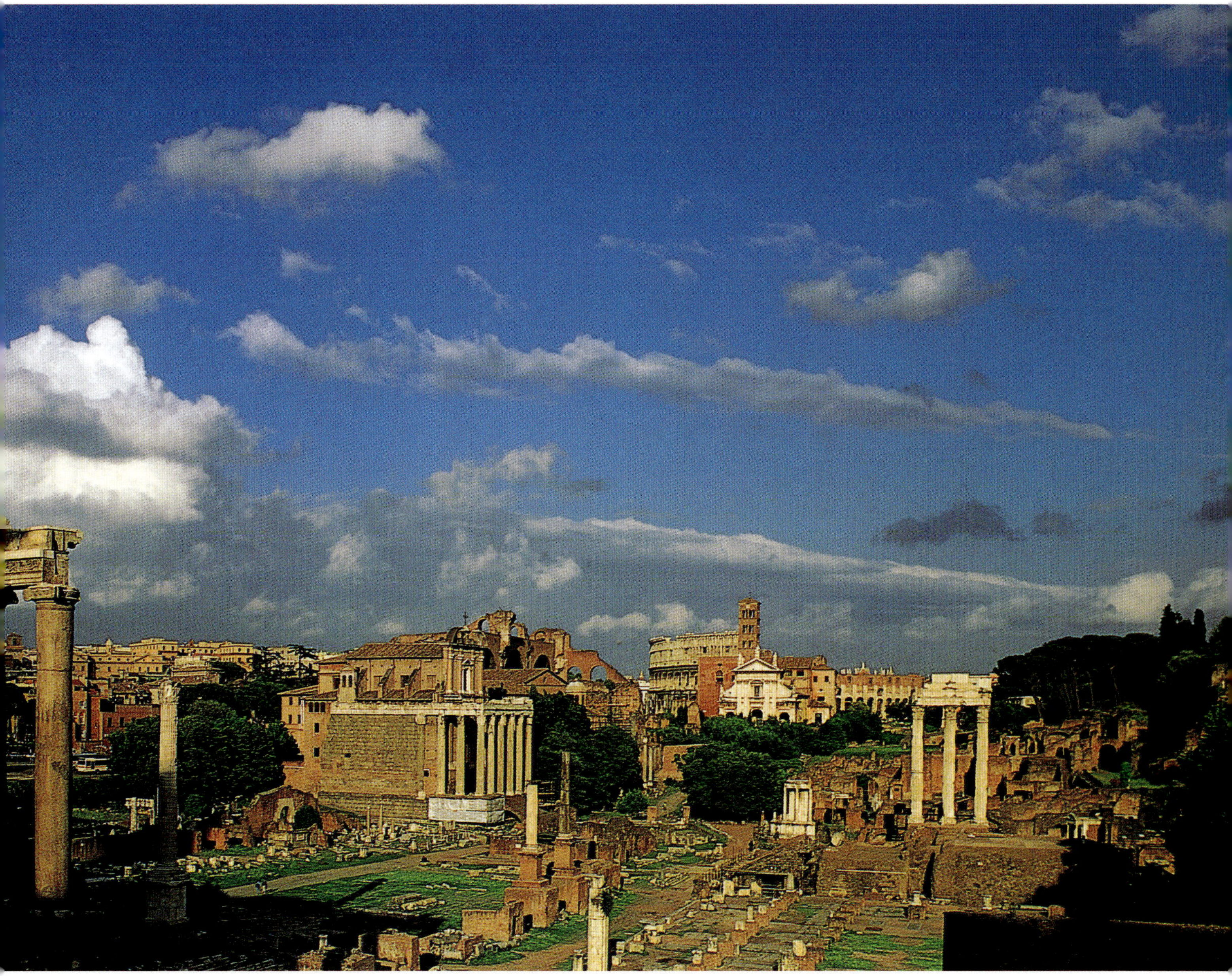

105 (top left) Among the most interesting monuments in the Roman Forum is the House of the Vestals, the residence of the priestesses who tended the sacred fire of Vesta, goddess of the household, which burned in the nearby circular temple.

105 (top right) The last and grandest basilica built in Rome was begun by Maxentius in AD *308 and completed by Constantine, who added a colossal acrolithic (a bronze body with marble extremities) statue of himself in one apse.*

105 (right) This section drawing reveals the huge proportions of the Basilica of Maxentius: it was 100 m (328 ft) long and 76 m (250 ft) wide. At the apex of the nave it was 53 m (174 ft) high and just under 25 m (82 ft) high in the two aisles.

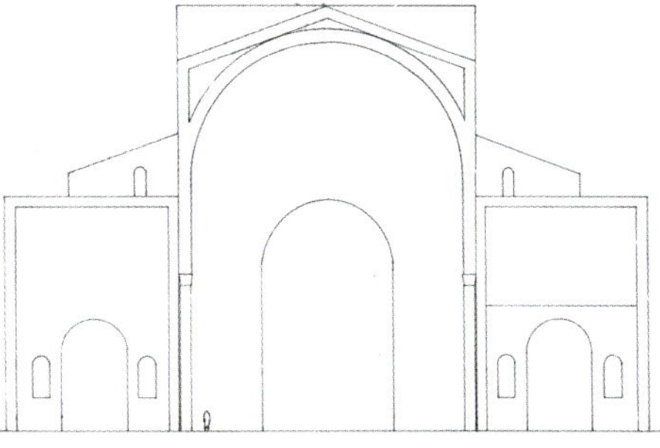

106–107 (overleaf) The Basilica of Maxentius in the 4th century AD*. The walls were covered in red and green porphyry with inlays of marble; it had superb box vaults with brightly coloured plaster. The statue of Constantine stands in the apse.*

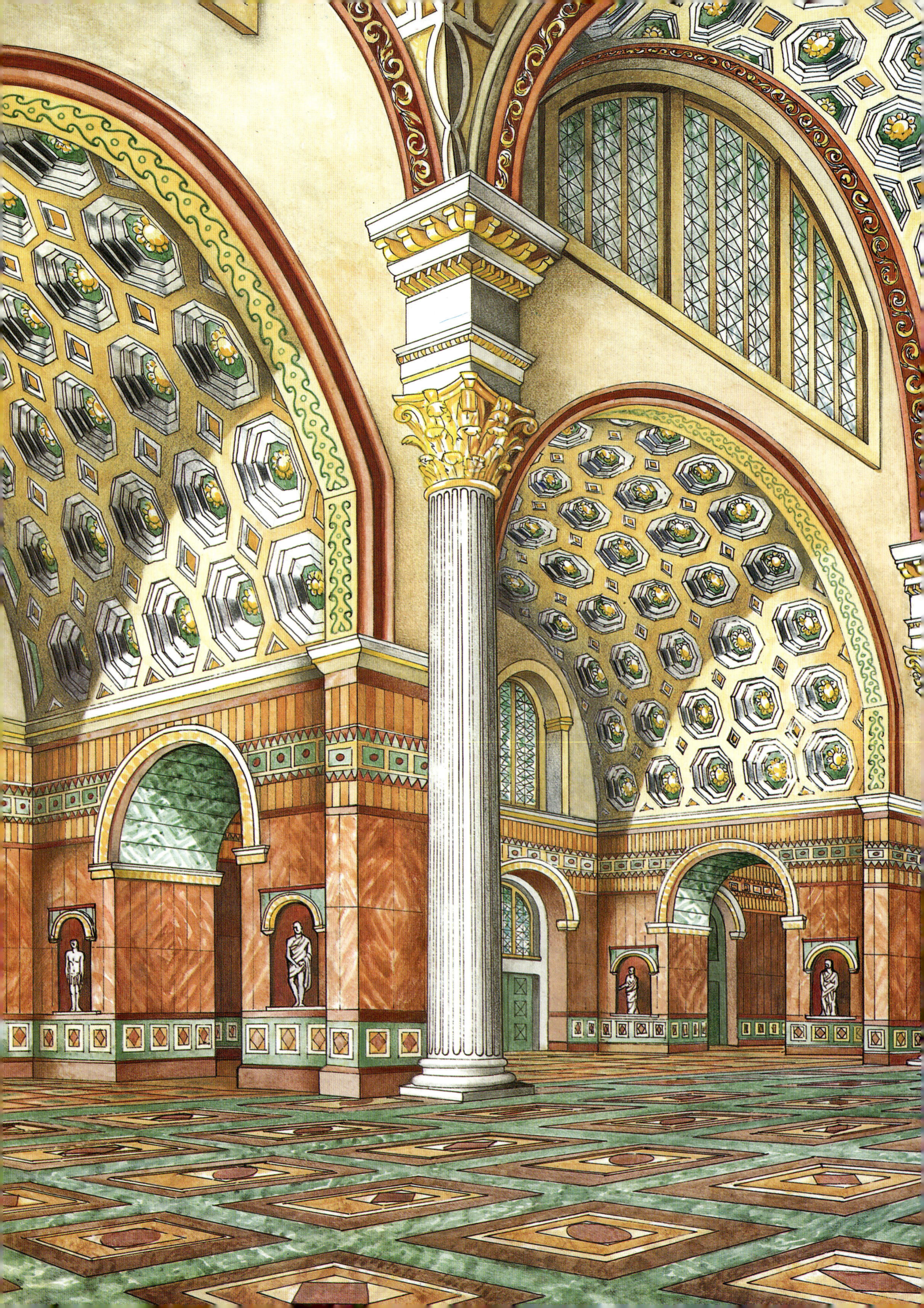

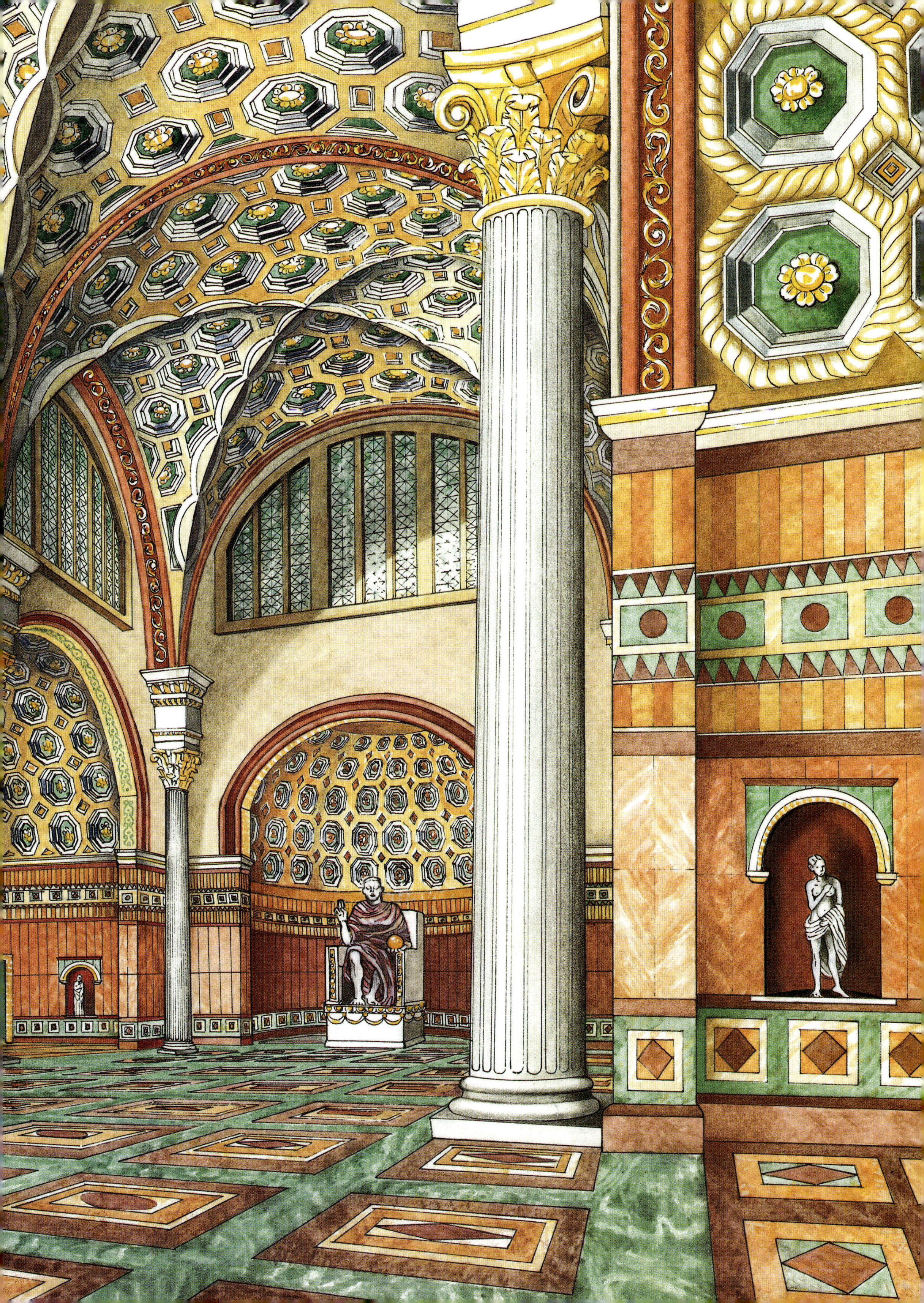

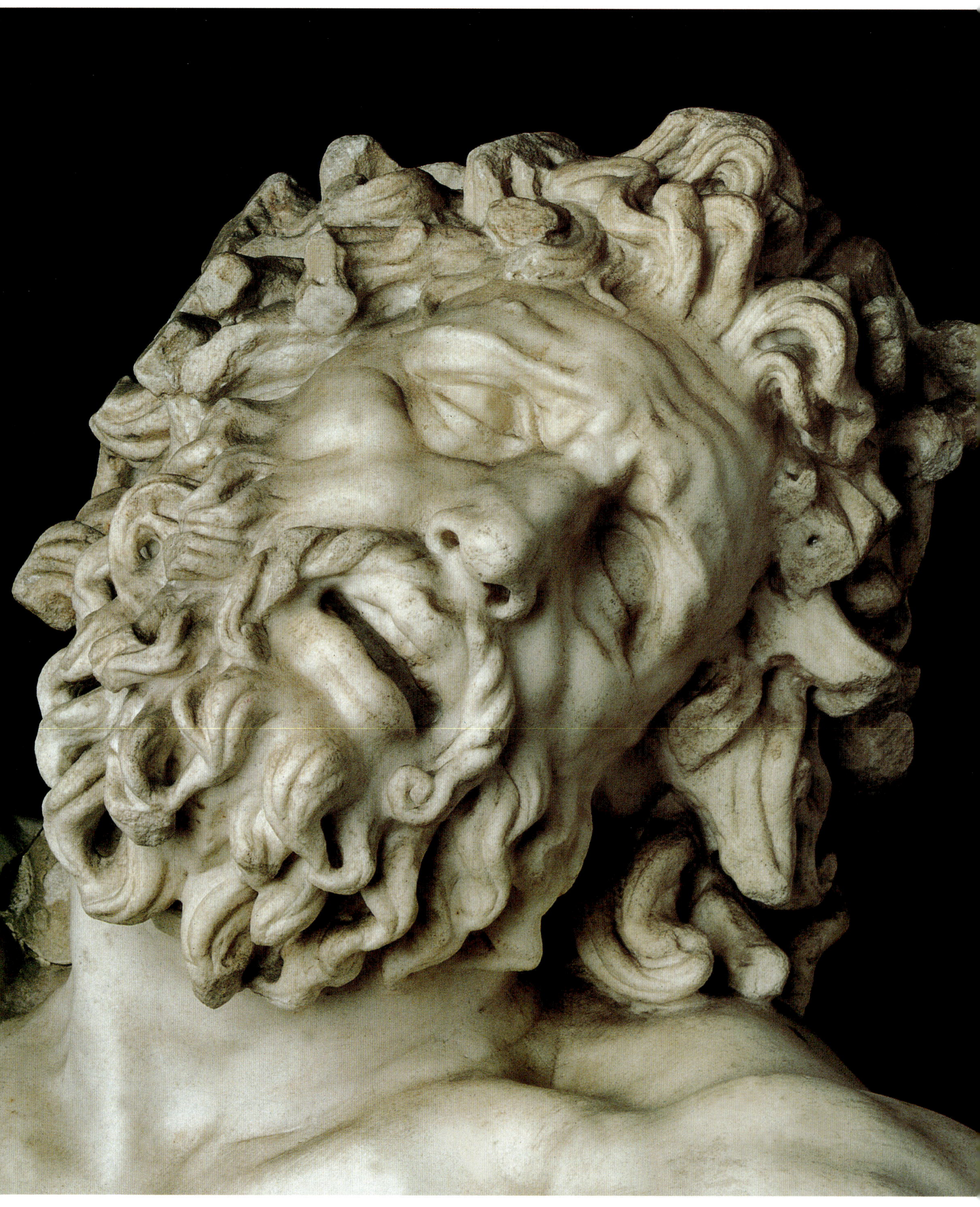

After the Carthaginian threat had been overcome a new construction boom began in the city, already divided into four regions (Collina, Esquilina, Suburana and Palatina). The commercial structures on the Tiber were improved; new buildings included the Emporium, the huge Porticus Aemilia, the impressive ruins of which can still be seen on the Testaccio plain, and the first *horrea* (food warehouses) made of masonry. The Circus Flaminius was erected on the Campus Martius, and the two oldest temples in the 'Largo Argentina' complex were built nearby. Between 184 and 170 BC, Porcius Cato, Aemilius Lepidus and Sempronius Gracchus built large buildings called basilicas on the

108–109 According to the Roman historian Pliny the Elder, the famous marble group of Laocoon once decorated the palace of Titus. The original Hellenistic work was attributed to the sculptors Hagesander, Polydorus and Athenodorus of Rhodes and perhaps stood in one of the monumental buildings at Pergamum. It was imported to Rome after Attalus bequeathed that kingdom to the Romans. Hailed by Pliny as a masterpiece, the great figural group, which illustrates the myth of the Trojan priest punished by Athena, demonstrates the great success which Greek statuary encountered in the Roman world from the 2nd century BC*. Copies of Greek originals were popular in the imperial age, and many Greek sculptors moved to Rome.*

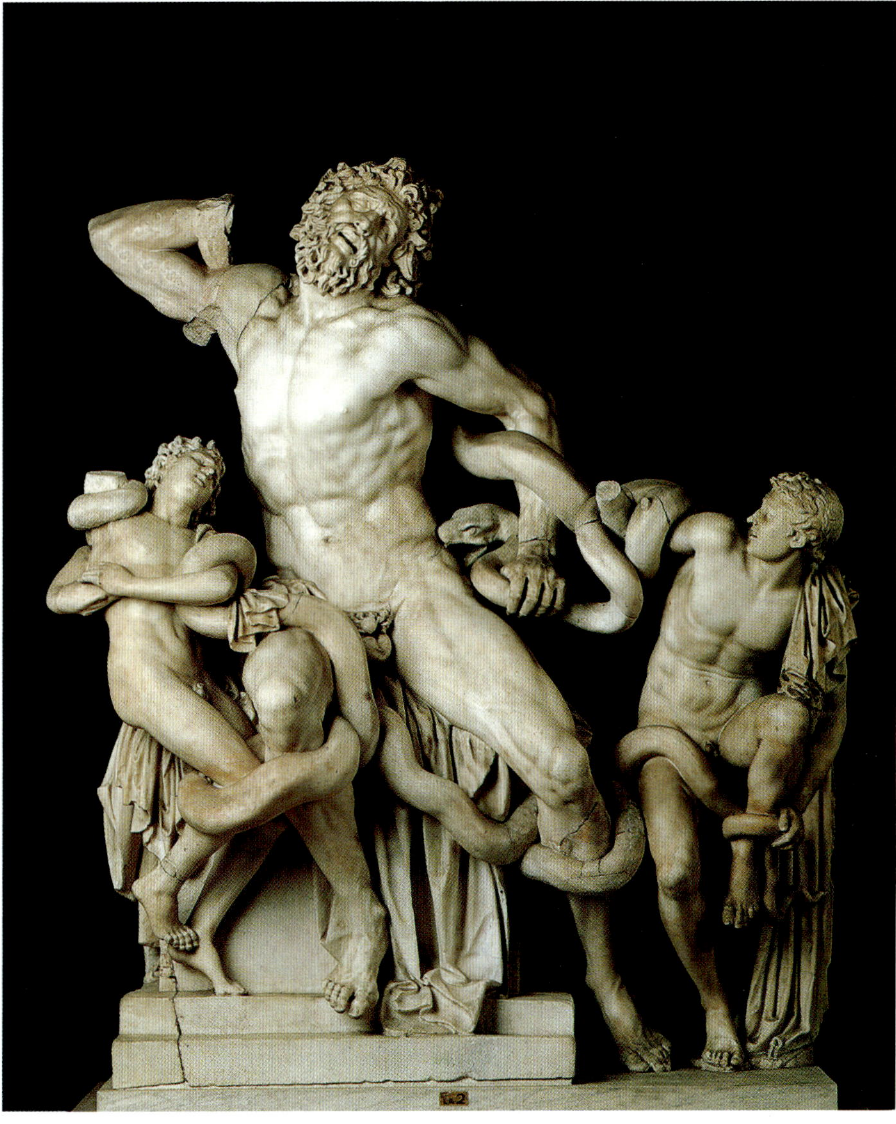

Hellenistic pattern to provide the city with suitable premises for discussing legal and business deals, which until then had taken place in the open in the forum. Numerous porticoes were also built. Aemilius laid the piers of the first masonry bridge over the Tiber, downstream from the Tiber Island; a few years later the piers were connected with supporting arches, thus introducing a type of construction later used to build aqueducts after the invention of *opus incertum*, a mixture of stones and mortar which facilitated bold architectural designs.

Contact with Greek colonies led to the import of sculptures, beginning the fashion for copying Greek originals which later became very popular. However, even the homes of the wealthiest Romans remained fairly modest, while those of the poorer classes, which were small and crowded together, were simple trelliswork structures of wood and brick. Lifestyles were generally austere; there were few slaves, and domestic life was very simple.

In the religious sphere, sacrifices were offered to the Lares (the tutelary divinities which protected the family and the house) on the household altar. Wax images of the Penates (the spirits of the ancestors) were jealously guarded, and displayed at funerals and the more solemn family ceremonies. Little by little, many gods such as Ceres, goddess of agriculture, Castor and Pollux (twin sons of Jupiter who, according to legend, fought at Lake Regillus with the Romans), Heracles, Aesculapius and others were introduced into public worship. Greek and Roman gods gradually were identified with one another, though the Romans still worshipped their traditional deities, and were suspicious of religions which might undermine their power.

Important ceremonies included the triumph, an honour reserved for generals who had made a major contribution to extending the borders of the state, destined to take on increasing importance over the centuries. The victorious general rode on a chariot drawn by four white horses along a route to the Temple of Jupiter Capitolinus. As the living image of a god, he was dressed in purple, crowned with a laurel wreath and held a sceptre surmounted by an eagle in his right hand. The procession was led by magistrates and senators. Then followed the booty, consisting not only of weapons and insignia, but also works of art, precious objects and exotic animals. Next came the sacrificial animals, the lictors with the *fasces*, and the veterans of the successful campaign, who sang songs and directed ribald jokes at their commander. Processions of prisoners and enemy chieftains, chained and wearing national costume, followed the triumphal chariot. Significant episodes of the war might be illustrated on large boards carried in the procession, as was a list of the towns and

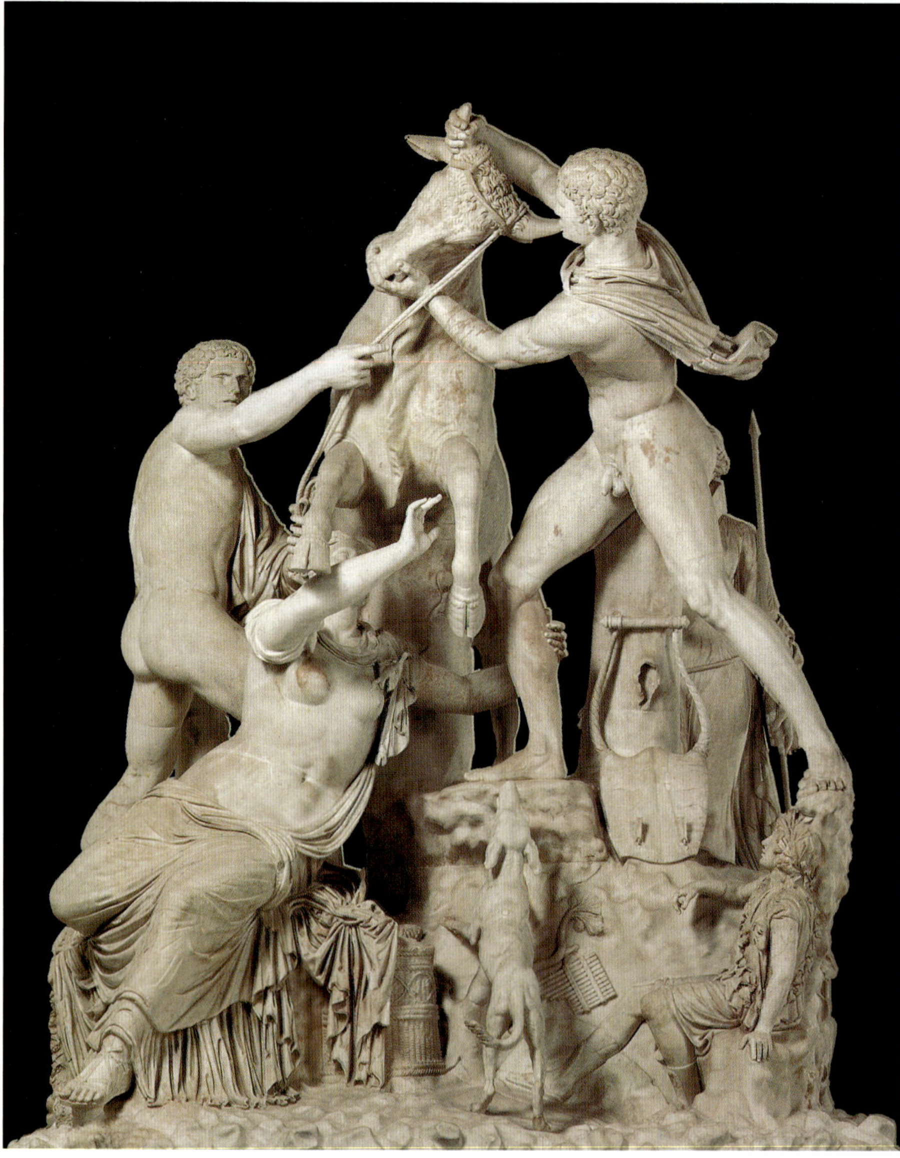

110 (above) One of the most outstanding of the many works of art which adorned the Baths of Caracalla was the famous marble group known as the Farnese Bull, a copy, dating from the Antonine age of a Greek original by Apollonius of Tralles. The sculpture portrays the myth of the punishment of Dirce, who was tied to a bull by Zethus and Amphion to revenge their mother Antiope.

111 (opposite) The statue known as the Dying Gaul is a Roman copy of a bronze original belonging to a votive group dedicated to Attalus I, King of Pergamum. The encounter with Hellenism was crucial to the birth of Roman art; however, at the beginning of the long creative process many ethical prejudices were expressed in Rome in conservative patrician circles.

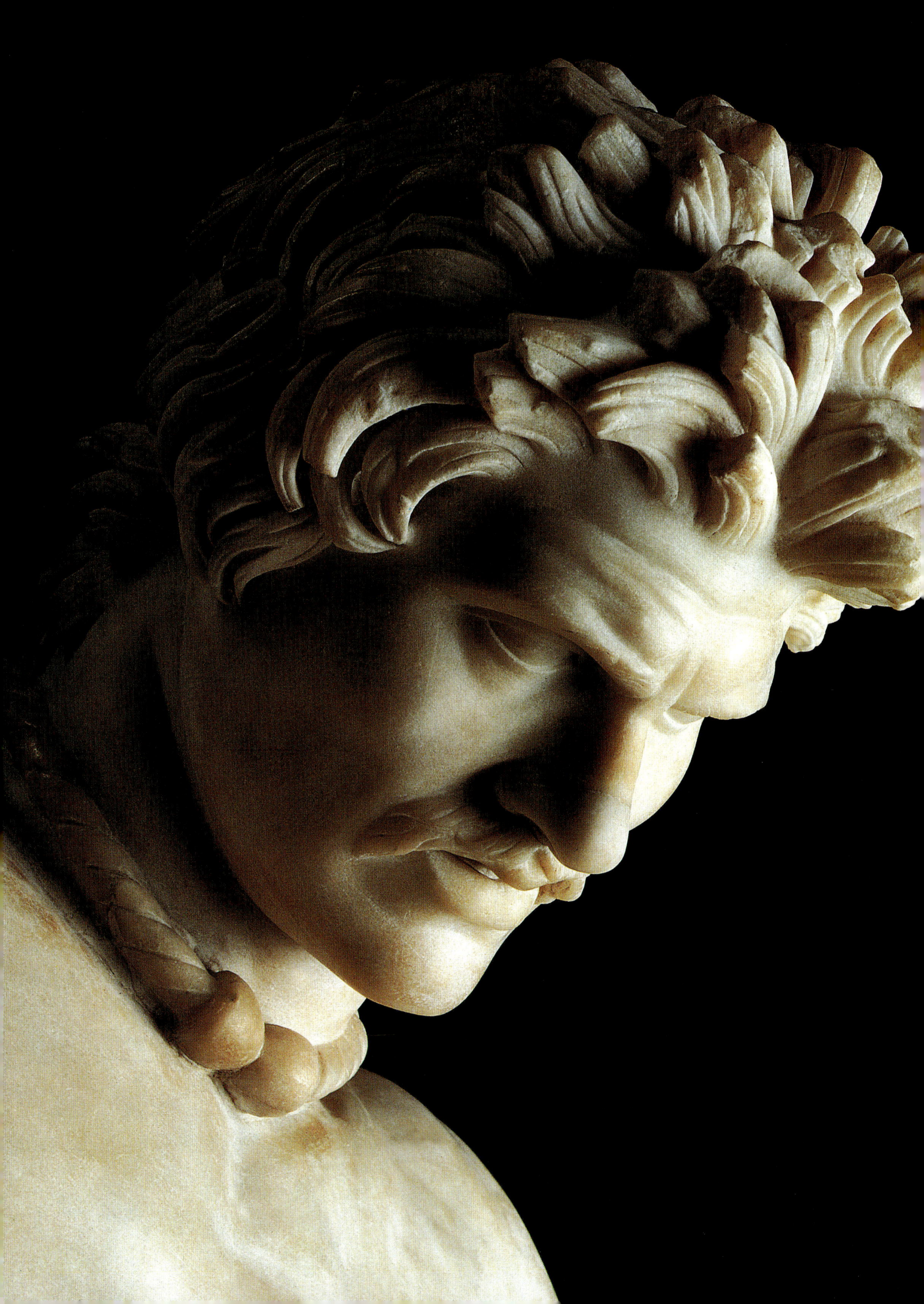

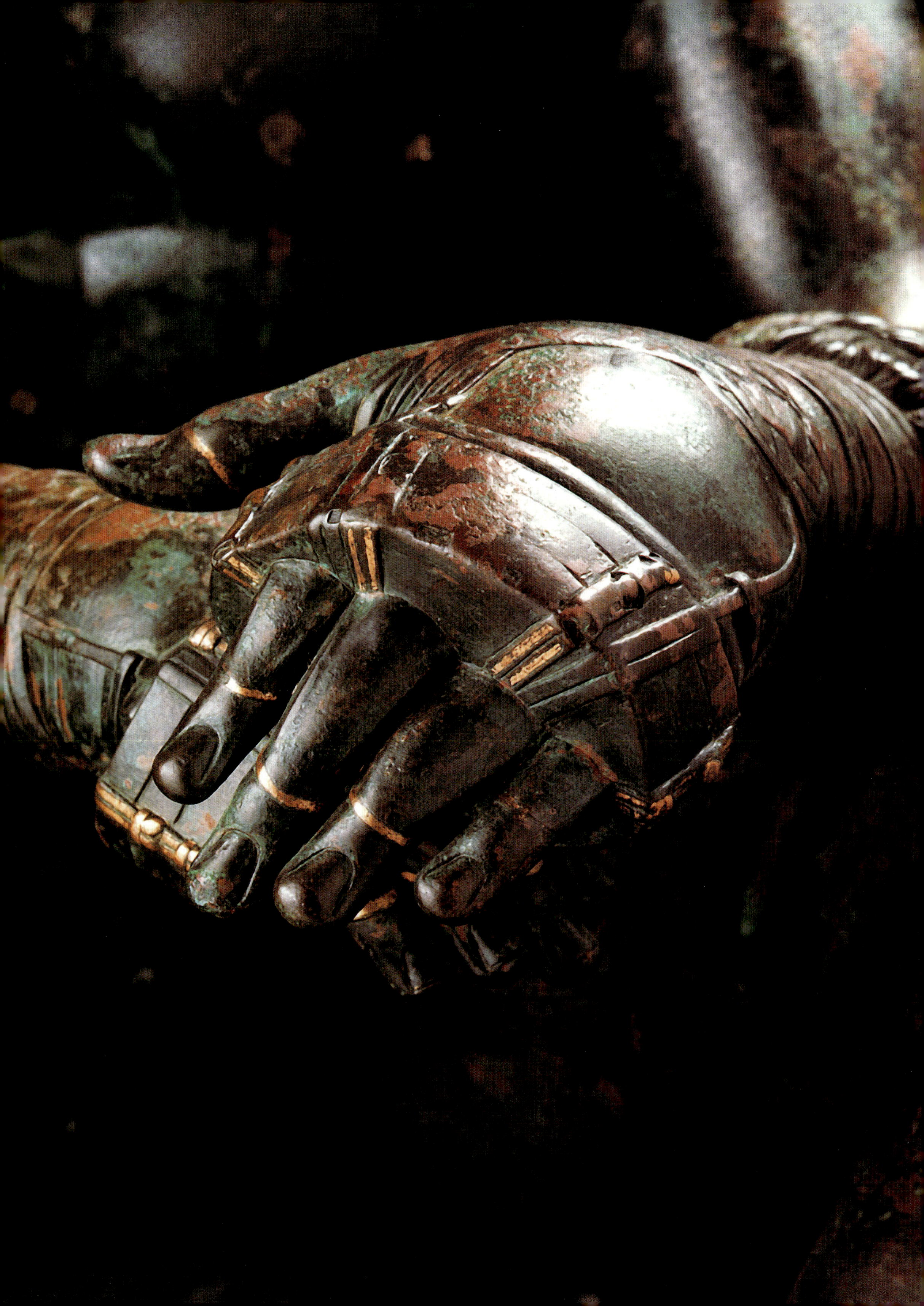

112 and 113 This splendid bronze of a boxer at rest was long attributed to Apollonius, one of many Greek artists who emigrated to Rome. Although this hypothesis has recently been disproved, there is no doubt that the statue was made to decorate a Roman building, perhaps a baths complex. The detail opposite shows the cesti, *a type of glove made from strips of leather and reinforced with lead.*

114–115 (overleaf) The Colosseum is the most magnificent monument of ancient Rome, and throughout the ages has been considered as the symbol of Rome's eternity. In the Middle Ages it became a quarry for building material. Its present state of preservation is due to Pope Benedict XIV who, in the mid-18th century, ordered the plunder to cease, declaring the building sacred in the mistaken belief that it had been stained by the blood of Christian martyrs.

populations subjugated, and the numbers of the enemy killed and taken prisoner.

Literary production was modest and consisted mostly of celebrations of military glories and songs sung at banquets lauding the feats of the ancestors. Theatrical performances, popular in tone, were mostly of rural origin. The ruling class cultivated the art of oratory for eminently practical reasons – politicians had to be skilled speakers, able to address their peers in the Senate and to win over the masses.

The age of the Punic Wars brought radical transformations in social and cultural life. The annexation of the Greek towns of southern Italy and numerous contacts made in the Mediterranean provided new influences. Hellenism – the literary and artistic civilization of the Greeks in the age of Alexander the Great – proved popular in Rome. Anything congenial to the ideology of the ruling class was accepted without hesitation. Thus oral literature and the sacred and popular forms of earlier periods were abandoned, and gradually replaced by the epic poem, tragedy, comedy and history.

Livius Andronicus, a Greek from Tarentum taken to Rome as a slave, gave the Romans, now beginning their Mediterranean ventures, the Latin translation of the *Odyssey*, while the Campanian Gnaeus Naevius composed a poem about the First Punic War in which he had fought. Fabius Pictor and Cincius Alimentus wrote historical works in Greek, a language by now known by many Romans. By imitating the literary forms of the Greeks, poets and historians created a Latin literature suitable to illustrate the main stages of Roman expansion. In religion there was a similar attitude of tolerance of different faiths. In 204 BC the cult of Cybele, a Phrygian divinity, was established in Rome. However, the rites in honour of Bacchus, the Bacchanalia, met with open hostility. Followers from different classes met secretly, and the fact that this religion crossed social barriers, although it had no political aims, was seen by the Senate as a threat to the existing order and a decree banned attendance at these meetings in 186 BC.

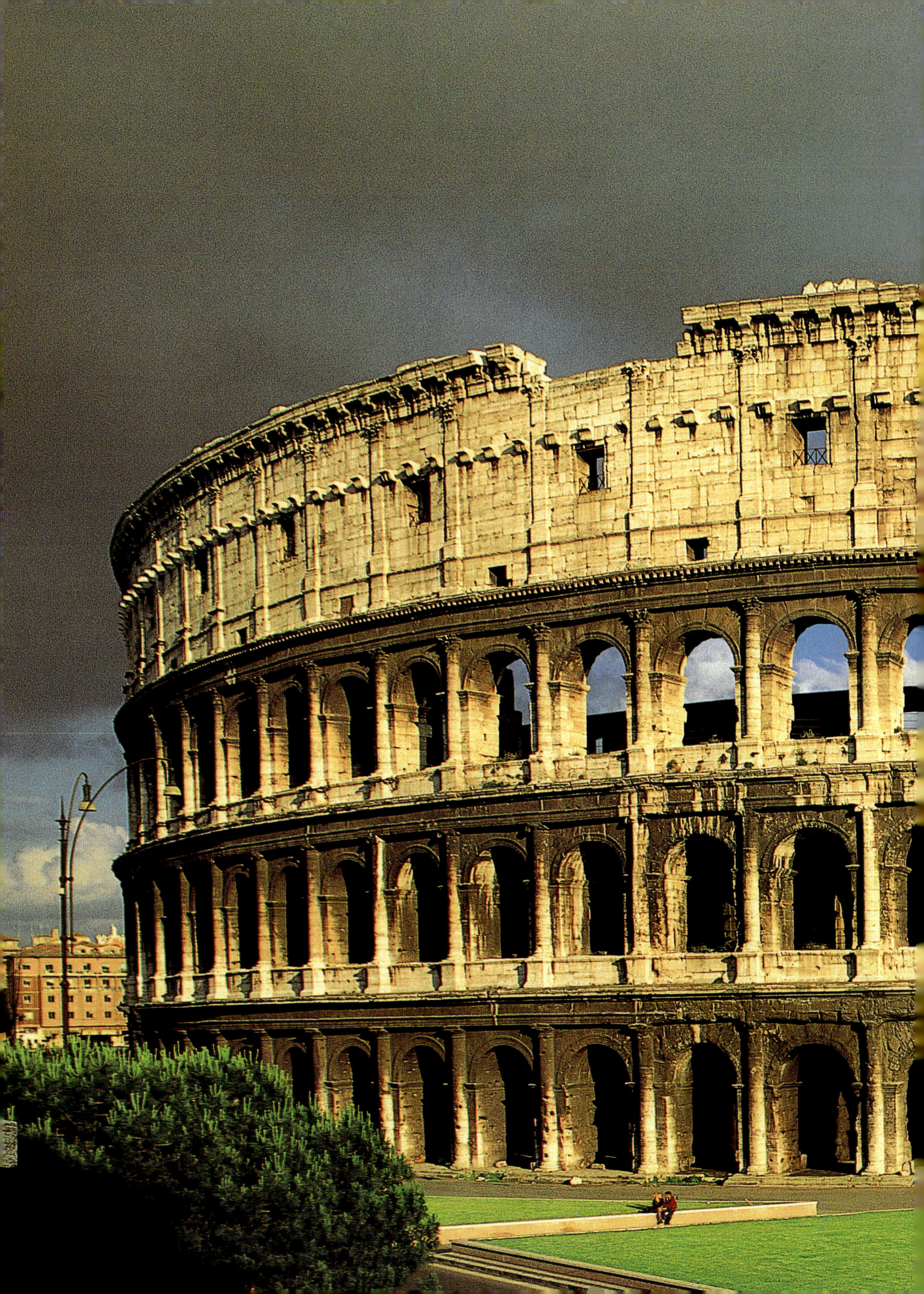

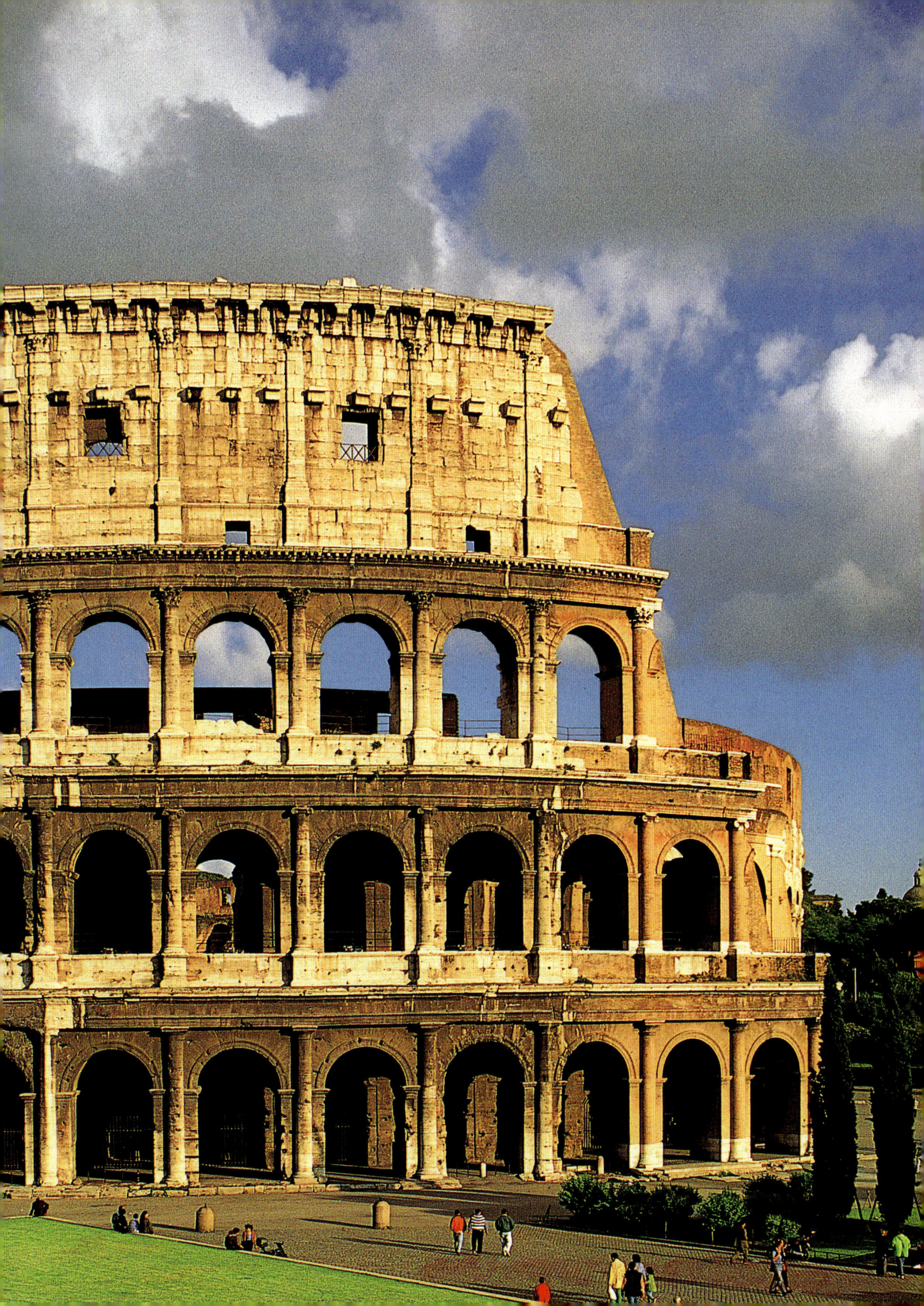

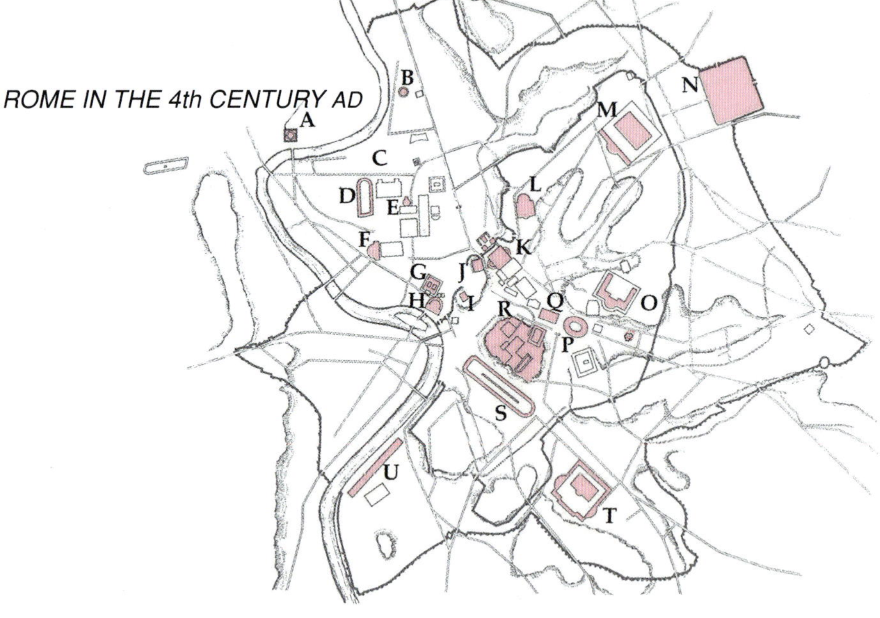

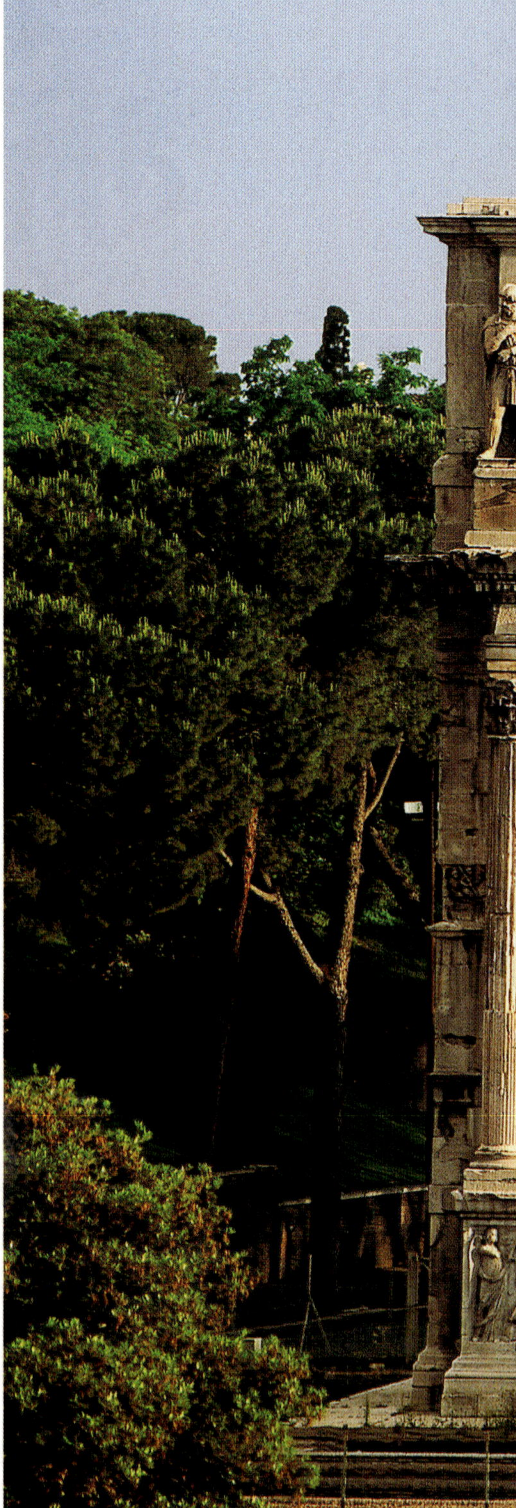

In the political sphere, Rome was dominated by the powerful Scipio *gens* (family). After the battle of Zama in 202 BC, seven Scipios were appointed consuls in ten years, while other magistratures were held by friends and relations. Both Scipio Africanus and Scipio Aemilianus were distinguished by their attitude to contemporary society. They used classical culture to enhance their prestige by founding a literary circle. Its members included the historian Polybius, the philosopher Panaetius, and the poet Ennius, the author of works exalting Rome's military glories, for which he was hailed as the Latin Homer. Terence, who came to Rome from Africa as a slave when still a boy and was freed and then adopted by the Scipios, brought the world of the middle classes into the theatre, replacing the realism of his predecessor Plautus (an author and manager of a company) with a more elegant style of comedy.

A faction of the nobility, led by Marcus Porcius Cato, jealous of the Scipios' leadership, was advocating a more rigid form of imperialism which was to triumph a few years later. Cato – a vehement defender of Roman tradition against Greek influence – was also an orator and author. He accused Scipio Africanus of illicit dealings and forced him to retire to his villa at Liternus in Campania, where he died in 183 BC, the same year that Hannibal committed suicide rather than fall into the hands of the Romans.

Towards the second half of the 2nd century BC, Rome began to take on a monumental appearance. Its architecture was transformed by the introduction of colonnades, beams and mezzanine floors made airier by the addition of galleries. Flat ceilings were replaced by arches, also used singly as triumphal monuments. Craftsmen from the Greek world worked in Rome, and copies of famous statues were commissioned from them to decorate private homes and public buildings. The art of portraiture was introduced and was original from the outset. People were not idealized but portrayed realistically, their features sometimes depicted quite unmercifully.

A Mausoleum of Hadrian
B Mausoleum of Augustus
C Campus Martius
D Stadium of Domitian
E Pantheon
F Theatre of Pompey
G Portico of Octavia
H Theatre of Marcellus
I Temple of Jupiter Capitolinus
J Arx
K Forum of Trajan
L Baths of Constantine
M Baths of Diocletian
N Praetorian Camp
O Baths of Trajan
P Colosseum
Q Temple of Venus and Rome
R Palatine Hill
S Circus Maximus
T Baths of Caracalla
U Porticus Aemilia

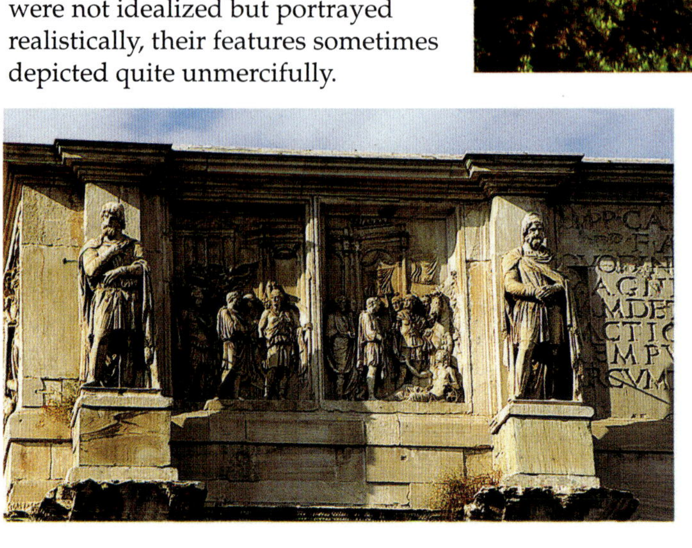

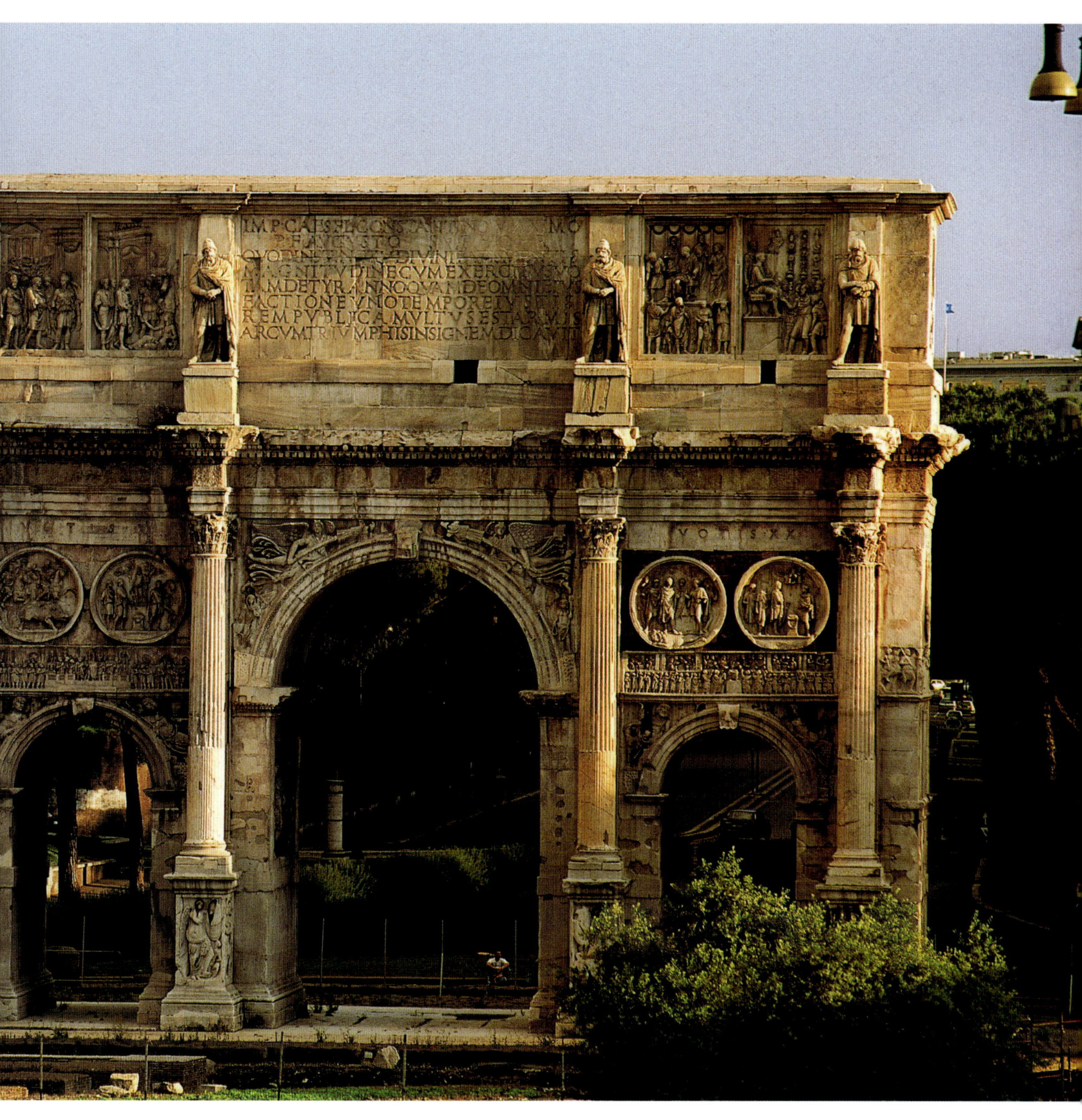

116 (opposite) Despite its varied origins, the Arch of Constantine is outstanding for its architectural harmony and pure proportions. Eight statues of Dacian barbarians crowning the arch certainly date from the age of Trajan, and eight of the ten roundels were also plundered from one of his monuments.

116–117 (above) The Arch of Constantine was erected in AD *315 to commemorate the emperor's victory over Maxentius at the battle of the Milvian Bridge. With its three archways, it stands alone near the Colosseum, 25 m (82 ft) high. Many of its friezes, statues and medallions were taken from buildings dating from the periods of Trajan, Hadrian and Marcus Aurelius. In particular, in the upper level the emperor Hadrian's head was replaced with Constantine's. The few reliefs made specifically for the monument are recognizable by their hasty workmanship, stiff formality and lack of perspective.*

118–119 (overleaf) According to legend, Romulus founded Rome on the Palatine Hill, where the emperors later built their palaces. In the foreground are the remains of the Domus Augustana of Augustus; in the centre is the Stadium of Domitian, designed for competitions and festivals.

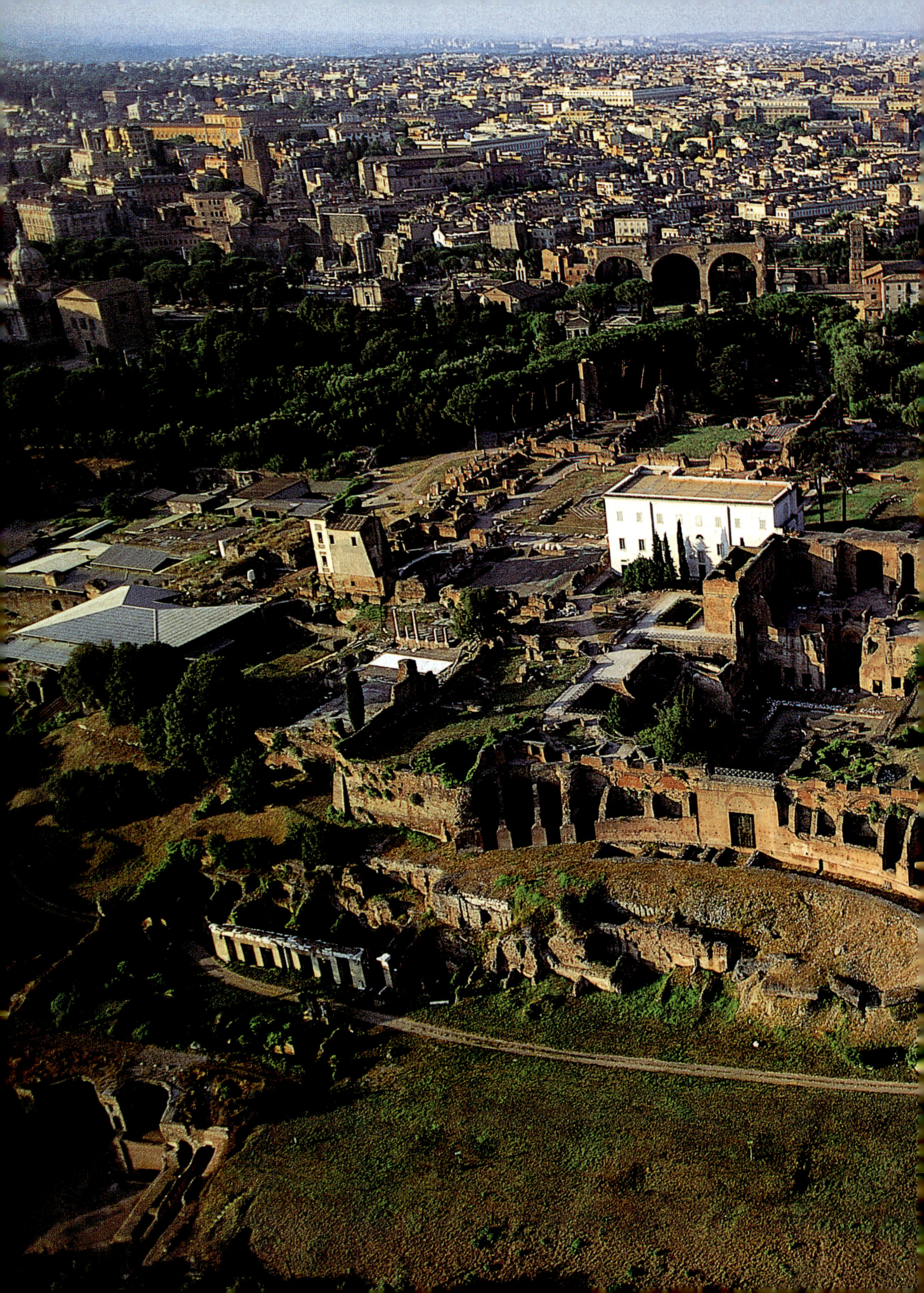

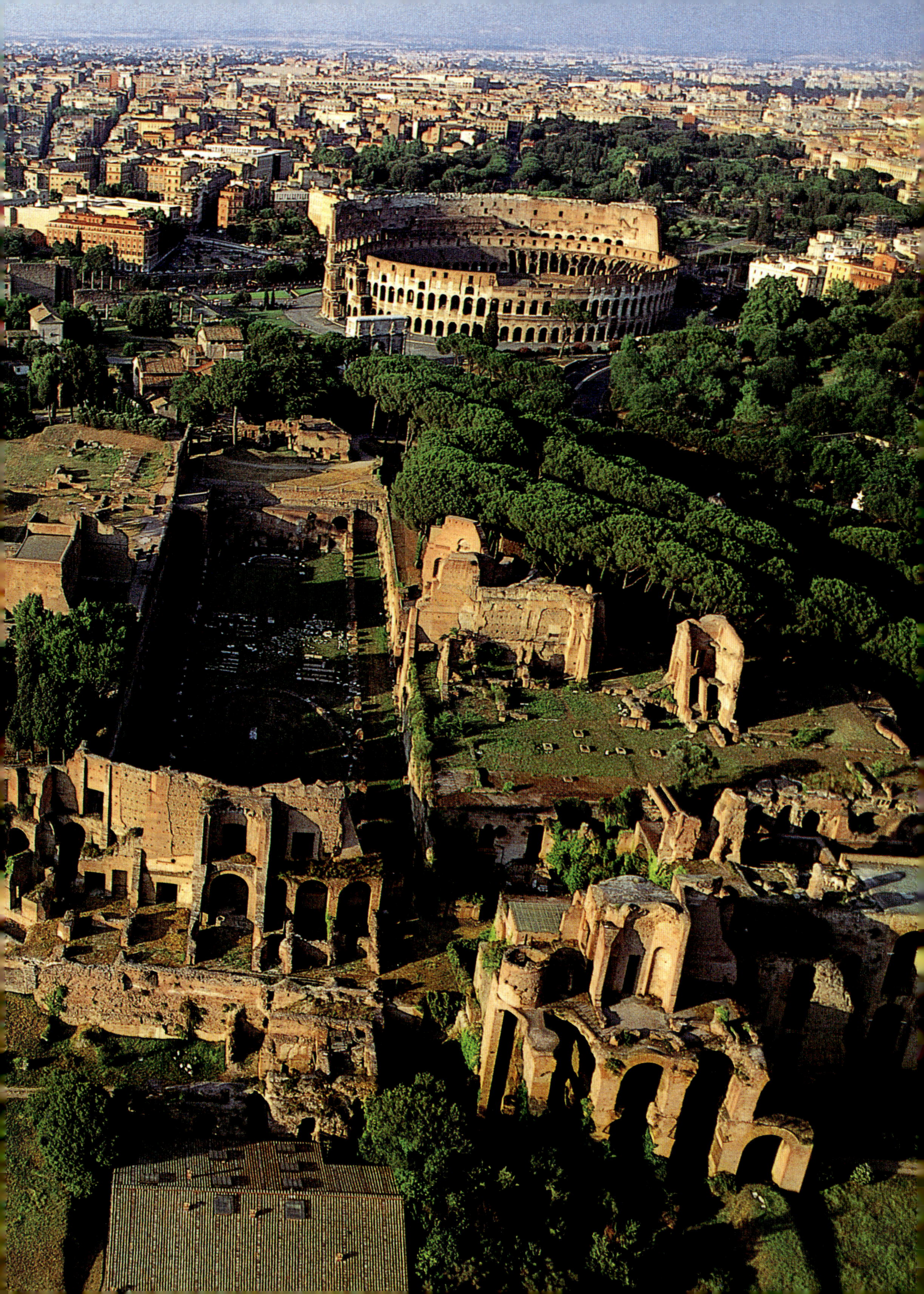

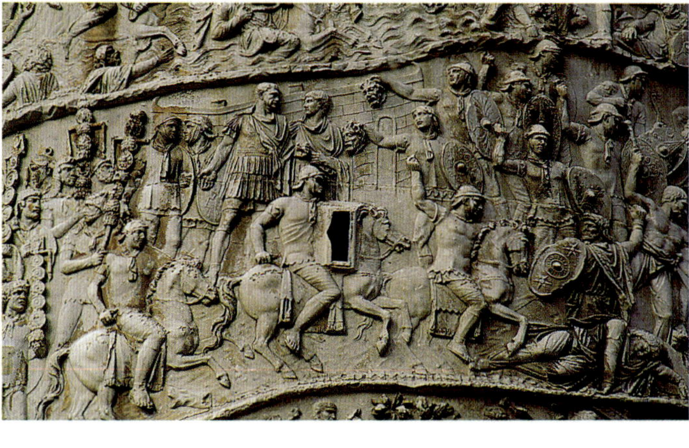

120 (right) The frieze spiralling round Trajan's column consists of some 2500 figures; Trajan himself appears around 60 times. Battle scenes alternate with peaceful activities and sacrifices to the gods to ensure the success of the military campaign.

120 (below) Trajan's Column, originally surmounted by a statue of Trajan, is now topped by one of St Peter, which was placed there in 1587. The column's podium, 10 m (33 ft) tall and covered in friezes, contained the emperor's funeral cella.

121 (opposite) The various episodes in the frieze around the column contain a wealth of technical and geographical details, though they would not have been visible to anyone at ground level. The monument was originally brightly painted.

A new literary genre now became popular – satire, reflecting a developing society in which contrasts between the old world and the new were evident. The creator of the genre was Lucilius who, in surviving fragments, seems to have been a faithful chronicler of his time.

The construction boom continued with even greater vigour in the age of Sulla. Marble was used for the first time in the construction of temples, and also, to a lesser extent, in patrician residences, the walls of which were colourfully painted. A typical example of the architecture of the period is the Tabularium, the state archives of 78 BC in the valley between the Arx and the Capitol.

The antagonism between Caesar and Pompey which influenced the political life of the period also had its affect on construction. Pompey's desire to associate his name with major public works to gain the favour of the populace led him to erect the first masonry theatre on the Campus Martius in 55 BC. It was surrounded with porticoes and decorated with Greek works of art.

A hall nearby, used as a curia (meeting-place) for the Senate, was the scene of the assassination of Caesar on the Ides of March in 44 BC. His violent death put an end to the intensive building activities of this great military leader, who had demonstrated his gift for town planning by building a second forum, on the Hellenistic pattern, in the middle of which was the Temple of Venus Genetrix, the tutelary deity of the Julian *gens*. He also began the extensive improvement of the republican forum; and built the Basilica Julia, to replace the now obsolete Basilica Sempronia. Projects he was unable to complete included a masonry theatre, finished by Augustus, who dedicated it to his son-in-law Marcellus. Caesar is also believed to have drawn up a town plan, the main aim of which was to divert the course of the Tiber in order to join Trastevere to the Campus Martius, which was to be used for private building.

An outstanding personality, Caesar was not only a shrewd politician but also a brilliant writer who recorded his military exploits in a clear, precise style, thus leaving important evidence not only of his conquests, but also of a crucial period in the social and political life of Rome.

At this time of great change and contrast, Roman society was striving towards a stability which would offer citizens greater harmony and tranquillity. While Latin spread throughout the west, Greek was studied by the sons of the ruling class. Oratory reached the height of its glory with Cicero, and historiography with Sallust and Caesar. Poetry reflected the spiritual aspirations of the time; while previously it had exalted the Roman state it now focused on the search for truth and inner peace, as in the verses of Lucretius, or was inspired by friendship and feminine love, as explored by Catullus.

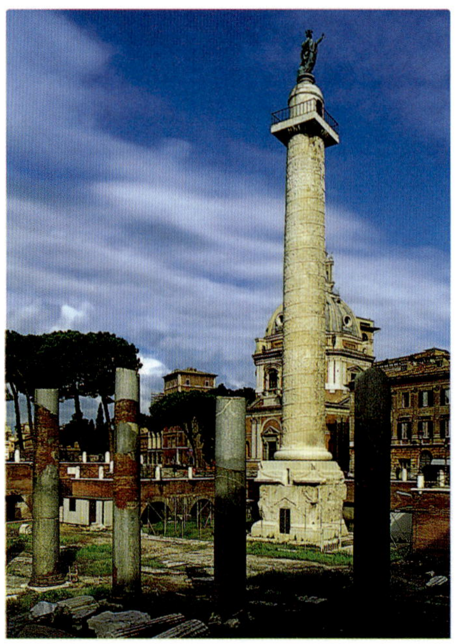

A gap between rich and poor was very evident, however; while the aristocracy lived in comfortable houses on the Palatine or in other residential areas, the poor were crowded into unhealthy districts of tall, narrow houses. The wealthy owned villas in the country or along the coast down to Naples. Women of high birth enjoyed a freedom and prestige unknown before, and marriages of convenience between wealthy families became more and more frequent. The proletariat consoled itself with shows, especially gladiatorial combats and the *venationes*.

Caesar's town plan was not implemented by his successor, perhaps because it was both too expensive and too radical. The more conservative Augustus carried out only improvements and restorations. He did abolish the old division of the city into four regions, made obsolete by the huge increase in its size. His reform of AD 7 divided Rome into 14 regions, each with several *vici* (districts). Eight regions were inside the old city walls and six outside, of which one, the 14th, was on the right bank of the Tiber, an

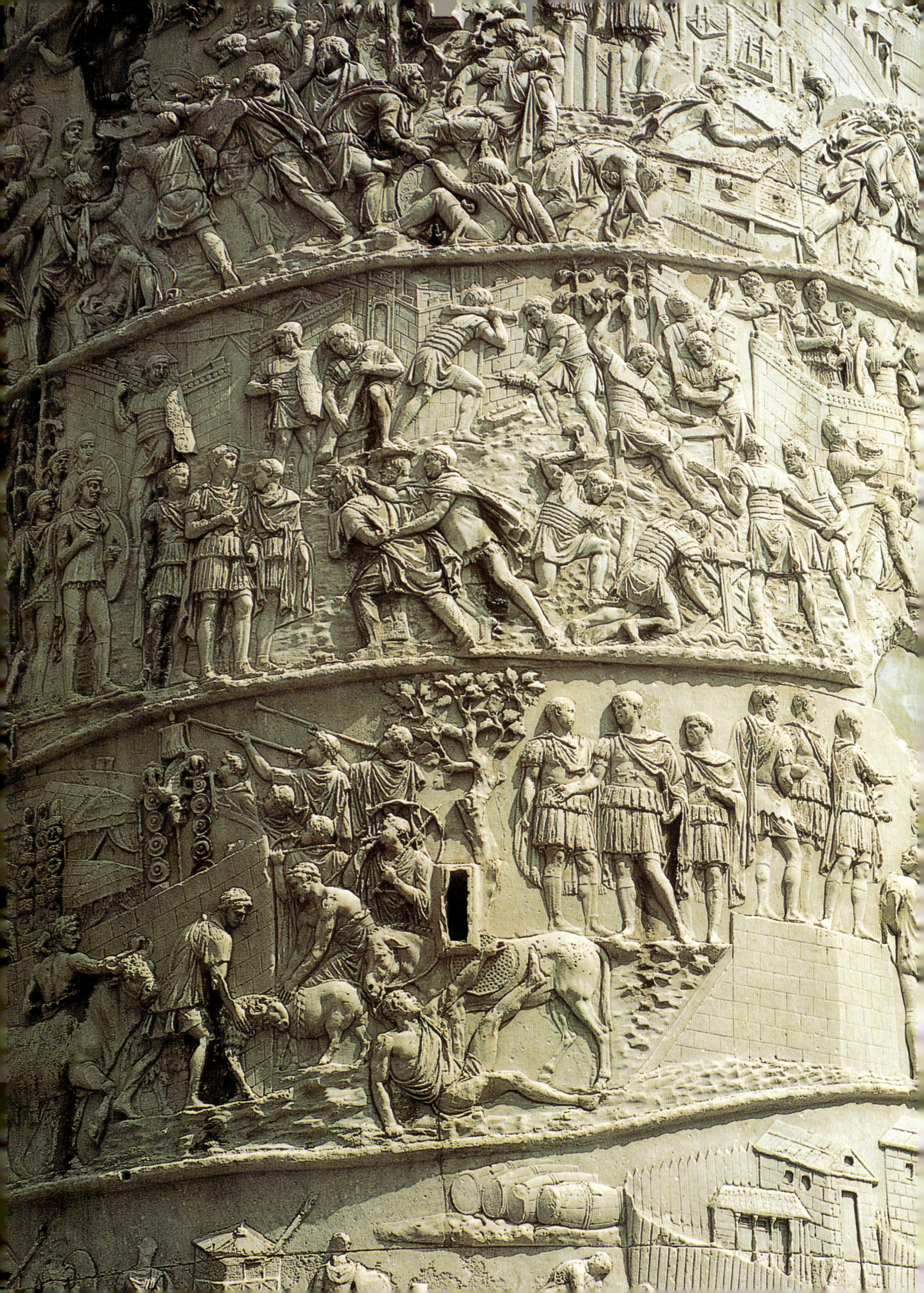

122 (below) The construction of the Pantheon, originally perhaps a temple dedicated to all the tutelary deities of the Julian family, was financed by Agrippa, Augustus' son-in-law, in 27 BC. After being destroyed by fire, it was rebuilt in its present form by Hadrian.

122–123 (right) The Pantheon is the best-preserved Roman building and one of the world's greatest architectural achievements. Its dome, with a diameter of 43.3 m (142 ft), is still the largest ever made without the use of reinforced concrete.

123 (opposite, below) The Pantheon's huge dome, representing a starry sky, is illuminated by the great central oculus 9 m (30 ft) wide, which symbolizes the Sun. The minimum thickness of this exceptional structure is 1.5 m (5 ft).

arrangement that survived until the late empire. At the time of Augustus, there were around 263 districts; each under the protection of a divinity, whose statue presided over main crossroads, and governed by 24 citizens (*vicomagistri*), elected from among the residents, and two senior magistrates. Houses were either the high-class *domus* or the multi-storey *insulae* for the lower classes.

To improve the quality of life, Augustus built numerous fountains and markets, installed lighting in the town centre and established the corps of the Vigiles and Urbaniciani to perform public services. Works for public benefit included cleaning the bed of the Tiber and the restoration of the old Appia, Marcia, Anio Vetus and Tepula aqueducts. Three new aqueducts were built during his reign: the Julia, Virgo and Alsietina. In the Roman Forum Augustus completed the Curia, the Basilica Julia and the Rostra. He renovated various temples, including the Temple of Castor and Pollux and the Temple of Vesta, the House of the Vestals and the Regia. He erected the Temple of the Divine Julius and built his own home on the Palatine Hill. Nearby, he constructed a temple consecrated to Vesta and one to Palatine Apollo, which he endowed with two libraries. A new forum dedicated to him, grandiose in its luxury, stood opposite Caesar's; at the centre was the huge Temple of Mars Ultor (the Avenger). He also developed the Campus Martius, reclaiming a large area of land. Here he built his Mausoleum, the *Ara Pacis* (Altar of Peace) and a solar clock. In the same area Agrippa, his son-in-law, funded the Pantheon, the Baths, the Basilica of Neptune and the Saepta, where the populace met as the *comitia centuriata*. Finally, the Theatre of Marcellus was completed, and a new bridge built over the Tiber. Many patrician villas rose on the Pincian, Palatine and Esquiline hills, and in Trastevere.

Literature reached its apogee under Augustus. Maecenas, a rich and cultivated man, brought writers like Virgil, Horace and Propertius into the emperor's circle. In the *Aeneid*, which became the national poem, Virgil recounted Rome's legendary origins, extolling the greatness of the city and Augustus. Horace, in his *Carmen Saeculare*, lauded the eternity of imperial Rome, while Propertius and Tibullus devoted elegies to personal themes. Other writers were Ovid, who described love in the setting of the capital, Livy who, in his 142-volume history of Rome, testified to the exceptional historical role of Rome, and Vitruvius, who wrote a detailed and valuable treatise on architecture.

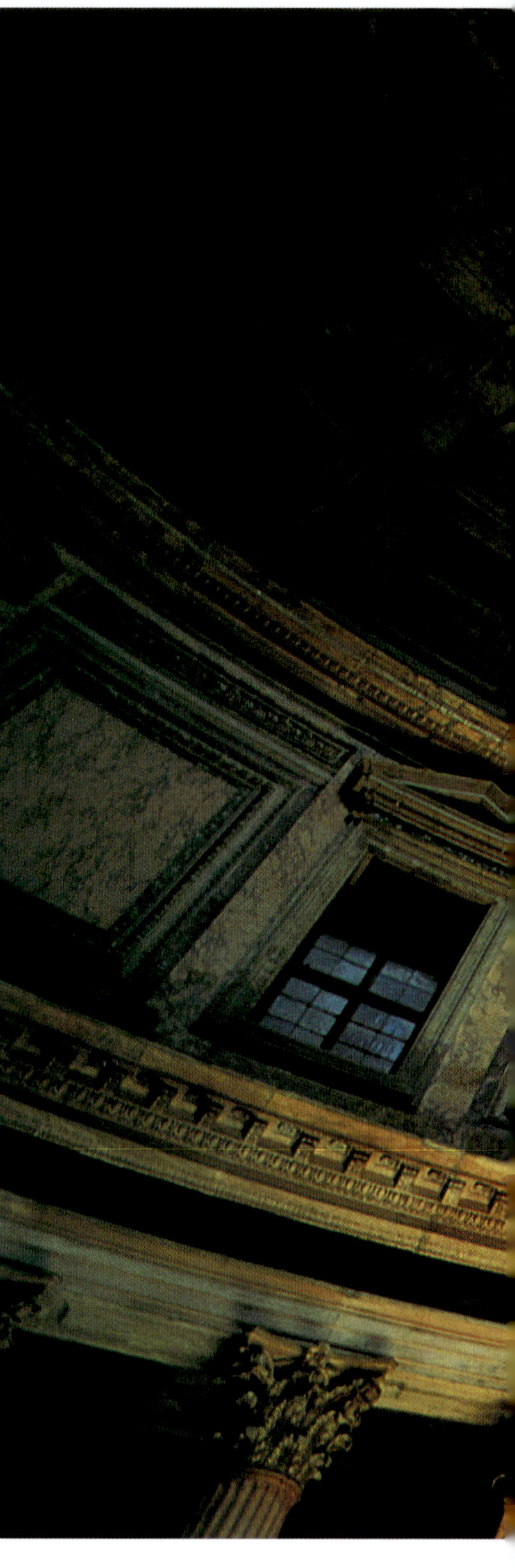

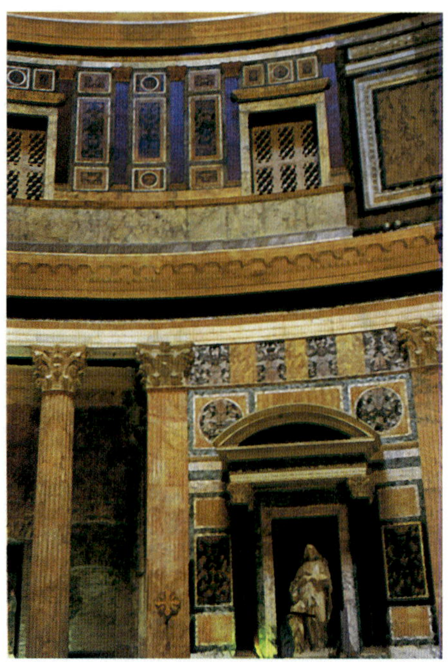

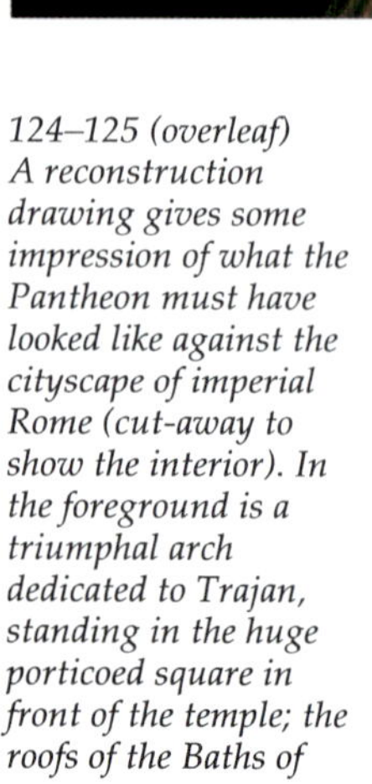

124–125 (overleaf) A reconstruction drawing gives some impression of what the Pantheon must have looked like against the cityscape of imperial Rome (cut-away to show the interior). In the foreground is a triumphal arch dedicated to Trajan, standing in the huge porticoed square in front of the temple; the roofs of the Baths of Nero are visible in the right-hand corner. Behind the temple a wing of the Basilica of Neptune, also rebuilt by Hadrian, can be seen in partial cross-section. At the top left is the Temple of Minerva, standing in the centre of the Saepta Julia, a great porticoed square originally designed for elections, which later became an art market.

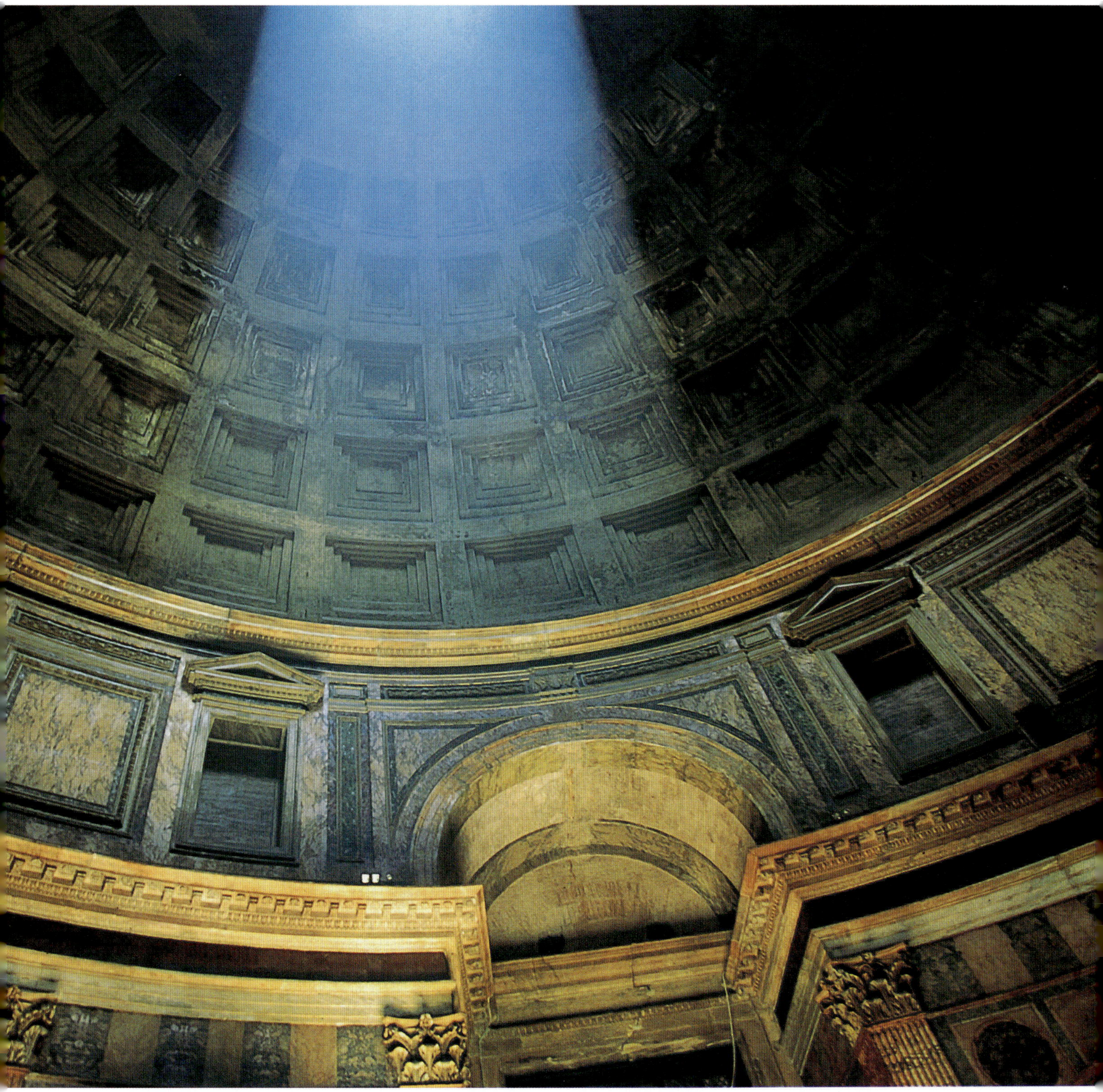

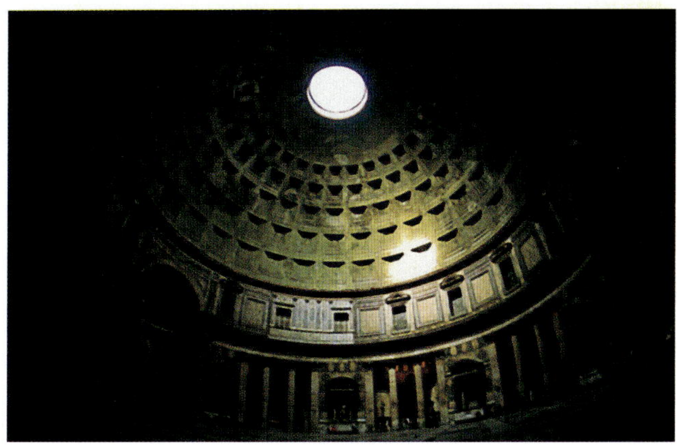

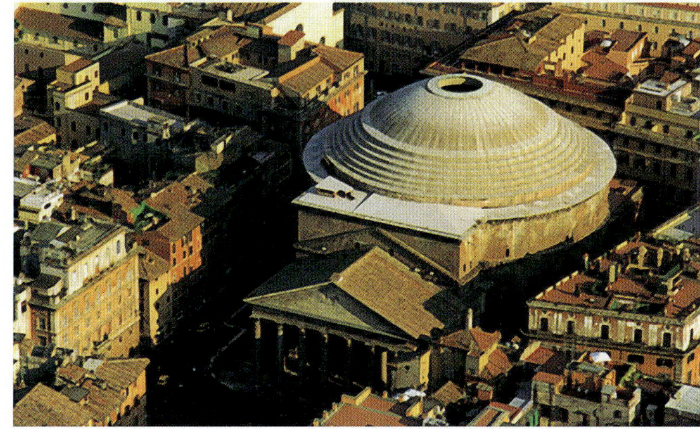

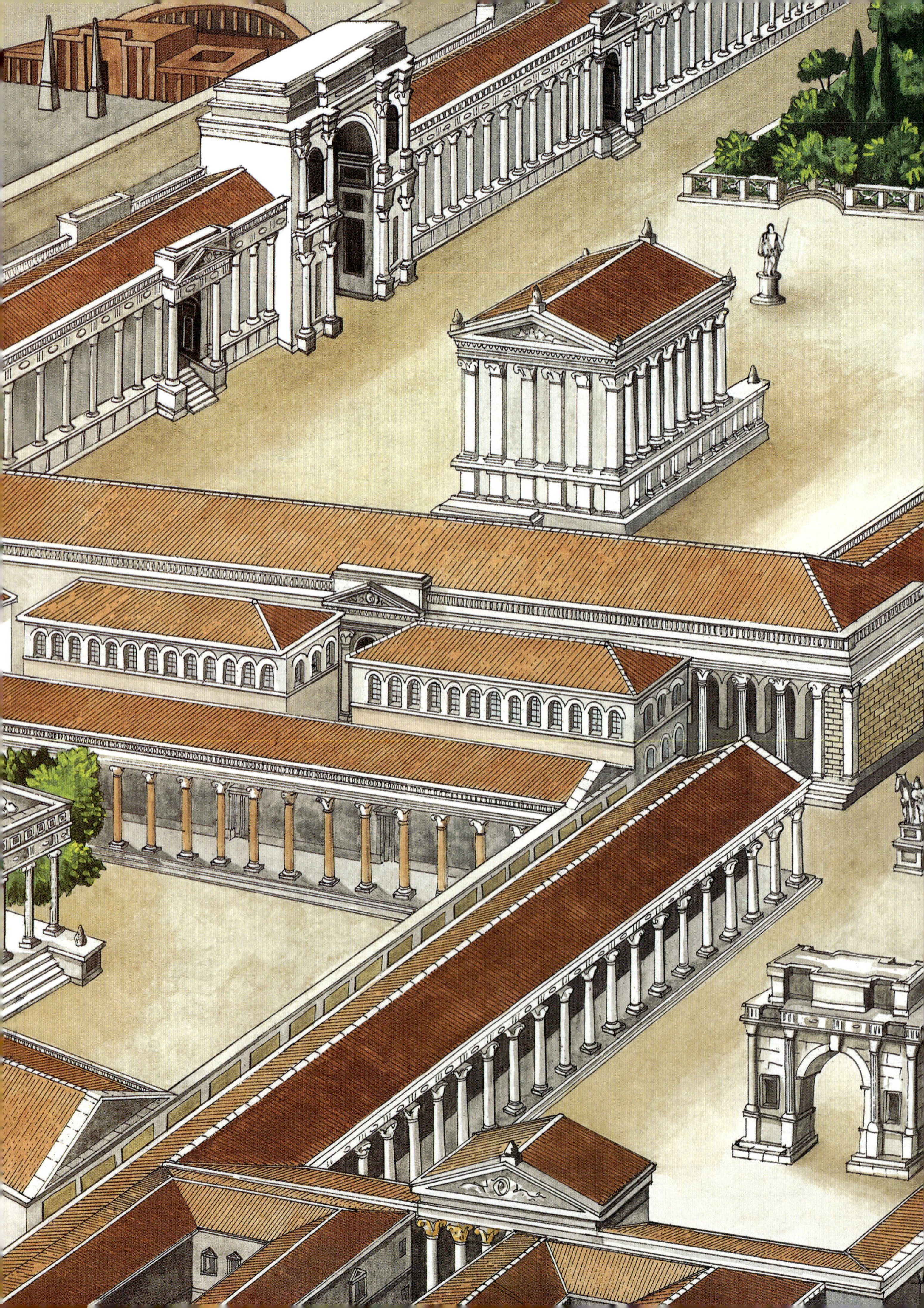

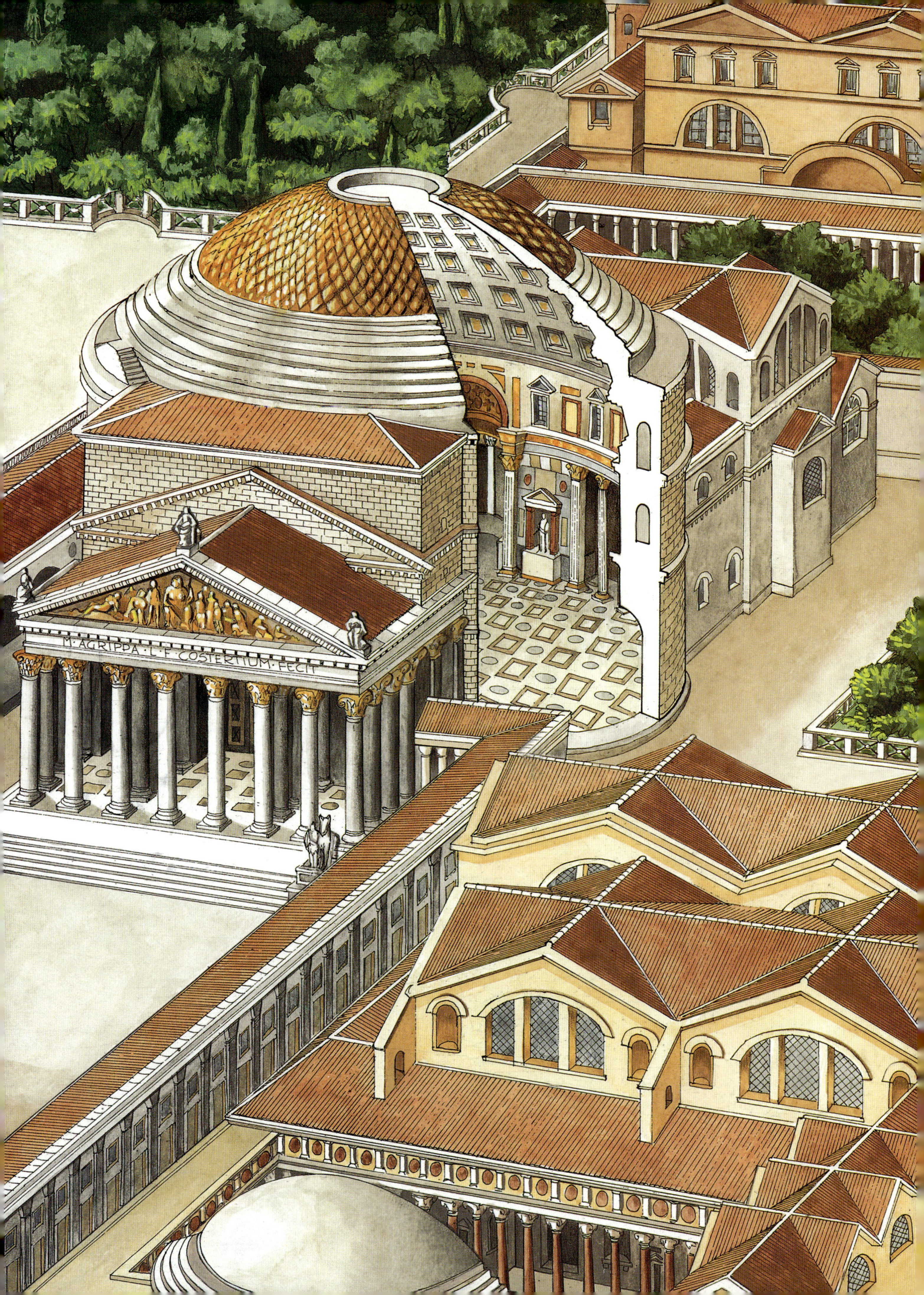
M·AGRIPPA·L·F·COSTERTIUM·FECIT

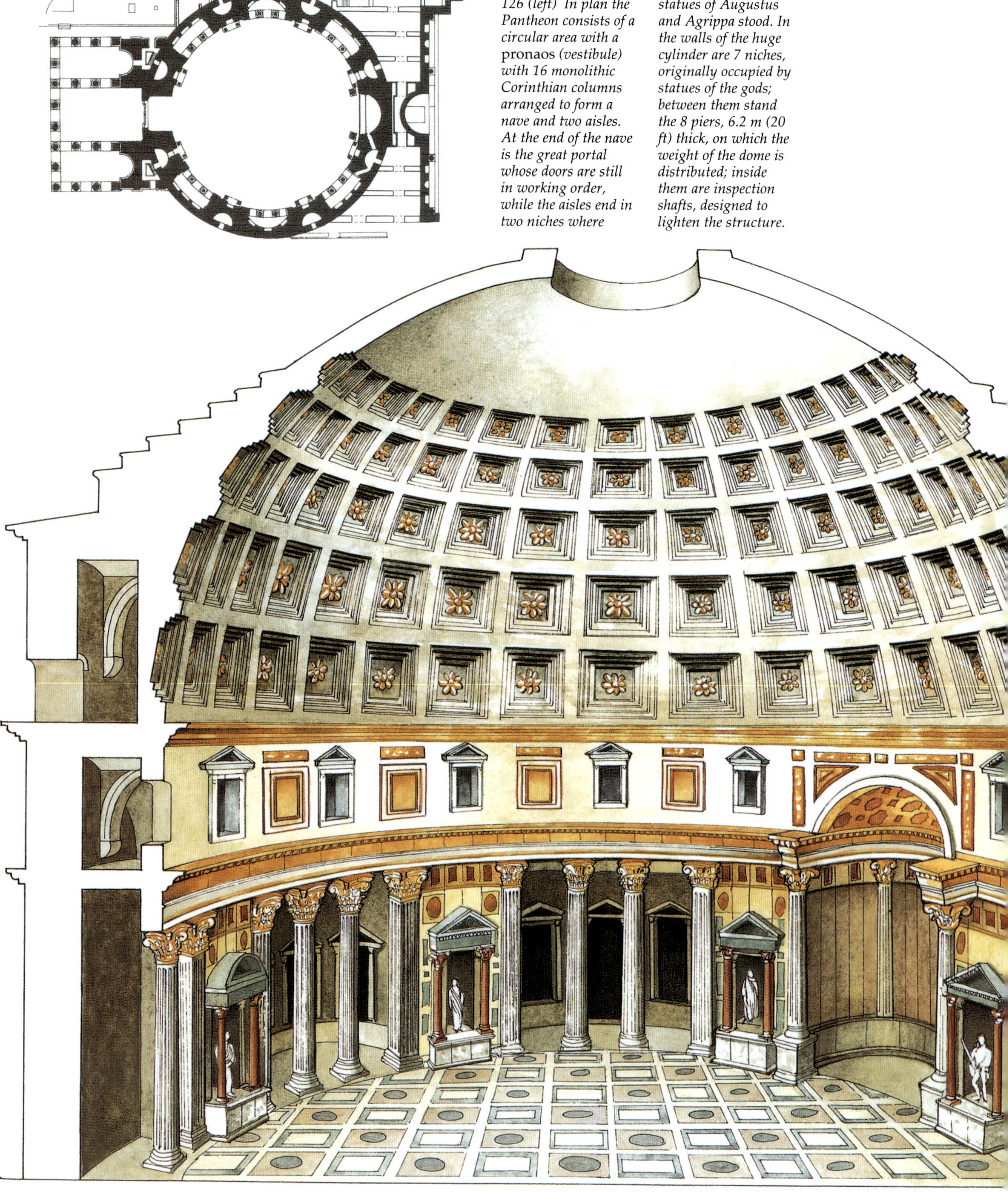

126 (left) In plan the Pantheon consists of a circular area with a pronaos *(vestibule) with 16 monolithic Corinthian columns arranged to form a nave and two aisles. At the end of the nave is the great portal whose doors are still in working order, while the aisles end in two niches where statues of Augustus and Agrippa stood. In the walls of the huge cylinder are 7 niches, originally occupied by statues of the gods; between them stand the 8 piers, 6.2 m (20 ft) thick, on which the weight of the dome is distributed; inside them are inspection shafts, designed to lighten the structure.*

126–127 (below) *Internally the height of the rotunda is equal to its diameter (43.3 m or 142 ft), so that the dome is a perfect hemisphere. Five rows of coffering lighten the weight of the dome. The structure is made of cement faced with brick, with horizontal rows of bricks and blocks of tufa. The materials become lighter towards the top.*

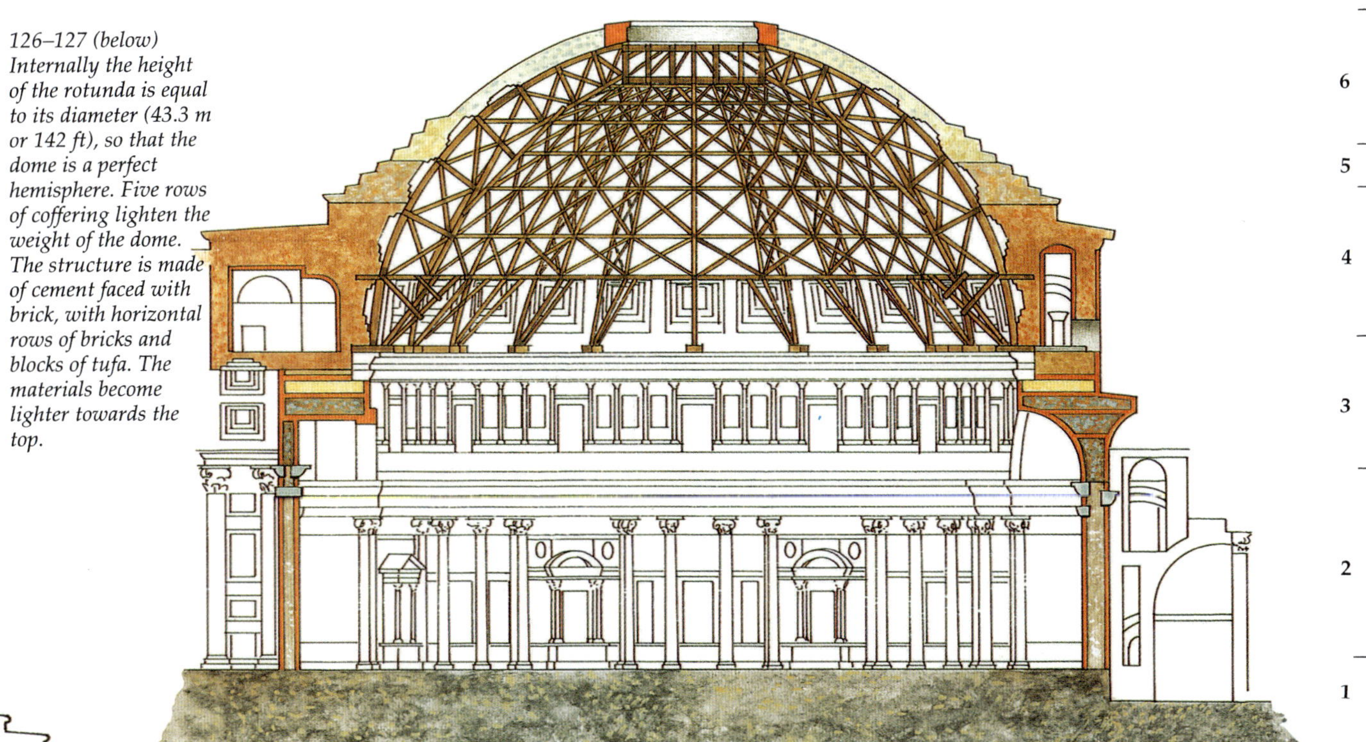

127 (above) *Six types of concrete were used in the construction of the Pantheon. The foundations, 4.5 m (15 ft) thick, are made of travertine chip concrete (1); the walls of the rotunda, from the floor to the first cornice, are made of concrete with tufa and travertine chips (2); another layer of* opus incertum *with tufa and bricks continues to the springing line (3); the first ring of the dome is made of concrete with brick fragments (4); the second ring is made of concrete lightened with tufa and brick fragments (5); and the cap is made of concrete bonded with pumice stone and blocks of tufa (6). The dome was cast on an extraordinary self-supporting wooden framework on to which the forms of the coffers, anchored in the masonry of the cylindrical section, were fitted.*

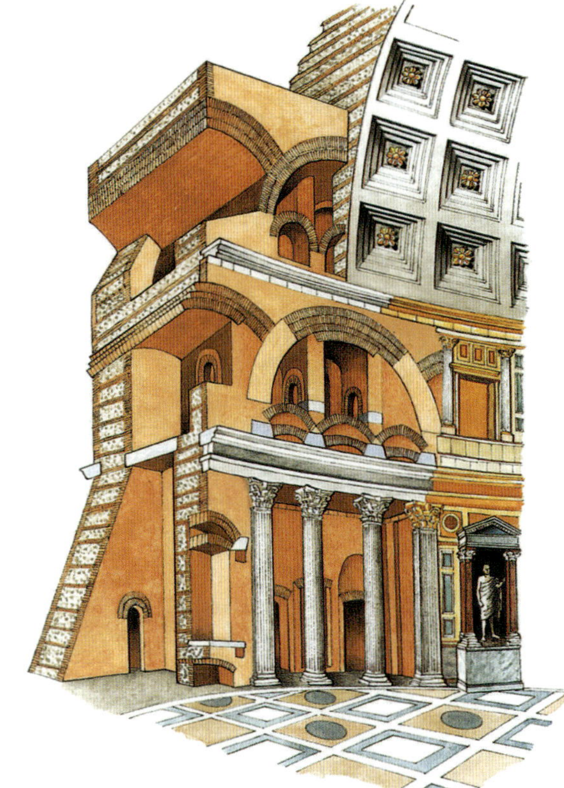

127 (right) *This cross-section shows the construction technique used for the Pantheon. The walls are faced internally with horizontal rows of bricks, used also as the formwork for casting the concrete which constituted the core. Above the niches the large relieving arches and flat arches resting on stone quoins direct the weight of the masonry on to the columns, preventing the horizontal beams from fracturing. The first ring of the dome, from the impost of the vault up to a height of some 12 m (39 ft), consists of great arches of brick embedded in concrete, which limit the thrusts and aid distribution of the weight of the cap between the 8 piers. Similar arches are visible in the outer masonry of the drum. In the dome, the only bricks used are in the ring of the oculus.*

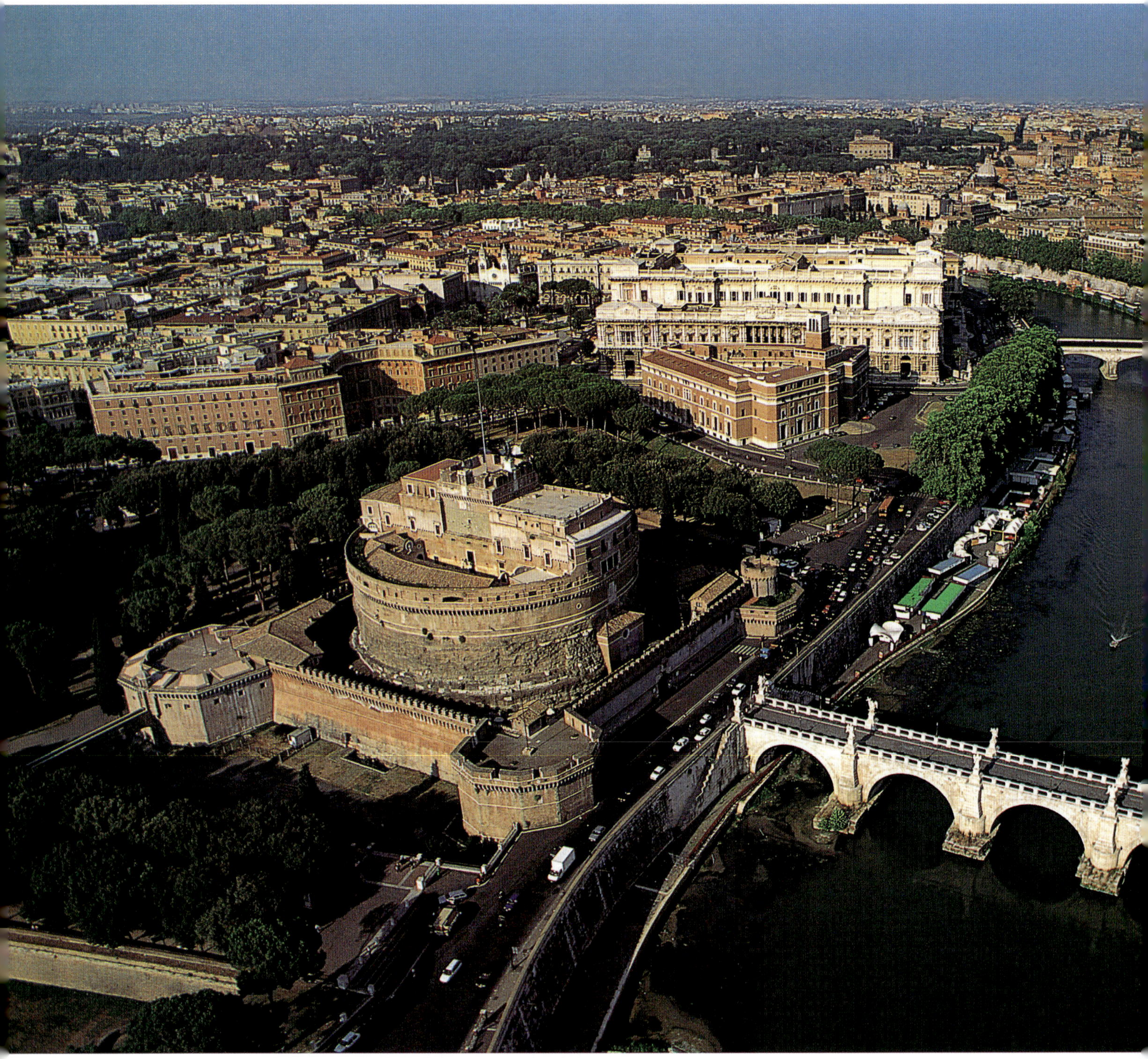

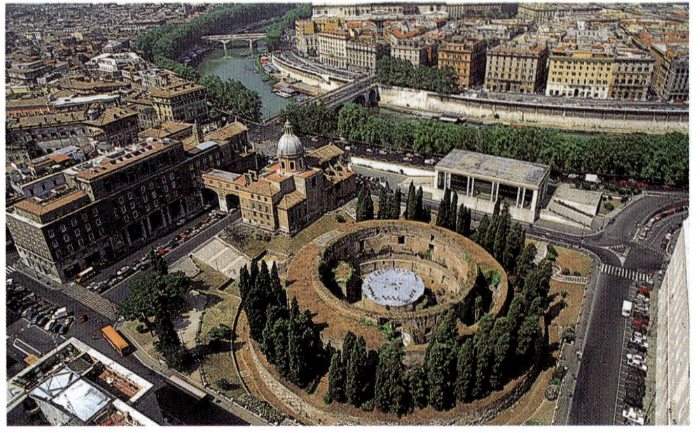

128 (left) All that now remains of the great Mausoleum of Augustus, which later became the sepulchre of the Julio-Claudian and Flavian dynasties, is a circular shell, 87 m (285 ft) in diameter. On the top was once a hillock planted with cypresses, at the centre of which was probably a cylindrical structure crowned by the gilded statue of the emperor.

128–129 (above) The impressive mausoleum Hadrian erected for himself and his successors was transformed over the centuries into what is now known as the Castel Sant'Angelo. Its great cylindrical form, once crowned by a mound of earth with cypresses, was surmounted by a high podium on which a statue group or a bronze quadriga stood.

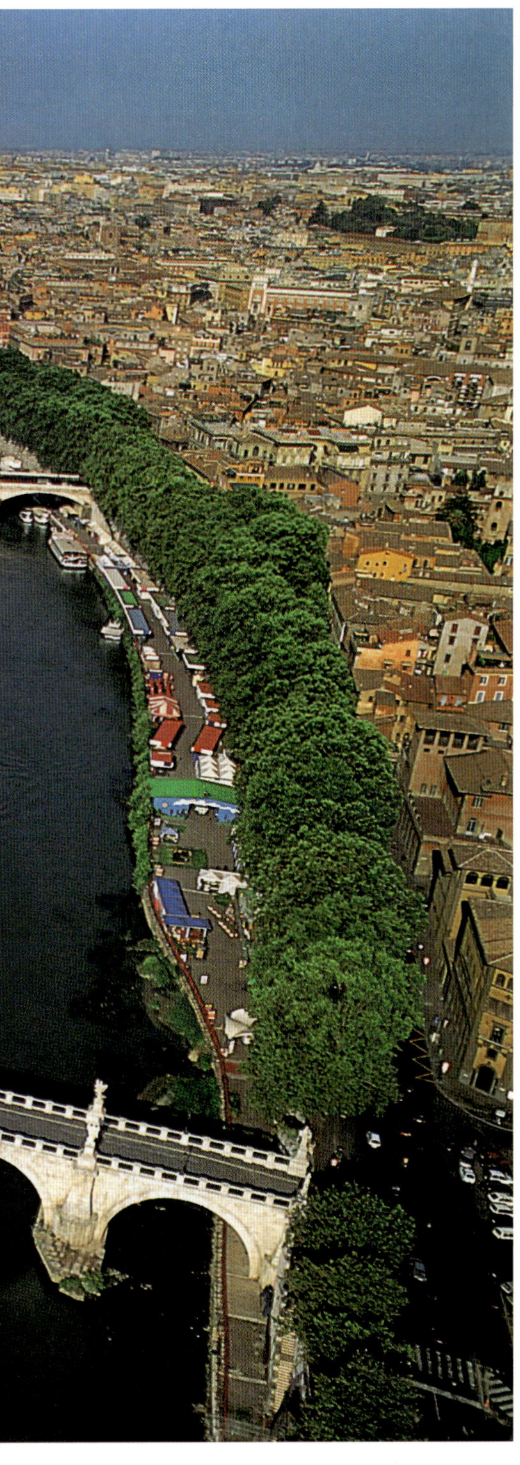

During the reign of Augustus' successor Tiberius no great public works were undertaken. His only major projects were his house on the Palatine Hill, the Domus Tiberiana, finished by Caligula, and the Castra Praetoria, the camp for the Praetorian Guard built on the advice of Sejanus, the praetorian prefect. Caligula built a circus in the Gardens of Agrippina in the Vatican. Nero later placed an obelisk, made in Egypt, on the *spina*. Claudius finished two aqueducts, the Claudia and the Anio Novus, and built the port of Ostia at the mouth of the Tiber, guaranteeing supplies to the Rome for over a century.

The reign of Nero is tragically famous for the terrible fire that raged through Rome for nine days in AD 64; three of the 14 Augustan regions were reduced to rubble, and seven others were badly damaged. The Oppian, the Esquiline, and part of the Aventine and the Caelian hills, and the Velia were devastated, including the Regia and the House of the Vestals; and several other monuments were affected. Many precious relics of ancient Rome were irretrievably lost, and thousands of inhabitants were made homeless. Nero drew up a complex, ambitious plan for reconstructing the city. The houses, limited in height, could no longer have party walls, and the fronts were protected by porticoes. These rules were not pursued with any real interest on the part of Nero (under Trajan large areas were still uninhabited), who gave all his attention to the Domus Aurea, his new imperial residence, in which unrivalled luxury and splendour ran riot. This 'Golden House' occupied the entire Palatine, much of the Caelian and Oppian hills, and part of the republican forum. Nero's only public building was a baths on the Campus Martius, near the Pantheon.

In the literary field, the patriotic and celebratory themes that had characterized the Augustan era were abandoned. Augustus' successors never succeeded in obtaining the same consensus on which the empire was founded; moreover, Caligula and Nero showed a clear inclination to promote the worship of themselves. Intellectuals therefore turned from politics and took refuge in introspection, exalting freedom of the spirit over the restraints of public life. Prominent writers included Seneca, who explored the qualities of the human soul in a search for dignified serenity, and Petronius who, in his *Satyricon*, paints a realistic picture of society, poking fun at the nouveaux riches – the freedmen – who indulged in brazen, vulgar luxury. Portraiture, idealized under Augustus, once more became highly realistic, as seen in portraits of Tiberius, Claudius and Nero.

The daily life of the people also changed; favourite entertainments were still gladiatorial combats and chariot racing at the Circus, but the custom of attending the baths, increasing numbers of which were built, also became popular.

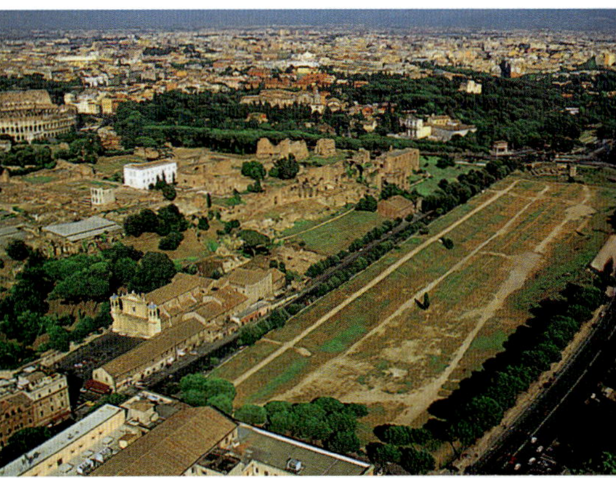

129 (right, above) The Circus Maximus was the largest structure designed for entertainment in Rome. It dates from the age of the Tarquins and was rebuilt on several occasions. In Trajan's time it was 600 m (1968 ft) long. Although estimates differ, it is believed to have housed 250,000 spectators and, in exceptional cases, up to 320,000.

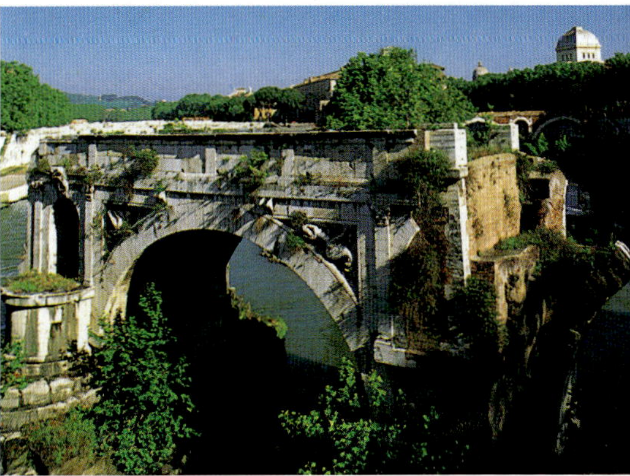

129 (right, below) Only a single span of the once-magnificent Aemilian Bridge survives, known as Ponte Rotto (broken bridge). A small arch, clearly visible in the massive left-hand pier, was designed, like other similar ones that once existed, to reduce the pressure of the water against the structure when the Tiber was in full spate.

The three Flavian emperors – Vespasian, Titus and Domitian – had the difficult task of reconstructing a city which, as Suetonius said, 'had lost its appearance because of ancient fires and ruins'. Many districts were entirely rebuilt, and numerous buildings were erected. The scene of the most radical work was in the valley between the Oppian and Palatine hills; the lake of the Domus Aurea was drained, and the monument which was to become the symbol of Rome was built there: the Flavian amphitheatre, better known as the Colosseum. This huge structure was inaugurated by Titus in AD 80, before its completion.

Under Domitian the restoration of many old buildings continued, and new ones were built. The Temple of Jupiter Capitolinus was rebuilt for the fifth time, and another temple, dedicated to Jupiter the Custodian, was erected. Work on the new imperial palace on the Palatine was completed, requiring great levelling and filling in of ground. The Domus Tiberiana and the Temple of Apollo were restored. In the forum a temple was consecrated to the memory of Vespasian and Titus, and the Arch of Titus, commemorating the conquest of Jerusalem, was built over the Via Sacra. On the Campus Martius, Domitian built the Stadium, with an Odeum next to it, stables for the four circus factions, the Naumachia (a lake for miniature naval battles), and a portico where Vespasian and Titus stood as they waited to celebrate the triumph of the Jewish War.

Domitian also completed the forum area; the saddle between the Capitol and the Quirinal Hill had been removed, the Forum Transitorium was built, and a new baths complex was constructed on the Oppian Hill. For the first time, Rome had a large-scale and above all rapidly implemented town plan. The Flavians ruled during a period of order and prosperity, except for the terrible catastrophe of the eruption of Vesuvius in AD 79, which destroyed Pompeii, Stabiae and Herculaneum, and killed the famous writer Pliny the Elder.

In the provinces, economic and social development led to the spread of Roman traditions throughout the empire; as a result, although it continued to attract intellectuals, Rome was no longer the only centre of cultural life. Many authors wrote in languages other than Latin – such as Arrian, Plutarch of Chaeronea, Appian and Flavius Josephus, who wrote about the Jewish War. A vivid portrait of life in the period is given by the Spanish poet Martial in his *Epigrams*. With Quintilian, the art of oratory regained some vigour, though it was now far removed from the splendours of the republican age.

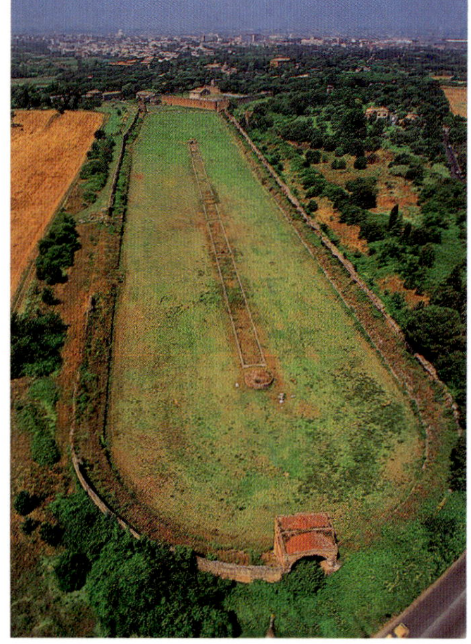

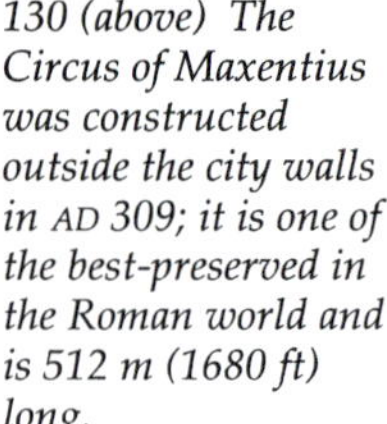

130 (above) The Circus of Maxentius was constructed outside the city walls in AD 309; it is one of the best-preserved in the Roman world and is 512 m (1680 ft) long.

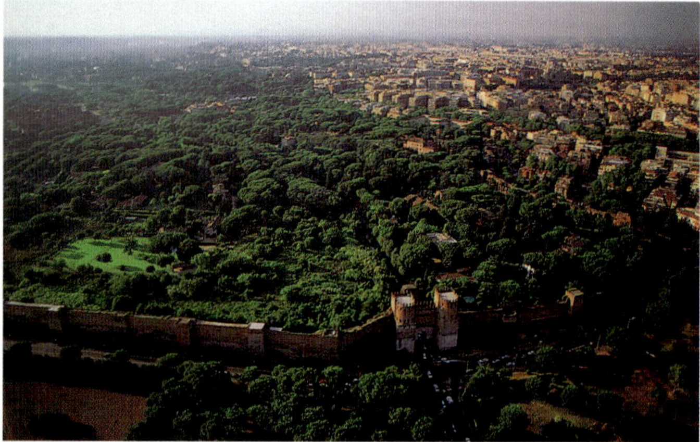

130 (right) The Gate of St Sebastian, with its single span flanked by crenellated towers, forms part of the Aurelian walls, 19 km (12 miles) long, which surrounded the city.

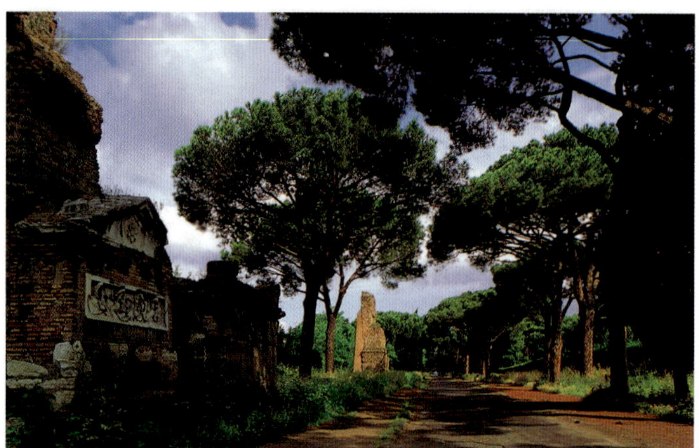

130 (centre) Built by the Censor Appius Claudius in 312 BC, the Appian Way connected Rome to Brundisium, a distance of 540 km (336 miles). Sections near the capital are lined with funerary monuments.

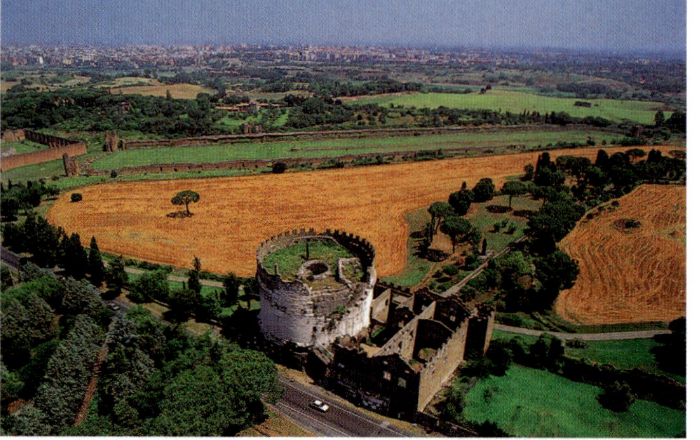

130 (below) The tomb of Caecilia Metella, daughter-in-law of the triumvir Crassus, is one of the most famous monuments on the Appian Way; it was converted into a fortress in the Middle Ages.

131 (opposite) The marble pyramid of Gaius Cestius, next to St Paul's Gate, is the highly unusual tomb of the praetor and tribune of the plebs who died in 12 BC. It is inspired by styles that became fashionable after the conquest of Egypt.

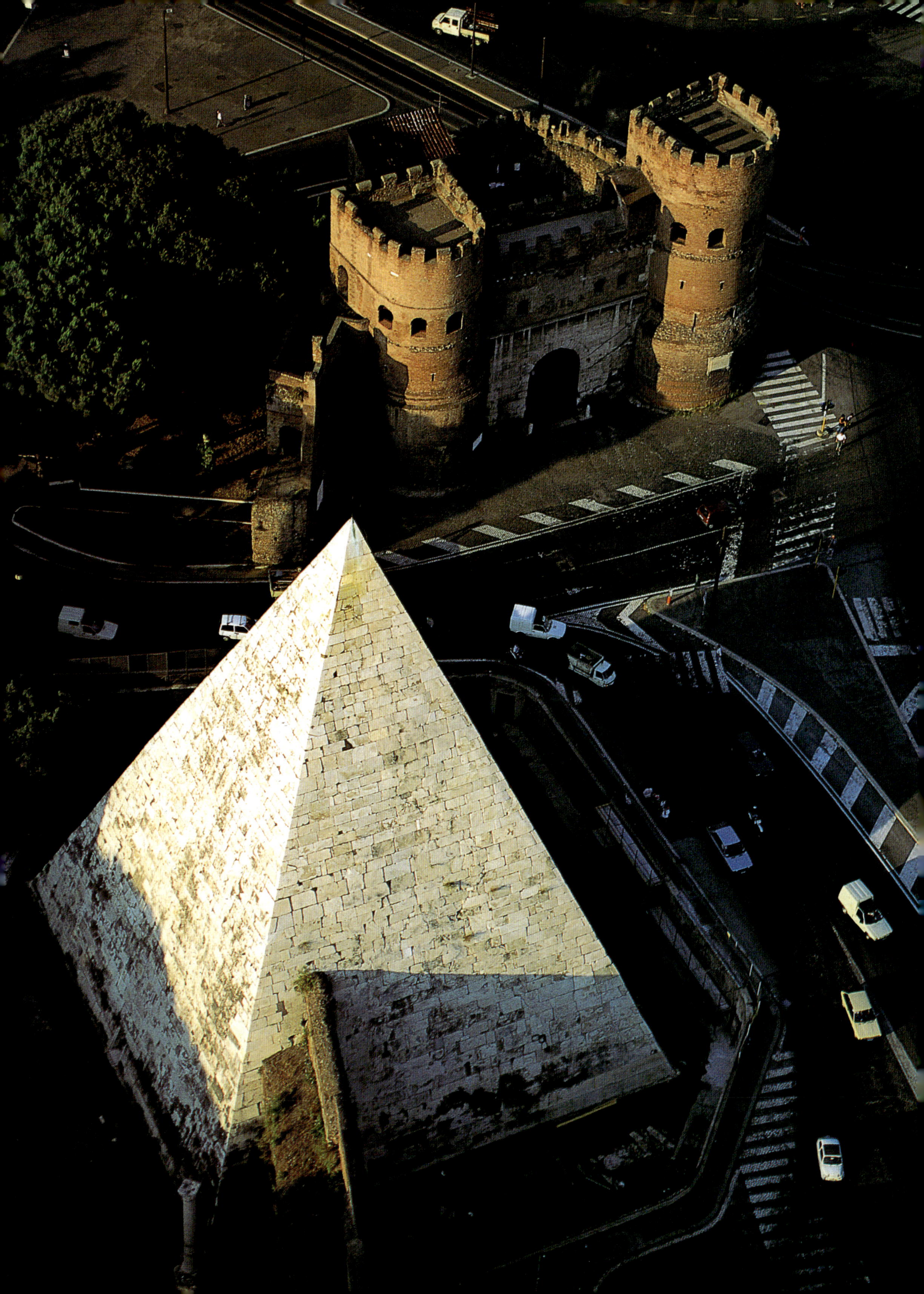

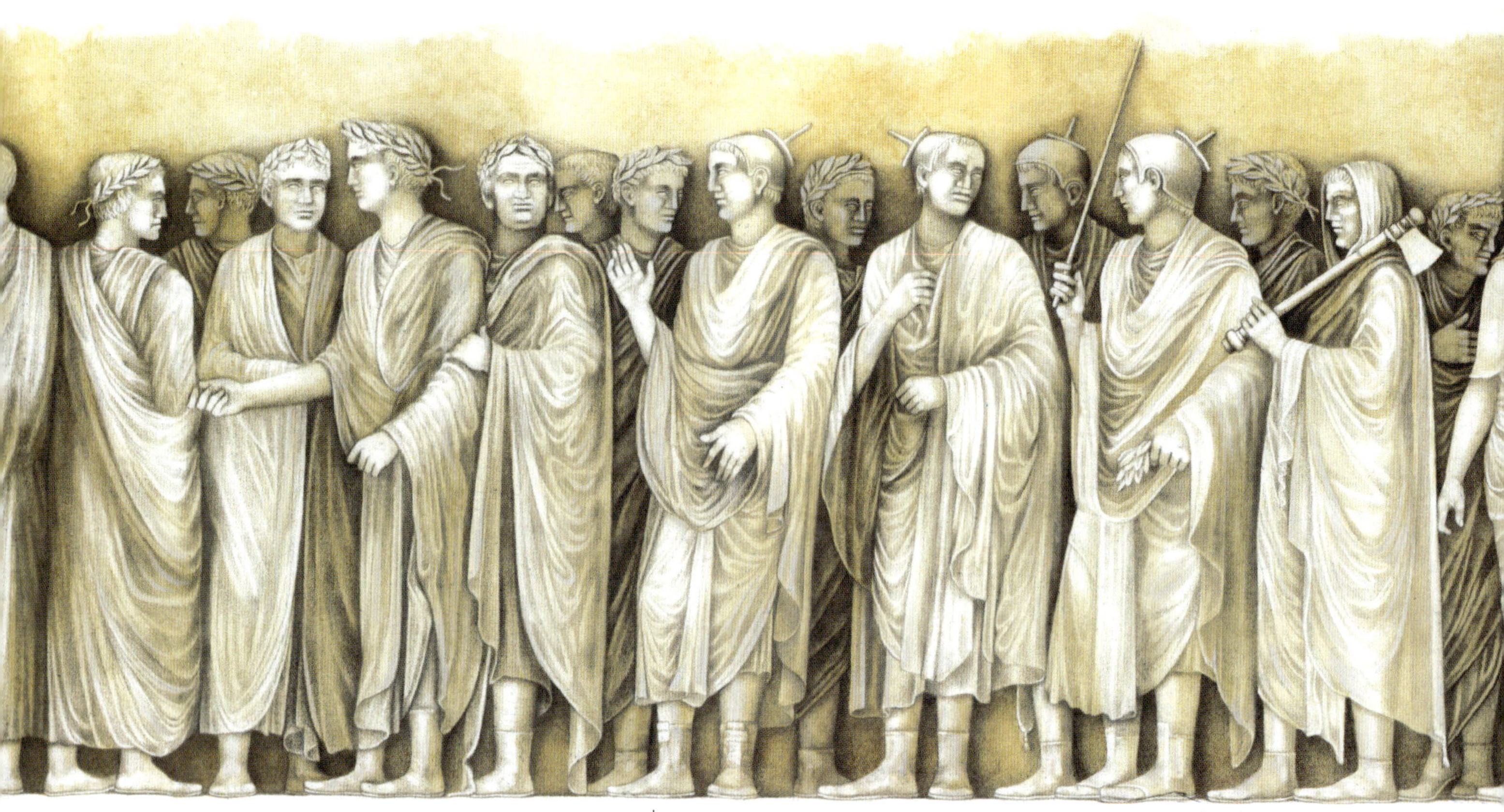

Consul Augustus Consul The four Flaminian priests Lictor

Trajan completed work begun by Domitian, especially in the forum and the baths, which were named after him. He finished restructuring the slopes of the Capitol and the Quirinal Hill and built the grandiose Basilica Ulpia; behind it, in the new forum, a Latin and a Greek library were erected opposite one another. Between the two buildings stood Trajan's Column. With its reliefs of episodes from the Dacian Wars this monument is of great interest both artistically, as it represents the best of Roman figurative art, and also in historical and documentary terms. It is also one of the few monuments which came through the Dark Ages unscathed. Near one side of the forum he built the Markets of Trajan. Trajan also gave the city a new and more efficient port, consisting of a magnificent hexagonal basin to replace that of Claudius, now silted up, and built the last great aqueduct to supply Rome with water.

Trajan's successor Hadrian gave the city two temples which came to symbolize Roman civilization: the Pantheon (founded by Agrippa but now dilapidated) and the Temple of Venus and Rome. On the right bank of the Tiber he built his mausoleum, joined to the opposite bank by a new bridge, the Aelian, still in use today. On the Campus Martius he erected a portico and a temple in honour of Marciana and Matidia, Trajan's sister and niece; Matidia was the mother of Hadrian's wife Vibia Sabina.

Apart from a column on the Campus Martius commemorating Marcus Aurelius' victories against the Germans and Sarmatians, the Antonine emperors did not build major works, merely completing those begun by their predecessors. The city was now full of monuments of all kinds, and the only buildings erected in later centuries were baths and porticoes. However, the state now showed particular interest in education – many libraries were opened, and state schools and professorships were financed. Increasing numbers of people were able to read and write, and many were bilingual in Greek and Latin.

In the age of Trajan the most vivid poetic voice was that of Juvenal, whose *Satires* give an unrelentingly realistic picture of contemporary society. The greatest historian was Tacitus, known for his biographies of the emperors, from Tiberius to Nero. Suetonius, who also wrote lives of the emperors from Caesar to Domitian, devoted himself to antiquarian study too. Other notable figures of the Antonine age were the medic Galen, Gellius, the rhetorician Cornelius Fronto, and the African Apuleius, author of the 'The Golden Ass', which symbolized the intellectual restlessness of the time, and a search for inner serenity which neither philosophy nor traditional religion could any longer fulfil.

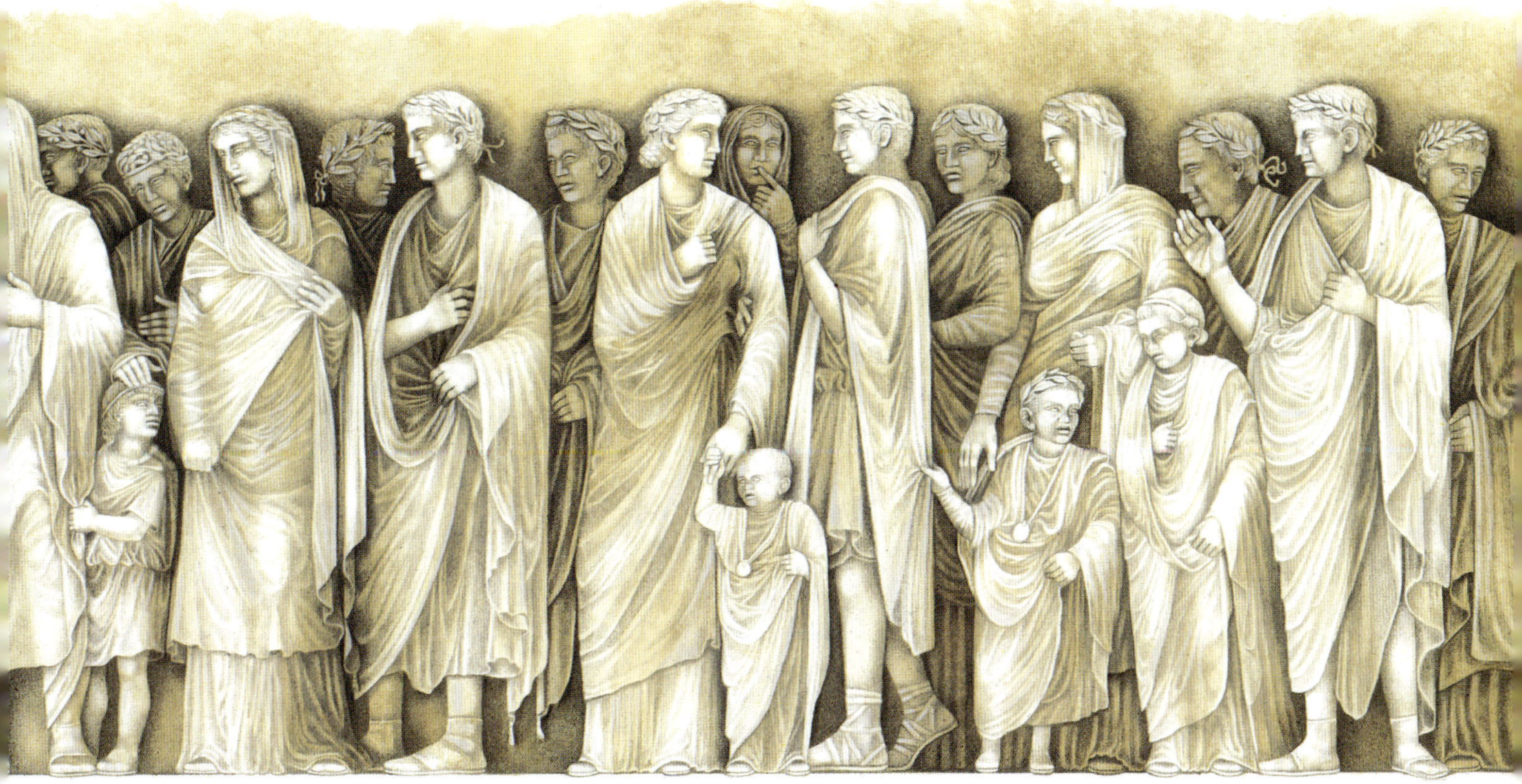

Agrippa | Gaius Caesar | Julia | Tiberius | Antonia the Younger | Germanicus | Drusus | Domitius | Antonia the Elder | Domitia | Domitius Ahenobarbus

132–133 The Ara Pacis Augustae, *a monument of outstanding historical and artistic value, was reconstructed in the late 1930s from fragments discovered as early as 1568. This 'Altar of Peace' was commissioned by the Senate in 13 BC to give thanks for Augustus' gift of peace to the entire Roman world after the victories in Spain and Gaul. It was consecrated on the Campus Martius in 9 BC with solemn ceremony. It consists of a rectangular marble precinct wall on a podium with two doors, each reached by a staircase. Inside, at the top of three steps, is the richly decorated altar. The precinct wall has magnificent sculptural decorations both inside – consisting of festoons with* paterae *(vessels) and* bucrania *(ox skulls) – and on the outside, where it is divided into two sections horizontally. The lower band has an elegant repeating frieze of acanthus volutes with swans and animals, while the upper band portrays four mythological scenes (one on each side of the doors) and the procession to mark the consecration of the altar, divided between the two shorter sides. While the one on the north side is badly damaged and less important, the group of characters on the south side is of great interest because it includes Augustus together with priests, magistrates and members of the imperial family. This illustration (which restores the gaps) shows the procession on the south side, with the exception of the first sector in which the reliefs are lost. The procession is headed by two of the lictors, followed by Augustus between two consuls; then come the four Flaminian priests and the Flaminian lictor; Agrippa, his son Gaius Caesar and the former's wife Julia, Augustus' daughter; Tiberius; Antonia the Younger (Augustus' niece) and her husband Drusus, Tiberius' brother, with his son Germanicus; Antonia the Elder (Augustus' niece) with her children Domitius and Domitia, and finally her husband, Domitius Ahenobarbus.*

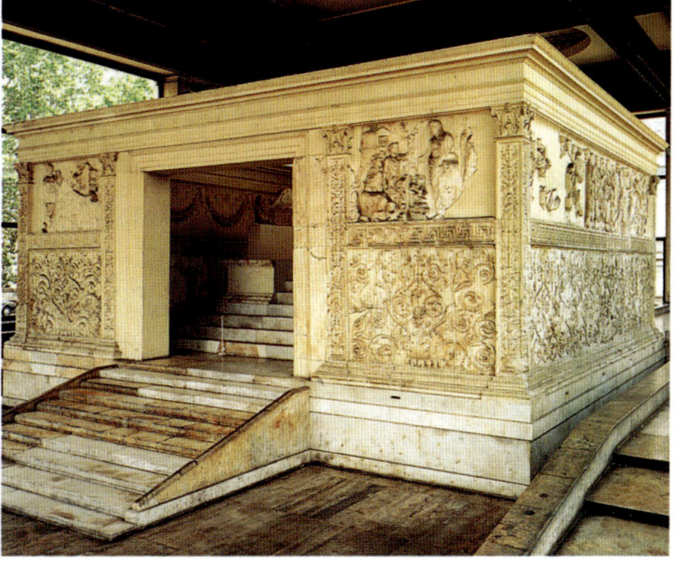

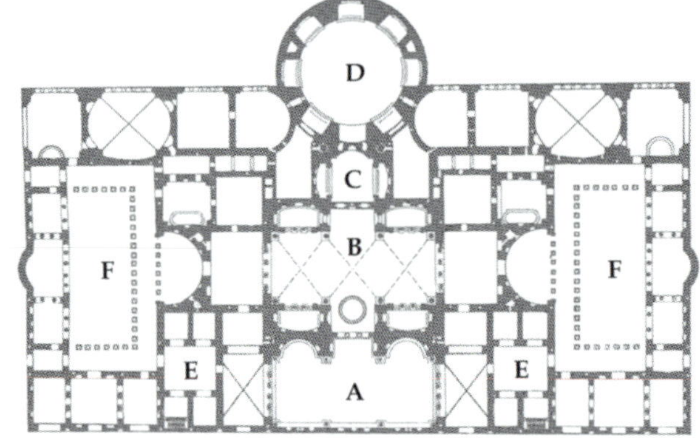

Septimius Severus was the first emperor of the following Severan dynasty. He mostly restored and completed existing buildings and his name is associated only with the construction of the Septizodium, at the foot of the Palatine Hill. This imposing structure, probably a nymphaeum decorated with statues and exquisite marbles, acted as a grandiose backdrop to the town section of the Appian Way, and greeted strangers arriving in Rome. Although Septimius Severus began the construction of the splendid baths later completed by his son Caracalla, after whom they were named, he devoted his attention not so much to the capital of the empire as to his birthplace Lepcis Magna in North Africa which he embellished with magnificent buildings.

Subsequent emperors are not associated with any particular monument, except for Severus Alexander, who built the baths on the Campus Martius; they were supplied by the new Alexandrine aqueduct, the last to be brought to Rome. Finally, at the end of the 3rd century AD, Aurelian began work on a mighty city wall which, though extensively rebuilt, still surrounds the city, with a perimeter nearly 19 km (12 miles) long.

Julia Domna, wife of Septimius Severus, was a patron of the arts and gathered leading personalities at court such as the historian Cassius Dio and the jurists Papinian and Ulpian. However, absolute imperial rule which had eliminated all free and spontaneous thought was not conducive to original literary production; rather it favoured the study and imitation of existing works. Religious tolerance allowed a profusion of Christian writings to circulate freely, and these are characteristic of the period. In this respect the works of apologists defending the new faith are important, especially those of the Carthaginian Tertullian, who upheld the Christian doctrine with great zeal and passionate moral rigour.

Diocletian and Constantine are responsible for the last period of extensive construction work in Rome. The grandiose baths at either end of the Quirinal and Helena's Baths on the Esquiline were built by these emperors. Maxentius erected a new basilica in the forum, and a large circus at his residence on the Appian Way. Constantine, who ruled the empire alone after the battle of the Milvian Bridge, restored many dilapidated public buildings, and also promoted the erection of new Christian basilicas. The Arch of Constantine near the Colosseum, a symbol of the pagan world, was built in his honour.

In the latter part of the 4th century AD, the old temples were gradually abandoned or converted into Christian churches. Only the walls and bridges were kept in efficient order. Despite the major restoration work on the city walls ordered by Arcadius and Honorius, they were unable to withstand the barbarian hordes led by Alaric, and in AD 410 the city was sacked and stripped of its greatest works of art. This event marked the beginning of the decline which accelerated in the second half of the 5th century, leading to the end of the Roman empire of the west.

Art also saw radical changes in the last period of the empire. In depicting the human figure artists passed from realism to increasingly marked stylization, reflecting the new image of power and its holders.

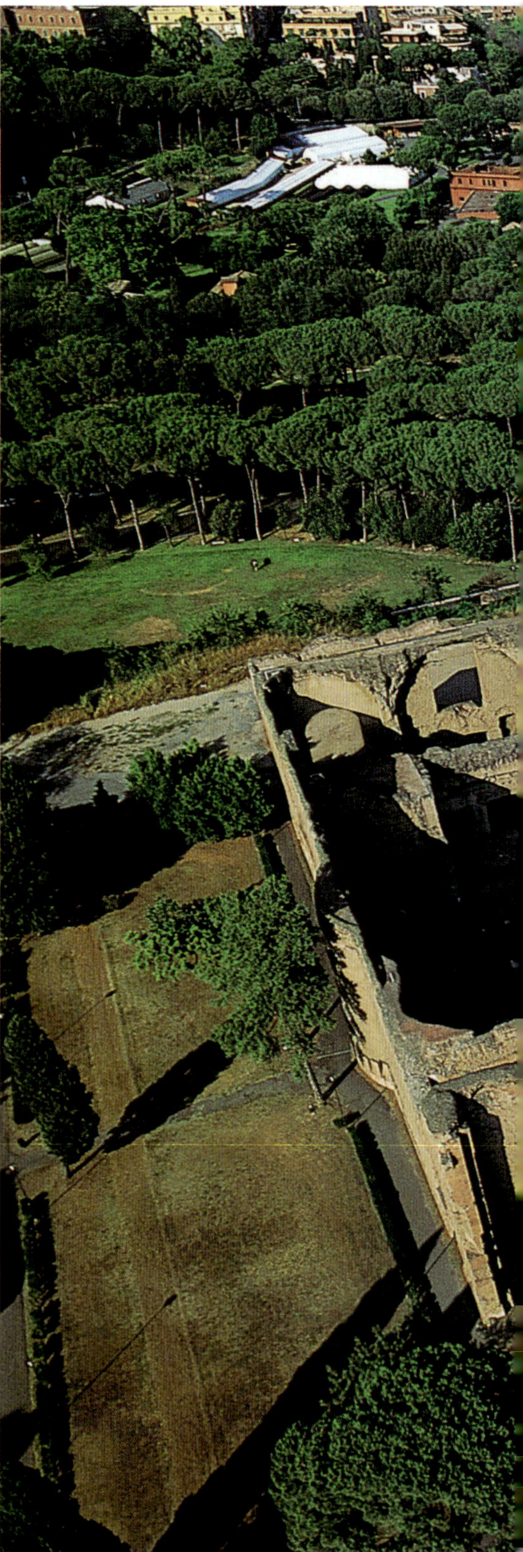

134–135 (above) Begun around AD 212 by Septimius Severus and inaugurated four years later by his son, after whom they were named, the Baths of Caracalla were considered the most magnificent in Rome. Covering a huge area, they could hold up to 1600 people engaged in various activities.

135 (right) The surviving mosaics do not do justice to the magnificence for which the Baths of Caracalla were once famous. They were also ornamented with priceless marbles, coloured plaster and statues. In addition to the bathing rooms, the huge complex included palaestrae for exercise, saunas, libraries and lounges.

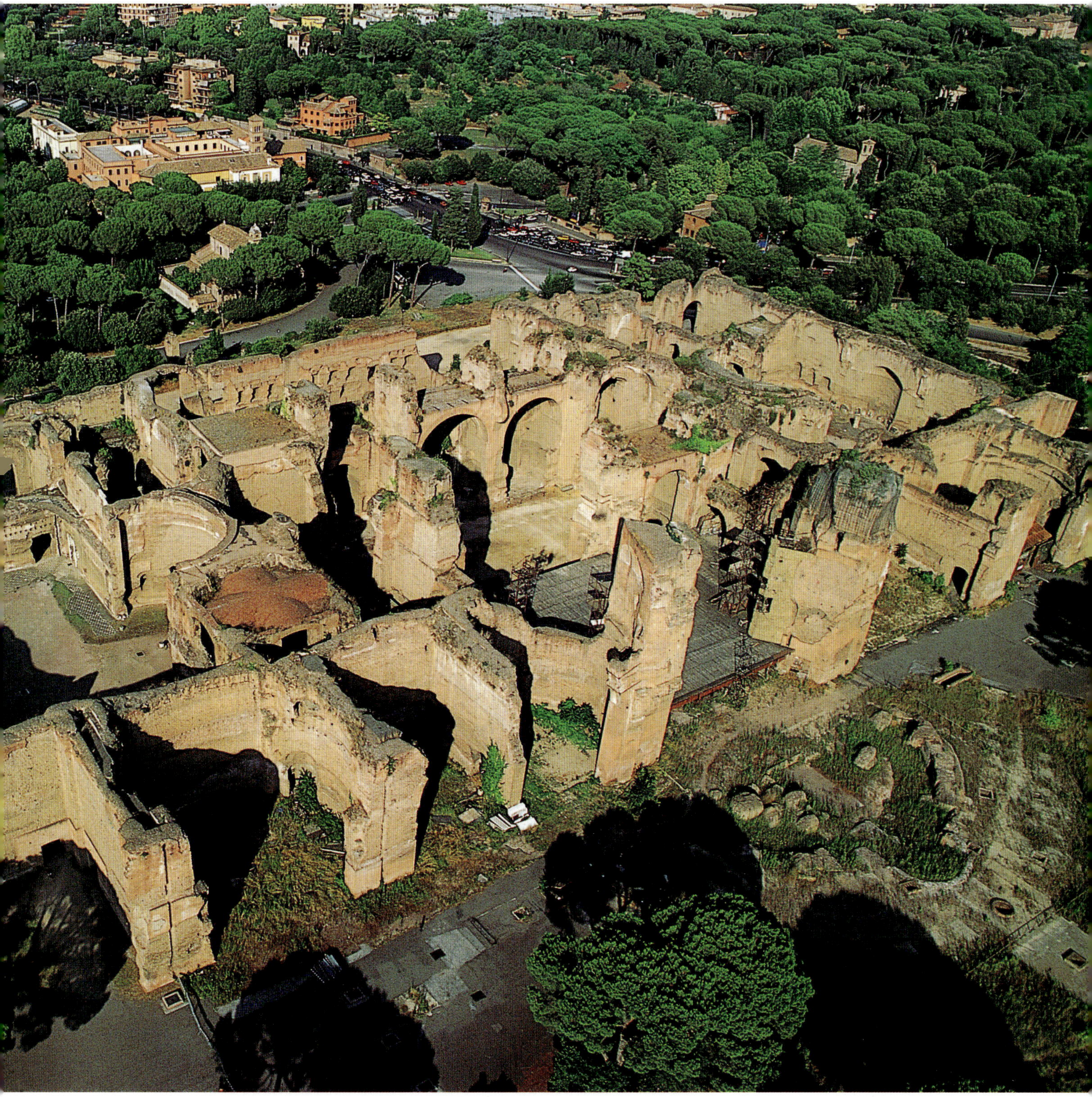

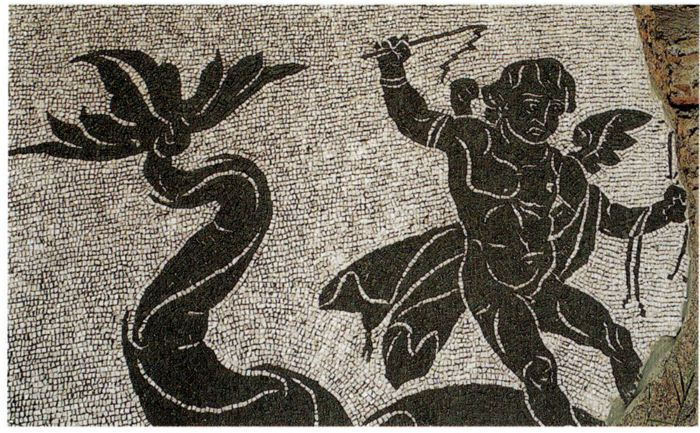

136–137 (overleaf) This reconstruction of the Baths of Caracalla shows the central area, in cross-section, with the swimming pool, the frigidarium, the tepidarium, and the caldarium, a circular room 35 m (115 ft) in diameter, which is now lost. Magnificent gardens surrounded the complex.

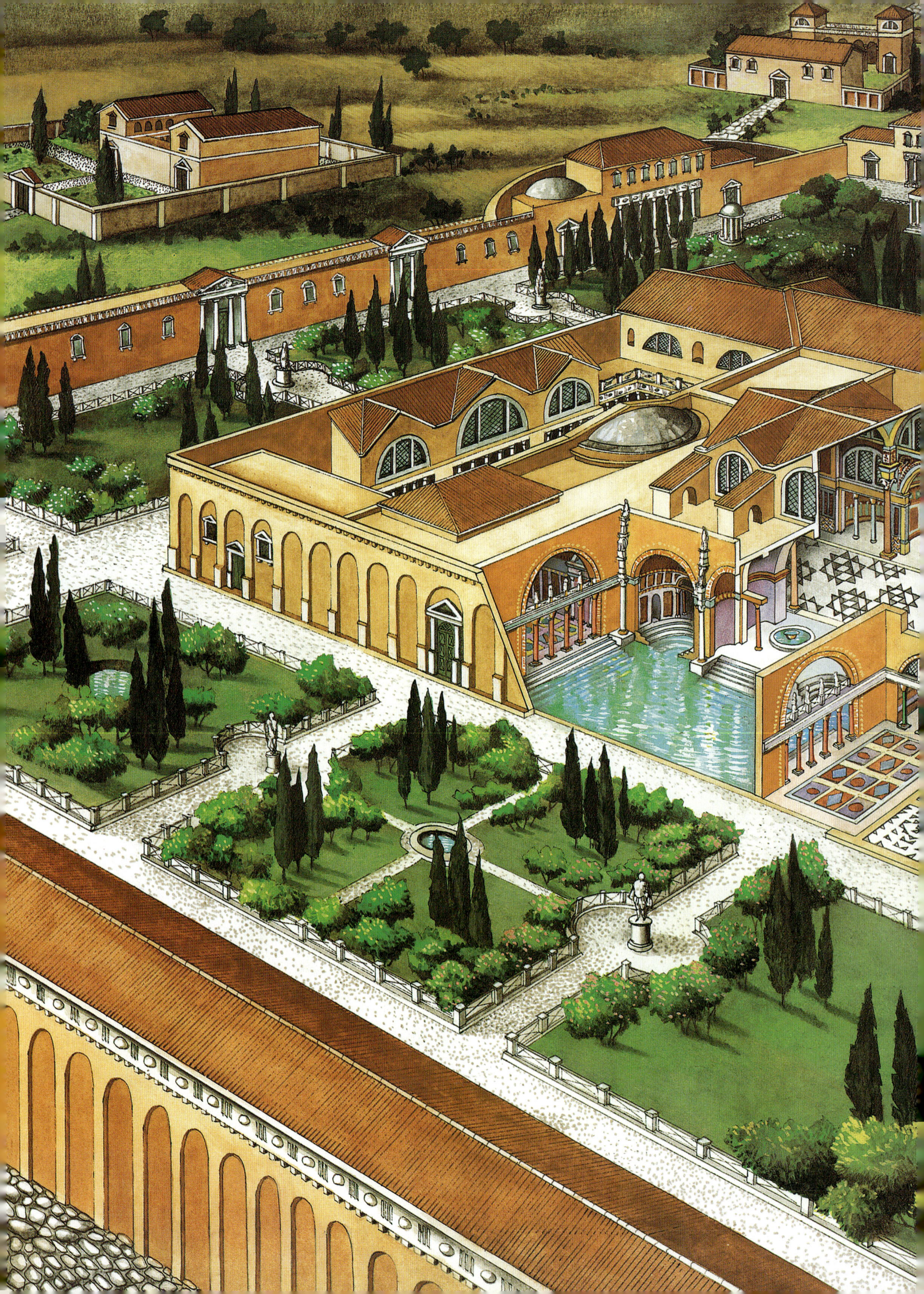

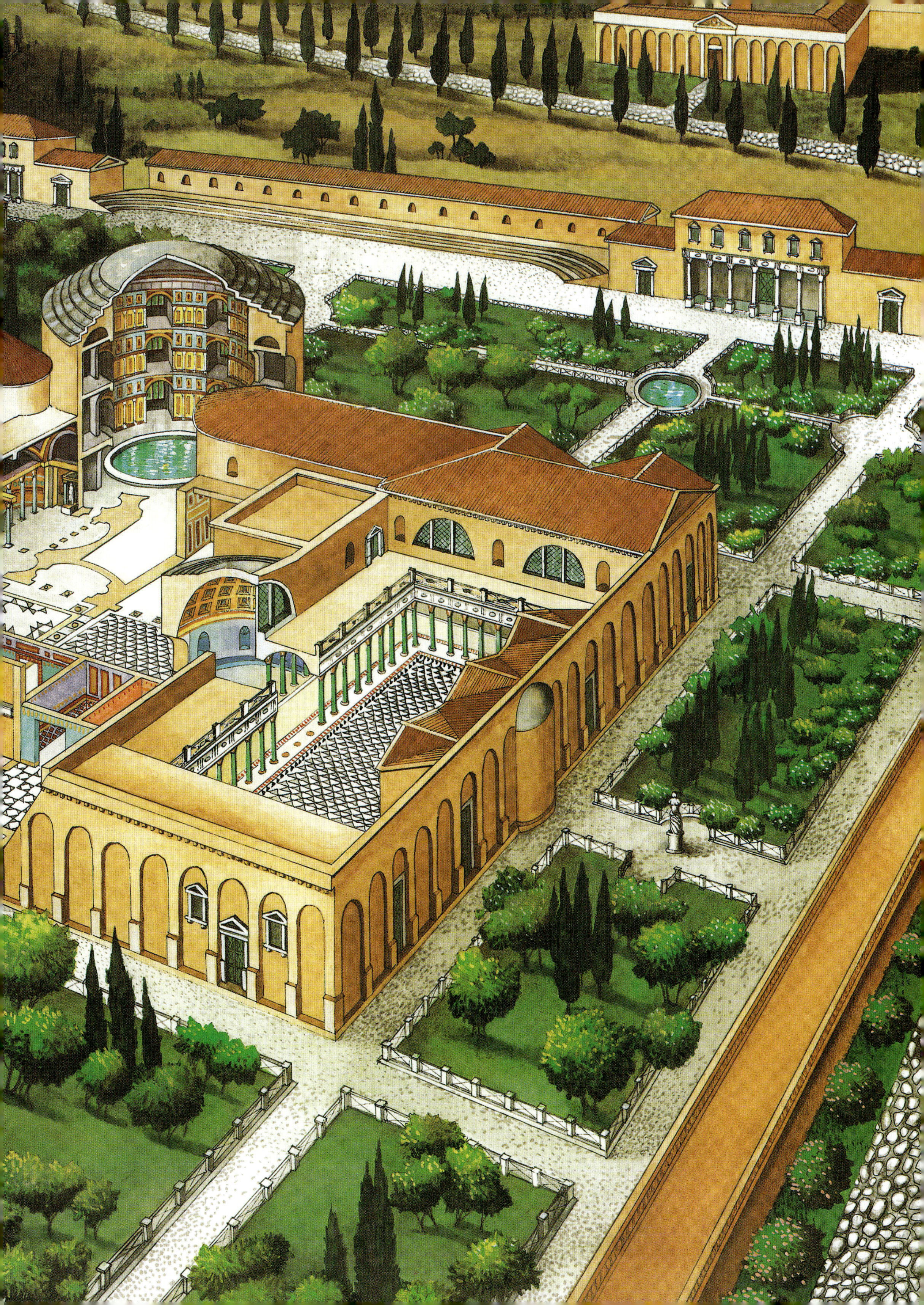

138 (right) The Basilica of Santa Maria degli Angeli was built in 1566 by Michelangelo, who adapted to this purpose the huge tepidarium of the Baths of Diocletian, the largest ever built in Rome. The façade of the sacred building, shown here, was one of the two apses of the caldarium, of which nothing else survives.

138–139 (below) The impressive size of the ruins of the Baths of Diocletian is revealed in this aerial view. The tepidarium, later converted into a church and modified by Luigi Vanvitelli in 1749, is 91 m (298 ft) long and 28 m (92 ft) high. The entire complex, built of brick between AD 298 and 306, could be used by 3000 people at once.

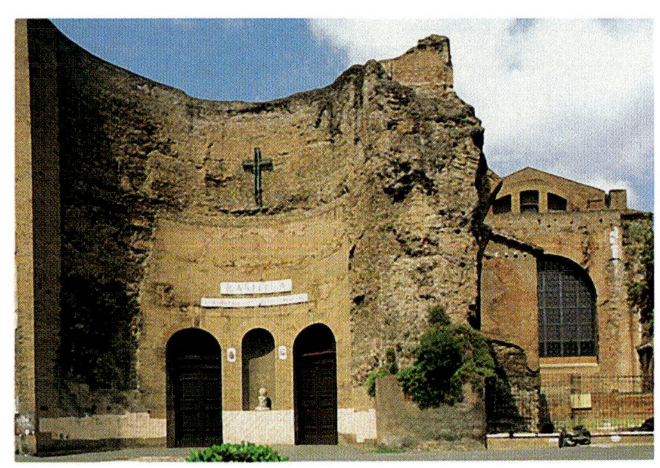

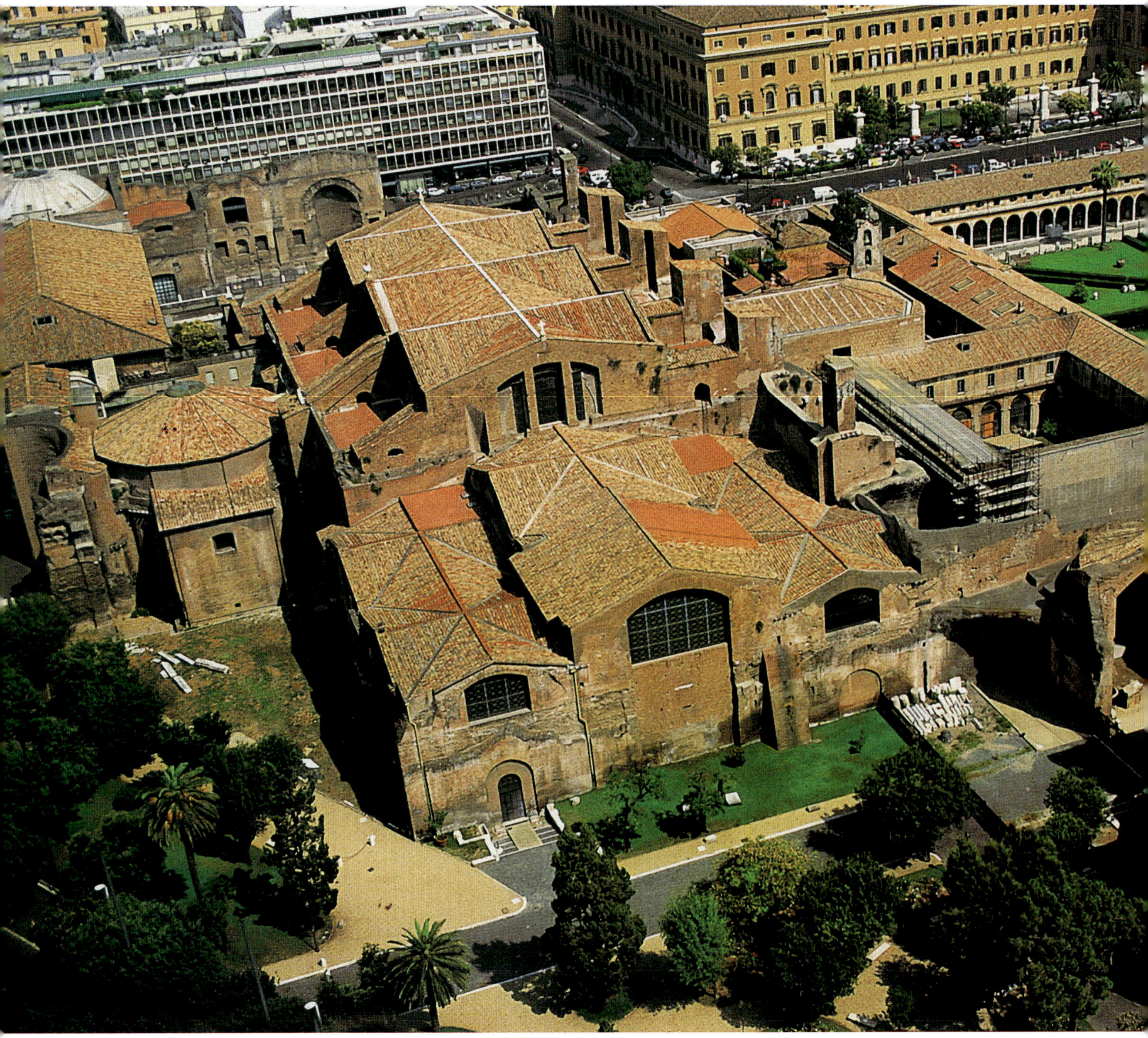

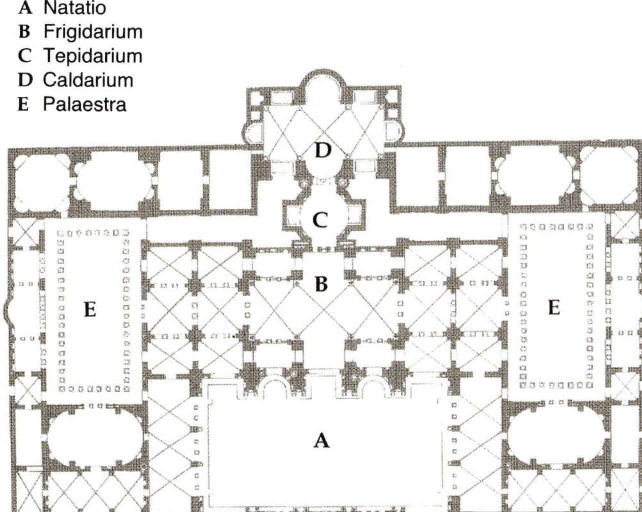

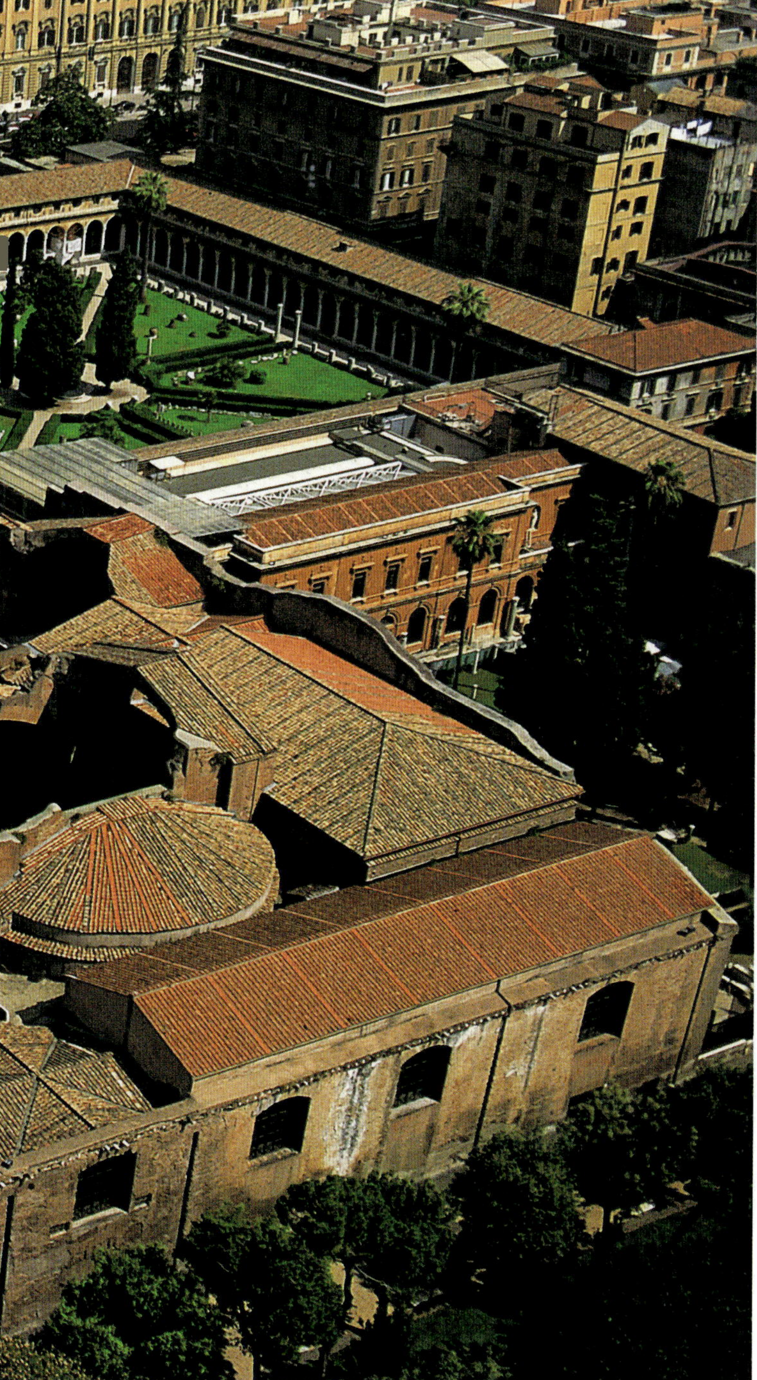

Sculptures are mainly represented by sarcophagi; some important mosaics also belong to this period, in which Christian themes featured more and more frequently.

However, in general the lifestyle of the Roman populace remained almost unchanged. The great public entertainments continued to be held whenever the imperial purse could afford them, though an inexorably advancing financial crisis forced everyone, including the court, to adopt a more austere way of life.

Under emperors like Diocletian and Constantine, support for literature continued. Works of this period were mostly studies of grammar and rhetoric, while the last followers of the pagan tradition vainly attempted to defend what was now a world in decline. There were many mediocre epitomizers and biographers who, following in the footsteps of Suetonius, wrote biographies of emperors. The only voice worthy of the historiographic tradition of the past was that of Ammianus Marcellinus. Christian culture led to the development of a new kind of intellectual who, while acknowledging the validity of past philosophical and literary traditions, accepted only those elements useful to the interpretation of Christianity. The greatest personality of the time was St Augustine, who explored the depths of the human soul with great insight. The last, grieving witness of the declining empire was Gallic poet Rutilius Namazianus who, in *De reditu suo*, narrates his return to his country, describing the sea voyage he took because the old roads were

139 (below) The National Museum in Rome, the entrance of which is shown here, is housed in a wing of the Baths of Diocletian. The plan of this complex followed the same system already used in the Baths of Caracalla in a more grandiose but basically unchanged form. Thermal baths were one of the most characteristic signs of Roman civilization, and buildings of this kind have been found in every province of the empire. There is certain evidence that there were ten monumental baths complexes in Rome alone, but written sources refer to at least six more, whose location is uncertain. The huge amount of water required by these structures was usually supplied by specially built branches of the main city aqueducts.

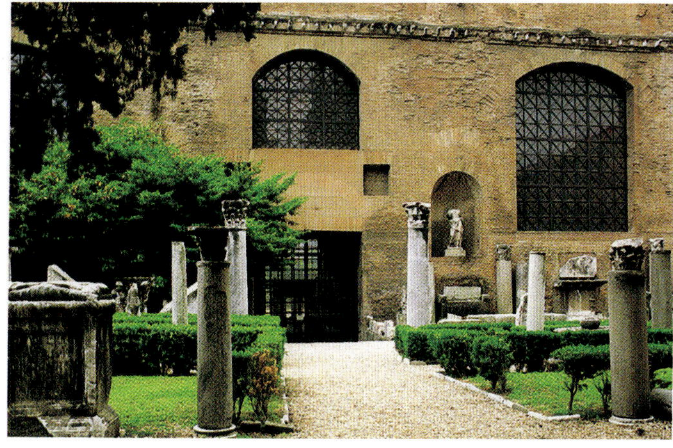

now impassable. Taking his leave, he addresses Rome: 'Hear, O beautiful queen of the world which is thine, O Rome now received among the celestial spheres! Hear, O mother of men and mother of gods, thou who, through thy temples, make us feel less distant from the heavens! We sing of thee and always of thee – as long as the fates allow, we sing... Thou hast created for people of every country a single fatherland; for lawless peoples it was great fortune to be subjugated by thee. In offering the vanquished the equality of thy rights, thou hast made a city of what once was the world...' (*urbem fecisti quod prius orbis erat*).

140–141 Roman art, was in many ways a tool serving the purposes of imperial political propaganda. However, as shown by these two portraits of children, which are delicate but academic, the more elegant themes of Hellenistic art were very popular with cultivated, wealthy individuals. They sometimes spent huge sums on decorating their villas with marbles and bronzes, an enthusiasm due more to snobbery than to any real appreciation of artistic values, however. In fact, the practice of art was never considered really worthy of a Roman citizen, and was willingly left to artists from Greece or Asia Minor who emigrated to Rome, or to plebeians and freedmen.

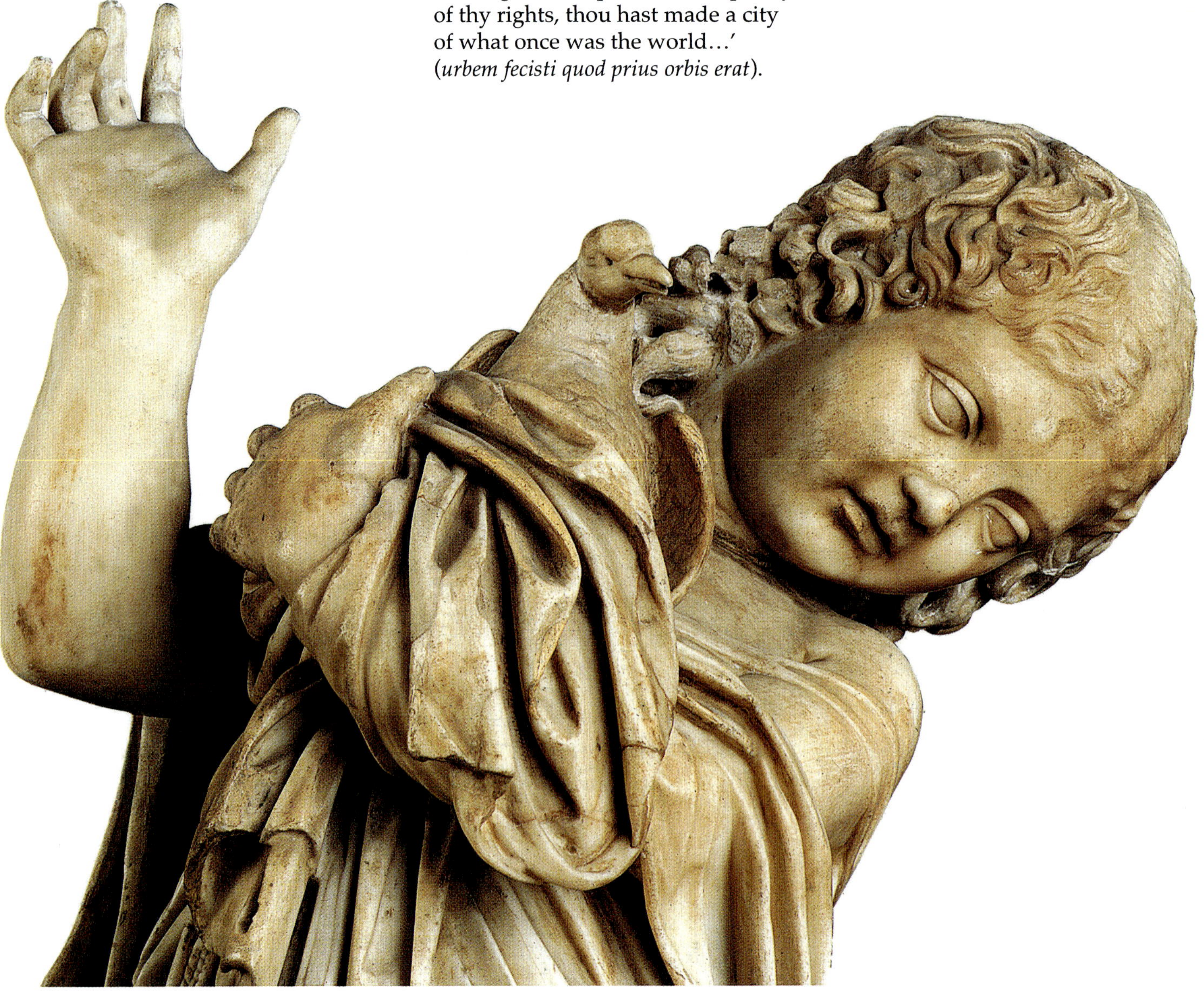

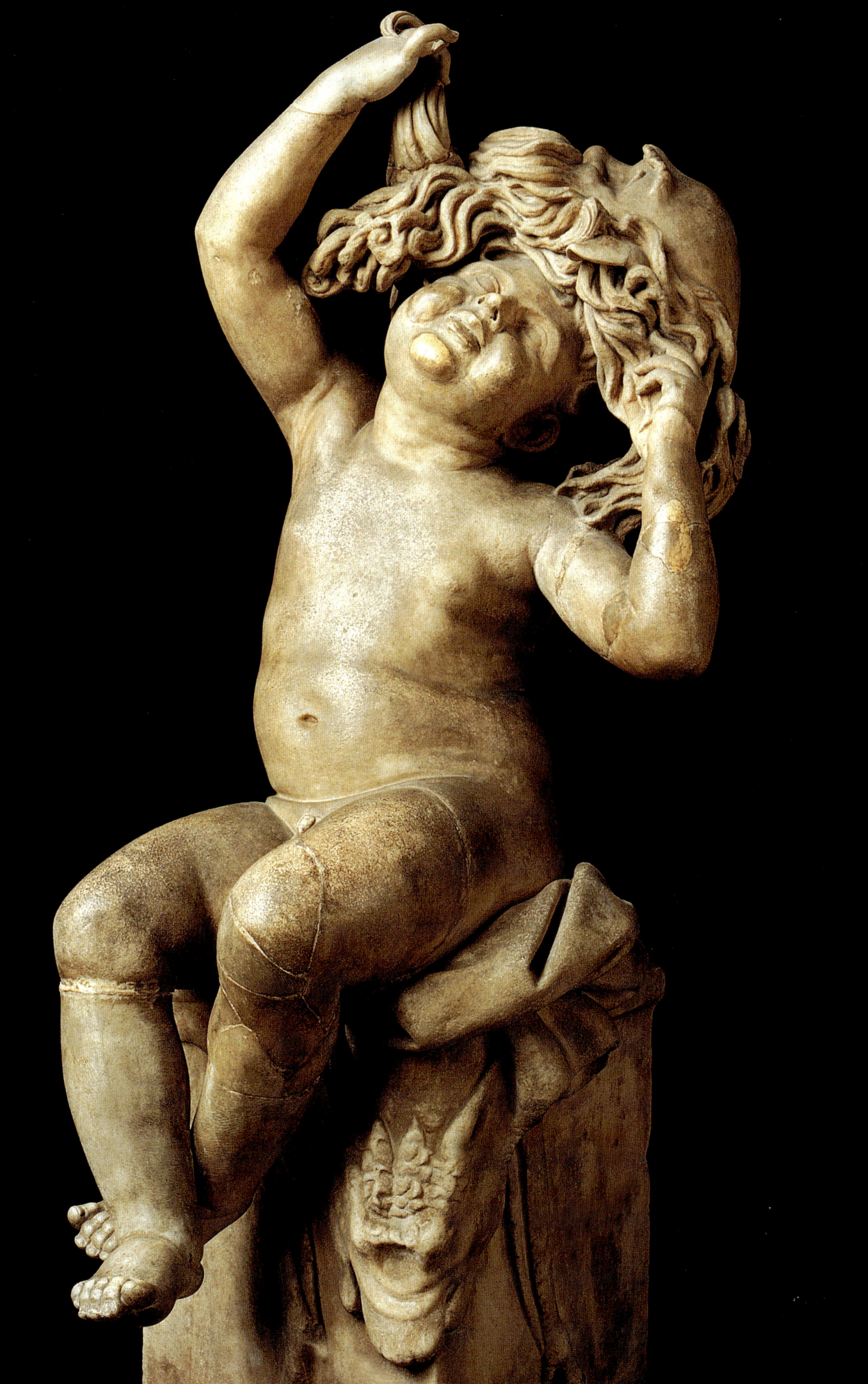

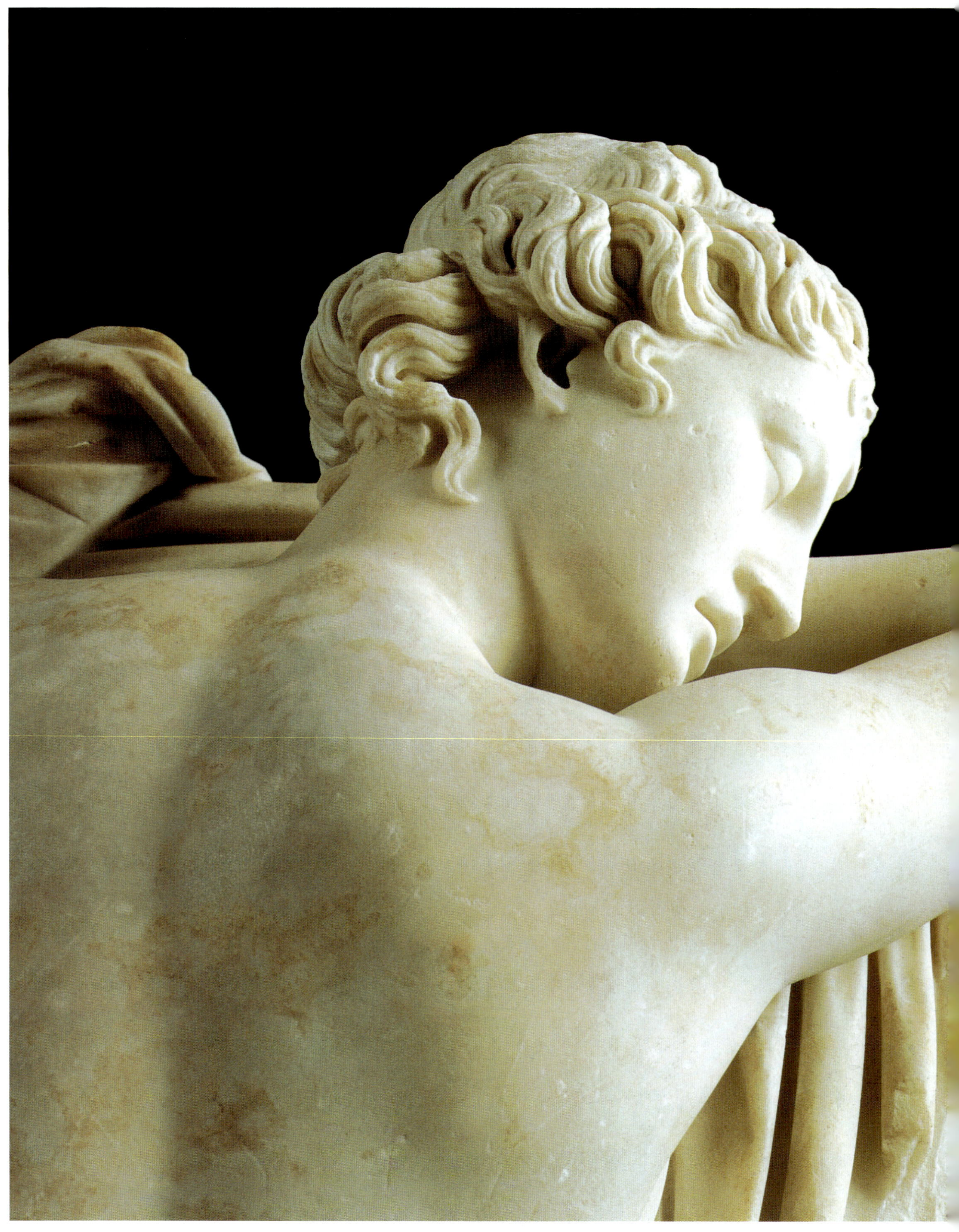

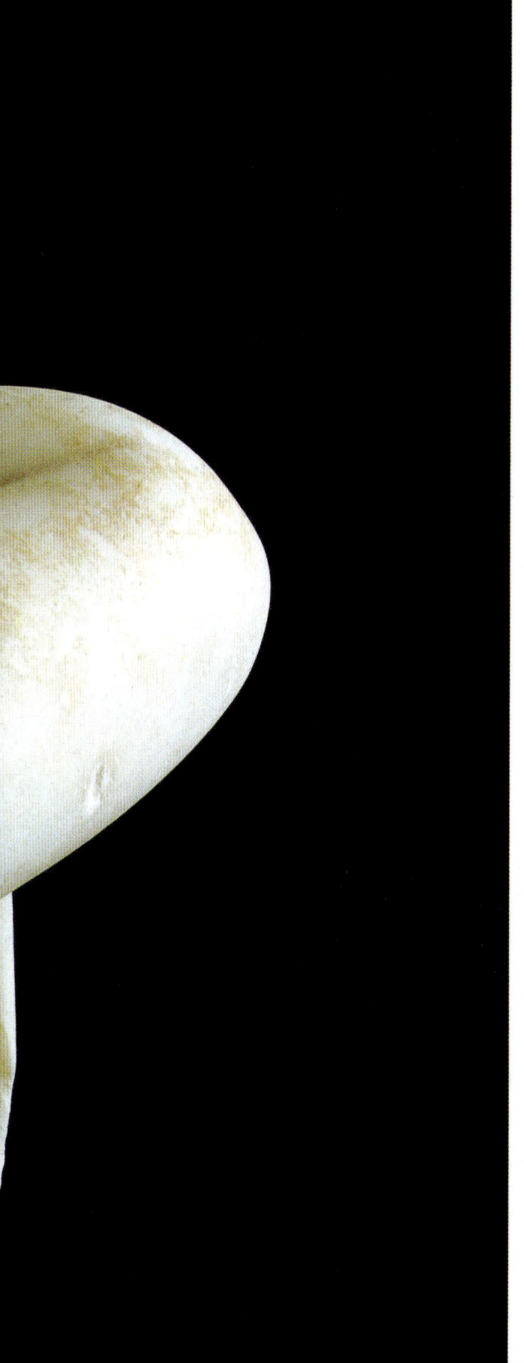

142 and 143 The encounter between the Roman world and Greek–Hellenistic art took place at a time when the former, which had until then concentrated on the initial stage of its expansionism, was beginning to show an enthusiastic appreciation of beauty as an end in itself, in part as the result of the arrival of great riches. The Greek world, on the other hand, had reached a stage of full maturity after centuries of development and was returning to certain archaic forms reminiscent of its former political and cultural supremacy. Rome was a willing importer of such models, and Roman figurative art was strongly influenced by them. However, official art continued to perform the utilitarian and celebratory function it had done since the origins of the republic. In practice, the Romans considered sculpture as having a decorative and ornamental function, which explains its success with wealthy citizens and in public architecture. Triumphal portraits continued to follow the lifelike models of historical tradition, sometimes interpreted in a virtuoso manner drawn from Hellenism. The field in which the Roman creative spirit was expressed with the greatest originality was architecture. Both the Capitoline Venus (below) and the Sleeping Hermaphrodite (left) are excellent Roman copies of Greek originals.

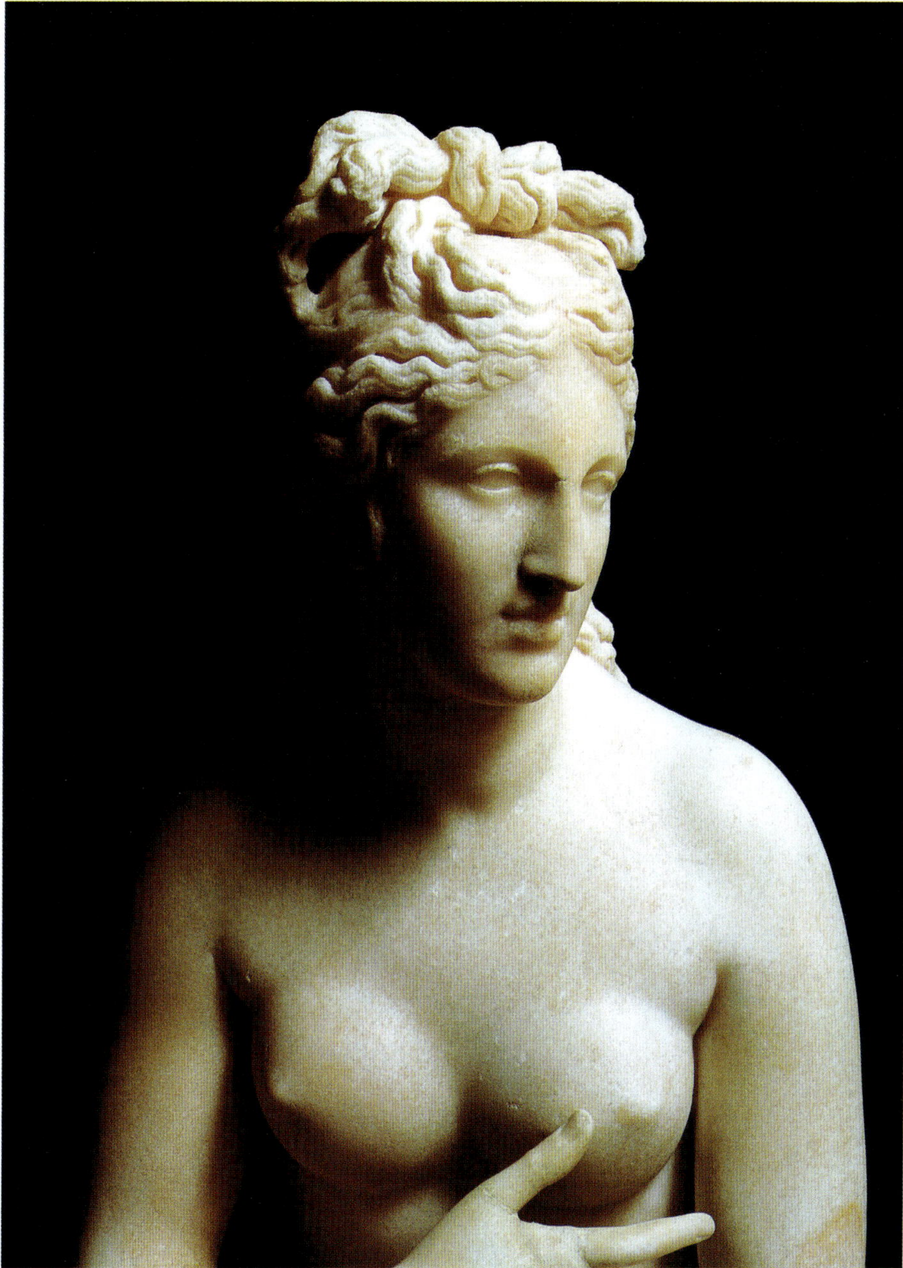

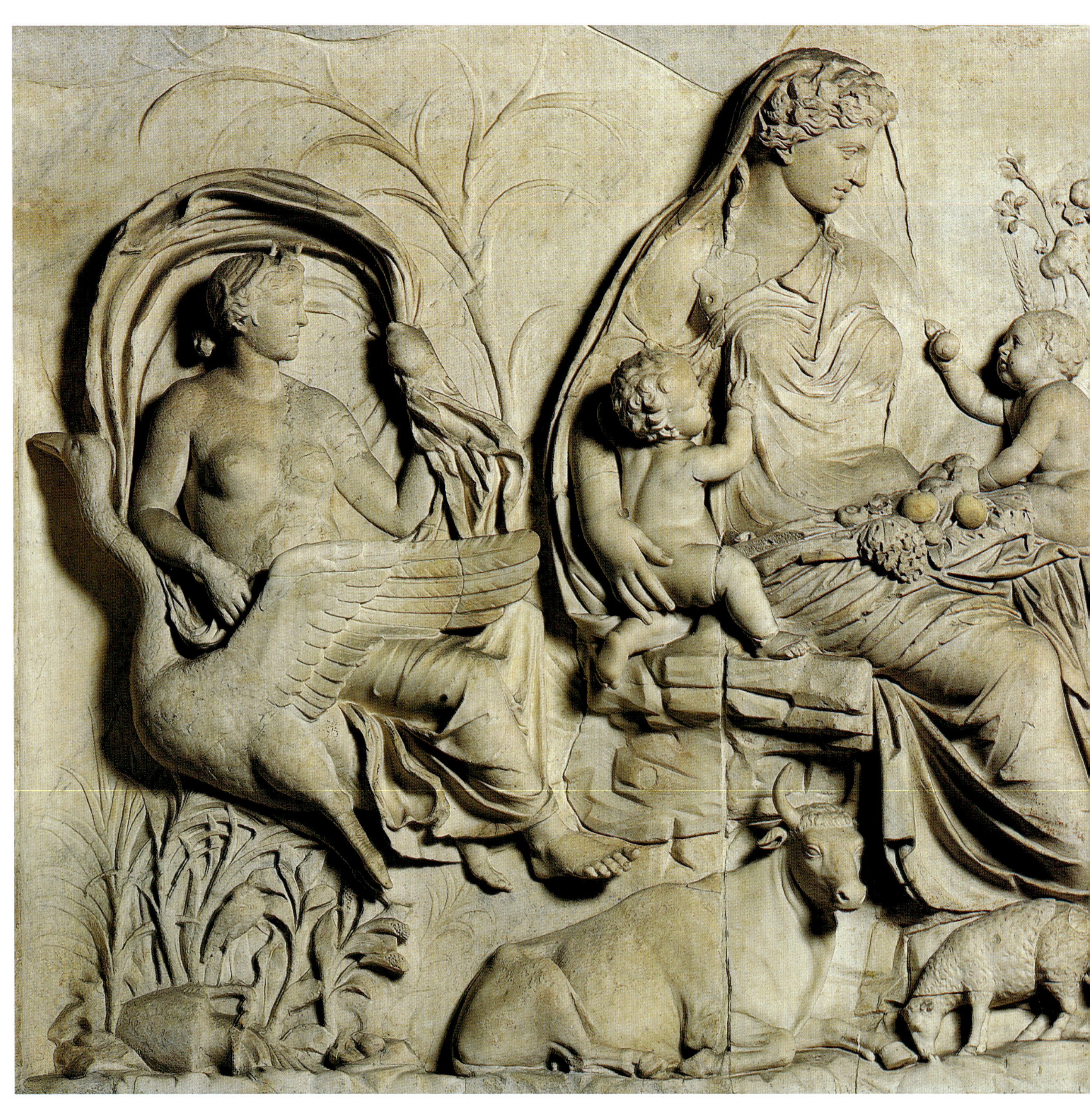

144–145 This relief, part of the outer decoration of the Ara Pacis Augustae, *shows Tellus, a female figure who personifies the fertility of the earth, with two nymphs symbolizing air and water. The scene represents the three elements of the world subjected to Roman power, and at the same time is an allegory of the peace and prosperity the rule of Augustus had brought to Italy. The monument is essential to the understanding of public art under Augustus. Its interpretation is aided by the valuable information provided by Ovid and by Augustus himself, in his autobiography* Res Gestae Divi Augusti. *Hellenistic influence can be seen in the outer decoration and the Tellus relief, while Neoattic taste is evident in the spatial composition of the two processions. At the same time, the clear propaganda purpose and the attention given to the historical details of the work are typically Roman. This eclecticism, together with the use of themes from Italic tradition, is characteristic of the art both of the late republic and, in particular, the early imperial age.*

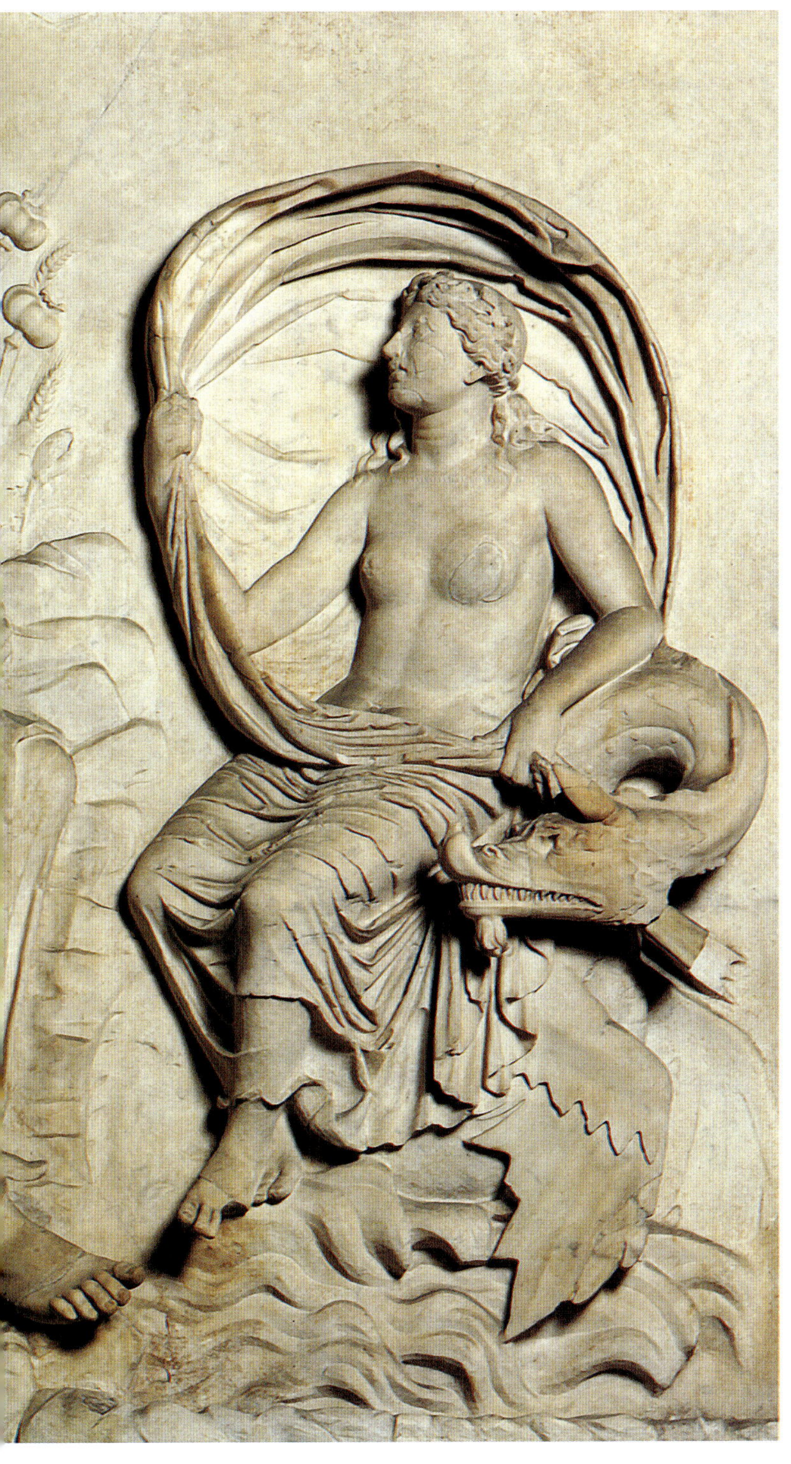

ROMAN CIVILIZATION IN ITALY

THE POLITICAL ORGANIZATION OF ITALY

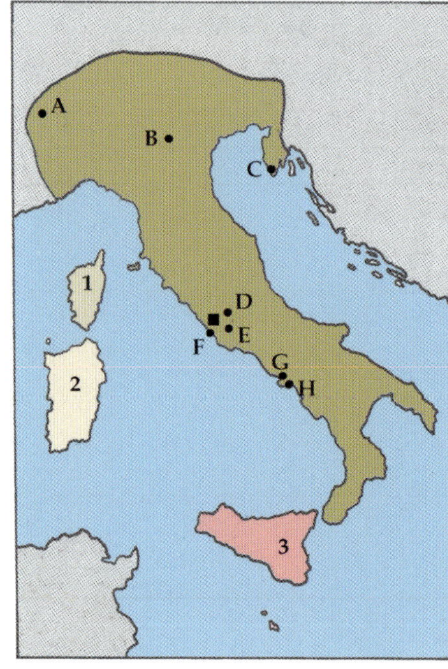

■ ROME
A AOSTA
B VERONA
C PULA
D TIVOLI
E PALAESTRINA
F OSTIA
G HERCULANEUM
H POMPEII

1 CORSICA (province from 227 BC)
2 SARDINIA (province from 238 BC)
3 SICILY (province from 241 BC)

Geographically Rome is located in the centre of Italy, a fact which meant that the Romans could nearly always confront their enemies separately. However, the gradual increase in conquered territories necessitated the introduction of a defensive system, which took the form of the typically Italic institution – the colony. Citizens and their families were sent to strategically crucial points, mainly already existing towns, not only to defend the new conquests but also to cultivate the land allotted to them. This land consisted of a third of the enemy territory, divided into small plots and redistributed in the form of private property. The citizens were called *coloni* (colonists), and the new communities were called *coloniae* (colonies). Colonists might be Latin or Italic allies or, far more often, Roman citizens who were equated with Latin allies or kept their rights of citizenship. From this came the distinction between *coloniae Latinae, coloniae Latinorum* and *coloniae civium Romanorum* – Latin colonies, colonies of Latins and colonies of Roman citizens. The oldest colonies were Latin ones: those on land conquered by the Latin League, some of which dated to the age of the monarchy. The foundation (*deductio*) of such towns, to which between 1500 and 6000 colonists were sent, continued even after the dissolution of the League in 338 BC; the last Latin colony in Italy was Lucca, founded in 180 BC.

These colonies, allied to Rome by a special treaty, had their own constitution, their own laws and their own magistrates. They paid no taxes to Rome, but had to supply military contingents in times of war. Founded to consolidate territorial advantages obtained during the Latin War, they were mainly formed by Roman plebeians who gave up their citizenship in return for ownership of a plot of arable land.

Latin colonies were mainly used to defend land borders, whereas in the case of coastal borders, Rome founded smaller colonies of Roman citizens. According to tradition, the first such Roman colony was Ostia, founded by Ancus Martius. The inhabitants of these colonies, usually numbering 300, retained the rights guaranteed by Roman citizenship and had their own magistrates. From 183 BC, Roman colonies began to replace Latin colonies in defence of territory. Modena and Parma in Cisalpine Gaul, and Saturnia in Etruria were founded in this period, when the number of colonists was increased to 2000.

When Rome was unable to send colonists to conquered territories, the inhabitants of the subjugated towns were allowed to enjoy Roman citizenship to a greater or lesser extent, and continued to live in their own homes. Thus the *municipium* (municipality) was introduced. The first *municipium* is believed to have been the Latin Tusculum, whose inhabitants were granted Roman citizenship in 381 BC.

The municipal system was applied on a large scale to Latin towns after the dissolution of the Latin League and at the same period to the towns of Campania. The inhabitants of the Latin towns obtained either

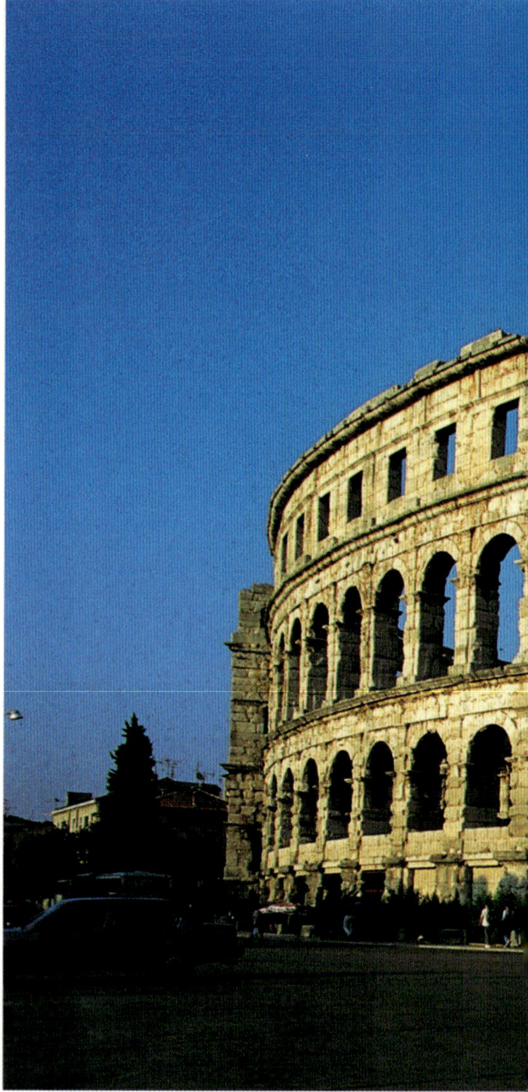

147 (opposite, below left) On the cliff which dominates the valley of the Anio at Tivoli stand the ruins of a round temple; it is usually called the Temple of Vesta, but was probably consecrated to Hercules. This building, dating from the late republican period, exerted great influence over 19th-century European architecture.

147 (opposite, below right) Verona, founded in a loop of the Adige river, was one of the largest Roman towns in northern Italy. Its amphitheatre, usually known as the Arena, dates from the first half of the 1st century AD. Though much restored, it is one of the best preserved in the world, and is still used for a renowned opera season.

146–147 (below) Pula, now a town in Croatia, on the Istrian peninsula, was a Roman colony from the mid-1st century BC. *Its amphitheatre has the unusual feature of four massive towers around the outer perimeter, which contain the staircases leading to the upper floors.*

147 (right) One of the most interesting of the numerous surviving Roman monuments in Pula is the funeral arch of the Sergia family, with a single archway between pairs of Corinthian columns. Dating from the third decade BC, *it is one of the oldest to survive intact.*

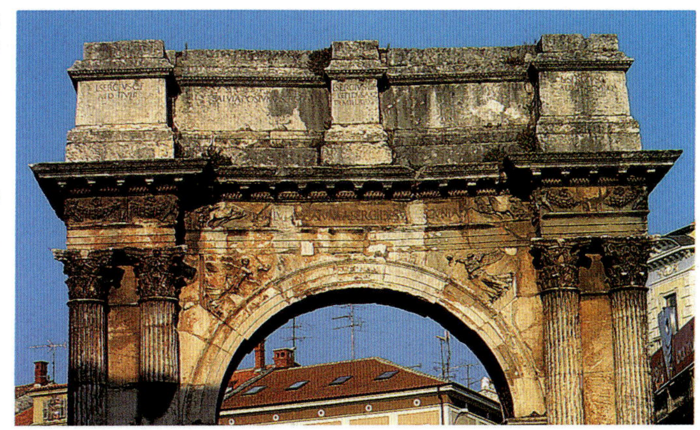

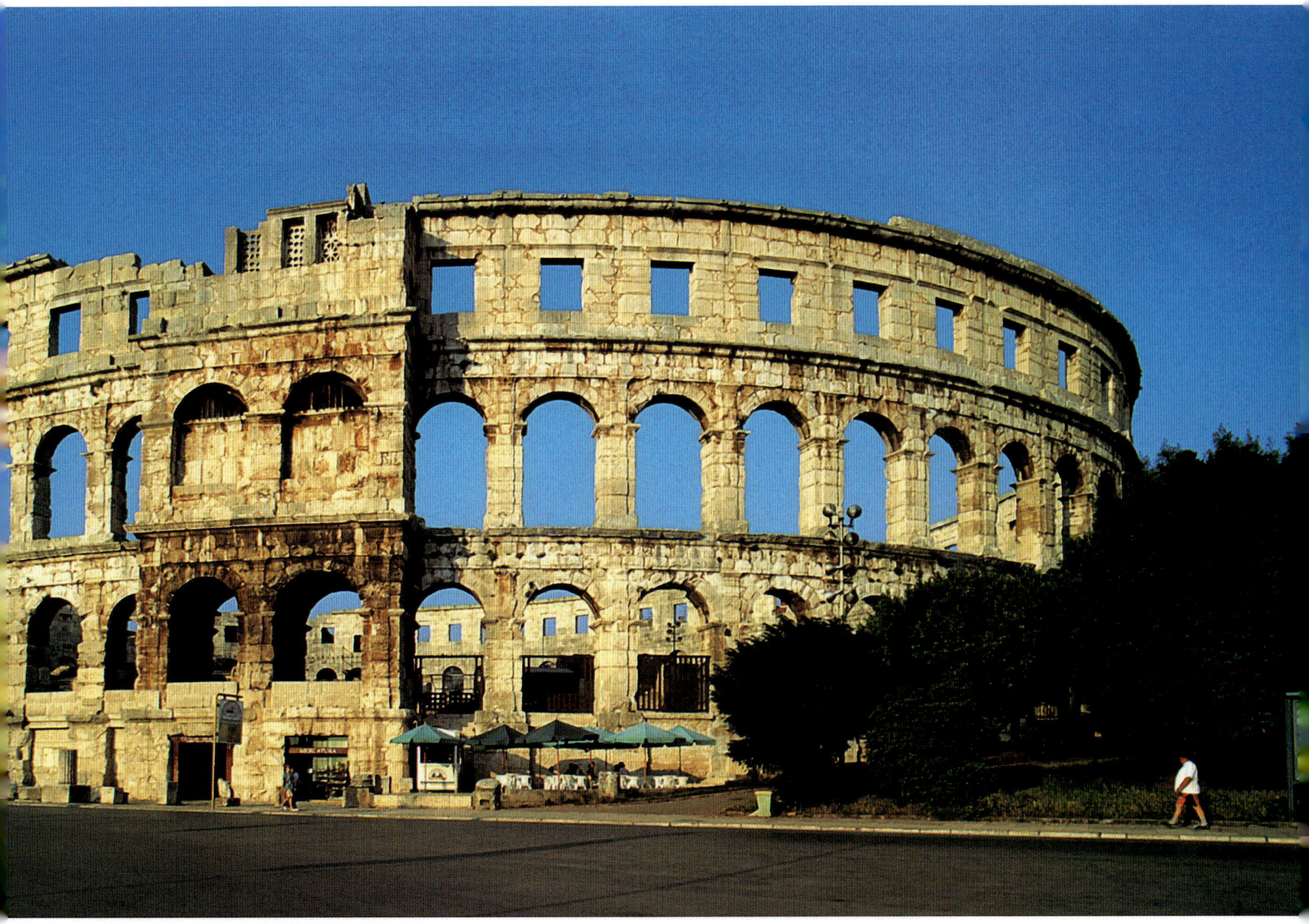

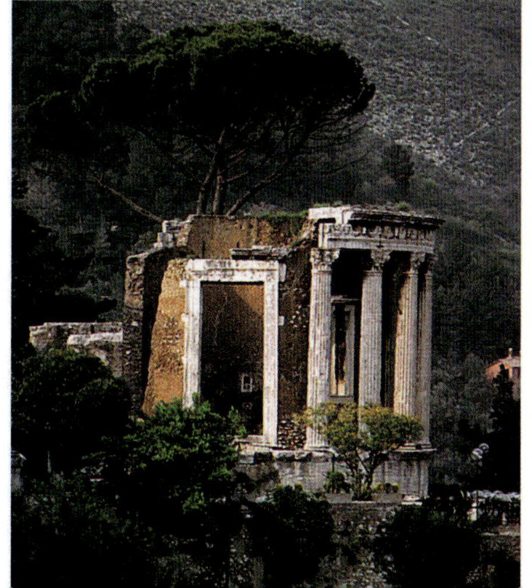

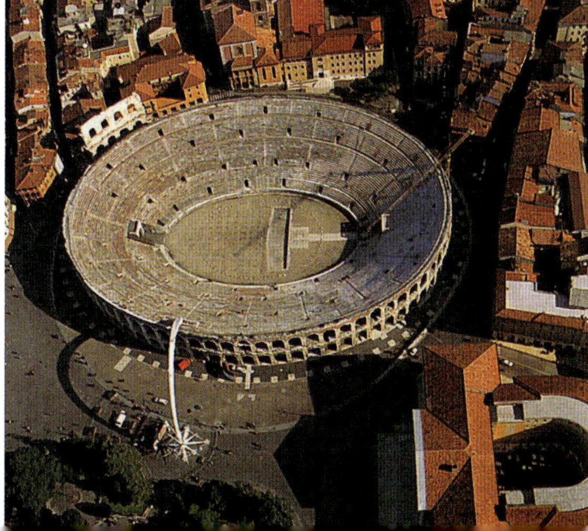

citizenship with full political rights or citizenship without the right to vote (*civitas sine suffragio*). This type of town belonged to a category of municipality of lesser status, known as *praefecturae* because they were under the jurisdiction of *praefecti* sent from Rome. There were also *civitates foederatae*, towns allied to Rome by a treaty, and retaining the title of sovereign state provided they did not dispute Roman supremacy. Almost all the towns in Etruria and Italy south of Vesuvius had this legal status.

In 123 BC Gaius Gracchus restored the institution of colonies, which by this time had lost much of their defensive role. His motive was to give land to the Roman proletariat; his attempt, violently opposed by the nobility, ended in bloody riots, during which he was killed.

The growing dissatisfaction of the Latin colonists and the allies in the Italic confederation, who had made an active contribution to the rise of Rome but were denied the status of Roman citizens, led to a full-scale armed conflict. The Social War of 89 BC resulted in the conversion of the remaining Latin colonies, which retained a solely legal function, and the grant of the prized *ius civitatis* to towns south of the Rubicon.

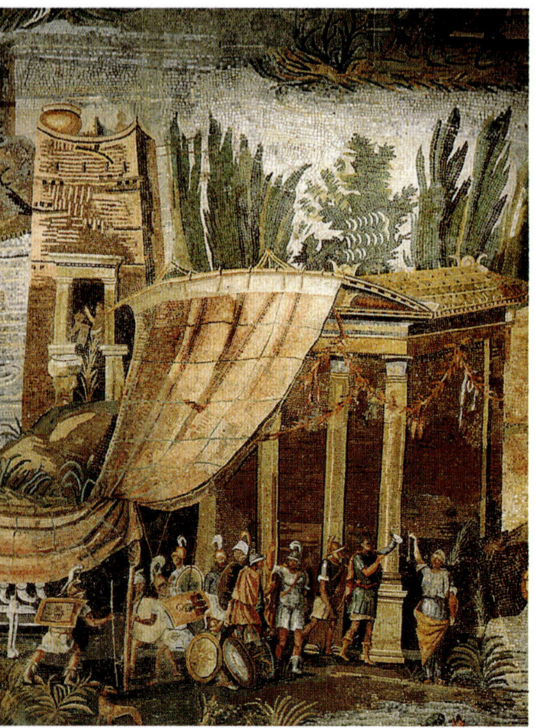

From then on, the municipal system was extended throughout Italy. The *municipium* had greater administrative independence and was long considered a perfect model of town organization. Supremacy was only regained by the colonies in the second half of the 1st century AD.

At the beginning of the 1st century BC, first under Marius and then under Sulla, the types of colony founded were increased in order to reward army veterans with grants of land; a practice that was later used by Caesar and Augustus. The land required for the new colonists was confiscated, as in the case of the 18 towns which had supported the conspirators against Caesar, or was purchased. The title of Roman colony became highly sought-after, and many emperors granted this status to numerous Italian towns.

All the towns described so far, despite various transformations over the years, modelled their constitutions on that of Rome, and increasingly came to resemble it. Rome adopted systems of governing that varied according to the period, the nationality of the new citizens and the treatment granted to them. The supreme magistrates of the colonies and municipalities in the imperial age were the *duoviri* or *quattuorviri iure dicundo*. Within certain limits they exercised civil and criminal jurisdiction, convened and chaired sessions of the council and people's assemblies, looked after the interests of the town, organized public works and ensured that religious duties were observed. All the magistrates were elected by the people in *comitia*, as demonstrated by electoral 'posters' which are still visible on the walls of Pompeii. Every town had its own budget to manage. Its income, consisting of miscellaneous receipts, had to cover a range of expenses: corn supplies, postal services, the billeting of troops, entertainments, and construction and maintenance of city walls, roads, aqueducts and public buildings. It was not unusual for wealthy citizens to erect public buildings or pay for entertainments out of their own pockets.

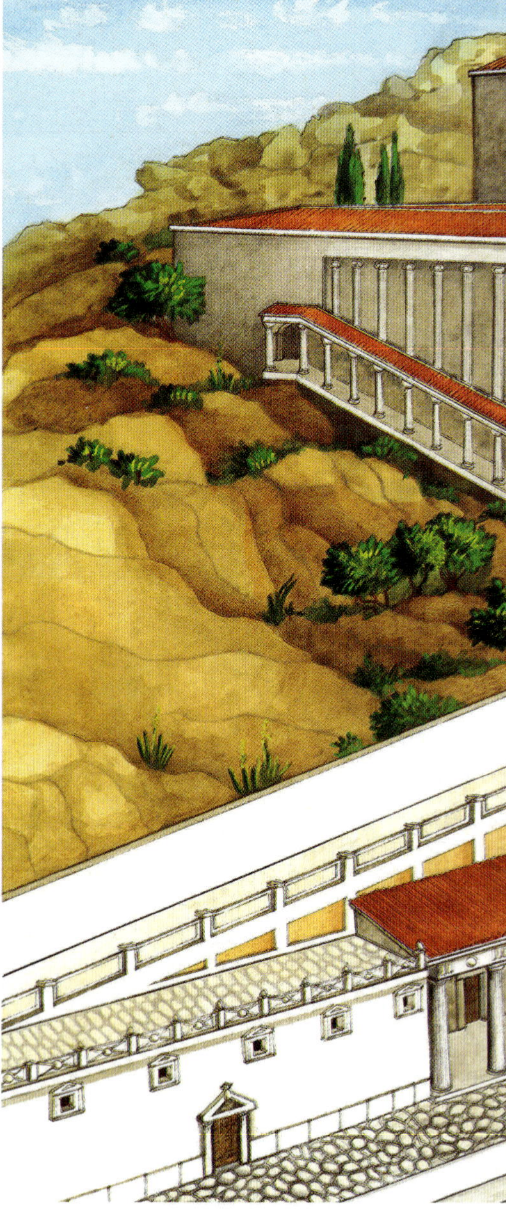

In town planning as in the organization of the political and social life of the colonies, the Romans showed a strong propensity for strictly ordering the spaces under their jurisdiction. When a colony was founded, the selected site, measuring around 70 sq. km (27 sq. miles), was measured from the town centre at the intersection of two roads, called the *cardo*, running north–south, and the *decumanus*, running east–west at right angles to

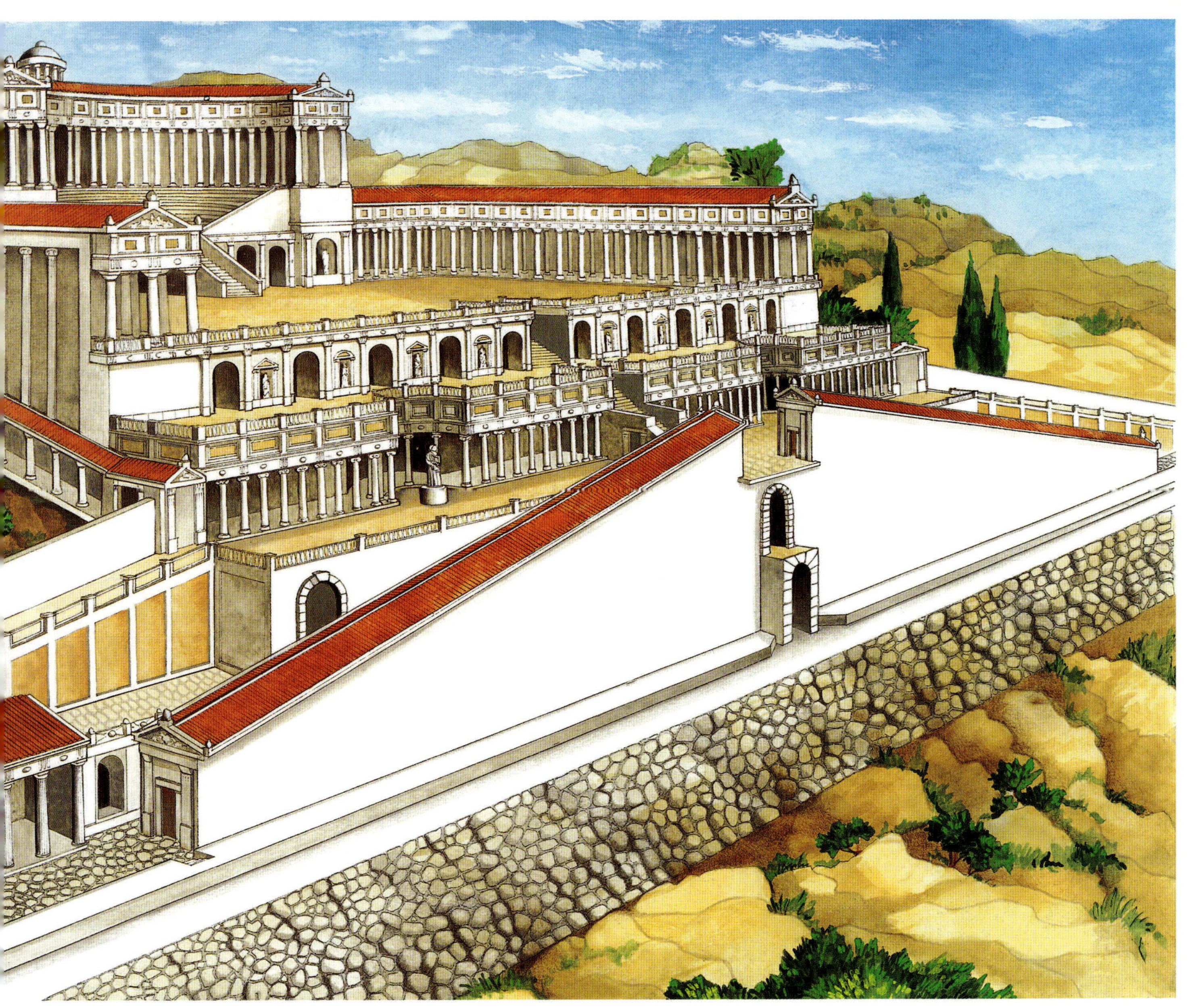

it. On the basis of these co-ordinates the land was divided into plots of 200 *iugera* (approximately 50 ha or 124 acres), constituting the basic cadastral unit. These plots were called centuries (*centuriae* – areas comprising 100 units of 2 *iugera),* and the division into centuries was called centuriation. Land could be divided *per strigas et scamna*, that is into rectangular strips, one running north–south and the other east–west. Each strip belonged to a single owner, with the result that a century was divided equally between a number of owners. In wooded areas or those crossed by streams, the necessary adjustments had to be made to ensure that everyone got a fair allotment.

The main tool used in surveying the land was the *groma*, and surveyors were therefore called *gromatici*. The *groma* was a cross-shaped instrument, with arms of equal length, fixed horizontally on top of a rod which was driven into the ground. Four plumblines were suspended from the arms so that perpendicular alignments could be established. When the *groma* had been placed in the centre of the land to be divided, two basic right-angled axes were drawn. Lines parallel to these were then defined at a distance of 20 *actus* apart, to obtain a regular grid. The *actus*, equal to 35.48 m (116 ft), was the unit of flat measurement, calculated on the basis of the area of land along which oxen could pull

148–149 The oracular sanctuary of Fortuna Primigenia in Praeneste (now Palaestrina) is one of the most important religious complexes of the Roman period in Italy. The group of buildings was extended further and further up the hillside from the 2nd century BC *to the age of Sulla. The main section of the lower part consisted of a colonnaded room; to the left was the cave of the oracle, and on the right was another, smaller room, the floor of which was decorated with a magnificent mosaic portraying the Nile in flood, shown opposite. In the upper part of the sanctuary the architects' imagination ran riot; they invented a highly pleasing arrangement organized around three terraces culminating in a large semicircle surmounted by a* tholos. *With its extraordinary anticipation of later architectural forms, Praeneste influenced the monumental buildings of the imperial age (including the design of Trajan's Column) and the religious buildings of the colonies.*

the plough in a single stretch. A plan of the land thus divided and allocated was drawn up, and a copy was sent to Rome. The division of the land into regular areas in accordance with a system of right-angled axes had pre-Roman origins, and was widely practised in Magna Graecia and Etruria, where it had religious associations. In much of the Italian countryside today, aerial photography reveals clear signs of the division into centuries, which is still visible in the courses of local roads, canals and boundaries.

A similar method of land division was used in the foundation of new towns. The town centre was laid out on the same plan as a military camp, with a rectangular or square shape and a chessboard pattern of roads aligned parallel to the *cardo* and *decumanus*. Inside the city walls, with guard towers at regular intervals, were the forum, the basilica, thc curia, the temples, the baths, the market, the theatre and, in the most recently founded towns such as Aosta, the amphitheatre.

Despite some variations due to the lie of the land, this pattern was always followed and it had long-lasting effects on the development of many towns of Roman foundation, even after the fall of the empire. In northern Italy in particular, where Roman architects had a free hand in planning the construction of new colonies established to control conquered lands, the regularity of the road networks of many town centres reveals their ancient origins. In Turin, Aosta, Como, Pavia and Piacenza, as well as Verona, Bologna and Lucca, the right-angled grid of the Roman town remained the basis of mediaeval town planning, and even influenced more recent building. In many cases, roads crossing the surrounding countryside followed the ancient routes, with few modifications. The imposing monumental remains still visible in these provincial capitals also demonstrate their flourishing economies and quality of life, only equalled and surpassed in modern times, over thirteen centuries later.

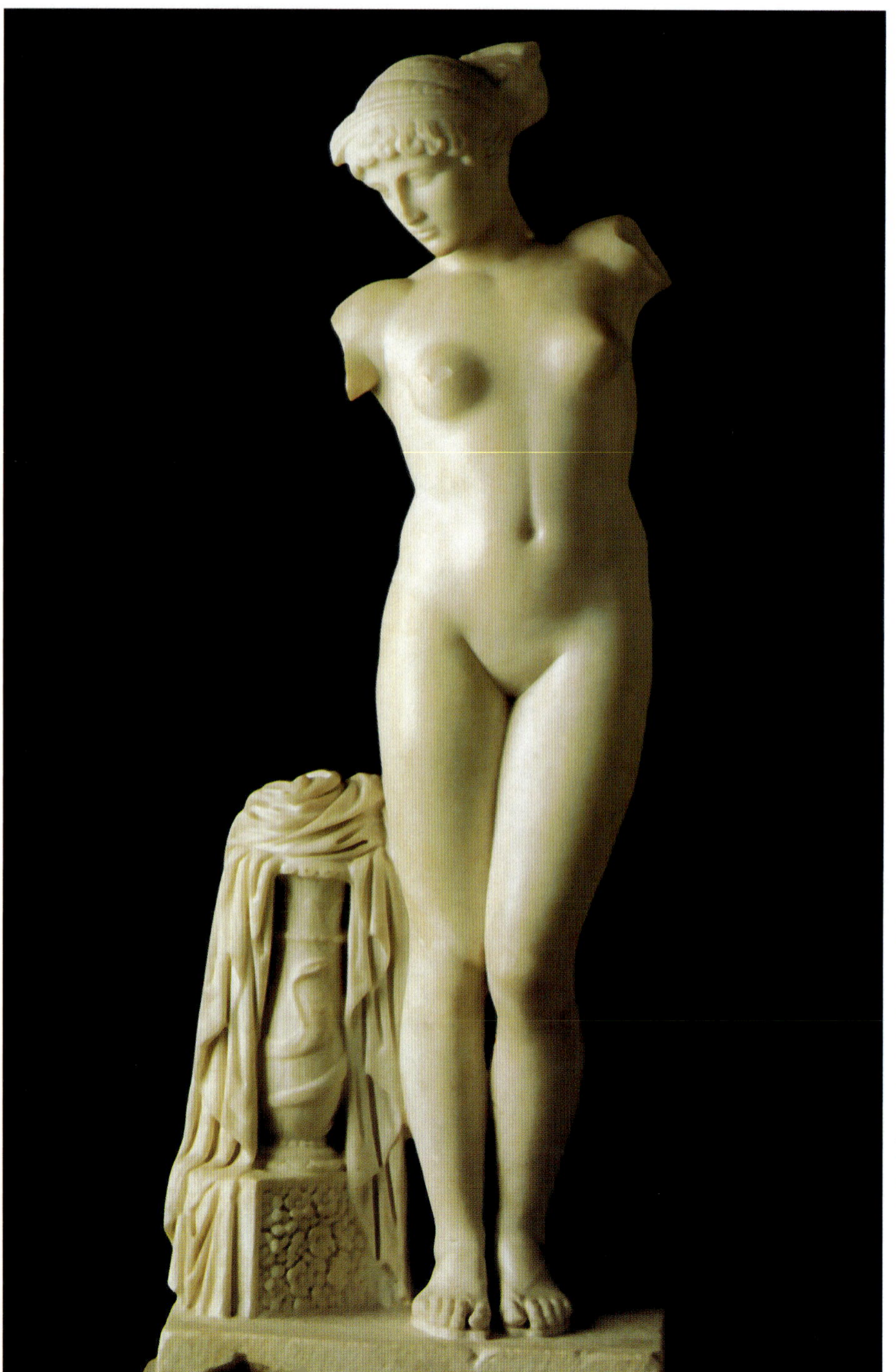

150 (left) The statue known as the Aphrodite of the Esquiline is an eclectic product, with superb results, of the last period of Hellenistic art. In this statue an archaic feel is cleverly blended with a naturalistic portrayal of the nude. Copies of Greek originals have been found in many parts of the Italian peninsula, demonstrating their great popularity. In official portraits the artists, often Greek immigrants, sometimes sculpted only the client's face in marble, and then fixed the head to mass-produced bodies inspired by famous works of the past. Wealthy Romans were enthusiastic collectors of art and antiques.

151 (opposite) This famous fresco fragment from Pompeii, dating from the 1st century AD, shows a newly married couple; the woman is holding a wax tablet, while the man holds a roll of parchment. He is considered by some to be the baker Pacuius Proculus, and by others to be an unknown city magistrate. Whoever he was, what is noteworthy is the evident wealth acquired in the early imperial age by the middle classes who, enriched by trade or public office, had become the true ruling class. The portrait also demonstrates the emancipation of Roman women, exceptional in the ancient world.

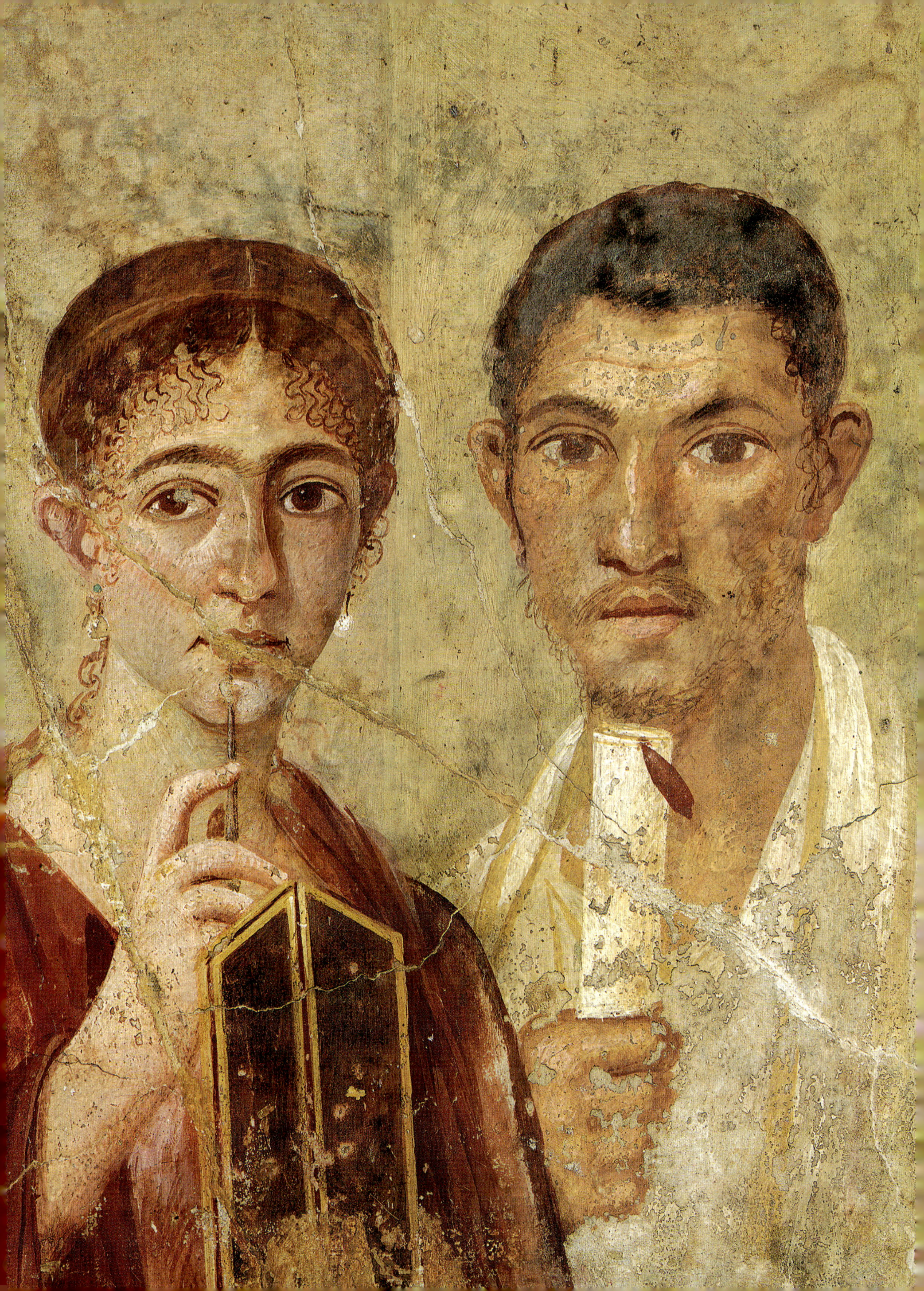

AOSTA, SENTRY AT THE FOOT OF THE ALPS

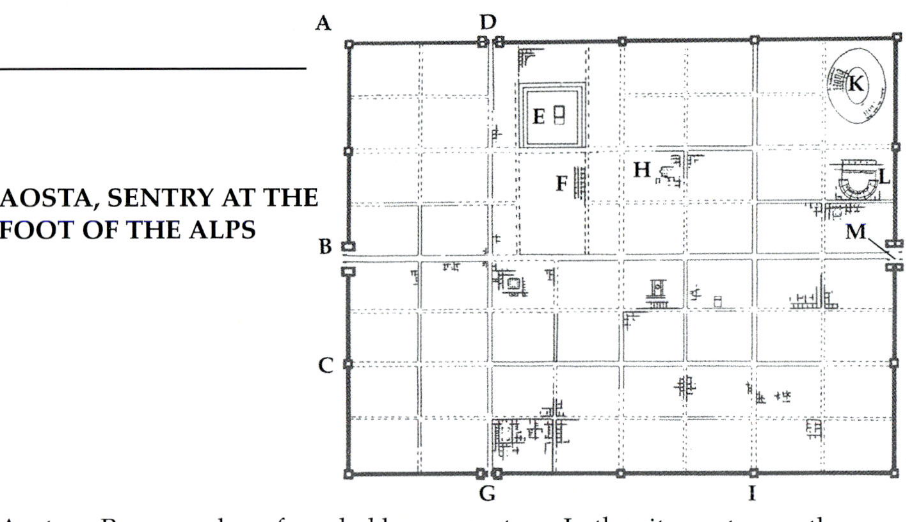

A Tourneuve
B Decumanus Gate
C Leper's Tower
D North Gate
E Sacred area
F Forum
G South Gate (Bramafam Tower)
H Baths
I Pailleron Tower
J Knight Commanders' Tower
K Amphitheatre
L Theatre
M Praetorian Gate

Aosta, a Roman colony founded by Augustus in around 24 BC and named Augusta Praetoria Salassorum, stands at the foot of the Alps, at the confluence of the Dora Baltea and Buthier, where the roads to Helvetia and Gaul began. It was built by 3000 discharged praetorians on the site of the military camp of Aulus Terentius Varro, who had quartered his troops near a major centre of the Salassi, the Celtic tribe he had been sent to vanquish.

Ancient Aosta had a very regular layout and is widely considered to be the Roman city that comes closest to the ideal model. Even today the city walls, just over 2.5 km (1.5 miles) long, seem complete, with several well-preserved towers, such as the Pailleron Tower and the Leper's Tower. The Praetorian Gate on the east side is one of the loveliest to have survived from ancient times. Consisting of two sections enclosing a huge courtyard, it has two massive square towers at the sides of a triple passage consisting of a large central supporting arch and two minor side arches. The height of the right-hand tower, now an exhibition area, was considerably increased in the 12th century. In the city centre are the remains of a temple in the area that was once the forum, surrounded by a large quadrangular cryptoporticus, an underground structure found in many forums in Gaul, probably used as a processional route.

The remains of the theatre and amphitheatre are situated not far from the gate, in the northeastern sector of the city. The grandiose back wall of the theatre auditorium, with its three tiers of arches and an intermediate row of rectangular openings, is very impressive. Excavations have brought to light various elements of the stage area, though only the lower part of a tier of steps has survived. Numerous features of the construction suggest that this was one of the few roofed theatres in the Roman world. Little remains of the amphitheatre, which, unusually, was situated inside the city walls. It was one of the first to be built in stone, a century before the Colosseum. Partly incorporated into a convent, it once held around 15,000 spectators. The triumphal arch of Augustus, standing alone not far from the Praetorian Gate, straddles the road which crossed the Buthier river on a bridge with a 17-m (56-ft) span. The arch has survived almost intact, except for the top storey which once contained the dedicatory inscription. It was probably built to commemorate the

152 (below) Among the most interesting antiquities in the Aosta Archaeological Museum is a silver bust of Jupiter Poeninus found at the Little St Bernard Pass, and a superb bronze baldric of the 2nd century AD.

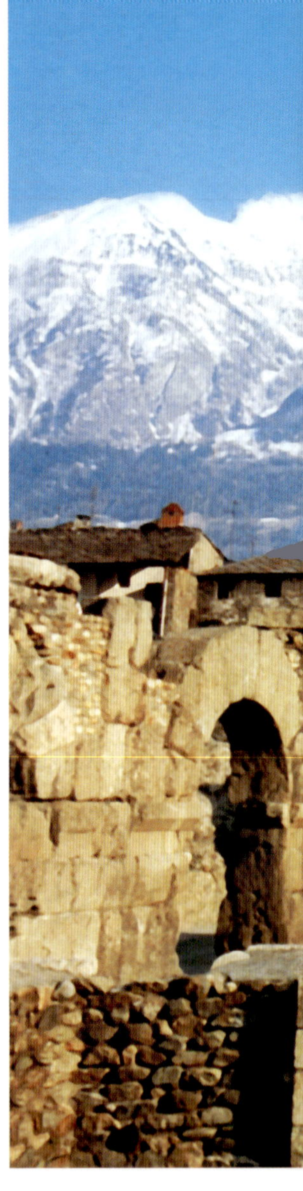

152–153 (right) Various features suggest that the theatre at Aosta, of which part of the end wall of the auditorium survives, was one of the few entirely roofed theatres in the Roman world.

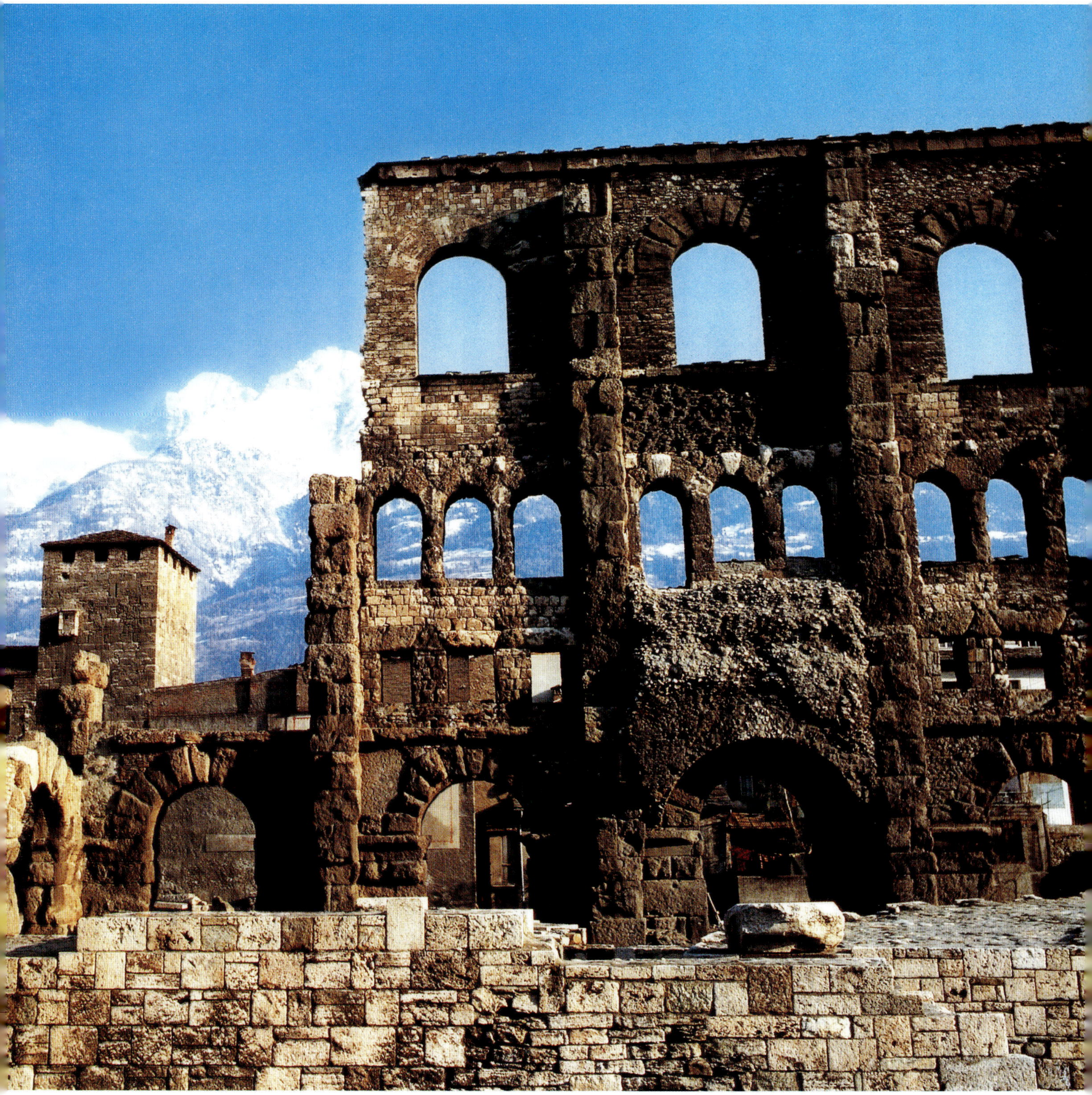

emperor's victories over the Alpine populations, especially the Salassi. It has a single supporting arch with a tall plinth on which stand half-columns, between which are rectangular niches.

Aosta is now a flourishing regional capital which, because of the remains that are perfectly assimilated into the life of the town, constitutes an area of international importance for research into Roman history and town planning.

153 (right) The Arch of Augustus at Aosta, made of carved stone blocks, is the oldest surviving freestanding arch. The construction of this impressive monument in a town relatively distant from the capital of the empire, was intended to intimidate the recently subjugated people, and to stir the pride of the new colonists.

154–155 (overleaf) Aosta, surrounded by countryside accurately divided into 'centuries', took the form of a rectangle measuring 724 x 572 m (2375 x 1876 ft). The mighty city walls guaranteed its defence, while the great public buildings met the rapidly growing population's desire for monumental constructions.

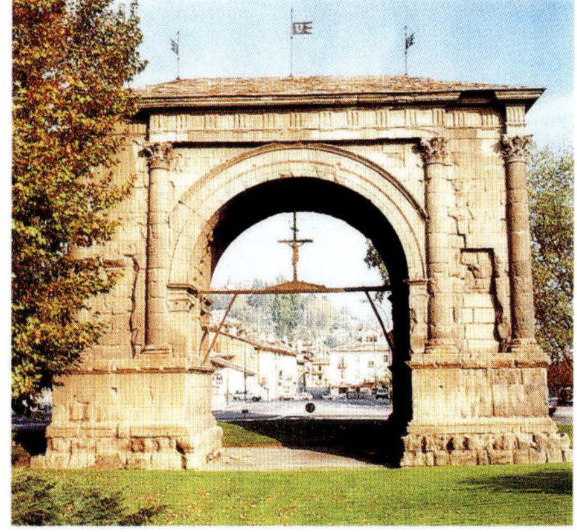

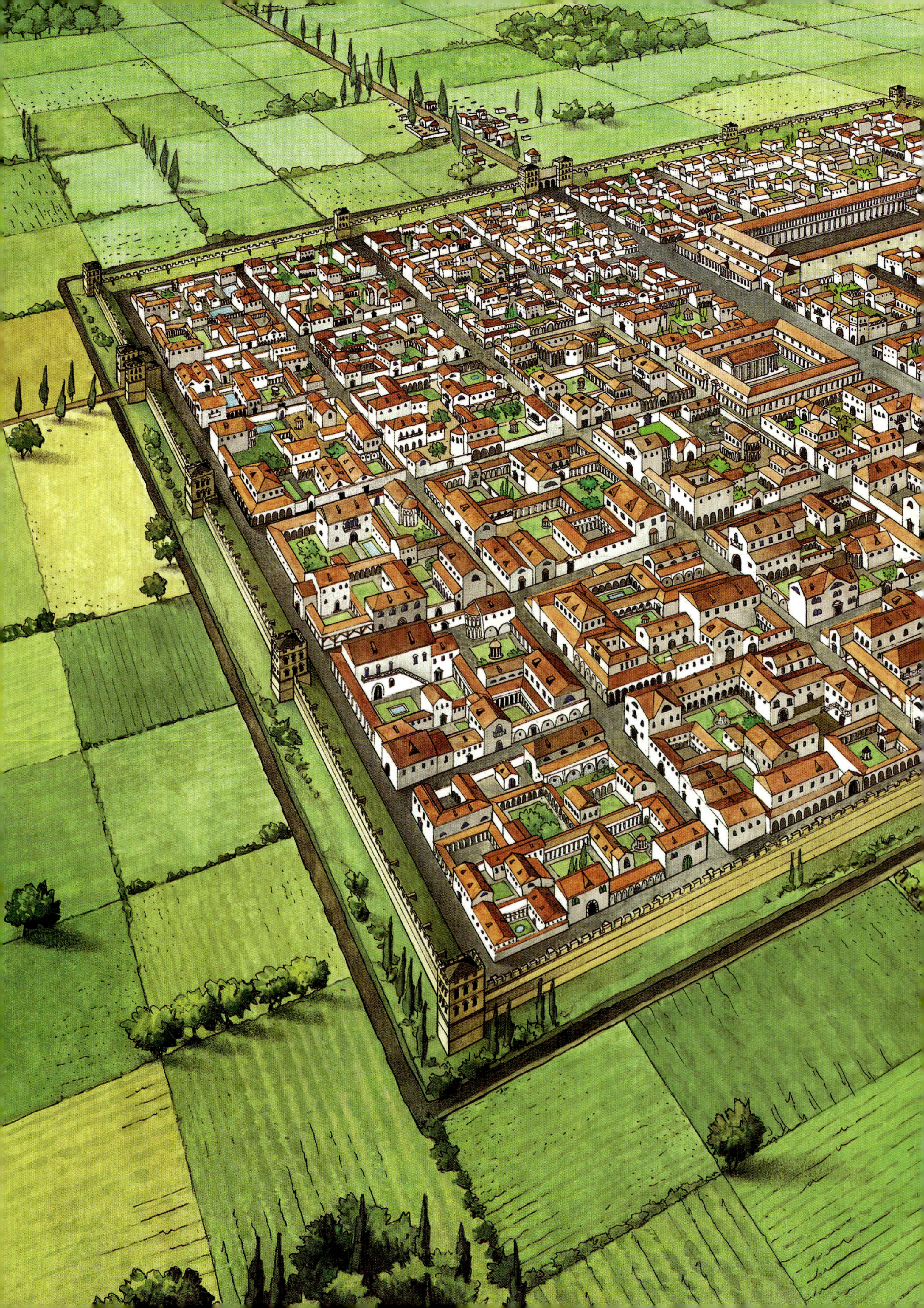

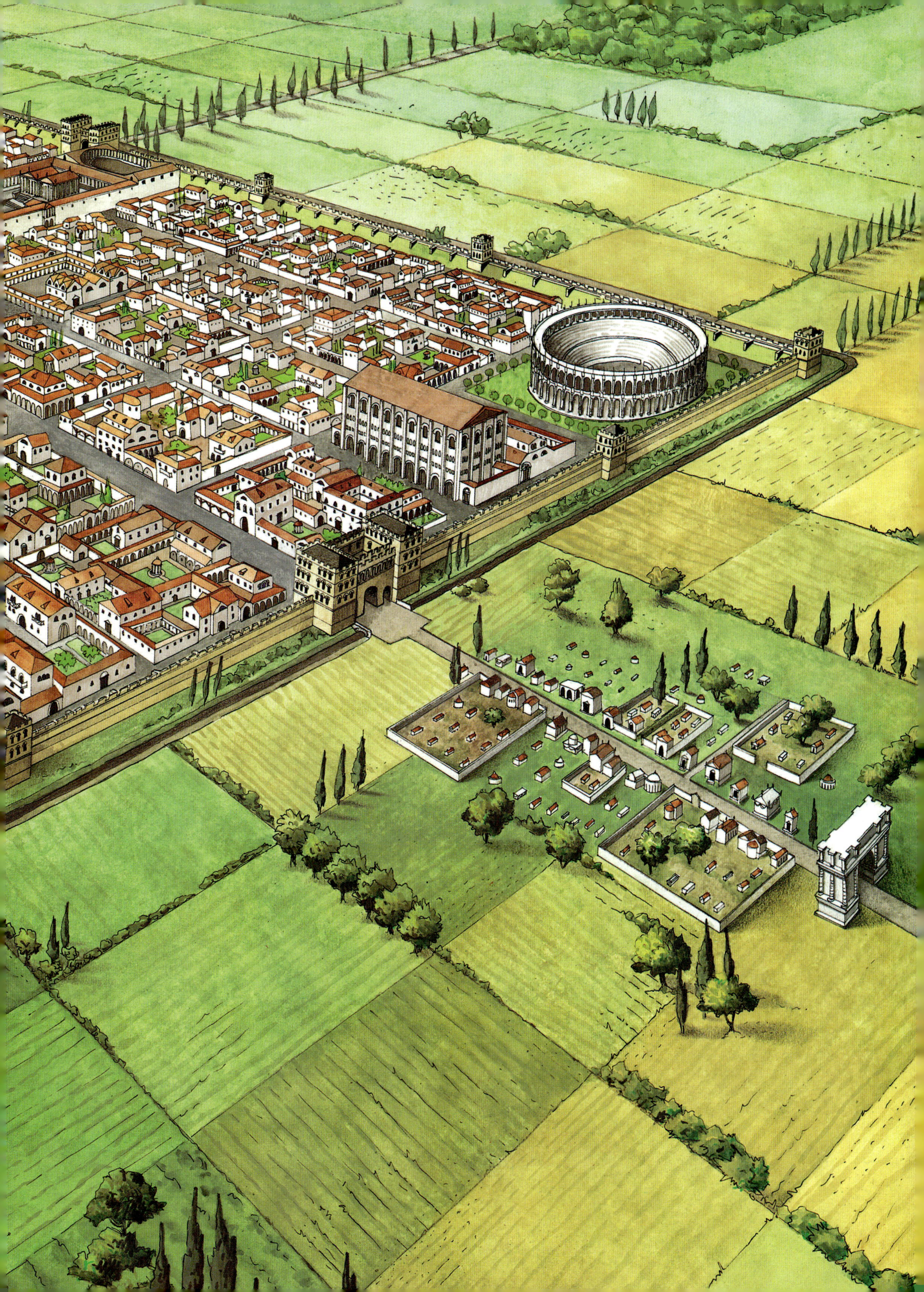

HADRIAN'S VILLA, A MAGNIFICENT IMPERIAL RESIDENCE

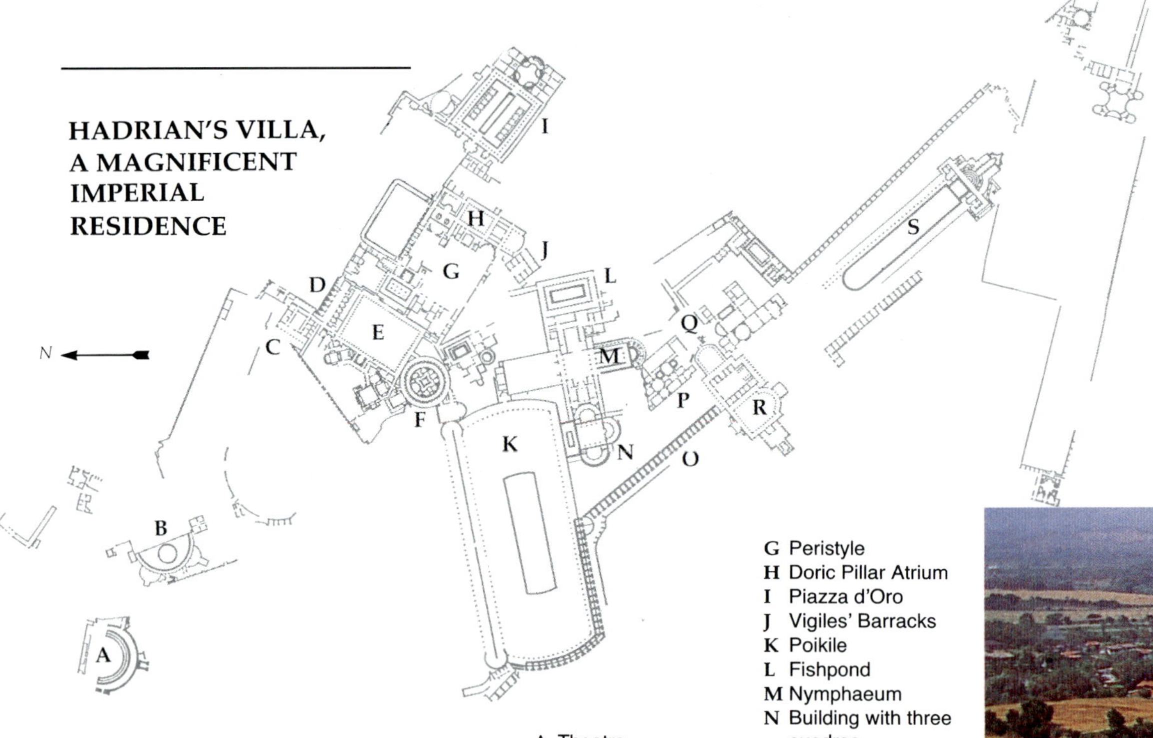

A Theatre
B Circular temple
C *Triclinia*
D *Hospitalia*
E Court of Libraries
F Maritime Theatre
G Peristyle
H Doric Pillar Atrium
I Piazza d'Oro
J Vigiles' Barracks
K Poikile
L Fishpond
M Nymphaeum
N Building with three exedrae
O 100 small rooms
P Small baths
Q Great baths
R Vestibule
S Canopus

Tivoli (the ancient Tibur) is situated to the east of Rome on the Via Valeria-Tiburtina near the Anio Falls. The city came under Roman influence early in the 5th century BC, but relations with Rome were by no means peaceful until the time of the Social War, when Tivoli became a *municipium* and obtained Roman citizenship. In the Augustan era it was one of the most fashionable resorts for wealthy Romans. Cassius, Maecenas, Horace, Quintilius Varro, Catullus, Sallust and Augustus all stayed in Tivoli, and Hadrian built his magnificent villa nearby. In addition to the natural beauty of the area there were ancient temples and sulphur baths in the plain below.

It is difficult to reconstruct the plan of the ancient city on the basis of the surviving monuments as little remains of the city walls and gates; the acropolis had its own wall. The area of the basilica and forum has been identified. On the south side of the forum are the well preserved remains of a rectangular building with a vaulted roof, probably the office for food supplies, as two *mensae ponderariae* (official standards used for measurements in trading transactions) were found there.

At the eastern end of the acropolis, facing the overhanging rock where the Anio forms the famous cascades, stand two temples: the rectangular, Ionic Temple of the Sibyl and the Temple of Vesta, which is circular with a Corinthian colonnade. Both date from the first half of the 1st century BC, and form picturesque features in their rural setting.

Outside the city walls, in the Grotta Oscura district, are the ruins of the grandiose complex known as the Sanctuary of Hercules the Victor. With its beautiful and pleasing layout, partly built on large terraces, it dates from the 1st century BC, although it was partly rebuilt in the Flavian era. This place of worship is closely linked architecturally with other contemporary sanctuaries in Latium, such as those of Jupiter Anxur in Terracina and Fortuna Primigenia in Palaestrina (Praeneste), and with the Tabularium in Rome. All are examples of the frenetic construction work carried out in the region around the mid-1st century BC.

Tivoli is now mainly famous for Hadrian's grandiose villa, situated on a large plateau on the Tiburtine Hills, to the southwest of the town.

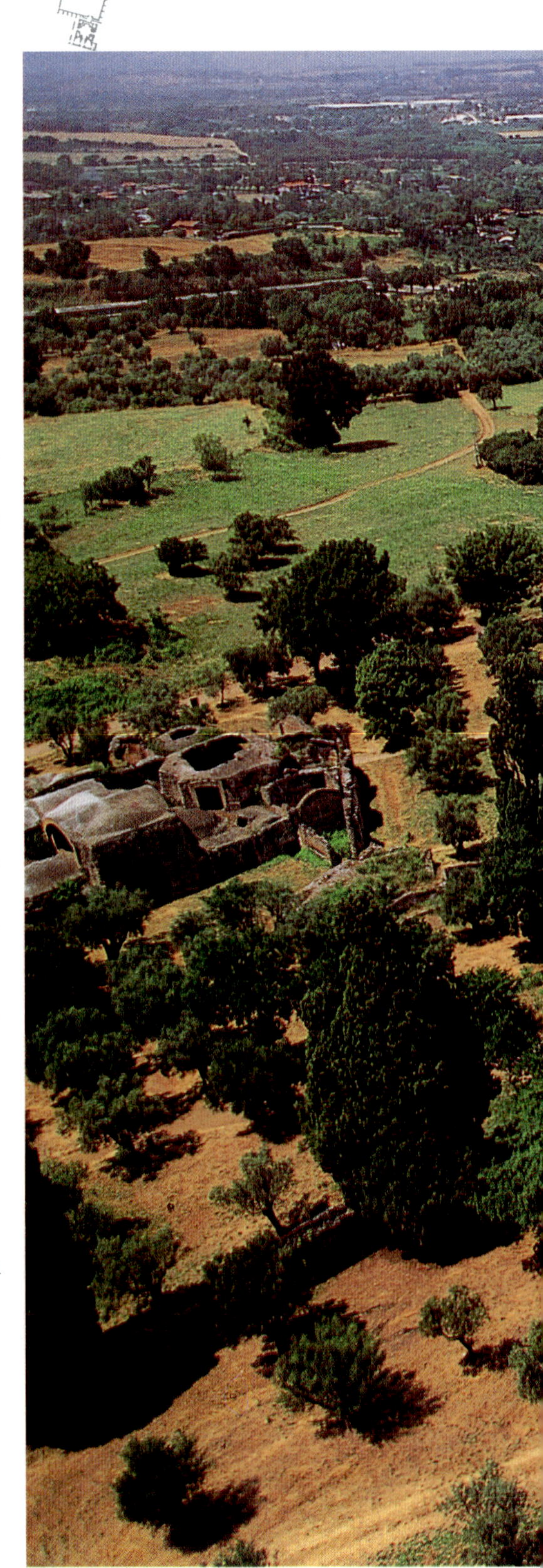

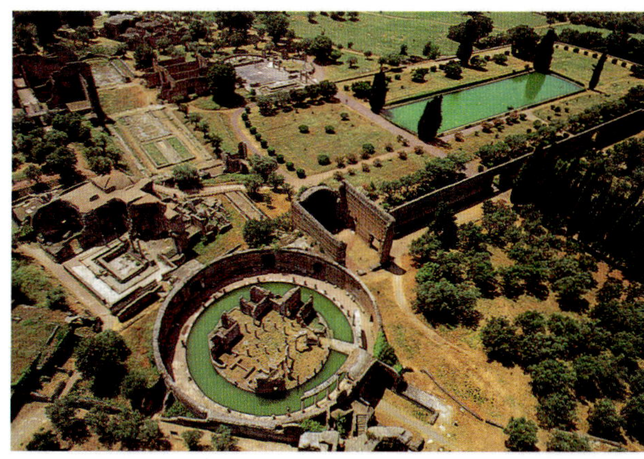

157 (left) The Maritime Theatre, surrounded by a portico and a circular canal, was actually a small villa to which Hadrian liked to retire to meditate alone, isolated from the rest of the world. The great swimming pool of the Poikile can be seen in the background.

156–157 (below) Hadrian built his villa near Tivoli between AD 118 and 133. He wished to recreate the places and monuments he had visited during his long travels. In the foreground are the ruins of the four-sided portico and what is called the fish-pond.

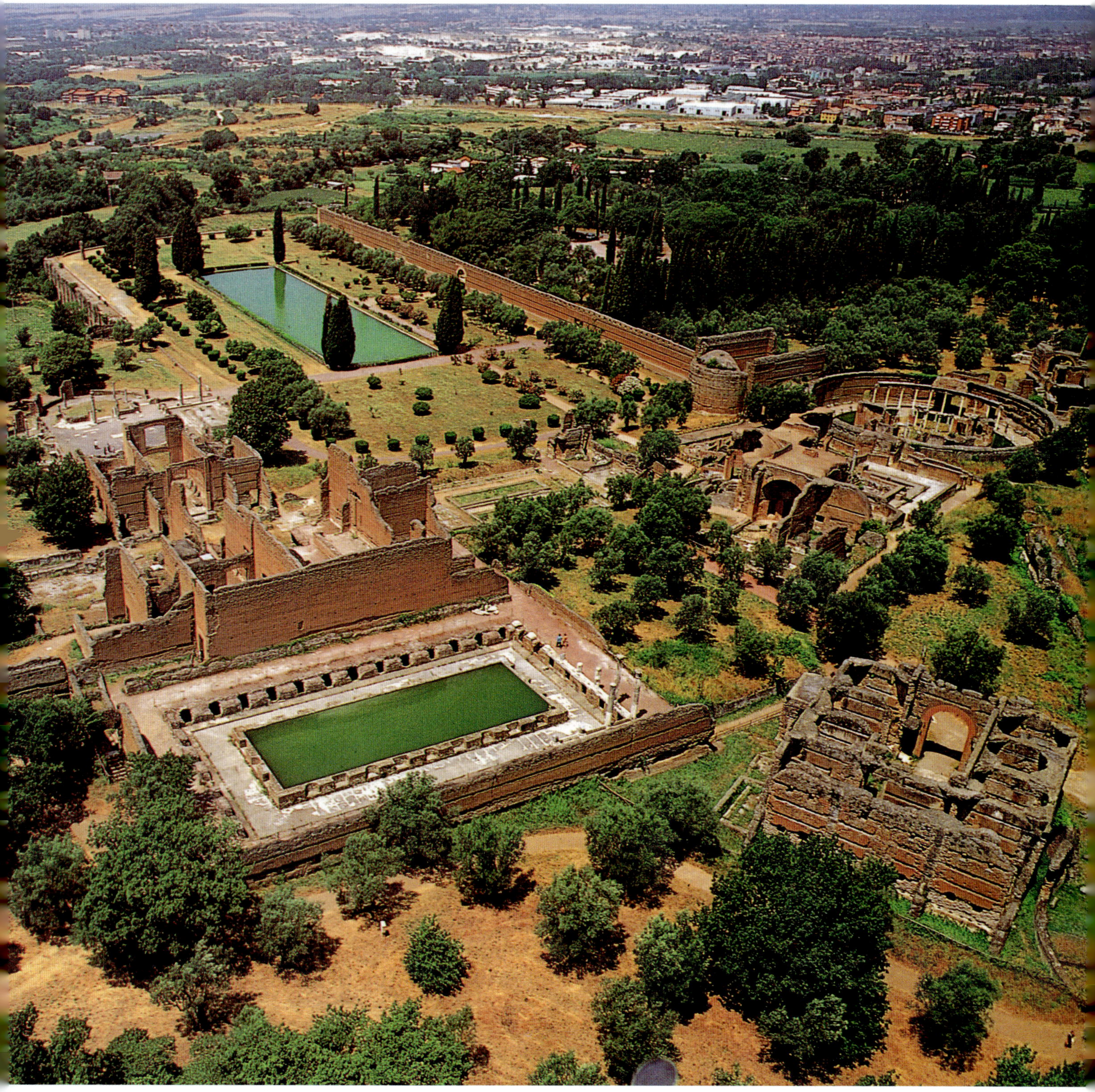

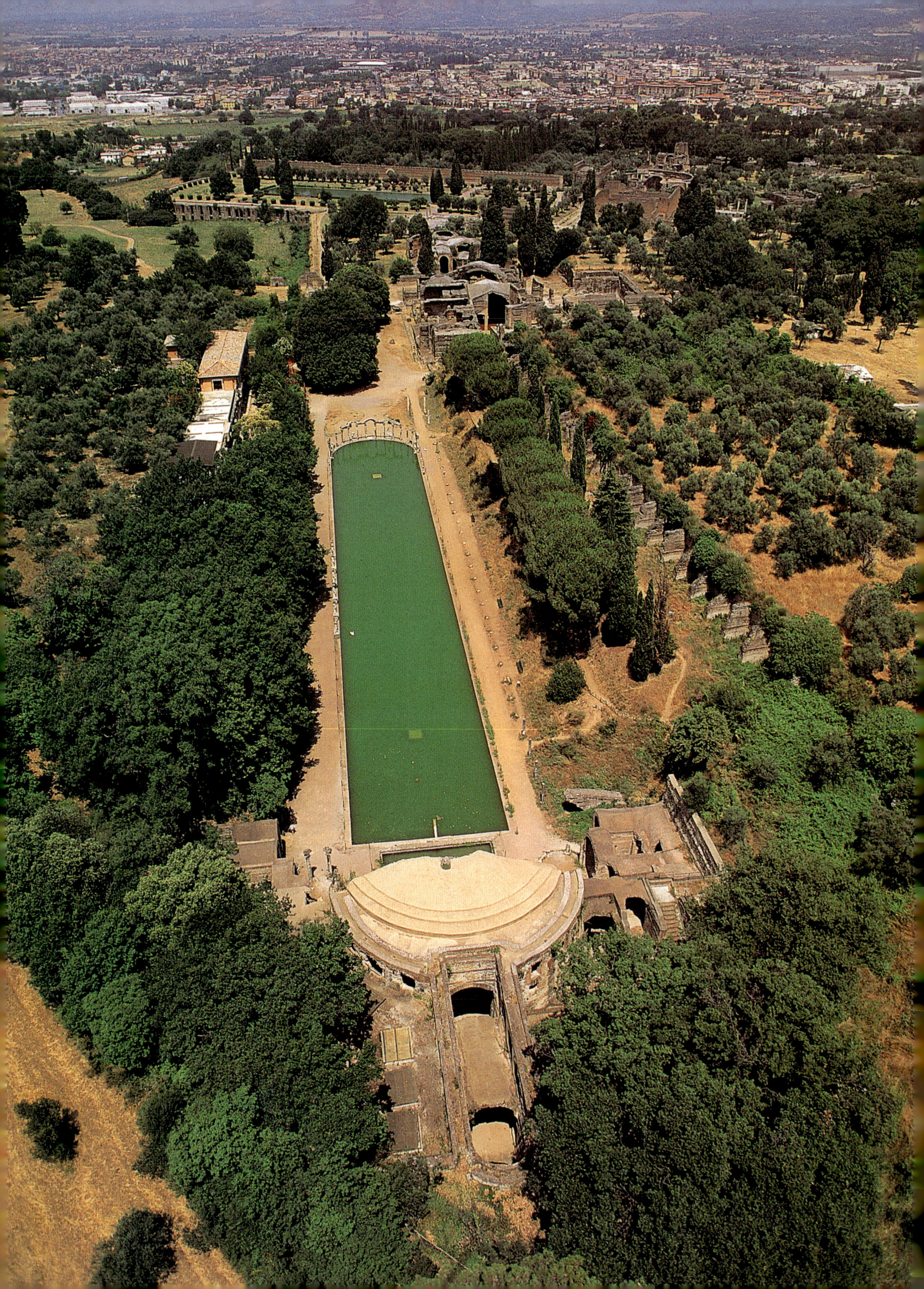

A huge complex of buildings, covering a site of some 120 ha (297 acres), it is one of the most interesting monuments in Italy. Built on a site previously occupied by a villa of the republican period, it fits perfectly into the surrounding landscape, apparently naturally but in fact following a precise design. Hadrian, a great admirer of the Hellenistic tradition, continued a practice introduced in the republican period of drawing on famous models for inspiration. When building his residence, therefore, he freely imitated places and monuments which had made the greatest impression on him on his travels through the empire.

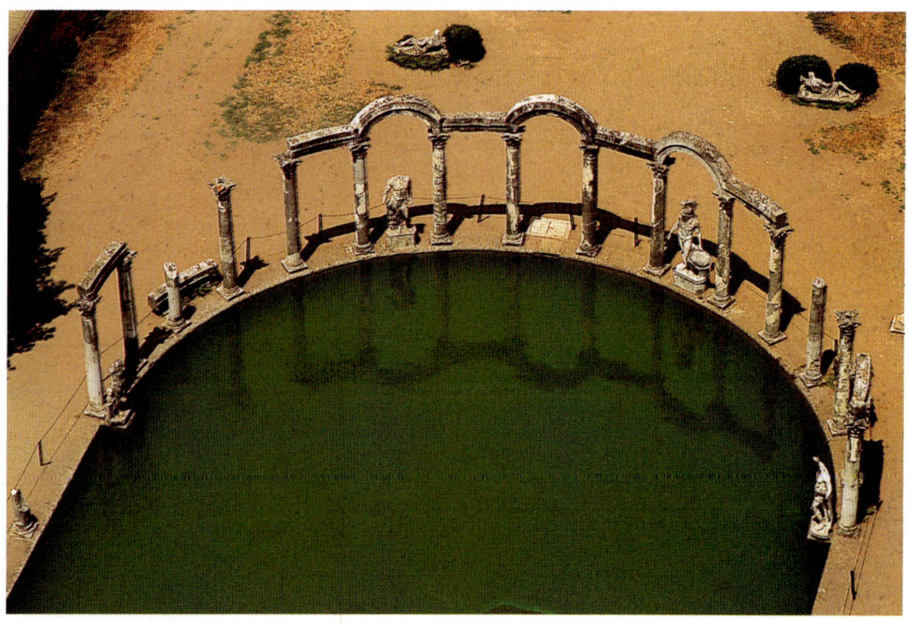

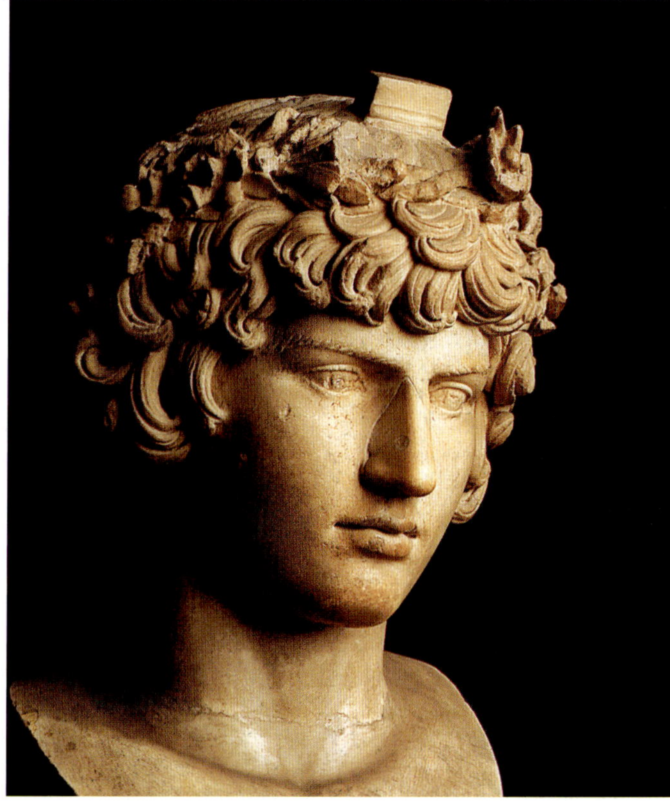

158 (opposite) Hadrian, a highly cultivated man, was keenly interested in art and architecture. This is evident in the layout of the Canopus, the most attractive part of the villa, which occupies an artificial valley to the south of the complex. The monument was designed to reproduce the Temple of Serapis at Canopus, in Egypt, and the canal which connected that town to Alexandria. The half-dome of the Serapeum stands out in the foreground.

159 (top) Around the edge of the pool in the centre of the Canopus was an elegant colonnade where numerous copies of famous Greek statues stood, including four copies of caryatids from the Erechtheum in Athens.

Hadrian's Villa is particularly famous for the number and variety of architectural forms represented, in particular the great range of vaulted ceilings, together with an interesting use of light and visual effects. Numerous sculptures, including the caryatids from the Canopus, imitating those of the Erechtheum in Athens, and other copies of originals by Pheidias and Polykleitos, have been brought to light by excavations. The complex was built between AD 118 and 133, with work initially limited to restructuring and extending existing buildings, to which baths, a gymnasium and a hall for official banquets were added. Everything else was built gradually, as the villa acquired its final monumental aspect. The entire area was served by a system of underground passages (some large enough for carts), designed to provide an independent service network, kept carefully separate from the luxurious upper levels.

The main access to the villa was on the north side, served by a road leading off the Via Tiburtina which ran alongside the Vale of Tempe, so called because it resembled the famous place of that name in Thessaly. Here stood the *Hospitalia*, a building used as dormitory for the

159 (left) Antinous was Hadrian's favourite who drowned in the Nile (perhaps intentionally) during a trip to Egypt. Numerous statues of him have been found in the Canopus area. Hadrian was consumed with passion for this young Bithynian, and deified him after his death. Some consider that the emperor's affection was aroused more by the sad, sensual beauty of the boy, which may have appealed to Hadrian's aesthetic, melancholy spirit, than by physical attraction. However it may be, in the classical period homosexual love was not considered scandalous; on the contrary, it was lauded by many poets.

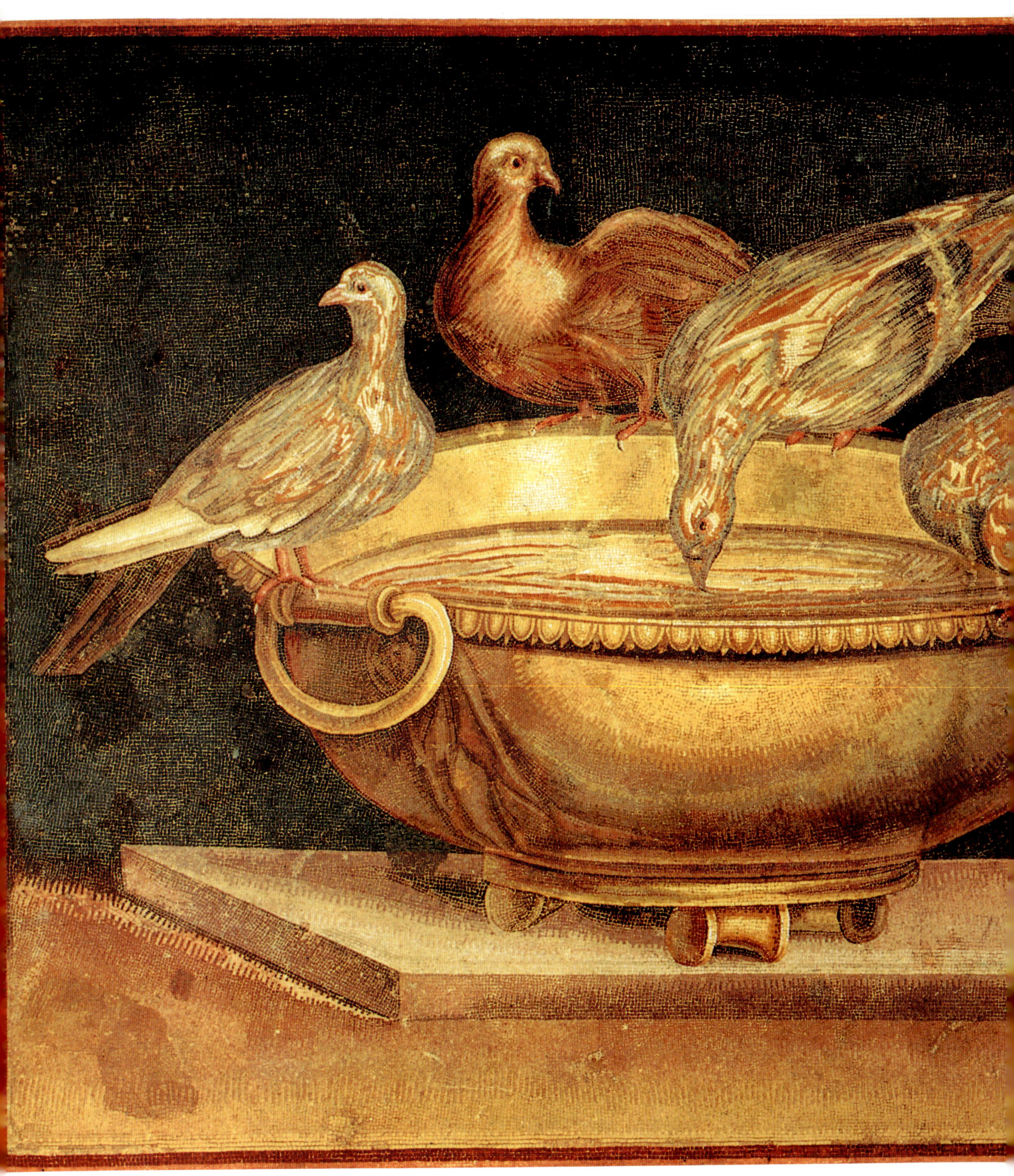

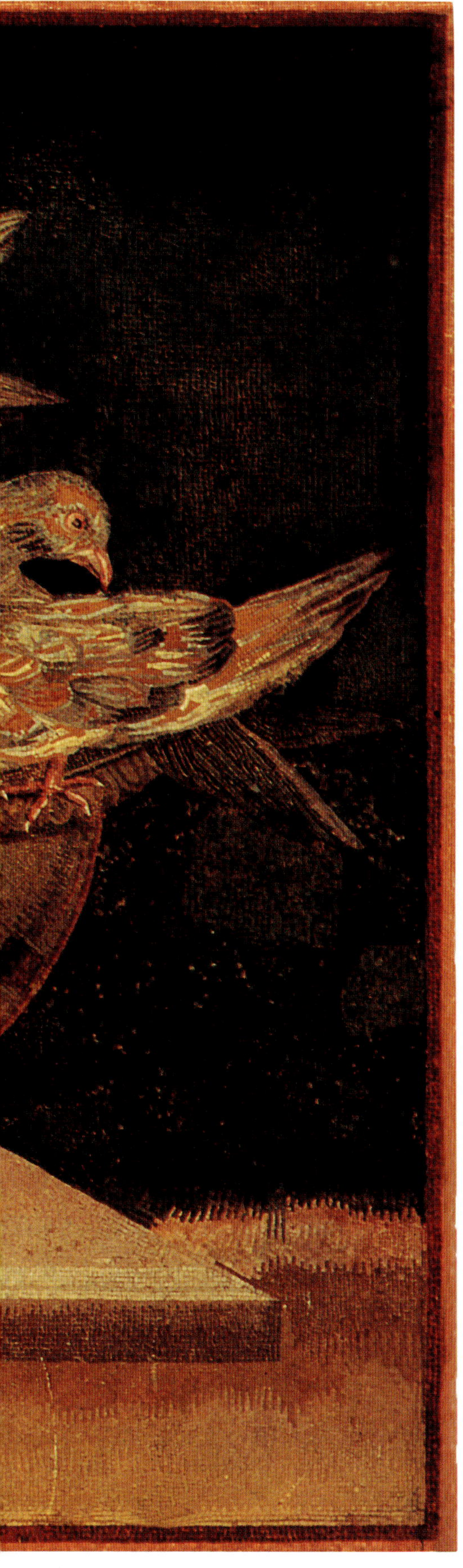

praetorians guarding the entrance. Nearby are two rooms known as libraries but which are summer *triclinia*, part of the older section of the building. One of the most attractive elements of the complex is the Maritime Theatre, which is reached through one of these rooms. A circular retaining wall with an inward-facing portico separates it from the rest of the villa. In the centre, a canal surrounded a circular islet, once reached by two small bridges. On this artificial island was a miniature villa designed for rest and seclusion, built around a courtyard with a fountain, and with its own small bath-house. Models are probably the residence of Augustus on the Palatine Hill, and, earlier still, the palace of Dionysius the Elder in Syracuse.

Beyond the Maritime Theatre is the central part of the villa, comprising the Court of the Libraries, the Palazzo, the Nymphaeum, the Doric Pillar Atrium with the barracks of the Vigiles at the side, and finally, the Piazza d'Oro, surrounded by a large peristyle and a portico with two aisles. The Doric Pillar Atrium, actually a basilica, leads to the Throne Room, a kind of palatial hall, used for solemn sessions of the imperial court. On the north side of the Piazza is a vestibule, octagonal in plan, the roof of which constitutes an outstanding example of a segmental dome. On the south side is a large, semicircular nymphaeum, possibly a summer *triclinium*. The Poikile is a large piazza surrounded by porticoes which formed a kind of *xystus* (a place for walks and learned conversation which formed an integral part of the gymnasia of Greek inspiration). It is built on to the west wall of the Philosophers' Room, near the Maritime Theatre. To the east is another set of buildings, including the so-called Stadium, and the summer *cenatio* (a dining room for official banquets).

The suite of rooms which follows includes the Small and Large Baths, the Vestibule and the Canopus, one of the most famous buildings of the ancient world. It occupies a long, narrow valley and consists of a canal with one rounded end lined by a colonnade with an architrave alternately arched and flat. Along the two longer sides run other colonnades, originally embellished with copies of famous Greek statues. The valley is closed by the Serapeum, a large semicircular apse or *exedra* surmounted by a half-dome with alternate flat and concave segments. A huge, Σ-shaped couch identifies the building as an elegant and impressive summer *cenatio*. Its plan is inspired by Egyptian temples and fits in with the adjacent lake. In antiquity Alexandria was linked by a canal to the city of Canopus, where a Temple of Serapis stood. The canal and town were famous for parties and banquets, an echo of which is visible in the Nile mosaic at Palaestrina. Antinous, the handsome youth who was Hadrian's favourite, drowned at Canopus, and Hadrian fell into a black despair. It is thus no coincidence that the loveliest statues of the young man were found here.

160–161 This exquisite mosaic from Hadrian's Villa is a copy of an original by Sosos of Pergamum, a Greek artist much admired by Pliny. The art of mosaics, imported from the Hellenistic world, was very popular among the Romans, and reached a high level of refinement during the imperial age. From the 2nd century AD *artists became so accomplished that they could compete with painters, seeking ever more subtle shades of expression. There were various styles and trends, but the main types were geometric and figurative and naturalistic. The tesserae were cubes made of stone or coloured glass paste, depending on how they were to be used. They were fixed to the backing with a layer of adhesive mortar on which the basic design was drawn out. The various kinds of wall and floor mosaics included* opus vermiculatum, *which used very small pieces and a wide range of colours to achieve highly detailed and delicate work, and* opus sectile, *which was made with larger, irregular, coloured marble pieces.*

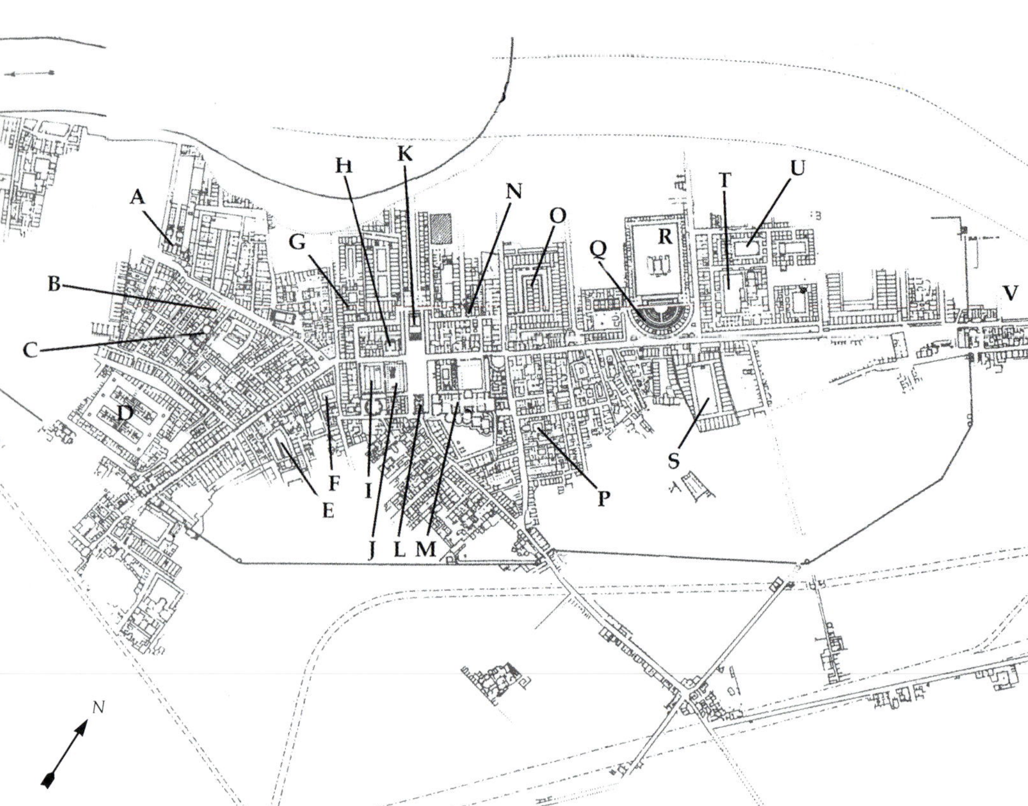

ANCIENT OSTIA

A Markets of Trajan
B House of Serapis
C Baths of the Seven Seers
D Houses with garden
E Schola of Trajan
F Macellum
G Horrea Epagathiana
H Curia
I Round Temple
J Basilica
K Capitolium
L Temple of Rome and Augustus
M Forum Baths
N House of Diana
O Large Horrea
P Domus of Fortuna Annonaria
Q Theatre
R Piazzale delle Corporazioni
S Horrea of Hortensius
T Baths of Neptune
U Vigiles' Barracks
V Porta Romana necropolis

The name of Ostia, the ancient port of Rome, derives from the word *ostium*, meaning entrance, as it was near the mouth of the River Tiber. According to tradition it was founded by Ancus Martius, but the oldest remains date from the early 4th century BC and relate to the original nucleus of the Roman colony. The town, built as a typical military camp (*castrum*) enclosed by rectangular walls and intersected by two perpendicular main roads, probably already had temples but no forum. In the mid-republican age Ostia was still basically a military outpost by the sea, although its port already played an essential role in guaranteeing Rome's corn supplies.

During the Punic Wars it served as a base for naval operations against Carthage and at one time had a permanent detachment of 30 ships. As with many other towns in Latium, Ostia was transformed from a military camp to a trading town during the republic, in the age of Sulla. The new city walls enclosed an area of some 69 ha (170 acres), 30 times the size of the original *castrum*, which increased slightly in the imperial age. This period saw a great construction boom, partly due to the introduction of new building techniques which were gradually adapted to the requirements of increasingly complex architecture. Many temples were built, including the grandiose Temple of Hercules. Homes of wealthy families – the typical Hellenistic-Roman *domus* with an atrium and, in the wealthier houses, a peristyle – were built along the main roads. In Ostia, unlike Rome, private houses have survived almost intact, so that their variety and development can be traced. The two basic types were the *domus* (a single-family house) and the *insula* (a large multistorey tenement block) which, from the 1st century BC, had *tabernae* (shops) on the ground floor selling all kinds of goods.

In the Augustan period Ostia also benefited from the great renovation taking place in Rome designed to enhance the dignity of the town. The important Temple of Rome and Augustus was built near the forum; with its elegant marble decoration, symbolizing a new architectural vision, it was the forerunner of the great monuments of the imperial age. The theatre, dating from the same period and influenced by similar buildings erected by Pompey

162–163 Ostia, once situated at the mouth of the Tiber on the coast, now lies several kilometres inland. It was the main port of Rome until the 2nd century AD, when it was gradually supplanted by the nearby Portus Romae. In the imperial age it was a rich, cosmopolitan city populated by a busy class of traders and businessmen; once abandoned it fell into ruin and was covered by the silts of the Tiber. It is now one of the most important archaeological sites in Italy.

163 (opposite, above) The great hexagonal port excavated by Trajan to extend one built by Claudius which was silting up, still survives, not far from Fiumicino airport. The new port area developed rapidly, attracting some of the workers from Ostia who soon moved there, founding a new town which was called Portus. Trajan's port covered an area of 32 ha (80 acres).

PORT OF TRAJAN

1 Port of Claudius (AD 42–64)
2 Lighthouse
3 Port of Trajan (AD 100–112)
4 Navigable canal
5 Course of the Tiber
6 Isola Sacra
7 Necropolis

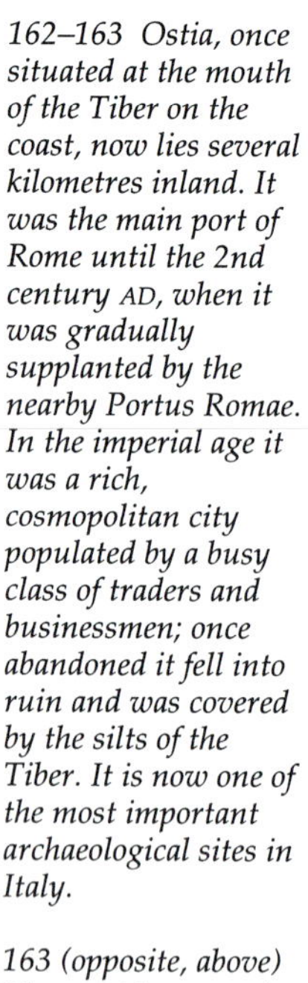

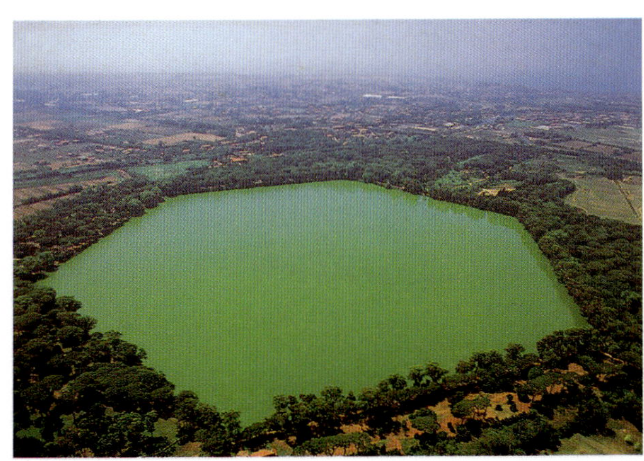

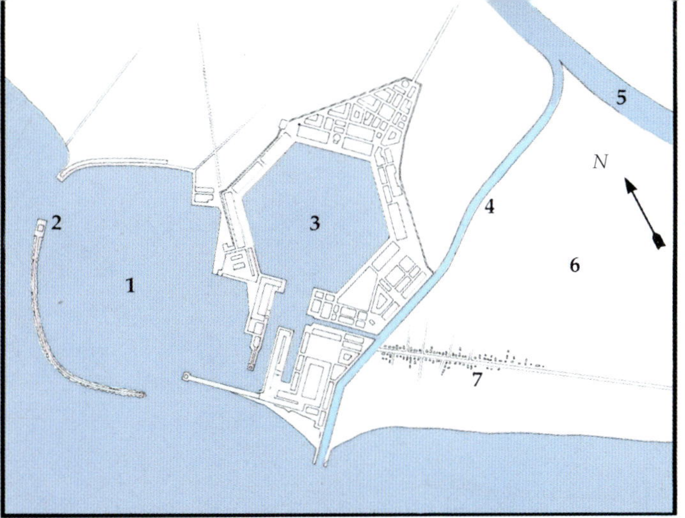
5
N
2
3
4
6
1
7

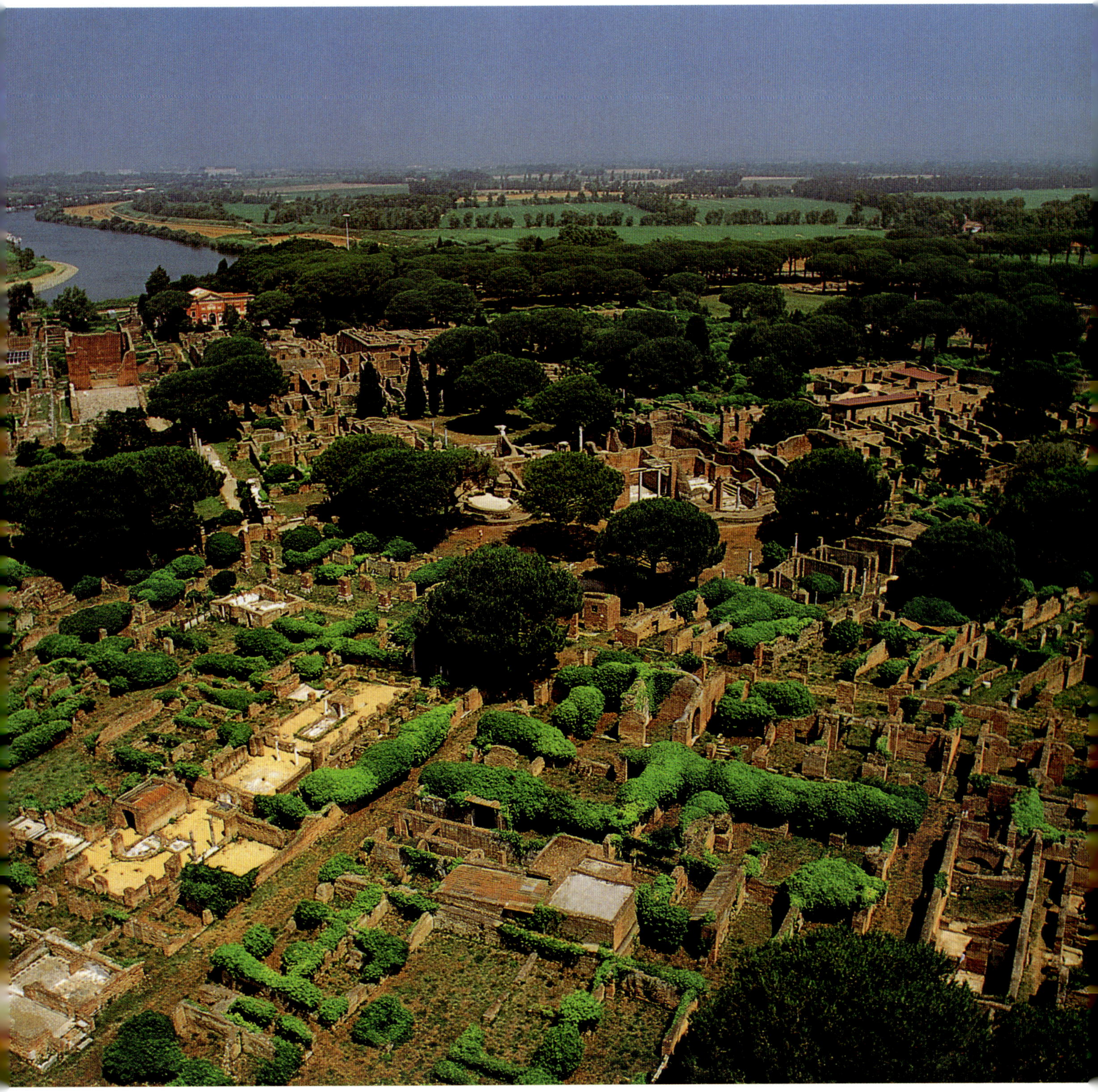

164 (below) The Piazzale delle Corporazioni was a huge quadrangular area surrounded on three sides by a portico in which the offices of trading and shipping companies were based; their businesses were advertised by mosaic signs.

164 (below, right) Ostia's theatre dates from the age of Augustus but was totally rebuilt under Septimius Severus. The auditorium, like the outer portico, was entirely reconstructed following modern excavations. Behind what remains of the scaena stands the Piazzale delle Corporazioni.

164–165 (right) Excavations at Ostia have uncovered numerous exquisite mosaic floors which decorated both public buildings and private homes.

and Marcellus, could hold 3000 spectators. Together with the Piazzale delle Corporazioni behind it, the theatre formed a magnificent complex. Increasing numbers of *horrea* (for storing corn and other goods) were built in various districts, demonstrating the growth of trading activity. Under Tiberius and Caligula Ostia was provided with an aqueduct, which allowed the construction of various baths.

Claudius ordered the creation of a port a few miles north of the mouth of the Tiber. Until then, the town's sea trade had been seriously hampered by the difficulty of access to the river port because of the treacherous sandbanks at the mouth of the Tiber. Large-scale urban renovation, necessitated by a constantly growing population, began in the reign of Domitian and was completed by Trajan. Trajan also had a large, perfectly hexagonal basin dug in addition to that built by Claudius, which was beginning to silt up, thus solving the problem of the port of Rome. The modern structure finally enabled the huge

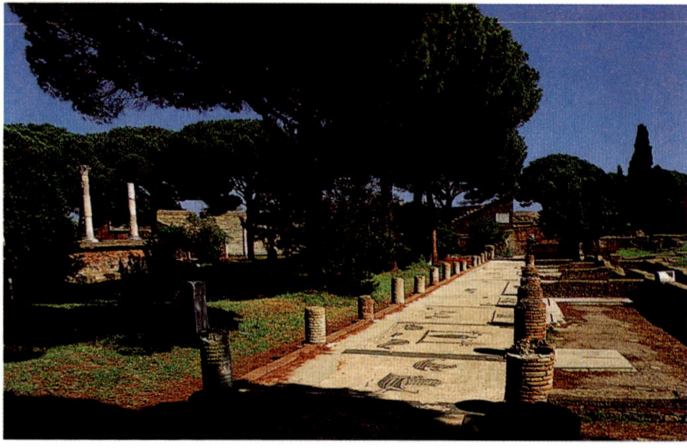

merchant ships of the Alexandrian fleet, which carried 150,000 tons of corn a year, and other ships which traded with the east, to dock at the mouth of the Tiber instead of Pozzuoli, near Naples, which until then had been the main port on Italy's Tyrrhenian Sea.

The small independent town which developed around the new dock was called Portus. Trajan also constructed a curia and a basilica in the forum, as well as numerous baths. At this time the town acquired a largely commercial role. Those products which could not immediately be absorbed by the Roman market, such as corn, oil and wine, were stored at Ostia. The cargoes of the great merchant ships were transferred to smaller boats (*codicariae*), which were towed up the Tiber to Rome by teams of oxen. Merchants were divided into guilds, which defended and promoted the interests of the various trades. Each had a headquarters (*schola*), where it held meetings and ceremonies.

Hadrian, like his predecessor, reorganized the town, giving the forum its final appearance; he built the great Capitolium (which stood between two wings of colonnades, like the Temple of Rome and Augustus in front of it) and constructed a residential district with services including the Baths of Neptune and the barracks of the Vigiles. The Garden House complex, built in a luxury residential district, also dates from this period.

The *domus*, symbols of the old aristocracy, were demolished in many districts to make room for tenement blocks for the up-and-coming new class consisting not only of rich, powerful traders but also of clerical and manual workers. This type of residence developed with the increasing use of brick and concrete which allowed the creation of innovative architectural forms. Numerous buildings survive, including the densely occupied, working-class dwellings. These had porticoed courtyards, around which the various rooms, often decorated with mosaics, were arranged. The

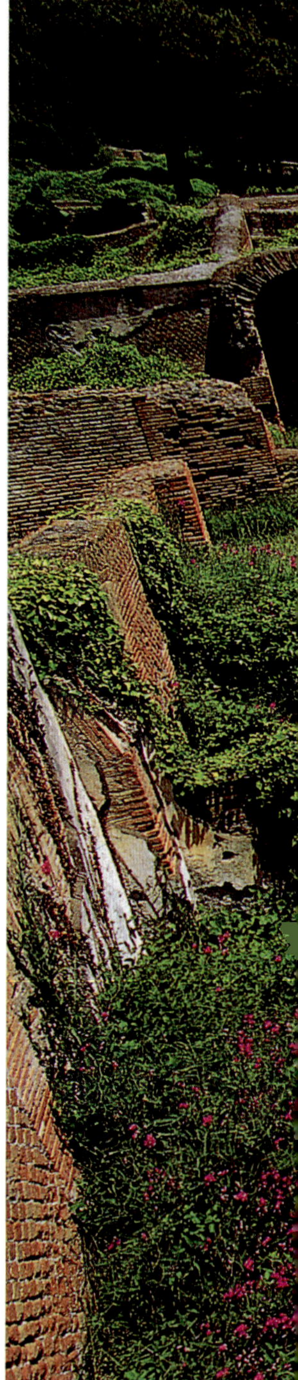

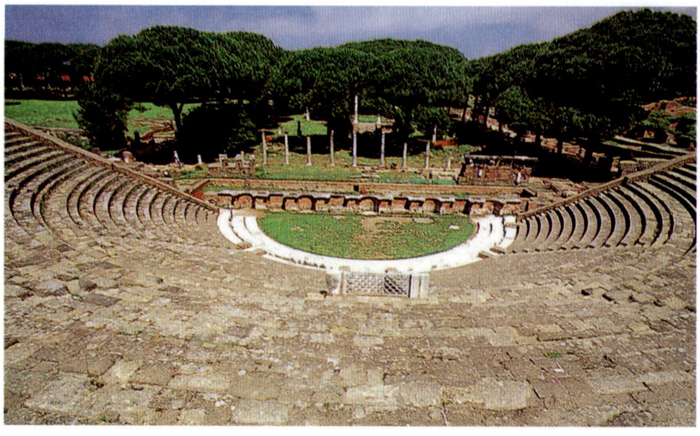

165 (opposite, below left) Many of the domus built in Ostia in the late imperial age were richly decorated.

165 (opposite, below right) In the middle of the forum stand the ruins of Hadrian's Capitolium (the largest temple in the city) dedicated to Jupiter, Juno and Minerva.

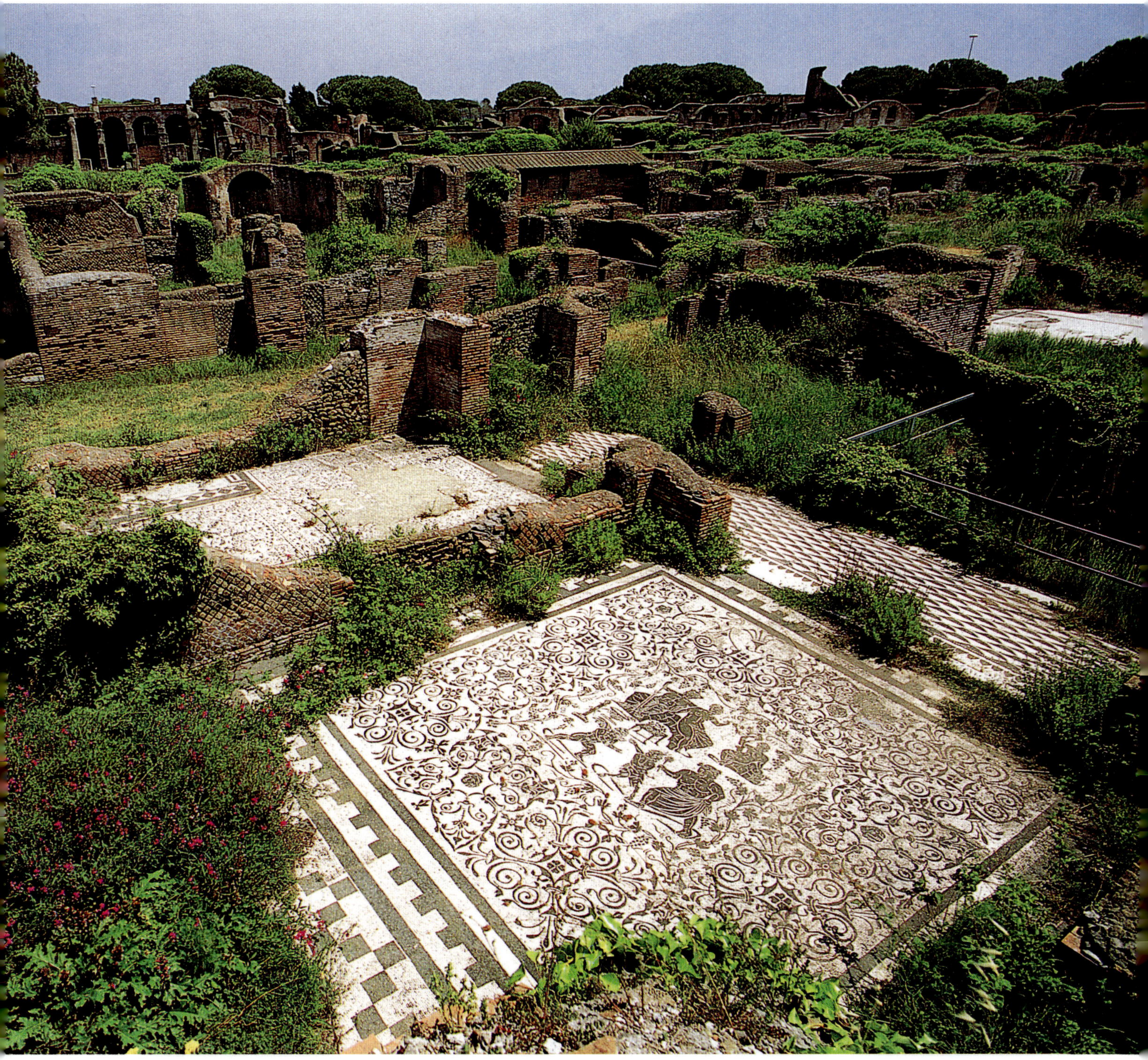

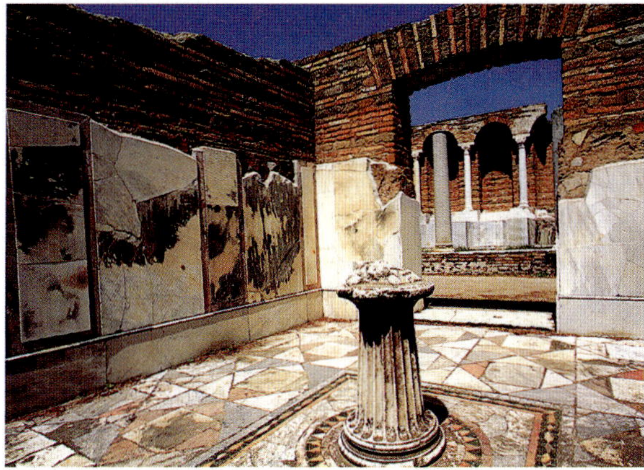

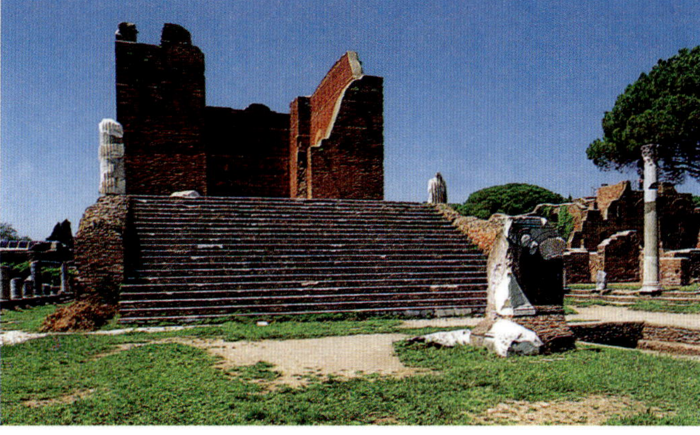

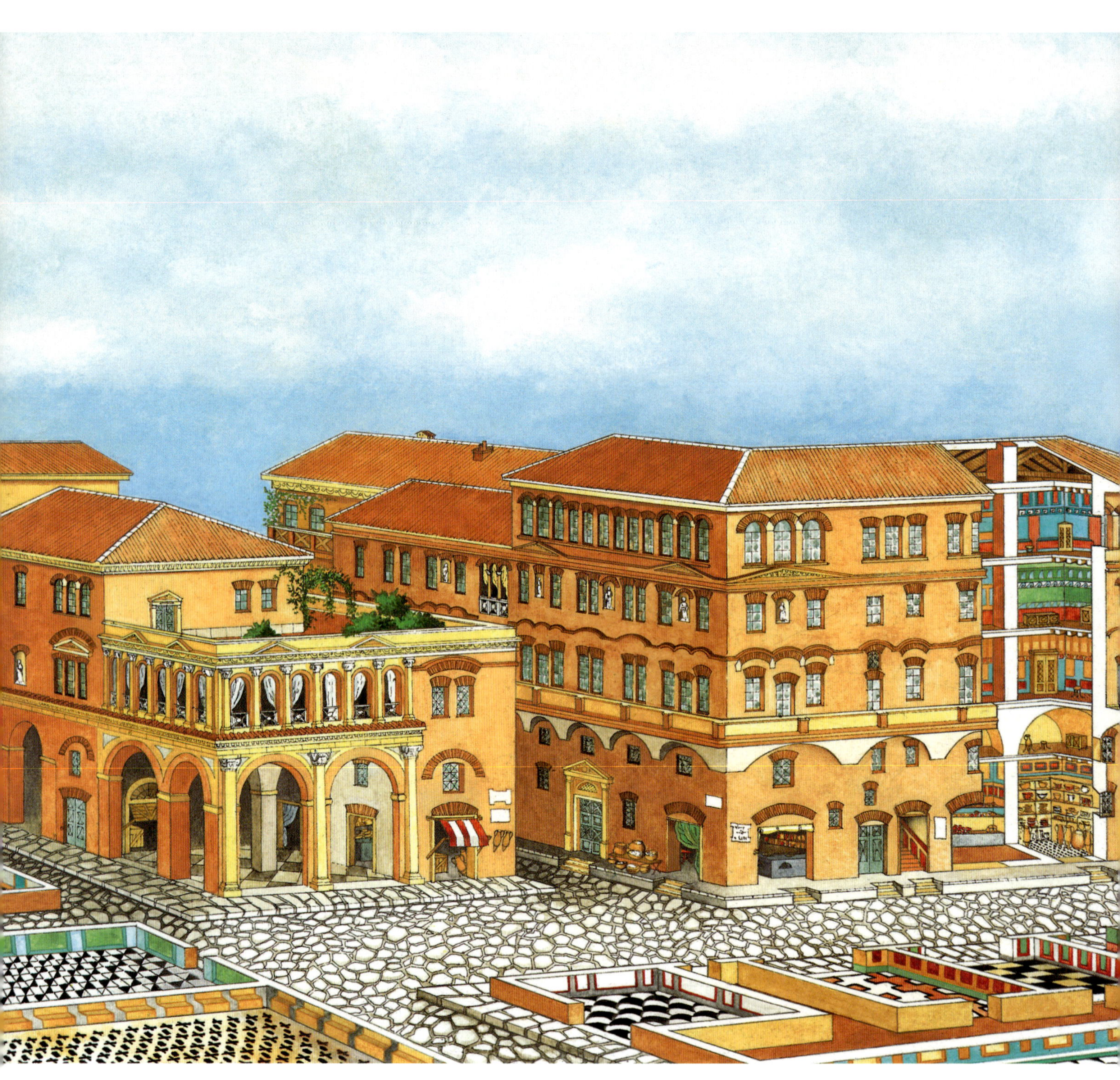

166–167 Various types of urban dwelling can be found in Ostia. In particular the insula, *which, with its appearance and the layout of living areas within it, can be said to be the forerunner of the modern apartment block, was very common and is well documented there. It usually had four or five floors, with the main façade on the road side and the secondary façade overlooking an inner courtyard or garden; there were numerous windows and balconies. Staircases led to the various apartments* (cenacula), *the entrances to which opened on to inner landings. The toilets were sometimes shared; they were usually situated on the ground floor or in suitable small rooms in the apartments, and served by the same sewage pipe. The* insulae *of Ostia, mainly for the middle classes, offered some degree of luxury; they were spacious and airy, decorated with wall paintings and mosaics, and possibly had running water, even on the upper floors. In some cases the remains of bath tubs have been found near the room used as a kitchen. This reconstruction is of the House of Diana and surrounding buildings. The ground floor was occupied by a row of shops; their attics, lighted by small windows let into the façade, were occupied by the owners. The decoration of the upper rooms is based on remains found in other* insulae *at Ostia, frequently consisting of simple squares of colour, interspersed with a few, rare figures or geometric patterns. The cross-sections of the structures opposite are not actual ones, but are intended to give a sample of wall and floor decorations found in Ostia.*

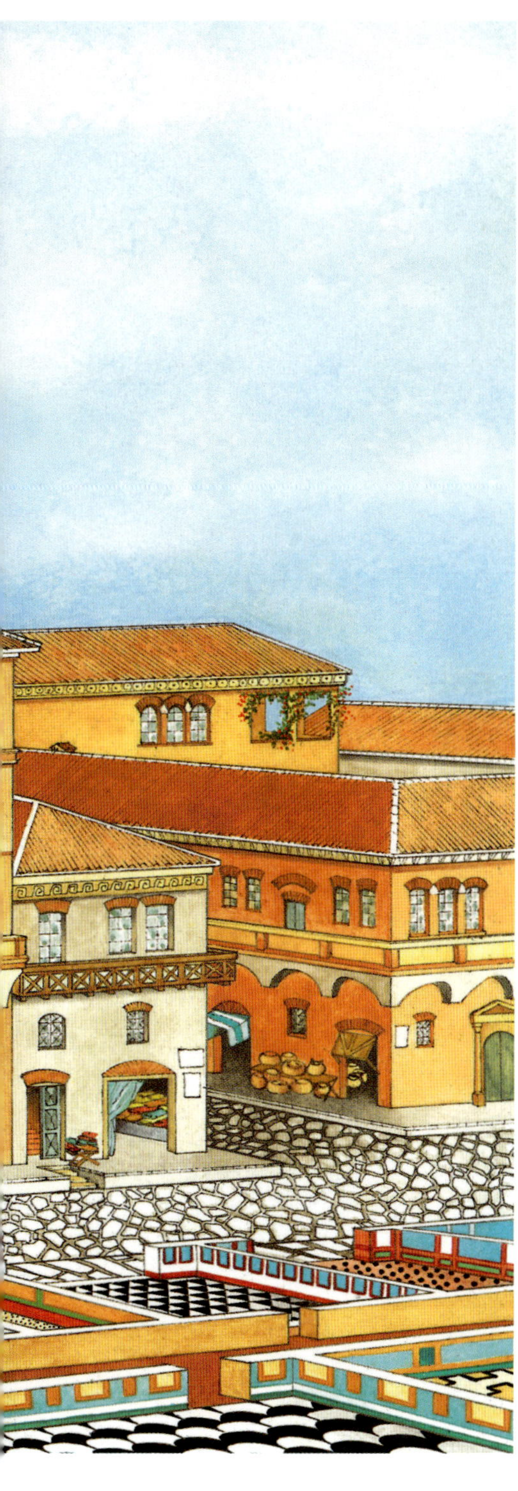

tabernae, over 800 in the 2nd century, were not only shops but also small workshops, with the owners often living in the attics.

Antoninus Pius completed the reconstruction of Ostia begun by Hadrian. By then the town was slightly larger than Pompeii, with 50,000 inhabitants. Major projects included the forum baths, the largest in the town, the imperial palace and tenement buildings, including the House of Diana and the Insula of the Charioteer.

Ostia, a coastal town, was open to foreign influences, including religious ones. Many oriental religions became popular under the Antonines, as shown by the presence of numerous shrines of Mithras. Commodus, the last of the Antonines, rebuilt the theatre and, having launched a new corn fleet, renovated the great *horrea* and built new ones. The town, which had reached the peak of its expansion, was enjoying a period of great prosperity. Building work came to a halt under the Severan emperors, who concentrated on restoration and reconstruction, with the aim of upgrading trade infrastructures. A new coast road, the Via Severiana, connecting the port of Terracina with Ostia, and Portus, was opened. A semicircular *emporium* on the Tiber, the extension of the *horrea* and the rebuilding of the Piazzale delle Corporazioni and its portico probably date from this period.

The unique mosaics of the Piazzale provide invaluable information about trade in Ostia. The motifs and inscriptions relate to shipowners and traders from towns all over the empire, as well as the local guilds. Among the new monuments were the Arch of Caracalla and a round temple, the last public structure in the town centre, possibly finished by the Gordian family.

A crisis occurred around the mid-3rd century, a time of serious political and economic disorder. In a few decades many buildings were abandoned. Much of the town's business activity was transferred to Portus, and the need for close control of supplies led to the concentration of all power in the hands of the prefect of Rome's food supply. Under Diocletian and Constantine the situation improved; by now, however, Ostia was no longer a flourishing trading town. Some buildings were constructed, but only along the main streets, whereas the inner districts were gradually abandoned. While the *insulae* began to empty, the *domus* of the nobility – secluded luxury mansions like the homes of the republican aristocracy – were being built again. From the 5th century the decline became irreversible. Building activity came to a standstill and wells were dug in the streets because the aqueduct had fallen into disuse. Ignored even by the Visigoths led by Alaric, Ostia now held nothing of interest. In the second half of the 6th century, in the Greek-Gothic war, it was used after the fall of Portus to send supplies to Rome. Its end finally came in the Saracen raids of the 9th century. Unlike Pompeii, Ostia suffered a slow, gradual decline, and its complex historical development, over at least nine centuries, can be seen in excavations.

HERCULANEUM, A CITY SHROUDED IN MYSTERY

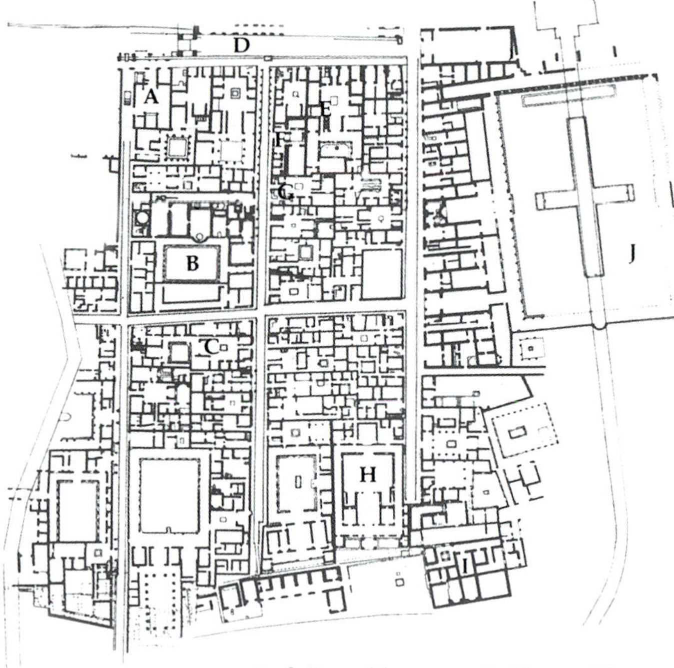

A College of the Augustales
B Forum Baths
C House of the Wooden Partition
D Basilica
E House of the Bicentenary
F House of Neptune and Amphitrite
G House of the Carbonized Furniture
H House of the Stags
I Suburban Baths
J Palaestra

Herculaneum (Ercolano), a town in Campania some 8 km (5 miles) east of Naples, was destroyed by the eruption of Vesuvius in AD 79. Its name derives from its legendary founder, Hercules. First Greek, then Samnite, it was subjugated by Rome in 307 BC; stormed by Sulla's faction in 89 BC during the Social War, it received the status of *municipium*, to which Roman colonists were sent. Many patrician villas were built in the republican period.

Far less badly hit by the hail of debris that destroyed Pompeii, Stabiae and Oplontis, it was long believed that Herculaneum was later covered by a vast mudslide that built up on the slopes of the volcano as a result of the violent cloudbursts following the cataclysm. It was therefore thought that most of the inhabitants had managed to escape, perhaps by sea, and very few skeletons were found during the excavations of the town. However, more recent studies and the discovery of hundreds of human remains in the port area show that the town was choked by a cloud of toxic gas and then buried under a flow of low-temperature lava. Only those who fled to Naples at the first sign of the eruption survived; the others, perhaps reluctant to leave their homes, hesitated too long, and when they eventually decided to flee, found it was too late. In a panic, they tried to escape in the boats still moored in the docks, but the increasing violence of the waves defeated them. In desperation they took refuge in buildings around the

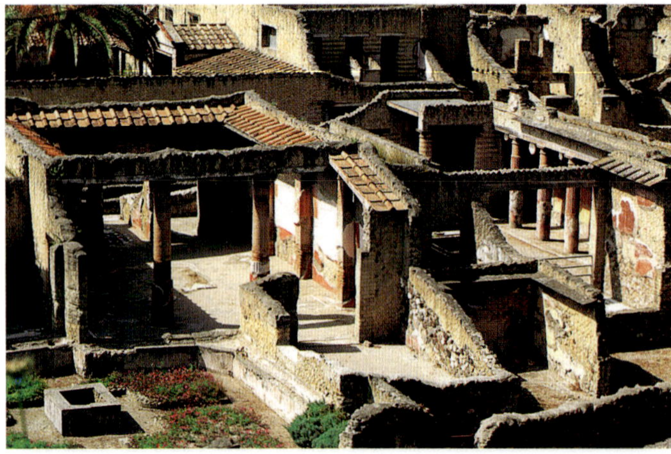

168 (centre left) In the House of the Gem, named after a cameo dating from the age of Claudius found there, the atrium with its impluvium *is well preserved; it led, via an* adytum *with two columns, to the* tablinum *and the garden behind.*

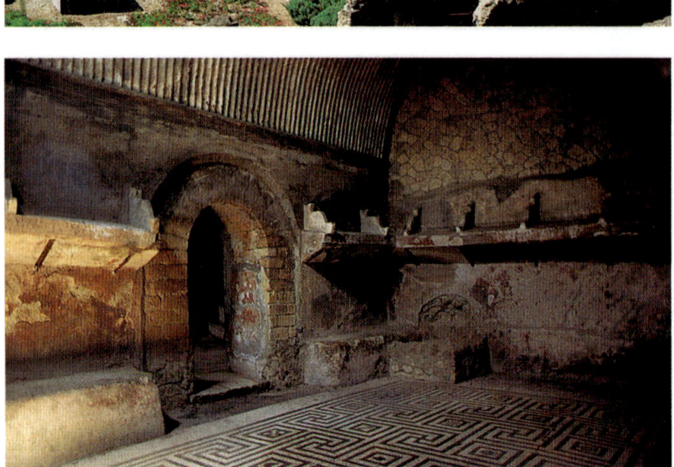

168 (bottom left) The Urban Baths, which stand in the centre of the town, date from the Julio-Claudian age and have a traditional design. The shelves where bathers placed their clothes can be seen along the walls.

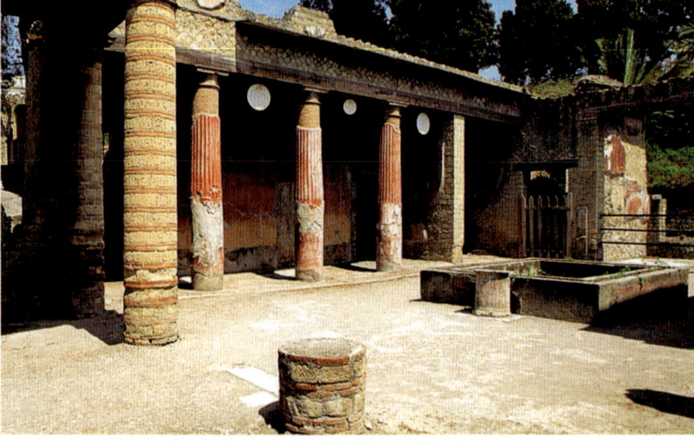

168 (centre right) The House of the Relief of Telephus was an aristocratic residence built on several storeys, with a very irregular plan. Its atrium featured bright red plaster and columns made of different materials.

169 (opposite) The Suburban Baths, dating from the Flavian age, are very luxurious, and had some innovatory architectural features, such as light and air shafts. An example can be seen in this vestibule, where light penetrates from an opening above the arches. The basin in the centre collected water from a spout concealed in the bust of Apollo.

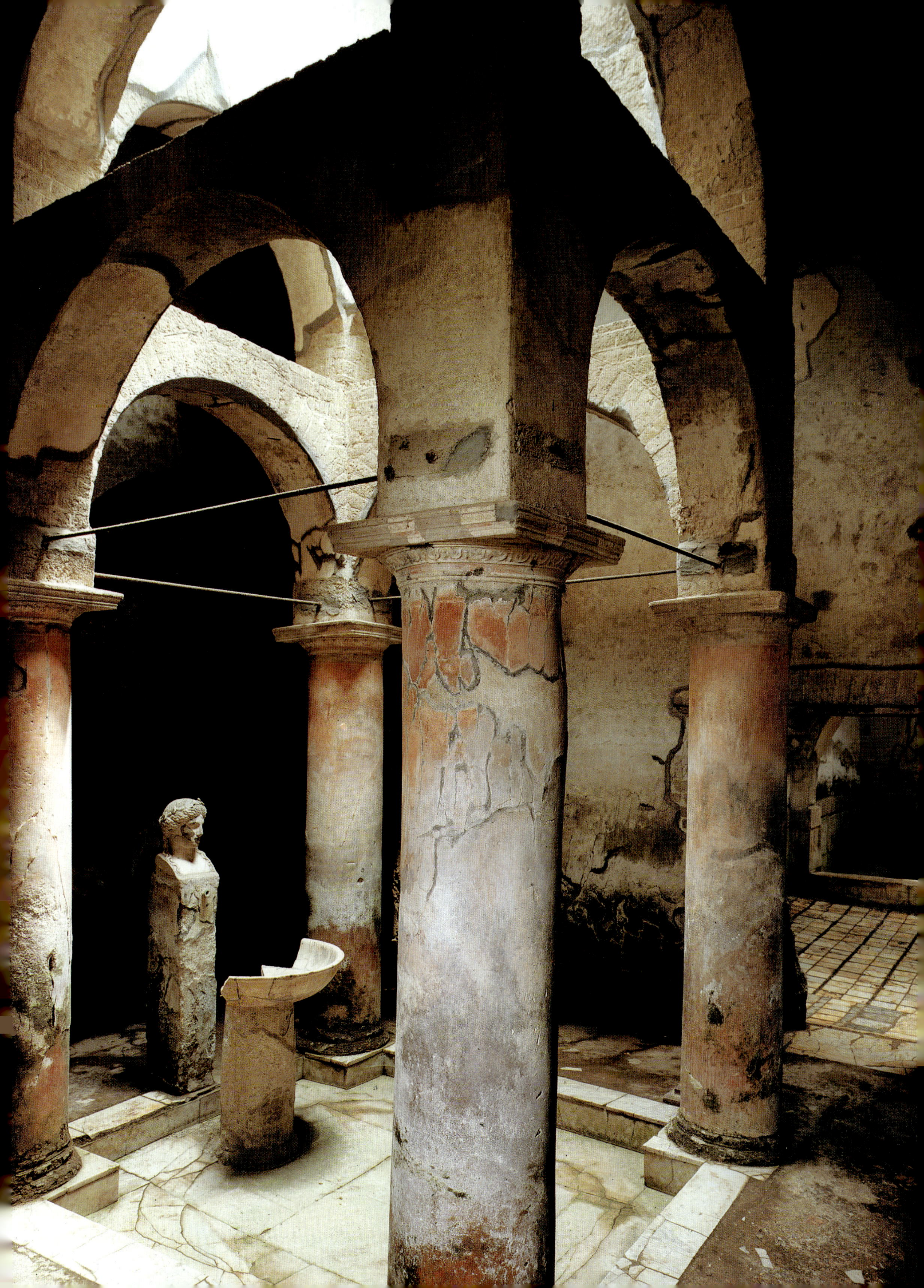

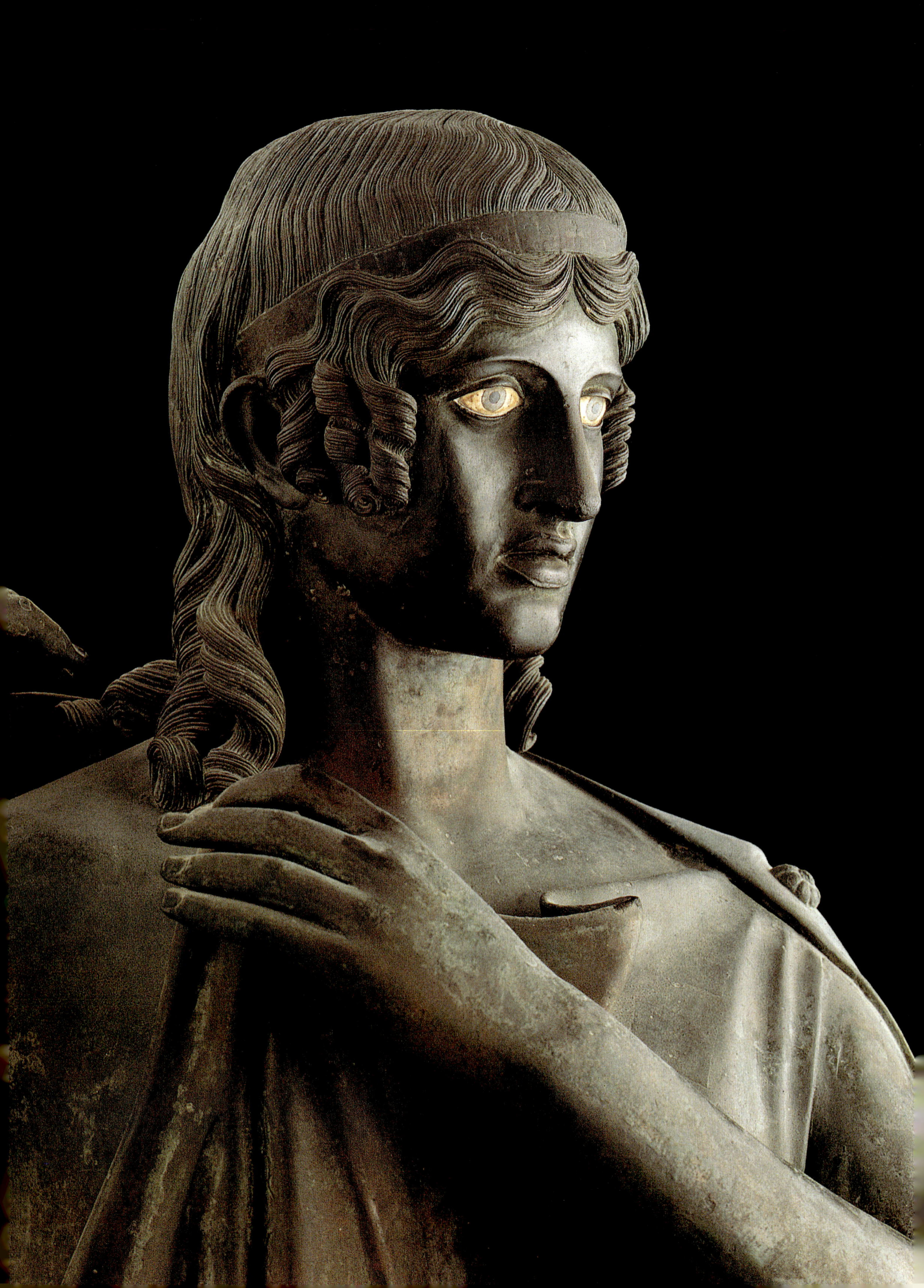

port, where they were overcome by the poisonous gases emitted by Vesuvius and died of suffocation. Their well-preserved skeletons (over 200 of them) provide invaluable material for the study of the lifestyles, diseases and diet of the ancient Romans.

In the days following the eruption the volcanic flow inundated the streets, reaching a depth of 16 m (53 ft) at some points. As it slowly dried, it solidified to the consistency of tufa and preserved everything it covered, including organic materials such as wood, leather, papyrus, vegetable fibres and food. This outstanding state of preservation has provided excellent material for the study of homes and furnishings; the exceptional discovery of written documents and literary manuscripts – the famous papyrus scrolls – is also due to this. The first excavations, in the early 18th century, led to the discovery of the theatre, which was stripped of its many statues of marble and bronze. Between 1738 and 1765, on the orders of Charles II of Bourbon, King of Naples, many shafts were dug which caused much damage but brought to light the magnificent Villa of the Papyri.

From 1828 to 1865 an attempt was made to uncover the entire town using the same techniques as at Pompeii, but work was abandoned because the volcanic rock was too hard. Later excavations were stopped because the modern town, built on the site of Herculaneum, was too close. Excavations were only systematically recommenced in 1927; to date, seven *insulae* have been uncovered, but much of the town,

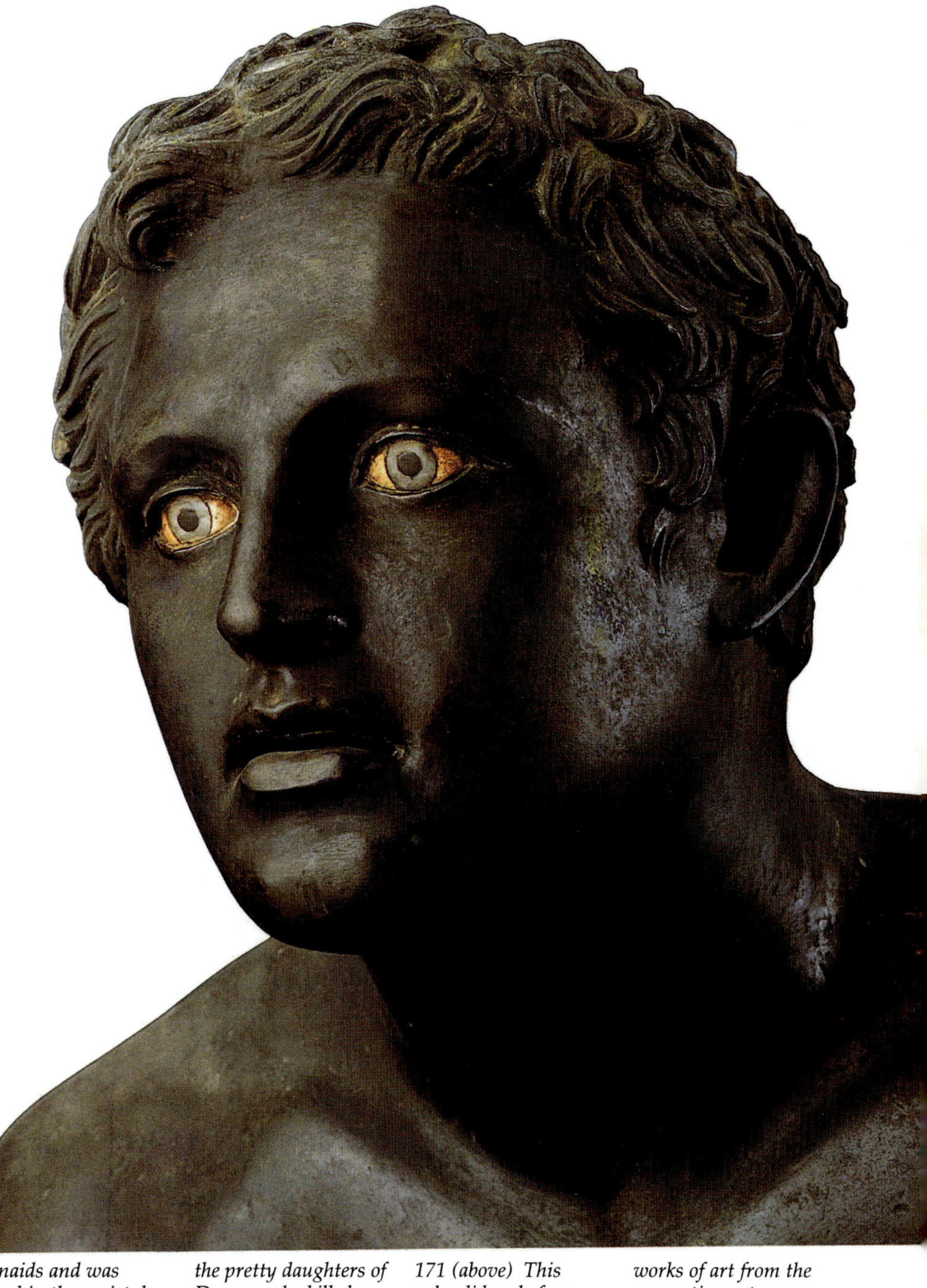

170 (opposite) An outstanding collection of works of art– some 90 bronze and marble sculptures including copies of classical and Hellenistic masterpieces, portraits of leading Greek personalities and decorative subjects – was found in the Villa of the Papyri, discovered in 1750. This magnificent statue is of one of the Danaids and was found in the peristyle of the wealthy residence together with four similar female figures. It was originally believed that the five girls were performing a religious dance, but it later became clear that they were carrying amphoras, now lost. The group was thus associated with the myth of the Danaids, the pretty daughters of Danaus who killed their husbands on their wedding night and were condemned in Hades to fill with water vessels with a hole in the bottom. Because of its exceptional luxury it is believed that the Villa of the Papyri belonged to Lucius Calpurnius Piso, Caesar's wealthy father-in-law.

171 (above) This splendid male face belongs to a statue of a wrestler in a struggle against an opponent, who was also portrayed in bronze. Also found in the Villa of the Papyri, the sculptural group is now on display in the Naples Archaeological Museum, where many works of art from the excavations at Pompeii and Herculaneum are exhibited. Recent investigations led to the rediscovery of this famous villa, which was originally explored by means of underground passages but was 'lost' when they were sealed in 1765.

including some major public areas, still remains to be uncovered.

Although the area excavated is quite small, it reveals a grid layout a fifth of the size of Pompeii. The town was originally surrounded by walls and built on terraces sloping down to the sea. Public buildings are well represented by the theatre, explored in detail by underground passages but still buried, the Forum Baths, the Suburban Baths and the gymnasium. The theatre, with a typically Roman layout, must have been very elegant; the *scaena* was beautifully decorated with exquisite marbles and giallo antico, cipolin and African marble columns, while the entire building was embellished with countless bronze statues and sculptures. The gymnasium, which was surrounded by porticoes and had a cross-shaped swimming pool decorated with a bronze fountain, must also have been monumental.

However, the true character of Herculaneum is revealed by a study of its houses. The *domus* was already beginning to show the vertical development that became widespread in later decades. Typical of this transitional period is the grid house, the classic apartment building that was cheap and rational in its use of space. The House of the Wooden Partition and the House of the Carbonized Furniture are particularly interesting.

Herculaneum was smaller than Pompeii but proportionately much more art was found there. Many bronze sculptures decorated public buildings and homes – especially the Villa of the Papyri, a mansion found 20–25 m (65–82 ft) deep in an area to the northwest of the present archaeological site. It is still buried under two petrified layers, the first was formed in AD 79, while the second was produced by an eruption of 1631. The great importance of the villa, explored by underground passages, lies in the numerous sculptures found – 58 bronze and 31 marble – and the library of papyrus scrolls. So far 1785 scrolls have been found, but many were lost in the mid-18th century when they were mistaken for lumps of coal. They contain philosophical writings, mostly by the epicure Philodemus of Gadara, and some Latin texts, including *De Bello Actiaco*.

Unlike Pompeii, Herculaneum was not primarily an industrial and trading town; its principal activities must have been crafts and the minor arts. This is demonstrated by the numerous surviving *tabernae*, including the workshops of potters and marble carvers, weavers and dyers, pasta makers and small wine producers.

Its peaceful nature and pleasant atmosphere, recorded by Greek geographer Strabo, probably made it a popular resort, frequented by the aristocracy of Rome and nearby Naples. Their luxurious peristyle homes were quite large, forcing the poorer citizens to extend their homes upwards; the result is a very interesting variety of types of dwelling. However, only further excavations, made extremely difficult by the conditions, will reveal the many secrets still concealed in the buried town.

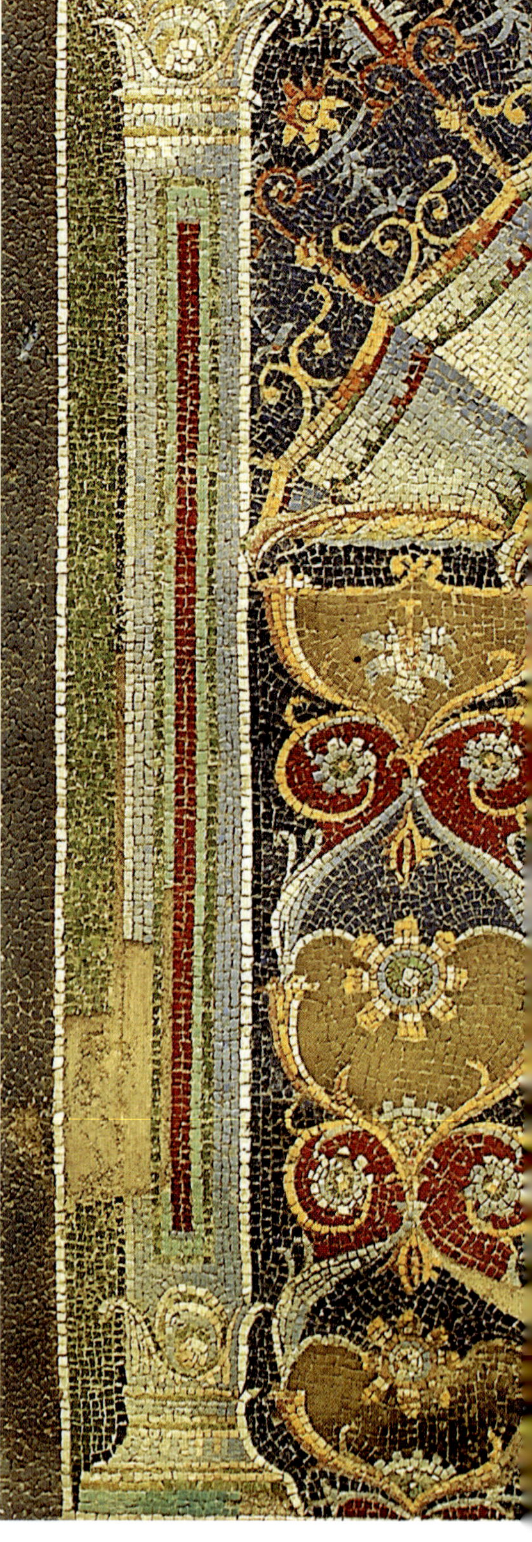

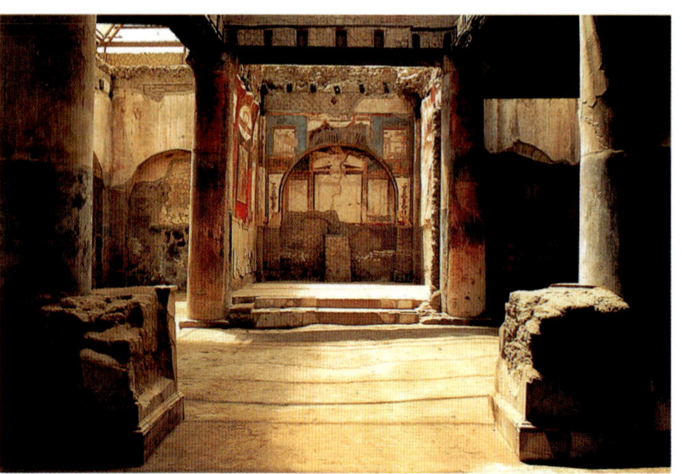

172 (left) and 173 (below) The huge inner rooms of the College of the Augustales (the priests who presided over the worship of the deified emperor and Rome) are decorated with magnificent wall paintings. The fresco depicting Hercules (the hero after whom the city was named) with Minerva and Juno is very fine.

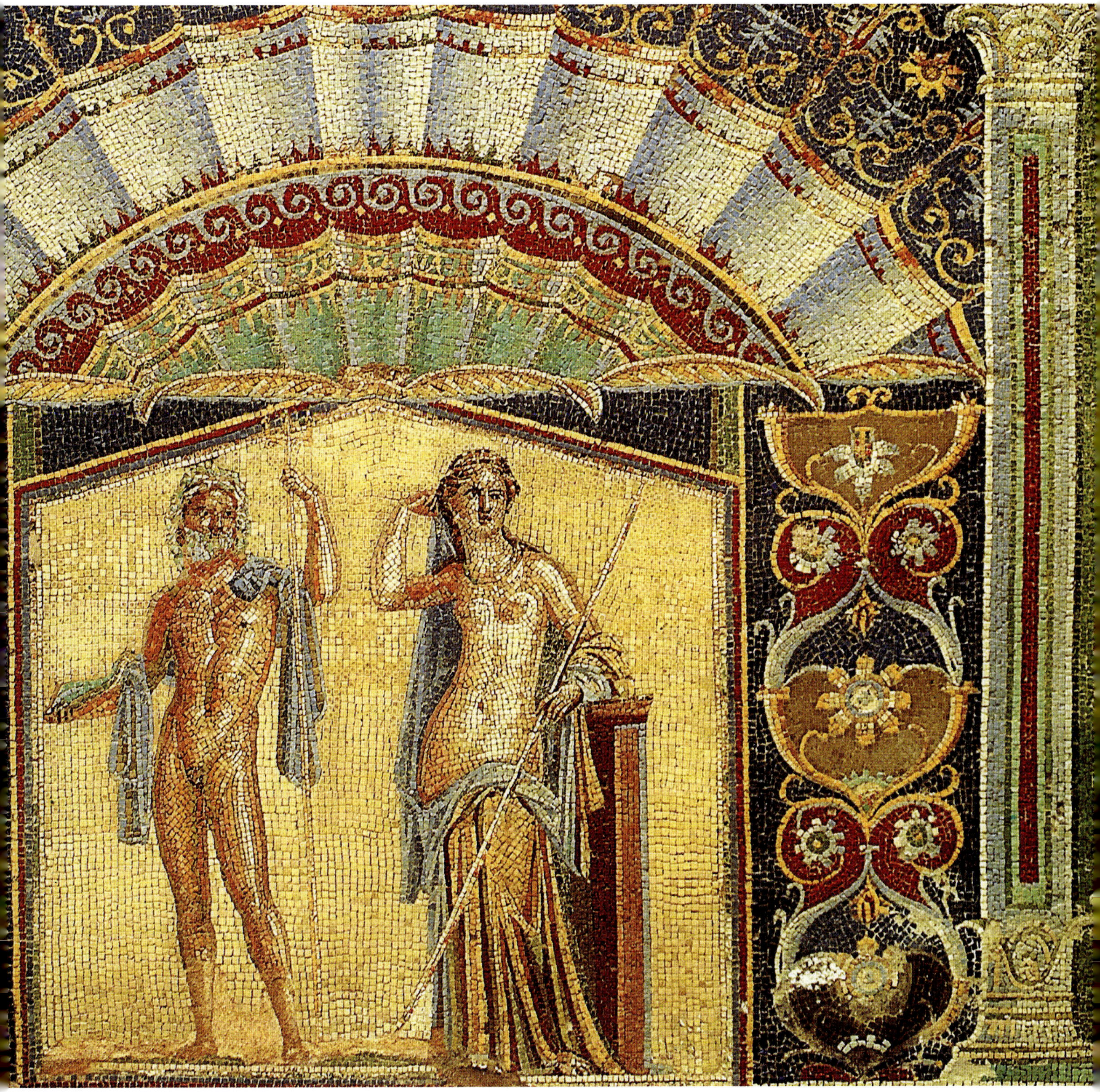

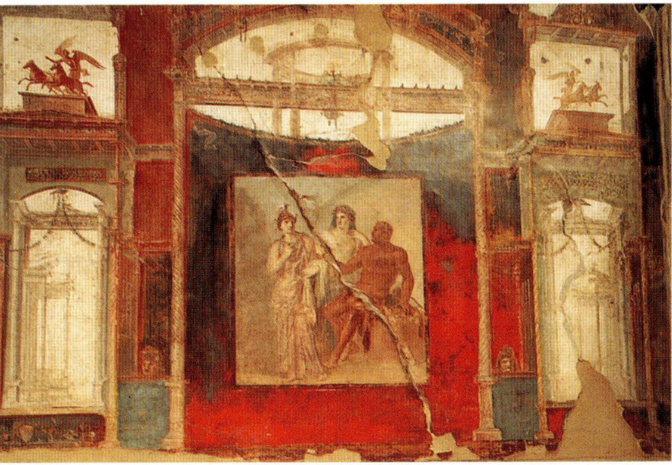

172–173 (above) The House of Neptune and Amphitrite is named after a splendid mosaic panel depicting two marine deities decorating one of the walls of the outdoor triclinium. *The house must have belonged to a wealthy merchant with elegant, rather sophisticated tastes, who was decidedly an art lover. This is demonstrated by the numerous bronzes and marble reliefs found in the various inner rooms and the luxurious decoration of the* triclinium. *Also, the fact that the subject of the mosaic was rare in the Roman world but was common in Greek art, indicates that the owner had aspirations to elegance.*

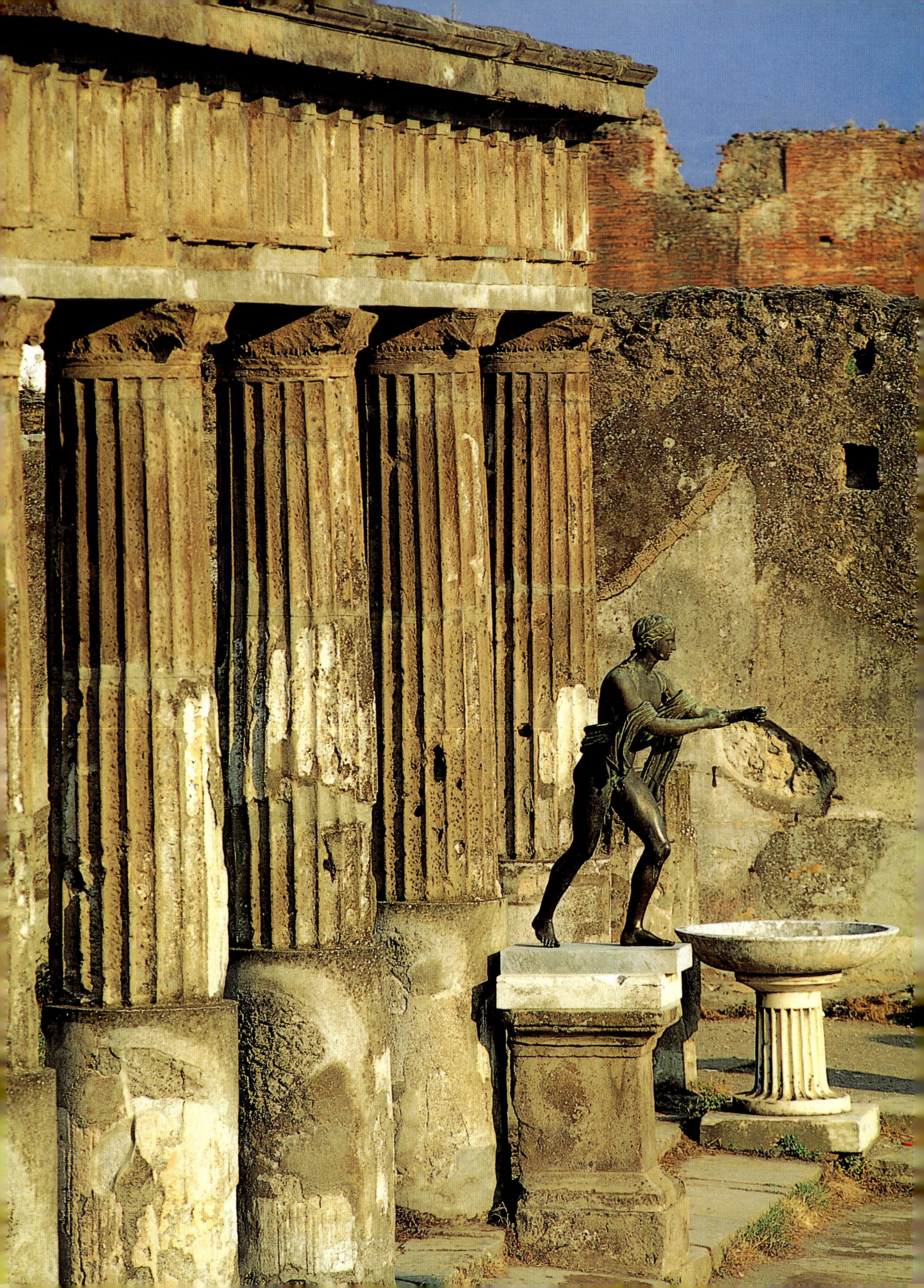

POMPEII, RISEN FROM THE ASHES

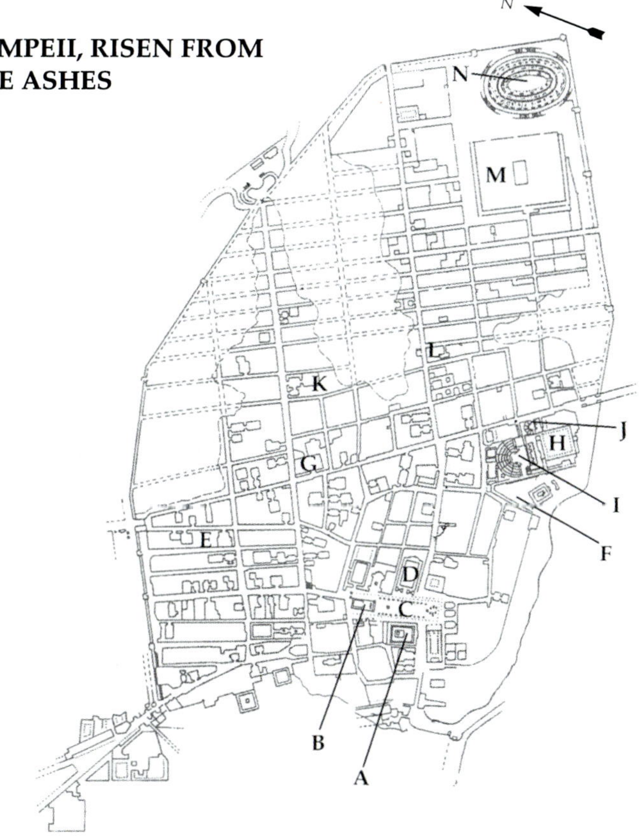

A Temple of Apollo
B Temple of Jupiter
C Forum
D Building of Eumachia
E House of the Vettii
F Triangular Forum
G Central Baths
H Gladiators' barracks
I Theatre
J Odeum
K House of the Centenary
L House of Pacuius Proculus
M Large palaestra
N Amphitheatre

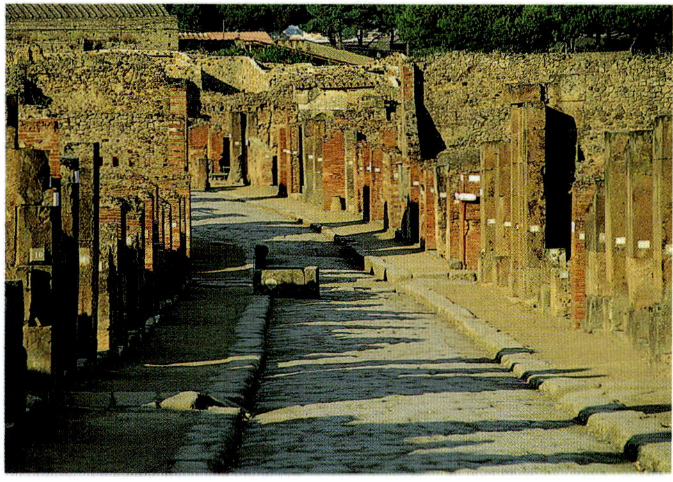

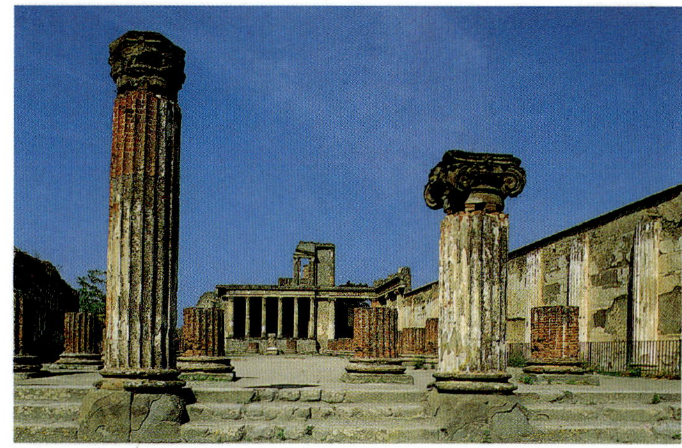

Ancient Pompeii was founded on the southernmost slopes of Vesuvius around the end of the 8th century BC by a community of Oscan peoples. It was later ruled by the Etruscans, and for a short time by the Greeks. Towards the end of the 5th century BC it fell into the hands of the Samnites, who ruled it until 310 BC, when it became allied to Rome. Following the Social War it was raised to the status of a *municipium*, and the inhabitants, belonging to the Menemia tribe, were granted Roman citizenship. In 80 BC, after the Civil War, it was made into a colony, named Cornelia Veneria Pompeianorum, by P. Cornelius Sulla, the dictator's nephew.

As a result of the patronage of Sulla's party, the town was renovated – major public buildings such as the baths, the odeum, the capitolium of the forum and the amphitheatre were erected, and the streets were paved. In time, the old and new inhabitants mixed, and the Oscan language was retained in addition to Latin, which became the official language of the colony. The

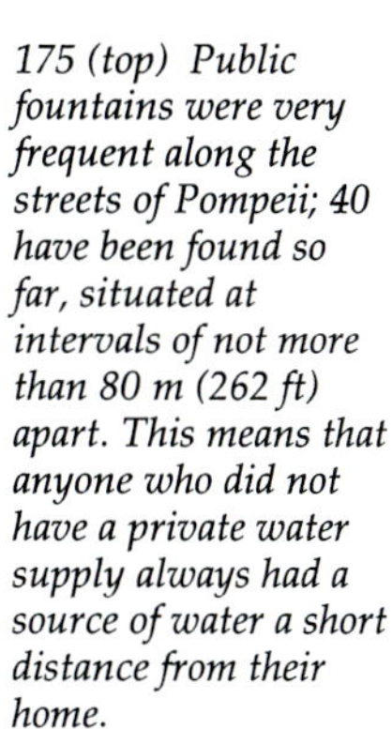

174 (opposite) The Temple of Apollo, of the 2nd century BC, stands near the forum, in a peristyle of 48 Corinthian columns. A bronze statue of Apollo holding a bow, now replaced by a copy, stood on one of the sides in front of the portico. The sanctuary was being restored after the earthquake of AD 62.

175 (top) Public fountains were very frequent along the streets of Pompeii; 40 have been found so far, situated at intervals of not more than 80 m (262 ft) apart. This means that anyone who did not have a private water supply always had a source of water a short distance from their home.

175 (centre) The ruins of the basilica, of the late 2nd century BC, stand at the western corner of the forum. This is one of the oldest surviving examples of this kind of building, used as a court-house and for business meetings. Later on it became characteristic of early Christian sacred architecture.

175 (bottom) The Great Theatre was built between the 2nd and 3rd centuries BC; although it was extended in the time of Augustus it is only slightly influenced by Greek building styles. The auditorium is built into the slope of a hill and not supported by masonry structures as was typical in later Roman architecture.

176 (below) At Pompeii the art of fresco painting reached great heights of expression. This is a room in the House of the Vettii, one of the most magnificent in Pompeii. When this domus *was restored after the earthquake of* AD *62, generous use was made of wall paintings in a blend of the Third and Fourth styles to create extraordinary effects of perspective with bright colours; mythological subjects alternate with architectural views.*

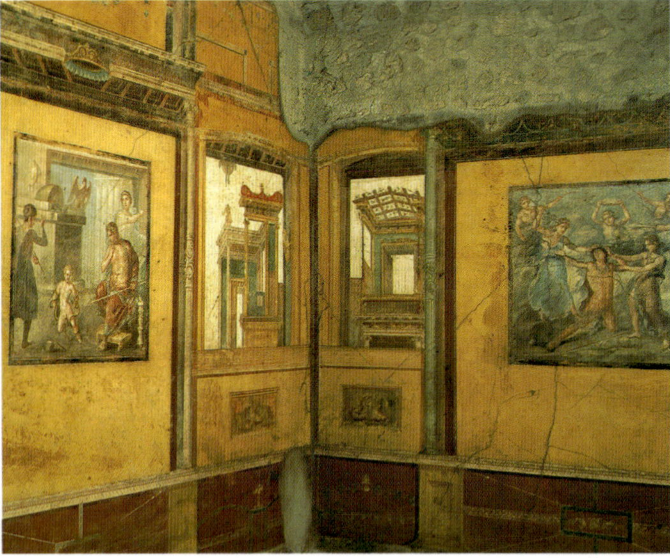

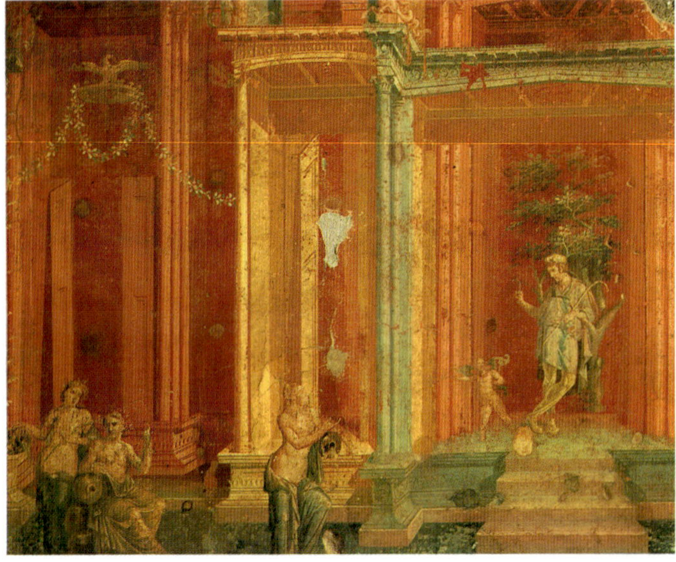

176 (above) Pinarius Cerialis was a skilled stone and cameo cutter who owned a small but tastefully furnished house. The frescoes on two walls of a cubiculum *on the ground floor are inspired by a theatre set. One portrays characters from* Iphigeneia in Tauris, *the tragedy by Euripides which inspired much Pompeiian painting, while the other (shown here) depicts the Judgment of Paris. It demonstrates a perfect technique and a great mastery of spatial organization. It is a great pity that artists did not sign their works – the only painter's name to have survived in the whole of Pompeii is that of one Lucius, of whom nothing more is known.*

town was administered by around a hundred decurions, aided by the duovirs and aediles, forming a kind of senate. There were also religious authorities, from the Augustales to the guardians of the cult of the *Lares compitales*. Like Rome, Pompeii was organized into districts, divided into *vici* and *pagi*, which had shrines to the Lares at the crossroads. The names of these districts are often recorded in the electoral posters painted on the façades of the houses.

From 27 BC a period of intense Romanization took place in Pompeii, leading to a reshuffle of the ruling political class. The supporters of Sulla were now excluded and new clans more closely allied with the imperial house predominated. In this political context, artistic and architectural styles derived from the official culture of Rome were introduced.

On 5 February, AD 62 a disastrous earthquake struck Pompeii and nearby towns, such as Herculaneum. A pictorial record of the earthquake survives in the reliefs on the *lararium* in the home of Lucius Cecilius Jocundus, which depict many of the town's buildings under the effect of the shock. The damage was so severe that it was still being repaired over ten years later. Trade, which until then had constituted the main activity in Pompeii, gave way to frenetic construction work, with associated speculation. But worse was yet to come.

One morning in AD 79, a cloud shaped like a pine tree blotted out the cone of Vesuvius. This was the warning sign of the terrible eruption which was shortly to wipe out the

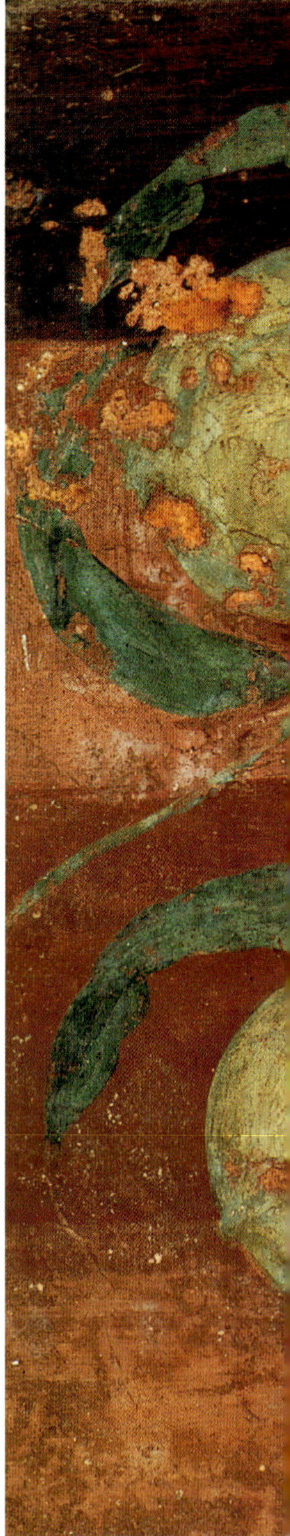

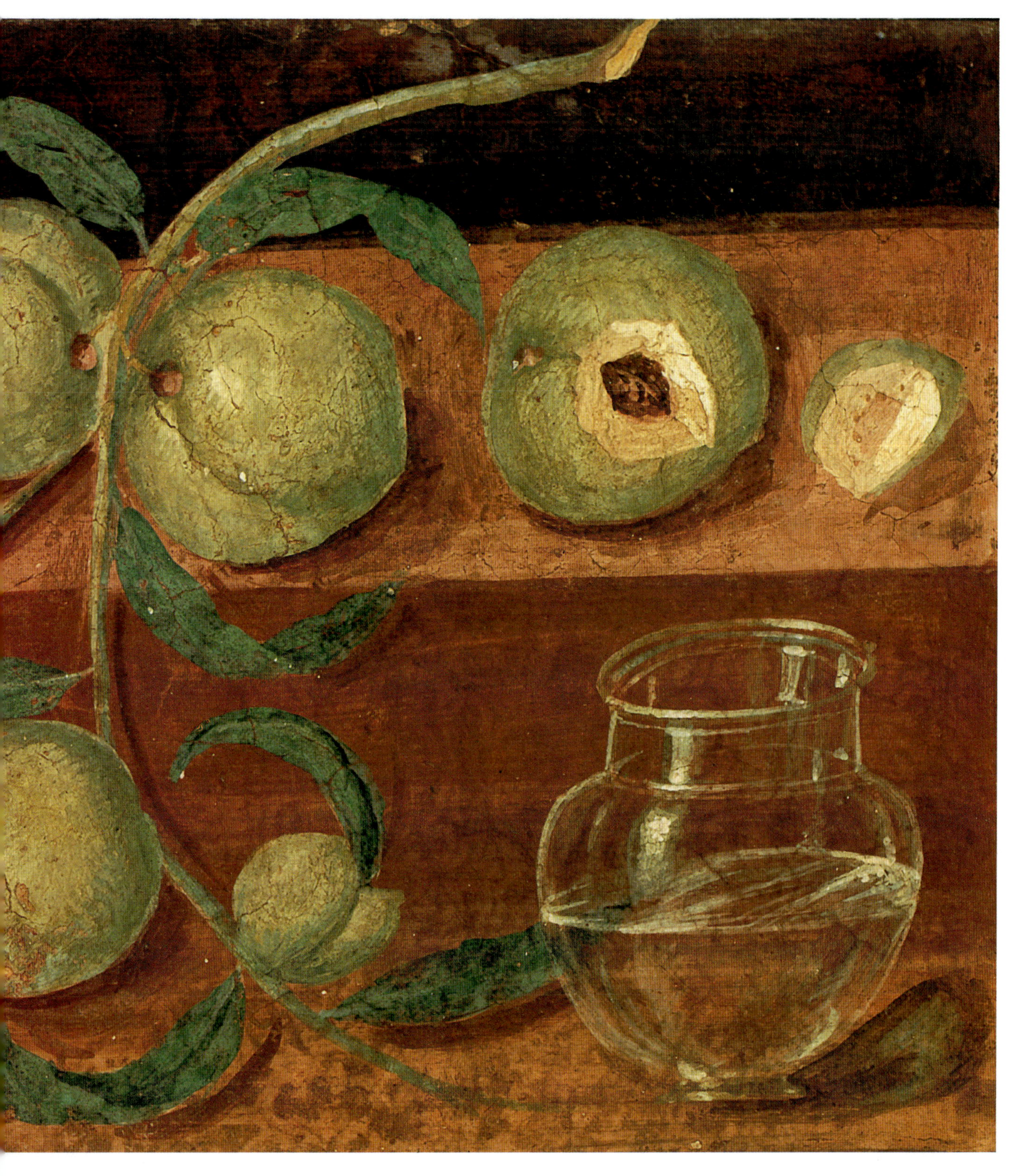

176–177 Still lifes, a common subject for artists, not only in Pompeii, demonstrate the sensitivity and expressive skill of the Roman painters. Oddly enough, wall painters were held in less respect than easel painters, and Pliny was of the opinion that only the latter were worthy of praise. Unfortunately, the materials used were highly perishable, with the result that very few examples of paintings on tablets have survived from the Roman age, and hardly any from Italic sources. With a few worthy exceptions, it seems the pictores parietarii *(wall painters) were skilled decorators with an inventive imagination rather than true artists.*

town, bombarded for four solid days by a hail of rock fragments that reached a depth of several metres, accompanied by toxic gas and a rain of ash, together with frequent tremors. Many of the people fleeing were suffocated, fell to the ground and were buried by the volcanic material. The hollows left by their decayed bodies in the hardened tufa were discovered by archaeologists and filled with plaster, forming the most dramatic evidence of the destruction of Pompeii. A detailed account of these tragic events was written by Pliny the Younger, an eyewitness to the catastrophe, in which his uncle, Pliny the Elder, admiral of the fleet at Misenum, died trying to observe the eruption and aid its victims on the beach of Stabiae. He recounted the terrible moments to Tacitus: 'You could hear the groans of women, the cries of children and the clamour of men; some loudly sought their parents, others their children, others again their spouses, and recognized them by their voices; there were some who, for fear of death, invoked it; many raised their arms to the gods, but still more said there were no more gods, and that this was the last night of the world...'

The buried town was rediscovered in 1748, and the first systematic excavations began in 1860. Restoration work followed, and over the years increasingly sophisticated techniques have enabled even the species of trees and bushes in the gardens of Pompeii to be identified.

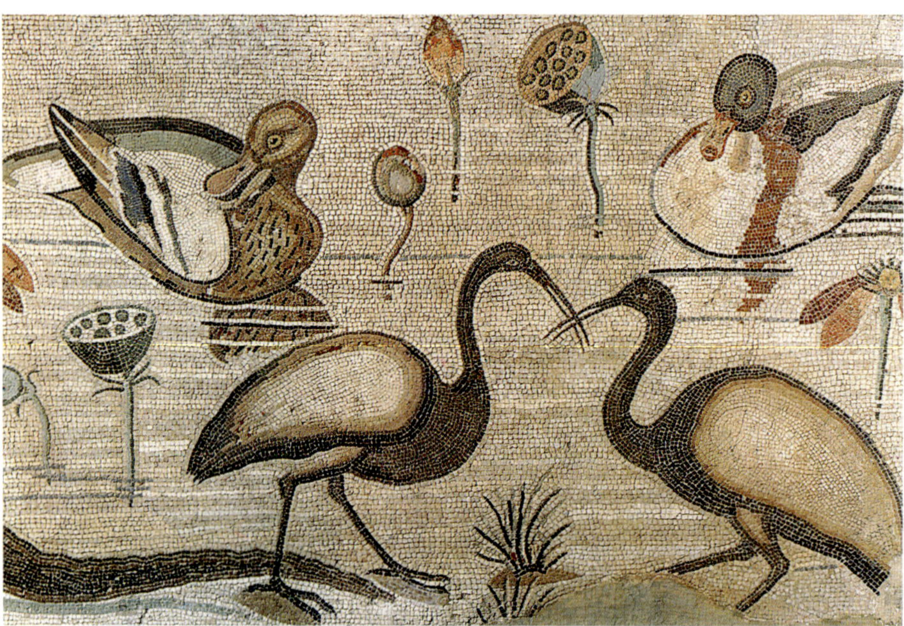

178 (above) Mosaic art reached great heights in the Roman world, as demonstrated by this Nile scene, discovered in a Pompeiian villa. For their subjects, the craftsmen were often inspired by famous paintings which were transferred in the form of large cartoons. The pieces forming the design were laid by museiarii, *and the background by* tessellarii.

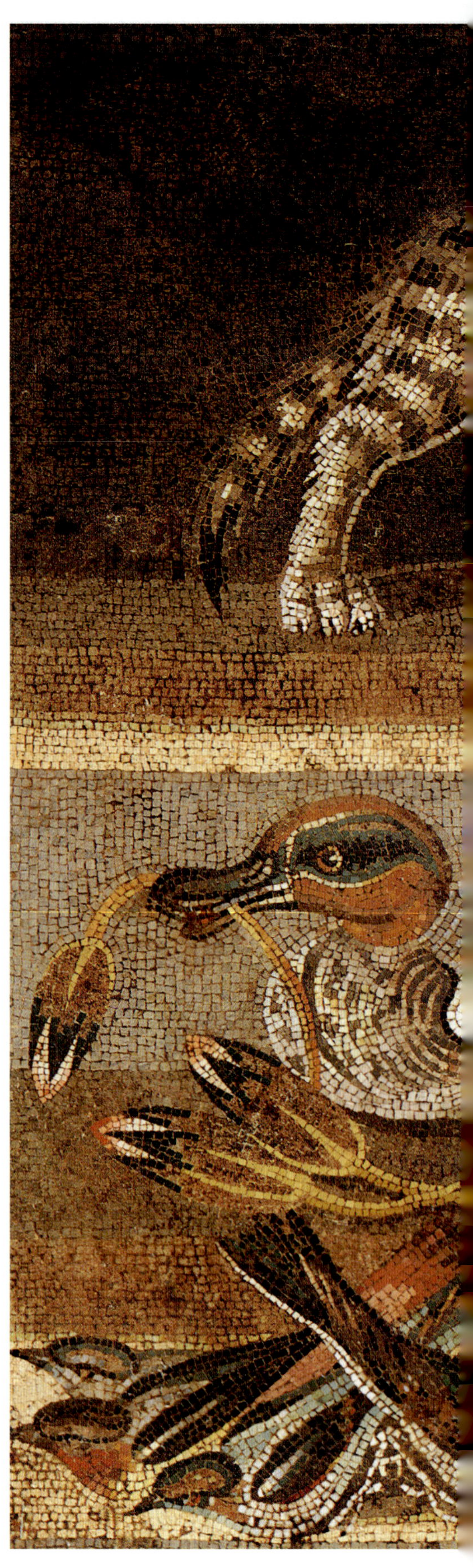

178–179 (right) Mosaic workers generally obtained the materials they needed for their art locally, but for shades of colour which could not be achieved using local stones they had to import materials. Tesserae made of glass paste, with which any shade could be obtained, overcame this problem. One of the first known examples of the use of this substance is in the House of the Faun – in the black background of the mosaic which shows a realistic picture of a cat pouncing on a quail. This practice became very common, especially for seascapes in shades of blue and the brightest green leaves.

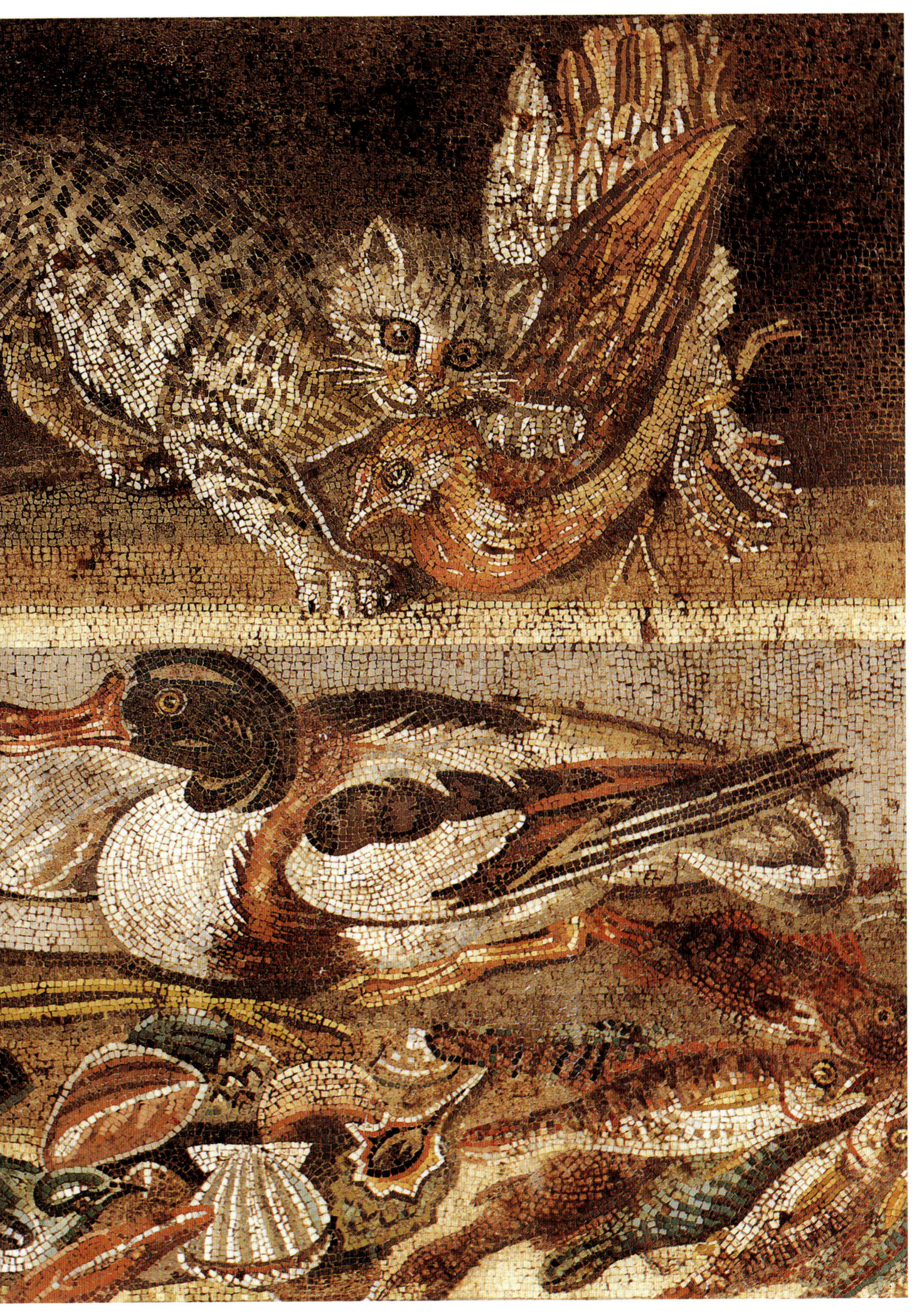

THE HOUSE OF THE CENTENARY

The House of the Centenary is so called because it was excavated in 1879, the 18th centenary of the eruption which destroyed Pompeii. It was a large residence, magnificently decorated with sculptures and oscilla *(marble and bronze discs with bas-relief decorations suspended from the architraves). The oldest part dates from the 2nd century* BC*; it was later altered on various occasions, and combined with an adjacent house. The walls of the large main atrium were decorated with small pictures in the so-called Fourth Style of painting. In the peristyle garden there was a marble fountain surrounded by rose bushes. A cross section of this* domus*, from the atrium to the peristyle, with its paintings and furnishings, is shown on the inner pages.*

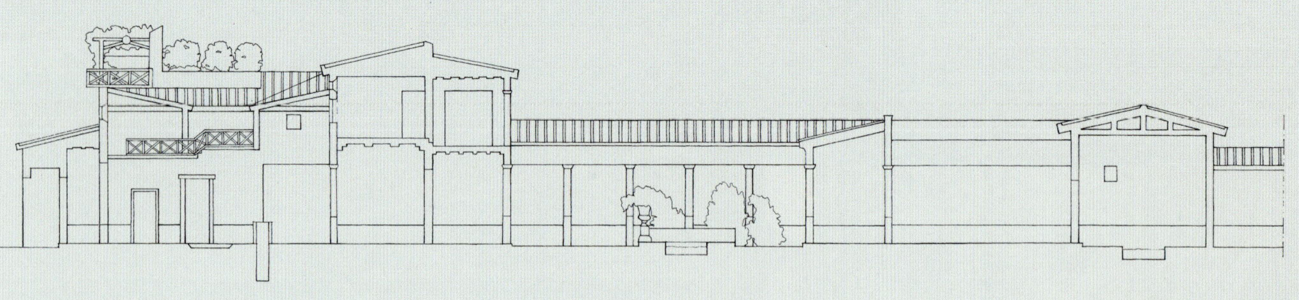

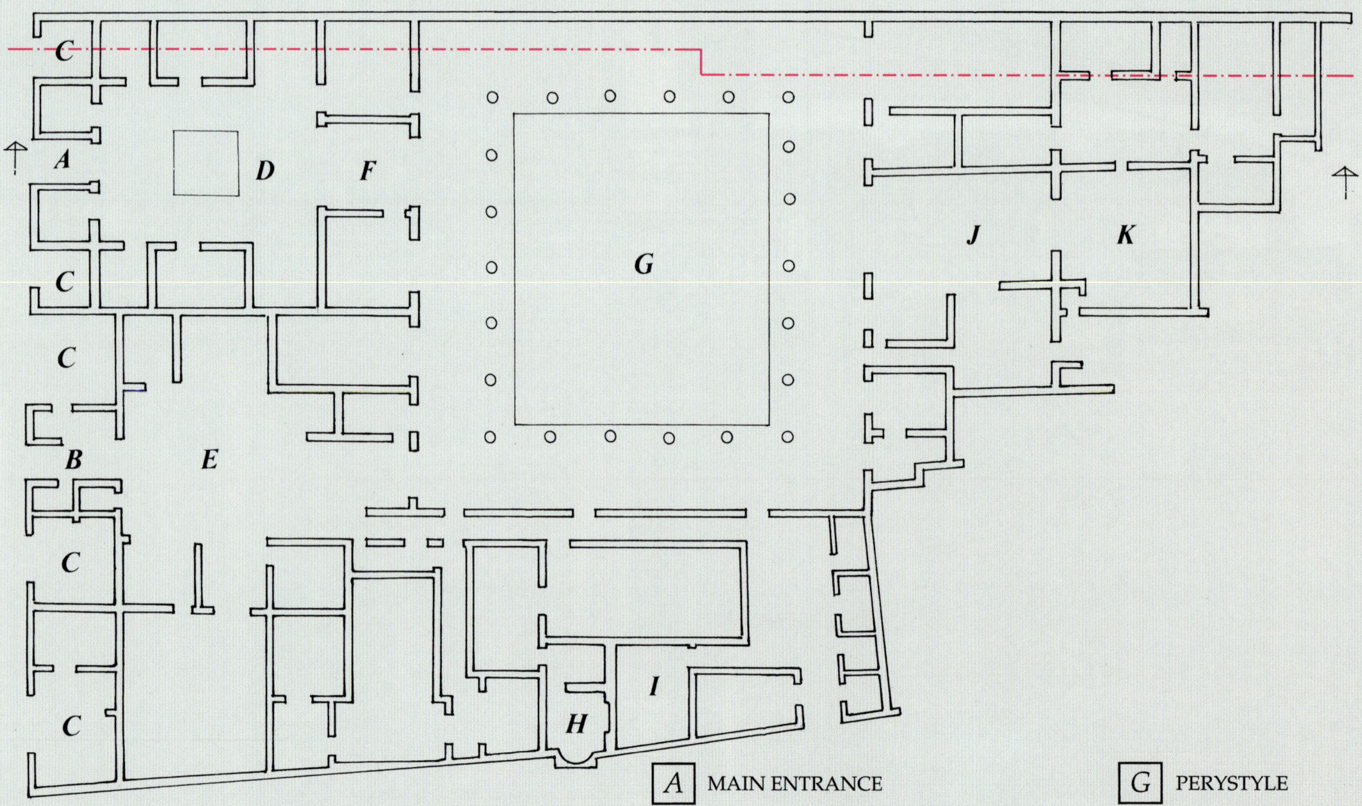

A MAIN ENTRANCE

B SECONDARY ENTRANCE

C *TABERNAE* (SHOPS)

D MAIN ATRIUM

E SECONDARY ATRIUM

F *TABLINUM*

G PERYSTYLE

H CALDARIUM

I KITCHEN

J NYMPHAEUM

K *VIRIDARIUM*

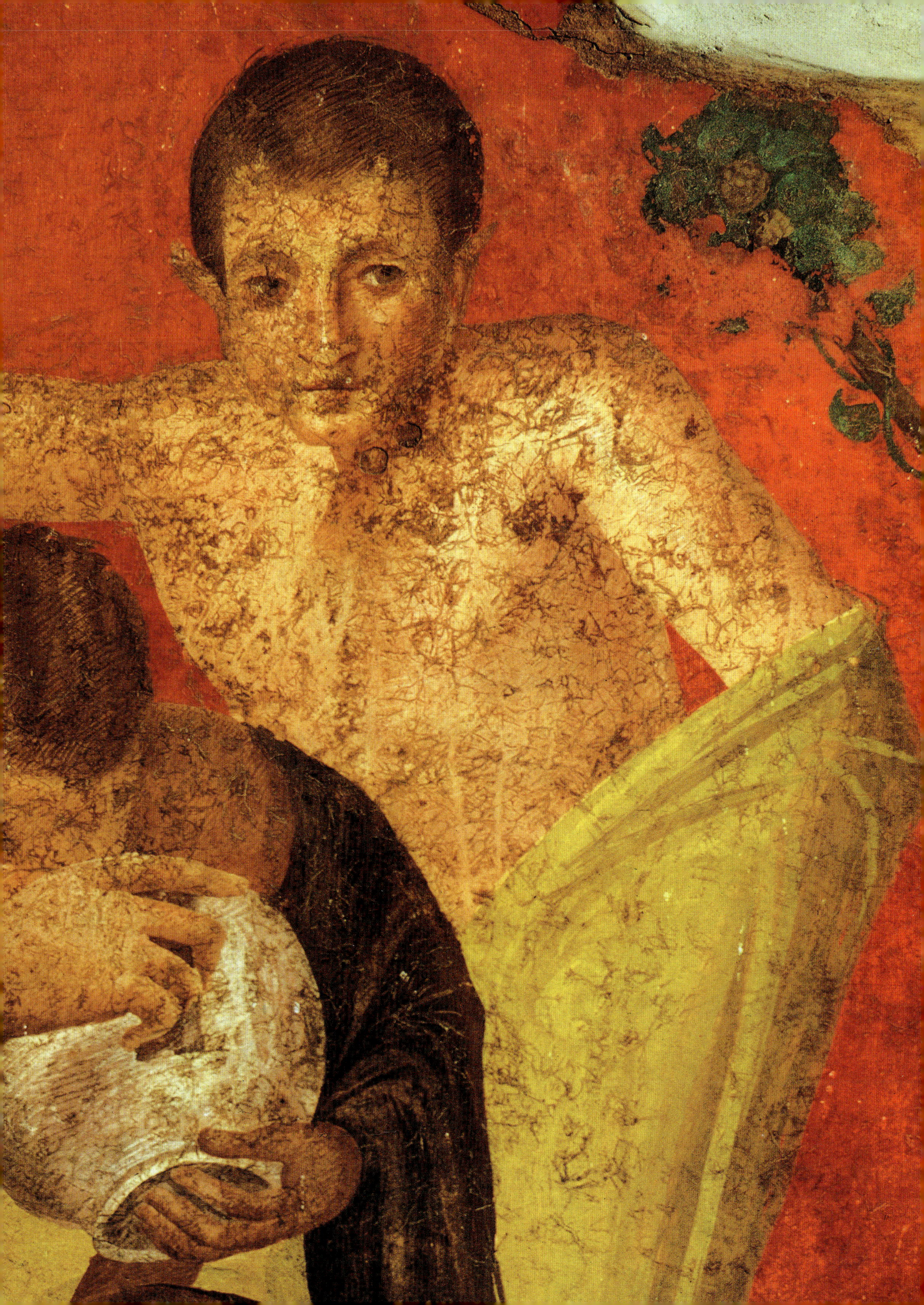

THE ROMAN EMPIRE AND ITS POWER CENTRES

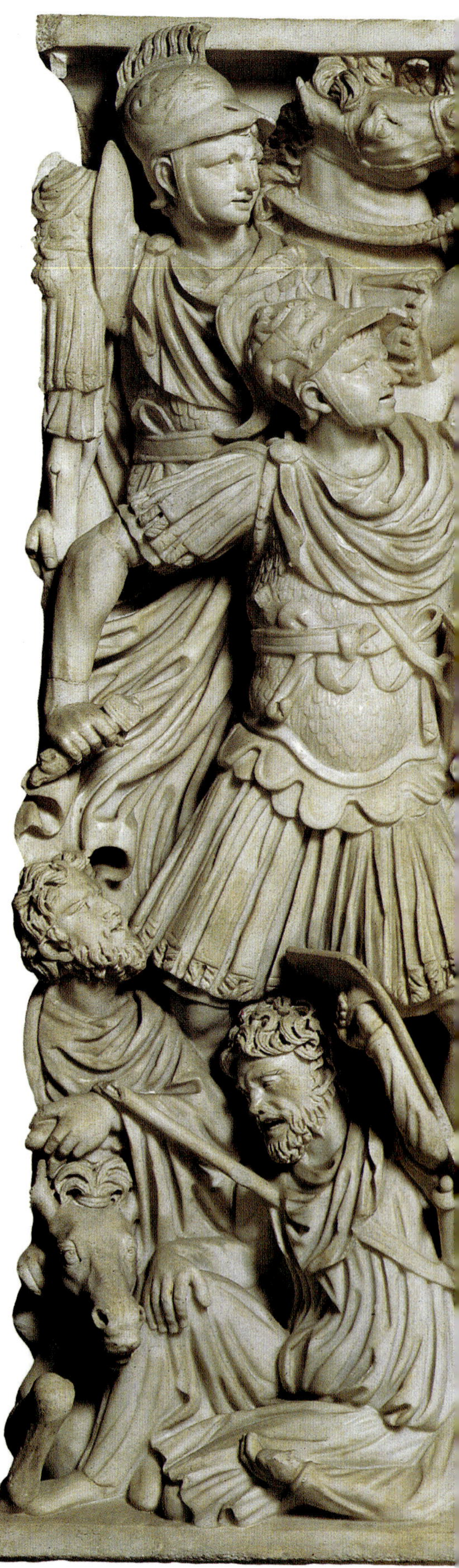

192–193 This lively scene of battle between legionaries and barbarians, a relief from what is known as the Ludovisi Sarcophagus, is a good illustration of the tireless Roman spirit of expansionism. Founded on a military discipline which developed into a veritable art form, and supported by a firm faith in its own cultural supremacy, Rome was able to build one of the largest and longest-lived empires in history. The frequency of battle subjects in Roman art is symptomatic of this warlike attitude. In this particular case, the Roman commander on horseback has been identified as Hostilian, the son of Decius who ruled from AD *249 to 251.*

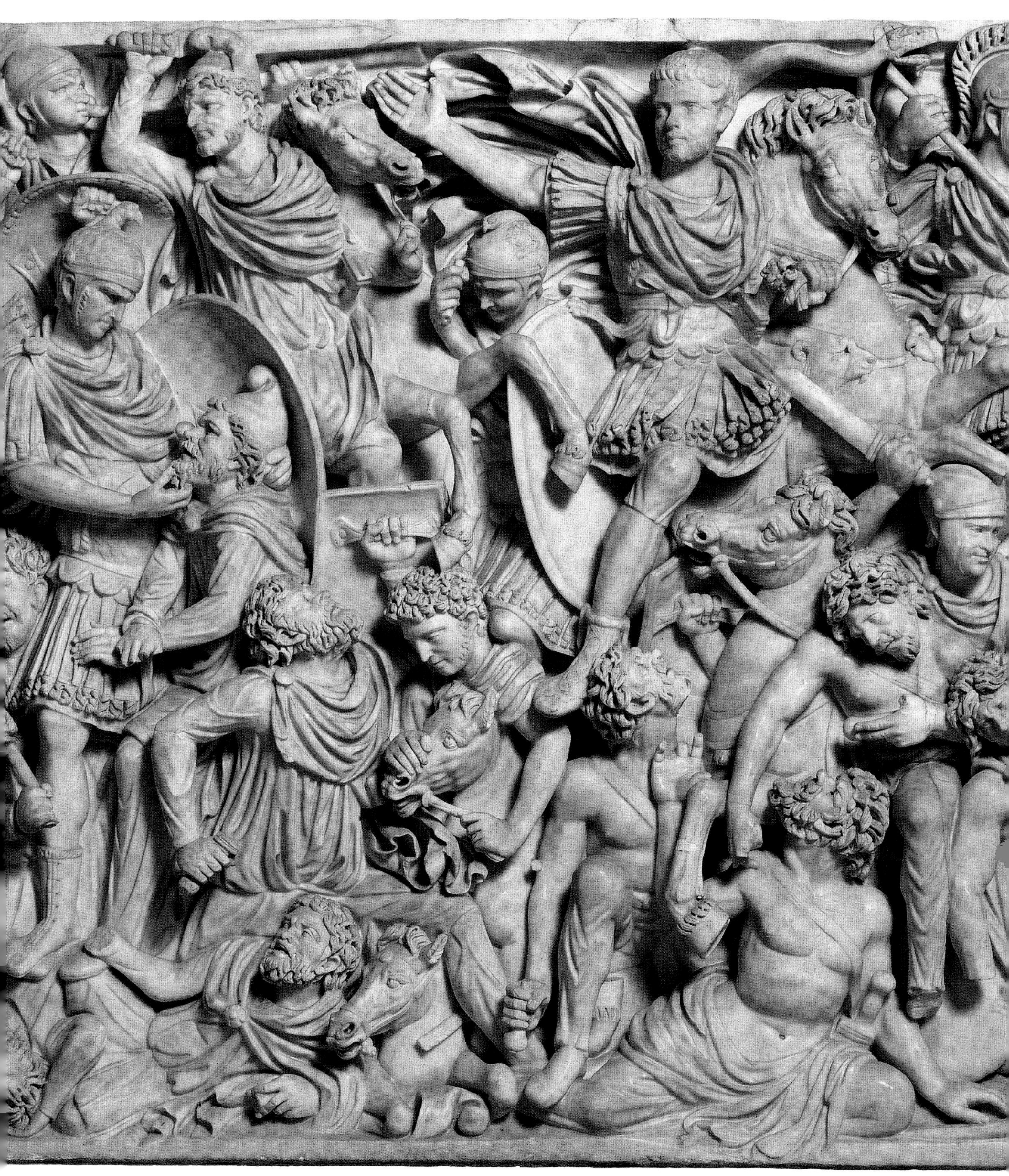

THE FORMATION AND ORGANIZATION OF THE ROMAN PROVINCES

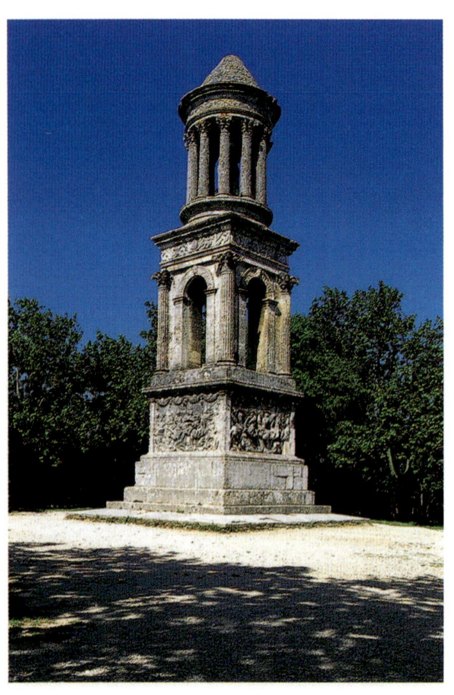

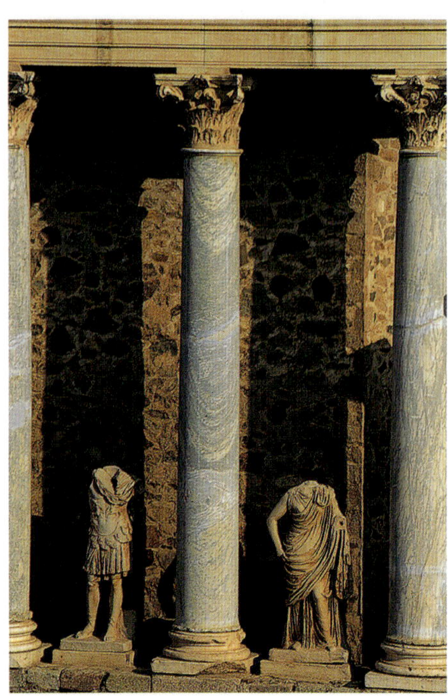

To the Romans the term 'province' generally indicated a territory outside Italy which had been annexed to Rome peacefully or by conquest and was under the jurisdiction of a magistrate of proconsular or propraetorian rank – that is a citizen of the senatorial class who had held the highest offices in the senatorial career. In republican times there was a sharp distinction between the legal status of the inhabitants of Italy, who enjoyed certain privileges, and that of all the other inhabitants of the empire, who had to pay a property tax. This difference was gradually reduced and Caracalla granted Roman citizenship to all inhabitants of the empire in AD 212. However, total equality was only granted under Diocletian, who placed the territory of Italy on a par with the provinces.

Rome's provincial dominion began with the acquisition of Sicily, Corsica and Sardinia between the First and Second Punic Wars. Hispania Citerior and Hispania Ulterior were soon added. Four new praetors, who held civil and military powers, were created to govern these territories. On taking office they issued an edict specifying the rules governing the administration of the province's cities and peoples.

In 146 BC Macedonia, comprising Illyria and Epirus, fell under the dominion of Rome. In the same year the province of Africa was created, comprising the territories of Carthage, after the destruction of that city. In 133 BC Rome inherited the kingdom of Pergamum from Attalus III, which became the province of Asia, and finally, around 120 BC, the province of Gallia Narbonensis was formed.

Such rapid expansion obviously required modifications to the existing administrative structure, which was unable to deal with the needs of territories further and further away from Rome or with the changing political conditions. The practice of extending a period of command after its conclusion (*prorogatio imperii*) was therefore instituted; by this system consuls and praetors became proconsuls and propraetors after holding office for a year, and thus continued to be part of government administration.

Between 133 and 31 BC, the year of the battle of Actium, a series of military operations led to the creation of the provinces of Pontus, Syria and Cilicia. In the meantime, the rulers of Cyrene and Bithynia had also bequeathed their kingdoms to Rome. At home, the internal political situation was deteriorating, and there was a real risk of dictatorship, which might easily have come about if a single person held major powers for too long. Pompey therefore established that a five-year interval must elapse between appointments as an ordinary magistrate and a promagistrate. From 58 BC Julius Caesar made extensive new conquests in his military campaigns. He defeated Numidia (which became Africa Nova) and Gallia Comata (central and northern France, with part of Belgium and Germany). In 49 BC he extended Italian territory by granting Roman citizenship to all inhabitants of Cisalpine Gaul (northern Italy).

194 (top) Saint-Rémy, ancient Glanum in Gallia Narbonensis, still preserves numerous Roman remains; one of the most interesting is the monument of the Julians, a three-storey cenotaph dating from the 1st century BC.

194 (bottom) The theatre of Merida, which dates from 15 BC, was donated to the rich Spanish city by Augustus' son-in-law Agrippa. After careful restoration the scaena *has been partly reconstructed and its original statues repositioned.*

195 (opposite) The Temple of Diana in Merida, from the end of the 1st century AD, is a magnificent example of a peripteral Corinthian temple, that is one that has at least one row of columns outside the cella, *which has not survived here.*

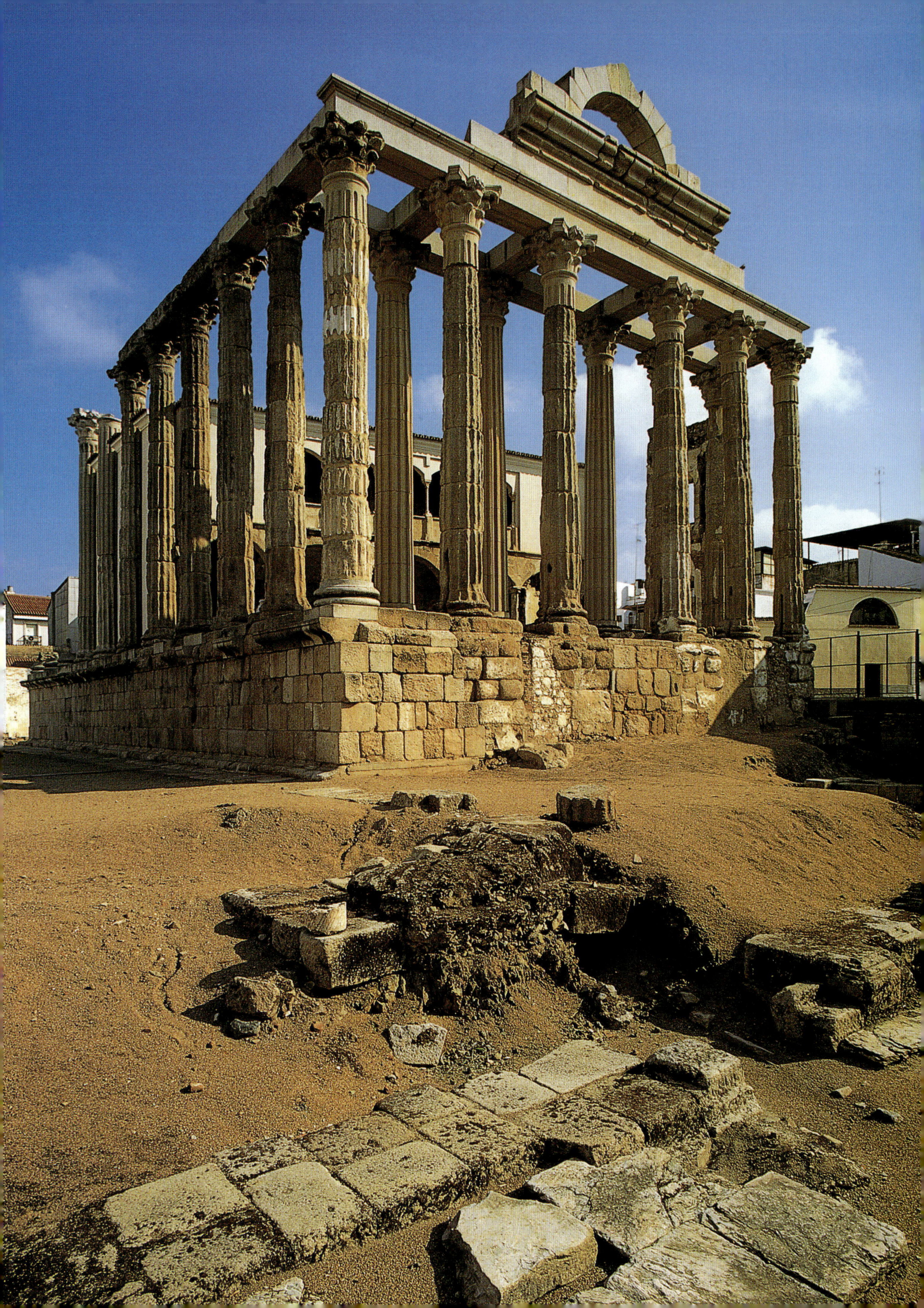

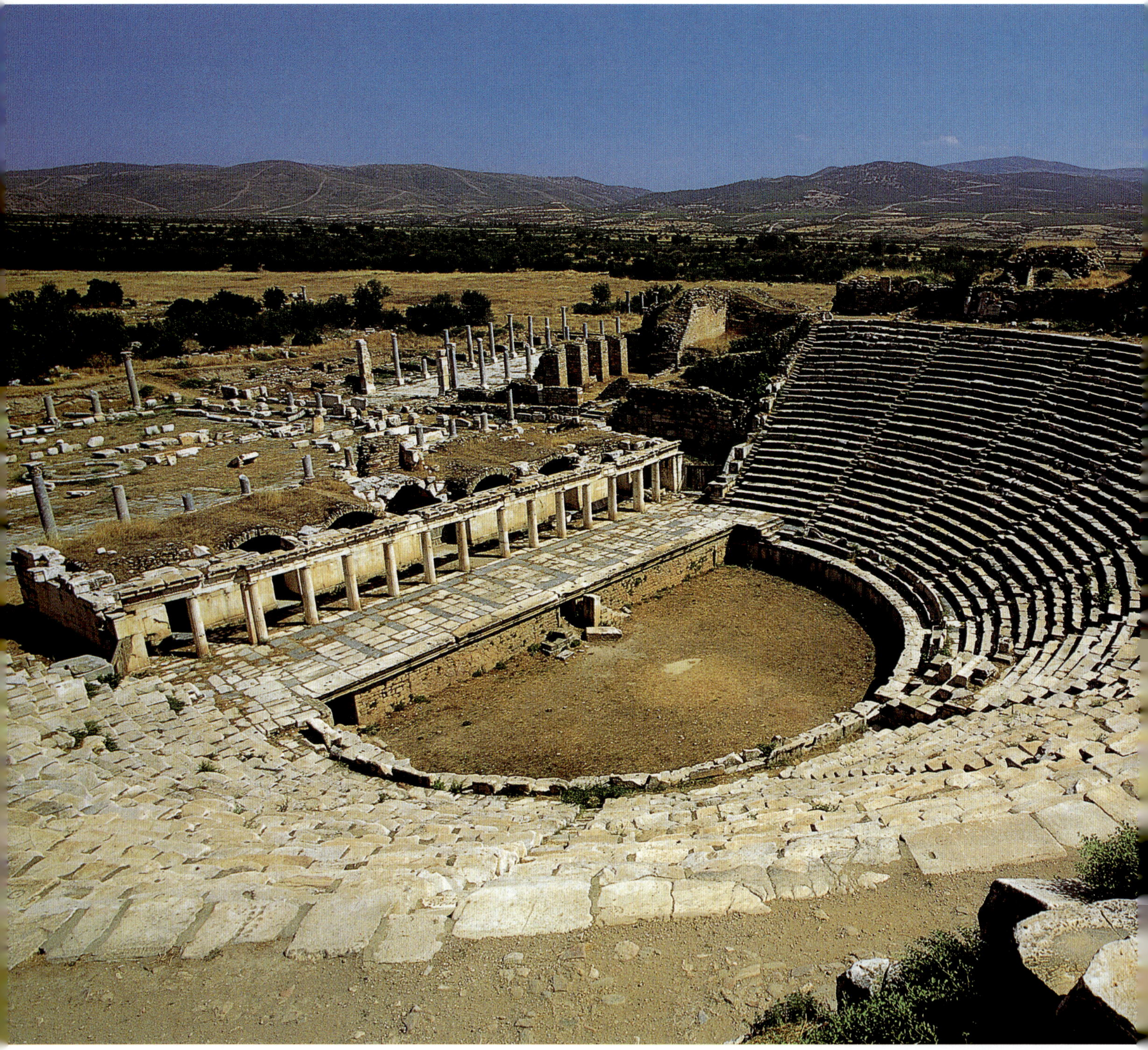

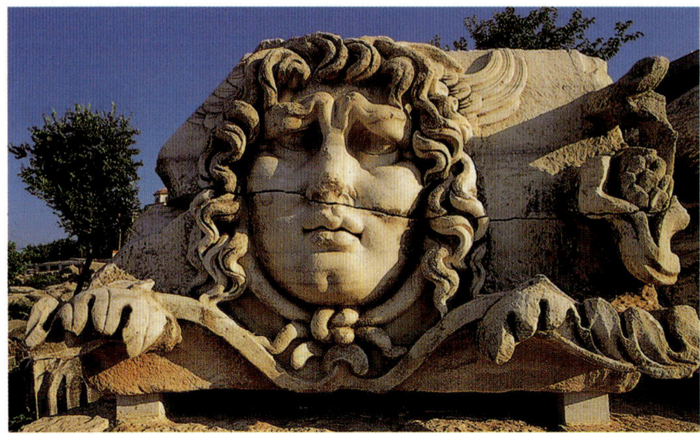

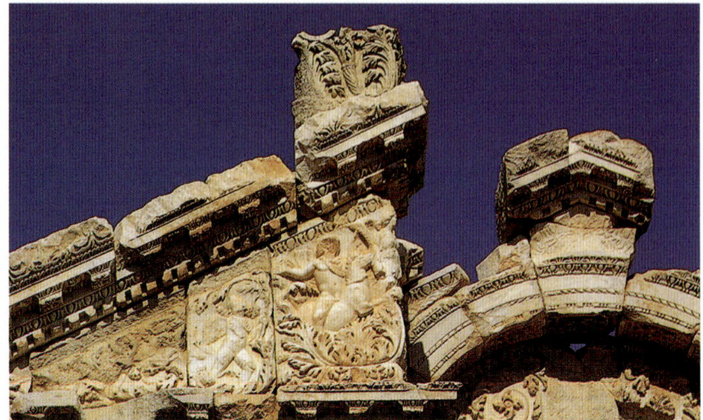

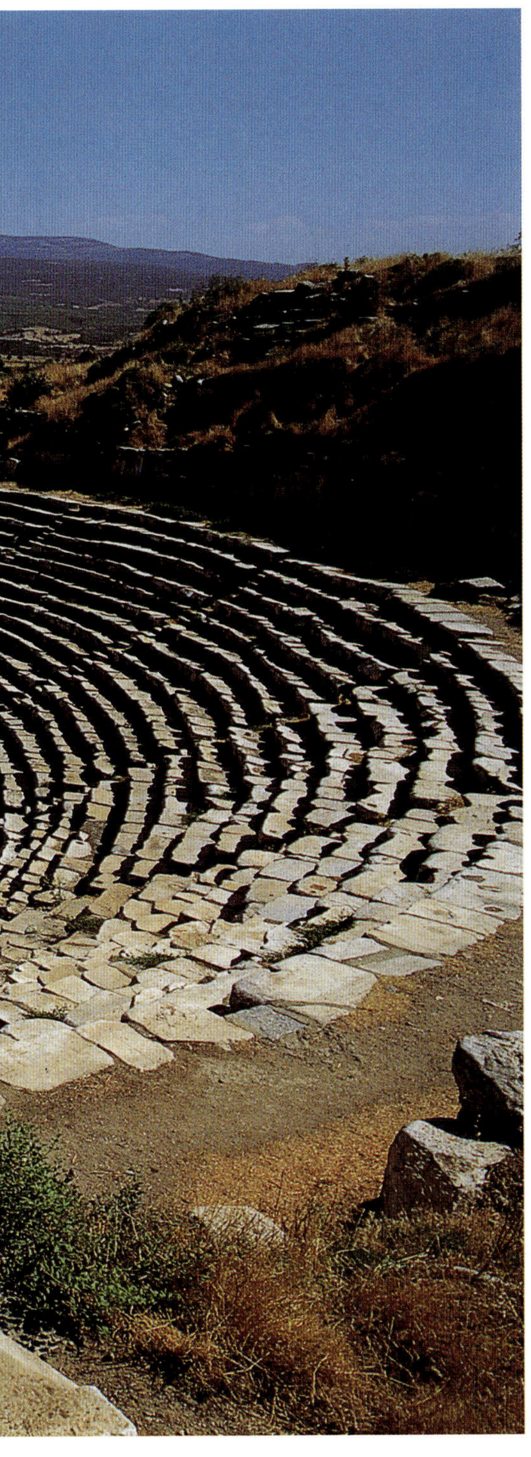

Under Augustus, the number of provinces increased considerably. After his victory at Actium, Egypt fell into the hands of Rome, soon followed by the Alpine regions (the Maritime Alps, the Cottian Alps, Raetia and Noricum), Dalmatia, Pannonia and Lusitania (present-day Portugal), and Galatia in northeast Anatolia. Provincial administration was radically modified: territories requiring a military garrison were placed under the direct control of Augustus, while all the others were left to the senate. The provinces were thus divided into two classes: imperial and senatorial.

In the case of the senatorial provinces, the senate chose the governors internally from former consuls (this was compulsory for the two prestigious provinces of Africa and Asia) or praetors. All governors, chosen by lot, received the title of proconsul, and held office for a year (unless extended), aided by a number of officials dealing with specific sectors. The emperor could influence the appointments by virtue of a special prerogative called *imperium proconsulare maius*, which placed him above all the governors.

Imperial provinces were ruled by magistrates called *legati Augusti propraetore*, chosen by the emperor from among the senators; former consuls were appointed for the provinces with the largest military contingents, and former praetors for the others. They too were aided by other officials, and the duration of their office was at the emperor's discretion. Other minor provinces were also placed under the direct control of Augustus; these were

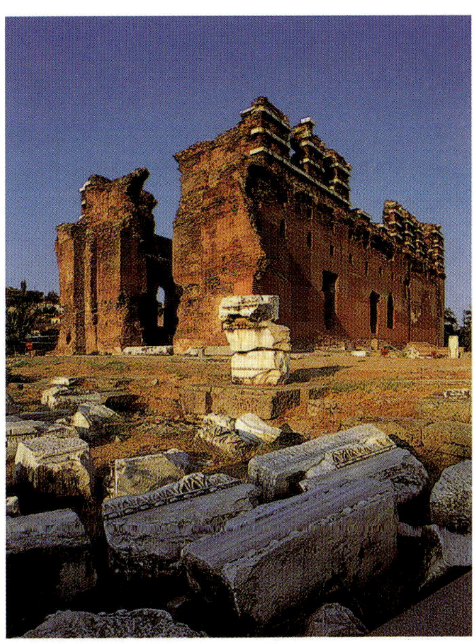

governed by members of the equestrian order, under the title of *procuratores*.

Egypt, which differed from the other provinces because of its special administrative, economic and cultural traditions was treated as if it were the emperor's private property. It was administered by an official of the equestrian order (a *praefectus*) who was given command of the legionary troops. Past experience had warned Augustus of the danger that Egypt could become a territorial power base for the senators, in opposition to imperial power.

Finally, Augustus left some regions to client kings, and allowed certain cities or sanctuaries to maintain a degree of independence. In various provinces particular towns had their own statutes or privileges, which fell into disuse with time. Tax exemptions existed, for example, in the *coloniae civium romanorum*, colonies to which military colonists had been sent, while other towns retained the titles of *liberae* or *foederatae*, although their inhabitants were not Roman citizens but *peregrini*.

The principles laid down by Augustus remained in force until the 2nd century AD, when the changes which were to lead to Diocletian's general reorganization began.

196–197 Theatrical performances, circus races and gladiatorial fights were some of the most typical social events in the Roman world and were very popular throughout the empire. As a result, buildings for public entertainment – like this superb theatre at Aphrodisias in present-day Turkey – are to be found in every province.

196 (opposite, below left) Miletus, an ancient city in Asia Minor, entered the Roman sphere of influence in the 2nd century BC and flourished during the empire. Nearby is the great sanctuary of Apollo, at Didyma, built in the Hellenistic era; the relief with the Gorgon's head is part of an extension built under Hadrian.

196 (opposite, below right) Aphrodisias was a flourishing metropolis in the province of Caria. The most original of the city's monuments is the tetrapylon *(a detail of which is shown here), a building in the shape of a four-sided arch supported by sets of columns rather than pillars. It dates from the mid-2nd century AD.*

197 (top) Pergamum, capital of the kingdom ruled by the Attalid dynasty, in Asia Minor, became Roman in 133 BC, and reached the peak of its prosperity in the imperial age, especially under Trajan and Hadrian. The Kizil Avlu, perhaps a basilica or a sanctuary consecrated to an oriental deity, dates from that period.

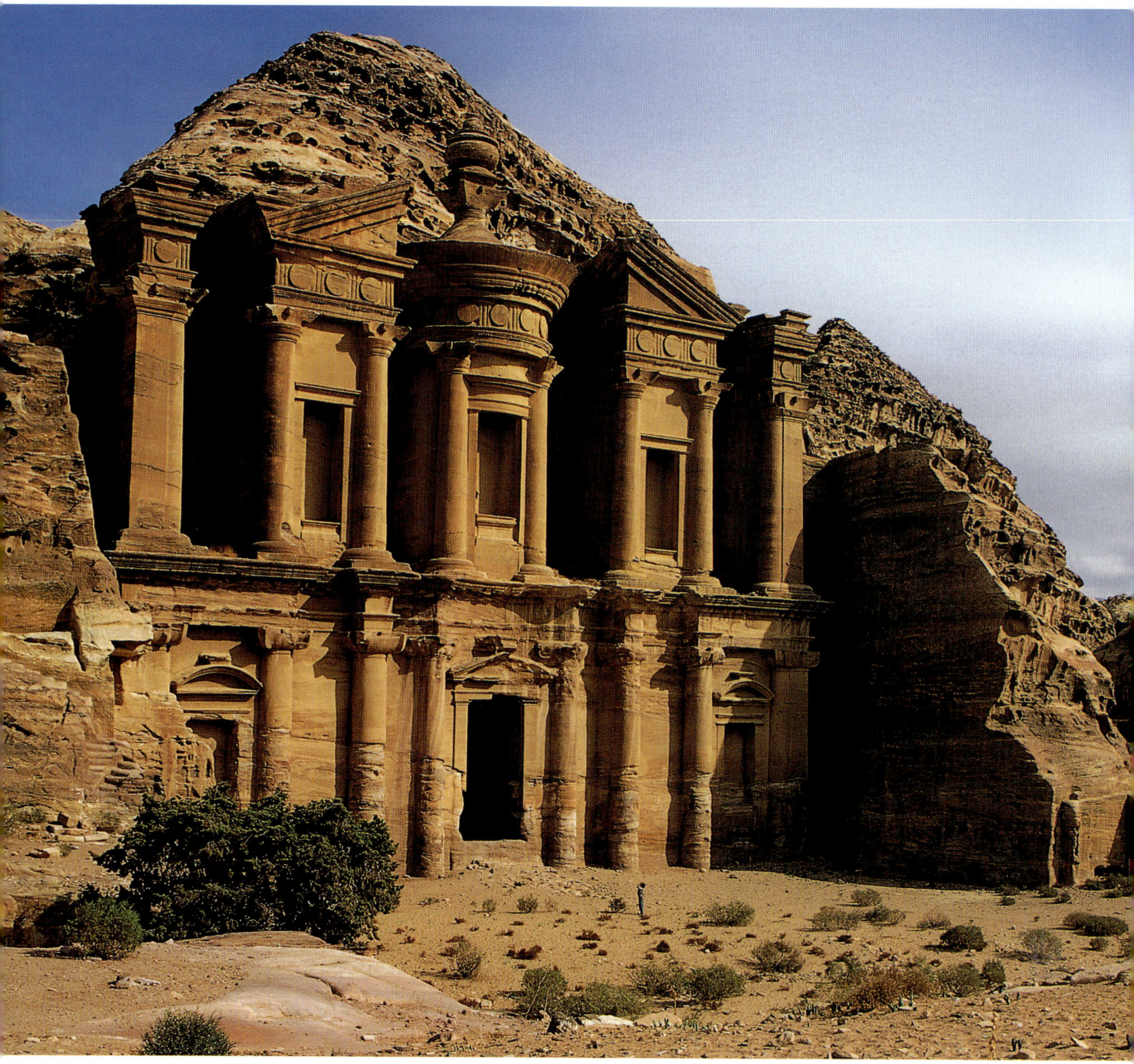

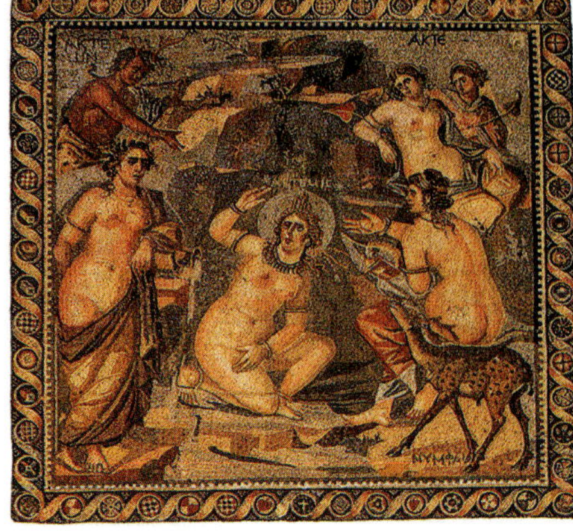

198–199 (above) Petra, the ancient capital of the kingdom of the Nabataeans in present-day Jordan, became the capital of the province of Arabia in AD *106. The city stood in a deep valley hollowed out by a river and because of the limited space, the main Nabataean monuments (mostly tombs and temples) were carved from the surrounding rock faces. Roman artistic influence can mainly be seen in the architectural façades constructed between the mid-1st century and the late 3rd century* AD. *The most spectacular monument in Petra demonstrating Roman influence is the building known as the Monastery, a temple with an imposing façade, 39 m (128 ft) tall.*

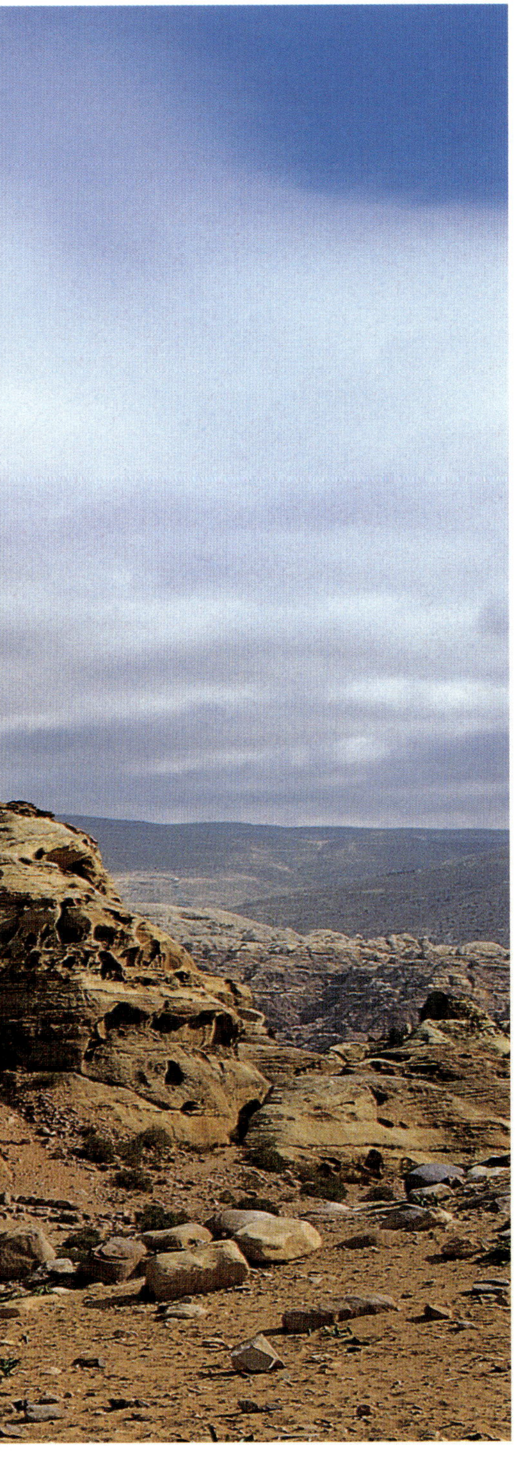

In the east, all features of independence which had so far been allowed in individual provinces disappeared; in the west, gradual Romanization took place, aided by the foundation of new colonies and the massive presence of legionary camps in border areas. Territorial extension during this period mainly came about through the defence or strengthening of borders. The two German provinces, Noricum and the Agri Decumates guaranteed the security of the Rhine–Danube border. Under Claudius, Britannia was conquered, and the provinces of Thrace, Lycia and Pamphylia were established. The province of Moesia was also founded in the Julio-Claudian era. Finally, Judaea, a client kingdom, became an equestrian province after its conquest by Titus. Trajan advocated a true expansionist strategy; after conquering Dacia, with its gold mines, he also declared Arabia, Assyria, Mesopotamia and Armenia Maior provinces.

Hadrian pursued a more prudent policy, preferring to abandon some of the territories conquered by his predecessor and concentrating instead on defence of the borders; Hadrian's Wall is one result. Under Septimius Severus, Assyria and Mesopotamia again became provinces and the province of Numidia was founded; Syria and Britannia were divided in half, and some regions were removed from Galatia making defence of the borders easier and preventing a governor obtaining command of too many legions.

Under Caracalla's Constitutio Antoniniana, Roman citizenship was granted to all subjects of Rome in AD 212. Conditions in the empire were particularly difficult at this time. In the east the Sasanians were growing in strength, while in the west the barbarian world was in upheaval. This barely controllable situation resulted in increasing political instability, combined with a serious economic crisis aggravated by continual wars. The unity of the empire was severely tested. A general of Gallienus, Postumus, founded an *imperium Galliarum* of Gaul, Britannia and Spain, and in AD 260 an independent kingdom was proclaimed in Palmyra by the sovereign Odaenathus, who took the title *dux orientis*.

A major reform of this period, generally attributed to Diocletian, led to the creation of a much more fragmented structure, designed to deal with the serious problems relating to border defence and the work of the provincial officers. For this purpose, the territory of each individual province was reduced, increasing their number to around 90; thus divided they were easier to manage, but lost their historical and cultural individuality. They were governed by a member of the equestrian order, the *praeses* or *corrector*, except for Africa, Asia and Achaea, which were still governed by a proconsul who reported to the emperor in person. Egypt continued to be governed by a *praefectus*. All that was left to the governor of each province was civil jurisdiction as military jurisdiction was handled by a *dux*, sometimes responsible for more than one territory.

The new provinces were grouped into 13 dioceses governed by *vicarii*, which in turn depended on the four prefectures of the praetor. The *vicarii* were directly responsible to the emperor, and the various governors,

198 (opposite below) This magnificent mosaic, of Artemis surprised while bathing, is in the museum of the Syrian town of Suweida, the ancient Dionysias. Many Hellenistic and Roman ruins are found here, once a flourishing caravan town, demonstrating the spread of western artistic influences in Syria.

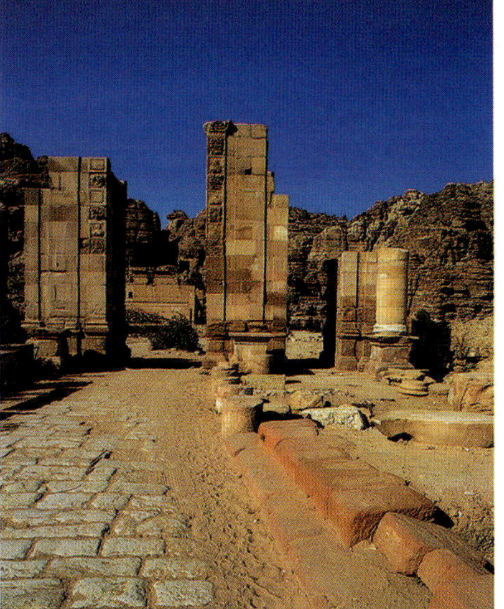

199 (right) In Roman times, Petra developed along the valley bottom after the river bed was filled in to make room for the forum, surrounded by various temples, a gymnasium, baths and shops. The main road was straddled by a triumphal arch with three archways, unfortunately destroyed by an earthquake.

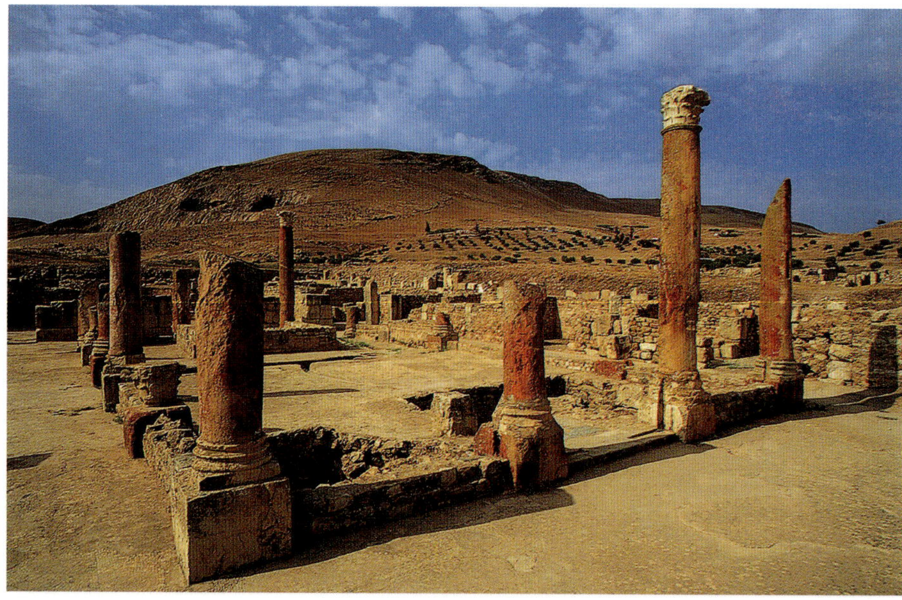

200 Bulla Regia, an attractive Roman town built on the steep slopes of Jebel Rabia in Tunisia, was promoted to the status of a colony by Hadrian. As well as numerous remains of public buildings, this town is famous for some large villas (a detail of the House of the Hunt is shown here), with the various rooms facing on to a central courtyard.

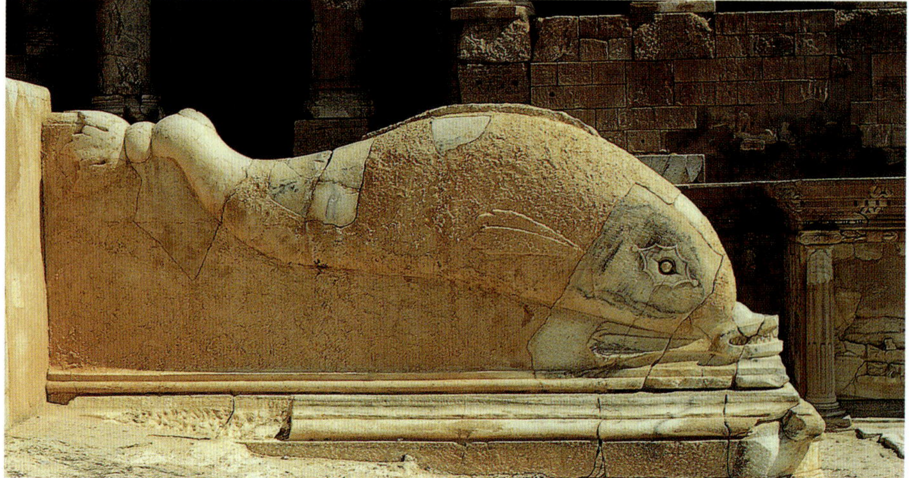

200 Sabratha, an ancient port of Phoenician origin in present-day Libya, became part of the province of Africa under Julius Caesar; it enjoyed great wealth and prestige until the late 3rd century AD, when its slow decline began. Monuments of exceptional interest such as the theatre (a decorative element from which is shown here) have been found at the archaeological site, which has not yet been completely excavated.

201 (opposite) Sufetula, a Roman town near present-day Sbeitla in Tunisia, was probably founded in the 1st century AD and flourished mainly under the Antonine and Severan dynasties. The most interesting of the important and well-preserved ruins, is the capitolium, with its highly original design, consisting of a set of three separate temples, each dedicated to a deity of the Capitoline triad.

now deprived of military power, became easier to control. In addition to aiding border defence, the separation of military and civil power was designed to prevent governors in major territorial bases with large garrisons being proclaimed emperor – generally elicited with gifts of cash obtained from illegal taxes. Italy was placed on a par with the other territories in the empire (losing a series of tax privileges), and divided into two dioceses, Italia Annonaria (northern Italy) governed by the *vicarius Italiae*, and Italia Suburbicaria (in the centre and south of the country), governed by the *vicarius Romae*. Diocletian's work was carried on by Constantine and his successors, who perfected the already complex bureaucratic system. The serious problem of territorial integrity and the financial resources needed to maintain an efficient army were their main objectives; the costs were borne by the inhabitants of the provinces, who were subjected to increasingly heavy taxation. The great barbarian invasions brought this complex provincial system to an end in the west, but it survived in the eastern empire, though radically modified.

One of the most interesting sources providing a detailed picture of the organization of the empire at this period is the *Notitia Dignitatum*. A richly illustrated manuscript, it presents numerous dating problems, but is generally believed to relate to

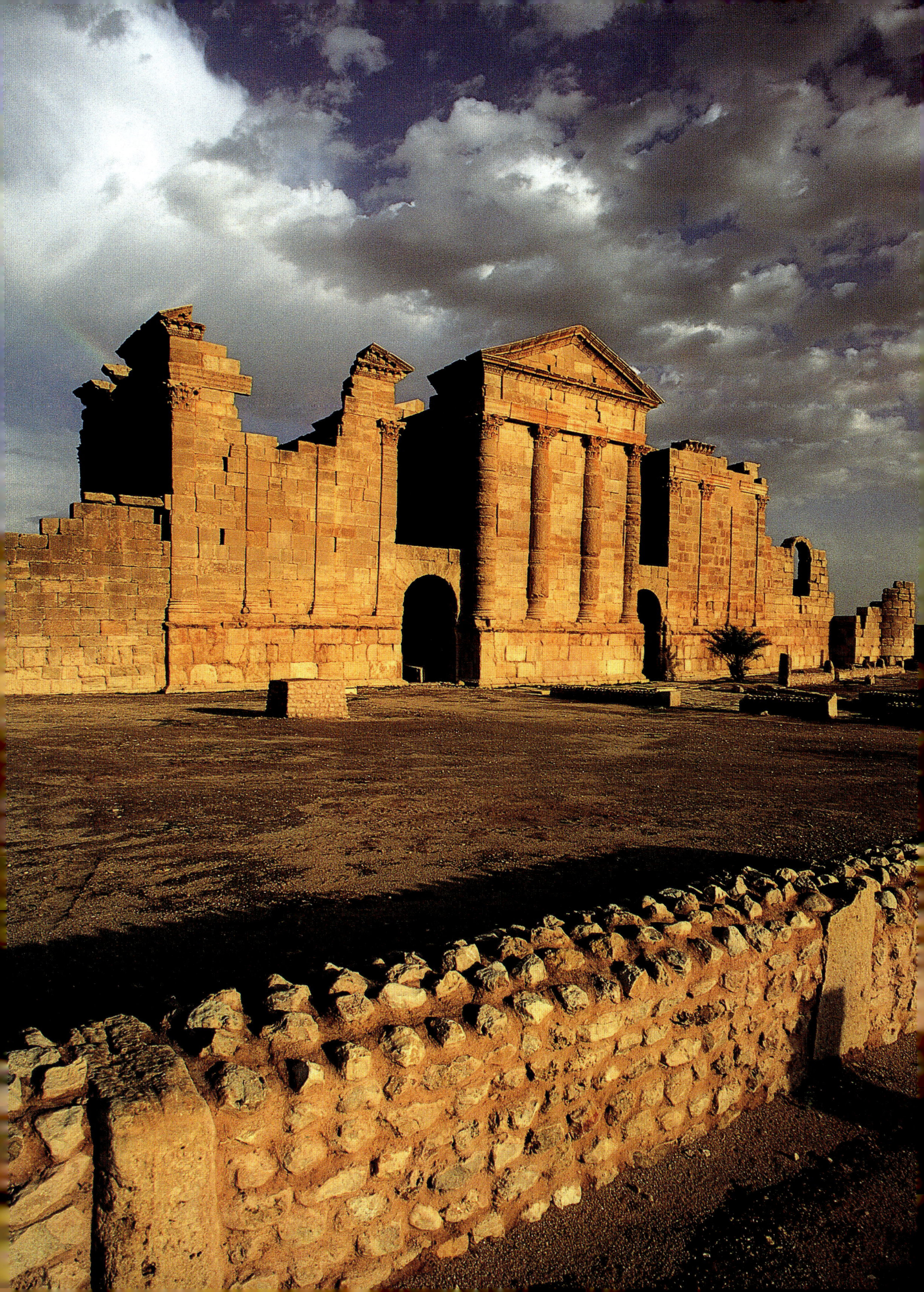

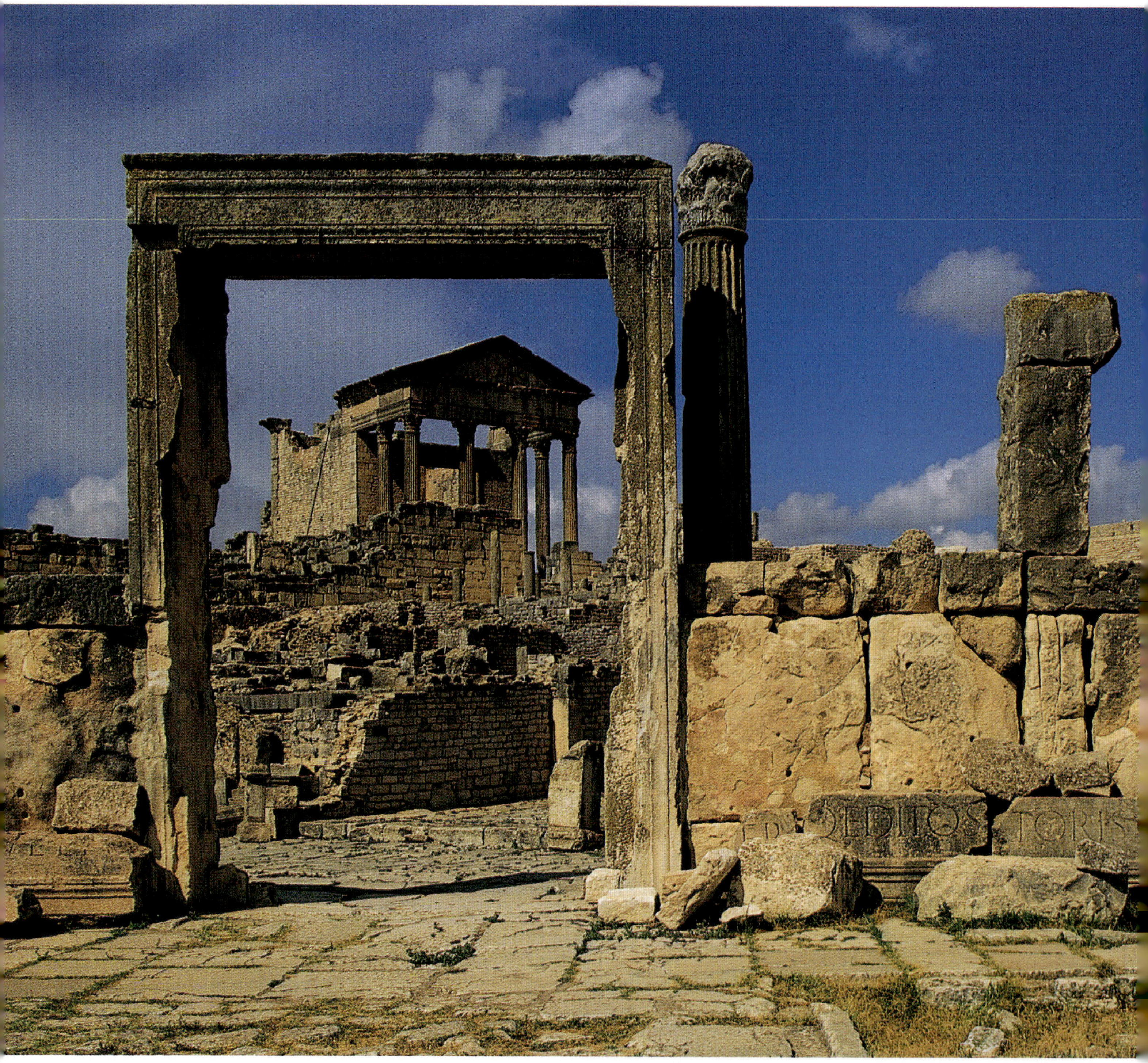

202–203 (above) *Dougga, the ancient Thugga, is one of the best-preserved Roman towns in the Tunisian Maghreb. Annexed to the province of Africa by Julius Caesar in 46* BC, *it became a* municipium *in* AD *105 and a colony in 261. The terraced layout and irregular plan of the town demonstrate its Punic origins, while the forum, the great theatre, the baths, the Temple of Caelestis, and the capitolium (shown here) are eloquent evidence of intensive Romanization. The town, which must have had around 5000 inhabitants, prospered as a result of the cultivation of the fertile surrounding plain watered by a wealth of springs.*

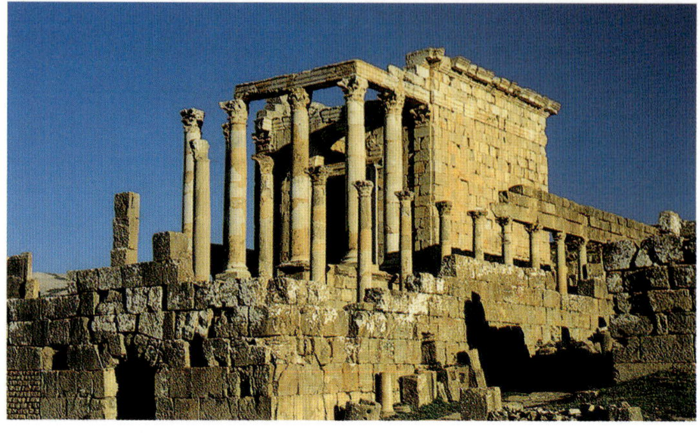

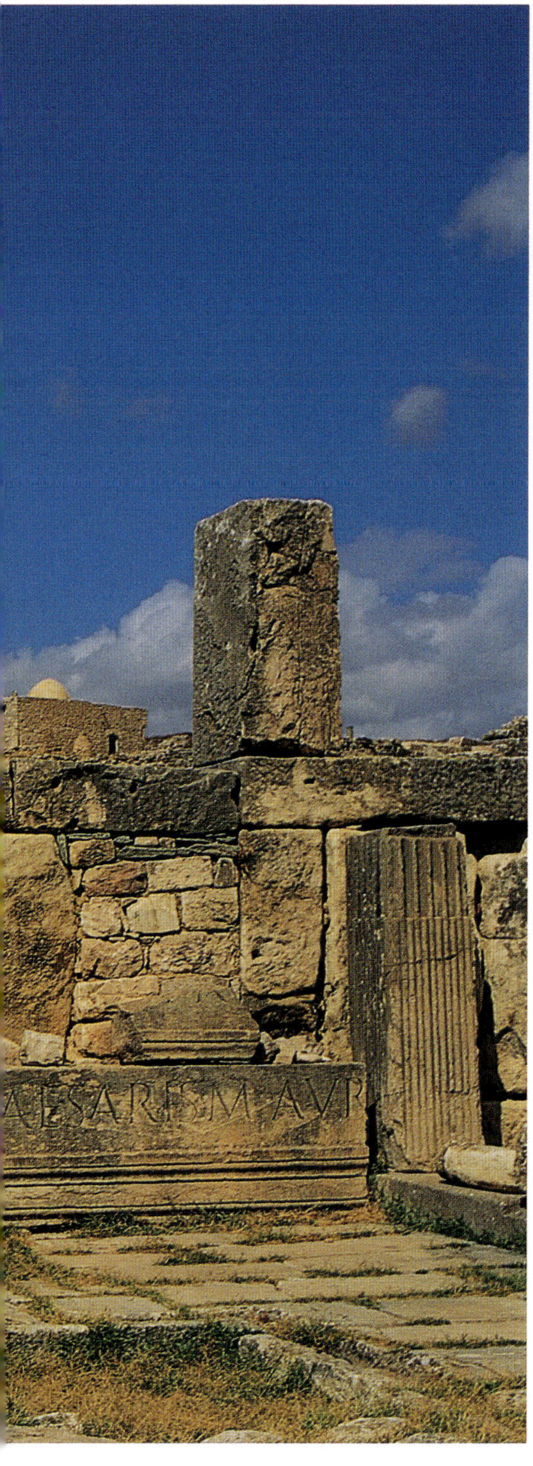

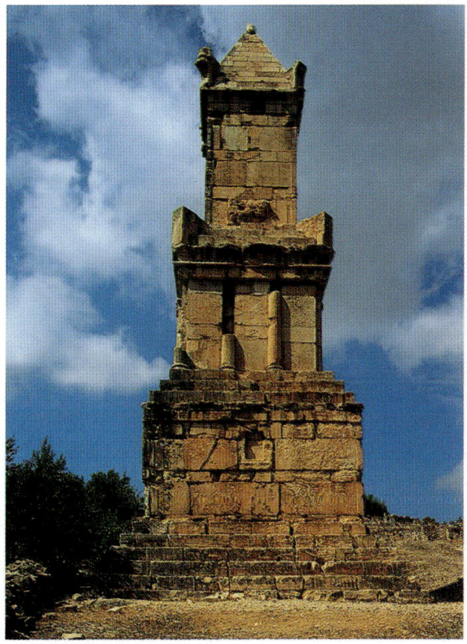

202 (opposite, below) Cuicul (now Djemila, in Algeria), which became a colony under Nerva, reached the height of its splendour between the 2nd and 3rd centuries. Mainly an agricultural town, it was fairly wealthy and was enriched with some impressive public monuments, including the temple of the Severan dynasty.

203 (above) Not far from Thugga stands a tower-tomb dating to the 2nd century BC. *Though of Punic origin, this monument is of great interest because the same architectural design is frequently repeated in mausoleums erected in numerous parts of the empire, confirming the heterogeneous and eclectic nature of Roman art.*

the mid- or late 4th century AD. It describes the civil and military offices of the eastern and western empires in minute detail, in order of importance, and lists the territorial divisions and structures and the military contingents responsible for organizing border defences.

In conclusion, the colonies, in many ways a territorial extension of the mother country, constituted the basic means whereby Roman civilization (language, customs, legal system, art and culture) spread beyond the narrow confines of Italy. In the other direction they acted as a conduit for absorbing and adapting all the external stimuli which made the Roman empire so unusual.

The colonies were symbols of power and the testing grounds of a complex society, which became increasingly sophisticated but also demanding and difficult to handle. They embodied a huge variety of experiences, externally manifested by monumental structures which evolved continually and were often more innovative than official ones. These experiences, transferred and assimilated to varying degrees, often influenced the development of tastes in the capital of the empire. Not only Roman architecture but also poetry, decorative arts, applied sciences and religion ceaselessly absorbed new influences, modified them and then transmitted them to the furthest corners of the empire in a continuous cycle. In spite of their differences, financial and intellectual exchanges between the various provinces were continuous. Olive oil produced in Africa was sold for high prices in Rome, tin from the mines of Britannia was exported widely, carts made in Gaul travelled the roads of the entire empire, and Greek and Jewish historians recorded the feats of Roman generals.

This ability to absorb such disparate elements, using them to reinvigorate itself, while retaining its own essential cultural features, was one of the distinctive features of Roman civilization, together with the tireless drive to extend its borders. Astute merchants and great travellers, the Romans journeyed as far as Zanzibar and Samarkand, traded with Begram, in Afghanistan, and along the Ganges, and reached the banks of the Huang Ho in China and the southernmost tip of India. In addition to spices and the finest fabrics, precious metals and objets d'art, a wide variety of ideas and stimuli flowed into Rome and other cities of the empire, which in turn influenced distant peoples and cultures. For example, a statue of Lakshmi, the Hindu goddess of fertility, was found in Pompeii, and archaeological excavations in China, India and southern Arabia have discovered Roman glassware, bronzes and coins carrying images of the Roman emperors.

Many modern countries that were part of the Roman empire still reveal their Roman heritage. Traces of Roman colonization remain in the place names of regions and towns, sometimes even of countries, in the languages and dialects spoken in Europe today (such as Romanian), in the presence of a large number of towns founded at the time of the republic or the empire, and even in the routes of many major roads still in use, from Scotland to Syria, from Spain to Hungary. The immense cultural, architectural and historical legacy of ancient Rome is thus tangible in numerous aspects of contemporary life, and details are still being discovered today by international research.

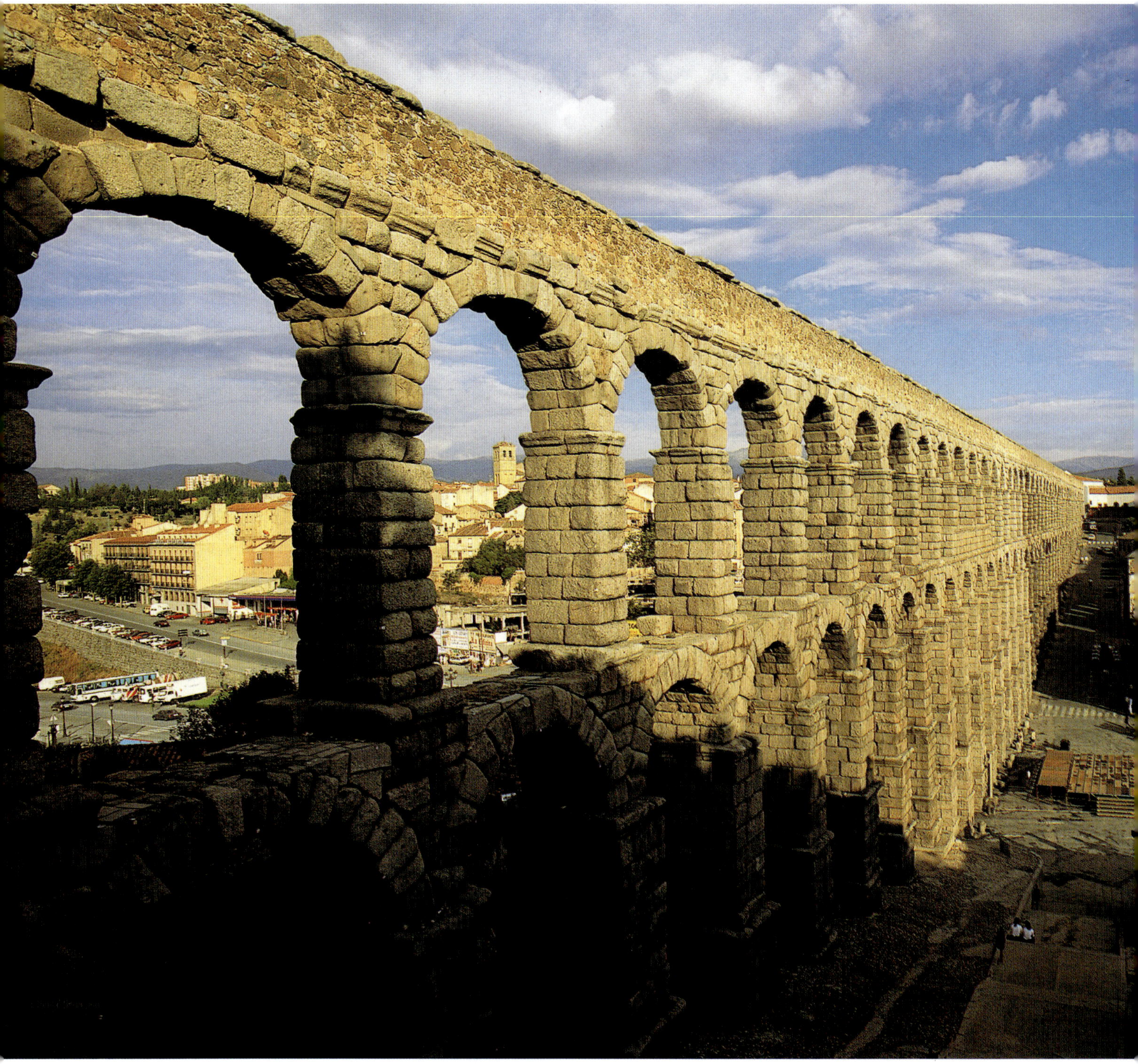

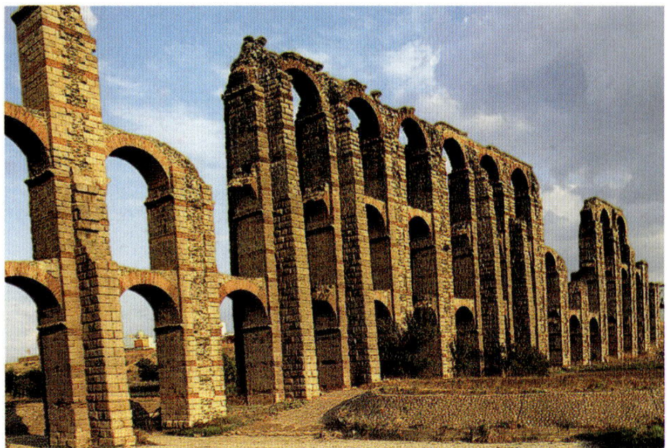

204 (left) The Los Milagros aqueduct at Merida is a spectacular example of Roman hydraulic engineering in the Iberian peninsula. Built in the 1st century AD, *it brought water to the town from a spring 5 km (3 miles) away, crossing the valley of the Rio Albarregas on a series of arches 830 m (2720 ft) long.*

204–205 (above) The Romans, who were skilled builders, solved the problem of the water supply for the various towns in the empire by diverting springs, some of which were some distance from the towns they served. Pipes ran inside masonry aqueducts which sometimes, as in the case of Segovia, had to cross valleys and natural depressions on a series of arches. The water was conveyed to a tank (the castellum aquae*), from which it was distributed under pressure to the town's water network. The Segovia aqueduct is one of the most grandiose in the Roman world; built of granite blocks fitted without mortar, it is 728 m (2388 ft) long and 29 m (95 ft) high.*

THE IBERIAN PROVINCES, LANDS WITH A HEALTHY ECONOMY

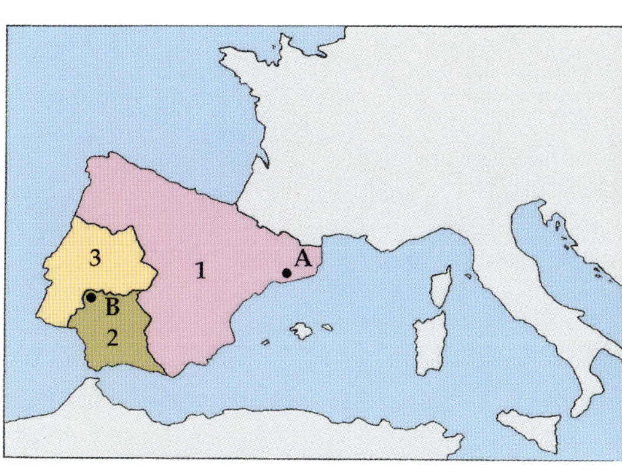

1 Tarraconensis
2 Baetica
3 Lusitania
A Tarragona
B Merida

205 (below) A marble portrait of Augustus, dating from the early 1st century AD, found in Merida is now in the local Museum of Roman Art. The emperor is shown in his capacity as Pontifex Maximus *(High Priest), the leading religious authority of the Roman state, with his head covered. He was appointed to this office in 12 BC when he had already obtained supreme command of the army as well as legal, political and administrative power.*

Roman dominion over the Iberian provinces had its origins during the Second Punic War. In the decades that followed, the Romans had to deal with numerous rebellions by the indigenous populations, culminating in the great uprising of the Celtiberians in 133 BC, which ended with the capture and destruction of Numantia by Scipio Aemilianus. The war against Sulla, in which Sertorius led troops of natives, Italics and Romans, was crucial to the Romanization of the peninsula. Caesar's victories in Spain, at Lerida in 49 BC and Munda in 45 BC, were important landmarks in the crisis which led to the final demise of the republic.

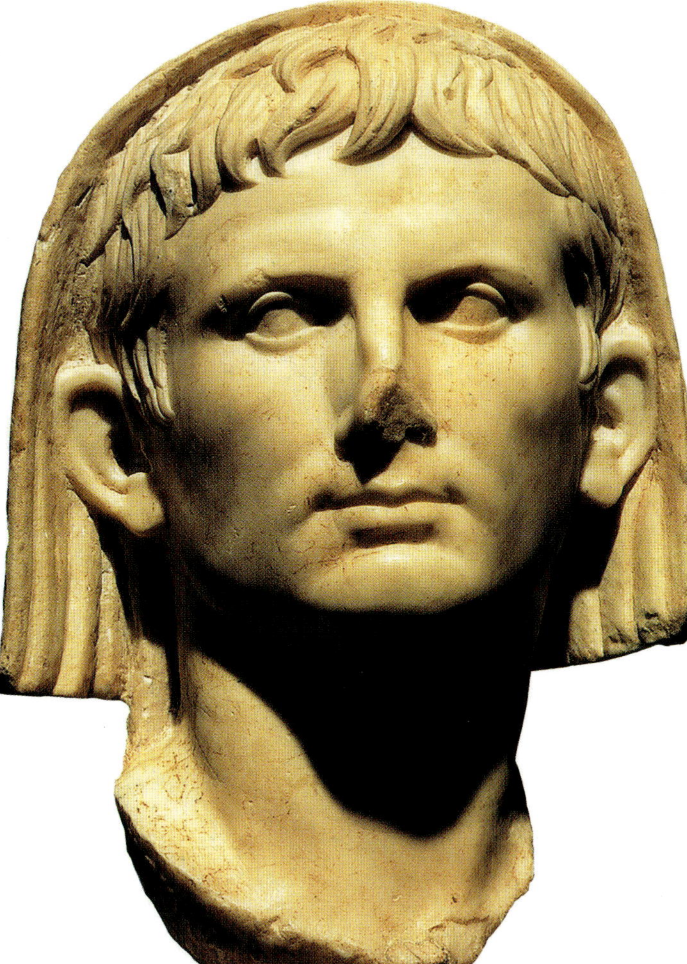

Clashes with tribes of the western Atlantic coasts and of the far northwestern regions of Cantabria, Asturia and Galicia continued for some time, until Augustus decided to put an end to them once and for all by sending Vipsanius Agrippa, one of his most loyal assistants. As life in the Spanish provinces was fairly peaceful under the empire, a single garrison was left there, manned by a legion stationed in Hispania Tarraconensis in a place named Legio after it (now León).

Numerous monuments and major public works in the peninsula demonstrate the widespread adoption of Roman civilization by the population, as well as the almost total dominance of Latin language and Roman religion. Some notable personalities came from Spain, including Seneca, Martial, Lucan, Quintilian and the emperors Trajan, Hadrian and Theodosius.

The Iberian provinces made a major contribution to the economy of the empire, mainly through their mineral and agricultural resources, but also (though to a much lesser extent) through the products of their industries. These included the salting of fish, which flourished on the southern and Atlantic coasts.

One of the main exports was oil, of which Baetica was a major producer. There was enormous demand for oil in the Roman world, for use not only in food, but also in personal hygiene and lighting. Spanish oil was imported to Rome between the 1st and 3rd centuries, carried by sea in amphoras of a roughly spherical shape and with an average capacity of 60–70 litres (13–15 gallons). They

206 (below) *Italica, founded by Scipio in 206* BC, *is the oldest Roman town in Spain. However, it was overshadowed by the more flourishing Seville (Hispalis) nearby, and became a* municipium *at a very late date. Two of the greatest Roman emperors, Trajan and Hadrian, were born here. Under Hadrian the town saw radical building work based on Hellenistic models. The magnificent town houses with mosaic floors uncovered by archaeologists date from that period.*

206–207 (right) *The amphitheatre at Italica, one of the largest in the Roman world, could hold 25,000 spectators and is part of Hadrian's extensive building works in the town. The rooms and service tunnels under the arena are well preserved.*

207 (opposite, below left) *The bridge over the Tagus near Alcantara was built by Trajan between* AD *105 and 106 at the expense of 11 Lusitanian* municipia. *The bridge, which has six arches (the longest of which has a 36-m (118-ft) span) is 143 m (469 ft) long, and was designed by the architect C. Julius Lacer to withstand the sporadic but violent flooding of the river.*

207 (opposite, below right) *Evora (Ebora), in Portugal, was one of the most important Roman colonies in Lusitania. Founded by Caesar under the name of Liberalitas Iulia, its greatest splendour came in the 2nd century* AD. *The Temple of Diana, of which 14 elegant Corinthian columns on a podium survive, belongs to this period.*

were often stamped with inscriptions indicating the capacity of the container, the exporter's name and the date. When the ships arrived in Rome the oil was decanted and the amphoras were destroyed as they were difficult to reuse. The Monte Testaccio (in Latin *mons testaceus*, or hill of sherds) is an artificial hill formed of amphora fragments, mostly of Spanish type, from the nearby river port. Monte Testaccio (not the only hill of sherds in Rome) is 30 m (98 ft) high and covers 20,000 sq. m (215,285 sq. ft), giving some idea of the scale of these imports. In the mid-3rd century Spanish oil, which was exported as far as Germany and Britannia, was replaced by African.

The Iberian peninsula was also a major producer of metals in the Roman world: gold, silver, iron, tin, copper and lead were exported in

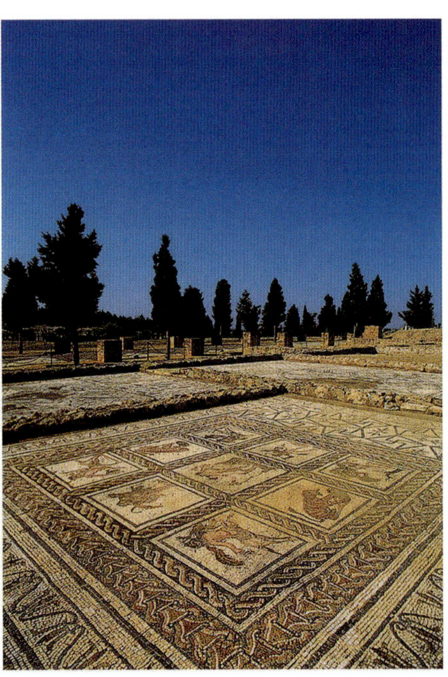

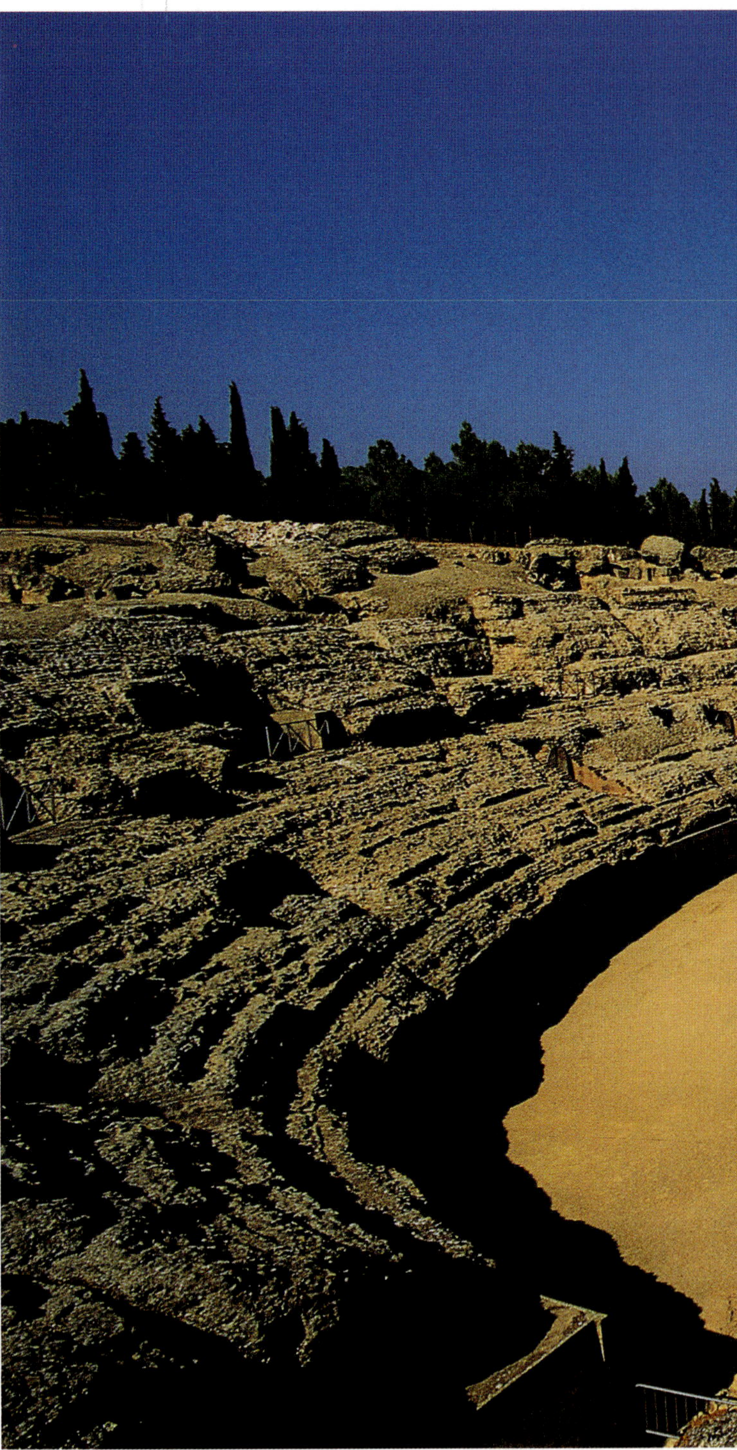

the form of ingots, not only to Rome, but also to other provinces. At the time of Polybius, 40,000 miners worked in the Cartagena silver mines. Spanish iron was of exceptional purity, allowing the production of high-quality weapons, which the Romans soon imitated. The law governing the copper and silver mines of Aljustrel in Lusitania (the *lex metalli Vipascensis*, dating to Hadrian) describes the exploitation of the Spanish mineral resources.

Recent excavations have revealed interesting technical information about the operation of the mines. In particular, the remains of some examples of the 'Archimedes screw' were found. This was a mechanical device used to drain underground water, extracting a huge amount of water with minimal effort. Large waterwheels, the remains of which have also been found, were used to increase the height and pressure of the water raised.

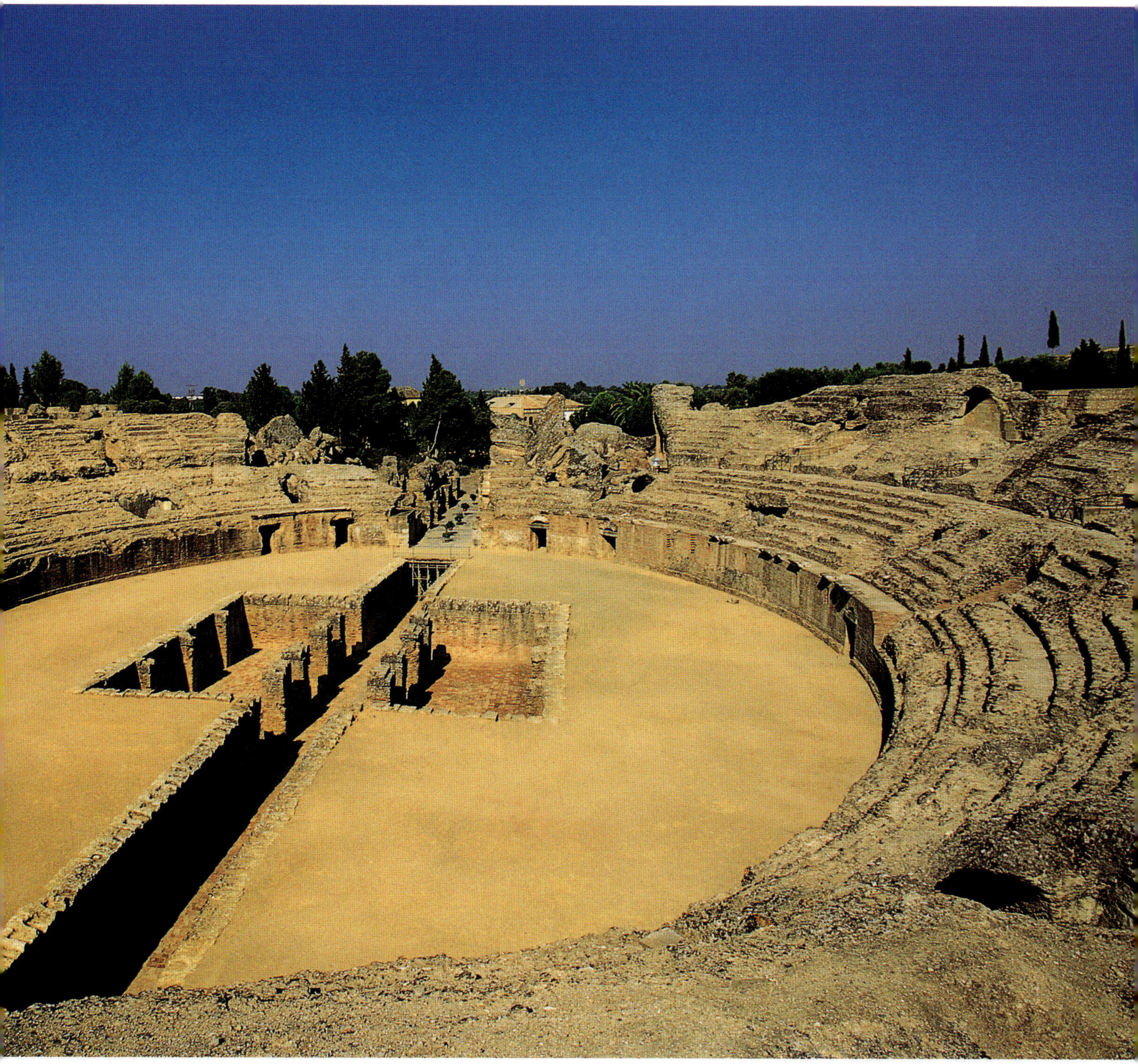

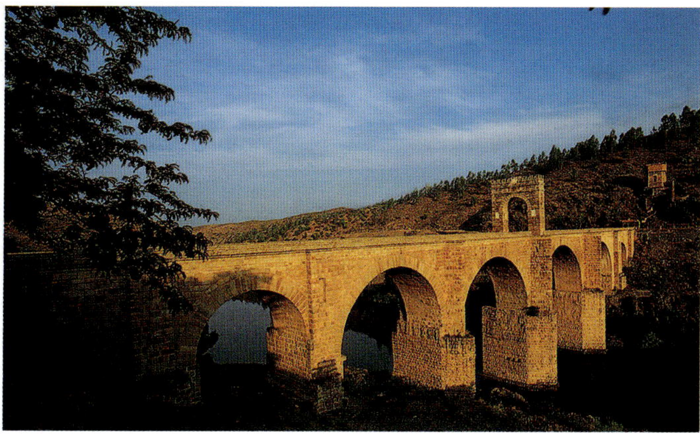

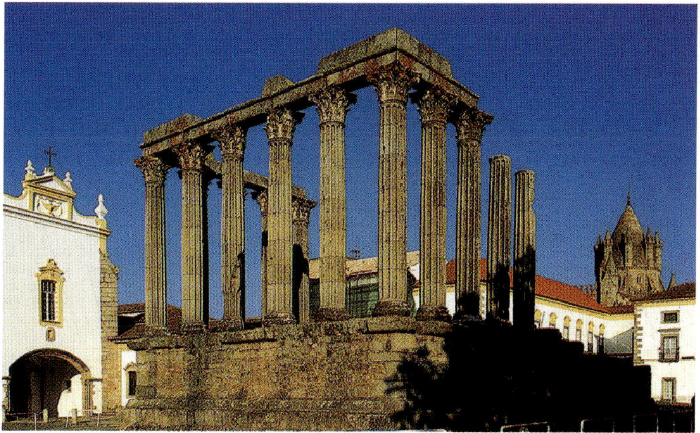

TARRAGONA, A PORT AT THE MOUTH OF THE EBRO

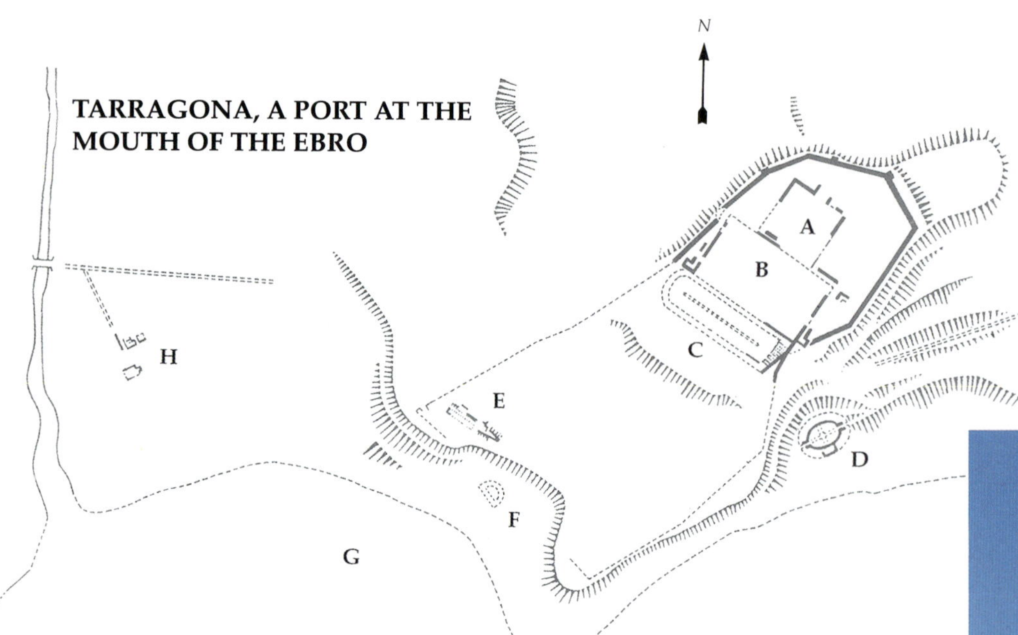

A Sacred enclosure
B Provincial Forum
C Circus
D Amphitheatre
E Urban Forum
F Theatre
G Port
H Necropolis

Ancient Tarraco, originally a city of the Hergetes, was the capital of Hispania Tarraconensis, also known as Hispania Citerior. It was already a colony under Caesar, and in 16 BC Augustus confirmed its status as capital of the region. Built near the mouth of the Ebro river, the Romans built a port which no longer survives.

In the port district are the remains of the theatre, the amphitheatre and a *macellum*, while the remains of the circus, the building known as Augustus' Palace, the forum, and what was probably the provincial governor's residence, dating to the second half of the 2nd century AD, are located in the upper town.

A temple dedicated to Augustus was built by Tiberius and restored under Hadrian and Septimius Severus. Other temples, such as that of Capitoline Jupiter and Minerva, are known almost solely from historical sources. What is believed to have been the governor's residential complex is very unusual; it is formed by the junction of the circus and the palace itself, joined at the eastern corner and located on the boundary of two town districts. Five aqueducts supplied Tarragona's drinking water; the main one, Las Ferreras, crosses a deep valley on two rows of arches. Various necropolises and the remains of numerous villas with mosaic floors are found around the town. The arch of Barà, built by Trajan's lieutenant Lucius Licinius Sura, is some 20 km (12 miles) from the town. Tarragona, an important centre of the imperial cult and an active trading centre for the wine and linen produced in the region, was seriously damaged by Franco-Alemanni raids in AD 260, and later devastated by the Arabs.

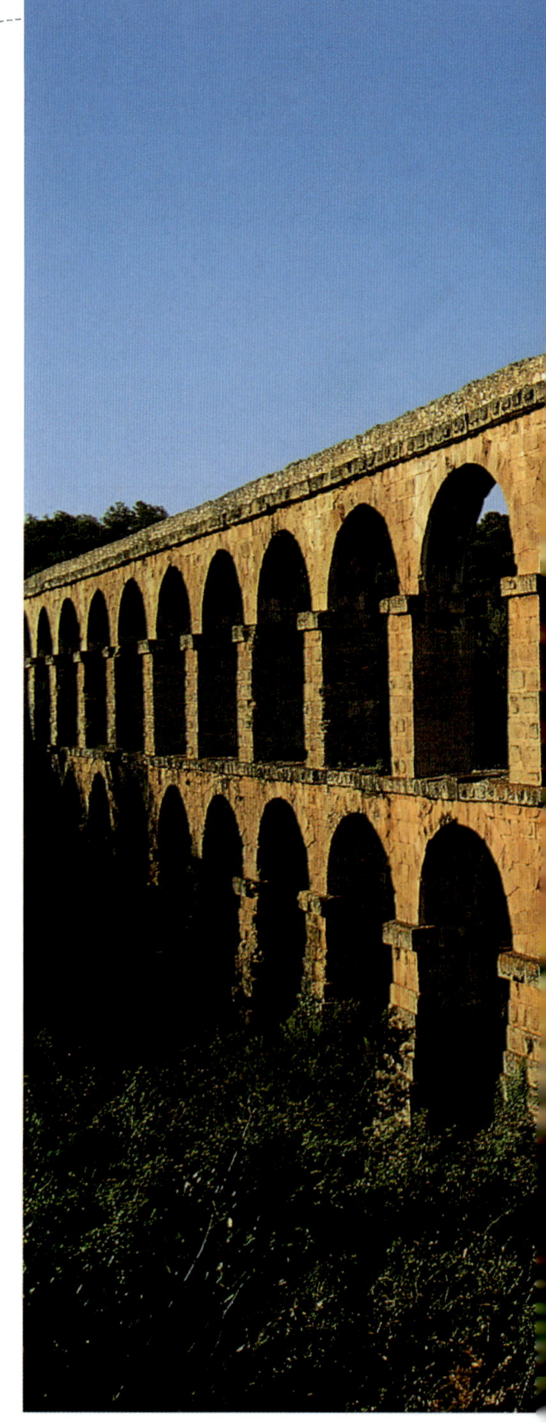

208–209 The Las Ferreras aqueduct, some 4 km (2.5 miles) from the town, is the most spectacular to survive in the eastern Iberian peninsula. It is 217 m (712 ft) long, and was built of stone blocks fitted together without mortar. At the top of the arches, the channel through which the water ran (the specus*) is still very well preserved.*

209 (opposite, above left) Tarragona was one of the few cities in Hispania to have an amphitheatre, confirming the social and political importance of this colony. The amphitheatre, dating from the first half of the 2nd century AD, was partially carved from the rock of the hillside which slopes down to the beach.

209 (opposite, above right) The circus, built in the late 1st century AD, completed the official programme of building work in ancient Tarraco. It was 325 m (1066 ft) long, and built in the style typical of this type of building, designed for chariot racing. A large part of the vaulted tunnels and some of the outer façade survive.

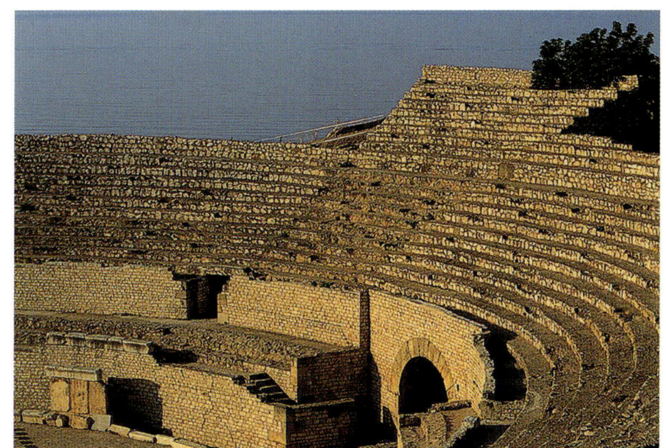

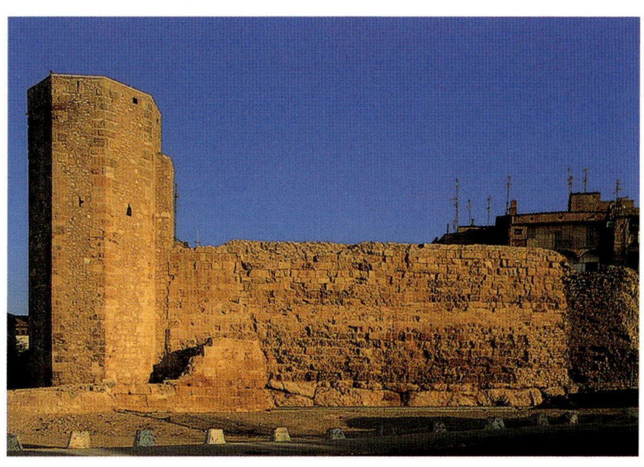

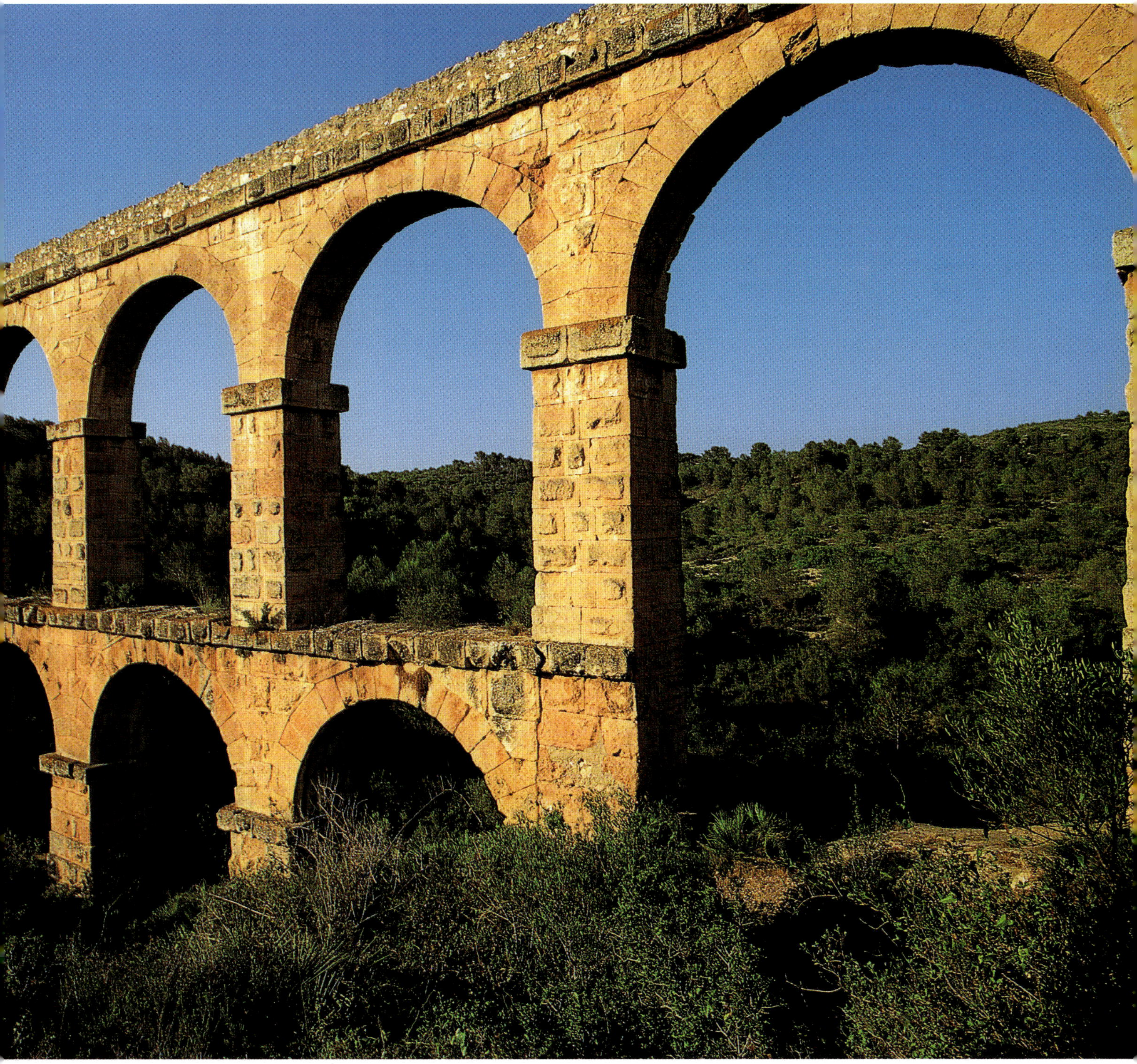

MERIDA, THE TOWN OF AUGUSTUS' VETERANS

A Bridge
B Arch of Trajan
C Temple of Diana
D Theatre
E Amphitheatre
F Circus
G San Lazaro Aqueduct
H Los Milagros aqueduct

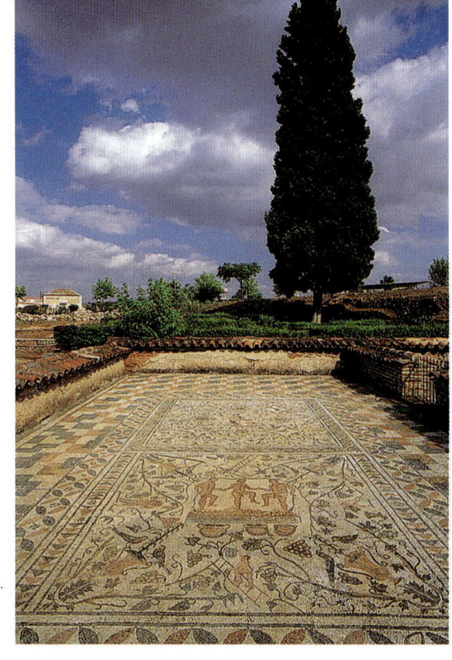

Emerita Augusta (modern Merida) was founded in 25 BC by a decree of Augustus and built by the veterans and emeritus soldiers of the 5th Alaudae and 10th Gemina legions as a military outpost. It became a flourishing trading centre, and, later, capital of Lusitania. Its impressive monuments make Merida one of the major archaeological sites in the Iberian peninsula. Its theatre, amphitheatre and circus, built in the same area outside the city walls, are well preserved. The entire *scaena* of the theatre has been completely rebuilt in recent years. A bridge over the Guadiana river, whose 60 arches span a distance of 792 m (2560 ft), is one of the longest surviving from the Roman period.

The town's water supply came from three aqueducts; large sections of the Los Milagros and San Lazaro have survived. The first, 25 m (82 ft) high, winds along an 830-m (2720-ft) route on 37 huge piers, made of alternating rows of granite and brick. It was supplied by a reservoir called Persephone's Lake, which has a large dam. An Arch of Trajan, the remains of a Temple of Diana and a small Temple of Mars, two mausoleums and a house converted into a Christian basilica can be seen in the town. Sections of the turreted city walls also survive. A sanctuary of Mithras has been excavated, bringing to light a group of marble sculptures, while others have been found in the necropolises and in the theatre.

Merida maintained its importance during the Christian and Visigoth periods, as shown by historical, artistic and epigraphic references.

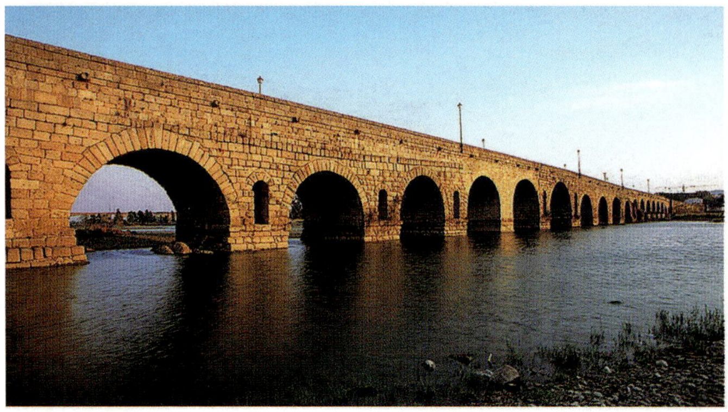

210 (top) Merida, founded as a military outpost for the control of Lusitania, soon became one of the wealthiest towns in the Iberian peninsula. This prosperity is demonstrated by the many archaeological finds in the urban area and the numerous monuments still visible today. This is one of the exquisite mosaics from a private house near the amphitheatre.

210 (centre) Three large aqueducts served the town; the one shown here is called the San Lazaro. In Merida, as in all the other cities of the empire, the operation of the aqueducts and all matters relating to water supply were handled by a magistrate called the curator aquarum.

210 (bottom) The bridge over the Guadiana is one of the most spectacular applications of the arch from the Roman age.

211 (opposite) Merida's magnificent theatre could hold up to 6000 spectators. After a long programme of rebuilding work on the scaena *(one of the loveliest in Europe) the building was restored to its original function, and now holds theatrical and musical seasons every year.*

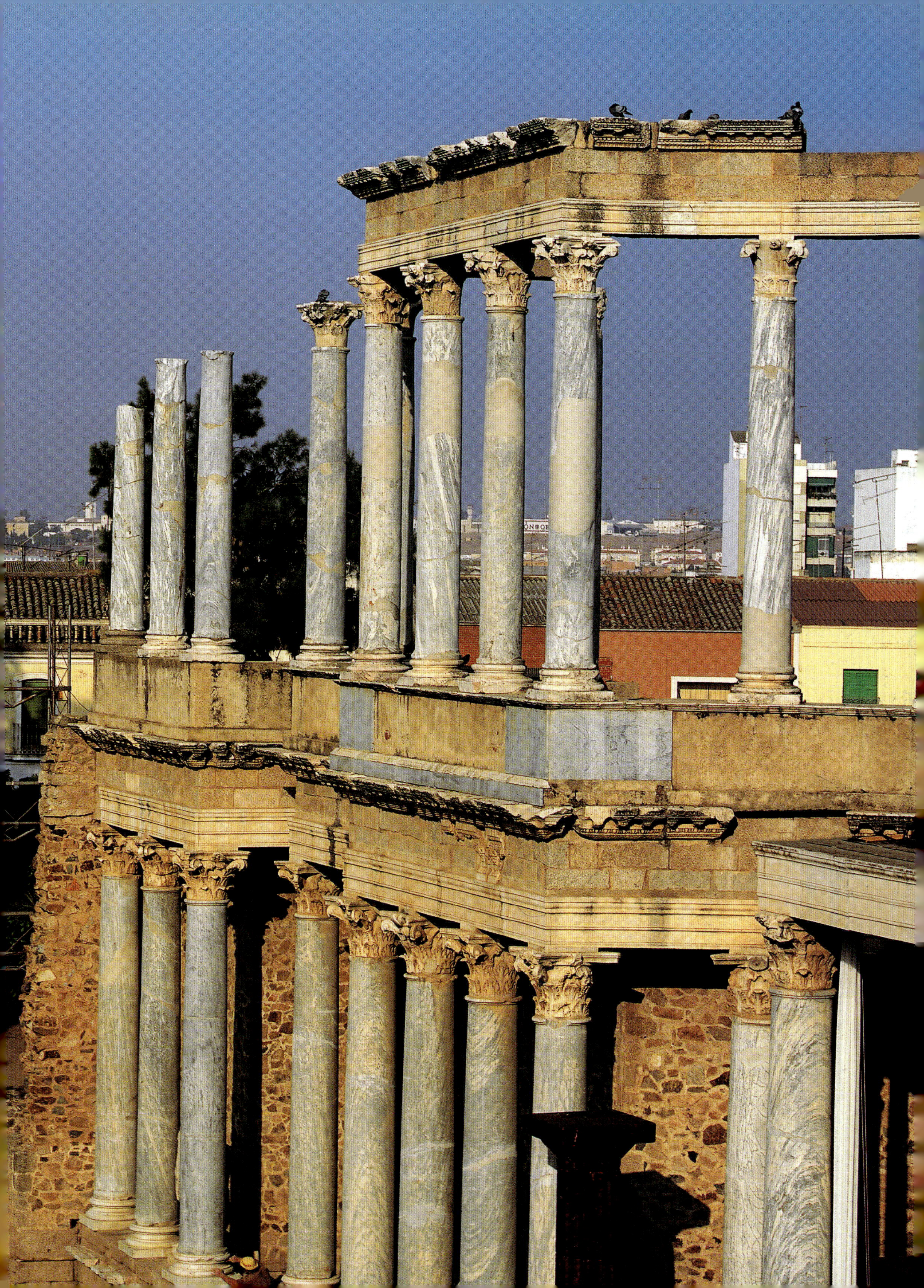

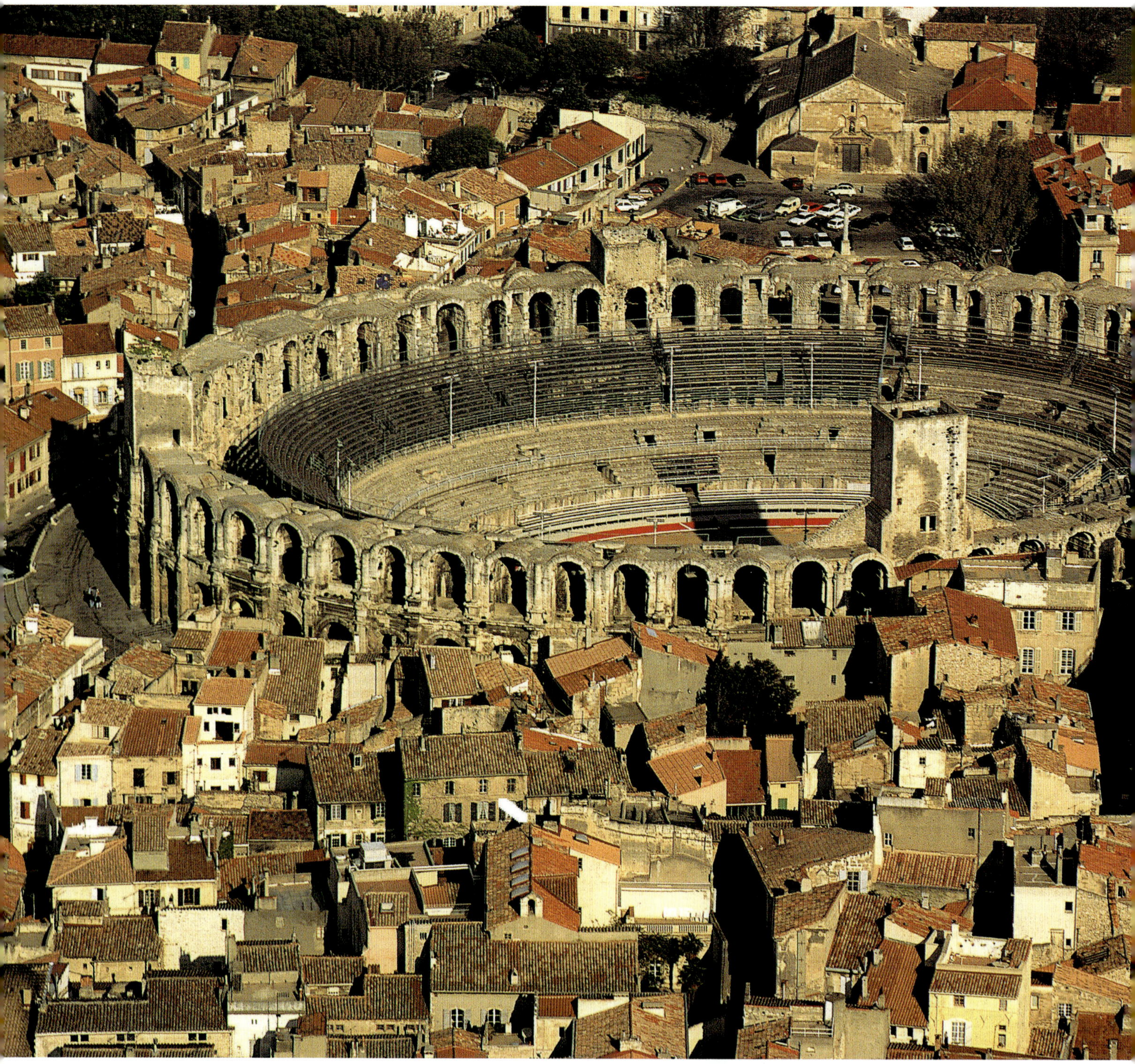

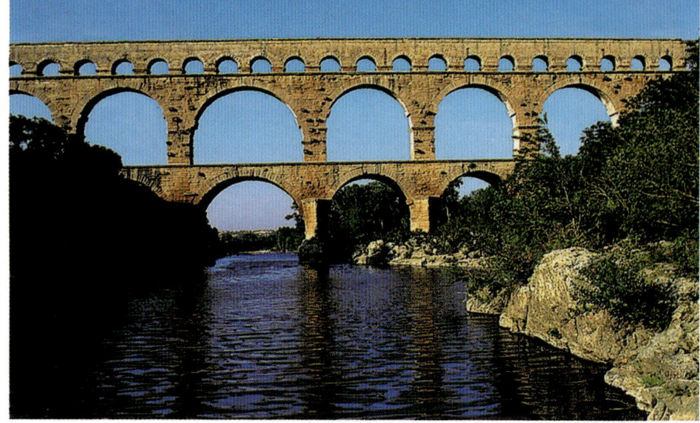

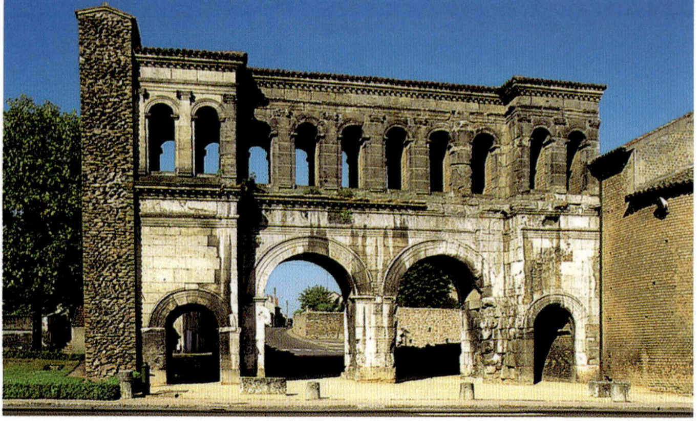

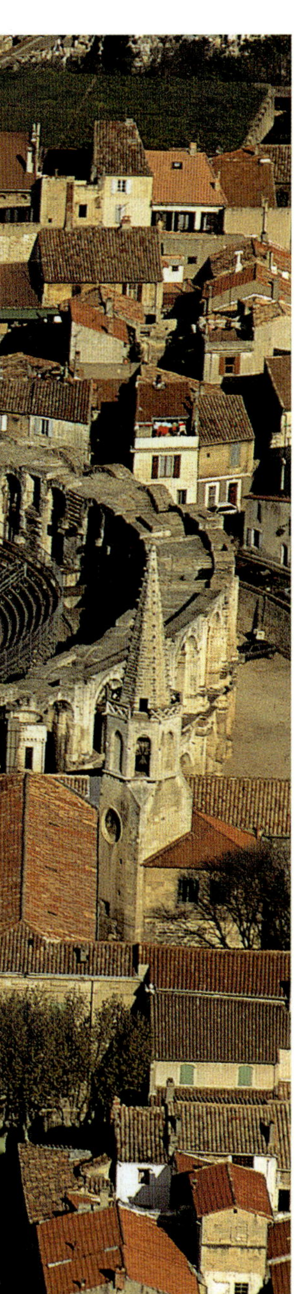

GAUL AND GERMANY, CORNERSTONES OF THE EMPIRE

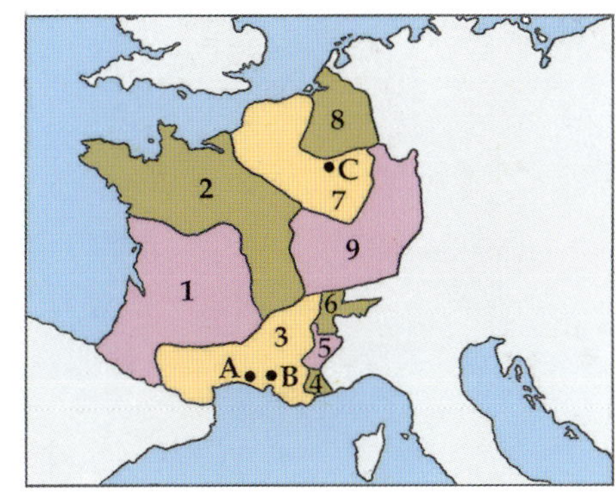

1 Aquitania
2 Lugdunensis
3 Narbonensis
4 Alpes Maritimae
5 Alpes Cottiae
6 Alpes Graiae et Poeninae
7 Belgica
8 Germania Inferior
9 Germania Superior
A Nîmes
B Orange
C Trier

Transalpine Gaul occupied the huge territory between the Atlantic, the Pyrenees, the Mediterranean, the Alps, the Rhine and the North Sea. The region had a mainly Celtic population, with Germans on the Rhine border and Iberian peoples in the area of the Pyrenees. Along the Mediterranean coast were numerous settlements of Greek origin, the main one being Massilia (Marseilles), a flourishing trading centre.

Society was feudal and based on a mainly agricultural economy. An aristocratic oligarchy held power, but the priestly caste of the Druids exerted considerable influence. The main deities, partly identified with the Roman pantheon, were Teutates, Taranis, Epona, Rosmerta and Cernunnos. Ethnic, religious and cultural unity did not prevent frequent rivalry and conflicts, exploited by the Roman conquerors. Their task was made easier also by the absence of towns, as the Gauls preferred villages and fortified hills.

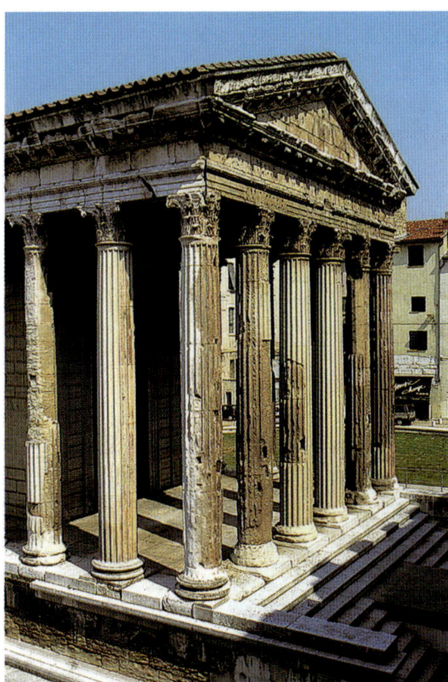

Contacts between Gaul and Rome began in the mid-2nd century BC, when Rome came to the aid of its ally, Massilia. The first colony (Narbo Martius, now Narbonne) was only founded in 121 BC, after a victorious military campaign against the Arverni tribe, which had attempted to set up a Gallic state. Shortly afterwards the province of Gallia Narbonensis (later called merely Provincia, hence the modern name, Provence) was set up, and trade and political and military alliances were encouraged.

There were frequent rebellions by various tribes, however, including uprisings by the Cimbri and Teutones, suppressed by Gaius Marius in 102 and 101 BC at the battles of Aquae Sextiae and the Raudian Fields. Caesar's victory over Vercingetorix at Alesia in 52 BC finally gave Rome possession of the whole of Gaul, which from that time on was strongly Romanized. Augustus permanently reorganized it, dividing the region into Gallia Narbonensis, Aquitania, Gallia Belgica and Gallia Lugdunensis, a system that lasted until Diocletian.

The population was divided into 64 *civitates*, corresponding to the original tribes. Every year their representatives attended the *Conventum Galliarum*, which met near the altar of Rome and Augustus at the confluence of the Rhône and the Saône, to discuss common affairs and exert a limited right of control over the Roman governors.

212–213 (left) The amphitheatre at Arles, dating from the late 1st century AD, is one of the best preserved in France, together with that in Nîmes. Its major axis is 136 m (446 ft) long and it can still hold 12,000 spectators.

212 (opposite, below left) An aqueduct conveyed water from a source near present-day Uzès to Nîmes. Over its 50-km (31-mile) length there is a difference in height of only 17 m (56 ft). To cross the Gardon river, the Romans built the Pont-du-Gard, 275 m (902 ft) long and just under 49 m (160 ft) high.

212 (opposite, below right) Autun, ancient Augustodunum, was one of the main cities in Lyonnese Gaul. In the 3rd century AD it was famous for its school of rhetoric. The town still has many Roman ruins, including the beautiful monumental gate of St André built into the city walls which date from the age of Augustus.

213 The Temple of Augustus and Livia, built c. 10 BC, is the most famous Roman monument in Vienne, ancient Colonia Iulia Vienna Allobrogum. Very similar to the one in Nîmes, it is also a Corinthian hexastyle temple (with six columns) on a tall podium.

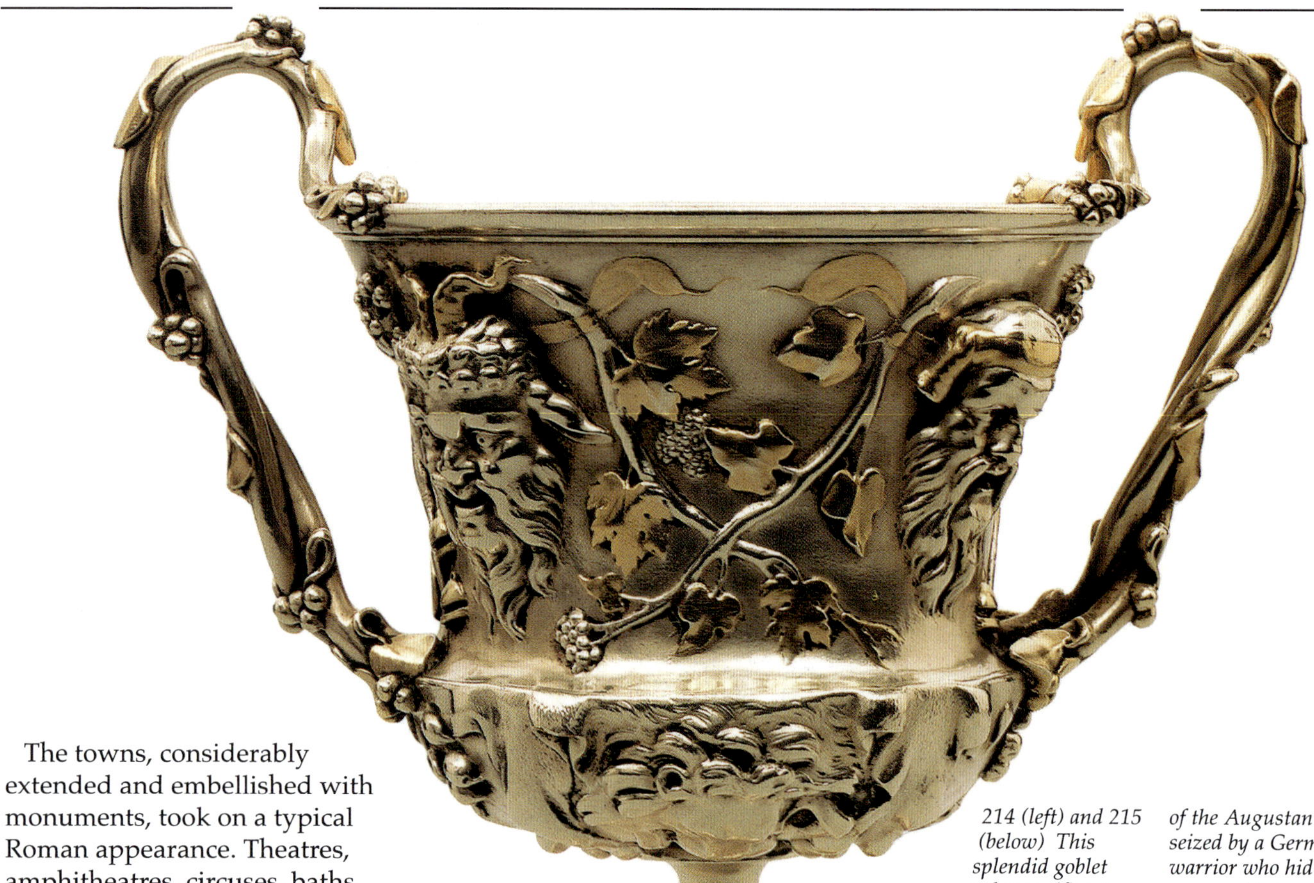

214 (left) and 215 (below) This splendid goblet and magnificent silver crater are part of the famous Hildesheim Treasure, found near the German town in 1865. Consisting of over 60 items, it was perhaps the travelling kit of a high Roman official of the Augustan age, seized by a Germanic warrior who hid it and was unable to retrieve it. From the 1st century BC the possession of silverware was considered a status symbol and represents another sign of the gradual Hellenization of Roman society and culture.

The towns, considerably extended and embellished with monuments, took on a typical Roman appearance. Theatres, amphitheatres, circuses, baths complexes, basilicas, arches, bridges and aqueducts, numerous remains of which survive today, were built throughout the region.

Gallo-Roman art was a strange hybrid of the Hellenistic-Roman experience and Celtic art. Unlike the art of other provinces it had its own independent features, such as funerary sculptures, the best-known examples of which consist of carved pillars portraying the activities of the deceased; special votive monuments dedicated to Jupiter, especially frequent in north and east Gaul; and, finally, the practice of decorating the entire surface of triumphal arches with sculptures.

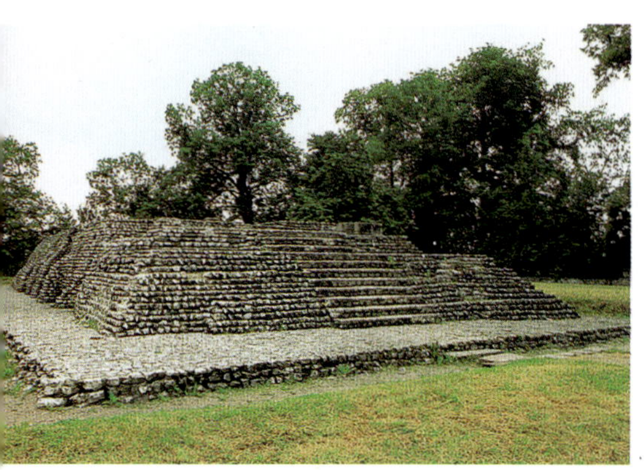

Gaul had a flourishing economy, based on the products of agriculture and industry and on trade between the north and the Mediterranean. Wines from Gallia Narbonensis were Rome's main export from the Flavian age, and a type of pottery called *terra sigillata* was very popular and traded throughout the empire. According to literary sources, gold was abundant; Gaul was one of the few countries of the Mediterranean able to mint its own gold coins.

The two provinces of Roman Germany comprised only a small part of the huge territory of that name. Caesar's campaigns in Gaul had taken the legions as far as the Rhine, to safeguard the Gallic provinces. Between 12 and 9 BC, Drusus fought courageously there, trying to lay the foundations of the unification of the various Germanic populations. Once pacified, they would meet at a religious and political centre, similar to the one established in Lyons for the Gauls, and Drusus consecrated a large altar for the federal cult, associated with the worship of Rome and Augustus, in the territory of the Ubii, on the left bank of the Rhine. However, his premature death first slowed and then jeopardized the conquest of these lands. Roman fortunes fluctuated, and its armies suffered some serious defeats at the hands of the warlike Germanic tribes, until the time of Tiberius. Particularly tragic was the defeat of Varus in AD 9 by the barbarian chief Arminius, when three legions were annihilated. Recent excavations have identified the site of the battle, in the Kalkriese area – helmets, fragments of breastplates, arrowheads, javelins and numerous Roman coins whose latest date is AD 9 have been found there. Interestingly, these remains coincide with a scene later witnessed by Germanicus, recorded by Tacitus: 'In the middle of the field, bones shone whitely, piled up or dispersed… scattered all around were fragments of arrows and limbs of horses; and human skulls were impaled on tree trunks. In the nearby sacred woods rough altars could be glimpsed, on which the Germans had sacrificed the tribunes and the leading centurions'.

Of the two Roman provinces, Germania Superior stretched from Lake Geneva to the confluence of the Vinxtbach and the Rhine, by way of Confluentes (Koblenz) and Bonna (Bonn). The only region on the far side was Taunus. Germania Inferior reached to the North Sea, including part of what is now the Netherlands. Opposite Colonia Claudia Ara Agrippinensium (Cologne) stood the fortified camp of Divitia (Deutz), acting as a bridgehead. In those sections where the Rhine did not form the border, a fortified *limes* protected the province against the barbarians. For 382 km (237 miles) it consisted of a *vallum* (rampart) reinforced by palisades with a ditch in front, and protected by fortified camps of various sizes. Many have been located and excavated, and the entire line of the *limes* has been traced. The Saalburg *limes* has been reconstructed and is well known.

The two Germanys were basically military provinces, as can be seen from the surviving monuments. With regards to their economy, glass was a characteristic product exported on a large scale to Rome. Some exquisite examples, from the workshops of Cologne, still survive.

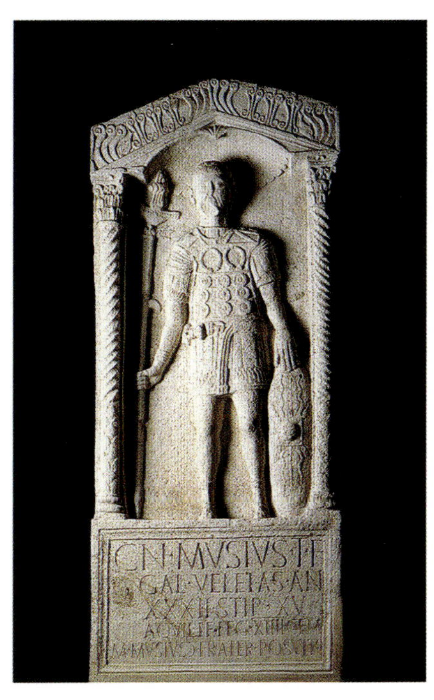

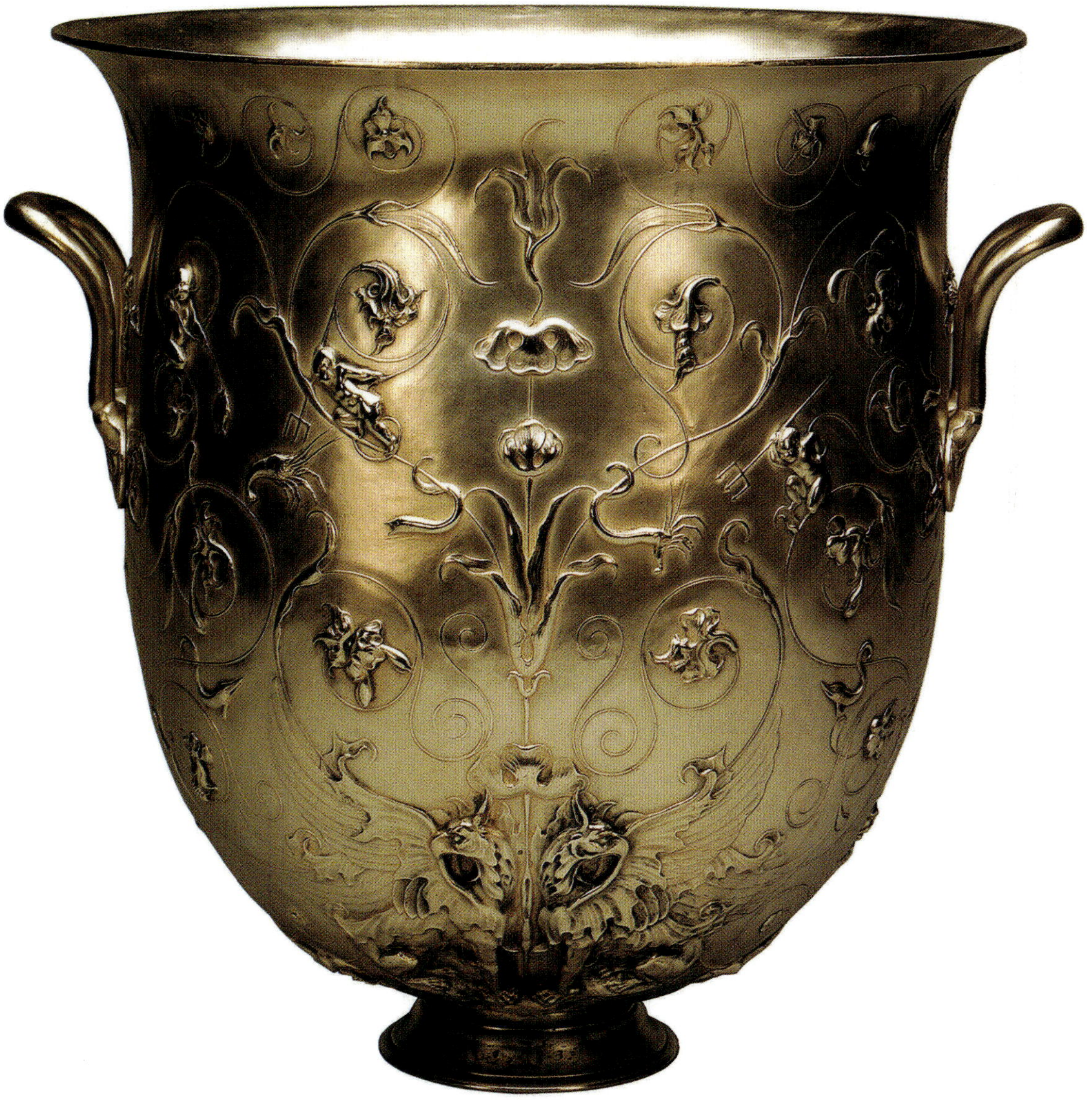

215 (above) The funerary stele of the legionary Gnaeus Musius is in the collection of the Mainz Landesmuseum. The town, known as Magontiacum, grew up around the military camp founded by Augustus near the confluence of the Main and the Rhine. The great fortress, manned by two legions, was an important base for the control of Germania Superior for a long period. Many similar steles have been found in the local military cemeteries.

214 (opposite, left) Augst, not far from Basle, was founded under the name of Augusta Raurica in c. 40 BC. It was situated at a strategic position at the intersection of the roads which crossed the Alps to connect Gaul with the Danube provinces. The major archaeological remains have been discovered around the forum and theatre area; illustrated here is the podium of a temple dating from the 2nd century BC.

NÎMES, THE PRIDE OF GALLIA NARBONENSIS

Nîmes, ancient Nemausus, named after a mythical son of Hercules, was a Latin colony of soldiers from Antony's army. Under Augustus it was called Colonia Augusta Nemausus, and was part of Gallia Narbonensis (Narbonnese Gaul).

It soon became one of the most flourishing and Romanized towns in the region and imposing remains of many important public monuments still survive. In the town itself, at the crossroads between the *cardo* and *decumanus*, near the site of the forum, is the Maison Carrée, one of the best preserved temples in France, initially dedicated to Agrippa, and later to Gaius and Lucius Caesar. South of the town is the large amphitheatre with two rows of arches, dating from the second half of the 1st century AD. It is very similar to the one in Arles and is still used for performances. No trace remains of the circus which must have been in the same area.

In the northwest part of the town is a huge monumental complex built around the sacred spring of Nemausus. There are the remains of the theatre, whose terraces exploit the natural slope of the hill, a nymphaeum and numerous temples.

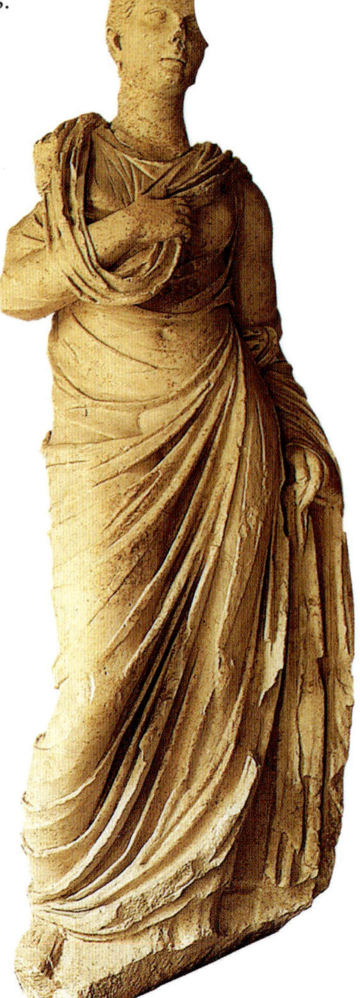

216 Nîmes was one of the most flourishing towns in southern Gaul; its prosperity is demonstrated by the outstanding collection of Roman art now housed in the local archaeological museum.

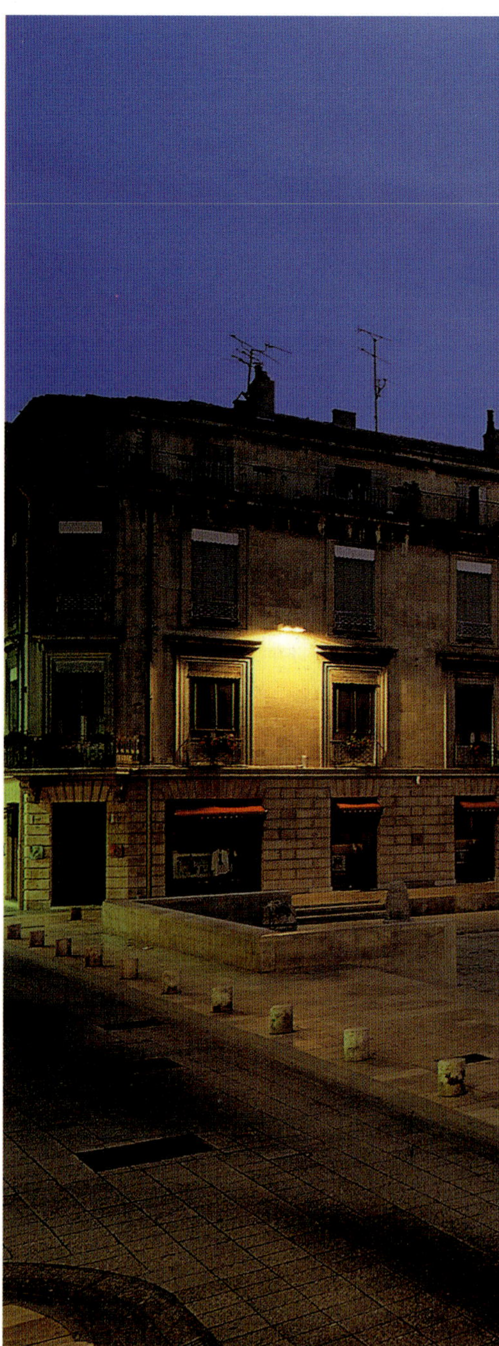

216–217 (right) The Maison Carrée is a perfect example of a Corinthian marble temple on a podium; it is the most complete of the comparable buildings surviving from the age of Augustus. Its excellent state of preservation is due to the fact that it was reused for various purposes from the Middle Ages on: it was converted into stables, then a church, and then the first city museum. It is now an exhibition centre.

The so-called Temple of Diana is of particular interest. Built in the Augustan period, it was extended and enhanced under Hadrian who set it in a scenic complex which wound around the slope of the hill.

Nîmes was supplied with drinking water by an aqueduct 50 km (31 miles) long, of which the spectacular Pont-du-Gard, with its three rows of arches, still survives.

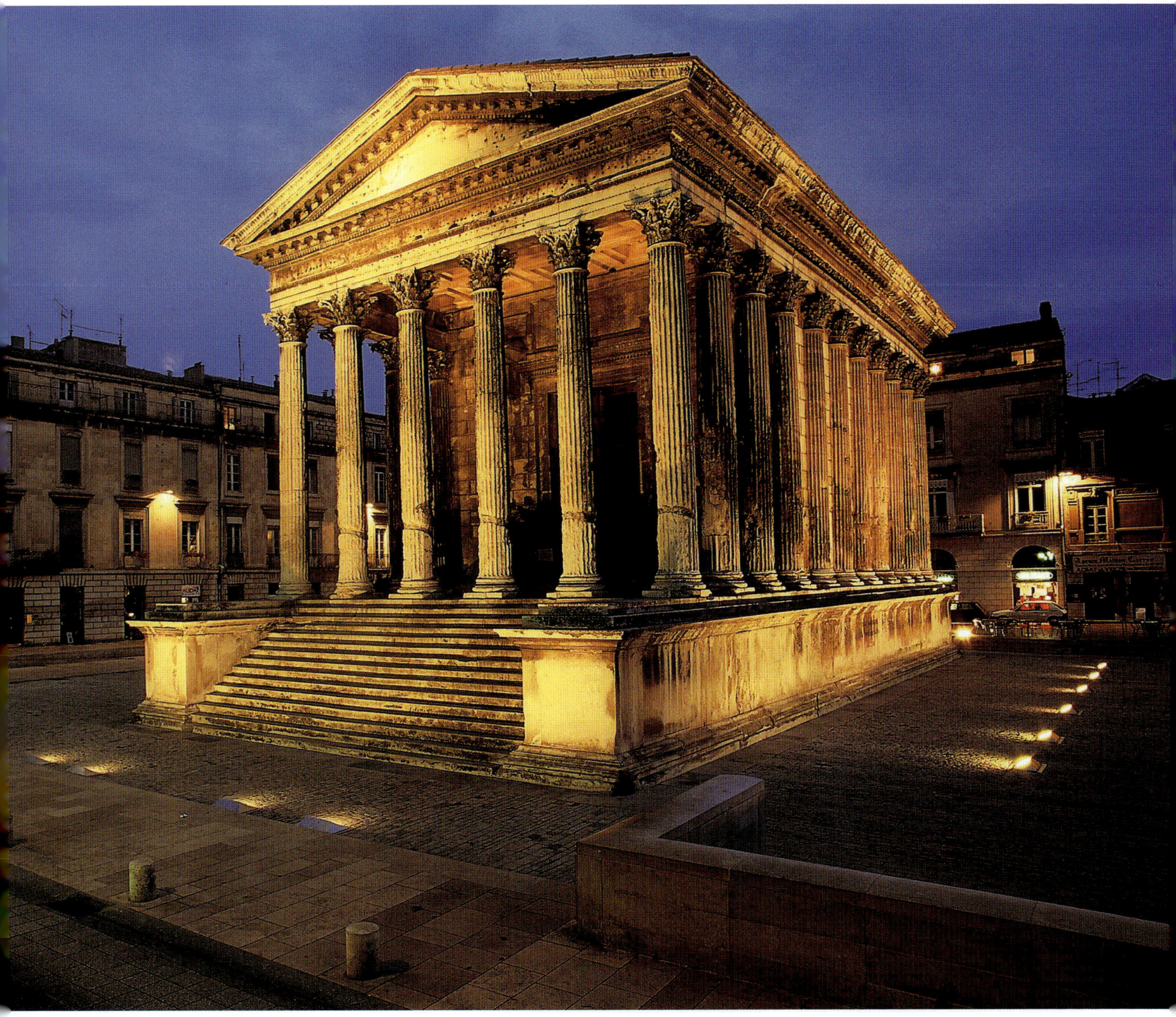

217 (below left) The amphitheatre at Nîmes, of the 1st century AD, was built using some advanced construction techniques. A total of 23,000 spectators could enter and exit quickly thanks to a system of five concentric tunnels at different levels, with passages and staircases in a radial pattern.

217 (below right) The Temple of Diana was part of the sacred complex around the Nemausus spring, built under Augustus. Part of the great barrel vault of the cella *survives. Due to the excellent state of preservation of its numerous monuments dating from the imperial age, Nîmes is often known as the 'Rome of France'.*

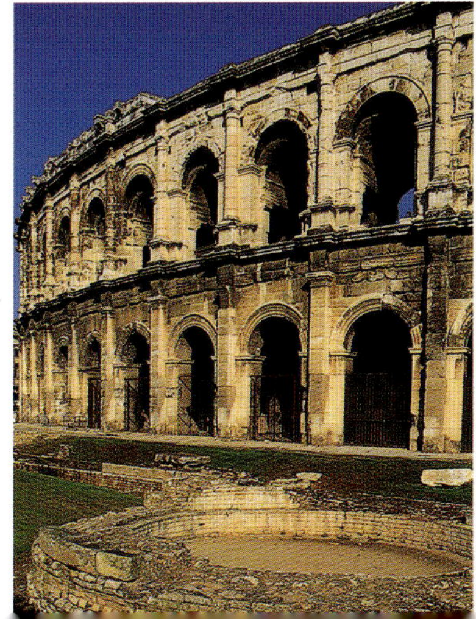

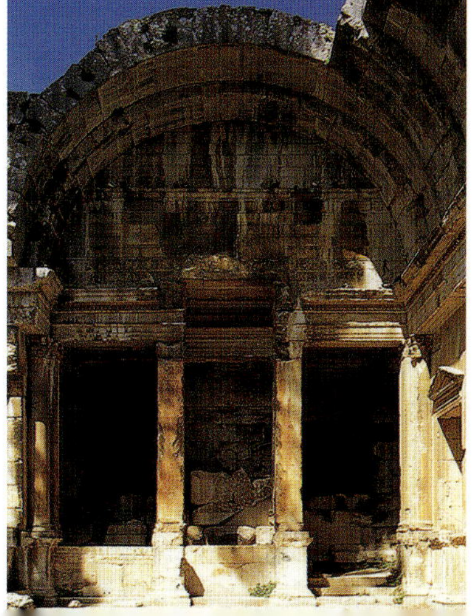

ORANGE, A COLONY FOUNDED BY JULIUS CAESAR

Under Julius Caesar, the town of Orange (Arausio) was the site of a colony of veterans of the 2nd Legion, commanded by Tiberius' father. To celebrate the founding of the colony a triumphal arch was built, one of the most impressive still surviving. It consists of a central archway with two smaller archways at the sides, 19.5 m (64 ft) across and 18.8 m (62 ft) high. A lively battle scene, war trophies, chained prisoners and a naval trophy commemorating Caesar's victory over Massilia (Marseilles) decorate it. The dedication, probably to Tiberius, was added later, after the suppression of the Sacrovirus revolt.

The other major Roman monument in Orange is its theatre, with an exceptionally well preserved *scaena*, the back wall of which is 103.15 m (338 ft) long and 36.8 m (120 ft) high. At the top, the brackets to support the poles of the *velarium* (protective awning) are clearly visible. The interior, which originally had three tiers of columns, features a wealth of decoration, including statues and friezes of centaurs, maenads, eagles and garlands. The outer façade is outstanding for its regular surface, while the auditorium still has acoustics of exceptional clarity.

Near the theatre are the remains of a large temple and a building with an *exedra* and parallel walls. This is perhaps the only example of a gymnasium discovered in Gaul.

The division of the territory of Arausio is documented by some very rare fragments of marble cadastral maps relating to the administration of the colony, which are housed in the local museum.

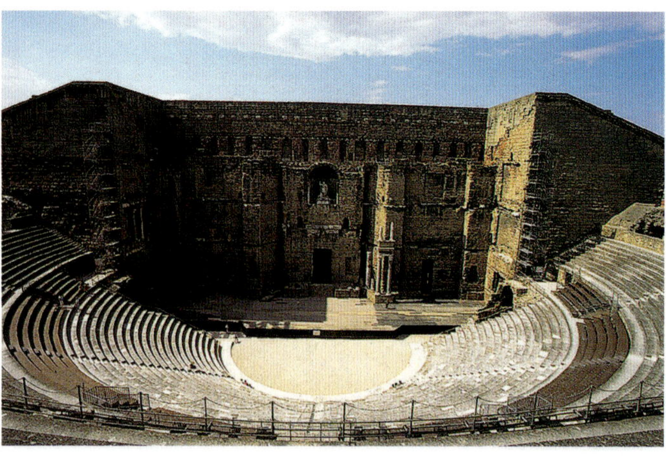

218 (top) The theatre at Orange dates from the end of the reign of Augustus and the beginning of that of Tiberius. It is particularly interesting for the exceptional state of preservation of the scaena *wall and the outstanding acoustics of the auditorium, which mean that theatrical performances are still staged here. A statue of Augustus 3.5 m (12 ft) high stands in the central niche.*

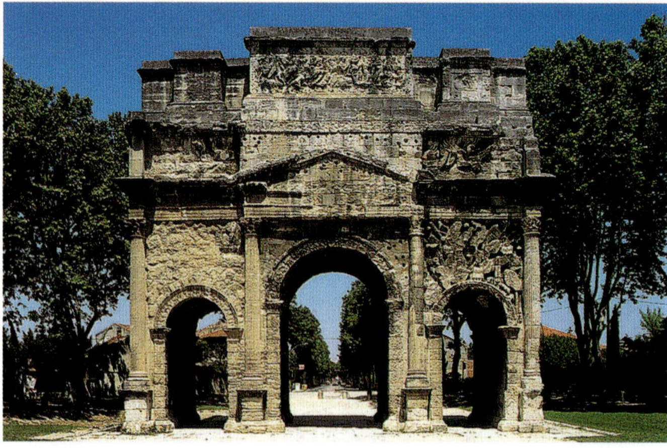

218 (centre) The triumphal arch at Orange was built in the northern area of the town to commemorate its foundation by Caesar.

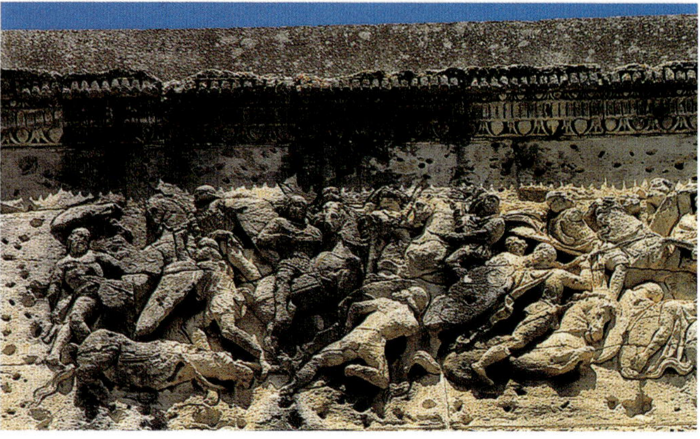

218 (bottom) Reliefs decorating the triumphal arch depict a battle between Roman soldiers and barbarian warriors, recalling the conquest of Gaul.

219 (opposite) The theatre at Orange is the only one in which the triumphal statue of the emperor has survived. It was found in fragments, but was pieced back together and replaced in its niche, which has a hemispherical vault.

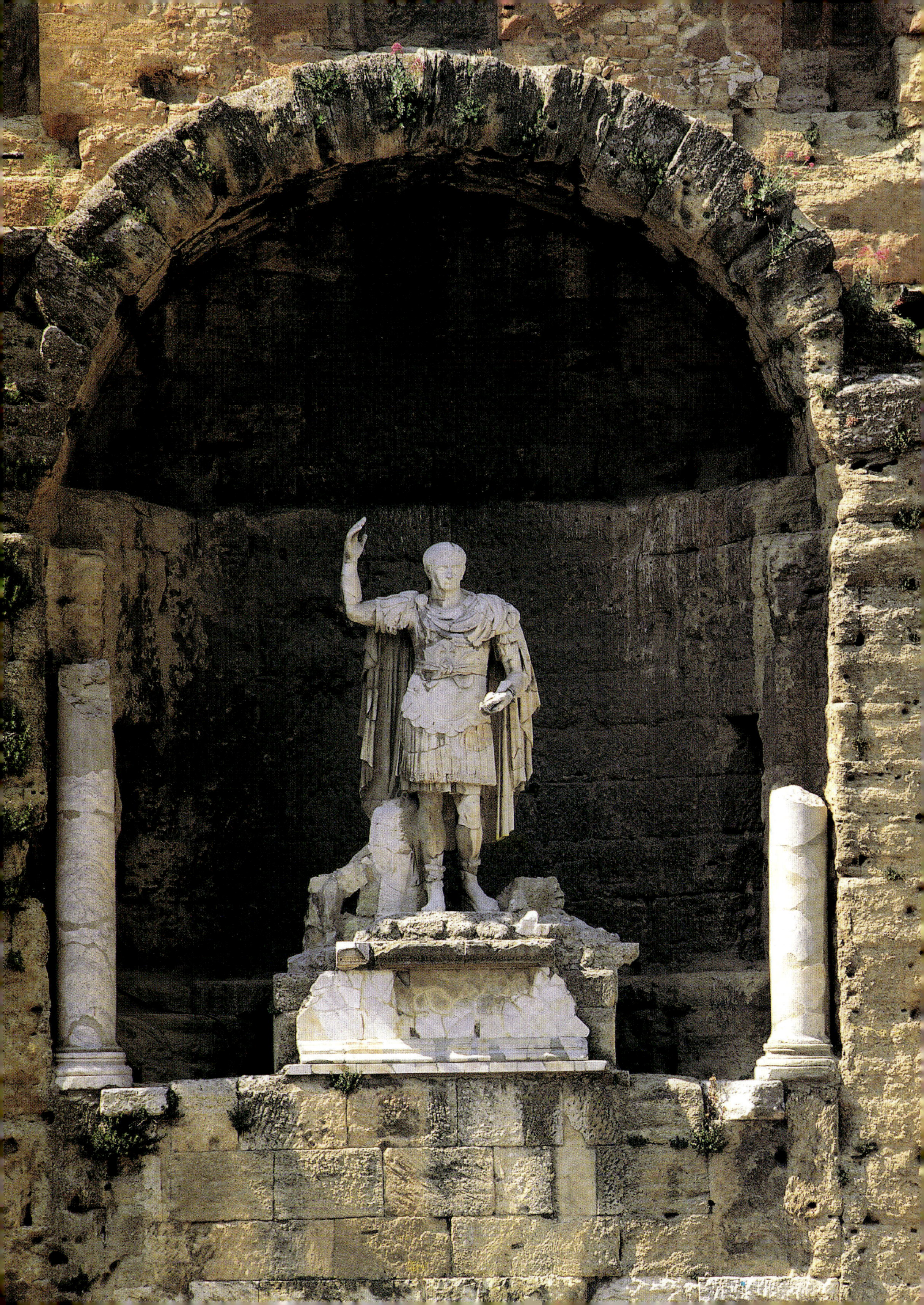

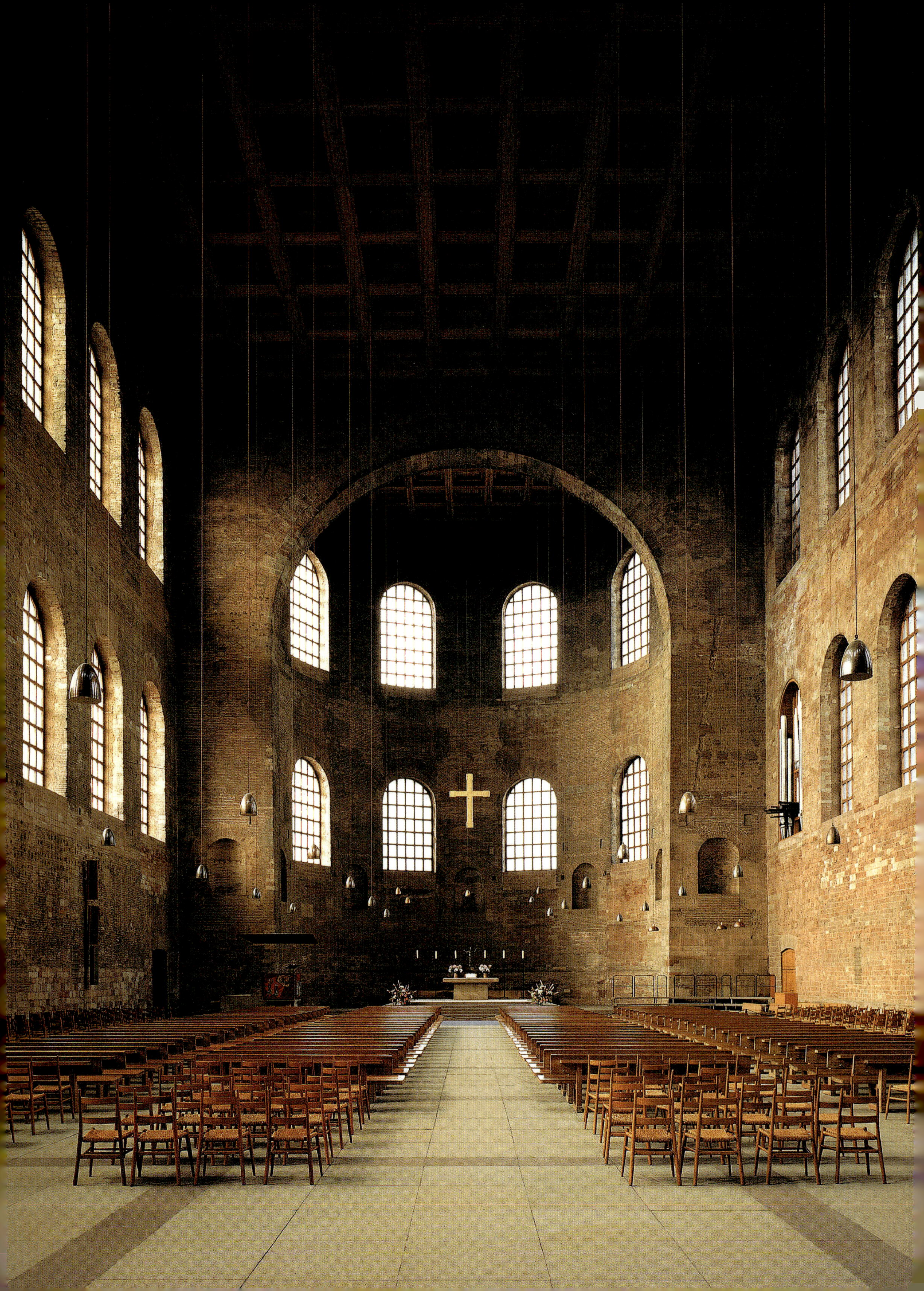

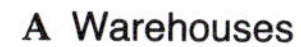

TRIER, A FLOURISHING TOWN OF THE LATE EMPIRE

A Warehouses
B Baths
C Forum
D Porta Nigra
E Palace of Constantine
F Aula Palatina
G Baths of Constantine
H Circus
I Amphitheatre

220 and 221 (right, top) The Aula Palatina, though much restored, dates from AD 310; it was the audience chamber of the Palace of Constantine.

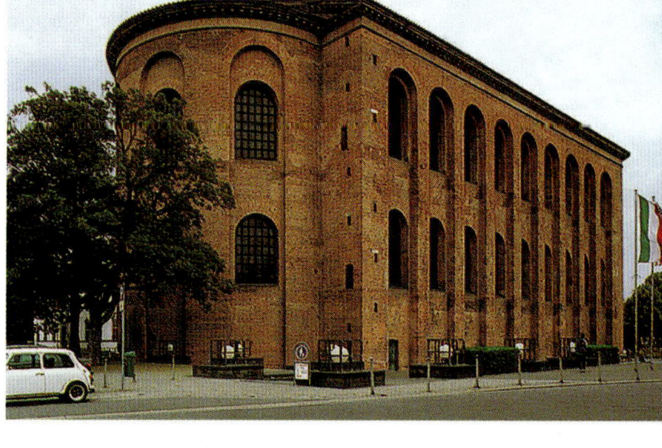

221 This fragment of a funeral monument, portraying a cargo ship carrying wine, comes from the town of Neumagen.

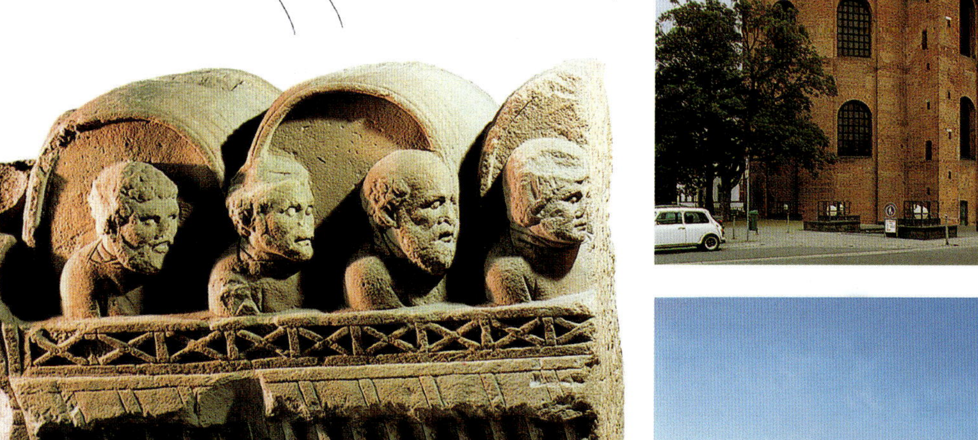

221 (right, centre) Porta Nigra, dating from the early 4th century, was built in the northern side of the city walls.

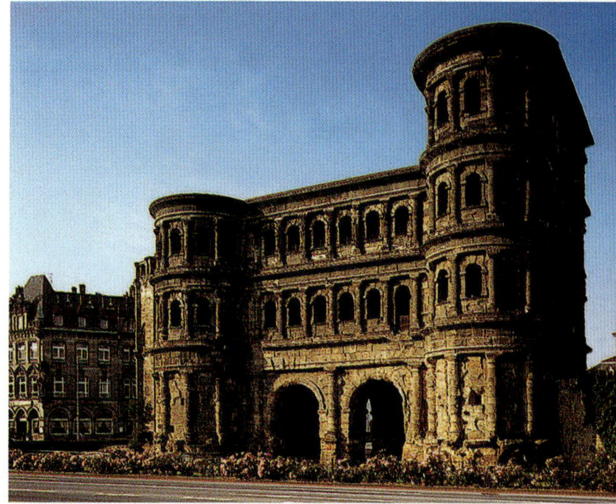

221 (right, bottom) The ruins of the imperial baths of Constantine were converted into a barracks in the 4th century AD, then reused in the Middle Ages as a church.

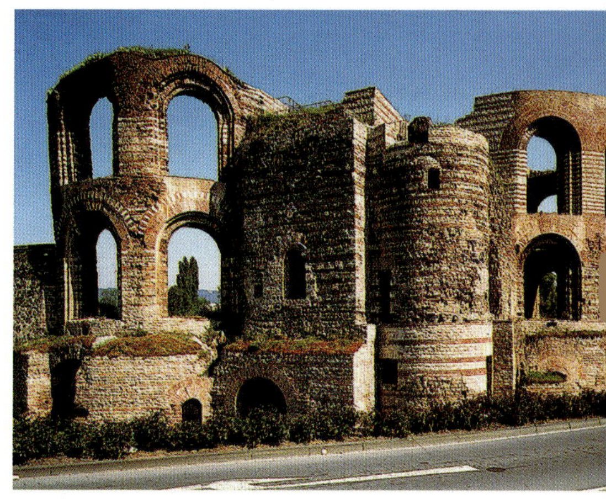

Augusta Treverorum (Trier) in Gallia Belgica was founded by Augustus between 19 and 16 BC. It was a very prosperous town which reached the peak of its glory in the late imperial period, when it became the residence of several emperors. Diocletian chose it as the capital of the western part of the empire in AD 287, and, under Constantine in particular, many major monuments were built there. Its decline began in the early 5th century AD, when the legions stationed on the Rhine were recalled to Italy.

Access to the town from the north is through the imposing Porta Nigra, dating from the 4th century, the best-preserved city gate. It had a large inner courtyard, enclosed between two towers connected by a twin gallery. The Aula Palatina is a grandiose basilica of Constantine, dating to AD 310. It consists of a huge rectangular room, with no aisles, and an enormous apse. The ancient brick building, surviving to the level of the roof, has two rows of tall arched windows. Nearby is the Imperial Baths complex, also built by Constantine though never finished, with a large palaestra. A nymphaeum formed the façade of the outer portico. Apart from the large residential villas in the vicinity of the town, other monuments include a bridge over the Moselle, a small amphitheatre dating from the 1st century AD, the richly decorated Baths of St Barbara, built near the end of the 3rd century, and the remains of a palazzo under the Cathedral, probably part of the residence of Constantine's mother Helena, where interesting panels with busts of women were found.

BRITANNIA, A PROVINCE UNDER MILITARY RULE

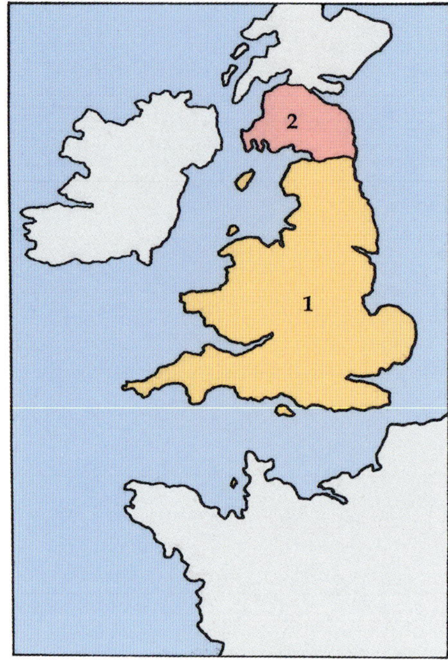

1 From AD 43 to 406
2 From AD 142 to 180

222 (below left) This series of niches belongs to the changing room of the baths at Cilurnum (Chesters), one of the 17 great fortified camps along Hadrian's Wall.

The Romans first came into contact with the people of Britannia in 55 BC, when Julius Caesar led a military expedition there, followed by a second one the following year. However, the region was only properly subjugated after AD 43, under the emperor Claudius.

The northern border, where Hadrian built his celebrated wall, ran from the mouth of the Tyne to the Solway Firth. Later, Antoninus Pius moved the *limes* further north, and ordered the construction of a second fortified line, which was operational only until the time of Commodus.

At the time of the Roman conquest, Britannia had a mainly agricultural economy, plus good mineral resources. The geographer Strabo listed the main products of the island as: 'wheat, cattle, gold, silver, hides, slaves and excellent hunting dogs'. Gold deposits were found in Wales, Scotland and Cornwall, and silver (obtained by refining lead), copper and tin were mined in many areas. Some mines in Cornwall produced copper associated with tin, which probably led to the local production of bronze. Other major copper mining centres were in north Wales. Tin was also important, at least until the 3rd century AD, when it was supplanted by Spanish ores. However, Britannia was famous mainly for its lead. The deposits were so rich that, as Pliny wrote, it was necessary to pass a law to restrict excessive production.

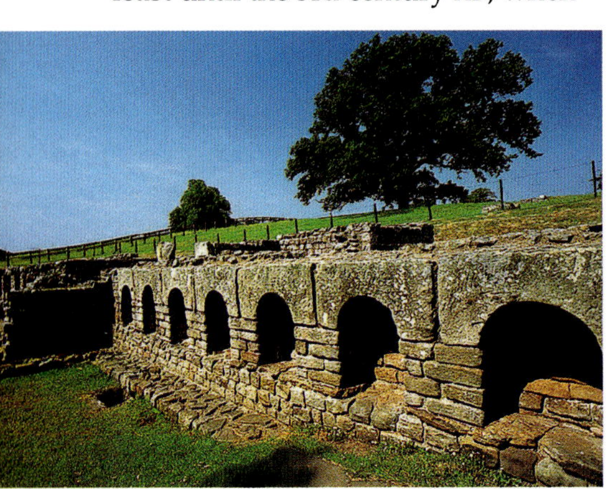

Roman interests in the products of Britannia were facilitated by the many landing places along its coast, especially in the south opposite Belgic Gaul, such as Dubris (Dover), Anderita (Pevensey) and Regulbium (Reculver). Colonization began in the Thames basin, where the most densely populated towns were located. Of these, Londinium (London), already an active river port, became the centre of the Roman road system. A busy route led east from here to Camulodunum (Colchester), an important colony and the headquarters of the imperial cult, then continued to Lindum (Lincoln) and Eboracum (York). Another commercial road was the one from Londinium to Calleva Atrebatum (Silchester) and the land of the Silures (Wales), where it reached Venta and Isca Silurum (Caerwent and Caerleon), with a branch to Glevum (Gloucester).

The problems facing the Romans in Britannia related mainly to security of transport across the Channel and the particular geographical conformation of the island, with its very uneven territory. Dealings with the local customs were aided by long experience acquired in Gaul, whose populations had strong cultural affinities to those of Britannia,

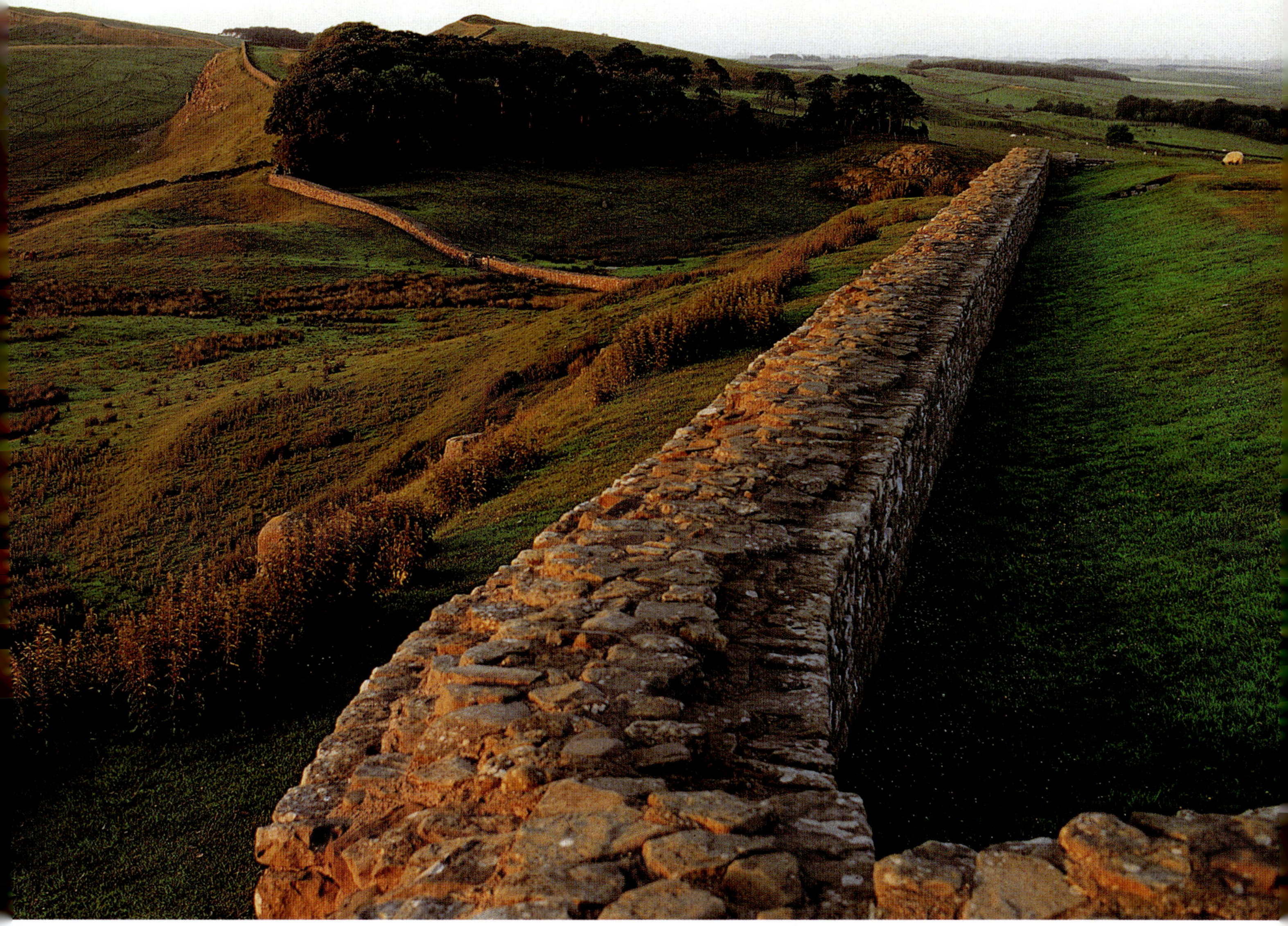

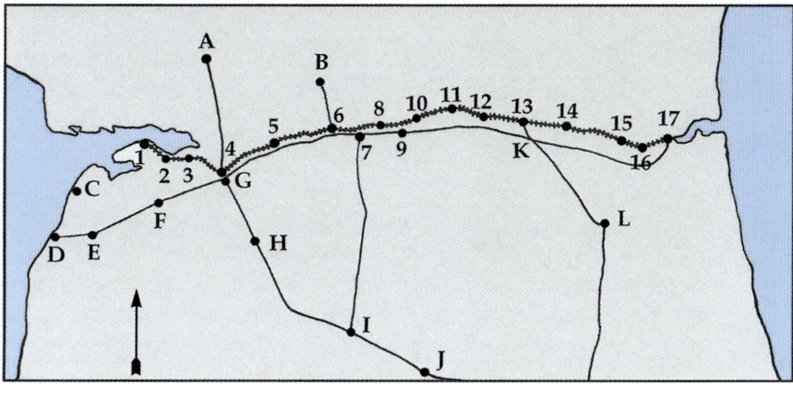

1 Maia (Bowness)
2 Congavata (Drumburgh)
3 Aballava (Burgh-by-sands)
4 Petriana (Stanvix)
5 Uxellodunum (Castlesteads)
6 Camboglanna (Birdoswald)
7 Magna (Carvoran)
8 Aesica (Great Chesters)
9 Vindolanda (Chesterholm)
10 Borgovicium (Housesteads)
11 Procolitia (Carrawburgh)
12 Cilurnum (Chesters)
13 Hunnum (Halton)
14 Vindobala (Rochester)
15 Condercum (Benwell)
16 Pons Aelius (Newcastle)
17 Segedunum (Wallsend)

THE DANUBE PROVINCES, REGIONS OF STRATEGIC IMPORTANCE

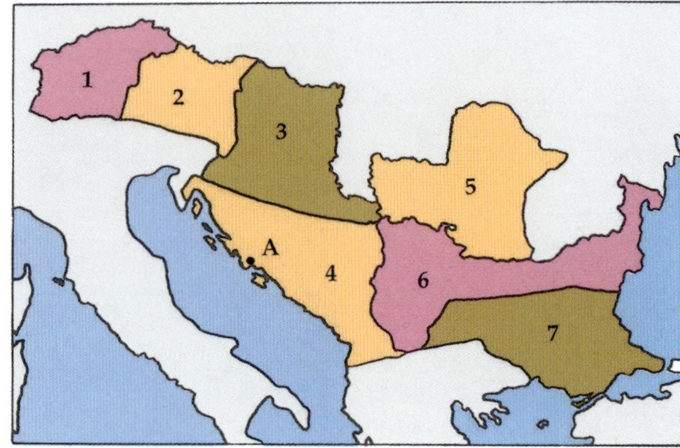

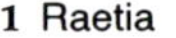

1 Raetia
2 Noricum
3 Pannonia
4 Illyricum or Dalmatia
5 Dacia
6 Moesia
7 Thracia
A Split

228 (below) The base of Trajan's Column is entirely covered with magnificent reliefs portraying Roman and barbarian weapons piled up in apparent disorder. Armour typical of the Dacian cataphracts, heavy-armoured horsemen, are recognizable by their 'fish-scale' appearance. Trajan's conquest of Dacia, made more difficult by the resistance of the warlike populations, was the last episode of Roman imperialism in the Danube region. Despite increasingly violent barbarian attacks, the last strongholds on the Danube were held until the 5th century.

229 (opposite) This large fibula (pin) made of gold and semiprecious stones, an exquisite product of what is known as Dacio-Roman art, is part of a treasure found at Pietroasa in modern Romania. The fibula, in the form of a stylized eagle, dates from the 4th century AD *and is clearly influenced by barbarian designs. The Danube regions, and Dacia in particular, were intensively Romanized, as demonstrated by the development of numerous towns. Local craftsmen were naturally influenced by styles imported by the Roman colonists, but then elaborated on them to produce wholly original styles, even after the withdrawal of the occupying troops.*

Bounded to the west by the German provinces, to the north by the Danube (except Dacia), to the east by the Black Sea, and to the south by Cisalpine Gaul and Achaea, the Danube province comprised a huge territory. It had seven regions: Raetia (Rhaetia), Noricum, Pannonia, Illyricum, Dacia, Moesia and Thracia (Thrace). Raetia, like Noricum, came into contact with the Rome as a result of trade through Aquileia.

The area was inhabited by Celtic populations, concentrated mainly in the Rhône, Rhine and upper Danube basins, which were organized in independent cantons. Largely because of the impenetrable terrain, the process of Romanization was not very effective and there were few major towns. Those that did exist included Augusta Vindelicorum (Augsburg), Cambodunum (Kempten), Brigantium (Bregenz) and Castra Regina (Regensburg). The real importance of these territories lay in the road network that crossed them, of great commercial and military value. Their few mineral and agricultural resources were scarcely sufficient to meet even local requirements.

Noricum was inhabited by Celtic-Illyrian populations. Before its subjugation the kingdom, with a capital at Noreia (Neumark), had friendly dealings with Rome for many years. Partly because of the high level of Italic immigration the province was fairly Romanized. The main wealth of the region came from metals, especially gold, lead and iron; the iron mines were the most famous in the entire Roman world in the imperial age. Ovid and Pliny also recount that exceptionally high quality steel was made there. Scholars think that a method of making steel using a percentage of manganese in the casting, probably unknown to the Greeks and Romans, was developed in Noricum around 500 BC. The art produced in this province in the Roman age was a combination of Italic and Celtic-Illyrian influences. In architecture, in addition to the sanctuaries of the Romanized Celtic deities, public buildings also closely imitated the Roman models.

Pannonia only became an independent province after the great insurrection of the Danube peoples, between AD 6 and 9, was put down. Various legionary camps were set up to defend the region against the barbarians from across the Danube, eventually becoming important centres of Romanization. In fact the main towns of the region developed from military camps and associated indigenous communities called *canabae*, consisting of craftsmen, merchants and camp followers.

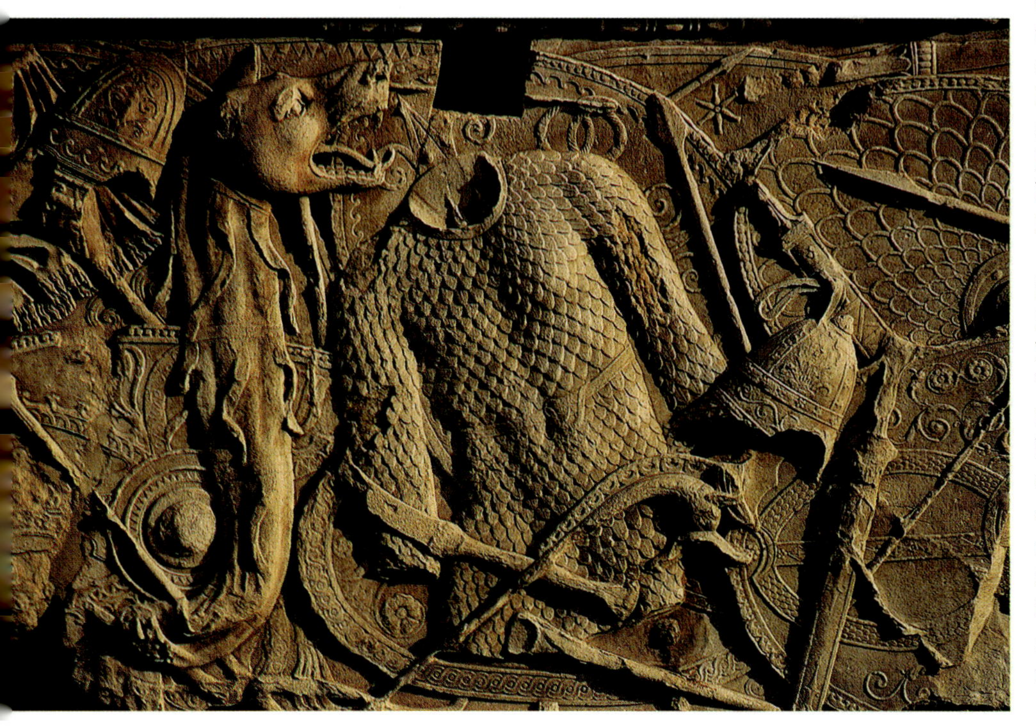

Although the economy of Pannonia mainly revolved around agriculture and mining, a flourishing business was also conducted by the traders who settled along the major roads crossing the province from west to east. Savaria (Szombathely), for example, was a major road junction from which routes led to Vindobona (Vienna), Brigetio (Szöny), Poetovio (Ptuj) and Siscia (Sisak), after which it was possible to continue on to Salonae (Solin) in Illyricum. An important role was also played by the major rivers, including the Danube, the Drava and the Sava.

Roman influence was strongest in the western part of the region, though it had to contend with a strong indigenous tradition, mainly Celtic and partly Illyrian, that had previously produced the La Tène civilization. The influence of this was still strong in the arts. There were also Greek influences in the eastern areas.

Illyricum, on the opposite shore of the Adriatic to Italy, had attracted the attention of Rome from the 3rd century BC because of the piracy of the indigenous tribes there. Wars designed to consolidate Roman rule over the Dalmatian and Liburnian tribes continued throughout the 3rd century BC, and much of the 2nd. The province was greatly extended under Augustus. From republican times the immigration of Italic traders who joined together in guilds led to the Romanization of the coastal towns and the islands. The coastal area was very different from inland, where the local populations assimilated Roman civilization far more slowly.

The main resources of this region consisted of iron, gold and silver mines, stock-rearing, and corn,

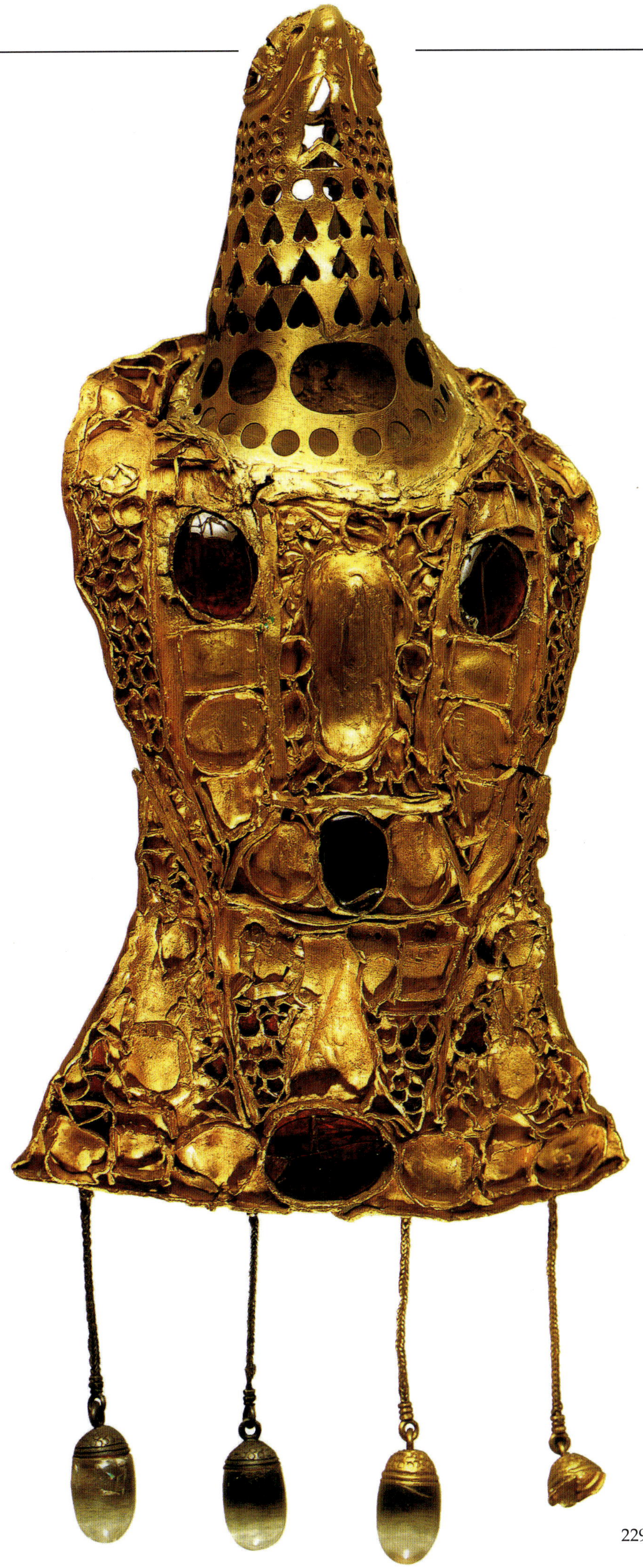

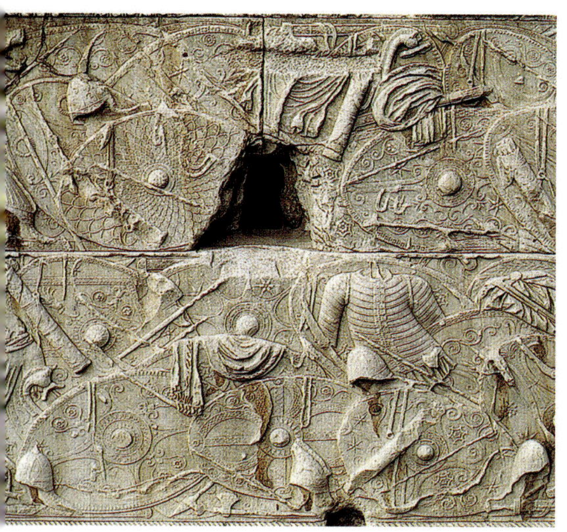

grape and olive growing. The major towns were Doclea (Duklja), Scodria (Skutari) and Salonae (Solin), the birthplace of Diocletian and an important ecclesiastical metropolis in the Christian era. Not far away Diocletian built his magnificent palace, around which the city of Spalatum (Split) grew.

Rome's military campaigns against Dacia began in the time of Domitian, following continual raids by local populations against the garrisons in Moesia. However, it was Trajan, in his two successive campaigns, between AD 101 and 107, who finally overcame the resistance of Decebalus, King of the Dacians, and conquered the region. The various stages of the Dacian Wars are vividly portrayed in the reliefs on Trajan's Column, which often show the Dacians with their characteristic headgear, the *pileus*. After the Roman occupation, numerous colonists flocked to the lands across the Danube, and it was mainly they, together with the legions stationed there, who helped make the region one of the most fully Romanized in the Empire.

Dacia's main resources were ores, especially iron, silver and gold; Trajan took back to Rome some 165,500 kg (364,000 lb) of gold and 331,000 kg (729,800 lb) of silver as war booty. The excellent quality of the surviving iron objects and the tools used to make them testify to the high level of technical expertise of Dacian metalworking. An extensive road network served the province, along which numerous towns developed, including Apulum (Alba-Iulia), Napoca (Cluj) and Ulpia Traiana (Sarmizegetusa), headquarters of the imperial legate. Dacia was abandoned by Aurelian in AD 270 under pressure from barbarian raids.

The Romans had to intervene in Moesia was to counter incursions of populations not subjugated by Rome into the conquered territories.

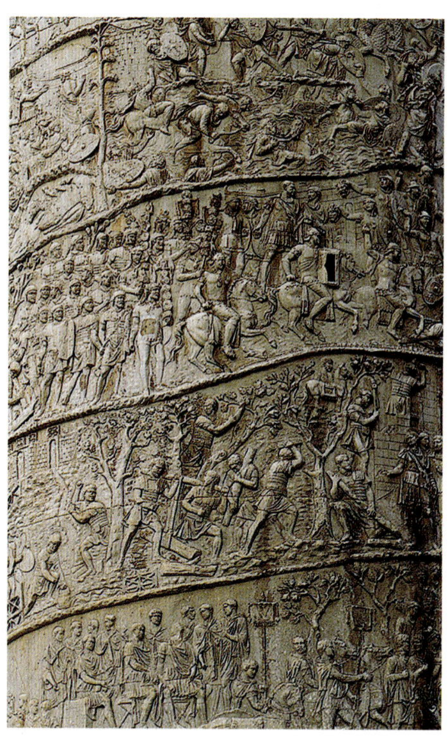

Military activity in the region was extensive, especially under the Flavians, and border security was always a major concern for the imperial legates. This province was one of the most mixed because of the variety of the land and the peoples who lived there, ranging from the Celtic-Illyrian tribes in the west to the Thracian tribes in the east, and the Greeks in the towns on the Black Sea coast. The variety of cultural traditions was overlaid by the effects of Romanization transmitted by the legions stationed along the Danube, with main camps at Singidunum (Belgrade), Noviodunum (Isaccea), Viminacium (Kostolac), Ratiaria (Arcar) and Oescus (Ghighen). Municipalities and colonies were few, and the province retained a rather rustic nature. The outstanding funerary and triumphal monuments of the region include the *Tropaeum Traiani*, near the village of Adamklissi (Romania), built to commemorate Trajan's Dacian conquests. The rich figured decoration of the impressive building is one of the most magnificent examples of provincial Roman art still surviving.

Thracia, formerly the kingdom of the tribe called the Odrisi, and later long disputed between Macedonia and Syria, was the last region on the near side of the Danube to become a Roman province, when Claudius took it in AD 46. Numerous towns, such as Flaviopolis, Hadrianopolis (Edirne) and Trajanopolis, were founded to promote the pacification process. Particular attention was also given to developing a road network to connect the Aegean with the Black Sea. Romanization was most intense in the coastal areas, already influenced by Greek civilization, whereas in inland areas the Romans had to contend with warlike local populations. Thracian tribal organization was maintained after the conquest, and most of the inhabitants retained their own customs and religion. Characteristic

230 (top) The reliefs, over 200 m (656 ft) long, that wind around Trajan's Column faithfully depict the various stages of the emperor's Dacian campaigns. They feature a wealth of detail which is invaluable to an understanding of Roman military organization. Legionaries are shown constructing fortified camps, sappers building a huge bridge over the Danube, and soldiers forming the testudo *or storming enemy towns with the aid of war engines. There are standard-bearers with the banners of the cohorts, buglers and horn players, and even field hospitals. It also portrays in great detail the various uniforms, weapons and models of breastplate worn at the time of the battles depicted.*

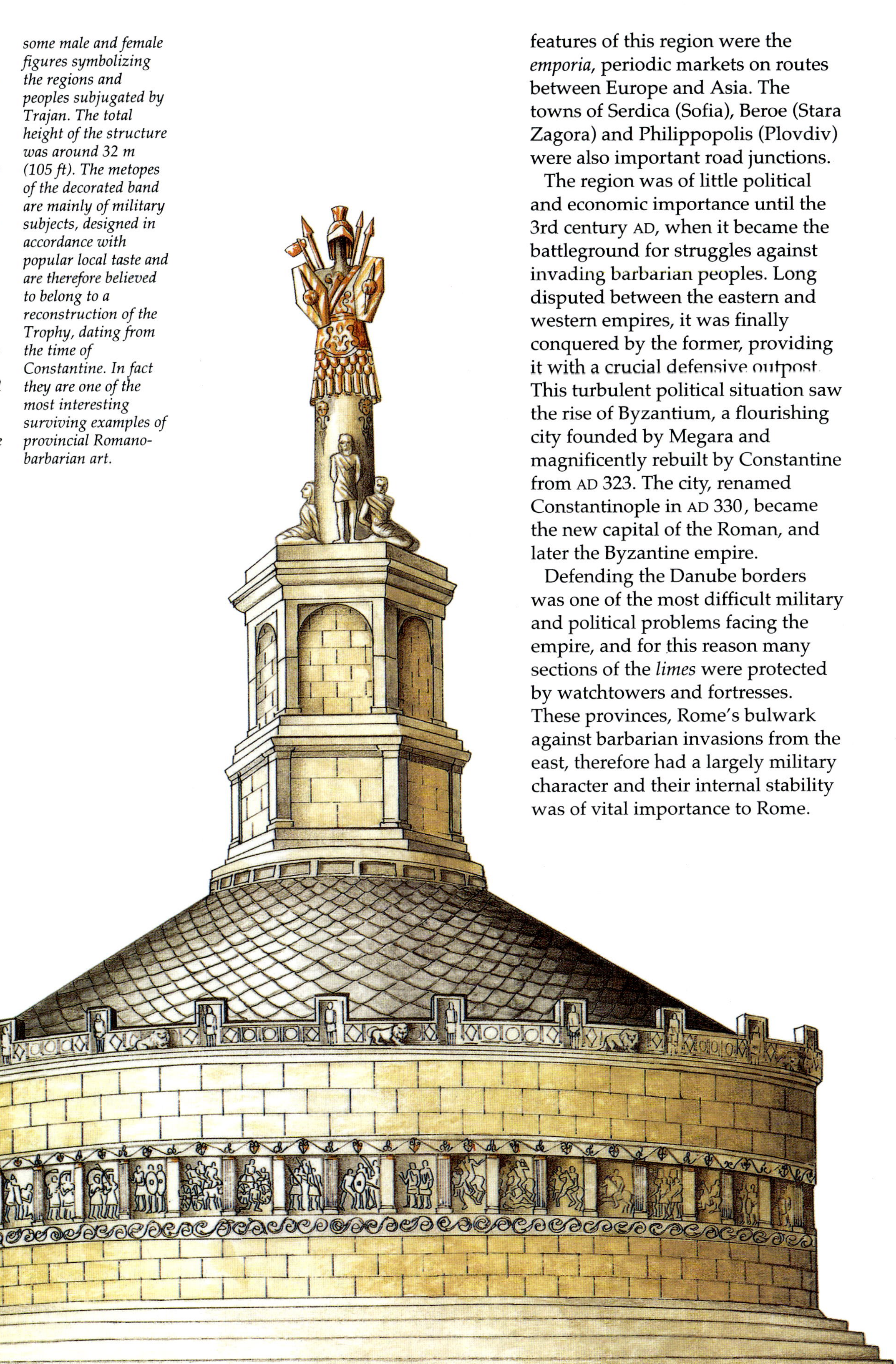

231 *The grandiose* Tropaeum Traiani *was built in* AD *109 in Lower Moesia (near modern Adamklissi in Romania) to commemorate Trajan's victories over the Dacians. It consisted of a massive cylindrical form made of concrete faced with blocks of limestone and decorated with a frieze, surmounted by a crenellated parapet. The conical roof was covered with fishscale-shaped stone tiles. A tall hexagonal pedestal at the top of the roof supported the great war trophy, at the base of which were perhaps some male and female figures symbolizing the regions and peoples subjugated by Trajan. The total height of the structure was around 32 m (105 ft). The metopes of the decorated band are mainly of military subjects, designed in accordance with popular local taste and are therefore believed to belong to a reconstruction of the Trophy, dating from the time of Constantine. In fact they are one of the most interesting surviving examples of provincial Romano-barbarian art.*

features of this region were the *emporia*, periodic markets on routes between Europe and Asia. The towns of Serdica (Sofia), Beroe (Stara Zagora) and Philippopolis (Plovdiv) were also important road junctions.

The region was of little political and economic importance until the 3rd century AD, when it became the battleground for struggles against invading barbarian peoples. Long disputed between the eastern and western empires, it was finally conquered by the former, providing it with a crucial defensive outpost. This turbulent political situation saw the rise of Byzantium, a flourishing city founded by Megara and magnificently rebuilt by Constantine from AD 323. The city, renamed Constantinople in AD 330, became the new capital of the Roman, and later the Byzantine empire.

Defending the Danube borders was one of the most difficult military and political problems facing the empire, and for this reason many sections of the *limes* were protected by watchtowers and fortresses. These provinces, Rome's bulwark against barbarian invasions from the east, therefore had a largely military character and their internal stability was of vital importance to Rome.

SPLIT, THE CITY THAT WAS DIOCLETIAN'S PALACE

N

A Private apartments
B Audience room
C Vestibule
D Mausoleum
E Peristyle
F Temple of Jupiter
G Silver Gate
H Iron Gate
I Offices and communal quarters
J Golden Gate

Ancient Spalatum developed in the 7th century AD around the palace Diocletian built as his residence from his abdication in AD 305 to his death in AD 313. As a result, many of the structures in the complex have been preserved and form a rare and magnificent example of a late empire residence. The general layout resembled a military camp, while the large portico overlooking the sea was inspired by contemporary fortified country villas.

Built on a trapezoidal plan, the palace had large walls of *opus quadratum* (squared blocks), at the corners of which stood strong square towers; only the southwest tower has not survived. Of the four gates, one in the middle of each side, the Gold and Silver gates are the best preserved, while that overlooking the sea was little more than a glorified opening. The southern part, now the most intact, contains an interesting complex comprising two areas – the imperial mausoleum to the east, converted into a cathedral in the Middle Ages, and a temple to the west, separated by what is called the 'Peristyle'. This is a huge, unroofed rectangular area edged with arcaded porticoes on the two longer sides and closed by a four-column *pronaos* (vestibule) with an interesting arched tympanum of Syrian inspiration. It was probably a hall used for open-air audiences.

From the exterior the mausoleum is an octagonal structure surrounded by a *peribolos* of columns with beams, while inside it is circular, with a series of alcoves separated by columns. The roof is pyramidal, and the building is raised to house the burial chamber. The temple, later used as a baptistery, sits on a tall podium; the well-preserved *cella* has a vaulted roof. The interior, like the frame of the main doorway, is richly decorated.

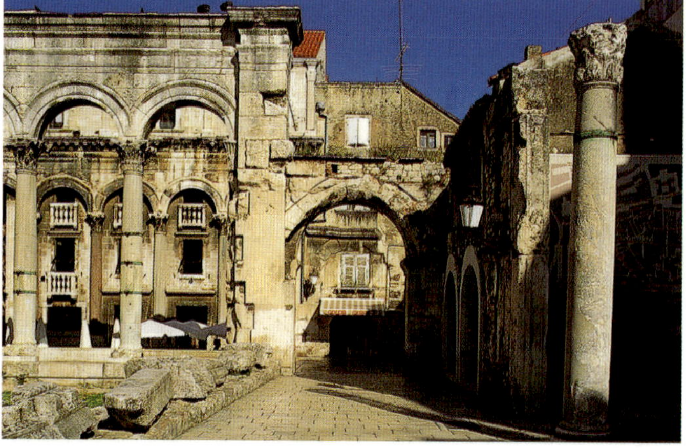

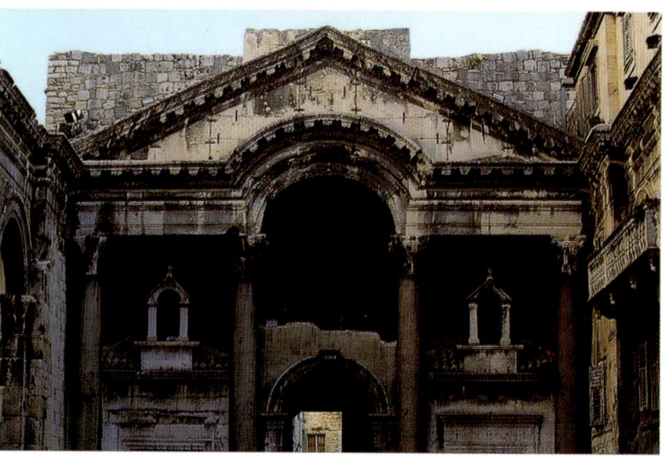

232 (right, above) Diocletian's Palace at Split is of exceptional interest because it is one of very few imperial residences to have survived from the period of the late empire.

232 (right, below) The Peristyle, now the most popular square in Split, is closed on the south by a pronaos *with four columns, surmounted by a triangular pediment with an arch on the two central columns.*

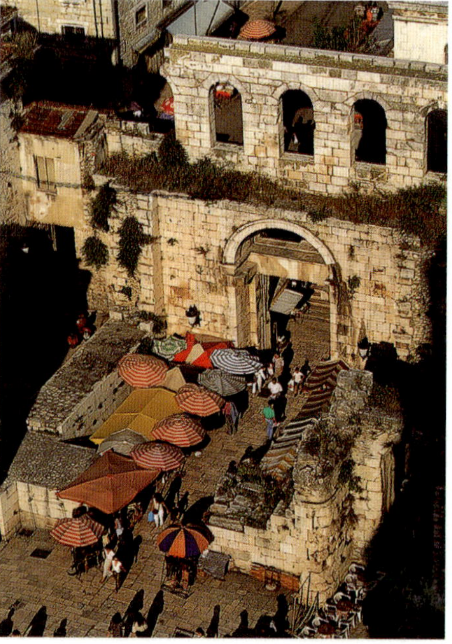

232 (far right) An aerial photograph shows the interior of what remains of the Silver Gate.

233 (opposite) Numerous blocks of hewn stone which once belonged to a colonnaded road are strewn around the area of the peristyle.

234–235 (overleaf) A reconstruction gives some impression of the huge size of Diocletian's fortified palace, which covered an area of almost 30 sq. km (12 sq. miles). It was surrounded by massive walls 3 m (10 ft) thick, and the interior space was divided by two right-angled avenues. The two quarters in the foreground must have been used as offices and barracks; next came the mausoleum, on the left, and the temple, perhaps dedicated to Jupiter, on the right. In the middle was the peristyle, followed by a vestibule and a rectangular hall leading to the imperial apartments. The section of the walls overlooking the sea was perhaps embellished with a hanging garden.

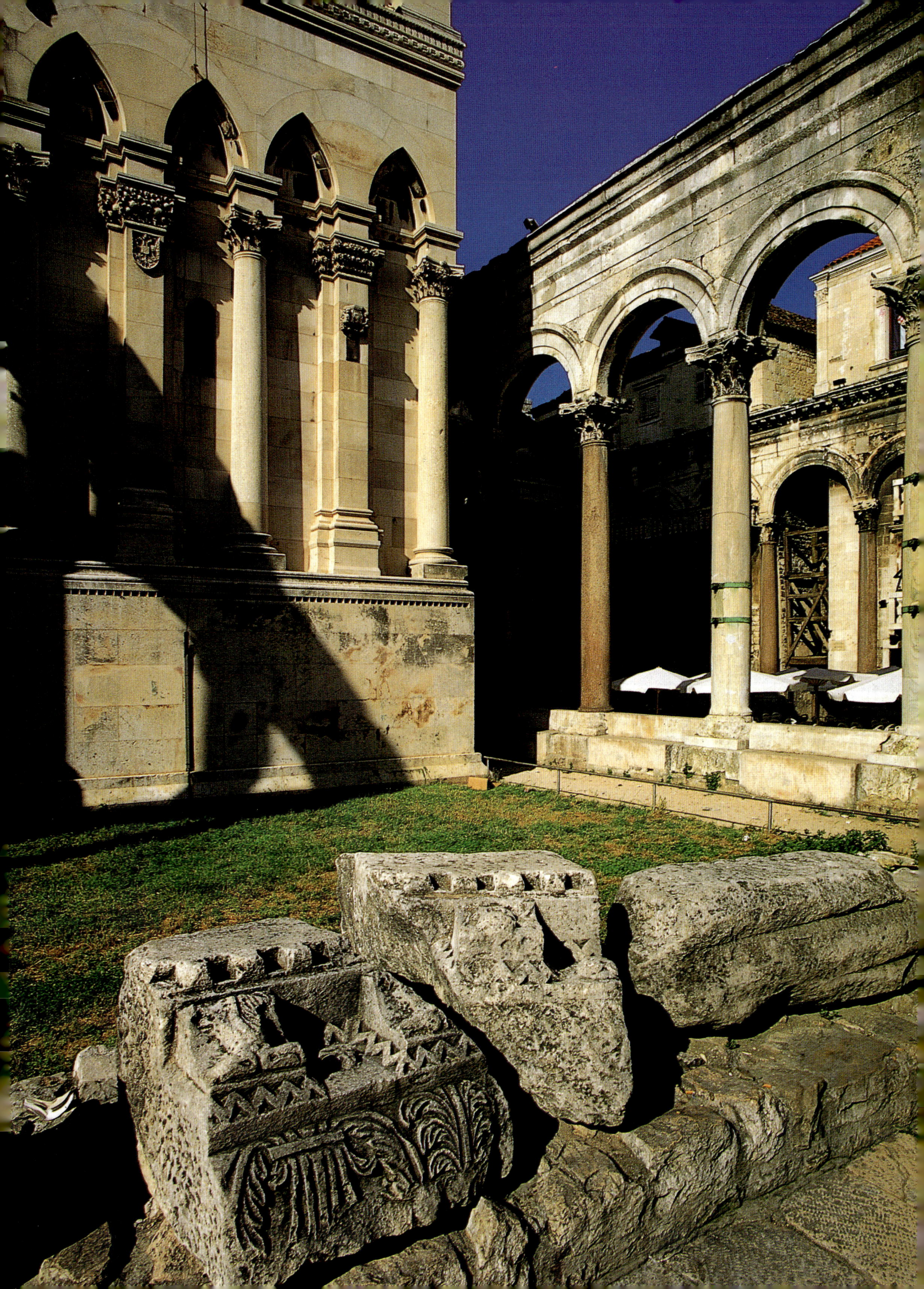

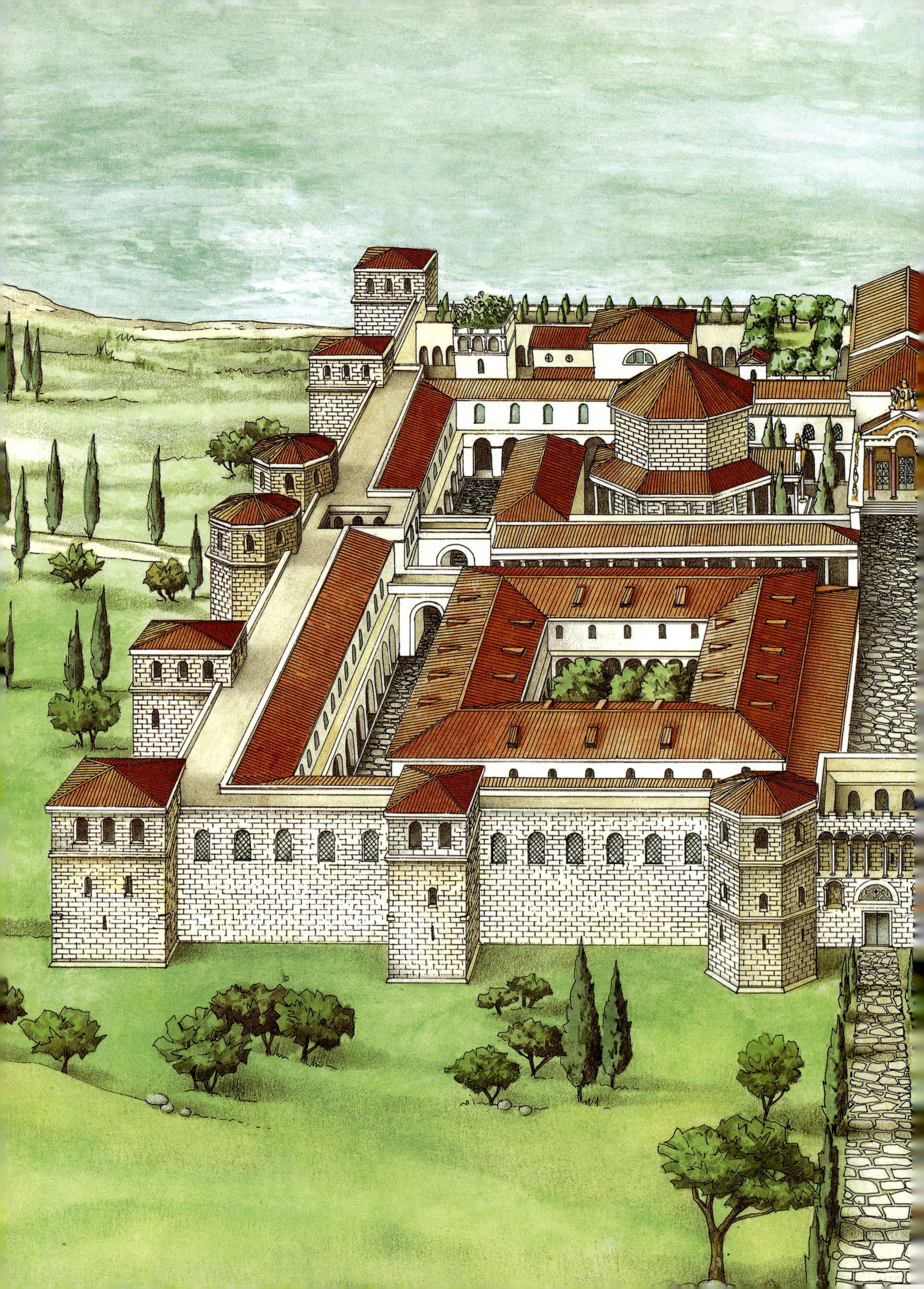

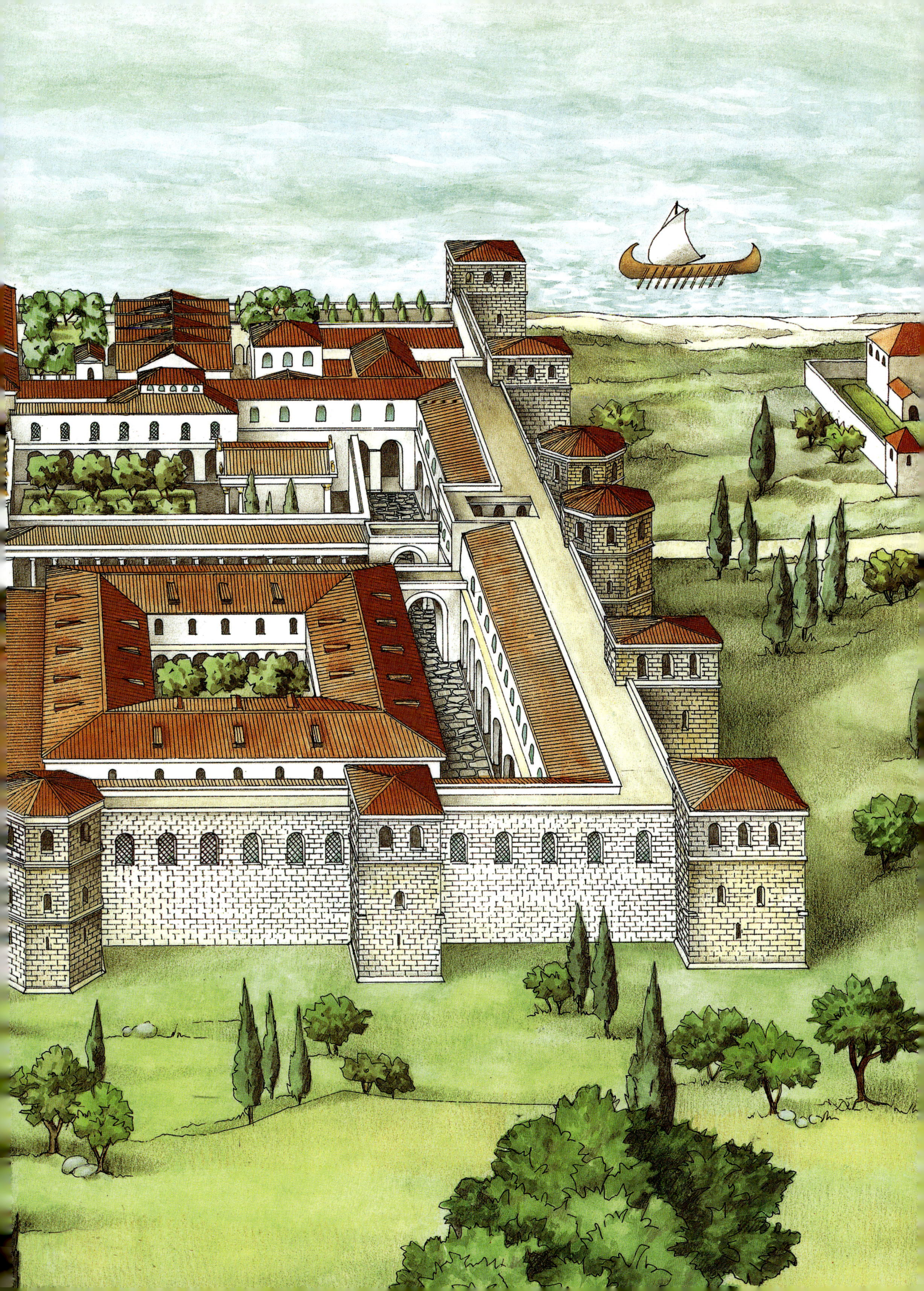

GREECE, IN THE FOOTSTEPS OF ANCIENT SPLENDOURS

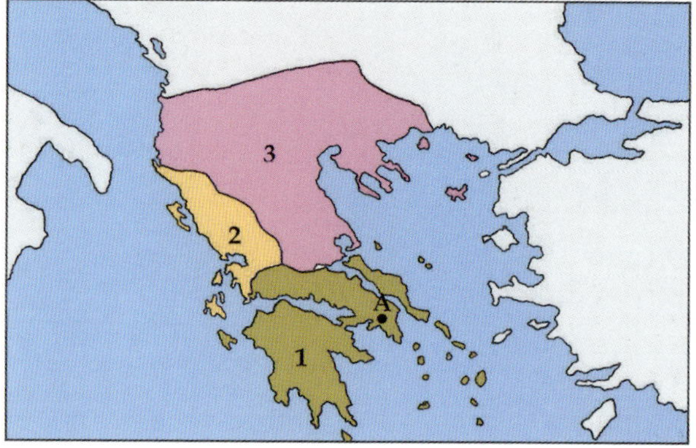

1 Achaea
2 Epirus
3 Macedonia
A Athens

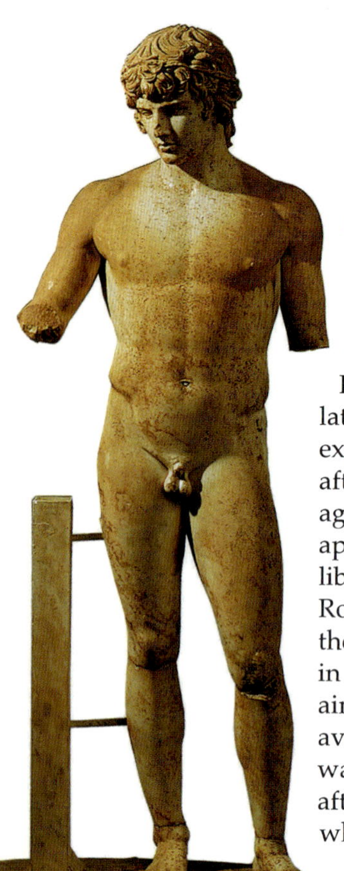

236 *A statue of Antinous found at Delphi, the work of a skilled local sculptor, is one of the many surviving portrayals of Hadrian's favourite. It exemplifies a marked return to the themes of classical Greek statuary in the treatment of the body, but the ambiguous beauty and markedly sensual face are typically Hellenistic.*

Roman intervention in Greece began in the 3rd century BC, at the time of struggles between the Macedonian kings and the Greek cities led by Athens.

Rome, called on to defend the latter, at first did nothing to exploit the supremacy it gained after victory at Cynoscephalae against Philip V and, at least in appearance, restored Greece to liberty. However, when the Roman legions finally defeated the Macedonian army at Pydna in 168 BC, Rome's expansionist aims became clear, and Greek aversion to their new conquerors was soon manifested. In 146 BC, after one of many rebellions, which tragically resulted in the destruction of Corinth, Greece was relegated to the status of a province, divided into Macedonia, Achaea, and also Epirus. In 88 BC, spurred on by the desire for freedom, Athens joined the anti-Roman campaign of Mithridates VI, King of Pontus, which ended disastrously two years later in the siege and sack of the city by Sulla. From then on, Greece was one of the most peaceful provinces, consoled by the remembrance of its glorious past and its fundamental role in Mediterranean culture.

Macedonia's economy flourished with the reopening of its gold and silver mines and better exploitation of its copper and iron resources. The Macedonian towns were allowed to keep their traditional form of government and were granted many immunities. Some, like Pella, Philippi and Dyrrachium, were colonized by Roman veterans. The Arch of Galerius in Thessalonica is an important monument, with its unusual form and rich sculptures.

Achaea, which in practice included the entire Peloponnese and the islands as far as Crete, together with the Cyclades, Attica, Boeotia and Euboea, gained new prosperity from its position at the hub of a busy system of sea routes leading to Piraeus, the ports of the Cyclades and the landing places on the Isthmus of Corinth. Under Caesar and Augustus numerous towns flourished once more, but the region enjoyed greatest status under Nero – who in AD 67 gave the Greeks their freedom and exempted them from paying tributes – and later under Hadrian, especially Athens.

Epirus, which only became an independent province in the 2nd century AD, played little part in the life of the empire, except for some coastal towns such as Actium – the most important port – founded by Augustus to commemorate his victory over Antony, and a few inland towns such as Dodona, with its Sanctuary of Zeus. With no major highways, the strategic value of Epirus lay in its naval bases.

Under Roman dominion, towns throughout Greece retained their traditional magistratures, and there were many free city-states such as Athens, Sicyon, Delphi and Thespiae. Sanctuaries and stadia continued to be active as centres of national gatherings. The most famous were those of the Isthmus, followed by Actium and Nicopolis, where Augustus instituted games. Under Hadrian, Athens was the headquarters of the Panhellenic amphictyony (a mainly religious association). Paradoxically, though subjugated Greece conquered Rome with the greatness of its culture, and its artistic traditions had an immense influence on Roman art.

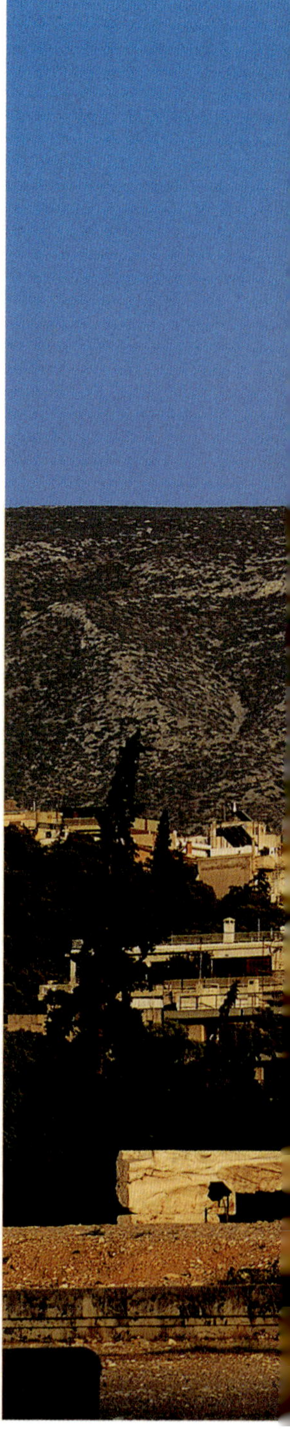

236–237 (above) The construction of the Olympieum in Athens, which began in the 4th century BC and was frequently interrupted, was completed by Hadrian c. AD 130. It was made entirely of valuable Pentelic marble, and was the largest Corinthian-style temple in ancient times.

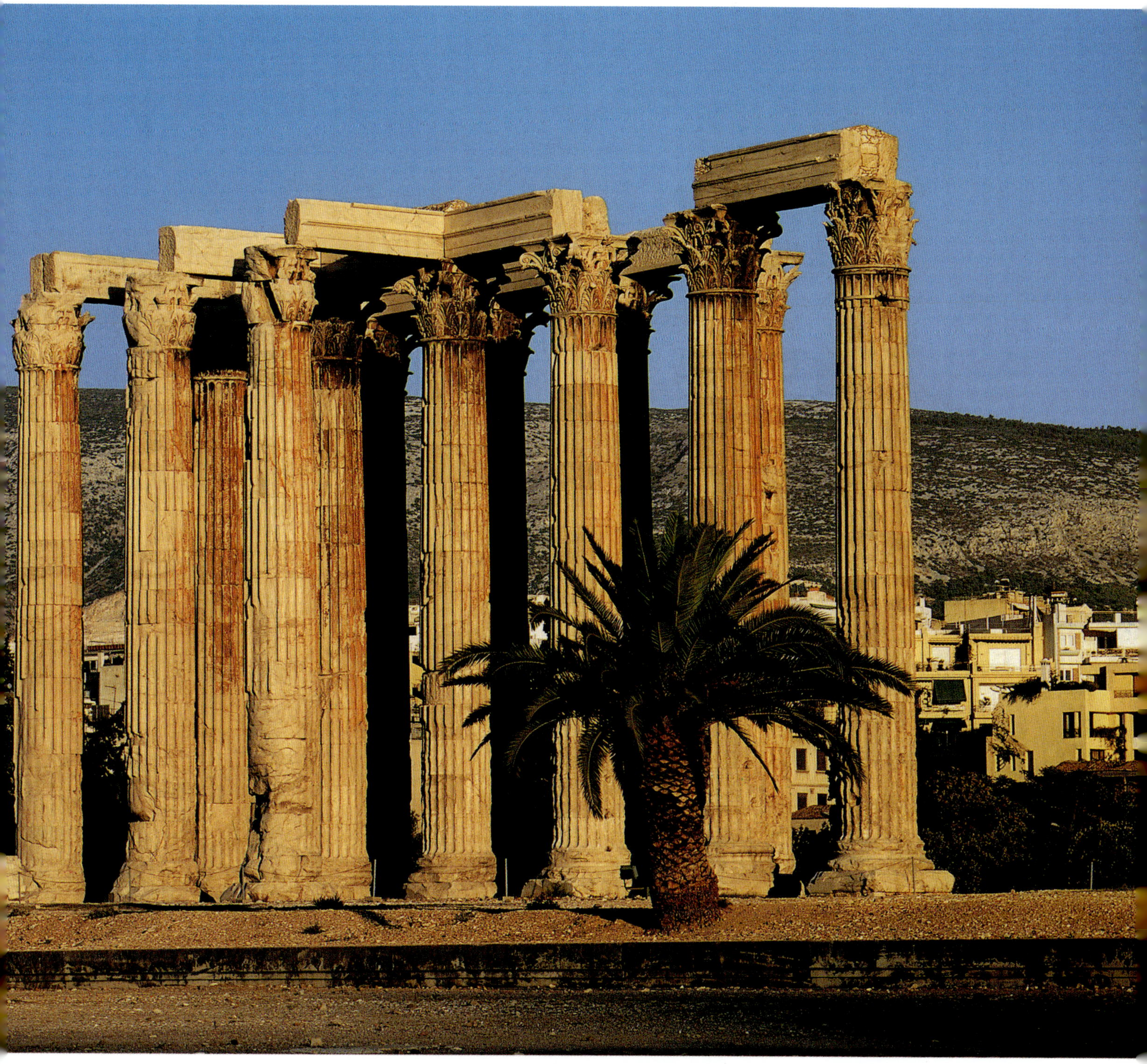

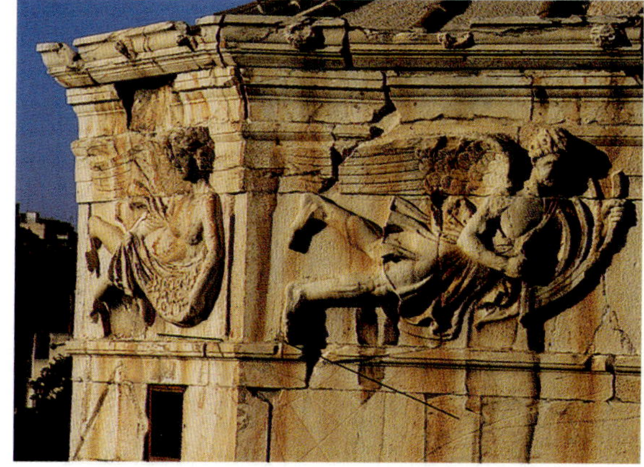

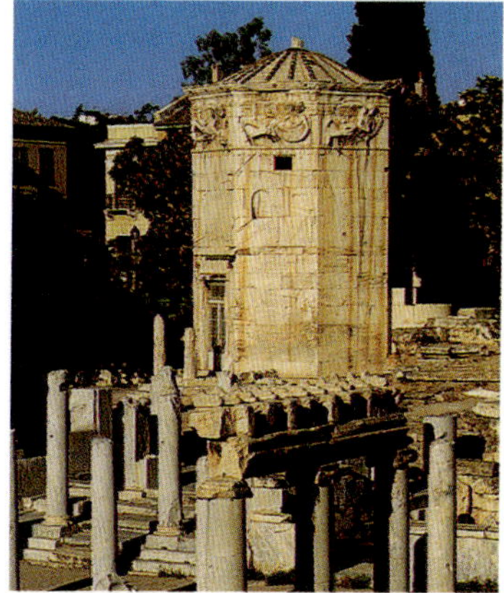

237 (right) The Tower of the Winds in Athens was built around the mid-1st century BC *to house the water-clock designed by Andronicus of Cyrrhus; its name is derives from the fact that it was topped by a bronze Triton which acted as a weather vane.*

ATHENS, THE BEACON OF CLASSICAL CIVILIZATION

Following its sack by Sulla in 86 BC and a period of unstable political equilibrium with Rome, Athens enjoyed the imperial favour of Augustus. Two other pro-Greek emperors, Nero and Hadrian, were particularly generous to the city, which had become a symbol of classical civilization. When the city was destroyed by the Heruli in AD 267, only the Acropolis survived, thanks to its strong walls. After this disaster, from which it never fully recovered, Athens regained a glimmer of its former glory under Theodosius. The university, still flourishing, was finally suppressed by Justinian in AD 529. Evidence of the Roman presence in Athens coexists with remains of the classical period, and can be traced in the form varying degrees of restoration work on nearly all the city's public buildings. Major monuments built under Augustus were the Odeum of Agrippa in the agora (market-place), the Temple of Augustus and Rome on the Acropolis, opposite the Parthenon, a stoa (colonnaded walk) in the Ceramicus district, and what is known as the 'Roman agora'. Little is known of building activity under the Julio-Claudian and Flavian emperors. The library of T. Flavius Pantainos and the funerary monument of G. Antiochus Philopappus, an Attic citizen and Roman consul, date from the age of Trajan. The generosity of Hadrian, celebrated as the second founder of the city, led to the construction of a stoa and a magnificent library to the north of the Roman agora, the completion of the Olympieum (the largest Corinthian temple in the ancient world), a gymnasium, and the restoration of the Theatre of Dionysius. The library, of which little remains, must have been truly magnificent; it had a portico with 100 marble columns, and the rooms had gilded ceilings and alabaster walls. A gymnasium and public buildings, including two baths, are part of what is still called the city of Hadrian, entered via his triumphal arch. Herodes Atticus restored the stadium, covering it with marble and built a new Odeum at the foot of the Acropolis at his own expense.

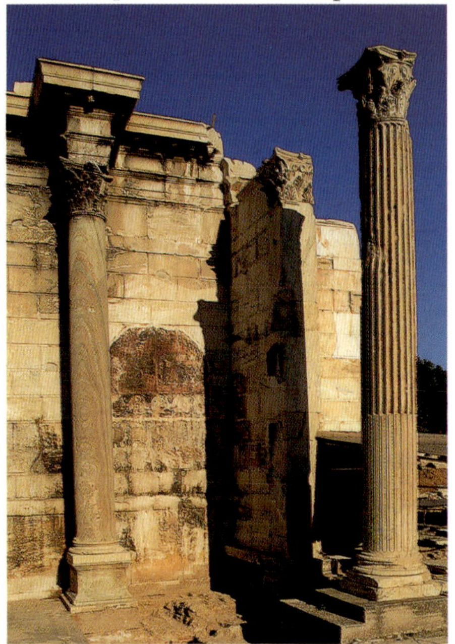

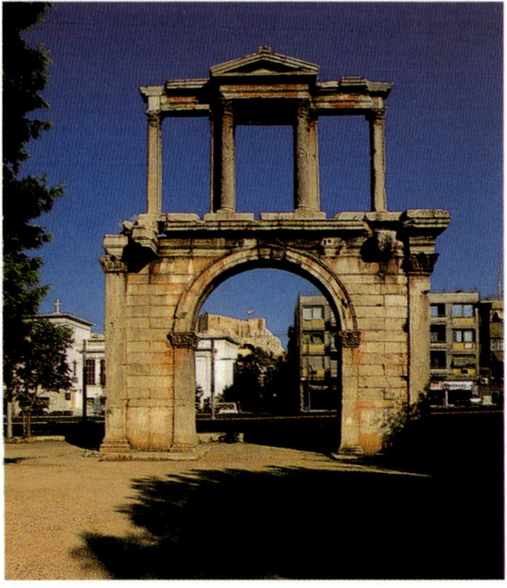

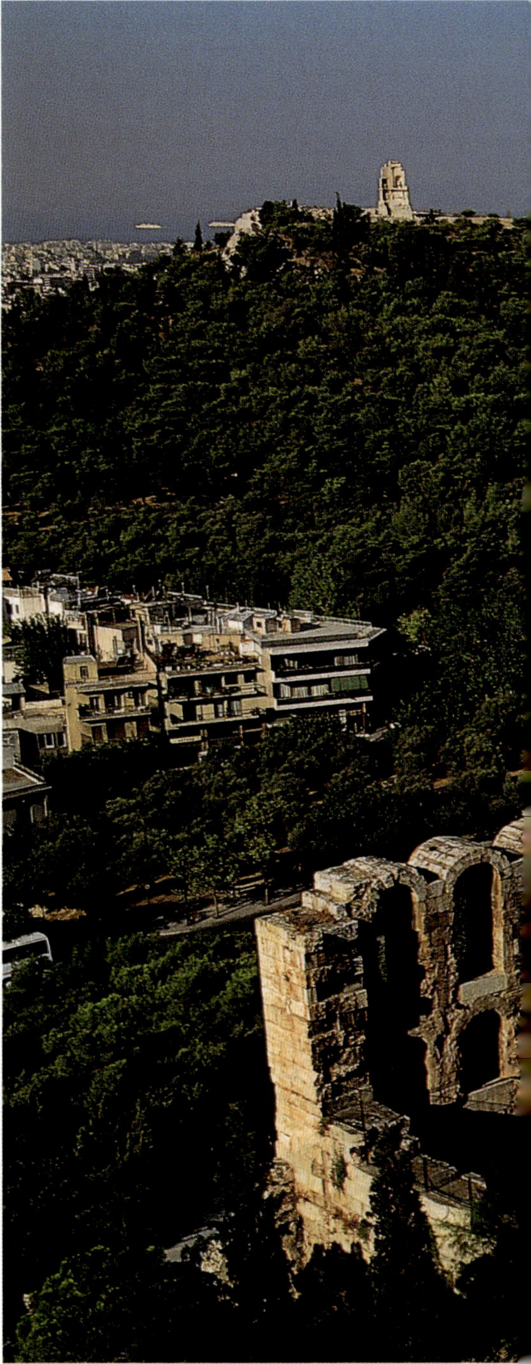

238 (left, above) The façade of Hadrian's Library consists of 14 Phrygian marble Corinthian columns surmounted by a perfectly balanced arrangement of columns and beams. Hadrian, a great admirer of Hellenism, embellished Athens with outstanding monuments, and lavished huge sums on their construction.

238 (left, below) On the border between the old part of Athens and the new Roman districts, the Arch of Hadrian, now stripped of the columns which flanked its archway and of the statues standing on the attic storey, broke away from the traditional form of this type of structure, evidence of a taste for Athenian architecture.

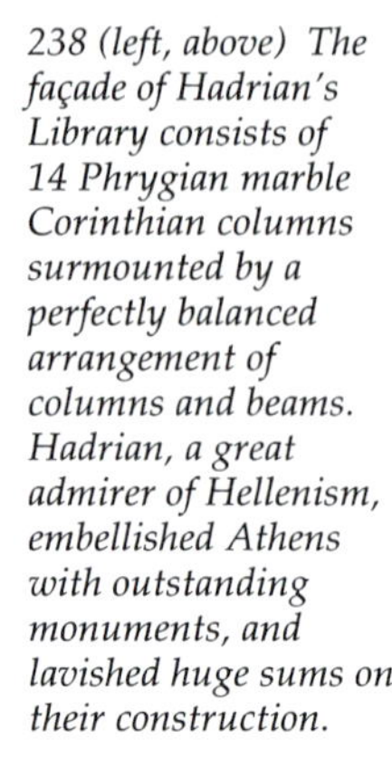

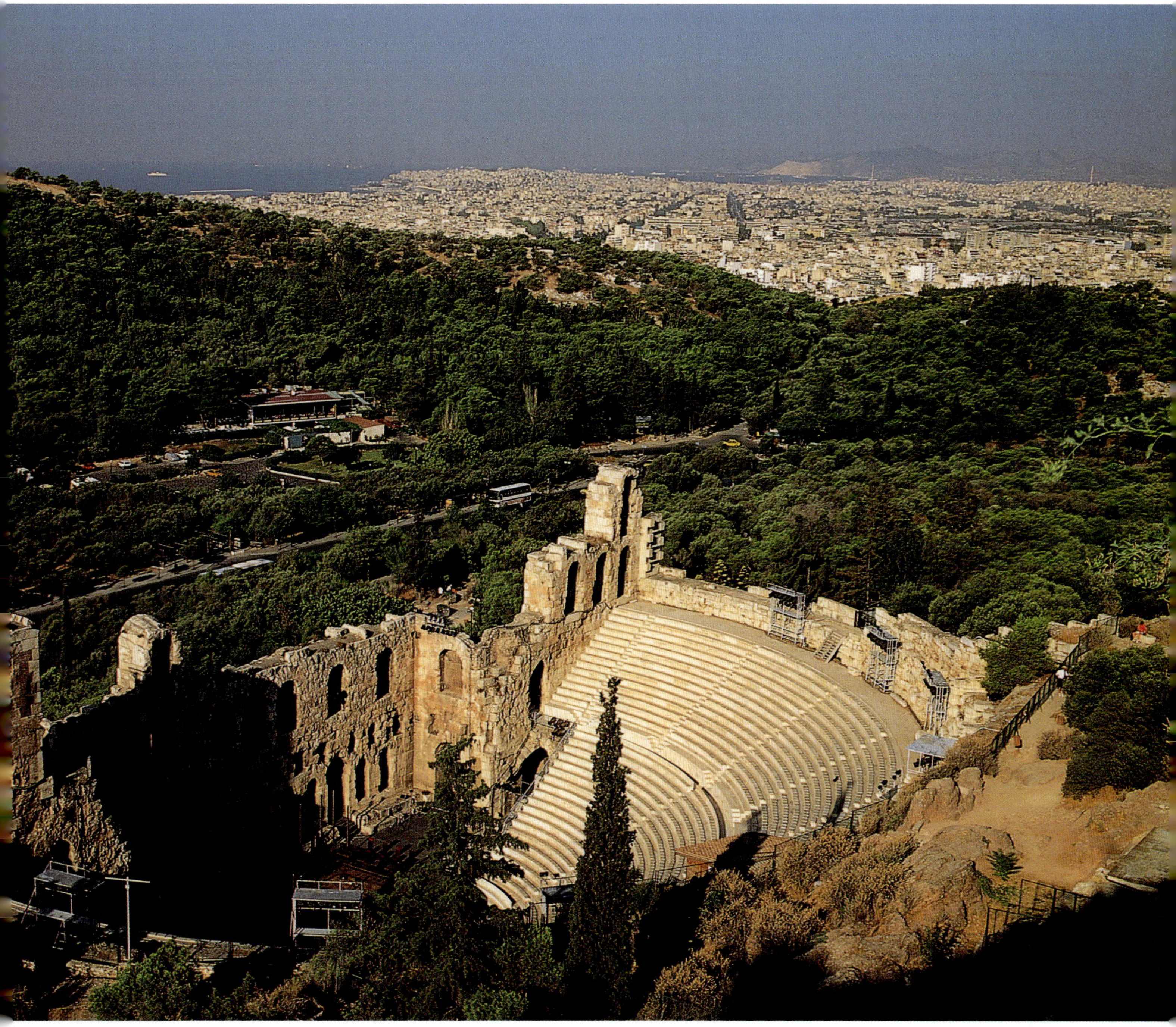

238–239 (above) Herodes Atticus built a magnificent Odeum at the foot of the Acropolis around AD *161, which is still remarkable for the extensive use of arches and vaults in its construction. These structural elements symbolize the change from rectilinear Greek architecture to curvilinear Roman architecture.*

A Roman Temple
B Odeum of Agrippa
C Library of Hadrian
D Roman Agora
E Tower of the Winds
F Theatre of Dionysus
G Arch of Hadrian
H Olympieum

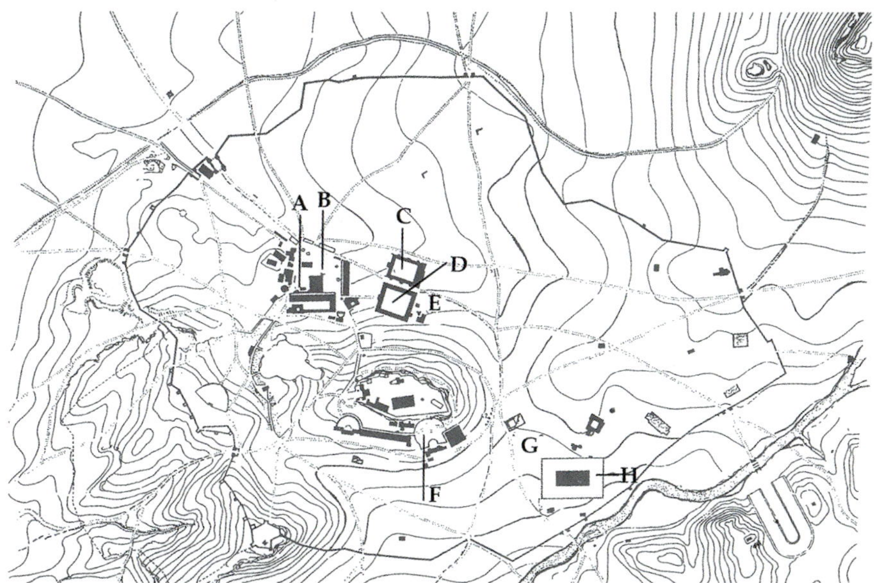

ASIA MINOR, THE LEGACY OF KING ATTALUS

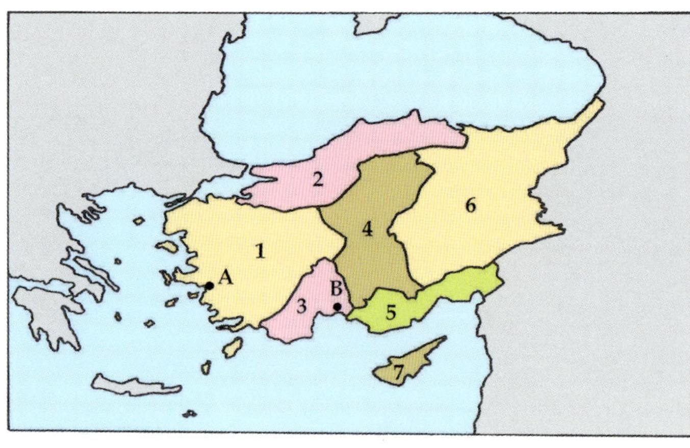

It was with the legacy of Attalus of his kingdom of Pergamum that the Roman dominion of Asia Minor began in 133 BC. It continued with the annexation of neighbouring kingdoms. The most important towns in the Asian provinces were the Greek colonies of Ionia, scattered along the coasts at the mouths of the great rivers. From the outset, the wealth of the region attracted large numbers of Italics, mainly tax collectors and traders, whose greed sparked off the discontent that led to a terrible revolt in 88 BC, in which 80,000 are said to have died. Unrest continued in the civil wars, and it was only with Augustus that the fortunes of Asia began to improve. A period of peace and prosperity began that lasted until the mid-3rd century AD, as seen in the numerous grandiose buildings found in all the towns of the province. Ruins of the Roman period are scattered over Asia Minor, not only in major towns such as Ephesus, Pergamum, Miletus and Halicarnassus, but also in flourishing minor towns. Sardis, Mylasa, Magnesia on the Maeander, Laodicea and Apamea are some of the best known.

Sanctuaries and religious centres carried on as usual, tolerated by the Romans, who merely introduced the worship of Rome and Augustus. In the artistic and cultural fields, the school of sculpture at Aphrodisias, with artists active in Rome and Africa, became very important. Literature and science, which boasted two major centres in the medical schools of Ephesus and Pergamum, were equally fertile.

The main sources of wealth in these provinces were agriculture and trade; priceless goods from the east were conveyed to the Mediterranean ports along the royal highways of the Achaemenids (Persians) and the new Roman roads. Purple-veined marble from the quarries of Synnada in Phrygia and the red marble of Chios were highly prized. Marble was transported on special ships called *naves lapidariae*, and unloaded at Ostia. It was carried up the Tiber to the depot at the foot of the Aventine, still called Marmorata (Marble Hill). It was usually moved in the form of rough-hewn blocks, to be finished at its destination. Asia Minor was also famous for sheep rearing and the production of wool and parchment which, together with papyrus, was the most common writing material in antiquity. Pergamum was renowned for its parchment, while most other towns were known for textiles and woollen garments, the quality of which was guaranteed by the weavers' and dyers' guilds. Fabrics dyed with a purple obtained from a mollusc were highly prized. At Hierapolis (Pamukkale) wool was washed in the natural hot springs to fix its colour. The region was also rich in ore deposits, especially silver and gold. The abundance of gold was the origin of the legend of Croesus (near whose kingdom the gold-bearing Pactolus river flows), and was noted in ancient texts, from the *Iliad* on.

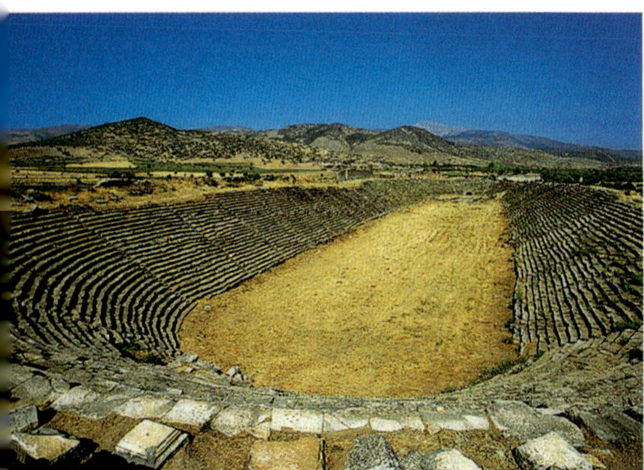

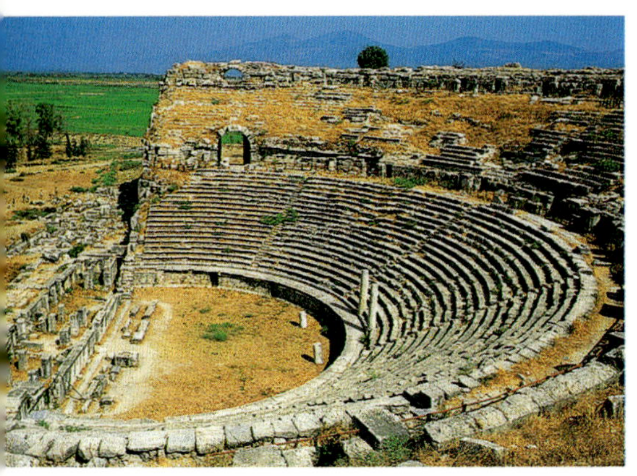

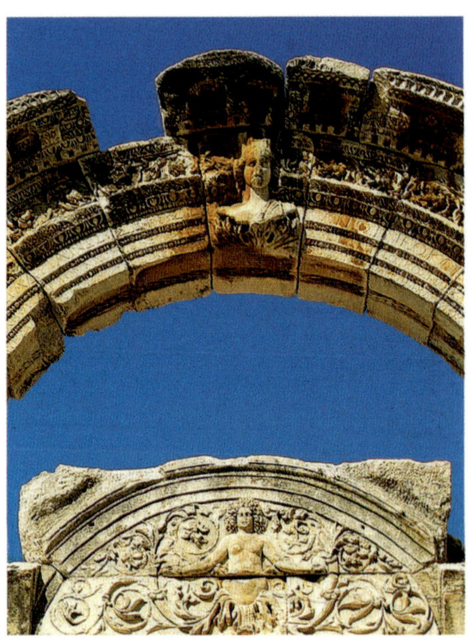

240 (left, above) In the imperial age the town of Aphrodisias was embellished with great public monuments, including a vast hippodrome.

240 (left, below) The present appearance of the theatre at Miletus dates to its rebuilding in the 2nd century AD.

240 (above) A detail of the magnificent Temple of Hadrian in Ephesus.

241 (opposite) The tetrapylon at Aphrodisias was the monumental entrance to the sacred area of the Temple of Aphrodite, patron goddess of the city.

242–243 (overleaf) The great theatre of Aspendos, built in the 2nd century AD, is the best preserved in Asia Minor. A Roman town as early as 133 BC, Aspendos prospered in the imperial age.

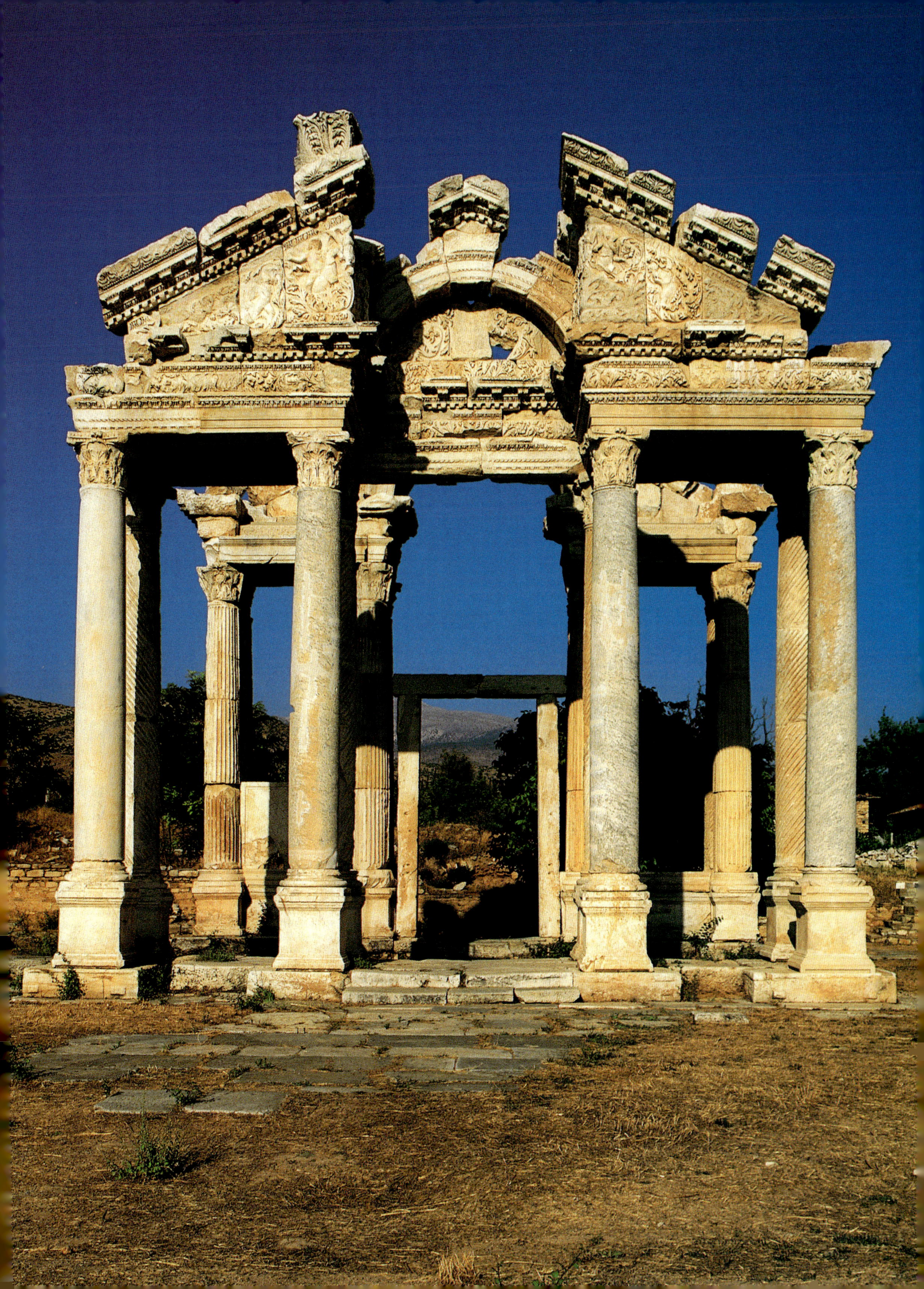

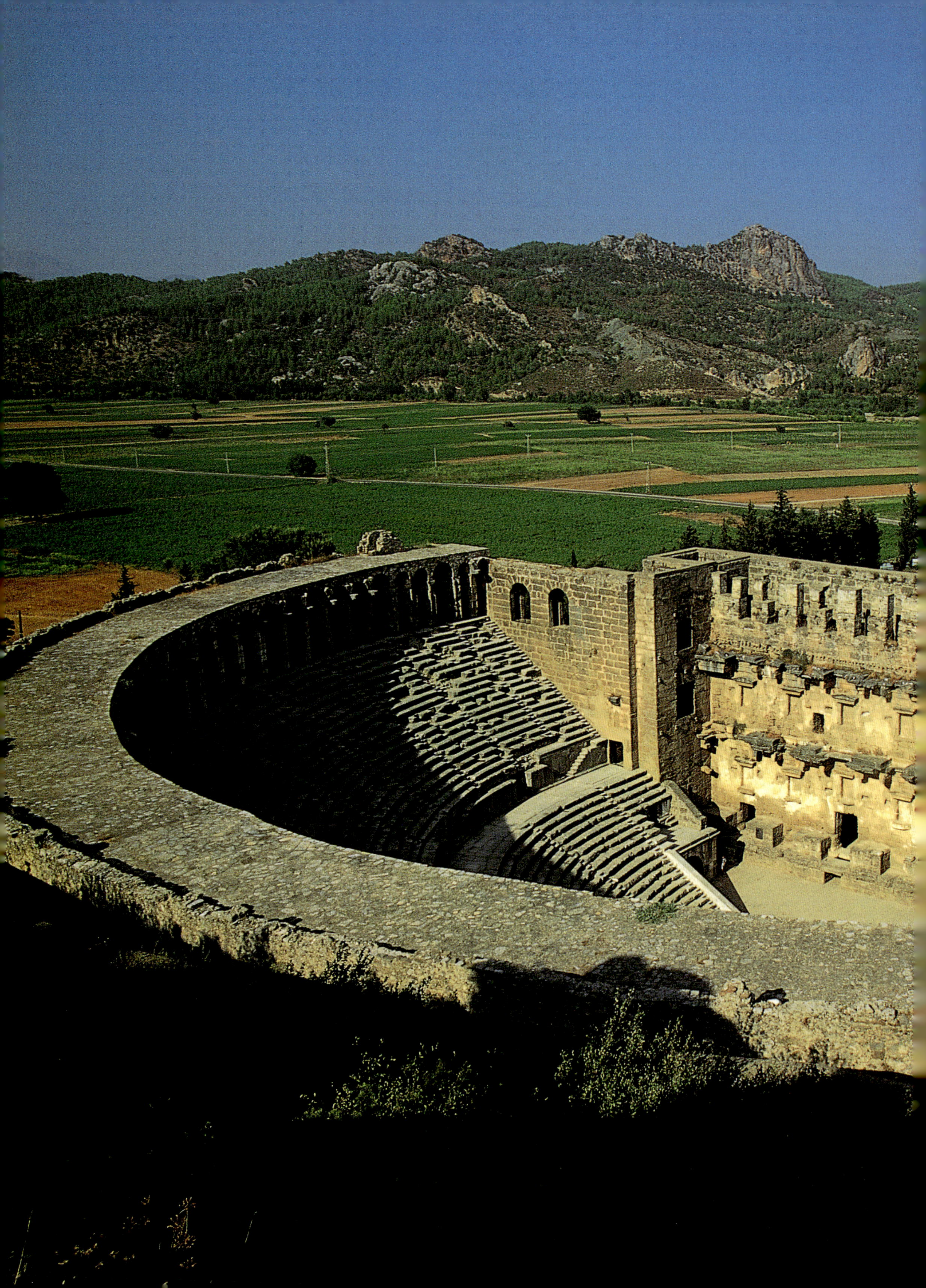

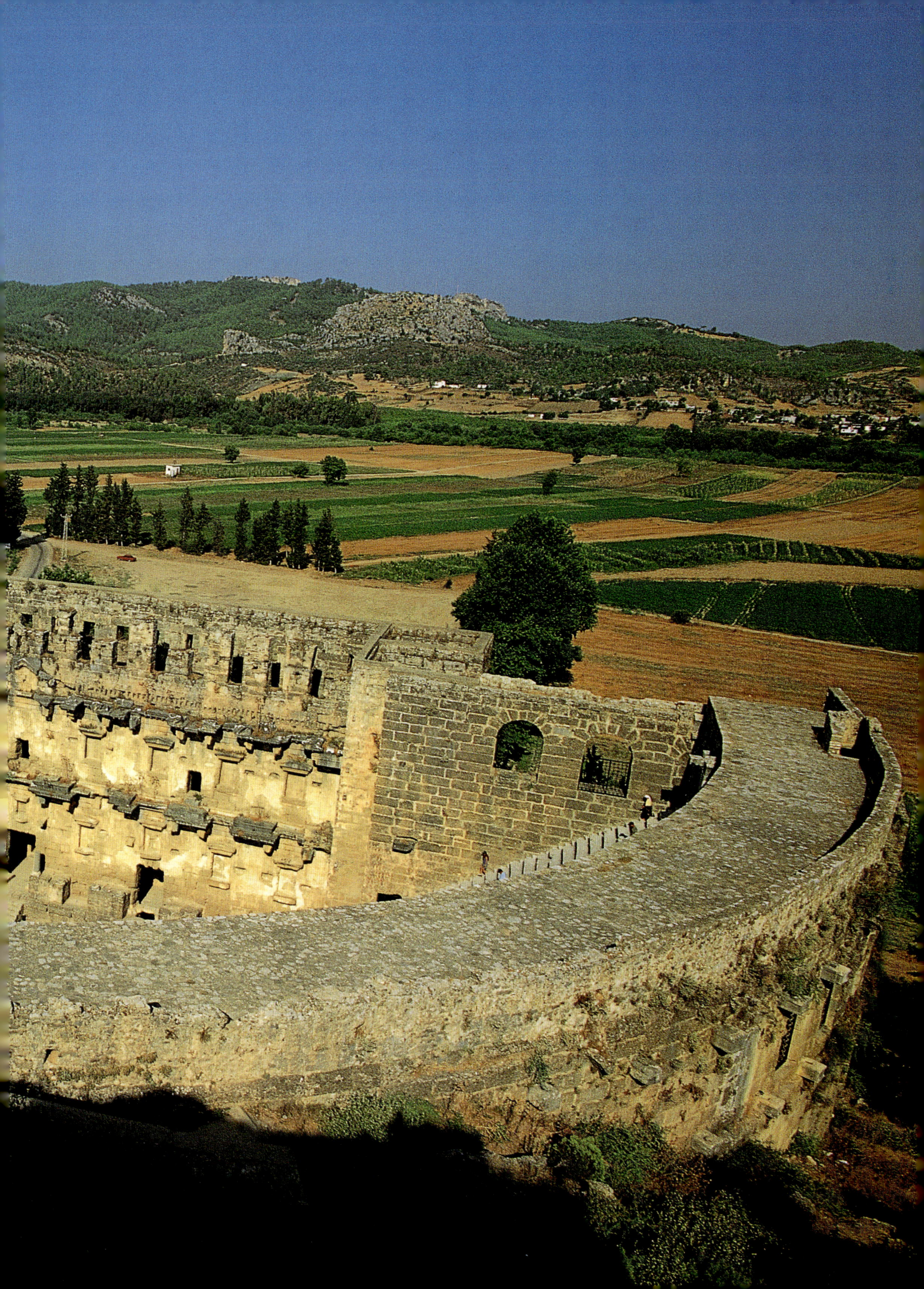

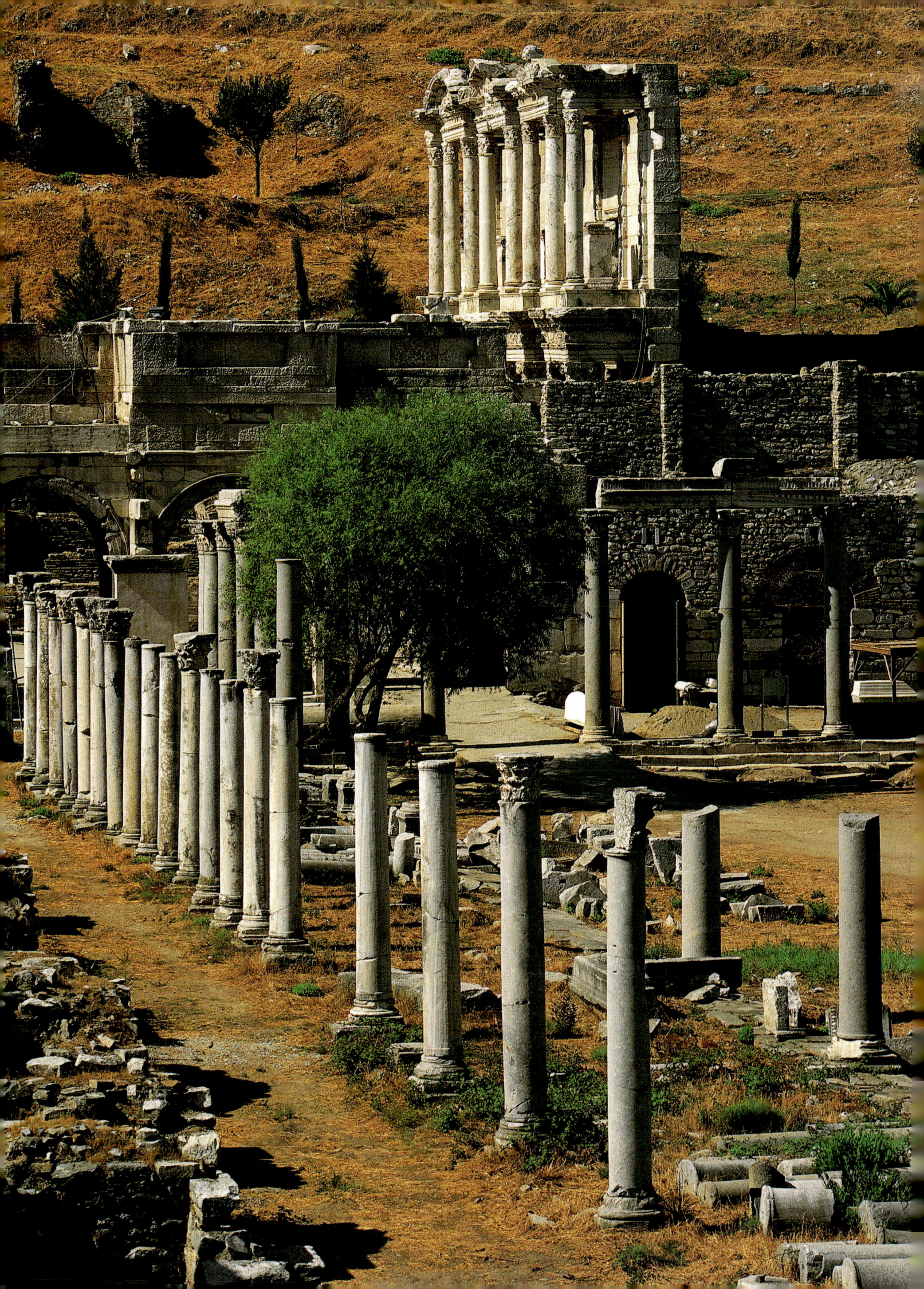

EPHESUS, BELOVED OF ARTEMIS

A Port
B Port baths
C Square of Verulanus
D Gymnasium of Vedius
E Stadium
F Theatre gymnasium
G Theatre
H Agora
I Library of Celsus
J Odeum
K Baths
L East gymnasium

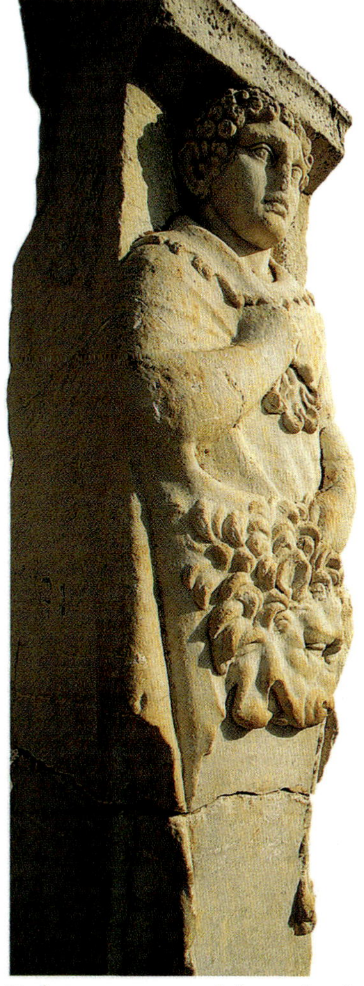

Ephesus, centre of the cult of Artemis and the birthplace of great philosophers, was one of the most populous and wealthiest cities in the ancient world. Built at the mouth of the Maeander, at the end of the great Royal Highway from the interior, it had a long and eventful history. Part of the kingdom of Pergamum, it was included by Attalus III in his legacy to the Romans, who made it the capital of the province of Asia. It maintained its primacy even after its sack by the Goths in AD 263. It soon recovered but was destroyed by the Arabs in the mid-7th century AD.

Although nothing remains of the temple of Artemis, one of the Seven Wonders of the Ancient World, restored for the last time in the Hellenistic period, the architectural heritage of Ephesus is still very rich. It was also clearly influenced by the long Roman presence in the area.

The town's main road was the Via Arcadiana (so called because it was rebuilt by the emperor Arcadius in the 4th century AD), which ran from the theatre to the port, lined with colonnaded porticoes. The theatre, of Hellenistic origin, was transformed during the empire. A similar fate befell the stadium, converted under Nero for use for gladiatorial games and wild beast hunts.

New construction work included numerous porticoes, built along the main roads, fountains and nymphaea, supplied with the water conveyed to the city by C. Sextilius Pollio at the time of Augustus. Among monuments dating from the Roman period are the Odeum (a small roofed theatre built by wealthy citizen P. Vedius Antoninus at the time of Antoninus Pius), the Serapeum (a grandiose temple dating to the 2nd century AD), the Temple of Domitian, the Temple of Hadrian (a small, elegant and richly decorated building) and the Library of Celsus. The latter, outstanding for its grandeur and luxury, was donated to the city by the benefactor Titus Julius Aquila Polemeanus in memory of his father, a senator under Trajan. The front, preceded by a stairway, has an unusual sequence of alternating doors, windows and niches with allegorical statues, in a complex, lively architectural form typical of Hadrian's era. Inside was a burial chamber containing the sarcophagus of Celsus Polemeanus – unusual in the Roman world as permission was only rarely given for particularly worthy citizens to be buried inside public buildings.

244 (opposite) The Library of Celsus (the upper part of which can be seen in the background) stands next to the agora, a large area surrounded by porticoes.

245 (left) The Gate of Hercules stood at the beginning of one of the main roads of the town. One of the reliefs, after which the gate was named, is shown here.

245 (centre) The commercial agora, *with numerous shops lining all four sides, was reconstructed in Corinthian style in the 3rd century.*

245 (bottom) Built in the 3rd century BC on the slopes of Mount Pion, the theatre was extended in the Roman age. It could hold 24,000 spectators and is still used for performances today.

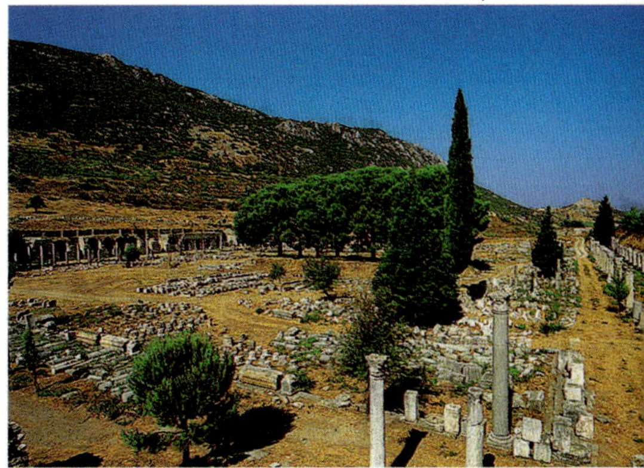

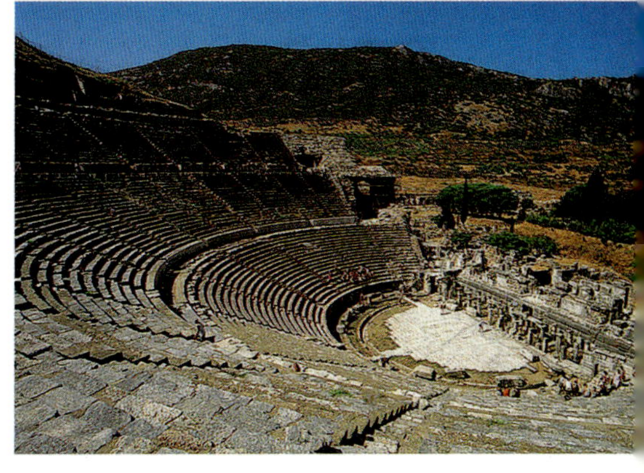

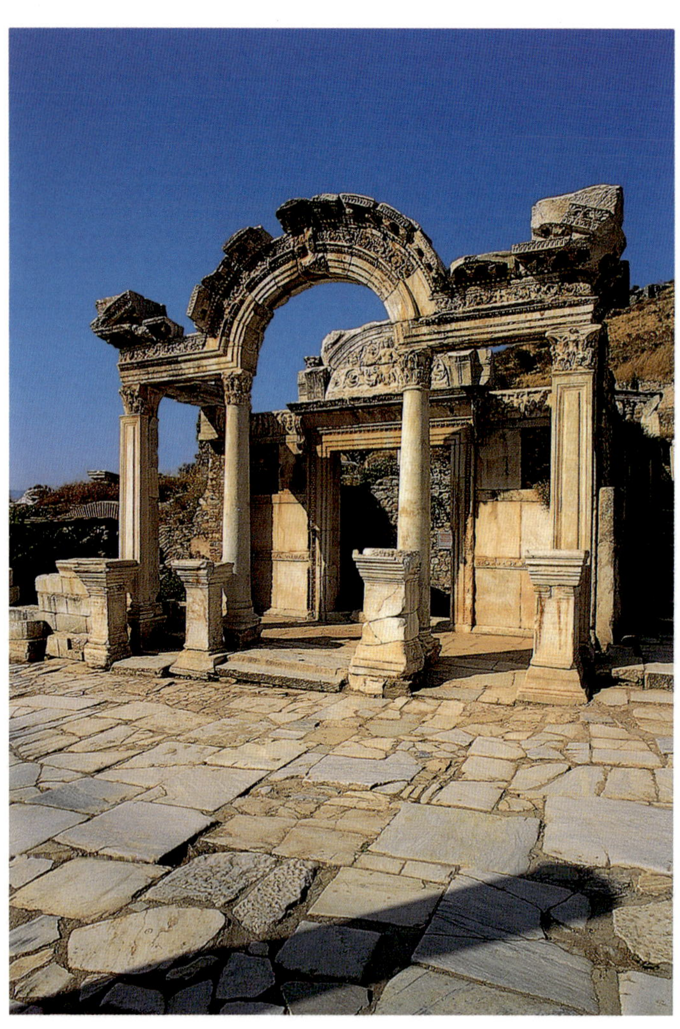

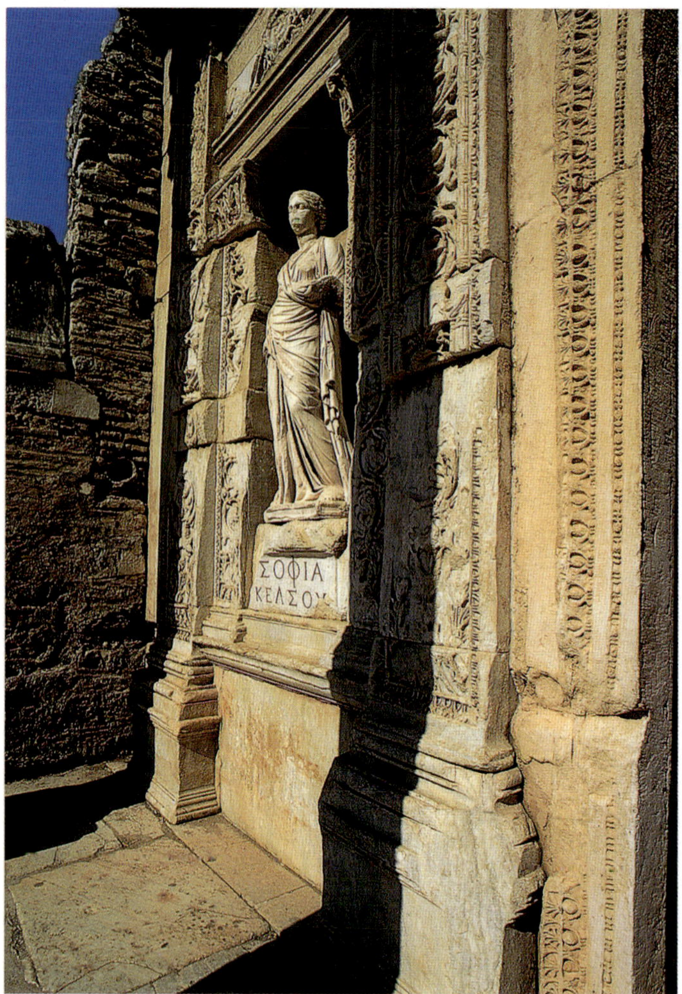

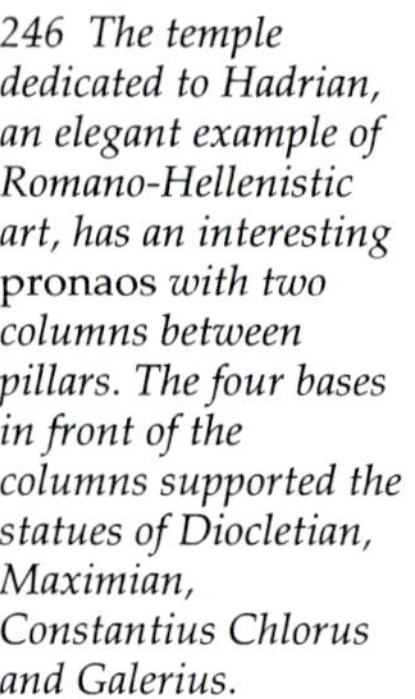

246 The temple dedicated to Hadrian, an elegant example of Romano-Hellenistic art, has an interesting pronaos *with two columns between pillars. The four bases in front of the columns supported the statues of Diocletian, Maximian, Constantius Chlorus and Galerius.*

246 Four niches in the façade of the Library of Celsus each contained a female statue, allegories of the principal virtues attributed to the famous man the building honoured. This is the personification of sophia *(wisdom). The entire building was restored between 1970 and 1978.*

247 (opposite) The magnificent Library of Celsus was built to commemorate Senator Julius Celsus Polemeanus – a magistrate of Ephesus – by his heirs, who also spent a large sum on the purchase of books. Unusually for a Roman public building, the library also contained the sarcophagus of the great man.

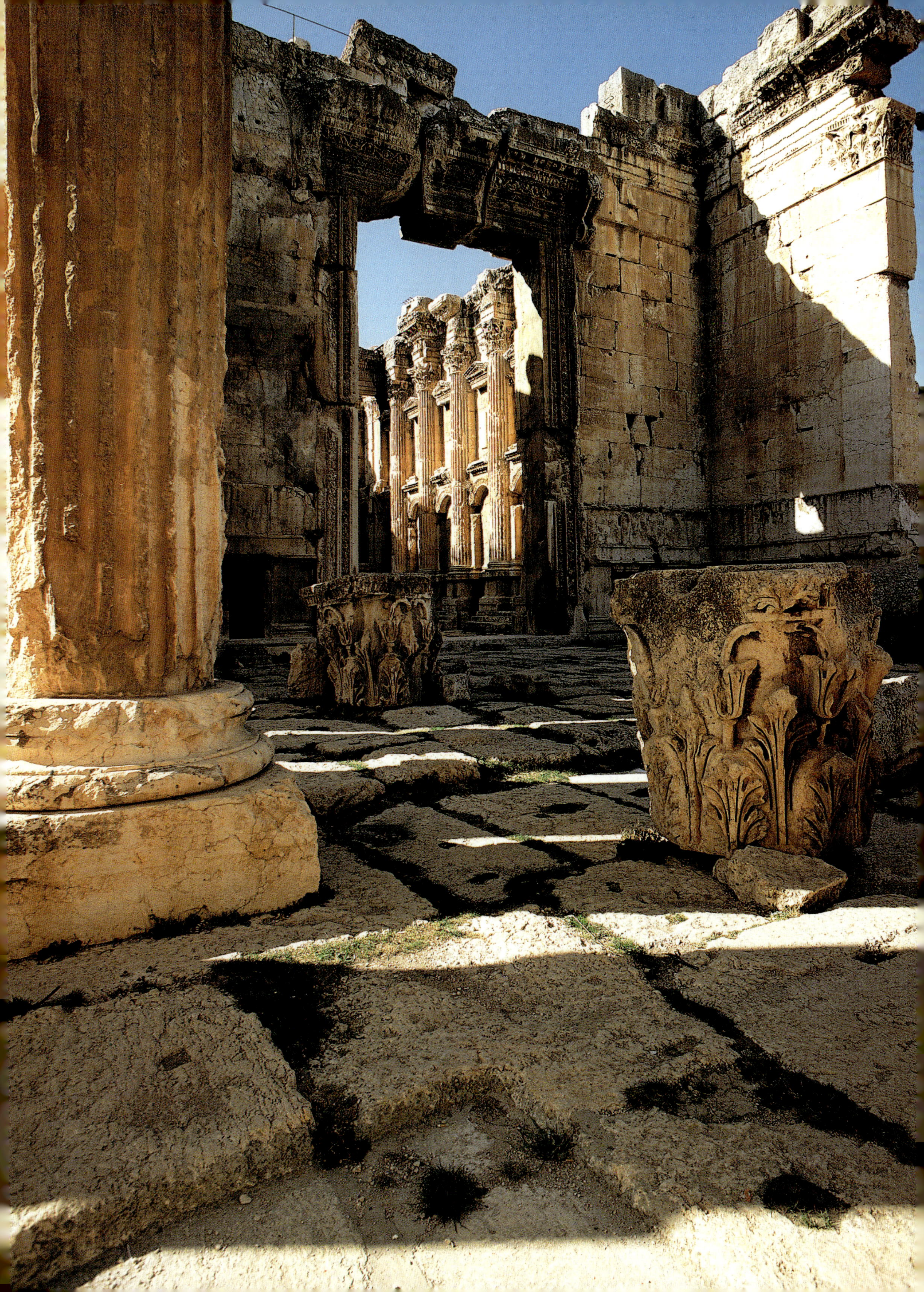

distances, paying tariffs and taxes as they went, sometimes escorted by armed troops to prevent attacks by bandits. These taxes had an affect on the price of the goods carried, which were therefore mainly products of limited size and high value. In addition to government taxes, tariffs were also payable to the various cities the caravans passed through, which offered a range of services to accommodate merchants, animals and goods. The 'Palmyra tariff', a bilingual stele in Palmyrene and Greek of AD 137, gives some idea of the goods commonly carried by the caravans: slaves, purple-dye, aromatic oils and spices, prostitutes, fabrics, salt and works of art.

Roman organization in these provinces was extremely efficient, especially the communications. The Romans improved and extended the existing road network, created by the Achaemenids and exploited by Alexander the Great, which connected the river and land routes along the Tigris and Euphrates and the caravan routes which led from Media and Persia to the Syrian ports and the interior roads of Anatolia. Towns furthest east, such as Nisibis (Nusaybin) and Singara, had military garrisons.

The Eastern Provinces were a melting-pot of different races and civilizations, where Greek, Semitic and Roman peoples came into contact with and influenced one another. Christianity spread rapidly here, and these regions became its main centre. This mixture of varied influences is demonstrated by the archaeological remains in numerous towns, such as Palmyra, Gerasa (Jerash), Philadelphia (Amman), Heliopolis (Baalbek), Damascus, Antioch, Apamea and Dura Europos, in which Roman, Hellenistic and Oriental elements blend to produce magnificent and often surprising results.

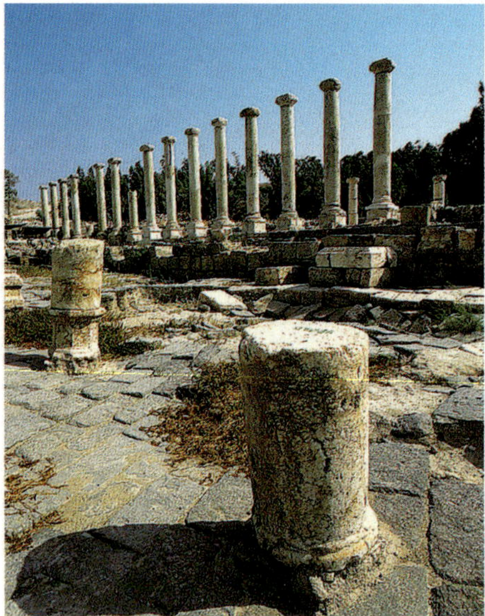

252 (top) Beth Shean, founded in the 5th millennium BC, is one of the oldest inhabited sites in Israel. The town was conquered in 63 BC by Pompey, who retained its Hellenistic name of Scythopolis; in the imperial age it expanded considerably, and major building work was carried out, including the construction of a large colonnaded road.

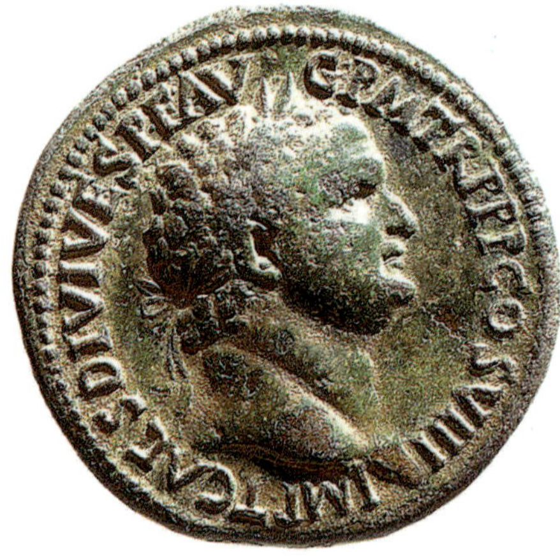

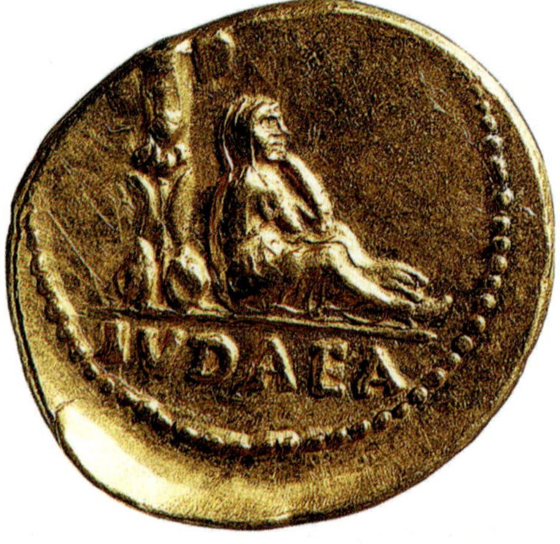

252 (centre) These two coins celebrate the final pacification of Judaea by Titus in AD 70; the bronze one bears the effigy of Vespasian, and the gold one portrays the region as a conquered woman. The Romans responded to the Jewish revolt which had broken out three years earlier by destroying the Temple of Jerusalem after the capture of the city by siege.

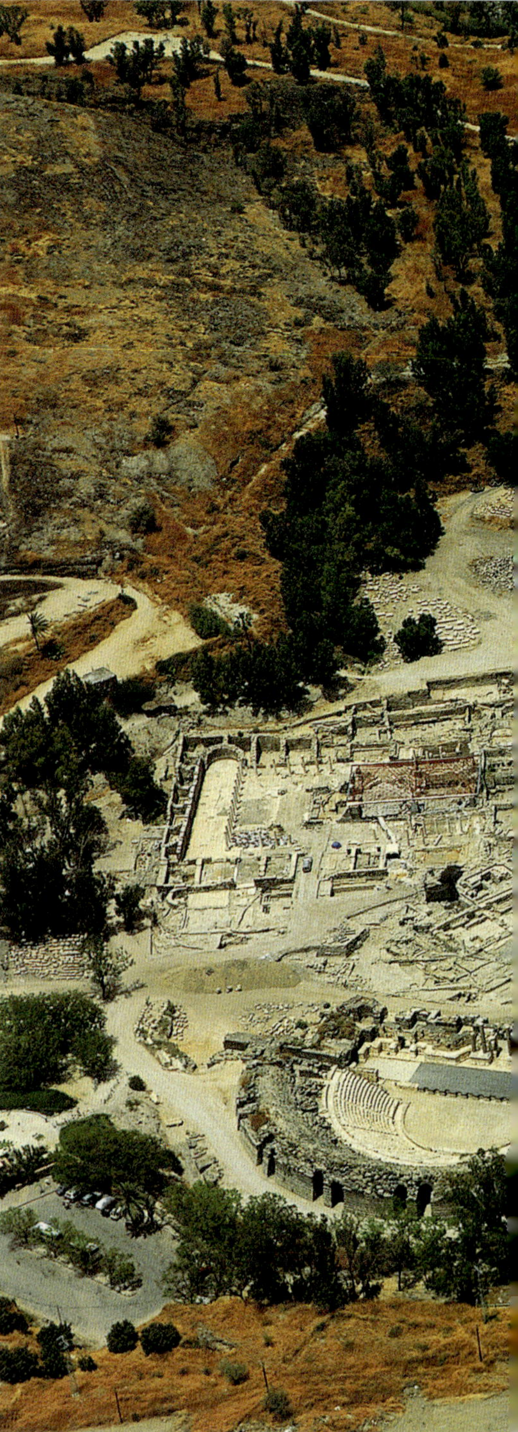

252–253 Beth Shean was originally built on the tell, visible at the top right, and expanded into the plain below in the Roman period. A road lined with numerous shops ran from the theatre and intersected another road; a temple and a nymphaeum were built at the crossroads.

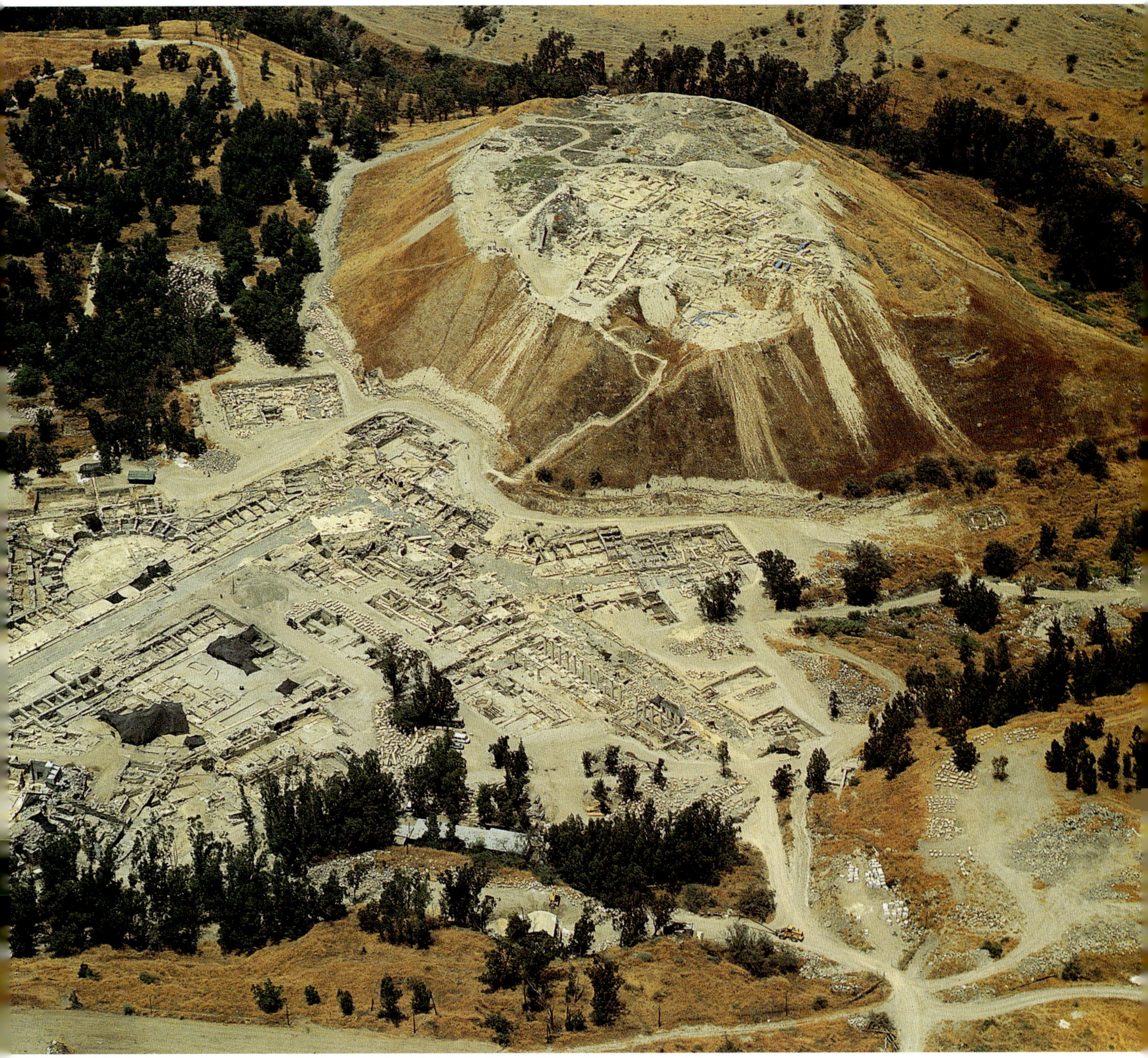

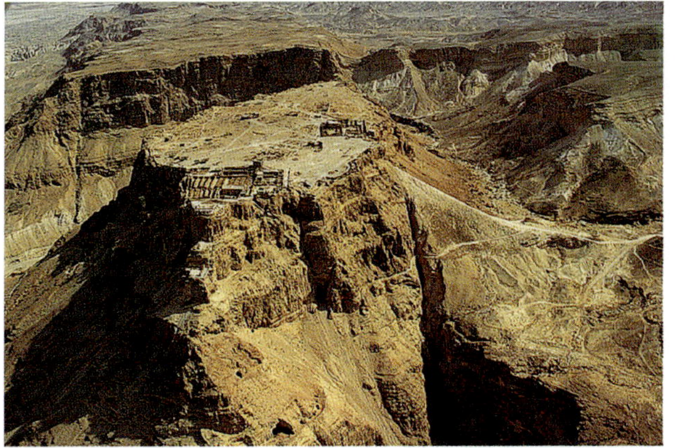

253 (left) The rock of Masada stands alone on the shores of the Dead Sea in Israel. The fortress on the summit was built by Herod the Great, who added two magnificent residences designed for the court and honoured guests, such as Augustus' legates. During the First Jewish Revolt against the Romans, the fortress was occupied by 960 Zealots who withstood the siege of the 10th Legion, commanded by general Flavius Silva, for three years. The stronghold was finally stormed in AD *73. with the aid of a huge ramp made of wood and crushed stone (visible in the right of the photo) which enabled the soldiers to breach the walls. All the besieged Zealots preferred suicide to capture.*

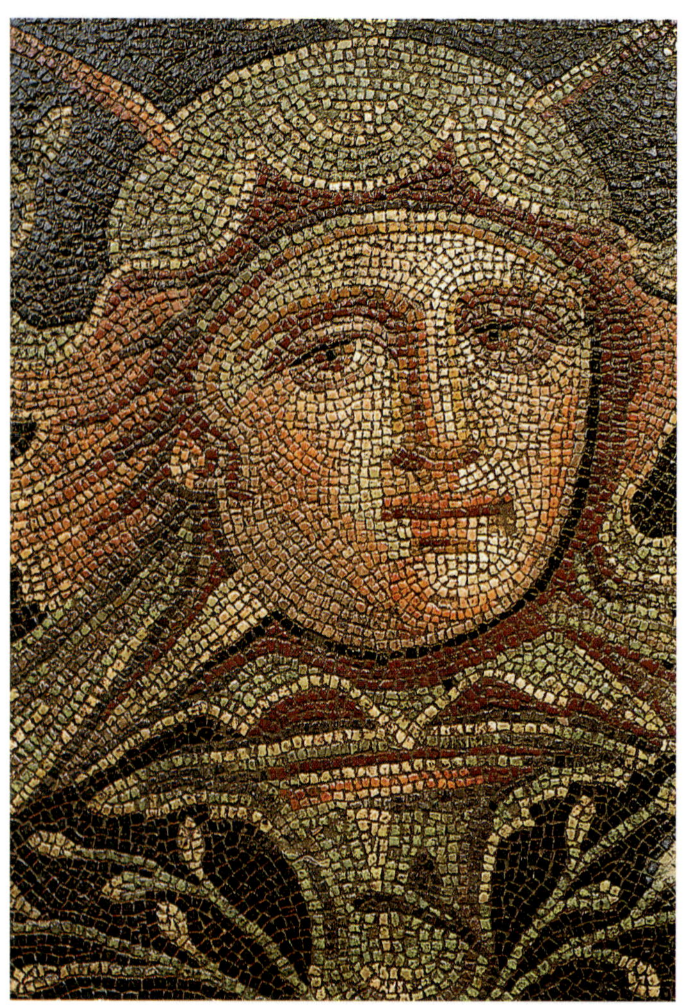

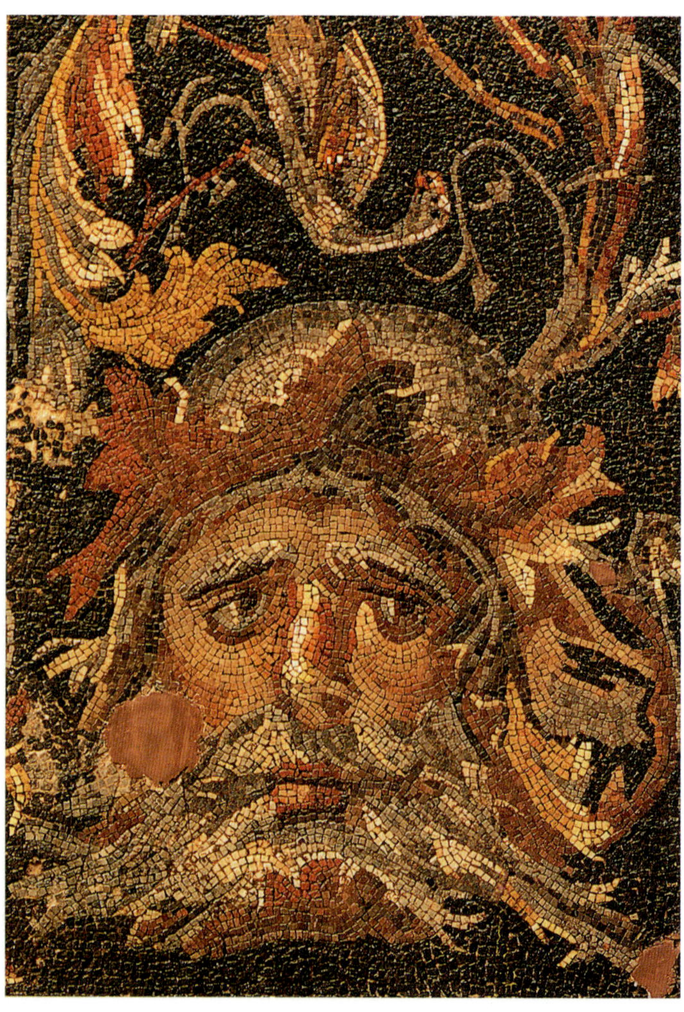

254 (left) Excavations at Hama (once known as Epiphaneia), an ancient town and caravan junction in central Syria, have brought to light some beautiful late Roman mosaics dating from between the 3rd and 4th centuries AD.

254 (right) This man's face, with its dramatic expression, is part of a mosaic dating from the mid-3rd century AD, *found in Suweida. Like all Syrian mosaics of the late imperial period it demonstrates great skill and a marked liking of colour, which is used in a wide range of shades.*

255 (opposite) The marriage of Peleus and Thetis, a magnificent detail from a large mosaic found in a villa at Philippopolis in the province of Arabia. The town (now called Shahba, in Syria) was founded around AD *244 by the emperor Philip the Arab, born in nearby Bosra. Syrian artists were strongly influenced by Hellenistic art and strove to emulate the results obtained by painters. They took the art of mosaics to a level of high refinement, using tiny tesserae and a wide range of colours. The subjects portrayed were drawn from Greek and Roman mythology, even in the late imperial period.*

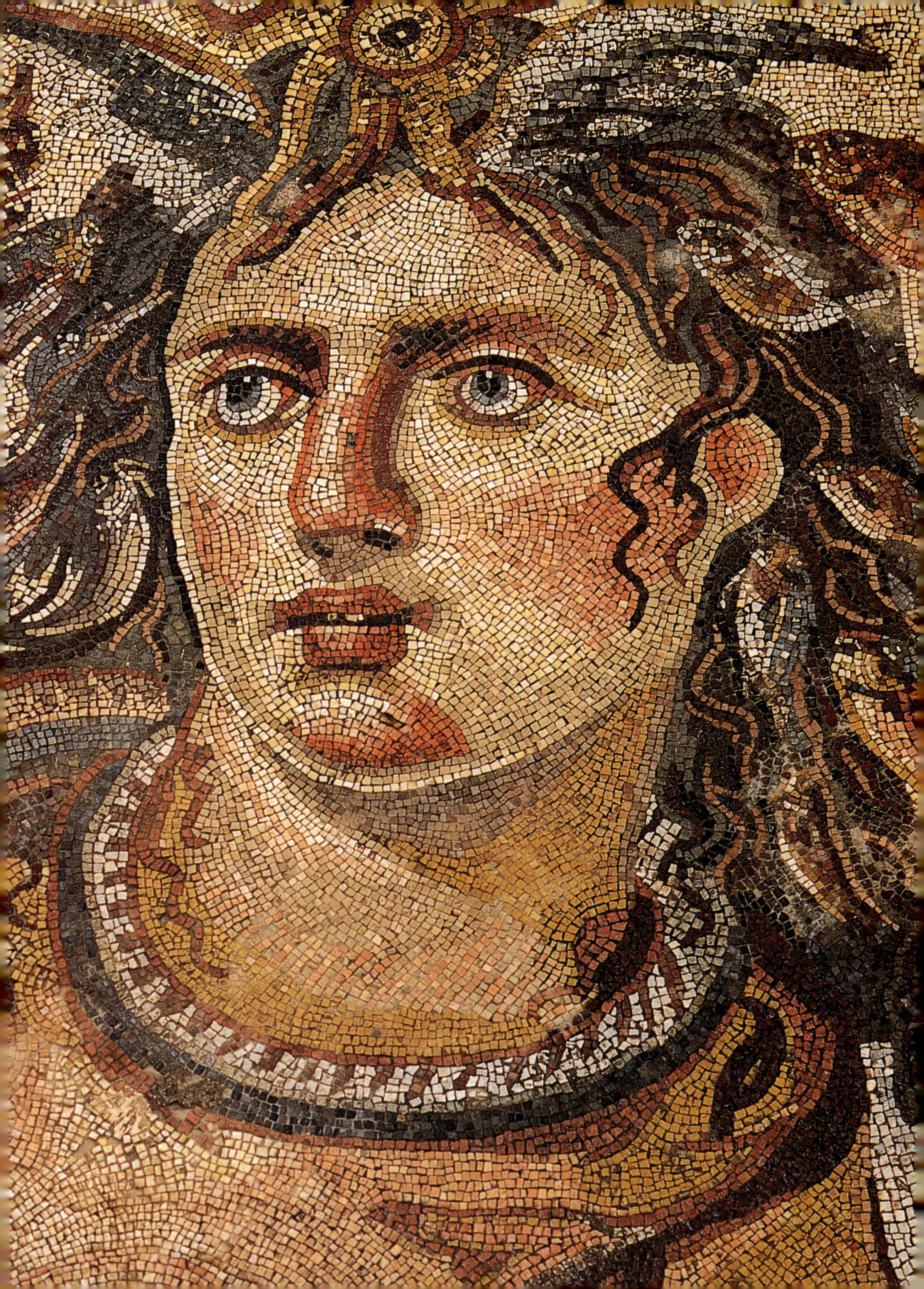

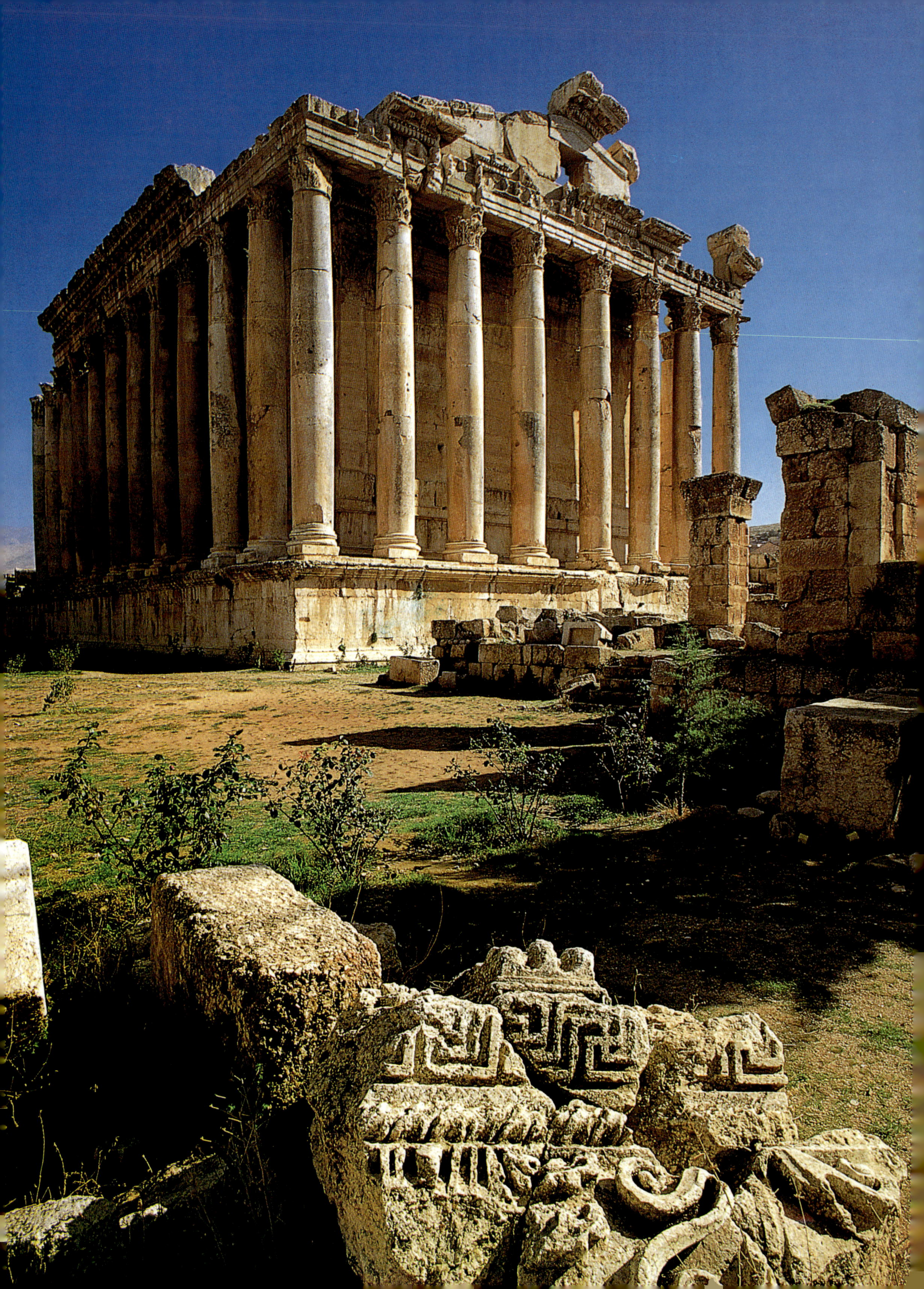

BAALBEK, DEDICATED TO THE HELIOPOLITAN TRIAD

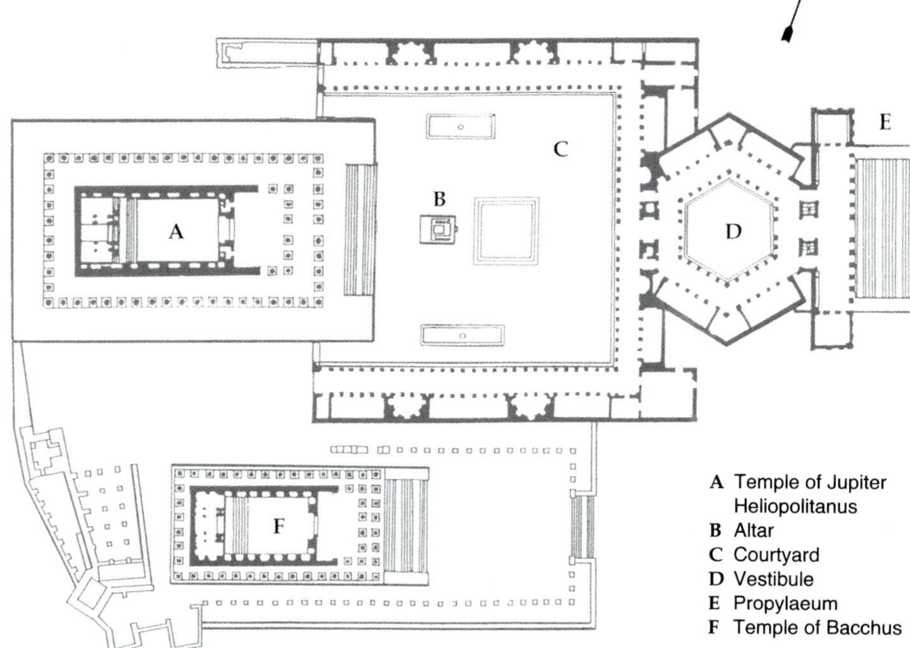

The earliest origins of Baalbek (in modern Lebanon) are obscure. Its present name – meaning 'city of Baal' – clearly refers to the god Baal; however, it seems that Hadad was originally worshipped there, who, in the Hellenistic era, was identified with the Sun and therefore with Zeus. As a result, the town was named Heliopolis (city of the sun). The city became a Roman colony and the site of a permanent garrison in the Julio-Claudian era, when it was called Iulia Augusta Felix Heliopolitana. Although the city played no active part in trade because of its distance from major routes, its religious role was fostered by the Romans. The fame of the Sanctuary of Jupiter Heliopolitanus is shown by the fact that Trajan consulted the oracle there before his expedition against the Parthians in AD 115. Heliopolis prospered until the first half of the 3rd century. Its temples were converted to churches under Constantine and Theodosius, and it became a bishop's see. The Arab invasion hastened its decline, and numerous earthquakes in later centuries reduced it to rubble.

The western part of the city was largely occupied by the impressive sanctuary of the Heliopolitan triad (Jupiter, Venus and Mercury), the ruins of which form one of the most important architectural sites of classical antiquity. Its main temple, dedicated to Jupiter-Hadad, was situated at the end of a complex of buildings, and stood on a podium 14 m (46 ft) high. Nearby is the much better preserved building known as the Temple of Bacchus, in fact dedicated to Mercury, divided internally by elegant Corinthian half-columns. The ruins of the small, round Temple of Venus are situated on the *decumanus maximus* of the city.

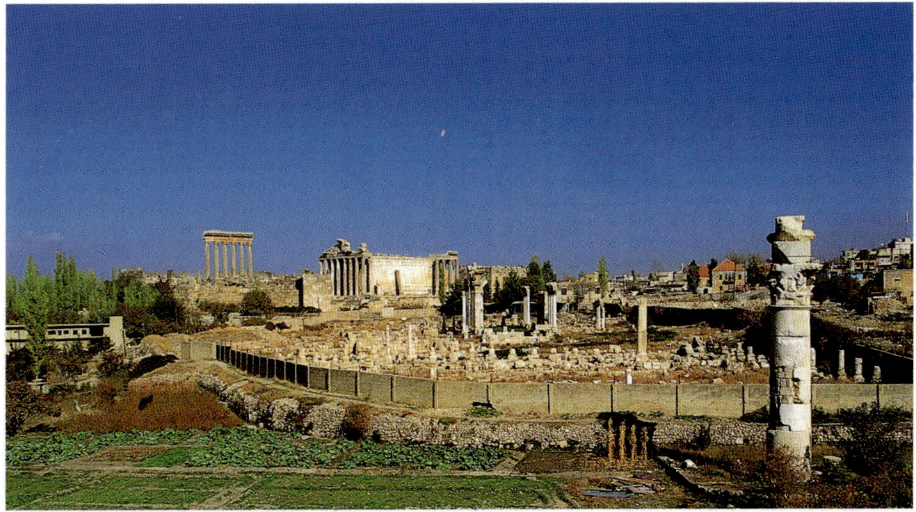

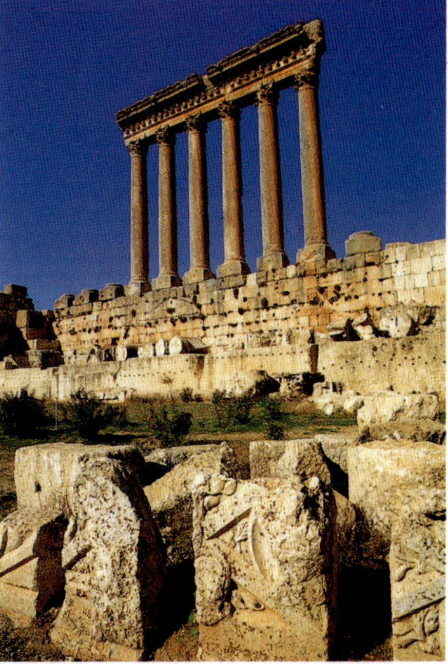

256 (opposite) This Corinthian-style temple, known as the Temple of Bacchus, was built between AD 150 and 200.

257 (above, left) The sanctuary of Baalbek is the most spectacular achievement of Syro-Roman art. For the construction of the Temple of Jupiter, Roman engineers found a method of cutting and transporting stone blocks weighing some 800 tons each.

257 (above, right) The six monolithic columns of the Temple of Jupiter, which date from AD 60, are 19 m (33 ft) tall.

258–259 (overleaf) A reconstruction of the interior of the Temple of Bacchus, one of the most magnificently decorated in the Roman world, shows its unusual construction features, such as the Corinthian half-columns, the canopy over the statue and the coffered ceiling.

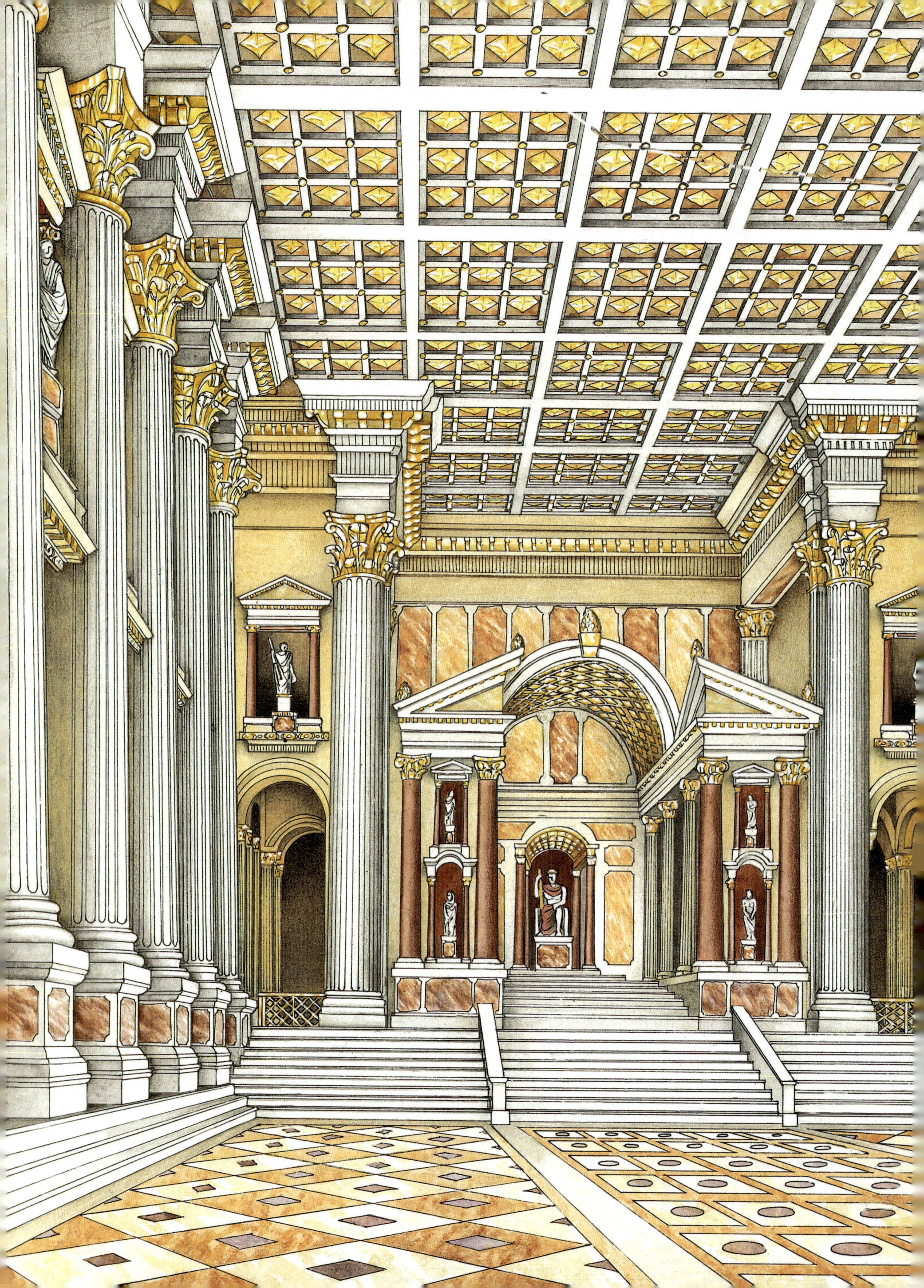

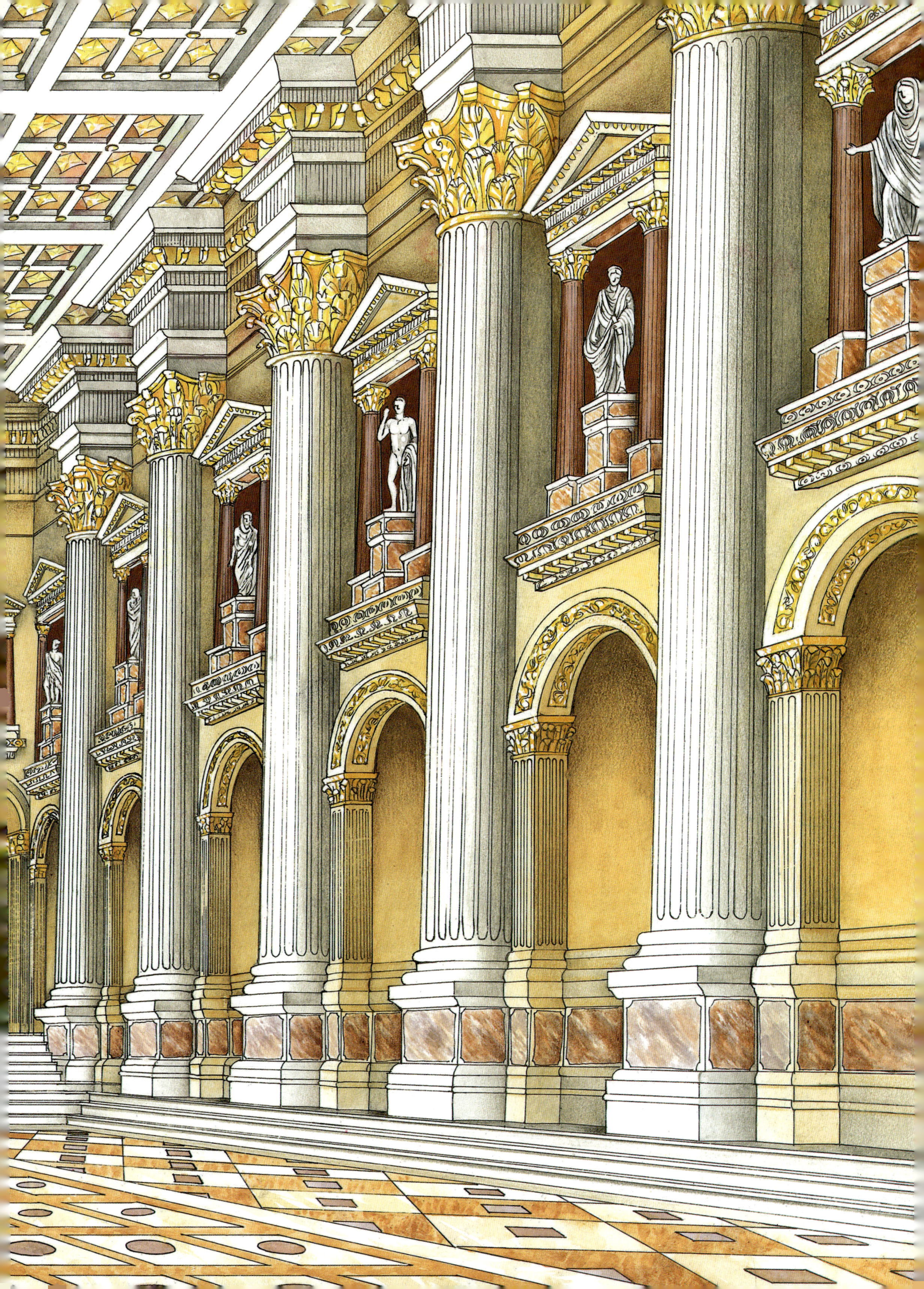

CAESAREA, THE PORT OF PALESTINE

A Theatre
B Herod's Palace
C Temple of Augustus
D Port
E Lighthouse
F Aqueduct
G Amphitheatre

Caesarea, a prosperous port on the coast of present-day Israel to the north of Haifa, was founded by the Phoenicians. In Hellenistic times it was known as Strato's Tower. The city was totally rebuilt between 25 and 9 BC by Herod the Great who, as part of his policy of friendly relations with Rome, called it Caesarea in honour of Augustus Caesar. The town, also known as Caesarea Stratonis, soon became the main port of the region and one of the busiest in the Mediterranean. After AD 44 it became the capital of the province of Judaea, later called Palaestina. It was the last Byzantine stronghold to withstand the Muslim invaders, who eventually stormed it in AD 640.

The city, extensively excavated recently, was built on the usual grid plan, and was enclosed by a perimeter wall 2.5 km (1.5 miles) long. Important monumental buildings include the amphitheatre, the hippodrome (where fragments of the porphyry obelisk which decorated the *spina* and the remains of the *metae* can still be seen), the baths and the theatre.

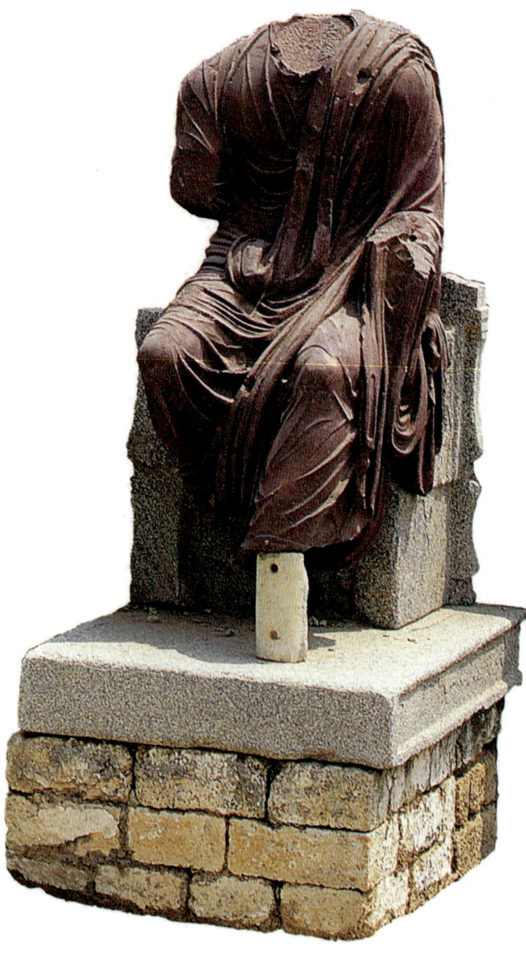

260 (above, right) The discovery in 1951 of this fragment of a red porphyry statue of the 3rd century AD revived interest in the archaeological exploration of the site of Caesarea.

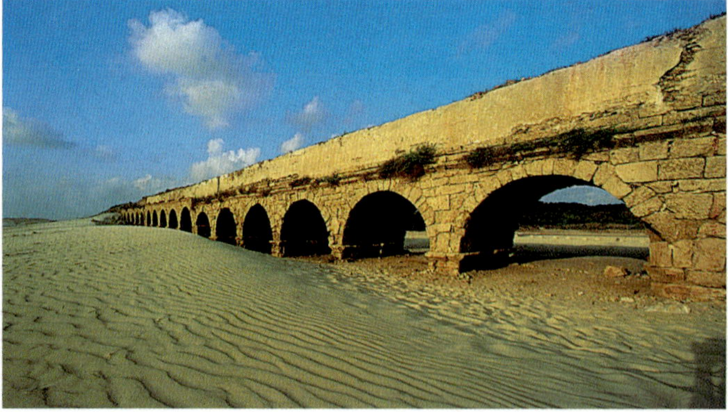

260 (centre) The system of water supply to Caesarea, consisting of two aqueducts, was one of the most complex in Palestine. The main pipe, which was 8 km (5 miles) long, mostly ran above ground on a series of arches, conveying water from springs at the foot of Mount Carmel to the city.

260 (left) The architecture and art of Caesarea were typical of many other towns all over the empire. Each structural element (like this composite capital) represented further confirmation of the supremacy of Rome. It was not mere chance that the town was dominated by the imposing shape of the Temple of Rome and Augustus.

261 (opposite) The shape of the artificial port built by Herod, now submerged, can be seen through the clear water of the bay. The ruins of the road built by the Crusaders with reused stone still emerge just above the surface of the water below the harbour. The promontory in the background, near the theatre, was once occupied by Herod's palace.

The auditorium of the theatre has been partly rebuilt, and is now used for concerts. The ruins of Herod's magnificent palace have been found on a promontory near the theatre. In the forum area stood a huge temple dedicated to Rome and Augustus, which was so large that it could be seen from far out at sea.

Caesarea was mainly famed for the great artificial harbour built by Herod, divided into two docks protected by massive jetties. A tall lighthouse stood at the end of one of the jetties. Two long aqueducts provided the town's water supply, diverted from springs at the foot of the Mount Carmel range. An inscription discovered on a pillar of the main aqueduct states that it was restored by the 10th Fretensis Legion in the reign of Hadrian. A significant find made during the excavations was a fragment of a stone inscription bearing the name of Pontius Pilate. The ruins of a synagogue with a mosaic floor are also interesting.

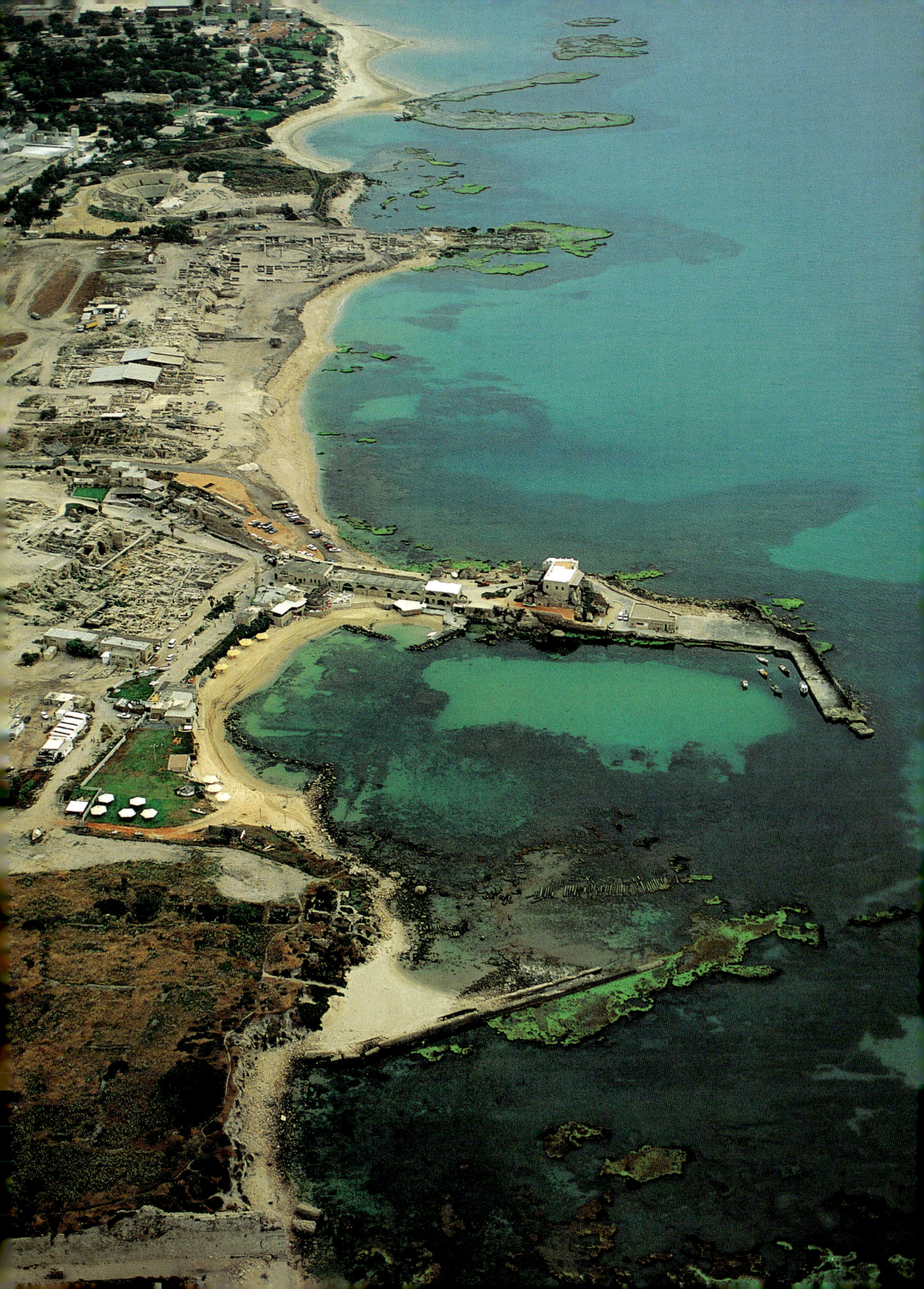

JERASH, A PROSPEROUS CARAVAN TOWN

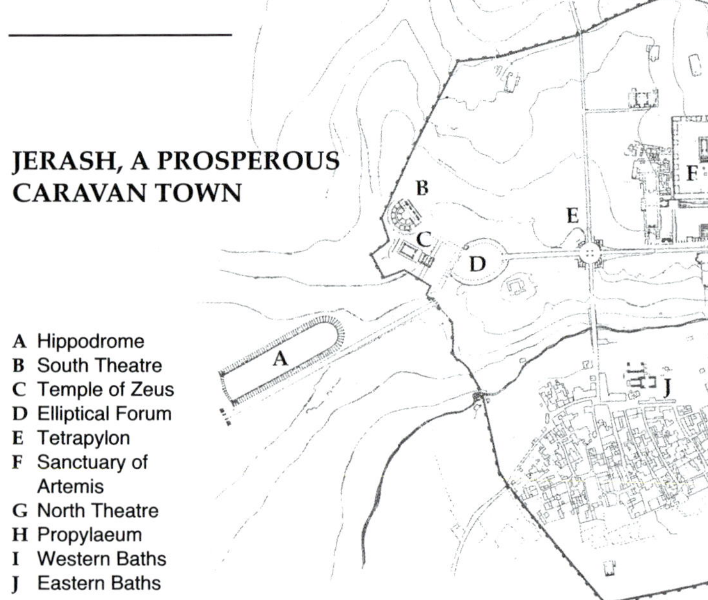

A Hippodrome
B South Theatre
C Temple of Zeus
D Elliptical Forum
E Tetrapylon
F Sanctuary of Artemis
G North Theatre
H Propylaeum
I Western Baths
J Eastern Baths

Jerash, ancient Gerasa, is situated in a wide valley on the banks of the Chrysorrhoas river in Jordan. Founded by the Semites, it was a Hellenistic city before becoming Roman. From the second half of the 1st century AD it prospered from the caravan trade, and reached the peak of its affluence in the age of the Antonines. After a period of decline between the 3rd and 4th centuries AD, Jerash flourished briefly once more under Justinian. Razed to the ground during the Crusades, it was abandoned and only repopulated after 1878. The excellent state of the preservation of its monuments is due to these centuries of oblivion.

The Roman town has a regular plan, with one road (the *cardo*) running north–south, intersected by two roads running east–west (the *decumani*), which crossed the river on two bridges in the centre of the town. Outside the south gate is a triumphal arch with three archways dating from AD 130, and next to it is a hippodrome, with a capacity of 15,000, dating to the 2nd or 3rd century. At the entrance to the city stands the Temple of Zeus, with eight columns in its façade, built in AD 163, and the south theatre, whose auditorium held 3000 spectators. Opposite the Temple of Zeus was the unusual city forum, which has a unique design. Instead of a rectangular plan it takes the form of an elliptical piazza with a long axis of 91 m (298 ft), and is surrounded by a portico with Ionic columns which housed a row of shops. It is believed that the forum of Gerasa played a mainly economic rather than political or religious role, and this hypothesis is supported by its position, decentralized in relation to the town plan. The Romans may thus have allowed the great

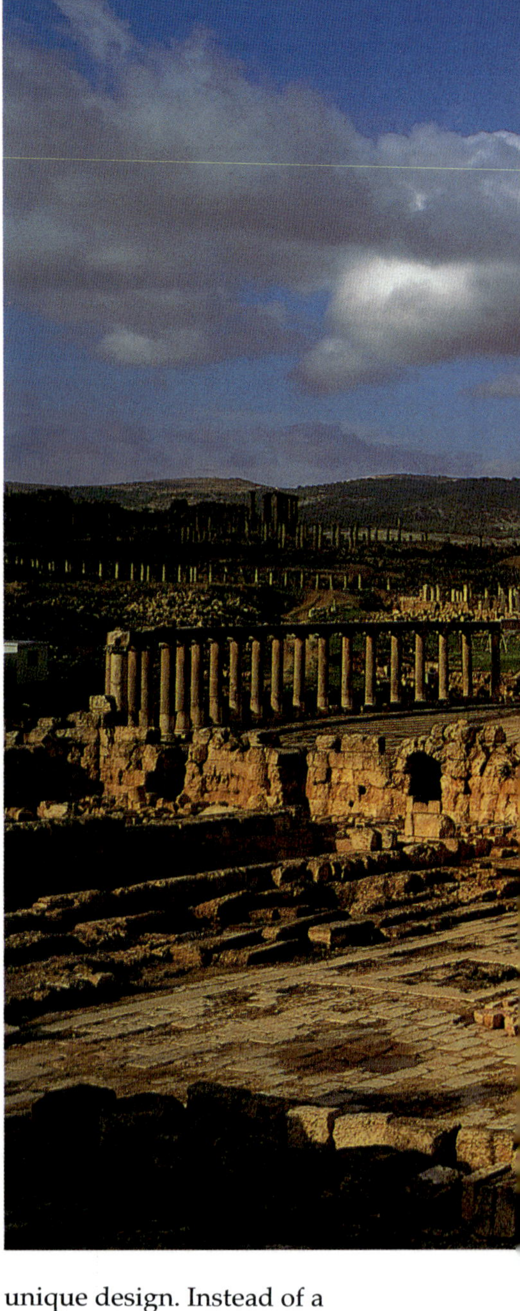

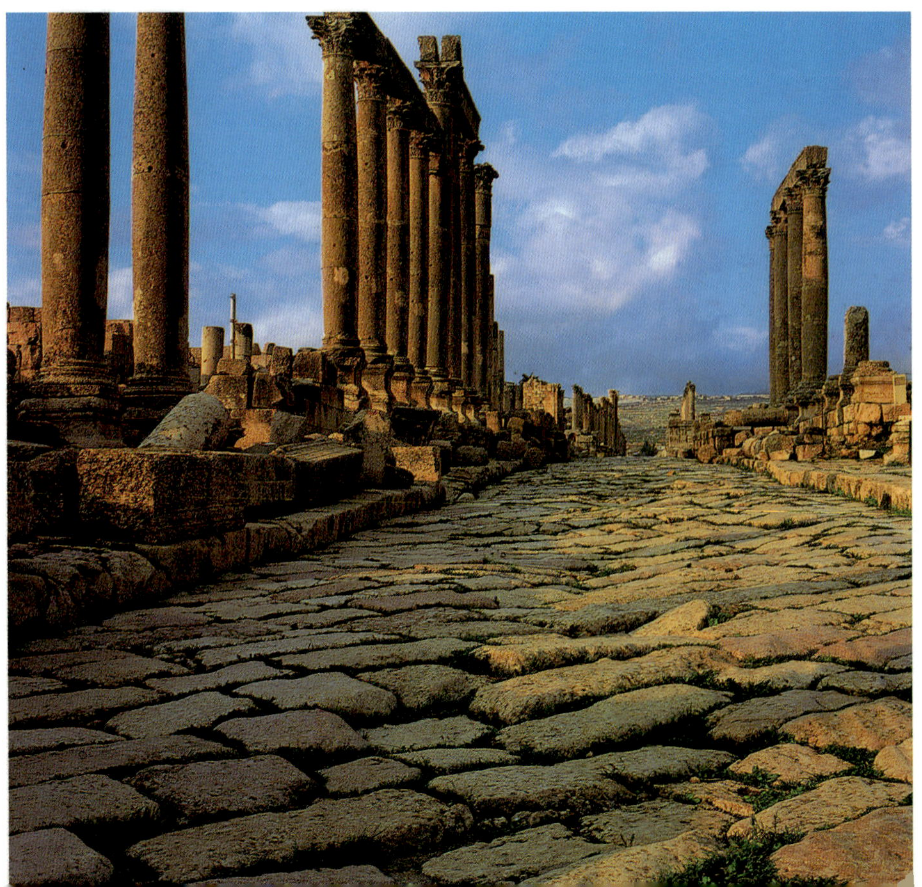

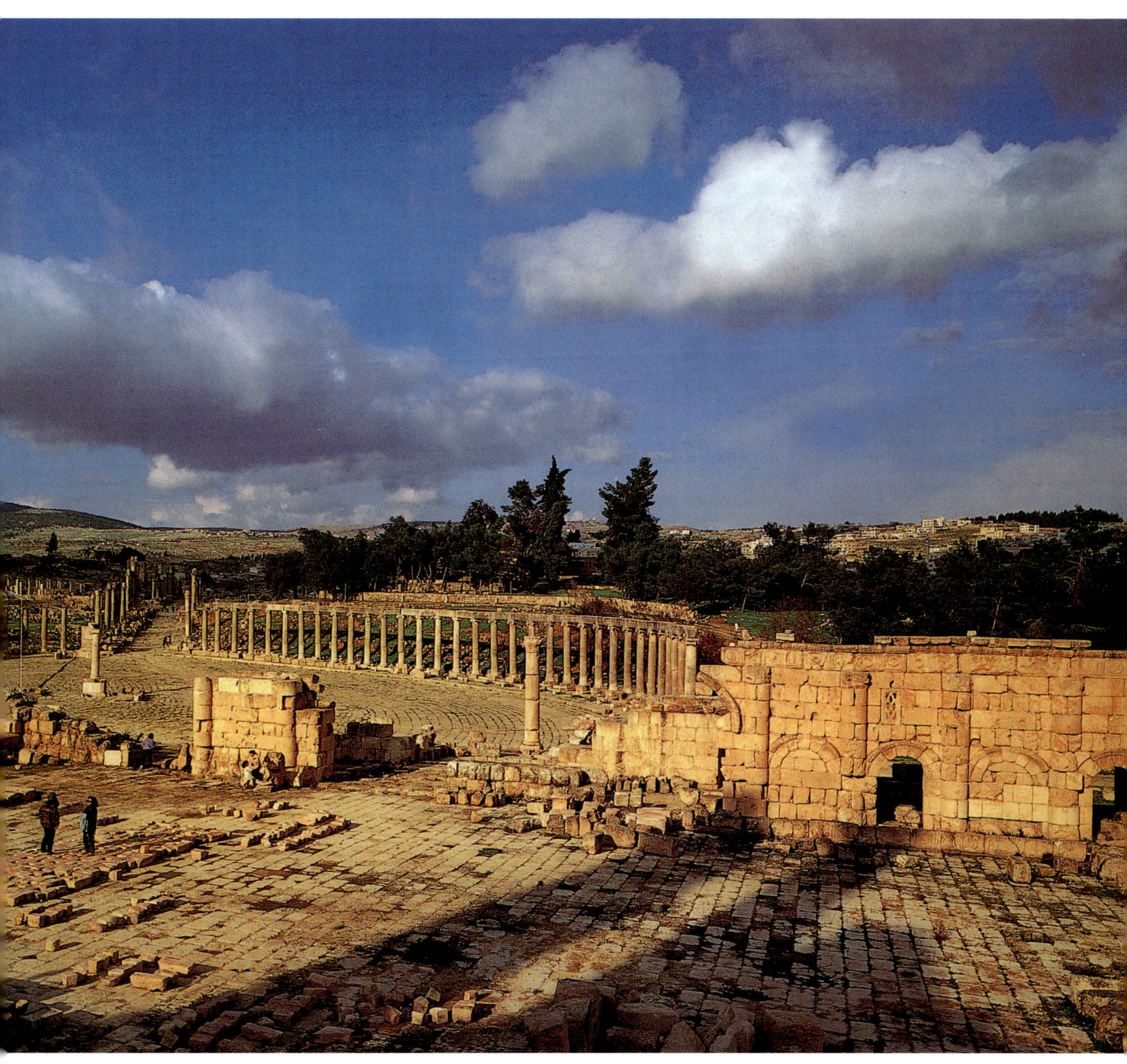

sanctuary of Artemis, situated right in the heart of the town, to retain its status as the focal point of the town's social and spiritual life.

The temple dedicated to the patron goddess of Jerash stands in the centre of a huge sacred enclosure, with an area of 34,000 sq. m (365,985 sq. ft), reached from a magnificent staircase leading from the *cardo maximus*. Other monuments dating from the Roman era were a second theatre built in the northern part of the town, two baths complexes, one on each side of the river, an impressive tetrapylon (four-sided arch) in the centre of a circular piazza on the *cardo*, and a similar, though less majestic example on the same road.

262 (opposite) Gerasa, an ancient town of Semitic origin, typifies the process of Romanization experienced by towns that became part of the empire. Its grid plan replaced the far less regular older layout, and monumental constructions were much in evidence along the colonnaded main roads.

262–263 (above) The elliptical forum, also known as the Oval Piazza, is certainly the most unusual monument in Jerash, and is an exception to the usual plan of this element of Roman public architecture. Built in Ionic style in the 2nd century AD*, it was used for business, rather than political or religious purposes.*

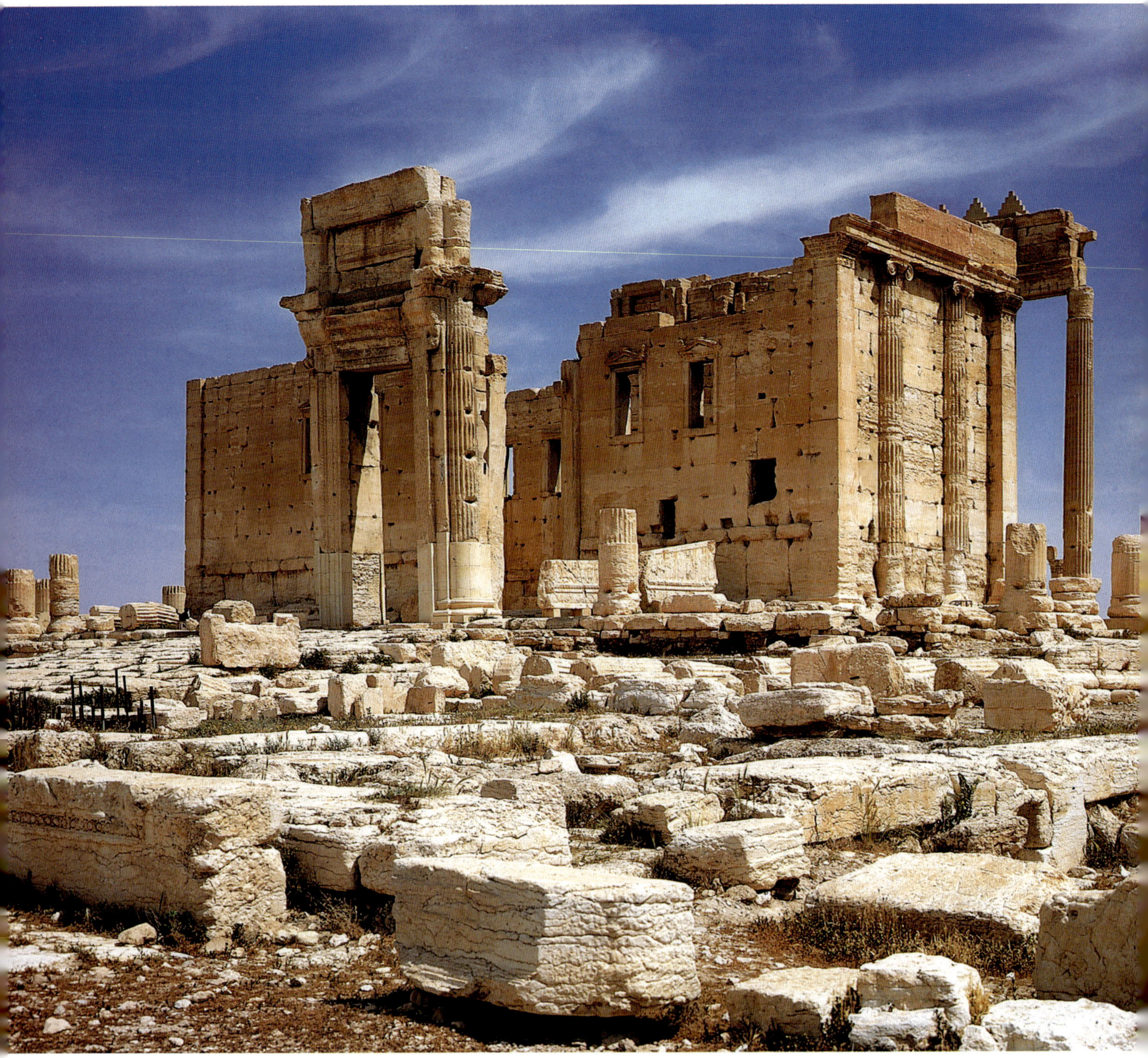

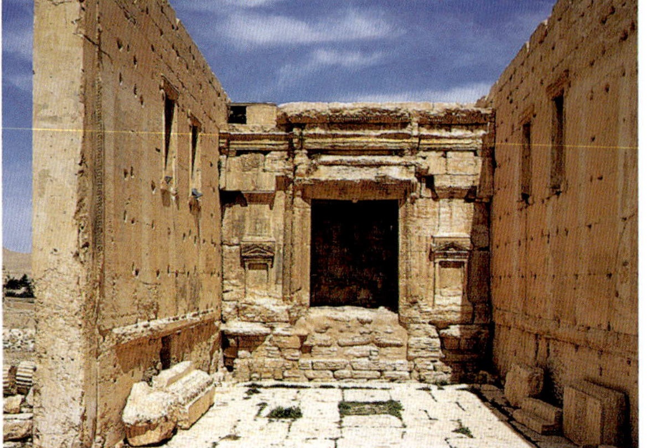

264 (left) A view of the cella *of the Temple of Bel reveals the most unusual features of its design – the entrance situated on one of the longer sides, and the presence of windows. In society, as well as in art, local customs continued to predominate, despite the fact that the Palmyrenes enjoyed Roman citizenship.*

264–265 (above) In the architecture of Palmyra western construction methods were used, though with a large degree of stylistic independence. For example, the plan of the great Temple of Bel is apparently not influenced by classical tenets but it is decorated with Ionic and Corinthian capitals.

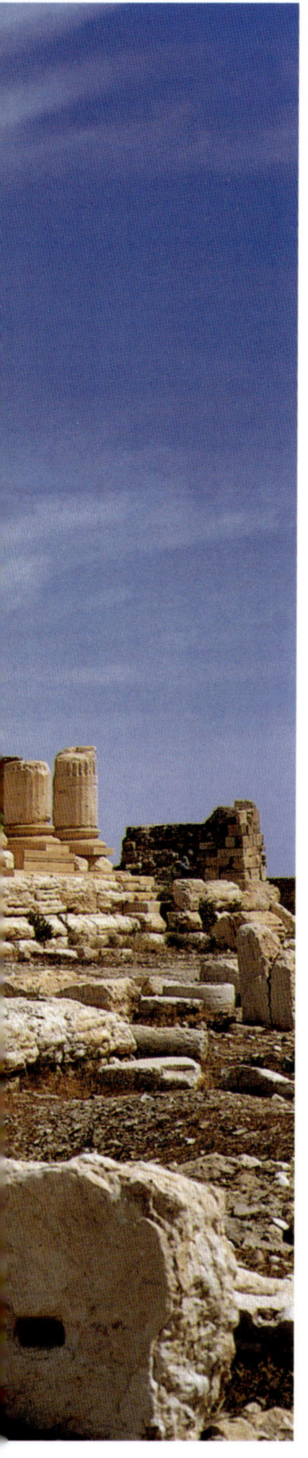

PALMYRA, A SPLENDID CITY IN THE DESERT

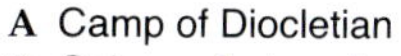

A Camp of Diocletian
B Colonnaded roads
C Forum
D Tetrapylon
E Sanctuary of Ba'alshamin
F Theatre
G Monumental arch
H Temple of Bel
I Monumental tombs

Ancient Palmyra stands in an oasis in the Syrian desert, midway between the Mediterranean and the Euphrates. It achieved a degree of affluence as early as the 4th century BC due to the local abundance of water, making it the pre-eminent caravan town in the region. It fell into ruin after its sack by Antony, but recovered, especially in the 1st century AD, when it achieved prosperity due to its neutral position between Rome and Parthia.

It became a Roman colony in AD 183, but was granted independence by Gallienus in AD 261 as a sign of his gratitude to Odaenathus, lord of the city, who had defeated the Persians. His widow Zenobia was hostile to Rome, however, and began an assertive policy of expansion in Asia Minor and Egypt. She was defeated by Aurelian, who destroyed the town in AD 272. The city was conquered by the Arabs in the 6th century, and was razed to the ground by the Umayyads. Palmyra is now one of the most famous sites in the Middle East, due to the excellent state of preservation of its monuments.

Palmyra's privileged position between east and west and its very mixed population have produced some unusual forms of art and culture, blending Aramaic, Semitic, Hellenistic, and, finally, Roman elements. Its architecture reflects this mixture, especially in the impressive temple dedicated to Bel, the Sanctuary of Ba'alshamin (which both have the unusual feature of a *cella* lit by windows), and the great colonnaded road on which stands an interesting triumphal arch with a triangular plan. The Temple of Bel combines elegant decoration and unusual structural features, such as the entrance situated on one of the longer sides, a cornice decorated with triangular crenellations, and the roof formed by a terrace with a turret at each of the four corners. By contrast, the theatre (also well preserved) and the Baths of Diocletian are typically Roman.

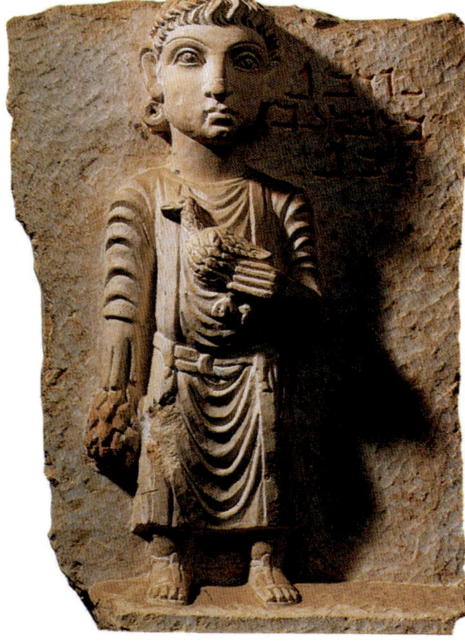

265 (above) Palmyrene art, which flourished between the reigns of Augustus and Gallienus, is a singular combination of local figurative styles and those imported from the Hellenistic–Roman west.

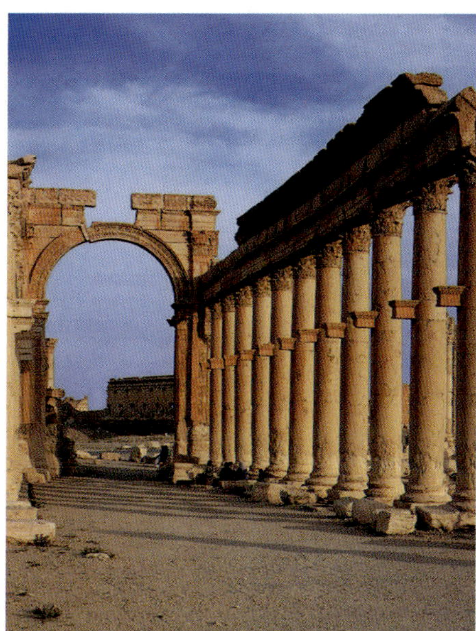

265 (left) The Great Colonnade, over a kilometre long, was erected in the 2nd century AD. Its most interesting feature is the addition, about halfway up each column, of a prominent shelf which supported statues of local dignitaries. This is a typically local element, combined with classical architectural styles.

EGYPT, CRETE, CYRENAICA, SPECIAL PROVINCES

A Aegyptus
B Cyrenaica
C Creta

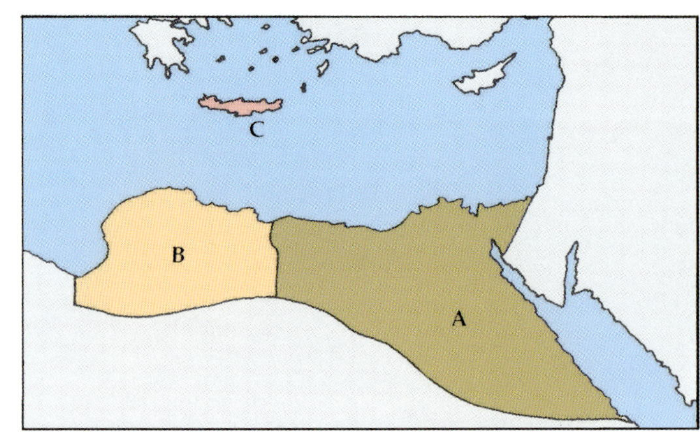

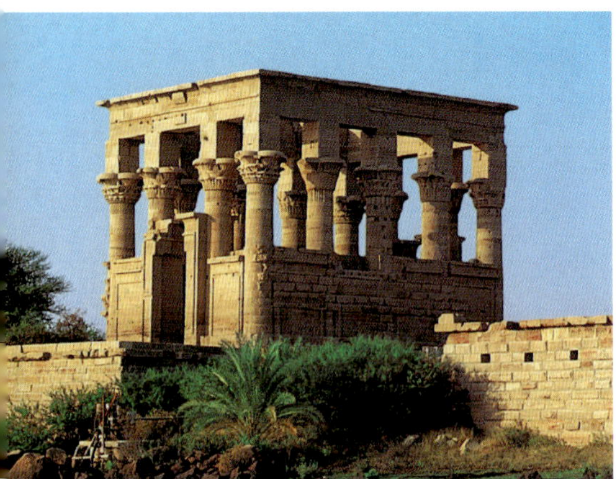

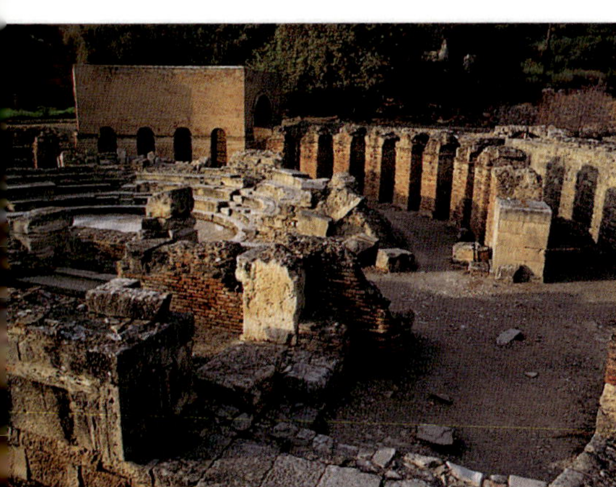

After the death of Cleopatra VII, who committed suicide following her defeat at Actium in 31 BC by Octavian, Egypt was the last of the Hellenistic kingdoms to come under Roman influence. Augustus made it into a territory directly ruled by the emperor, who governed it through a *praefectus Aegypti*. From the outset the Roman rulers, who had inherited the privileges of the Ptolemies, had to deal with problems caused by conflict between the Greek community (which enjoyed legal and tax privileges) and the Jewish community. The latter in particular instigated numerous rebellions, the bloodiest of which took place under Claudius and Trajan.

Roman culture had a rather limited impact on this region, whereas Egyptian art and religion in particular exerted considerable influence on the Roman world. This is demonstrated, for example, by the great success which the worship of Serapis, Isis and Osiris encountered in Rome. The new rulers enthusiastically – if amateurishly – emulated the architectural and figurative themes of the local traditions – one example is 'Trajan's Kiosk' on the island of Philae. Perhaps the most original form of art in the Roman period in Egypt were the so-called Fayum portraits, which were painted on wooden panels and placed over the faces of mummies.

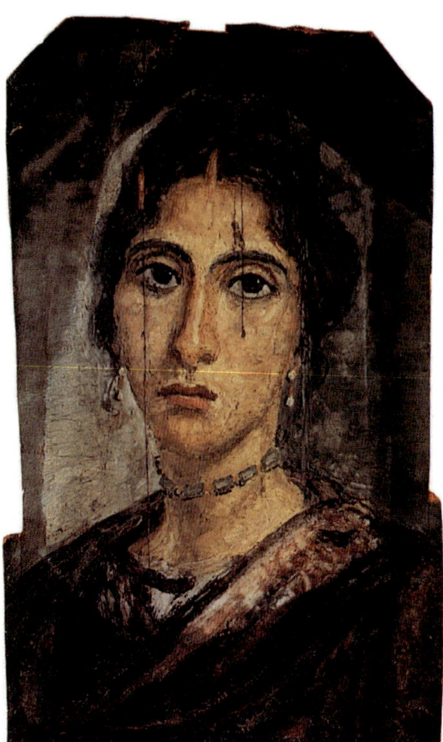

Very few new towns were founded, and those that were built were mainly military outposts or trading stations in strategic positions. They include Babylon, a fortress dating from the time of Trajan, now engulfed by the modern city of Cairo, and Antinoopolis, built by Hadrian to commemorate his favourite, Antinous.

Egypt played a significant economic role within the empire. Large amounts of corn produced in the province, together with valuable raw materials and luxury articles were shipped from Alexandria. The goods exported included various types of stone: pink 'obelisk' granite from the quarries of Syene (Aswan), grey granite from Mons Claudianus and red porphyry from Upper Egypt. The country also held the monopoly in the papyrus trade, and was famous for its wool, which clothed much of the Roman army.

Camels were of great strategic value in the military field. From the 2nd century AD, camel-mounted units were set up in the region, and these robust animals were also used in Europe, as demonstrated by numerous finds of bones in various parts of Gaul, the German provinces and even Britannia.

Trade with Nubia and Ethiopia flourished on the southernmost borders of Egypt, which were occupied by legionary garrisons. Various *emporia* on the Red Sea carried on a flourishing trade with India, from which rare and precious goods arrived; Berenice, for example, was famed as the port used by ships bringing olivines (green gems prized by the Romans) from Zavargad.

Numerous caravan routes crossed the desert and followed the coasts towards Arabia, Petra and Palestine, or towards Cyrenaica. The latter region was declared a province in 74 BC, but Antony later gave it to his daughter by Cleopatra. Augustus restored its status as a senatorial province in 27 BC, annexing it to the island of Crete. Governing Cyrenaica presented the same difficulties as Egypt, because of the violent clashes between the Jewish and Greek communities. The damage caused by a particularly bloody Jewish rebellion in AD 116 was partly repaired by Hadrian. However, the country's economy, which had begun to recover from the time of Augustus, was irreparably damaged by the slaughter and devastation committed by both sides. Cyrenaica remained famous, however, for its thoroughbred horses, which were still being exported at the end of the 4th century.

Crete was far more peaceful, and the history of the island includes no particularly outstanding events. As a result, Roman military presence was limited to a few garrisons. In both regions Rome pursued a very liberal policy towards the towns, which enjoyed numerous immunities.

266 (opposite, top left) Trajan's Kiosk was built in AD 105 on the island of Philae, in Egypt, next to a sanctuary of Isis.

266 (opposite, centre) Cyrenaica, an old and prosperous Greek colony, entered the Roman sphere in 74 BC, and was made a joint province with Crete by Augustus.

266 (opposite, bottom left) Gortyn became the capital of the province of Crete in 67 BC. These are the ruins of the Odeum.

266 (opposite, bottom right) The best-known artistic relics from Roman Egypt are portraits painted on wood or linen which were placed over the face of the deceased.

267 (above) Portrait of a man on canvas, from Antinoe, from the 3rd century AD; its sober lines clearly demonstrate the influence of Roman pictorial styles. Apart from their funerary use, portraits of the same artistic quality must have been common throughout the empire in other contexts.

AFRICA, THE GRANARY OF ROME

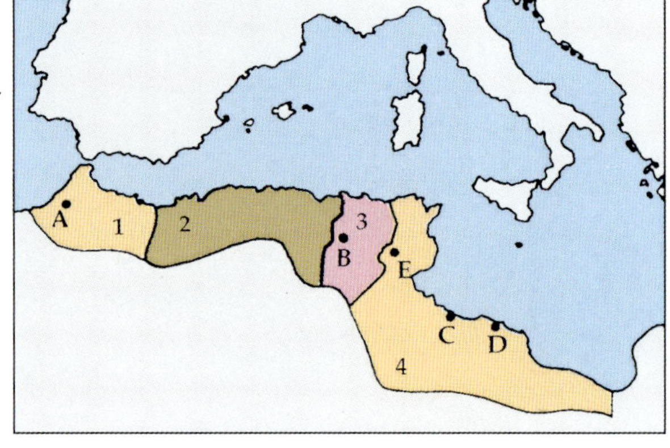

1 Mauretania Tingitana
2 Mauretania Caesariensis
3 Numidia
4 Africa Proconsularis

A Volubilis
B Timgad
C Sabratha
D Lepcis Magna
E Sufetula

Roman penetration into the African continent began after the destruction of Carthage in 146 BC. The first provinces were Africa Proconsularis and Africa Nova or Numidia, to which Mauretania Caesariensis and Mauretania Tingitana were later added. The African border, which stretched from present-day Morocco to Libya, was by far the longest in the empire, some 4000 km (2485 miles) long, and bounded a territory whose immense geographical variety was matched by the widely differing cultures and lifestyles of the local populations. Roman interest in Africa was due both to the strategic position of its ports, control of which guaranteed domination of the Mediterranean routes, together with its immense agricultural wealth. For this reason the Romans encouraged the development of the ancient maritime towns of Carthaginian and Greek origin, and built new ones. At the same time they gained control of the hinterland and the trade in valuable goods from the interior by extending existing caravan towns and building many more, as in the case of Timgad. An excellent road network connected the towns to the coastal ports, where goods destined for Rome were loaded on to cargo vessels.

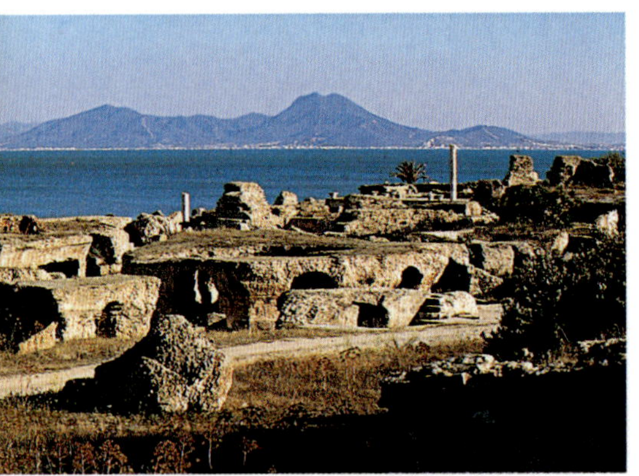

In the countryside around the towns, scattered over a vast radius, were the farms of the rich local landowners. Numerous dams, traces of some of which still remain, collected the seasonal water which rushed down the wadis. It was then collected and distributed for irrigation purposes by complex systems of channels.

The prosperity of cities like Sabratha and Lepcis Magna was based mainly on their enormous production of corn and olive oil. The corn trade, which gave Africa its nickname of 'the granary of Rome', was far more strictly controlled by the government than trade in other products. Even at the time of Augustus some 150,000

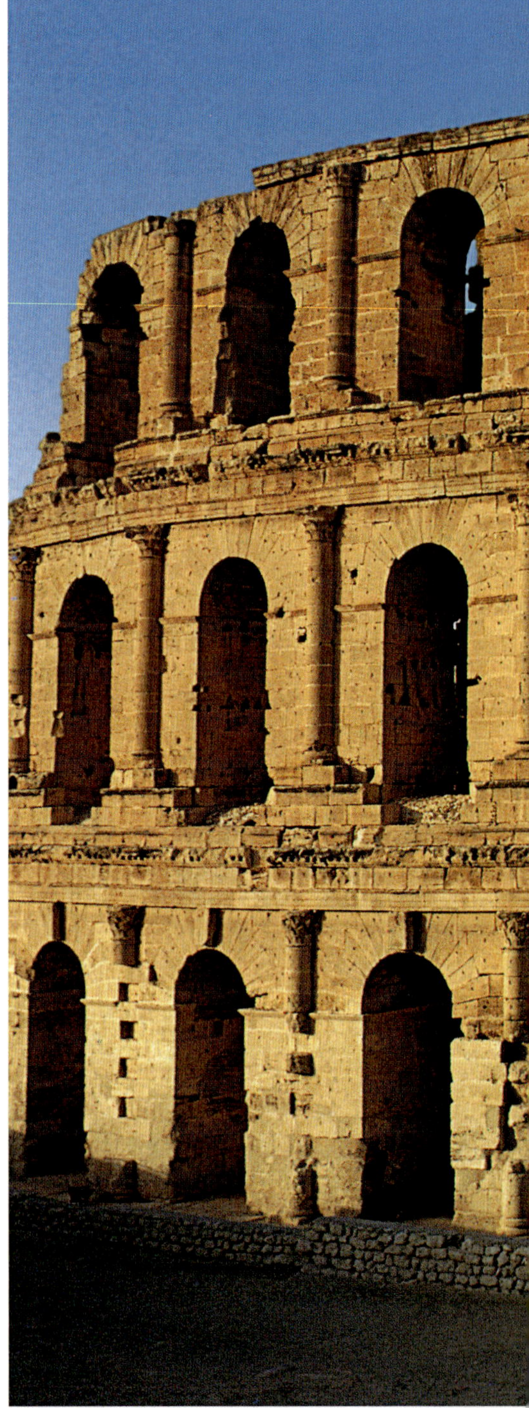

plebeians received the public corn dole, so the importance of a regular supply of this staple to Rome was partly political. Carthage was the main corn shipping port, and Augustus ordered its reconstruction. Oil exports also acquired great importance, especially from the 2nd century AD; the oil was shipped in cylindrical jars, made in the coastal towns of Tunisia, which were also used to store *garum*, a popular sauce

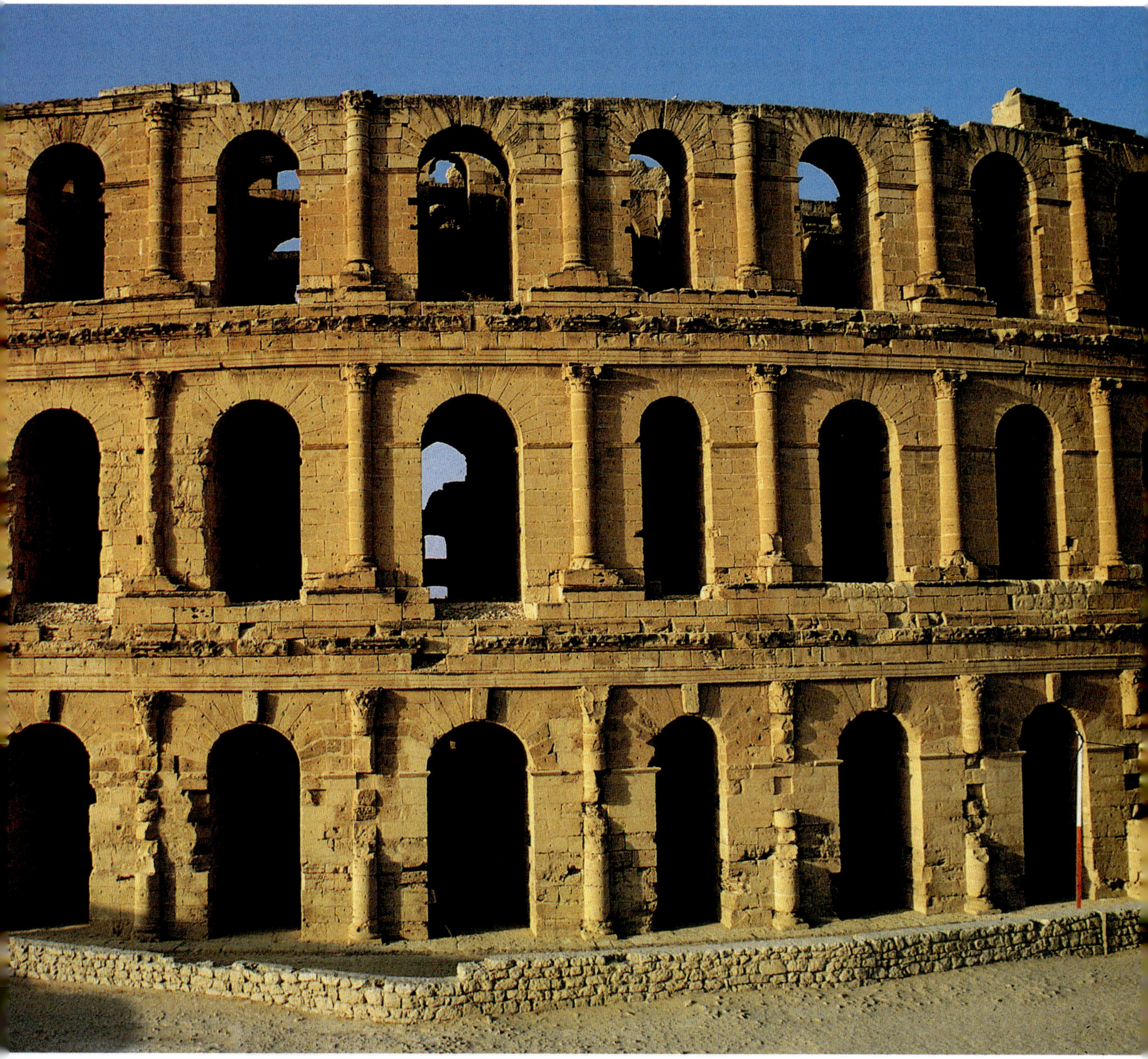

268 (opposite, above) Carthage, razed to the ground in the Third Punic War, was rebuilt on the orders of Augustus.

268 (opposite, below) The province of Africa was often portrayed as a woman wearing a headdress in the form of an elephant's head, as on this plate, found in Boscoreale, of the 1st century AD.

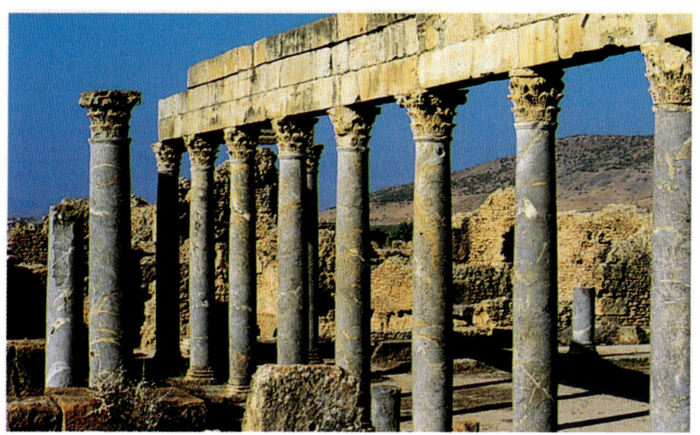

269 (left) Thuburbus Maius, founded on the site of an earlier Berber settlement, reached the peak of its splendour under the Antonines. Like all the Roman towns in Tunisia, it owed its wealth to olive growing. This is a view of the portico of Petronius, dating from AD 225.

268–269 (above) The amphitheatre of El Djem, in present-day Tunisia, was the second largest in the Roman world after the Colosseum. Ancient Thysdrus, around 40 km (25 miles) from the sea, flourished in the 2nd and 3rd centuries as a result of the production and sale of olive oil.

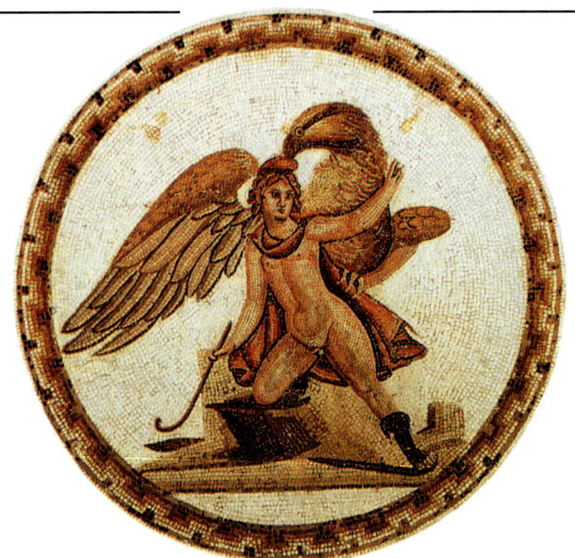

270 *Zeus, disguised as an eagle, carries off Ganymede, 'the most beautiful of mortals', to make him the cup-bearer of the gods. This mosaic, dating from the 3rd century* AD, *was found in Sousse, in present-day Tunisia. Many of the Sousse mosaics are now housed in the museum in Tunis.*

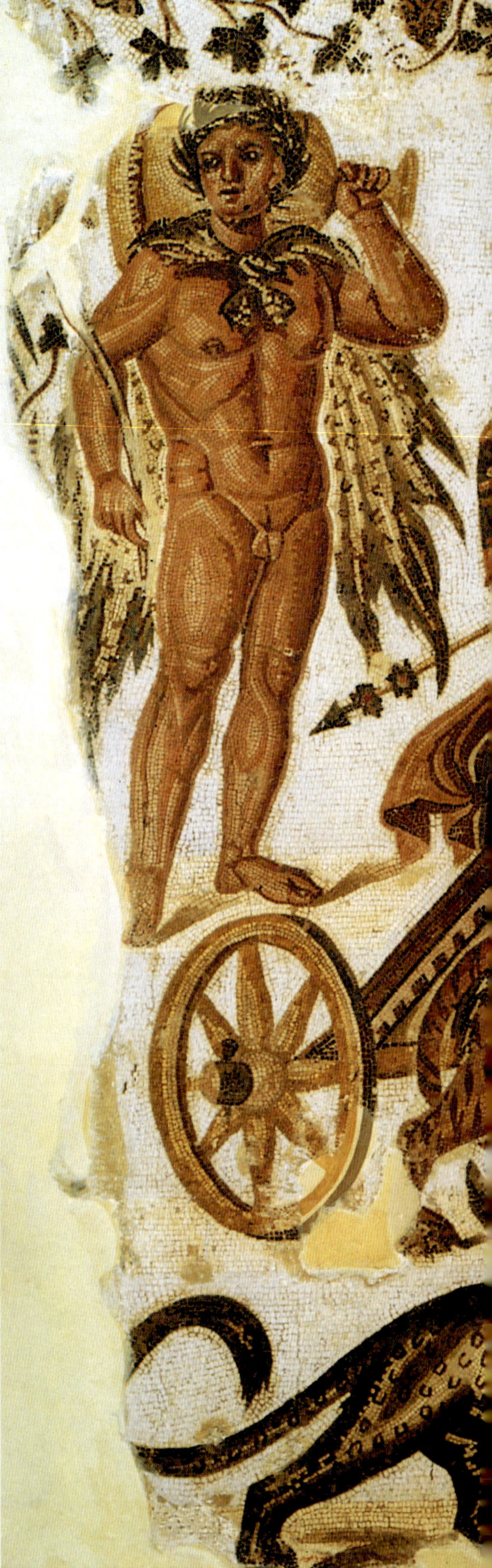

made of salted and fermented fish, which was the basic ingredient of Roman cuisine. Africa was the largest supplier of this condiment, which was also made in numerous centres along the Mediterranean and Atlantic coasts.

Wild animals formed another important export from the African provinces – horses for the circus races, and beasts, lions, leopards and elephants for the games held in the amphitheatre. They were captured in hunting expeditions and then transported on special ships to destinations far and wide.

The introduction of Roman civilization into Africa had wide-ranging results, as demonstrated by the many monuments which have survived to the present. In particular, both the official language and religion were always Roman, although rural people continued to speak Punic and worship Baal and Tanit, though identified with Saturn and Caelestis. The African provinces reached the height of their glory at the time Hadrian's journeys, and the construction, cultural and economic programmes promoted by the Severan dynasty.

From the 2nd century on, local people also had a major influence on the political and intellectual life of the empire. Emperors like Septimius Severus, jurists and writers like Fronto and Apuleius, and the group of Christian apologists (especially Tertullian and St Augustine) are representatives of the outstanding contribution made by Africa to the development of pagan and Christian cultures in the Roman empire.

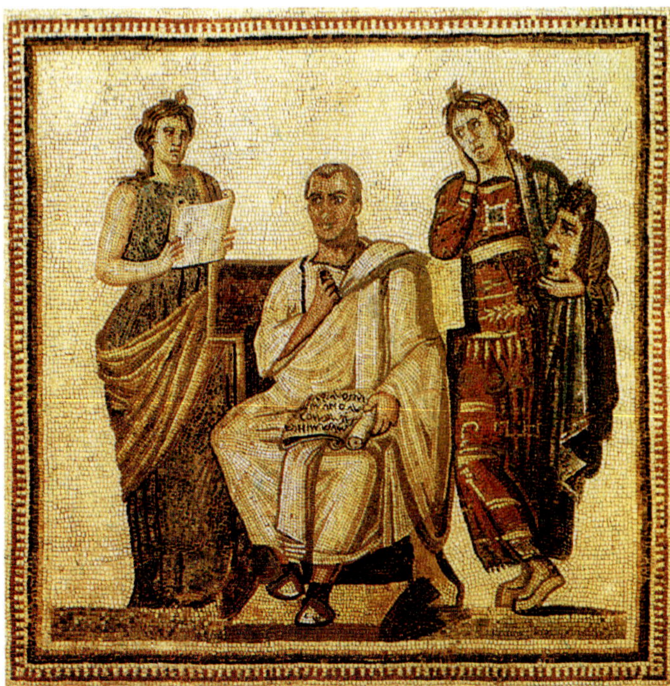

270 *This famous mosaic portraying Virgil was found in a villa at Sousse and dates from the 3rd century* AD. *The seated poet is holding an open papyrus scroll on which the eighth verse of the* Aeneid *can be read. On his right is Clio, the muse of history, and on his left stands Melpomene, the muse of tragedy. Culture played a very important role in the Roman world because it brought social status.*

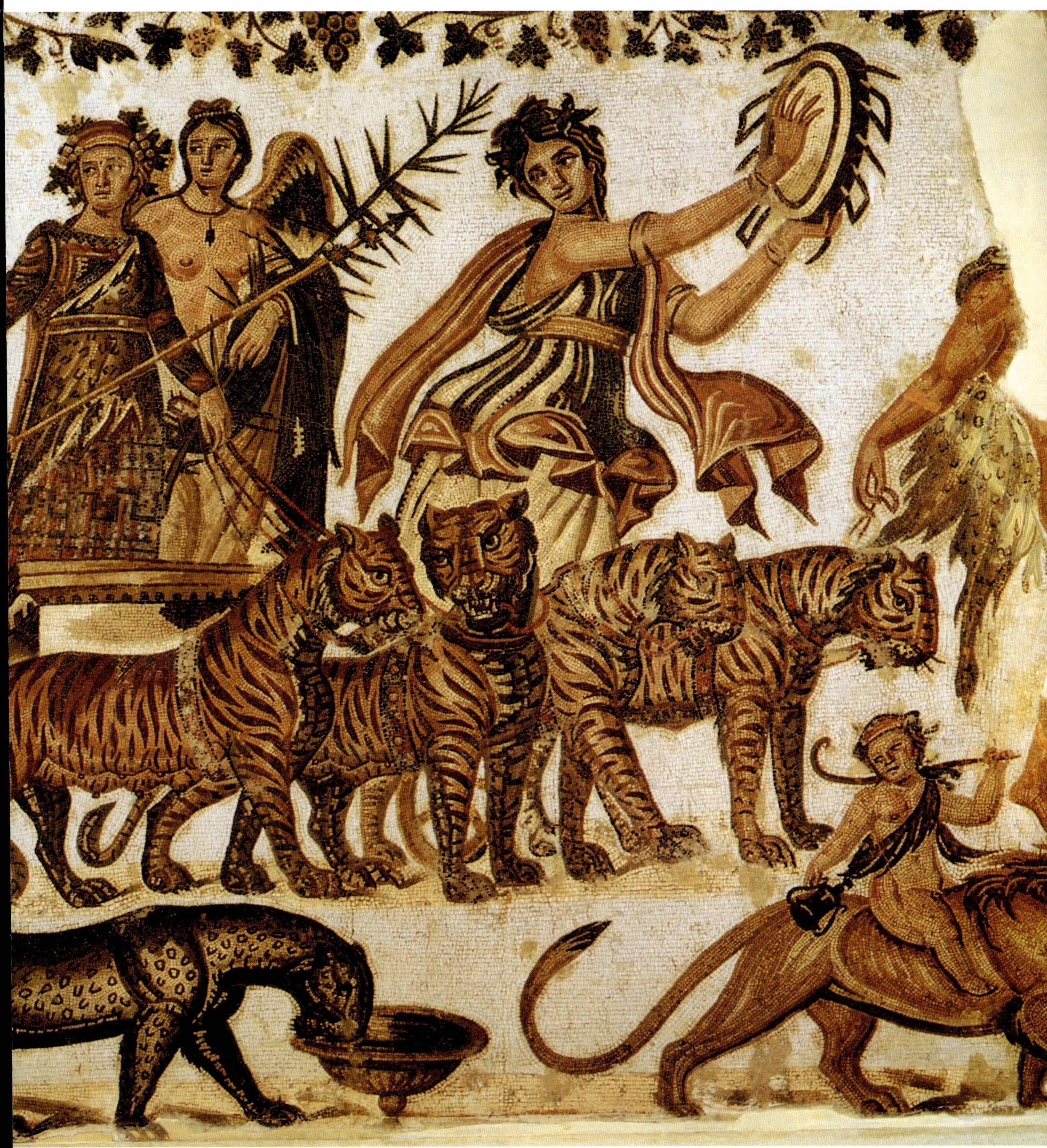

270–271 This detail of a mosaic floor, found in Sousse and housed in the museum in Tunis, confirms the high artistic level achieved in the African provinces. It shows a scene celebrating the triumph of Dionysus in his capacity as master of the forces of nature and lord of the wild beasts. The mosaic dates from the 3rd century AD, *when the port reached the peak of its development as a result of trade with the interior and shipments of olive oil to Rome in great cargo vessels. Little or nothing has survived of Hadrumetum, apart from the mosaic floors of the wealthy local villas.*

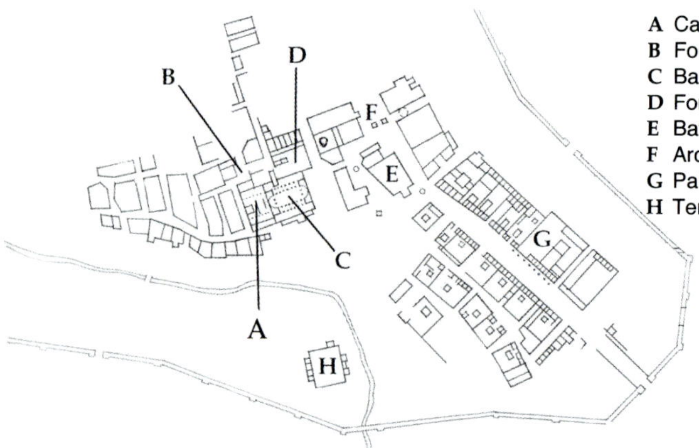
B
D
F
E
C
A
G
H
A Capitolium
B Forum Baths
C Basilica
D Forum
E Baths
F Arch of Caracalla
G Palace of Gordian
H Temple

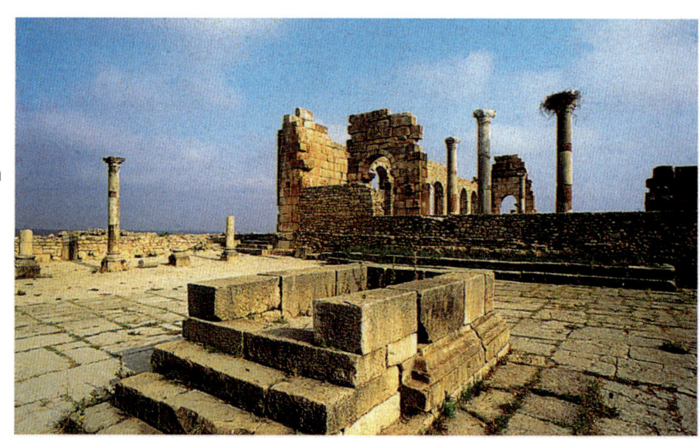

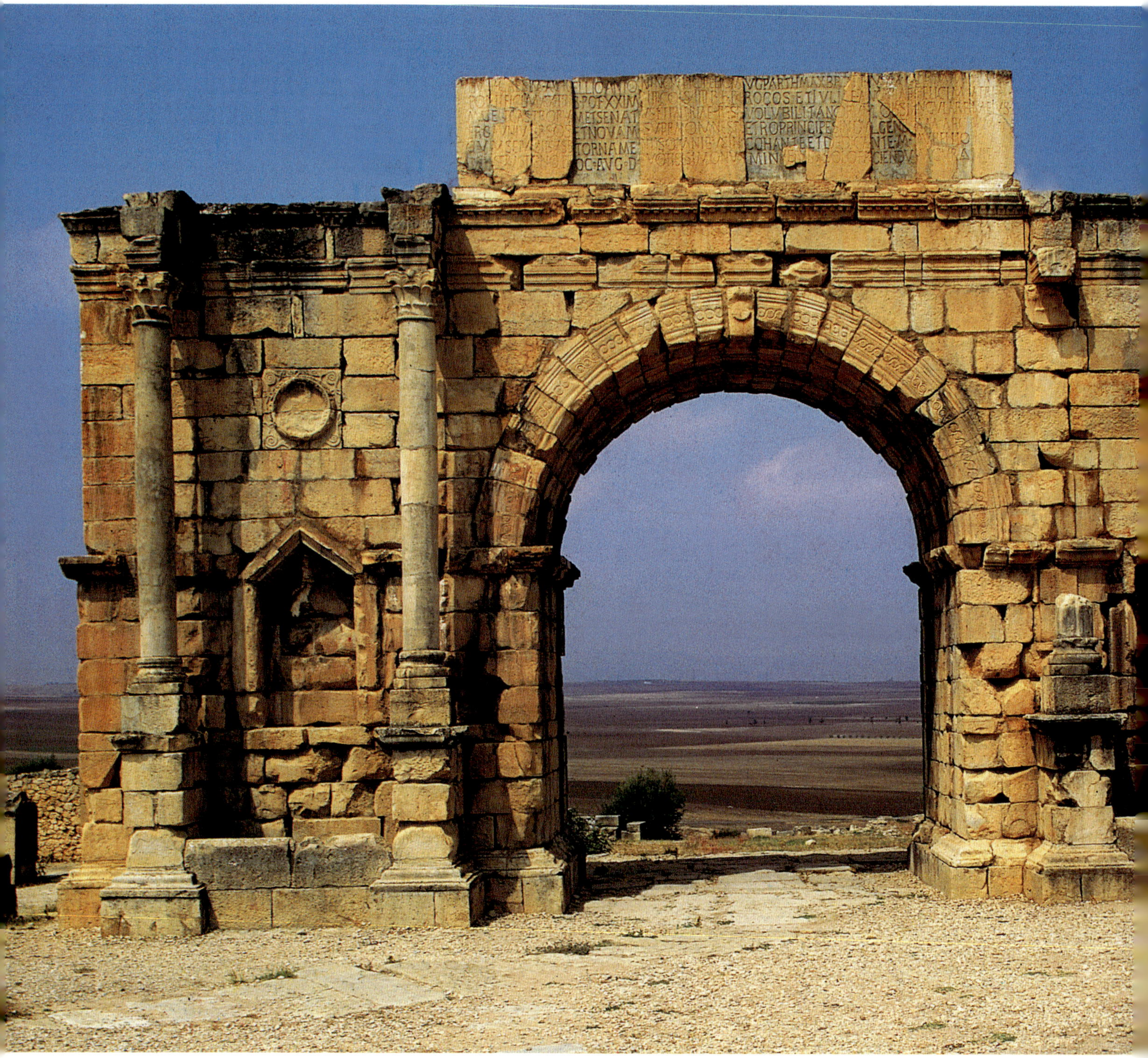

VOLUBILIS, A COLONY ON THE OUTSKIRTS OF THE EMPIRE

Volubilis, a town of Mauretania Tingitana in modern Morocco, was a settlement of some importance from the 2nd century BC, and probably was the residence of King Juba II. After falling under Roman influence, it became the headquarters of the imperial procurator. Claudius granted the town Roman citizenship in AD 44, giving it a new lease of life. Volubilis expanded rapidly in the 3rd century, and even after the region was abandoned under Justinian it maintained a semblance of wealth before falling into ruin.

The town consists of an original, irregular nucleus, and the Roman districts, designed according to the usual grid plan. Situated on a plateau sloping steeply south, it is enclosed by walls dating from the time of Marcus Aurelius. The forum, a huge square with porticoes on four sides, renovated last at the time of Antoninus Pius, is on the boundary between the original town and the new districts. On the eastern side is the basilica, with two apses and three entrances; small rooms on one of the longer sides were possibly used as offices. The capitolium (built under Macrinus in AD 217) stands on a tall podium to the south, facing on to a small square with porticoes providing shade for a row of rooms, possibly housing colleges. In another square stands the triumphal arch dedicated to Caracalla; its main archway was flanked by two small niches, possibly for fountains. Two baths, an olive-processing works and a number of kilns were found in the town, and a sanctuary was located outside the walls. A partly underground aqueduct provided water, and supplied a fountain at the northern baths. Private buildings demonstrate the high standard of living of the local bourgeoisie, enriched by industry and commerce; some of their homes were fitted with baths. 'The Palace of Gordian', a large private house on the *decumanus maximus*, was probably the residence of the provincial governor. The town's many mosaics, in particular ones with geometric patterns, seem to have influenced the decoration of Berber carpets still made today.

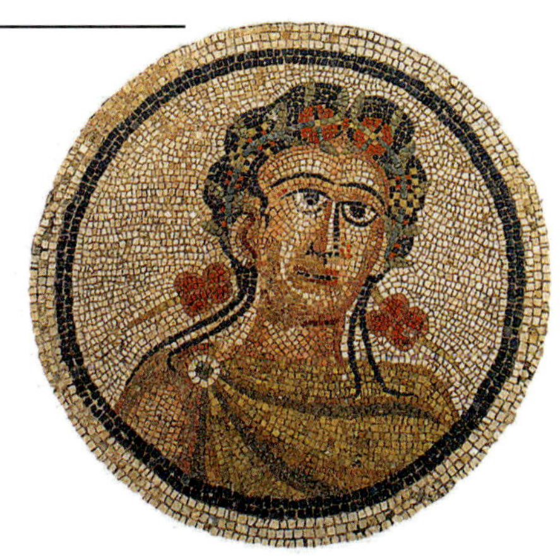

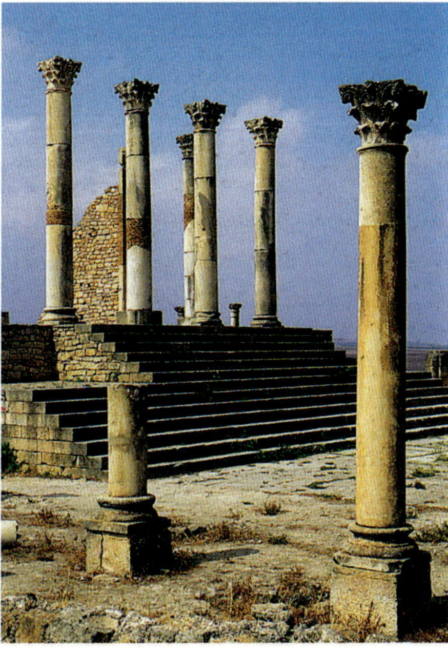

272 (opposite, above) After Mauretania was annexed to the Roman empire, Volubilis retained its status as capital, and new monuments were erected. The basilica stands on the east side of the forum.

272–273 The Arch of Caracalla is one of the best-preserved structures in Volubilis. The basin under each of the side niches suggests that two fountain statues stood in them.

273 (top) Many houses in Volubilis retain a wealth of mosaic decoration, which demonstrates the presence in the city of a large and affluent middle class of mercantile or industrial origin.

273 (centre) All that remains of the capitolium is the wide access staircase and the columns of the pronaos, *surmounted by Corinthian capitals. Volubilis flourished under Septimius Severus, and later, until the 3rd century AD.*

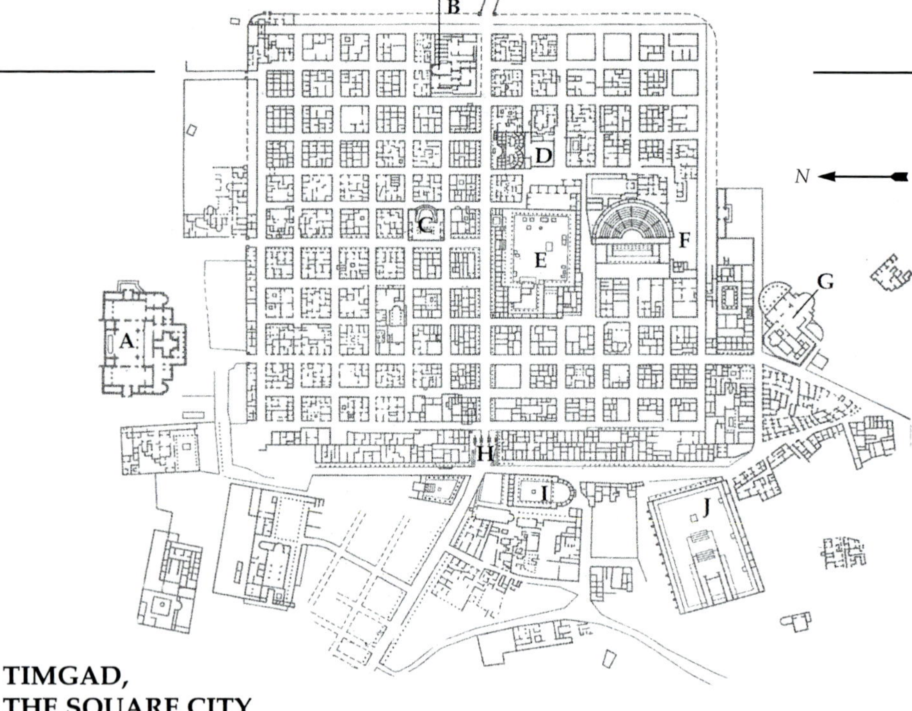

TIMGAD, THE SQUARE CITY

Timgad, in Numidia, was founded in AD 100 by Trajan's veterans and called Marciana Traiana Thamugadi. It may have stood on a site formerly occupied by an indigenous settlement, but no trace of this now remains apart from the name. The layout of the city, with its right-angled axes, reflects that of a typical military camp. It was originally enclosed by city walls, which soon fell into disuse, as demonstrated by various buildings, including the capitolium, which were outside the original grid and not aligned with it.

The perfectly square city of Timgad was divided in half by the east–west *decumanus maximus*. The *cardo maximus* divided the northern part of the city in half, but the southern area was largely occupied by the forum and public buildings, including the theatre, which exploited a natural depression in the land. The completely straight city streets were paved with limestone slabs, and a number of fountains were installed at the crossroads. The city's three main gates stood at the ends of the two main roads, each flanked by porticoes, while traces of a secondary entrance next to a minor *cardo* remain on the south side. A magnificent, sumptuously decorated triumphal arch of Trajan, with three archways, formed the west gate. The road to Lambaesis (Lambesi), the headquarters of the military commander and governor of the province, ran from this gate, while the road to Cirta (Constantine), the capital of Numidia, began at the north gate. The forum occupied a huge quadrangular area, with porticoes all round, behind which were the buildings connected with the public life of the city: the curia, the basilica and the rostra. At the centre were numerous triumphal monuments, only the bases of which remain. Inside the original city walls was a market, with two semicircular courtyards along which were found various shops, no fewer than 14 baths complexes and a library. Facing on to the *cardo maximus*, the library was a small rectangular building with a semicircular room, the wall of which was divided into a number of alcoves for the cupboards to hold the books, consisting of long strips of rolled parchment.

Two temples, dedicated to Ceres and Mercury, stood to the west of the theatre, while the Temple of Saturn was situated in the northern suburb. The temple dedicated to the Capitoline deities was not near the forum as usual, but outside the city perimeter. It stood alone on a tall podium, and had a *pronaos* (porch) of six Corinthian columns. There was a large sanctuary to the south of the town, near a spring, in an area later occupied by a Byzantine fortress. Also outside the urban quadrangle, towards the west, was another, very large market.

Residential building is well represented, and the wealthier examples reflect the typical layout of the African house, with the addition of elements partly of Hellenistic and partly of Roman origin. Fullers' shops, potteries and other industrial works have also been found. Built mainly of stone, with little use of valuable marble, Timgad is especially famous for its mosaics, featuring geometrical and plant motifs and found in nearly all its public and private buildings. Structures dating from the Christian era demonstrate that Thamugadi still prospered in the late empire.

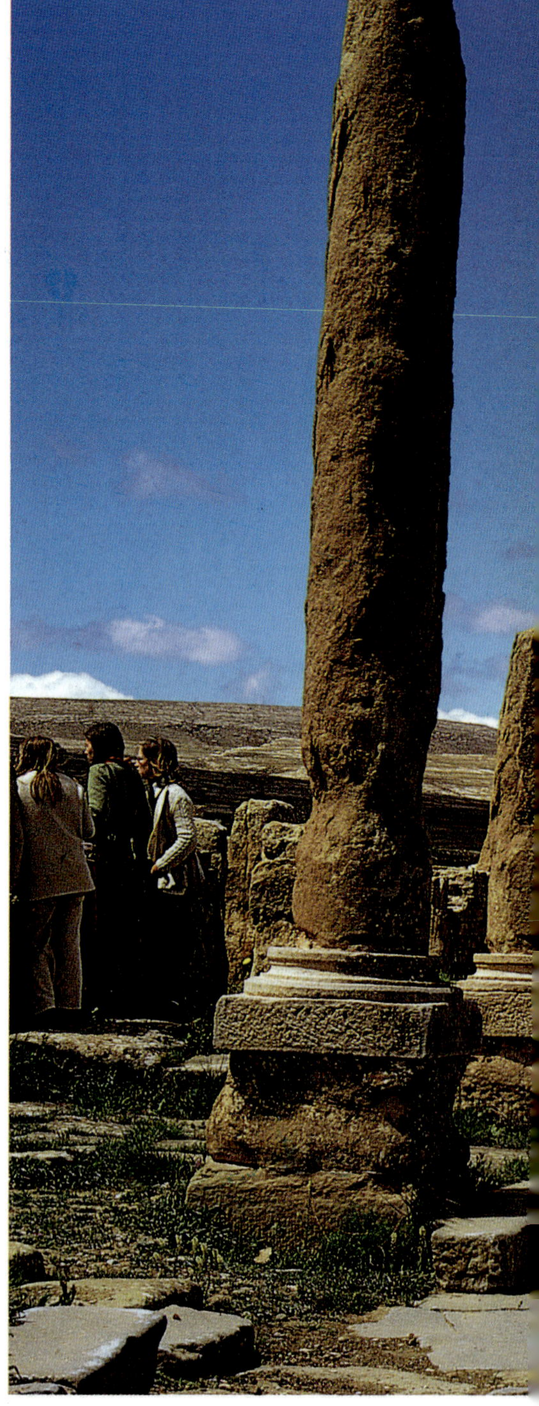

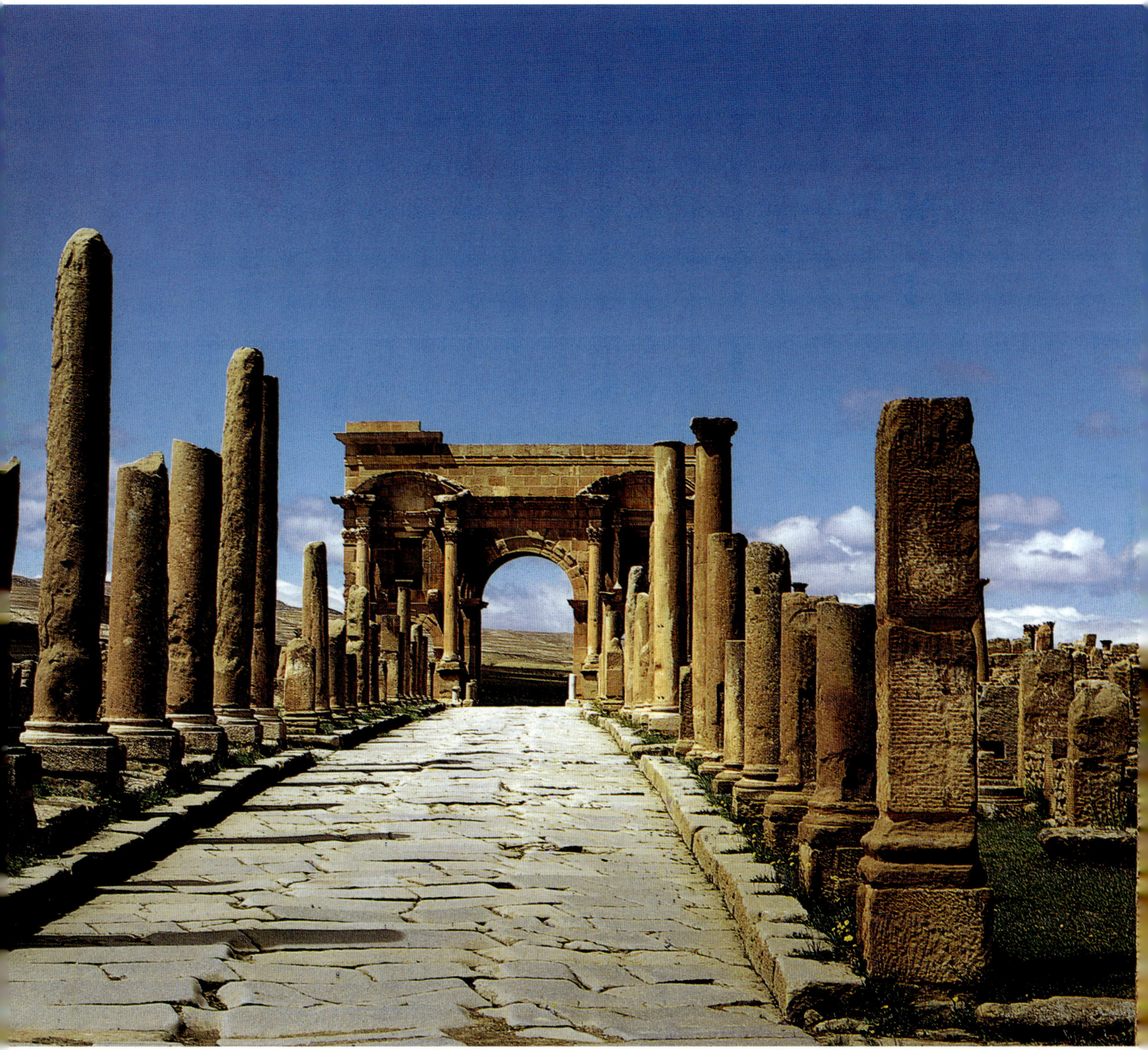

A Northern baths
B Eastern baths
C Public library
D East market
E Forum
F Theatre
G Southern baths
H Arch of Trajan
I Market of Sertius
J Capitolium

274–275 Timgad, founded by Trajan as a colony for veterans of the 3rd Augustea Legion, soon became a rich agricultural market, whose prosperity increased hugely, under the Severan dynasty in particular. Its strictly perpendicular layout reveals its origins as a military camp.

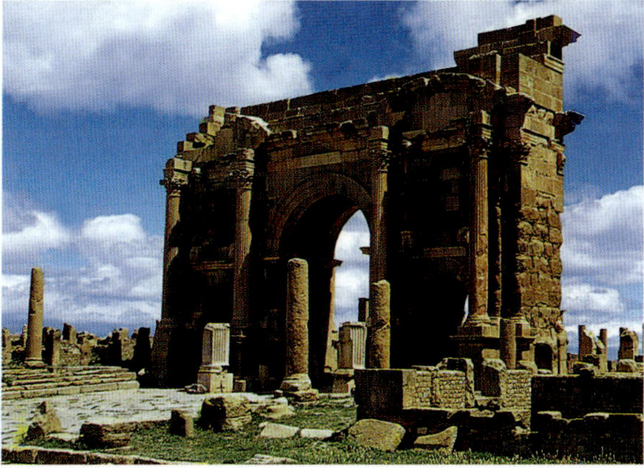

275 (left) The Arch of Trajan, with its three archways, formed the western access to the city. Though on the edge of the empire, Timgad was embellished with all the great public monuments common to the other Roman cities, though with only sparing use of costly marble.

SABRATHA, CITY OF MONUMENTS

276–277 The theatre of Sabratha, built between the late 2nd and early 3rd centuries AD, is one of the best preserved in Africa. The stage front has three tiers of columns, while the platform of the scaena *is decorated with elaborate reliefs.*

277 (opposite, above left) The columns in the foreground were part of the peristyle of a wealthy villa built in the 2nd century AD in the vicinity of the theatre, whose partly restored structures can be seen in the distance.

277 (opposite, above right) Some columns that were part of the vestibule of the curia have been re-erected in the forum area. The curia, found in all Roman towns, was the senate house in which citizens met to discuss local affairs.

Sabratha, an ancient city on the coast of Libya, fell into Roman hands in 46 BC, when Caesar deposed the King of Numidia. Already thriving under Augustus, it reached the peak of its prosperity under the Antonine and Severan dynasties, mainly as a result of its trading activities. Many of the surviving buildings belong to this period. Still flourishing at the beginning of the 4th century, decline soon set in due to the increasingly frequent raids by populations from the interior, culminating with its sack by the Vandals after AD 455. After a brief period of recovery in the Byzantine age, it was occupied and plundered by the Arabs and fell into a state of total neglect. The port and part of the northern area of the town were later swept away by the sea.

Archaeologists have revealed the city's monumental appearance, the layout of which was influenced by the tortuous, untidy nature of the earlier Phoenician town. The oldest part of Sabratha is occupied by the forum, overlooked by the ruins of the capitolium, the curia, the Temple of Serapis and the Temple of Liber Pater, one of the most popular deities in the African provinces.

The capitolium is a typical Italic temple; it stands on a tall podium and is entered by a side staircase. A large basilica stood on the south side of the huge forum square; not far away was the temple dedicated to Antoninus Pius. The grid design of the eastern part of the city dates from the mid-2nd century AD; here stood the Temple of Hercules, the Baths of Oceanus (named after the subject of a mosaic in the tepidarium) and the theatre, whose *scaena* is one of the best preserved in the Roman world. To the northeast of this impressive building, on the sea front, is the sanctuary of Isis, whose temple stood in a large courtyard surrounded by Corinthian columns. The amphitheatre is built in a former quarry, some way east of the town.

Sabratha is also famous for its Christian monuments, as outstanding as its Roman ruins, in particular the Basilica of Justinian, with its splendid mosaics.

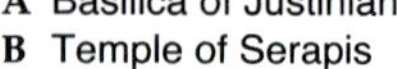

A Basilica of Justinian
B Temple of Serapis
C Capitolium
D Forum
E Basilica
F South Temple
G Temple of Antoninus Pius
H Temple of Liber Pater
I Forum baths
J Baths
K Temple of Isis
L Theatre

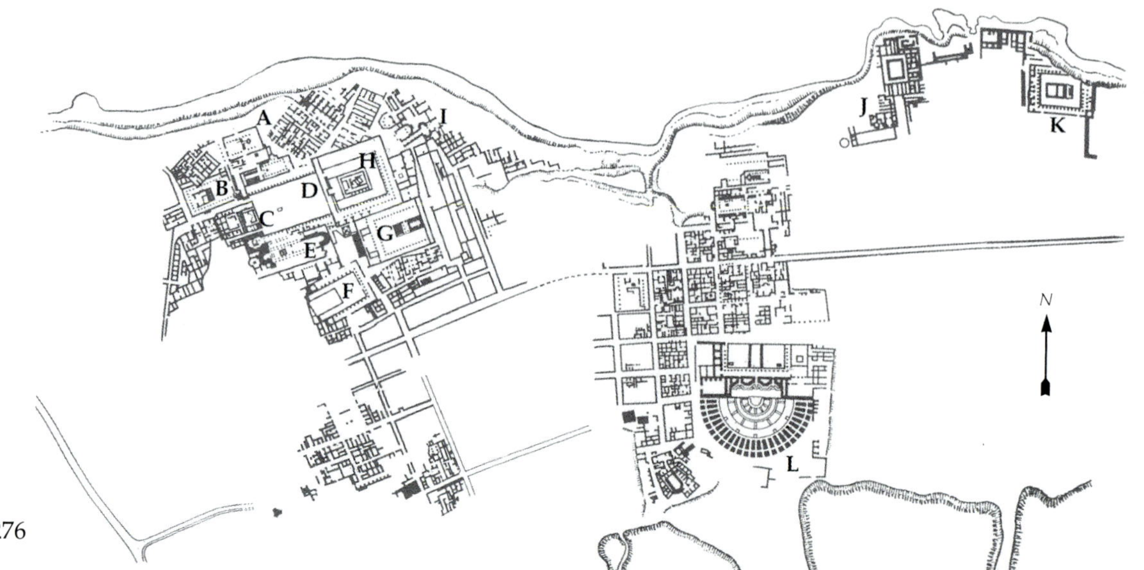

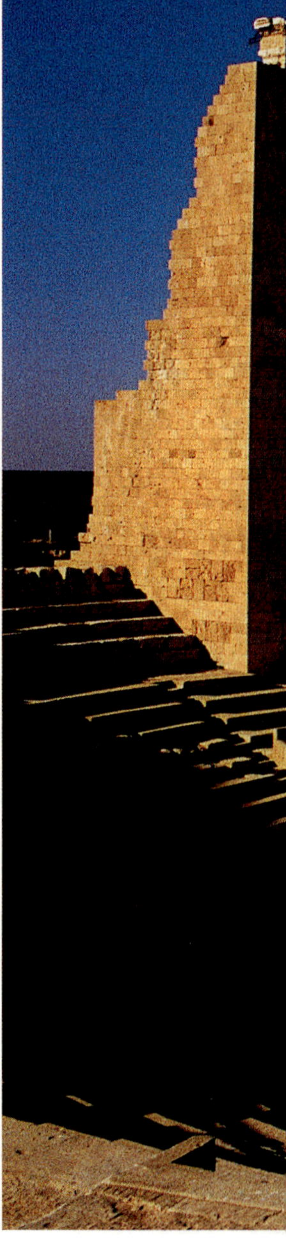

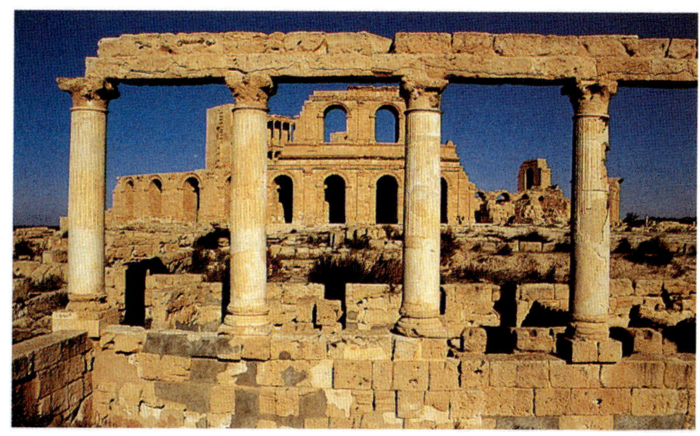

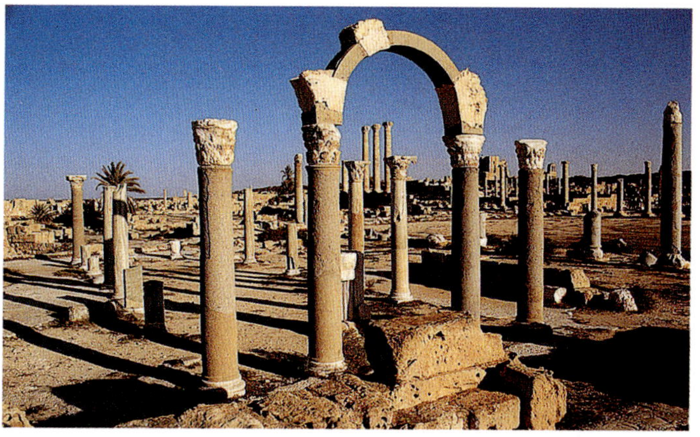

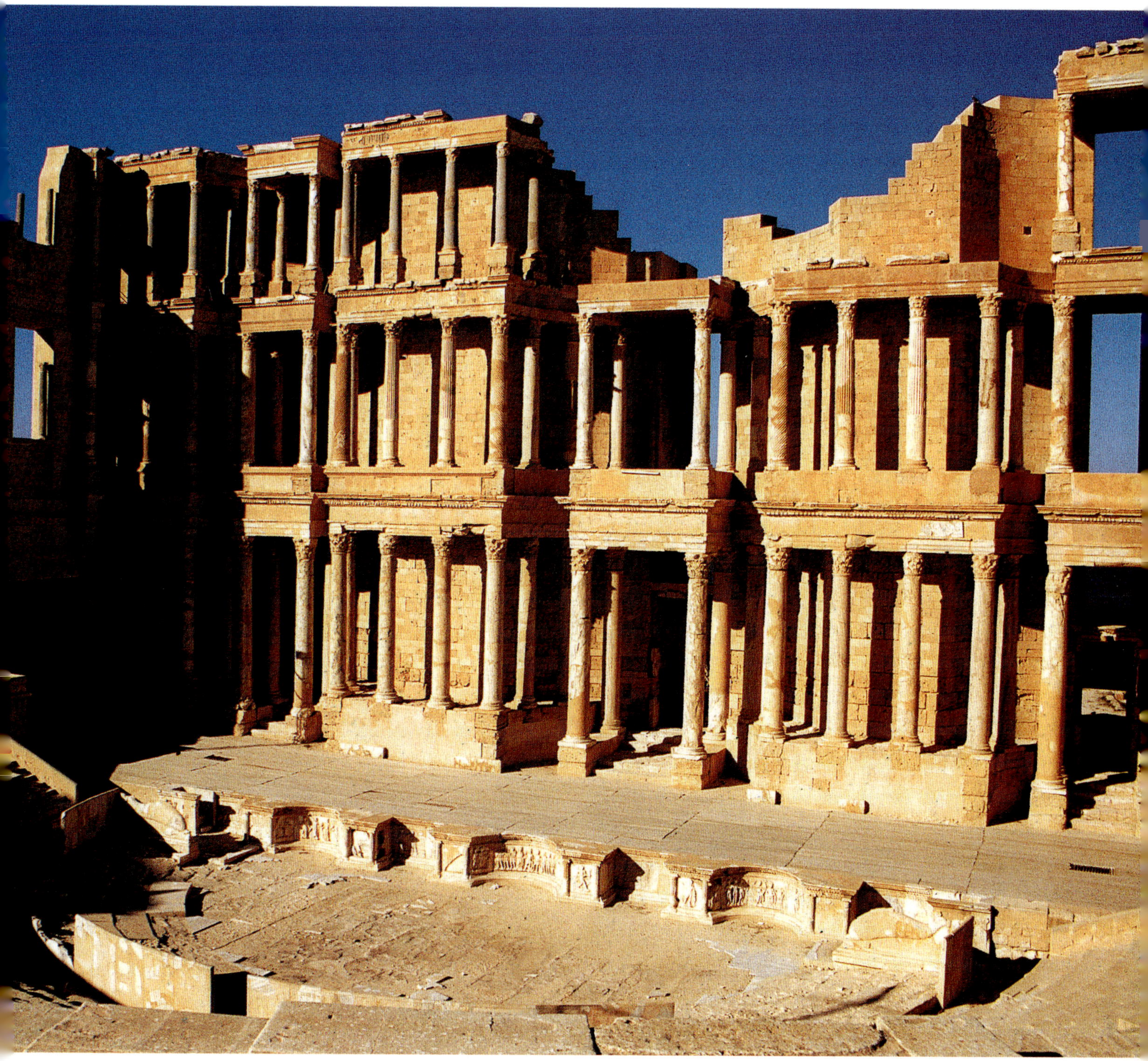

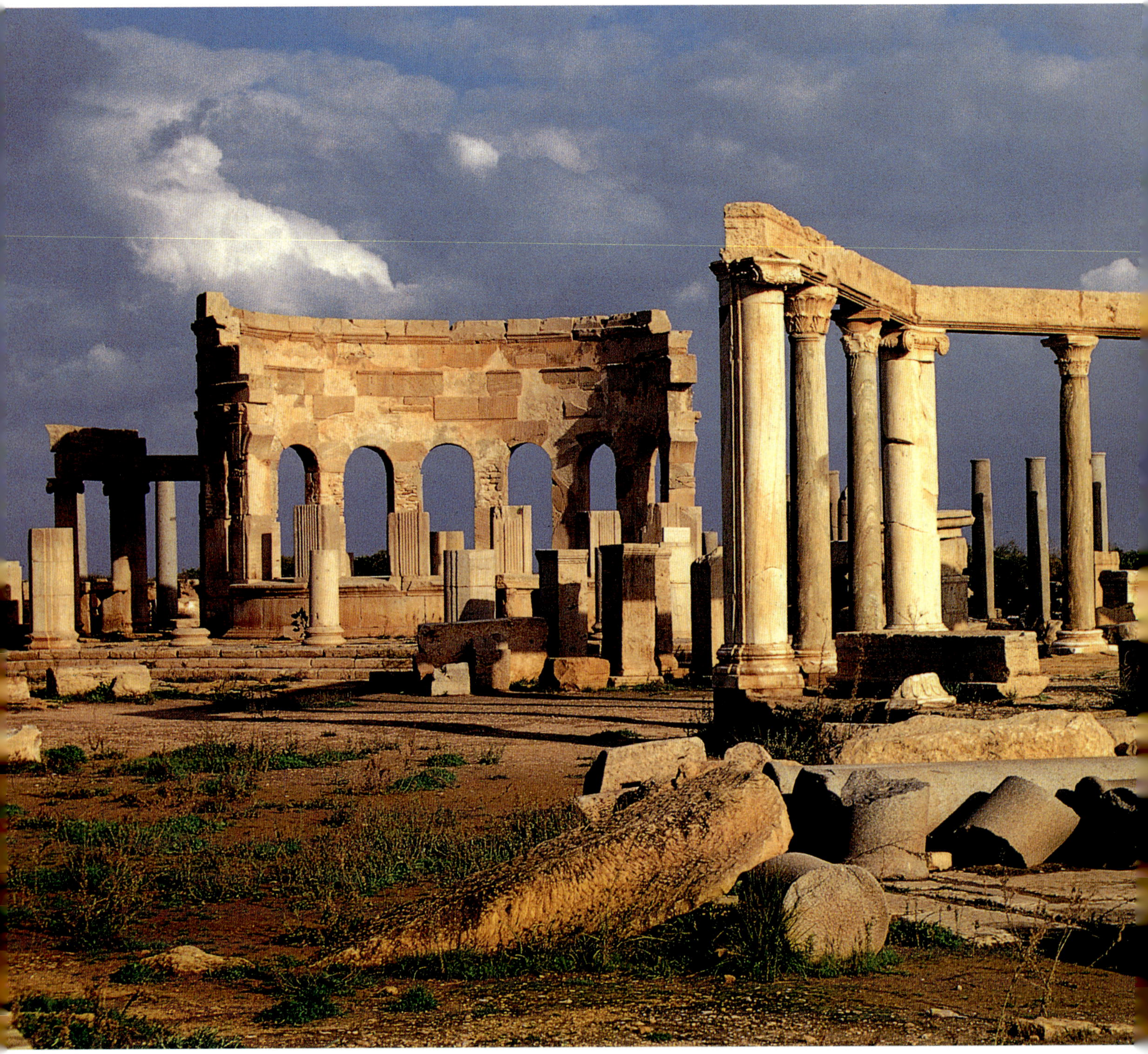

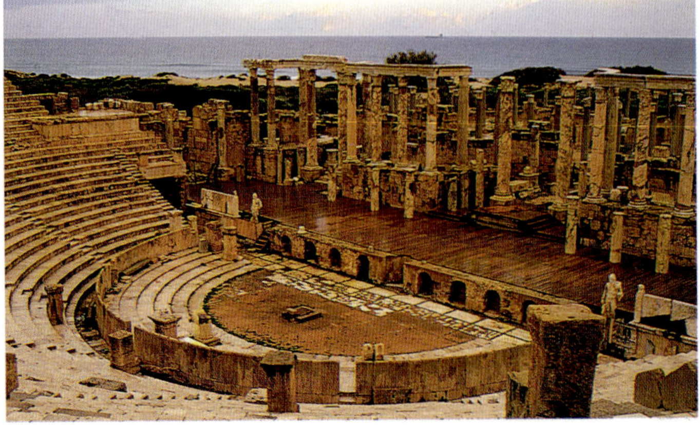

278 (left) The theatre of Lepcis Magna, built in the time of Augustus, was financed by a local merchant. It was partly built on a natural slope, but the upper part had support structures filled with crushed stone. The richly decorated stage front was added at the time of Antoninus Pius, in the 2nd century AD.

278–279 (above) The market of Lepcis Magna was one of the most flourishing in Africa; caravans from the interior of the continent brought valuable goods, slaves and exotic animals, while huge quantities of olive oil arrived from the country and high-quality garum and salted fish were brought from the coast.

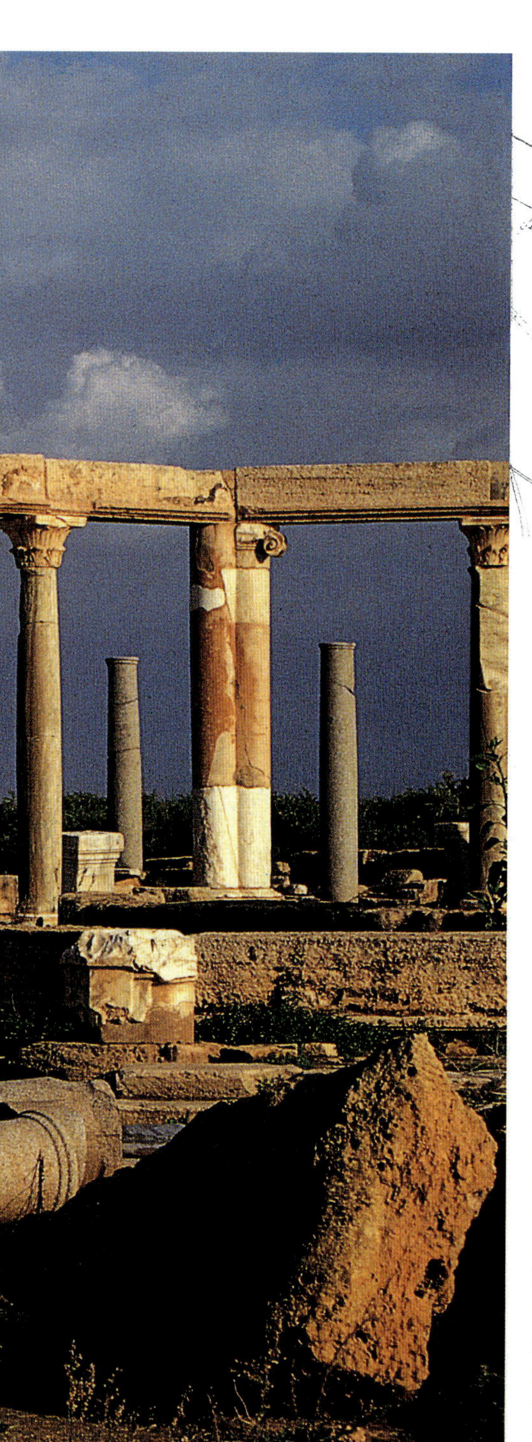

LEPCIS MAGNA, A SUPERB MARBLE METROPOLIS

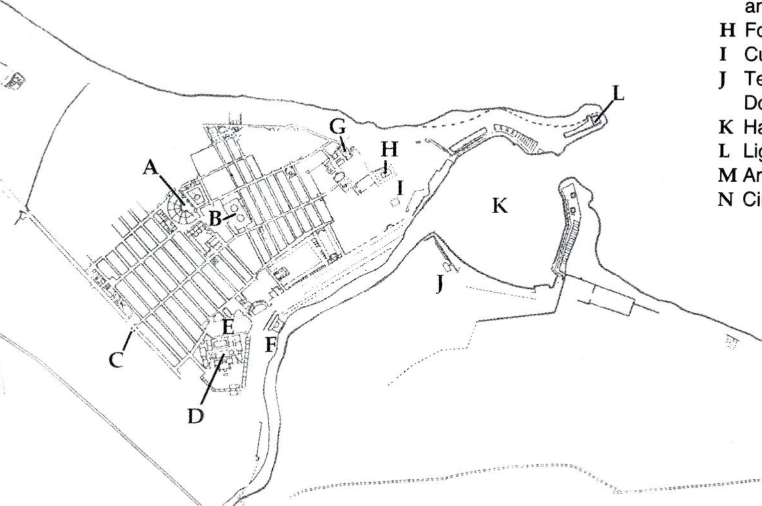

A Theatre
B Markets
C Arch of Septimius Severus
D Baths of Hadrian
E Palaestra
F Nymphaeum
G Temple of Rome and Augustus
H Forum
I Curia
J Temple of Jupiter Dolichenus
K Harbour
L Lighthouse
M Amphitheatre
N Circus

Lepcis Magna, a flourishing city of Phoenician origin in Tripolitania, was the main port between the two gulfs known as the Syrtes. It became part of the province of Africa in 46 BC after the battle of Thapsus. Trajan made it a colony in AD 110 and it reached the height of its splendour in the reign of Septimius Severus, born there in AD 146, who carried out extensive building work. The metropolis, with its splendid monumental aspect, became one of the richest in the Mediterranean, its wealth based on the export of valuable goods from the interior – ivory, precious gems, slaves and exotic animals – and local products. Tuna salting and *garum* production prospered in Lepcis, which was also famous for its olive oil.

The city's decline in the 4th century was due both to raids by tribes from the interior and a rapid silting of the port caused by a serious error in the design of the dock built by Severus. Subsequent invasions by the Vandals badly weakened it, and, after a brief period of recovery under Justinian, it finally fell into ruin.

The basic design of the city's plan, around two diverging main roads west of the Wadi Lebda, was already evident as early as the Augustan age. Generous local benefactors endowed the city with numerous monuments in the 1st century, including the Old Forum (with the curia, a basilica, the Temple of Liber Pater, the Temple of Hercules, and the Temple of Rome and Augustus) and a large market. An interesting structure, the market was formed by a rectangular area bounded by porticoes, in the middle of which

279 (right) A number of Ionic columns that were part of the Temple of Hercules, built in the early 1st century AD, stand in the area of the Old Forum. The square in front, which was given its first monumental buildings by Augustus, was the heart of the city until it was renovated under the Severan dynasty.

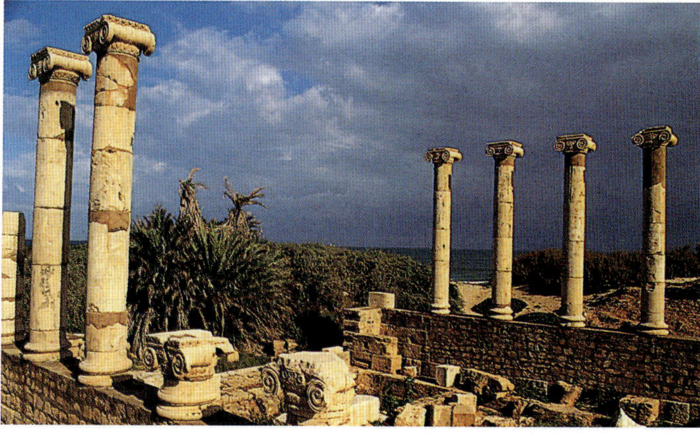

stood two round pavilions set in octagonal porticoes. Nearby was the theatre (almost as early as Pompey's Theatre in Rome) and the Chalcidicum, an elegant building for trade of AD 11. In AD 126 Hadrian added to the splendour of Lepcis with a huge baths complex, including a palaestra. Septimius Severus' extensive building programme was carried out in the area between the *cardo maximus* and the Wadi Lebda, which was diverted outside the city. A new and grandiose urban highway was built. An impressive colonnaded road, 20 m (65 ft) wide, it began near Hadrian's Baths with a gigantic nymphaeum and led to the docks. On the west side of the road stood the New Forum and the Basilica of Severus, with its splendid marbles, statues and relief decorations of acanthus volutes, animal protomes and mythological scenes. The same taste for magnificent baroque ornamentation is evident in the large four-sided arch at the crossroads between the *cardo* and the *decumanus maximus*. It features pilasters decorated with friezes similar to those of the basilica, and sculptural decorations, including political and religious scenes, which, in terms of style, already herald Byzantine art.

280–281 Styles of architecture under the Severans were luxurious and elaborate, with an evident fondness for apses, niches and colonnaded façades. A good example is the avenue outside the Severan Basilica and adjacent to the Old Forum, interesting for the elegant chromatic effects obtained by using different materials.

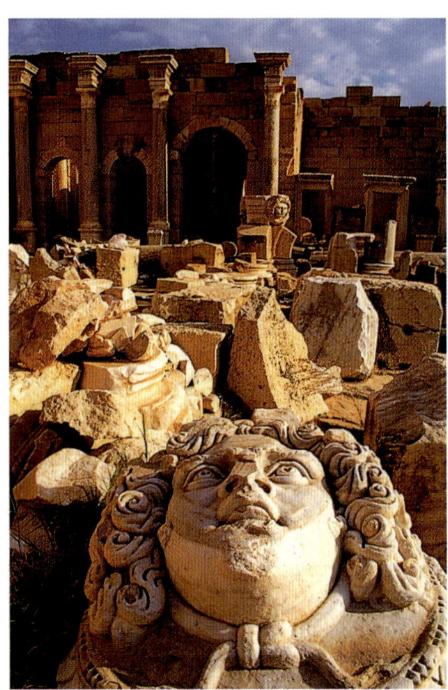

280 An intensive building programme by Septimius Severus, a native of the town, transformed Lepcis Magna into a magnificent metropolis. This is one of the Medusa medallions decorating the Severan Forum – a good example of the use of sculpture to emphasize the play of light and shade, to great dramatic effect.

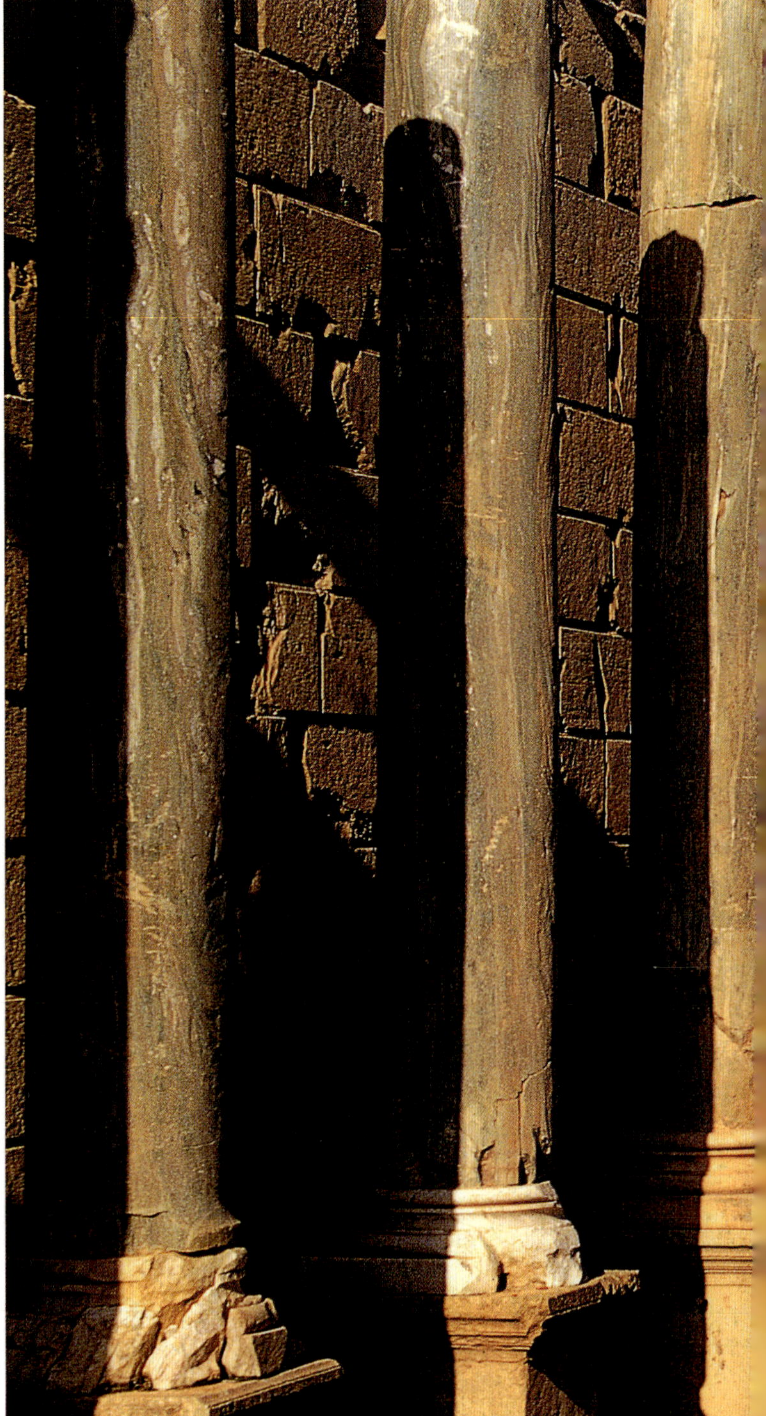

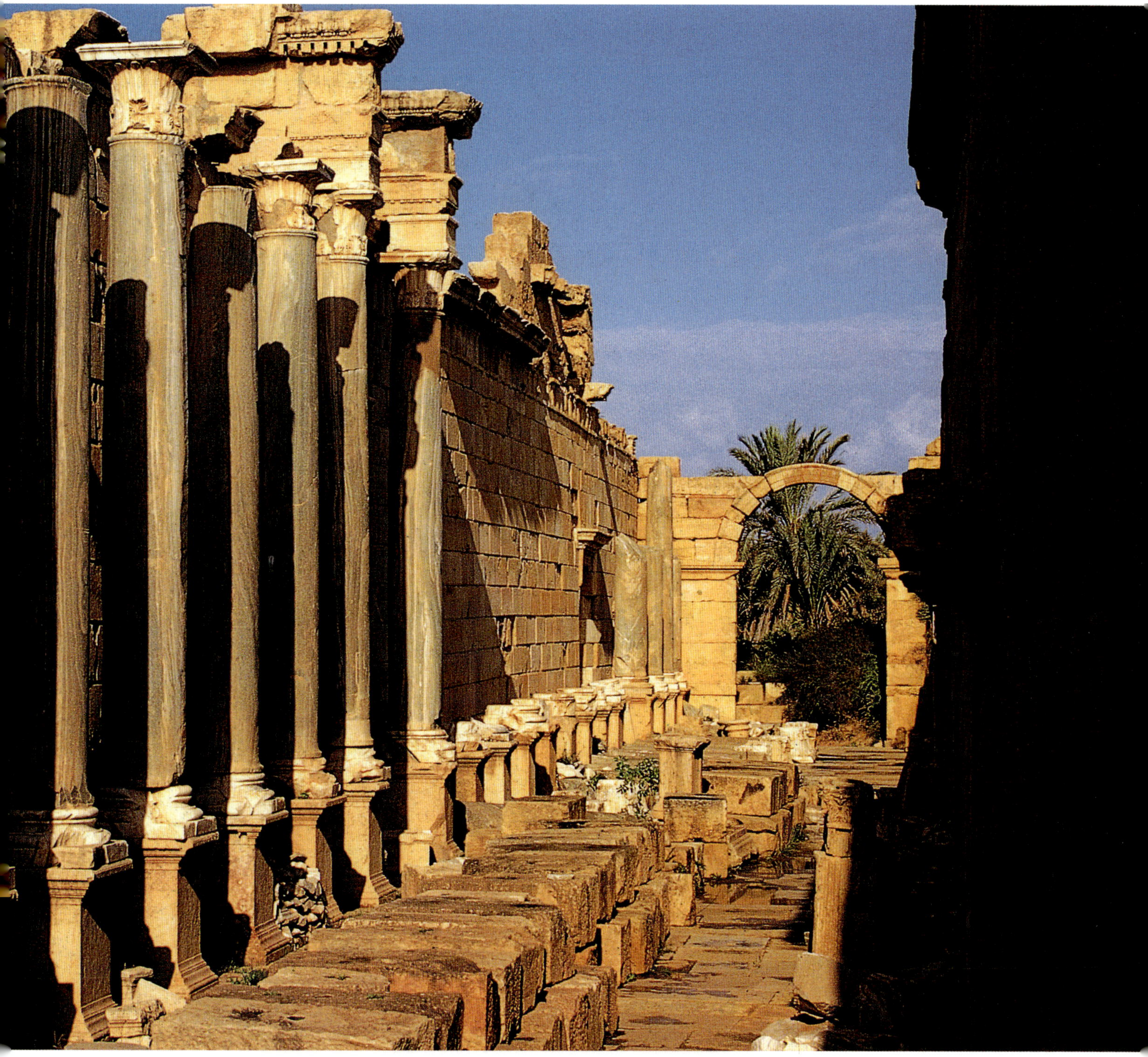

281 (right) The basilica of the Severan Forum is representative of the new styles which came into vogue in the late 2nd century AD. The columns are made of red granite with white marble capitals, and the pillars framing the apse are decorated with acanthus volutes. Numerous niches relieve the solidity of the masonry.

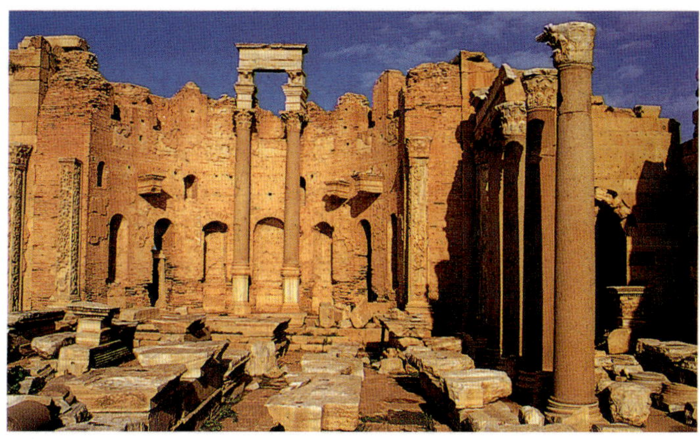

282–283 (overleaf) A reconstruction of Lepcis Magna at the peak of its splendour: the great colonnaded avenue, with the Severan nymphaeum, sloped down to the port, near which stood the Old Forum. Next to the theatre were the Chalcidicum and the market. The Baths of Hadrian are in the foreground, with the Severan Forum behind.

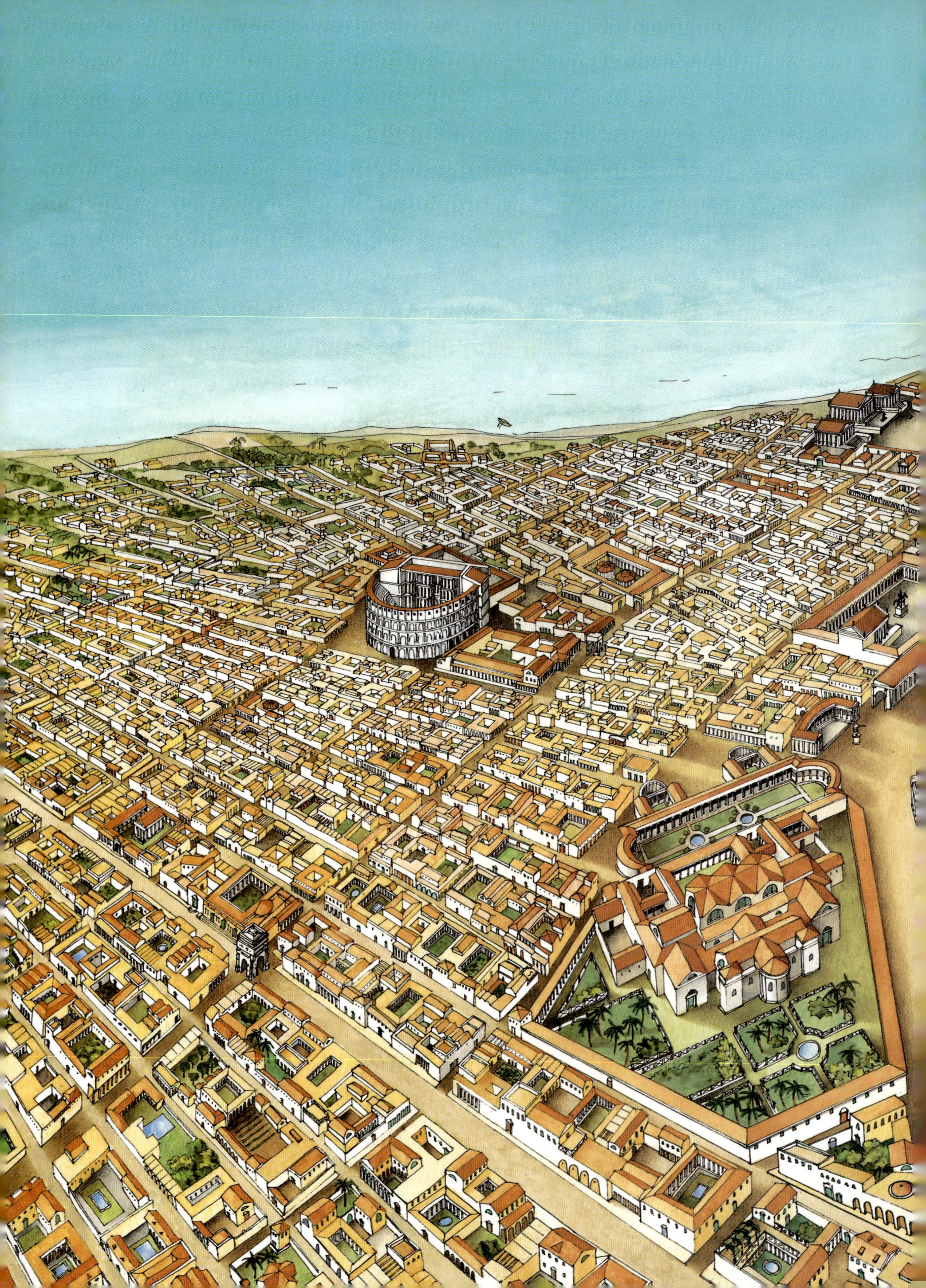

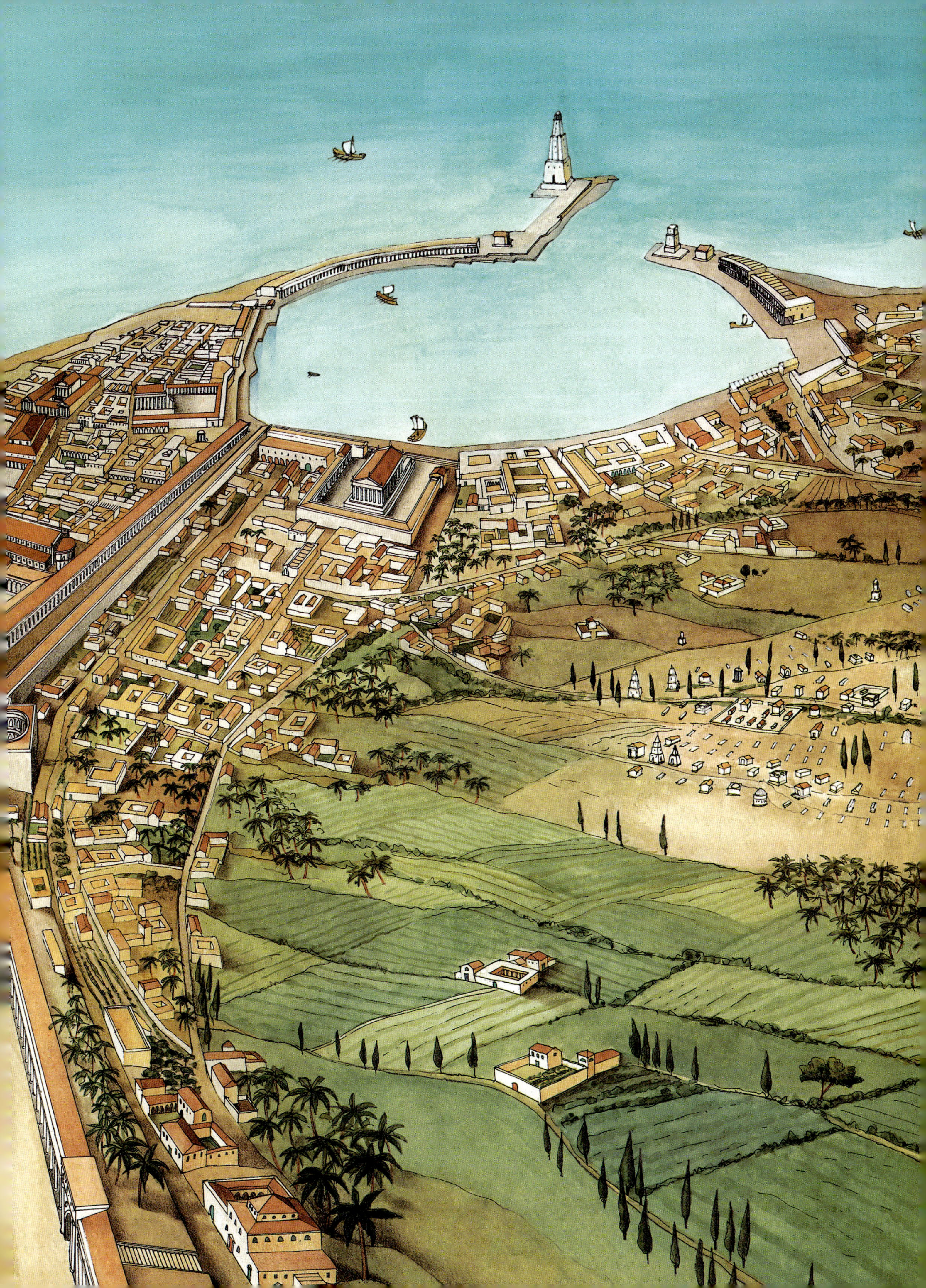

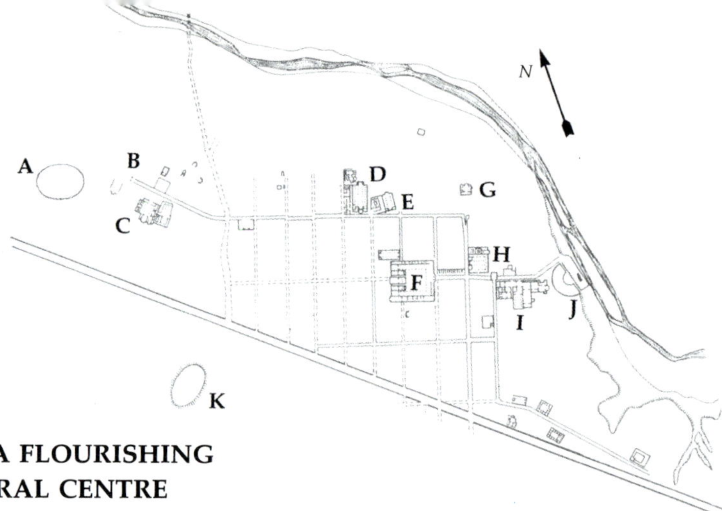

A Amphitheatre
B Arch of Septimius Severus
C Building of the Seasons
D Basilica of Vitalis
E Basilica of Bellator
F Forum and Capitol
G Baths
H Basilica of Servus
I Great Baths
J Theatre
K Mound and stele dedicated to Saturn

SUFETULA, A FLOURISHING AGRICULTURAL CENTRE

The history of Sufetula, a Roman town near Sbeitla in what is now Tunisia, is not recounted in any written source. Archaeology, however, supports the hypothesis that it was founded in the second half of the 1st century AD following a military campaign against a local tribe. The town grew up around the crossroads of major highways which brought it into contact with the main cities of the region. Enriched by olive growing and oil production, Sufetula reached the peak of its splendour between the 2nd and 3rd centuries AD, when many impressive monuments were built. It became a bishop's see and prospered in the Byzantine period until it was stormed and sacked by the Arabs in 647. Excavations have brought to light much of the urban area and the subdivision of the centre into *insulae* is clear. Major monuments include the forum, a square with porticoes on three sides and three tetrastyle temples forming the capitolium on the fourth. These were joined by arches to present a single façade. Opposite this complex stands a triumphal arch with three archways, built into the wall surrounding the forum and dedicated to Antoninus Pius, under whom Sufetula particularly flourished. Other buildings include an amphitheatre with an unusual, almost circular plan, a theatre built on a hillside and a large baths complex. An arch dedicated to Septimius Severus, now destroyed, and another to the first Tetrarchs, marked the southern and northern boundaries of the town. Water was supplied by an aqueduct crossing a wadi on a bridge still in a good state of repair. Five large basilicas, with signs of restoration, survive from the Christian era.

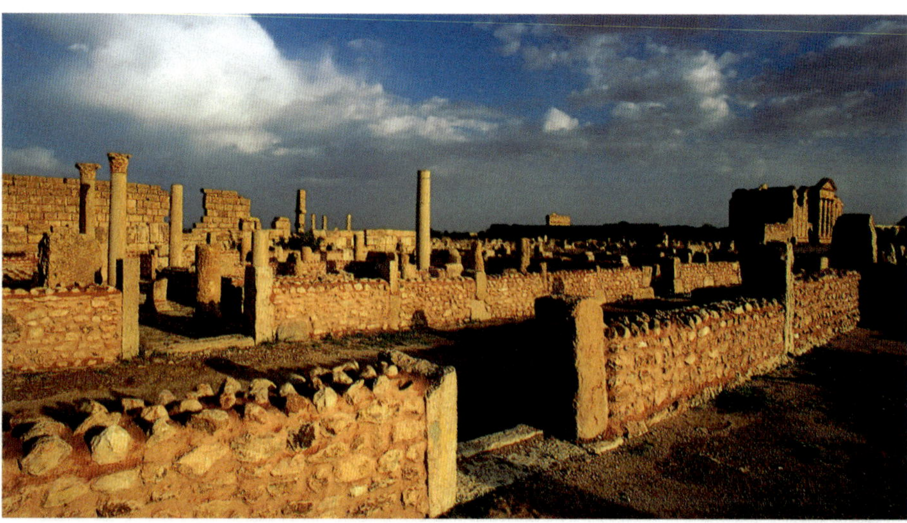

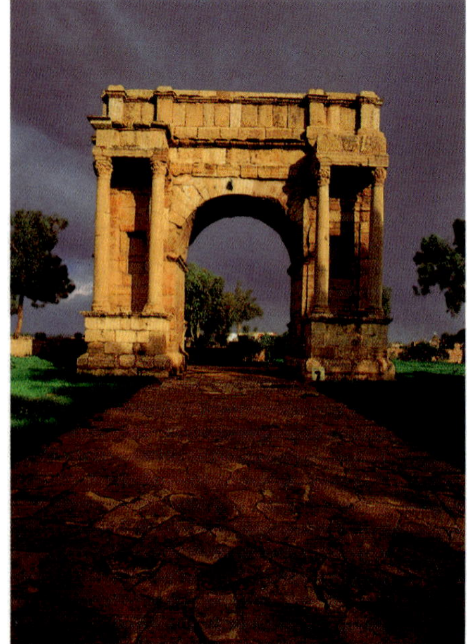

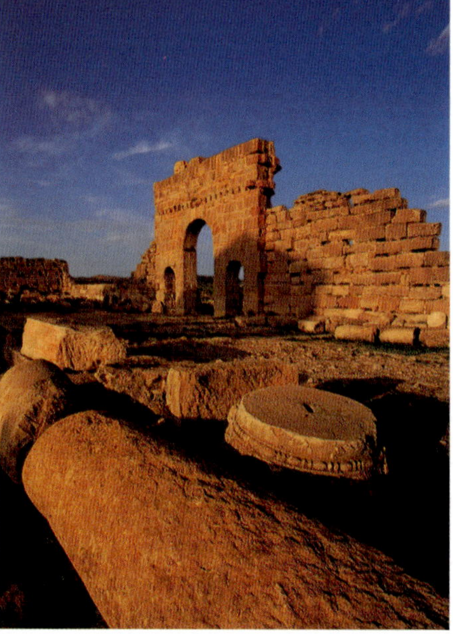

284 (top) The centre of Sufetula was organized according to the typical division into 'centuries', with the insulae *built on a rectangular plan and the forum in a dominant position. The borders of the town, which was not surrounded by walls, were marked by two triumphal arches.*

284 (above left) The triumphal arch dedicated to the Tetrarchs has a single archway with a niche framed by columns on each side – a style which was quite common in Africa. The design of this kind of monument varied from province to province.

284 (above right) The forum area was bounded by a wall which contained a triumphal arch dedicated to Antoninus Pius, dating from AD 139, in the form of a monumental gateway.

285 (opposite) Unusually, the capitolium of Sufetula is formed by three separate buildings, joined by arches to form one façade.

286–287 (overleaf) The Arch of Antoninus Pius was reached along a colonnaded avenue lined with shops.

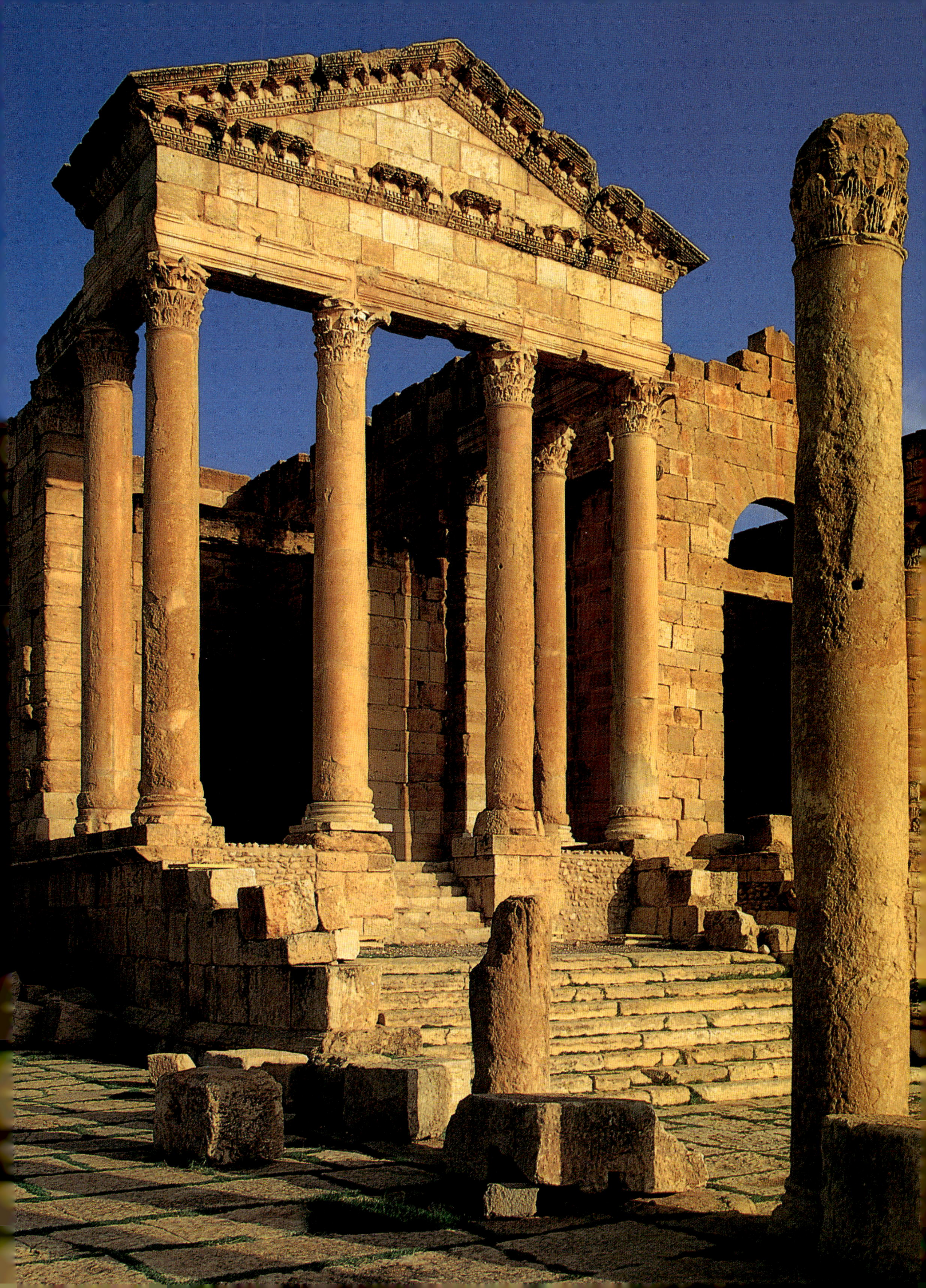

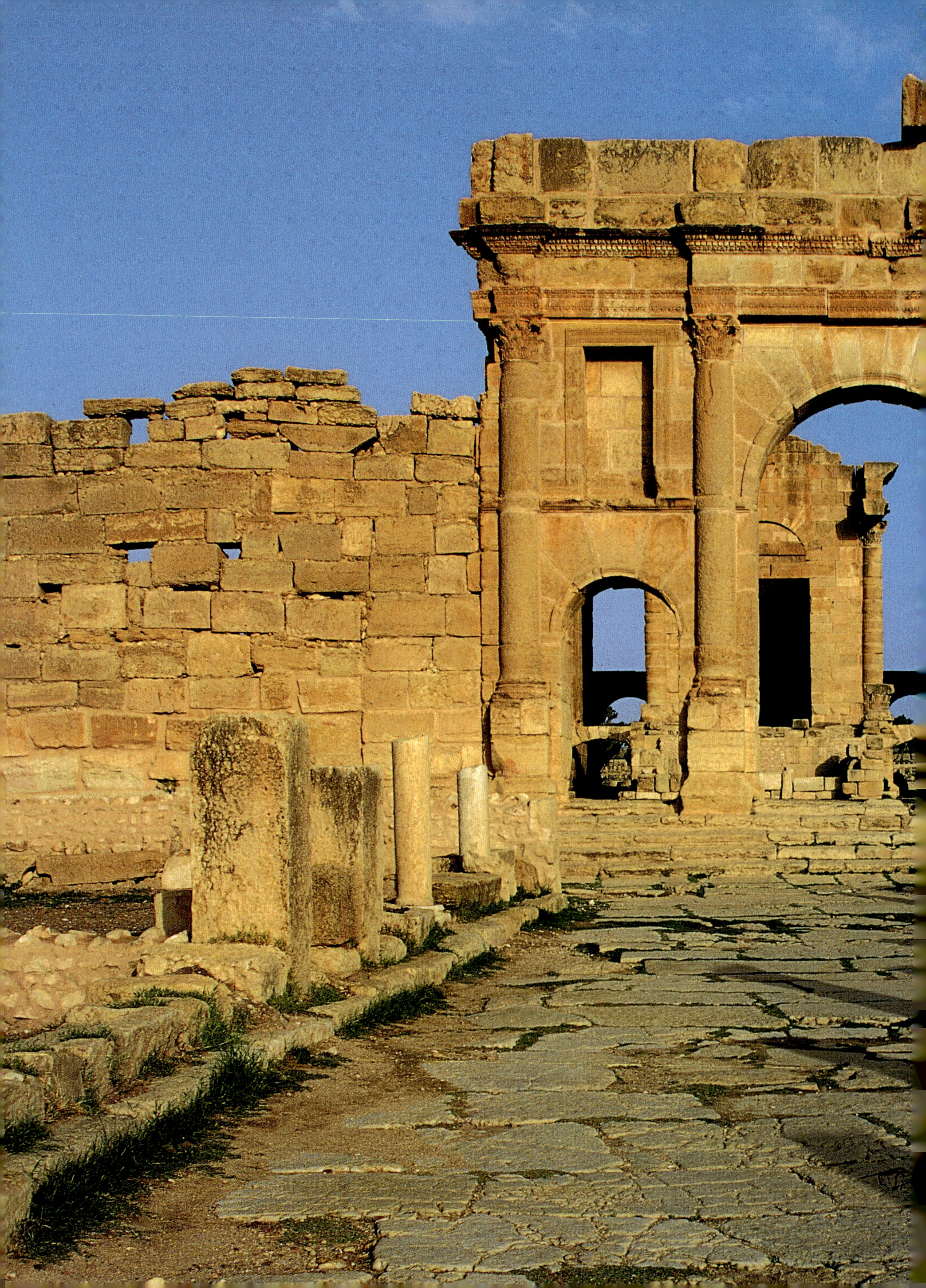

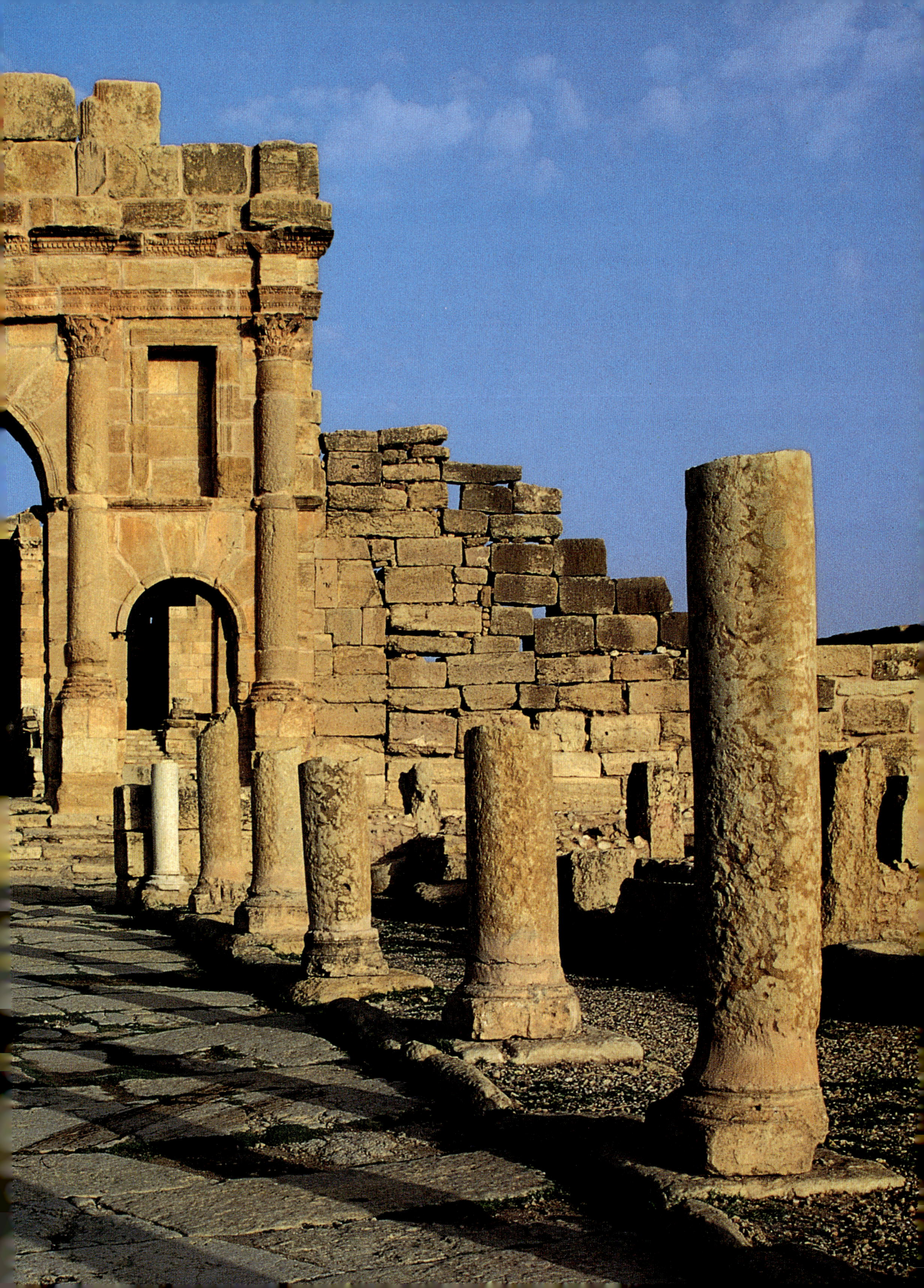

SELECT BIBLIOGRAPHY

HISTORY AND CIVILIZATION

Astin, A.E., Walbank, F.W., Frederiksen, M.W. & Ogilvie, R.M. (eds), *Cambridge Ancient History, Vol. VIII: Rome and the Mediterranean to 133 BC*, 2nd ed. Cambridge 1989.

Barnes, T.D., *The New Empire of Diocletian and Constantine*, Cambridge MA 1982.

Barrett, A.A., *Caligula. The Corruption of Power*, London 1989.

Birley, A., *Marcus Aurelius. A Biography*, London 1987.

Birley, A., *Septimius Severus. The African Emperor*, London 1987.

Carcopino, J., *Daily Life in Ancient Rome*, Harmondsworth 1973.

Cary, M. & Scullard, H.H., *A History of Rome*, London 1975.

Connolly, P., *Greece and Rome at War*, London 1981.

Cook, S.A., Adcock, F.E. & Charlesworth, M.P. (eds), *Cambridge Ancient History, Vol. X, The Augustan Empire, 44 BC–AD 70*, Cambridge 1934.

Cook, S.A., Adcock, F.E., Charlesworth, M.P. & Baynes, N.H. (eds), *Cambridge Ancient History, Vol. XI: The Imperial Peace, AD 70–192*, Cambridge 1936.

Cook, S.A., Adcock, F.E., Charlesworth, M.P. & Baynes, N.H. (eds), *Cambridge Ancient History, Vol. XII: The Imperial Crisis and Recovery, AD 193–294*, Cambridge 1939.

Cornell, T. & Matthews, J., *Atlas of the Roman World*, Oxford & New York 1982.

Crook, J.A., Lintott, A. & Rawson, E. (eds), *Cambridge Ancient History, Vol. IX: The Last Age of the Roman Republic, 146–43 BC*, Cambridge 1994.

Cunliffe, B., *Rome and Her Empire*, London 1978.

Ferrill, A., *The Fall of the Roman Empire: the Military Explanation*, London 1990.

Ferrill, A., *Caligula. Emperor of Rome*, London 1991.

Gibbon, E., *History of the Decline and Fall of the Roman Empire*, London 1776. New edition, London 1994.

Grant, M., *The Emperor Constantine*, London 1993.

Grant, M., *The Roman Emperors. A Biographical Guide to the Rulers of Imperial Rome, 31 BC–AD 476*, London 1996.

Griffin, M., *Nero: the End of a Dynasty*, London 1985.

Jones, A.H.M., *The Later Roman Empire, 284–602: a Social, Economic and Administrative Survey*, Oxford 1964.

Jones, B.W., *The Emperor Titus*, London 1984.

Jones, B.W., *The Emperor Domitian*, London 1992.

Keppie, L., *Understanding Roman Inscriptions*, London 1991.

Lane Fox, R., *Pagans and Christians*, Harmondsworth 1986.

Levick, B., *Claudius*, London 1990.

Millar, F., *The Roman World and its Neighbours*, London 1981.

Millar, F., *The Emperor in the Roman World*, 2nd ed. London 1992.

Moatti, C., *In Search of Ancient Rome*, London 1993.

Scarre, C., *The Chronicle of the Roman Emperors. The Reign-by-Reign Record of the Rulers of Imperial Rome*, London & New York 1995.

Scarre, C., *The Penguin Historical Atlas of Ancient Rome*, Harmondsworth & New York 1995.

Scullard, H.H., *From the Gracchi to Nero. A History of Rome 133 BC to AD 68*, 5th ed. London & New York 1982.

Syme, R., *The Roman Revolution*, Oxford 1939.

Walbank, F.W., Astin, A.E., Frederiksen, M.W., Ogilvie, R.M. & Drummond, A. (eds), *Cambridge Ancient Hsitory, Vol. VII, pt. 2: The Rise of Rome to 220 BC*, Cambridge 1989.

Webster, G., *The Roman Imperial Army*, 3rd ed. London 1985.

Wheeler, M., *Rome Beyond the Imperial Frontiers*, London 1954.

Williams, S., *Diocletian and the Roman Recovery*, London 1985.

Williams, S. & Friell, G., *Theodosius: the Empire at Bay*, London 1994.

ART AND ARCHITECTURE

Adam, J.-P., *Roman Building*, London 1994.

Boëthius, A., *Etruscan and Early Roman Architecture*, Harmondsworth 1978.

Doxiadis, E., *The Mysterious Fayum Portraits. Faces from Ancient Egypt*, London & New York 1995.

Henig, M. (ed.), *A Handbook of Roman Art. A Survey of the Visual Arts of the Roman World*, London 1983.

Higgins, R., *Greek and Roman Jewellery*, London 1966.

Lepper, F. & Frere, S., *Trajan's Column*, Gloucester 1988.

Ling, R., *Roman Painting*, Cambridge & New York 1991.

Ramage, N.H. & A., *Roman Art*, London 1995.

Richmond, I.A., *Roman Archaeology and Art*, London 1969.

Rossi, L., *Trajan's Column and the Dacian Wars*, London 1971.

Sear, F., *Roman Architecture*, revised ed. London 1989.

Smith, R.R.R., *Hellenistic Sculpture*, London 1991.

Strong, D., *Greek and Roman Gold and Silver Plate*, London 1966.

Strong, D., *Roman Art*, revised ed. Harmondsworth & New York 1988.

Trevor Hodge, A., *Roman Aqueducts and Water Supply*, London 1995.

Walker, S., *Roman Art*, London 1991.

Ward-Perkins, J.B., *Roman Architecture*, London 1988.

Ward-Perkins, J.B., *Roman Imperial Architecture*, Harmondsworth 1981.

Wheeler, M., *Roman Art and Architecture*, London 1964.

ARCHAEOLOGICAL SITES

Bisel, S.C., *The Secrets of Vesuvius*, Sevenoaks 1990.

Breeze, D.J. & Dobson, B., *Hadrian's Wall*, 3rd ed. Harmondsworth 1987.

Browning, I., *Palmyra*, London 1979.

Connolly, P., *Pompeii*, Oxford 1990.

De Franciscis, A., *The Buried Cities: Pompeii and Herculaneum*, London 1978.

Drinkwater, J., *Roman Gaul, the Three Provinces, 58 BC–AD 260*, London 1983.

Grant, M., *Cities of Vesuvius, Pompeii and Herculaneum*, Harmondsworth 1976.

Holum, K.G. & others, *King Herod's Dream – Caesarea on the Sea*, New York & London 1988.

Johnson, S., *Hadrian's Wall*, London 1989.

Keay, S.J., *Roman Spain*, London 1987.

King, A., *Roman Gaul and Germany*, London 1988.

MacDonald, W.L. & Pinto, J.A., *Hadrian's Villa and its Legacy*, New Haven & London 1995.

Maiuri, A., *Herculaneum*, Congleton 1989.

Maiuri, A., *Pompeii*, Congleton 1989.

Meiggs, R., *Roman Ostia*, 2nd ed. Oxford & New York 1974.

Potter, T.W., *Roman Italy*, London 1987.

Potter, T.W. & Johns, C., *Roman Britain*, London 1988.

Raven, S., *Rome in Africa*, 3rd ed. London & New York 1993.

Richardson, L., *A New Topographical Dictionary of Ancient Rome*, Baltimore 1992.

Richmond, I.A., *Roman Britain*, London 1973.

Salway, P., *The Oxford Illustrated History of Roman Britain*, Oxford & New York 1993.

Stern, E. (ed.), *New Encyclopedia of Archaeological Excavations in the Holy Land, Vols I–IV*, Jerusalem 1993.

Wightman, E.M., *Roman Trier and the Treveri*, London 1970.

Williams, H. & C., *Roman Turkey*, London 1989.

Wilson, R.J.A., *Roman North Africa*, London 1990.

Wiseman, F.J., *Roman Spain: an Introduction to the Roman Antiquities of Spain and Portugal*, London 1956.

ANCIENT SOURCES

Caesar, *The Gallic War*, trans. H.J. Edwards (Loeb ed.). Cambridge, MA 1986.

Caesar, *The Civil War*, trans. J.F. Mitchell. Harmondsworth 1976.

Juvenal, *The Sixteen Satires*, trans. P. Green. Harmondsworth & New York 1974.

Martial, *Epigrams*, trans. D.R. Shackleton Bailey (Loeb ed.), 3 vols. Cambridge, MA 1993.

Res Gestae Divi Augusti. The Achievements of the Divine Augustus eds P.A. Brunt & J.M. Moore. Oxford & New York 1967.

Suetonius, *The Twelve Caesars* trans. R. Graves, revised M. Grant. Harmondsworth & New York 1989.

Tacitus, *Annals* trans. J. Jackson (Loeb ed.), 3 vols. Cambridge, MA 1934 & 1937.

Tacitus, *Histories* trans. C.H. Moore (Loeb ed.), 2 vols. Cambridge, MA 1935 & 1931.

INDEX

Note: numbers in *italics* indicate captions

ILLUSTRATION CREDITS

PHOTOS

Antonio Attini / Archivio White Star: 146–147, 147 top, 194, 195, 196, 197, 198–199, 199 bottom, 200 top, 201, 202–203, 203 top, 204, 205, 206, 207, 208, 209, 210, 211, 212 bottom, 213, 216, 217, 218, 219, 232, 233, 237, 238, 239, 240, 241, 242–243, 244, 245, 246, 247, 248, 249, 250, 251, 252 top, 256, 257, 262 top, 269 bottom, 272, 273, 284, 285, 286–287.

Marcello Bertinetti / Archivio White Star: 55 top, 105 top right, 123 bottom left, 252–253, 253 bottom, 263, 268–269.
Marcello Bertinetti / Archivio White Star 'Italian Air Force General Staff permit no. 316 dated 18/8/1995': 128–129, 128 bottom, 129 top, 130 top, 138–139, 156–157, 157 top, 158, 159 top, 162–163, 163 top.
Marcello Bertinetti / Archivio White Star 'Italian Air Force General Staff permit no. 325 dated 1/9/1995': 2–3, 18–19, 98–99, 100 top and centre, 101, 123 bottom right, 130 bottom, 131, 134–135.

Massimo Borchi / Archivio White Star: 222 bottom, 226–227.

Luciano Ramires / Archivio White Star: 212–213.

Giulio Veggi / Archivio White Star: 35 right, 67 top left, 96 bottom, 100 bottom, 104, 104–105, 105 top left, 114–115, 116, 117, 118, 119, 120, 121, 122 bottom, 122–123, 129 bottom, 130 centre bottom, 135 bottom, 138 top, 139, 164, 165, 168, 172, 173, 174, 175, 221 top right, 230, 266 top.

AKG Photo: 220, 221 top left, 221 bottom.

R. Bouquet / Diaf: 266 bottom left.

British Museum: 94 top, 224, 225.

Bruce Coleman: 200 bottom, 223 top.

Stephen Coyne / Bruce Coleman: 250 bottom.

Giovanni Dagli Orti: 6–7, 8, 20–21, 22 top, 24 top right, 36, 43 bottom, 60 top, 67 top left, 70, 71, 72, 73, 76 top, 92 bottom, 93, 98, 148, 160–161, 169, 176, 178, 187, 188, 189, 190–191, 229, 236, 264, 265, 267, 270, 271.

Araldo De Luca – Rome: 4–5, 9, 12–13, 14–15, 23, 25, 26 centre, 35 right, 35 centre left, 35 centre, 35 centre right, 39, 40 bottom, 43 top, 44 top, 45, 46 bottom, 48, 49, 50, 51, 54, 55 bottom, 56–57, 58–59, 60–61, 62 bottom right, 63 top, 63 bottom, 66, 67 bottom, 75 bottom right, 76 centre and bottom, 78 bottom, 78–79, 82–83, 84, 85, 89 top, 89 centre top, 89 centre bottom, 92 top, 96 top, 108, 109, 110, 111, 112, 113, 133 bottom, 140, 141, 142, 143, 144–145, 150, 151, 159 bottom, 170, 171, 180, 181, 192–193.

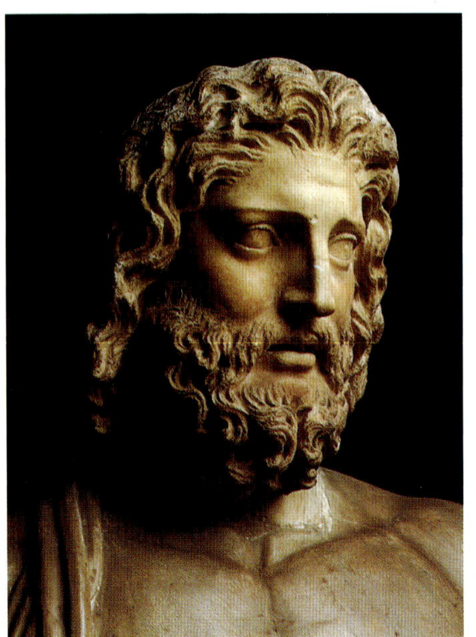

F.M.R.: 26 centre left, 27.

Fotografica Foglia: 86, 87, 88, 89 centre, 89 bottom, 90, 91.

Cesare Galli: 266 centre, 276, 277, 278, 279, 280, 281.

Jean Paul Garcin / Diaf: 255, 268 top, 274.

Cesare Gerolimetto: 147 bottom, 228, 262 centre and bottom.

Giraudon / Archivio Alinari: 17.

Johanna Huber/ SIE: 262, 263.

Archivio IGDA: 46 top, 94 bottom, 152 top.

Jürgen Liepe: 266 bottom right.

Rene Monjoie: 67 centre left, 152–153, 153 bottom.

Photo Nimatallah / Ag. Luisa Ricciarini: 16 bottom, 44 bottom, 62 top, 63 centre left, 63 centre right, 63 bottom, 67 centre right.

Andrea Pistolesi: 222–223.

Zev Radovan: 47 bottom, 252 centre and bottom.

Photo R.N.M.: 268 bottom.

Ag. Luisa Ricciarini: 62 bottom left, 64, 75 bottom left.

Roemer- und Pelizaeus Museum: 214 top, 215 bottom.

Rossenbach / Zefa: 221 centre.

Archivio Scala: 10–11, 22 bottom, 24 left, 24 bottom right, 26 left, 26 centre right, 26 right, 38, 40 top, 41 top, 42, 46, 47 top and centre, 58, 60 bottom, 68, 78 top, 152 bottom.

P.G. Sclarandis / SIE: 198 bottom, 254, 255.

Alberto Siliotti / Archivio Image Service: 202 bottom.

Emilio F. Simion – Milan / Ag. Luisa Ricciarini: 41 centre bottom.

Foto Ubu / Ag. Luisa Ricciarini: 176–177, 178–179.

MUSEUMS AND GALLERIES

Antiquarium of the Forum, Rome: 23 bottom right.

Archaeological Museum, Delphi: 236 top.

Archaeological Museum, Hama: 254 left.

Archaeological Museum, Herculaneum: 86, 87, 88, 89, 90, 91.

Archaeological Museum, Nîmes: 216 bottom.

Archaeological Museum, Palmyra: 265 top.

Archaeological Museum, Sousse: 270 top, 270–271.

Archaeological Museum, Suweida: 198 bottom, 254 right.

Bardo Museum, Tunis: 270 bottom.

292 Jupiter Optimus Maximus was the supreme deity in the Roman pantheon, lord of the sky and light, thunder and lightning; a great temple was dedicated to him on the summit of the Capitol in Rome.

Bibliothèque Nationale, Paris: 1, 17, 35 centre left, 37, 40 bottom, 43, 49, 50, 66, 84, 85, 96, 111, 140, 141, 143, 159.

British Museum, London: 94 top, 224, 225.

Capitoline Museums, Rome: 20–21, 43 bottom, 47 top right, 47 top left, 150, 160–161, 292.

Egyptian Museum, Cairo: 266 bottom left.

Israel Museum, Jerusalem: 47 bottom, 252 centre and bottom.

Kunsthistorisches Museum, Vienna: 16, 44 bottom, 46 top.

Landesmuseum, Mainz: 94 bottom.

Louvre Museum, Paris: 93, 267, 268 bottom.

Mosaics Museum, Shahba: 255.

Museo Archeologico, Aosta: 152.

Museo Civico La Rocca, Riva del Garda: 67 top left.

Museo della Civiltà Romana, Rome: 60 top, 62 bottom left, 64 top, 70 bottom.

Museo Gregoriano Profano, Vatican: 58, 60 bottom.

Museo Nazionale Romano, Rome: 12–13, 22 top, 26 left, 36 bottom, 58–59, 63 bottom, 76 top, 98, 112, 113, 142–143, 192–193.

Museo Pio Clementino, Vatican: 26 right, 41, 45, 108–109, 109.

Museo Prenestino Barberiniano, Palestrina: 48.

Museo di Villa Giulia, Rome: pages 22 bottom, 23, 24 top, 24 bottom left, 25, 38.

National Archaeological Museum, Florence: 40 top.

National Archaeological Muesum, Madrid: 70 top, 71, 72–73, 73.

National Archaeological Museum, Merida: 205 bottom.

National Archaeological Museum, Naples: 8, 26 centre, 39, 67 bottom, 75, 76, 78–79, 82–83, 67 centre right, 78 top, 110, 151, 170, 171, 176–177, 178–179, 178, 180, 181, 188–189.

National Archaeological Museum, Venice: 26 centre right, 41 top.

National Archaeological Museum, Taranto: 75 left.

National History Museum, Bucharest: pages 92 bottom, 229.

National Museum of Abruzzo, l'Aquila: 62 top.

Private numismatical collection F. Bourbon: 35 right.

Roemer- und Pelizaeus Museum, Hildesheim: 214, 215.

Uffizi Galleries, Florence: 63 top left, 63 centre.

Vatican Museums, Braccio Nuovo, Vatican: 9.